Rod Laver's
TENNIS DIGEST

Second Edition

Edited by
Rod Laver
and
Bud Collins

**In Cooperation with
World Tennis Magazine**

DIGEST BOOKS, INC. NORTHFIELD, ILL.

TENNIS DIGEST STAFF

EDITORS
Rod Laver
Bud Collins

PRODUCTION MANAGER
Wanda Sahagian

ASSOCIATE PUBLISHER
Sheldon L. Factor

Cover photo by John C. Russell

Rod Laver's TENNIS DIGEST is a publication of Digest Books, Inc., 540 Frontage Rd., Northfield, Illinois 60093.

ISBN 0-695-80527-4

Library of Congress Catalog #72-97511

TABLE OF CONTENTS

PLAYING INSTRUCTION

5 How to Read a Tournament Story
17 Are Coaches Dead Wrong? *by Julius Heldman*
33 Groundstroke vs. Volley Reflexes *by Don Klotz*
38 The Most Common Faults in Tennis (and How to Cure Them)
46 Think of the Ball as a Clock *by Julie M. Heldman*
59 A Better Way to Practice *by Don Klotz*
84 Why Your Volley Isn't Improving *by Gladys M. Heldman*
93 "I'm Ready" *by Marcia Ames Key*
105 No Second Bounces *by Don Klotz*
110 A Classic Doubles Point *by Julius Heldman*
120 The Axioms of Tennis *by Colin MacArthur*
130 A New Look at the Forehand *by Julius Heldman*
143 Teaching Youngsters to Serve *by Ed Collins*
144 Concentration, Early Preparation and Balance *by Fred A. Earle, Jr.*
154 How to Practice: Plan Your Workouts *by Gladys M. Heldman*
157 The Key to Good Footwork *by Dennis Van der Meer*
171 Checkpoints for Intermediate Players *by Gladys M. Heldman*
176 All About the Two-Handed Backhand *by Julius Heldman*
191 The Topspin Forehand *by Guy Cognen*
202 A Tournament Point *by Julius Heldman*
209 "What's Wrong With My Backhand?" *by Pancho Segura*
221 How to Practice *by Dennis Van der Meer*
222 Lessons from the Master *by Barbara Breit Gordon*

FEATURES

10 Mixed Doubles Moves Out of the Closet *by Bud Collins*
24 The Intersexual Saga of Tennis *by Bud Collins*
31 The King vs. Riggs Story *by Jean and Cliff Drysdale*
42 Hail and Farewell to the Softest Touch in Tennis *by Bud Collins*
49 Ramona: It Sang Out a Different Song of Love *by Neil Amdur*
60 Around the Tennis World *by Bud Collins*
90 How I Won the Singapore Open *by Bob Golton*
103 A Tennis Dictionary *by Lance Tingay*
106 Biography of a Backhand *by Roy Johnson*
115 The Poet Laureate *by Linda Timms*
116 A Centennial Primer: The Way It Really Was *by Bud Collins*
138 Married Doubles or You take the Backhand, Mr. Hyde *by Marlene Fanta Shyer*
161 Celebrity Tennis—Show Biz on the Court *by Candace Mayeron*
188 Moon-Balling on the Moon *by E.K. Hammond, Sr.*
200 Japan, Land of the Rising Tennis Boom *by Jean Drysdale*
259 Good Afternoon, Folks—Welcome to the U.S. Open of 2001 *by Bud Collins*
268 A Pedal Nudist on the Joys and Trials of a Barefoot Contester *by Bud Collins*
270 Where Angels Fear to Tread *by Candace Mayeron*

TACTICS AND STRATEGY

36 The Numbers Racket *by R.I. Smith-Johannsen*
48 How to Combat the Jitters *by Ed Collins*
88 The Imaginative Player *by Pancho Segura*
96 Poaching *by Julius Heldman*
122 Tips on Winning Matches *by Pancho Segura*
136 Analyzing an Opponent *by Gladys M. Heldman*
152 Trigger Your Concentration *by Don Klotz*
184 The Return of Serve in Singles *by Gladys M. Heldman*
197 How to Adapt to New Surfaces *by Gladys M. Heldman*

PERSONALITIES

20 Nastase *by Rex Bellamy*
52 Althea Gibson is Alive and Well *by Neil Amdur*
97 Tom Gorman—A Wee Bit O'Irish *by Rex Bellamy*
100 Olga the Volga Volleyer *by Bud Collins*
126 Mike and Flo—Hero and Heroine of the Highchair *by Bud Collins*
140 On Playing Tennis for Your Country *by Julie M. Heldman*
146 The Reminiscences of Rod Laver *by Rod Laver*
166 Ashe in South Africa *by Richard Evans*
173 Where Have You and Your Game Gone, Whitney? *by Bud Collins*
180 Meet Alex Mayer *by Mike Lupica*
192 Pilgrimage to Barellan *by Bud Collins*
204 The Real Durr *by Rex Bellamy*
214 We Remember You, Billie Jean *by Bud Collins*
263 Thru the Years With Rod Laver

STYLES OF PLAY

150 The Tanner Serve *by Julius Heldman*
212 The Ashe Forehand *by Julius Heldman*

MISCELLANY

34 The Joys and Horrors of Playing the Circuit
55 Everything You Want to Know About Equipment *by Julius Heldman*
108 Tennis Camps Come of Age *by Candace Mayeron*
112 Tennis Etiquette *by Gladys M. Heldman*
124 Improving Your Tennis Brain *by Julie M. Heldman*
133 A Century of Tennis
158 Tennis Test: Rating for Beginners and Intermediates
164 Denver Cooks Ol' Mother Freedom's Goose *by Mike Lupica*
272 Championship Rolls: USLTA & Wimbledon Winners
288 America's Tennis Immortals

How to Read a Tournament Story
A Beginners' Key to Tennis Terminology

This glossary is designed to help you understand the players and the experts when they comment on matches and/or tournaments. Glance through it before reading this book and use it for reference when reading tennis stories in the sports section of your newspaper. It will also be of help to you when listening to tennis commentary on television.

ACE: A serve that the receiver is unable to touch, much less return. A near-ace is a serve which the receiver barely touches but is unable to hit back.

Ad: See *Scoring*.

All-court Game: There are two kinds of games—baseline (hitting groundstrokes) and net (hitting the ball before it bounces, called "volleying"). The all-court player excels both from the backcourt (or baseline) and from the net. Therefore the all-court player has a good serve, forehand and backhand, as well as a good volley and overhead.

Alley: A narrow area on either side of the court that is "good" only in doubles. It is called the "tram" in England. See *Court Diagram*.

Angle: This usually refers to the sharp angles on the court, and these are made by hitting sharp, *short* crosscourt shots. A *deep* crosscourt shot has only limited angle. Very few players can hit a sharp, short crosscourt when standing on the baseline; it is much easier to hit the shot when standing close to net (inside the service box). In the diagram below, the lines show the sharp, short crosscourts, which have a great deal of angle, and the deep crosscourts, which have much less angle.

Approach Shot: A groundstroke hit by a player on his way to net. It is often a chip on the forehand and a slice on the backhand.

Attack: One can either attack from the baseline by hitting very hard, deep shots that are well placed (obsolete) or one can attack by coming to net on a good serve or a deep return, thus forcing the opponent to make a very good shot to stay in the point. In general, the word "attack" refers to *coming to net* on a good serve or a deep, forcing return. Some players will attack solely on "bluff", hoping by their massiveness or agility to press the opponent into a weak return or error.

Backcourt: This is the area around the baseline (see *Court Diagram*).

Backhand: A groundstroke hit on the left side of the body. (Lefthanders hit backhands on the right side of the body.)

Backhand Volley: A volley hit on the left side of the body (righthanders) or on the right side of the body (lefties). There are also backhand dropshots and backhand overheads. See *Dropshot, Overhead* and *Volley*.

Backswing (or wind-up): That part of the stroke that comes before the hit. On forehand and backhand groundstrokes, it is *usually* a rather full motion, with the racket moving back behind the body and then swinging forward toward the ball. N.B.: There is very *little* backswing on volleys, except in the case of the *drive volley*.

Big Four: See *Grand Slam*.

Block: A return hit with almost no backswing or follow-through. Fast serves are frequently *blocked* back since there is no time for a backswing.

Block Volley: A volley hit with almost no follow-through, usually because there is no time for the net man to do anything but block the ball.

Bonne Bell Cup: An international competition between Australian and American women, played along the same lines as a Davis Cup match (see *Davis Cup*).

Breaking (or breaking serve): This refers to the receiver winning his opponent's serve. In good tennis there are very few service breaks, and many times there is only one service break per set. It is rather rare in top men's tennis to see three service breaks in a set; it is slightly more frequent in top women's tennis.

Call: A ball is called "out" or called "fault" or called "let." A linesman never calls a good shot (he indicates it by putting his hands out, palms down).

Chalk: The boundary lines of a court are painted with chalk on grass courts and are often painted with chalk on clay. When a ball hits the line, the chalk literally "flies." On occasion, the ball can hit near the line but not on it and the chalk will still fly. Therefore balls that bring up chalk are not automatically good.

Change-over: The players change sides after the odd games of each set (1, 3, 5, 7, 9, etc.). In match play the time limit allowed on the change-over for toweling off or sipping water is 60 seconds.

Chip: A short-backswing drive with very little backswing and an underspin follow-through (see *Underspin*). It greatly resembles the volley action. Players use chip shots against hard serves or to approach the net.

Choking: Tightening up (getting nervous) at any point (or all) during a match.

Chop: A drive with a volley action, very much like the chip but used in backcourt exchanges (the chip is generally used to approach net, whereas the chop need not be followed to net). The chop was quite popular many years ago but it is not often seen today.

Circuit: A series of consecutive tournaments with players generally signing up for the series, viz., the Dewar Cup Circuit (played in Britain in the Fall), the Sugar Circuit (played in South Africa in the Winter), the Virginia Slims Circuit (played in the U.S. by Women Pros), etc.

Corners: The baseline corners of the court. A player who "hits the corners" (Chris Evert, for example) is a mighty tough player to beat.

Crosscourt: Diagonal shots from one side of the court to the other. See *Angle Chart*.

Davis Cup: A series of men's team

matches between different nations played over the course of many months each year. The formula for each tie (round) is four singles and one doubles match, but the singles are played by only two men on the team (each of the two men plays each of the two opponents). It is an elimination tournament played in zones (two zones in Europe, one in America and one in the Far East, with the zone winners playing off in the semis and finals).

Defensive Shots: When a player is forced by deep, hard or wide shots, he often hits a defensive shot, viz., a high, deep ball, so he can get back into position again. Good defensive play means excellent court coverage as well as returning the ball deep and high.

Depth: A ball that has good depth bounces within 2 to 3 feet of the baseline. A serve that has good depth bounces within 6 inches of the service line.

Deuce: See *Scoring.*

Down-the-line: A shot that parallels the sideline (see *Court Diagram*). If both players are righthanders, then Player A's forehand down-the-line would go to Player B's backhand. Player A's backhand down-the-line would go to Player B's forehand. It is the opposite of the crosscourt.

Doubles: Tennis with two players on each side.

Double-fault (or "doubles"): A player is given two chances to get his serve into the proper service court. If he fails, he has served a double-fault or, he has "served doubles."

Drive: A groundstroke, forehand or backhand.

Drive Volley: A volley in every sense of the word (hitting a ball before it bounces), but the volley is stroked like a groundstroke rather than punched. This is usually done only on high balls.

Drop Shot: A ball hit with so much underspin and control that it barely clears the net and then dies (bounces low with very little or no forward motion).

Drop Volley: Similar to a drop shot but the player hits it from the net as a volley.

Experience: A term used by tournament players which refers to the playing of many, many tournaments under a variety of conditions. An "experienced" player has competed on grass, clay, cement, carpet and composition courts, good and bad, on hot and humid and cold and windy days. He has played under lights, in the shadows and in the rain, with no linesman and with a full crew of linesmen, on back courts and in packed arenas, against attackers, lobbers, stallers, needlers and good sports. He has had the gallery cheering for him and cheering against him, has been an underdog and a favorite, he has had great days and bad days, he has been down 0-5 in the third and won and he has been up 5-0 in the third and lost. He has suffered from at least four of the following: leg or hand cramps, heat fatigue, tennis elbow, tennis shoulder, a bad back, knee or leg, sprains, muscle tears, broken bones and, above all, tournament jitters. He knows what it is to play his best and to play his worst, to be keyed up and to be stale, to dream for a week about a match lost on one crucial point, to have "feel" and to lose "feel," and to play on wet grass and cracked clay with Dunlops, Pirellis, Wilsons, Tretorns and every other imaginable ball. He has been congratulated for his good play after he has lost 6-0, 6-0 and has been booed by an unknowing crowd when he walked up to the umpire's chair to see if there would be new balls for the third set. He has been housed by tournament committees in attics, dorms, private homes, motels and luxury resorts. He has played for peanuts as an amateur and for big money as a pro, and he has won and lost under both circumstances. There is nothing on the court that he hasn't experienced, and this adds "15" to his game (if he doesn't succumb to nerves) when he plays an inexperienced player who is every bit as good as he.

Fault: A service that is not good be-

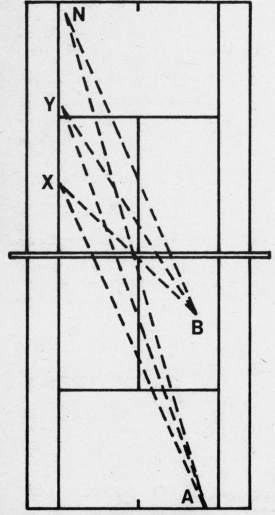

ANGLE CHART
A-to-N and B-to-N are simple crosscourts without much angle.
A-to-Y and B-to-Y are good angle shots.
A-to-X (an extremely difficult shot) and B-to-X are the very sharp angle shots.

cause it fails to go in the proper service box or because the player has foot-faulted.

Flat Shot: A ball hit without any spin.

Foot-fault: A fault by virtue of stepping on the baseline or inside the baseline or over the center mark on the baseline before the ball is hit.

Forcing Shot: A ball which, by its depth, pace or angle, puts the opponent on the defensive.

Forehand: A groundstroke hit on the right side of the body if one is a right-hander. See *Backhand* and *Backhand Volley*.

Forest Hills: A term often used to denote the U.S. Open Championships, which is held at the West Side Tennis Club in Forest Hills, L.I., N.Y.

French Championships: Traditionally, one of the three biggest tournaments in the world (the others are Wimbledon and Forest Hills). The French Championships are played on clay and the winners of the men's and women's titles are generally recognized as the best clay court players in the world.

Grand Slam: Until a few years ago, the Grand Slam (winning the Big Four—Australian, French, Wimbledon and U. S. titles in the same year) was the measure of tennis greatness, and this feat was only accomplished by Don Budge, Rod Laver (twice), Maureen Connolly and Margaret Court. Recently the Australian title has lost much of its luster since so few of the top players regularly compete for it. The Women Pros now consider the $100,000 Virginia Slims Championships at Boca Raton as their fourth tournament in the Grand Slam.

Grass Courts: Tennis is played on grass in only a very few countries, viz., Australia, New Zealand, Great Britain and the U.S. There are very few grass courts in the U. S., and they are primarily in clubs on the Eastern Seaboard. They are extremely expensive to maintain and, unless they are near perfect as at Wimbledon and Australia, one gets bad bounces (or no bounces at all). Many top players today feel that grass is an anachronism, particularly Forest Hills grass.

Groundstrokes: Forehands and backhands hit after the ball has bounced once.

Heavy Ball: A ball which, because of the pace, depth and/or spin im-

parted to it, feels "heavy" on the racket of the receiver.

Holding: This refers to holding serve, viz., "Arthur Ashe held to win the set."

ILTF: This stands for "International Lawn Tennis Federation," an all-male organization which claims authority over all women.

Junior: A player who will not reach his 19th birthday until October of the calendar year (the date used to be January 1 of the following calendar year).

Junior Wimbledon: A tournament for Juniors of different nations held during the second week of the Wimbledon Championships and generally watched (until the finals) by mothers, fathers and coaches. Only one player from each country may be selected.

Last 8: The players in the quarter-finals.

Let: A call to indicate that the point should be replayed. A let is called on serve when the ball ticks the net but still falls in the correct service court. Lets can also be called for interference (a dog running onto the court or a ball from the next court rolling over), to correct a call (a linesman calls "out", then changes his mind) and because the receiver was not ready for the serve (the receiver may not make any movement or attempt to return the ball).

Lob: A high ball designed to go over the net man's head. A short lob is a set-up which the net man can easily put away. An offensive lob either catches the net man by surprise because of its disguise or it has enough topspin to jump away from the net man trying to chase it down. A defensive lob is a very high ball, sometimes hit in desperation and sometimes be-

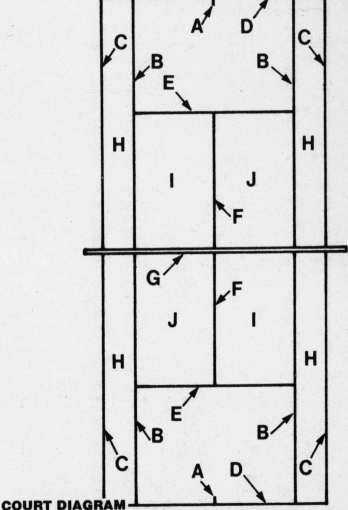

COURT DIAGRAM

A: The center mark on the baseline. The server must stand to the right of it when serving into the forehand court (I) and to the left of it when serving in the backhand court (J).

B: The sideline boundary in singles.

C: The sideline boundary in doubles.

D: The baseline.

E: The service line.

F: The center service line.

G: The net.

H: The alley. Balls hit in the alley are "out" in singles. Hitting in the alley is allowed in doubles except on serve.

cause the player does not know how to lob offensively (with disguise and spin).

Length: Another word for depth.

Linesman: The official who calls balls out or hand-motions that they are good. See *Officials*.

Love: Zero in tennis scoring.

Low Shot: A ball that bounces low. Chips and underspin backhands, if hit properly, will bounce low and are extremely effective against players who don't like to bend or who hit low balls "up" (too high, thus giving the net man a set-up).

Match Point: One of the players need only win one point to take the match. In the case of the 9-point tie-breaker, there can be double-match-point if the tiebreaker score is 4-4 in the final set.

Net Cord: Any shot that ticks the net. If it happens on serve, the serve is played over (a let). On any other shot the point is continued without interruption.

Net Cordsman: The linesman who sits right by the umpire's chair with his hand on the net. His duty is to call lets on service "not up" when a player hits a ball after it has bounced twice. He also keeps a duplicate score card. Additionally he has the responsibility of measuring the net during the first change-over after each set.

Net Player: The man at net who volleys. A net player is also someone who volleys at every conceivable opportunity.

New Balls: In most tournament play, new balls are provided when the match starts and again for the third set if the match goes to three sets. In major tournaments, new balls are provided more frequently, viz., on "7 and 9." Because the players warm up before starting the match, new balls are provided after the 7th game and thereafter every 9 games.

"Nothing" Ball: A high or fairly high ball that has nothing on it (no spin and no pace). The opponent therefore has to manufacture his own pace.

Not Up: A call that indicates the ball has bounced twice before the player hits it.

Officials: The officials at a tournament are the Tournament Director (he organizes the event), the Referee (he schedules play, calls play—because of rain or darkness—and he is the final judge on any court disputes), the Umpire (he sits on a chair by the net, calls the score and runs the match), the linesmen (sidelinesman, baselinesman, service linesman and net cordsman) and the footfault judge (he sits on a chair next to the baselinesman and must sprint across the court every two games to sit by the baselinesman on the other side).

Overhead: A ball that is hit in the air several feet above the player's head with a service-like motion. The overhead can either be hit before it bounces or after it bounces (a bounce overhead), but most players prefer to hit it before the bounce if possible.

Pace: The sting of a ball on a player's racket. Pace is speed or speed combined with spin (sidespin produces sting).

Passing Shot (or Passer): A ball that passes the net man. The three passing shots are crosscourt, down the line and over the head (lob).

Percentage Tennis: This is playing the right shots at the right time. Some of the basics of percentage tennis are: 1) always get your first serve in when playing doubles, 2) hit all approach shots deep, 3) on a forehand approach shot, hit it deep to the opponent's backhand unless you can make an outright winner on the crosscourt, 4) in the forehand court, never serve to the opponent's forehand unless a) you can pull him into the fence, b) you are 0-0 or 40-15 or, possibly, 30-30, c) he has the all-time "choke" forehand.

Placement: A groundstroke or volley that the opponent cannot reach. An ace is a service placement.

Racket Face: The strings of the racket.

Rally: An exchange over the net, usually when both players are on the baseline. When it is said that "there were no rallies," it means that almost all the exchanges were short (viz., a serve and a return of serve placement *or* a serve and a return of serve error *or* a serve, a return of serve and a put-away volley). The statement "Let's rally" means "Let's hit a few balls and groove our strokes." "Rally" should not be confused with "volley." One never says "Let's volley a few" (a volley is a ball that is hit before it bounces).

Ranking: A classification (sometimes arbitrary) of players according to their records on the basis of the previous year's performance. This classification is an honor given by a tennis association or society or sports writer and does not carry with it any financial compensation. Further, national rankings arouse more ill feelings than gratitude, except in the case of the No. 1, and frequently seedings (see *Seed*) in a particular tournament are not based on the rankings but on current performance, thus enraging the No. 1 ranked player.

Return of Serve: The return of service (just as it sounds).

Scoring: In tennis there are points, games, sets and matches. There must be at least 4 points to a game, but because one must win the game by two points, there can be 10 or 20 or even 30 points in a game. The points are scored as love (0), 15 (one point), 30 (2 points), 40 (3 points) and game (the last point). 15-30 means 1 point to 2; 30-15 means 2 points to 1. If one player gets to 40-30 (3 points to 2) and loses the next point, the score is not called 40-all (there is no such term except in VASSS No-Ad), but "deuce" since one player has to win by 2 points. The next point after "deuce" is "ad" (for "advantage"). If the player who has the ad loses the next point, the score reverts to deuce; if he wins it, he has the game. Frequently there will be a game that has 8 or 10 deuces and ads before one of the players can win 2 points consecutively. Sets are a minimum of 6 games; there used to be no maximum until the tiebreaker was introduced a few years ago, and since a set in those days had to be won by two games, there were commonly sets of 9-7 or 12-10 or, very rarely, 20-18. Now a tiebreaker is usually used when games are 6-all. The most common tiebreaker is the best of 9 points, but WCT (see *WCT*) uses a tiebreaker of 12 points and the winner must win by 2 points. A match is composed of the best of three sets, although some tournaments use the best of five sets in men's matches.

Service: The stroke that starts the point. It is almost invariably hit by throwing the ball up with one hand to a point approximately 3 to 4 feet above the head, whereupon it is struck with the racket which is held in the other hand. The racket and arm hopefully form a straight line at the moment of impact.

Service Court: See *Court Diagram*.

Set-up: An easy put-away shot, provided you are a good player. Set-ups (for good players) are high, short serves, any high, short shot, any drop-shot that is poorly executed and bounces high, high balls within easy reach of the net man and short lobs. A good player who misses a set-up has nightmares for a week if it cost him the match.

Seed: In a tournament the two best players may be placed in opposite halves of the draw so that they don't meet in the first or second round (they are "seeded" Nos. 1 and 2). The next two best players are put in opposite quarters of the draw from Nos. 1 and 2 (they are "seeded" Nos. 3 and 4). There can be one seed for every 8 players, according to USLTA rules. In a draw of 64, therefore, there can be 8 seeds. "Seeding" should not be confused with "ranking" (see *Ranking*). The seeds are the result of the Tournament Committee's prejudgement on the caliber of the field.

Serve-and-Volley Game: The description of a player who relies on a big serve and a net game. He is also called an attacker.

"7 and 9": See *New Balls*.

Sidespin: A spin achieved by making the racket come across the ball with both a forward and toward-the-body motion. The result is a "heavy" ball. The masters of the sidespin forehand were Jack Kramer and Maureen Connolly. Today the best exponent is Kerry Melville. For some reason, players simply are not using this forceful weapon anymore.

Slice: On the serve, slice is imparted by making the racket face come across the right side of the ball (for righthanders) rather than hitting it flat or with topspin. "Slice" is also another term for "underspin" (See *Underspin*).

Smash: See *Overhead*.

Spin: The motion created by racket on ball which causes the ball to bounce in an unusual manner. Spins are created by coming over (topspin), under (underspin) or across (sidespin) the ball. Lefthanded spins are particularly obstreperous, and there is a current movement among right-handers to have them barred from the game. Spins are used for control: when one hits a flat ball, only gravity brings the ball into court; controlled spin forces the ball to the left, the right or downwards.

Stalling: Taking too much time between points or on the changeovers. This is manifested by slow, despondent movements in returning to the baseline, the constant inspection and re-tying of shoelaces, thorough toweling of all appendages, prolonged ad-

justment of wrist, arm or knee bands, meticulous inspection of glass and pitcher as well as slow consumption of the liquid therein, etc. Stallers are the nemesis of players, umpires and spectators. While the rest of us will go to heaven by jet, stallers will be delivered in ox-carts.

Steel Elbow: See *Choking*.

The Second (or The Third): This refers to the second or third set, viz., "Billie Jean led 4-2 in the second."

Tarpaulin: A court covering frequently used at clubs holding major tournaments which either leaks or does not quite cover the entire court, thus permitting unlimited seepage. It is designed to reassure spectators during a heavy downpour that play will one day be resumed.

Tiebreaker: A system designed to terminate sets at the 6-all level.* Then the contestants either play the best of 9 points with "Sudden Death" coming on the 9th point if the points go to 4-all, or the best of 12 points, with one of the players having to win by 2 points (this is not Sudden Death).

Topspin: This type of spin is created by having the racket face come up and over the ball, as well as moving forward at the same time. Heavy topspin is created by pulling the racket up sharply without coming forward as much; light topspin can be achieved by starting with the racket head low and finishing well in front of the body with the racket head high. Topspin, unless excessive, makes it easier to control the ball. After the ball bounces, it jumps forward faster and higher than a flat ball.

Two-Handed Shot: Although one can go through a lifetime without seeing a two-handed serve or overhead, one cannot go through a Wimbledon or Forest Hills without spotting a two-handed backhand. Exponents of this shot are Cliff Drysdale, Chris Evert, Jeanne Evert, Mike Belkin, Frew McMillan (on forehand, backhand and volley), Jimmy Connors and a large group of top Junior Girls from Florida and points north.

Underspin: The racket face, instead of being perpendicular to the ground, tilts so that the bottom edge of the racket is further forward than the

top edge. The effect, when the racket meets the ball, is to make the ball spin backwards, thus slowing it up and making it rise. Underspin is therefore necessary when hitting a very low ball close to net (the ball must rise up to go over the net). Underspin is used by players on the backhand on approach shots or down the line shots (for control). It is not recommended on passing shots simply because the ball slows up and rises, giving the net man a better crack at the ball. Underspin is used on almost all volleys, the exception being drive volleys.

USLTA: An exclusive stag club whose members claim they represent the different sections of the country. They regularly elect each other to office and just as regularly they suspend the members of the WT Women's Pro group.

U.S. Open: One of the two most important tennis tournaments of the world, played at the West Side Tennis Club in Forest Hills, L.I., N.Y.

VASSS: The Van Alen Simplified Scoring System(s). One is the 9 point tiebreaker and the other is No-Ad. "Deuce" and "ad" are eliminated, and a game can be won by one point (at "40-all", the next point wins the game).

Virginia Slims Circuit: The players in this group are members of the WT Women's Pro Tour. They hope to form their own Women's International Tennis Federation (they anticipate taking in a "token" man). Before the formation of this circuit, prize money for the women annually was under $75,000; within two years it became $650,000. Their motto: "You've come a long way, baby!"

Volley: A shot hit before the ball bounces, usually from a position close to the net. It should not be confused with "rally" (See *Rally*).

WCT: A Pro organization headed up by Lamar Hunt (owner) and Mike Davies (Executive Director).

Wightman Cup: A competition between women representing Great Britain and the U.S., played annually. The matches comprise 5 singles and 2 doubles.

Wimbledon: The most famous tennis tournament in the world. It is almost impossible to get tickets for this event unless you "know somebody." It is held at the All-England Club at Wimbledon near London the last week of June and the first week of July. ●

---

*Wimbledon, to be obstinate, starts the tiebreaker at 8-all and only uses traditional scoring in the final set.

Mixed Doubles
Moves Out of
The Closet

BY BUD COLLINS

IS THERE ANY redeeming social value to mixed doubles? I mean, if the people involved are consenting adults, who feel they're finding fulfillment without hurting anyone else? Or is it just another dirty game that should be banned by the Supreme Court?

I'd heard arguments pro and con, and I wondered about it as I flew the unfriendly skies of some airline or another—they're equally bad these days, aren't they?—toward Dallas to witness something called the 1974 Spalding International Mixed Doubles Championship. At least they didn't call it a "classic," the most overworked word in sport since "great."

I decided to poll the people on either side of me in the plane: "Who was the greatest mixed doubles player of all time? By great I mean great, not just good, okay?" The answers came winging back: Henry VIII...Catherine the Great...Tommy Manville...Elizabeth Taylor...Brigham Young...Lana Turner...Mickey Rooney...Zsa Zsa Gabor...

"No, no. I mean mixed doubles in tennis."

"Tennis? Mixed doubles in tennis?" the woman next to me screwed up her face. "That's a game? Mixed doubles in tennis? I thought you meant..."

At least they'd heard of tennis, these fellow travelers. But they didn't associate mixed doubles with tennis.

Who would have, really, until a guy we reckoned to be a misguided—as well as misplaced—Aussie, name of John Gardner, shamelessly put mixed doubles right out there in public on the Southern Methodist University Campus, where thousands of voyeurs could watch. Nay, not thousands—millions—because Gardner permitted television coverage of the first International Mixed. And he even had the blessing of the landlord, Paul Hardin, president of Southern Methodist. Can you imagine Methodists sanctioning such goings-on at their school?

Yes, heterosexual tennis had come out of the closet during the first week of a new year. Once a back street affair, relegated to out-of-sight courts, mixed jumped right out there with the respectable elements of the game—men's singles and doubles, women's singles and doubles. It was being flaunted brazenly on the legitimate sporting stage of

Moody Coliseum, home of the male pro singles championship presented annually by WCT.

Before that wondrous January week, mixed was something that came in a plain brown wrapper. You might have indulged in it with your spouse or sweetheart, but you did it in private and mentioned it to nobody. You realized that the English think highly of mixed, but the English are kinky in that respect. A bit mad. If you ever see them huddled beneath blankets and heavy coats, resisting freezing 55 mph gales off the ocean at Bournemouth while they relish four people nobody ever heard of in an orgy of mixed, well, you'll know all you need to know about English tennis voyeurs.

The French believe mixed was invented by the Marquis de Sade, and that it should be undertaken at the Charenton Asylum, not on a court where it might attract attention at Roland Garros. The Italians and Australians have removed mixed from their national championship program altogether. And the Americans sheepishly throw together a draw at the last minute at Forest Hills, from which most of the pairs self-consciously withdraw before they actually have to perform.

But John Gardner, apparently, didn't know any better. He hasn't been around that long. An innocent, not quite 25-years-of-age, he was smuggled into Dallas from Albury a few years ago on a tennis scholarship at SMU, and has become the varsity coach, as well as a laborer in the university's fund-raising vineyard. A slim, serious, even worried-looking (which he had every right to be) young man, Gardner was in the market for a tournament to support his SMU varsity, which ranked fourth among American college teams in 1973. Why not, he mused, establish a mixed doubles tournament for the exceptional pros? Gardner was convinced that mixed is high on America's list of intersexual fun-and-games. But could he get anybody to admit it—by either playing in the tournament or purchasing a ticket to watch?

"Billie Jean King was target No. 1," says Gardner. "After she was intrigued by the idea and signed a contract to appear—the day before she beat Bobby Riggs—everything else fell into place." That is a little like Christopher Columbus saying, "After I sold Queen Isabella on the idea,

Owen Davidson watches partner Billie Jean King return serve (far court) and begin to move in against Cliff Drysdale and Francoise Durr. It might be a lob because Durr has stopped on the way into net behind her service.

it was all smooth sailing." Oh sure.

Target No. 2 was Rod Laver, "who signed as a favor to me," says Gardner.

Target No. 3 was the team of Chris Evert and Jim Connors, the epitome of mixedness. Though Connors' agent, Bill Riordan, signed a contract on Jimmy's behalf, Jimmy decided to protect his investment in a diamond ring by following Chris to Australia. That contract-jumping didn't please Gardner. Nor should it be taken lightly by anyone in tennis, lest the game descend to the level of other pro sports in which signatures on contracts are meaningless.

But Gardner, willing to forgive in the name of romance, hopes Chris and Jimmy, or Mr. and Mrs. Connors, or whoever they are by then, will sign up (Jimmy thus honoring his commitment, if belatedly).

Cohabitation of a tennis court no longer seemed the hush-hush perversion of other tournaments and other days because of one salient item: money. The eight couples who came to Dallas to do their swinging were paid beyond the fantasies of such mixed champions as Bunny Ryan, Hazel Wightman, Doris Hart, George Lott, Vic Seixas, Ken Fletcher—and even Xaviera Hollander.

Sixty thousand dollars was what made mixed suddenly look like a proper diversion. Rod Laver hadn't played mixed for nearly 14 years. His coach, Charlie Hollis, had caught him at it and made him promise never to do it again. But would Rodney Laver expose himself once again in this cus-tomarily furtive enterprise merely for a shot at 10 grand? You bet he would.

"Sixty thousand…sixty big ones?" O.K. Davidson nearly swallowed his mustache when he heard John Gardner quote the figure. For years O.K. (that's Owen Keir) Davidson has been the king of mixed doubles—a distinction of about the same eminence as being king of mixed drinks at a convention of the Women's Christian Temperance Union. Not only that, but Davidson revels in his deviance. "Yes, I like mixed doubles," he defiantly declares in a tone of voice that indicates "Don't knock it if you haven't tried it." He is well aware that such talk gets him needled and marked as some sort of sexual freedom nut in his native Australia. But Davidson has had so much success at mixed that he doesn't care who knows it. Few knew or cared until he and Billie Jean King wrapped up the $20,000 first prize with a ringing 6-2, 4-6, 6-3, 6-4 triumph over Rosie Casals and Marty Riessen.

O.K. still didn't believe it when he arrived in Dallas. "I'm one of those chaps," Davidson admitted, "who would play mixed for short money, and play hard." Can't help himself, poor fellow. "But $60,000? Bloody wonderful. Do you realize that for winning both Wimbledon and Forest Hills Billie Jean and I got a total of $1,600 apiece? And here in Dallas the first round losers get $1,500 each!"

"It's the most money I ever made in a half-hour," grinned The Spider Man—Frank Froehling—after he and Kristien

Eager crowds of more than 7,000 filled Dallas' Moody Coliseum—one of the best arenas in the world for indoor tennis—to see the first big-money mixed tournament. Wimbledon champions Billie Jean King and Owen Davidson carried off $10,000 each.

Kemmer were flushed, 6-4, 6-1, by Casals and Riessen opening night. Suddenly the International Mixed had joined WCT's doubles championship in Montreal in the narrow society of rich doubles tournaments.

"Dallas," says boy promoter Gardner, "is a sophisticated sports city. You have to give them the best. They're tennis mad, but if you're going to promote at Moody, where Lamar Hunt puts on the pro singles championship, you've got to come up with the names. Would the big names play mixed here, when they hardly ever do anywhere else? I thought so if we could make the money appealing enough. With the names, I knew I could sell tickets."

I wondered. I was feeling sorry for Gardner as I flew the cramped and crammed skies of some airline or another. Sure, tennis is thriving. Certainly, he had some lustrous boxoffice names (King, Laver, Casals, Gunter, Emerson, Richey, Riessen, Drysdale, Durr). But...mixed doubles? Would people pay to watch that? I hoped so, and I empathized with the handful I expected to show up because I've always thought mixed a delight.

By far the most entertaining match I monitored was a semi-final mixed at the French Open: Francoise Durr and Jean Claude Barclay over Kristien Kemmer and Frank Froehling, 7-5, 6-4, a smorgasbord of psychedelic stroking. Barclay's form makes Durr and Froehling's seem lyrical. Everybody was bashing backhands with both hands except Froehling, who hid his completely. In that Parisian mud they appeared to be Creatures from the Red Lagoon, and I asked myself if Kristien Kemmer were my daughter, would I approve of her indulging in mixed with The Spider Man? There were only two spectators: me and a demented, displaced Englishwoman, who thought that, because it was cold and raining, she was in Bournemouth.

Yes—if you must know the truth—I, too, am a mixed degenerate. But you will never get Bonnie Mencher, Joan Silbersher, Meg Wilson, Karen Susman, Belmar Gunderson, Donna Fales, Joyce Williams, Tex Montgomery Rindfuss, Kitty Stanton, Janet Hopps Adkisson, Bobby Goldberg, Cannonball Connolly, Ruth Jeffrey, Gail Hansen, Rosie Casals, Jeannie Kirkpatrick, Carol Aucamp, Midge Fremont-Smith, Pat Stockton, Big Red Crawford or Edy McGoldrick to confess that they shared the intimacies of a tennis court with me. Those are liaisons of the past each wishes she could annul from memory and blot from faded draw sheets.

So I had a soft spot for the tournament and Gardner. But, after all, my appearance involved no financial risk. I was on assignment for *World Tennis* and the Public Broadcasting System. Gardner was in much deeper. True, he had partial sponsorships (Spalding and the *Dallas Morning News*), but if he was to avoid financial disaster, he had to sell most of 35,000 seats. And—bravo for him, and hurrah for mixed—Gardner did just that. Twenty-six thousand paid admissions were counted for four sessions, and Gardner was able to autograph the laborers' checks, assured they wouldn't bound as high as a Davidson kicker.

Obviously there are a lot of mixed freaks living in Texas. Didn't Texans set the all-time tennis attendance record of 30,742 for Billie Jean's mixed singles waffling of Bobby at the Astrodome? And isn't one of the state's most popular games the shooting of wives by husbands and vice versa? It figured then that men and women firing tennis shots at each other would have significant attraction in the Lone

E. J. Holtke

Roy Emerson practiced saying "Sorry, Wendy...Sorry, Wendy..." before partnering Wendy Overton. They reached the semi-finals.

Rod Laver leaps to take a lob over the head of Lesley Hunt with his high, lefty backhand volley. She ducks so that he can hit the ball down and she won't get in the way. Lesley defaulted in the Australian Open doubles to make it to Dallas on time.

Star State.

Gardner knew his territory. However, he didn't know the ways of that very small universe beyond Texas called the tennis world and the men who run it—or think they do. "It took me six months to even get a sanction from the ILTF (International Lawn Tennis Federation), and a lot of grief in getting it," says Gardner. "I couldn't believe it." Believe, man, believe—and be thankful it took only six months. Sounds like an ILTF speed record to me.

More appalling was the conduct of the ATP (Association of Tennis Pros, the men's union). "World Team Tennis was going to sponsor us originally," Gardner recounts. "They were coming in for $45,000 which meant we'd only have to do $15,000 at the gate to break even. No problems." It was a natural for WTT, what with mixed to assume a prime position in their format and with such WTT'ers involved as King, Davidson, Casals, Emerson, Froehling, Durr.

No problems until ATP contacted Gardner and told him that, unless he shed WTT sponsorship, no ATP players would be available. Hence no tournament. This is known as a shakedown in less civilized precincts where the tactic originated. Because of its questionable opposition to WTT, ATP was willing to kill a tournament that offered exceptional employment opportunities to ATP members. Is that what a labor union is supposed to do—eliminate jobs? Thank goodness the ATP has now taken a more moderate posture and no longer threatens to eject from membership those players who sign with WTT. WTT may present difficulty and conflict, but it also offers jobs—for as long as the league lasts. Can a union deny its members a chance to work?

John Newcombe, who signed with Houston and faced ATP expulsion, said it well and eloquently to ATP boss Jack Kramer: "I'm sick and tired of being banned, and the public is sick of it, too. Do you mean to tell me that if Henry Kissinger can bring China and the United States together, and negotiate peace in Vietnam and the Middle East, that we can't find a solution to the problems of our game?"

John Gardner, swacked in the middle of the ATP-WTT conflict, had no choice. He gulped, held back the tears and said thanks, but no thanks, to WTT's cash. "We were prepared to go it alone at the gate...and hope. Then," says Gardner, "we thought we had Sunbeam as a sponsor. But that fell through. Finally the *Morning News* pitched in, and Larry King got Spalding for us, but we still had to do most of it by selling tickets. We found out what I prayed would be true—we had a product people wanted to watch. Tennis players identify more with doubles than singles, and mixed is a big game with the ordinary players, the backers. But they never get a chance to see it played really well."

Marty Riessen, who has had—shall we say—substantial aid from Mighty Mama, Margaret Court, in winning several major mixed doubles titles, agreed. Riessen, coming off his and Rosie Casals' final round loss, glowed, "I haven't had so much fun in a tournament in years. Mixed is generally the third event at a tournament, forgotten, left until nightfall on a back court. By then the players are tired after singles and doubles—and who cares? Here it was center stage. The ball kept moving like you never see in the usual singles, or even doubles. The money was big, and so was the pressure, yet there was a relaxed good spirit.

"People wondered if the women could take a best-of-five sets final (the first ever for mixed). Hell, they were sharper for it than the men. They knew they could play doubles with the men. I don't mean they're as strong or necessarily as good. But they knew they could hold up their end of the bargain, and they sure did. It was interesting tennis, and above all, fun for us and the spectators. I've never heard such enthusiastic applause. We get so wrapped up in ourselves and our singles on the pro tours that often a lot of the fun is lost. It's a business, sure, but it should be fun, too."

In 1960 Rod Laver won the Wimbledon mixed for the second straight year linked to Darlene Hard. ("She made it clear she'd take her overheads, and I didn't mind because she hit them harder than I did. She was probably stronger than I was.") Despite that success, Laver heard from his coach, Charlie Hollis: "Forget mixed. You'll never win the singles until you do. You can't waste strength on a third event." Laver gave up mixed and won the Wimbledon singles four straight times (1961-62, 68-69).

"That 1960 final was weird," Rod remembers. "We were down a set and 5-3 in the second to Maria Bueno and Bob Howe. Just then, with them about to serve for the match, Darlene got sick or something. She ran off the court and disappeared through the door to the dressing room. Everybody wondered what's going on. The referee came down and asked what was wrong. I didn't know. He couldn't follow her to the dressing room. Bueno and Howe were furious, and I felt uncomfortable, but what could we do? We waited. Was the referee going to default a Wimbledon final one game from the end? In about 10 minutes, Darlene came back, said nothing—and we broke serve and went on to win it in three. Howe is still cheesed off."

Laver had another blonde accomplice, Lesley Hunt, and she was enthused about their new alliance. "I didn't know what to expect because most of the men I've played with haven't really tried. I realized they think of mixed as a second-class event, but it's no fun to play with somebody going through the motions. Rod was just great. What a thrill to be on the same court with him and watch him up close."

"I went for a few balls I shouldn't have," sighed Laver, "and when I didn't hit them well enough, I left a big hole open. That hurt us."

Lesley was forgiving, "Any time you have a chance to go for a winner, who am I to complain?" Hunt and Laver had a struggle in beating the sister-brother act of Nancy Gunter and Cliff Richey, 6-3, 2-6, 7-6. But their tiebreaker good fortune ran out in the semis against Casals-Riessen, 2-6, 6-2, 7-6.

It is my contention that the female wins mixed matches and the male loses them. This was confirmed by that semi, turning on Casals' splendid lobs that drove Laver to costly overhead errors. "If Laver has a weakness," said TV commentator Hurricane Donna Fales, "it's his smash on mid-court lobs. Sometimes, anyway." This may be like faulting Sophia Loren for having an ingrown toenail, but Laver does occasionally blow those overheads. At six-points-all in the tiebreaker, Hunt serving to Casals, Rosie lofted her return over netman Laver. It's the standard mixed return for us hackers, and it worked: Rod belted the ball beyond the baseline, then Rosie served it out, scoring the match point with a stinging volley that Laver netted.

"It was enjoyable to play mixed again with the good players," said Rod. "I had intended to rest this week, but Gardner's idea caught my fancy. You like to help out on something new that adds variety to pro tennis and is well run. Lesley," he asked, turning to his partner, "how did it feel to play with 155 pounds on your back?"

Said Hunt, "Is that all you weigh?"

With King and Casals in the lineup, the tournament should have been subtitled the Equality Bowl. They've been on an "equal pay for equal work" campaign for years, and what could have been a better platform for the liberated woman than tending her half of the court for an even split of the goodies? "This tournament," said Billie Jean, "shows you why team tennis will succeed. People love mixed doubles, men and women as partners and opponents. I can understand why the men have brushed mixed off in the past. Like with Laver at Wimbledon, if a guy has a chance in singles and doubles, he doesn't need the mixed. He's usually tired at the end of the day and wants to go home. Women have historically tried harder in mixed, maybe to impress the guys, or show we could play with them. But here everybody's all out. It's great."

Not everybody thought so. Feminist King received a protest from a feminist organization called Women For

Marty Riessen puts away a high, swinging forehand volley. The extent of the follow-through indicates he didn't just punch the ball. Marty and Rosie Casals lost in a four-set final.

Change, asking her to drop out of the tournament. The reason: profits were to defray expenses of the all-male SMU varsity. You can't win.

But Billie Jean—and second banana Davidson—won just the same, though they were two points from defeat in their 6-2, 3-6, 7-6 (9-points-to-7) opener against Francoise Durr and Cliff Drysdale, and had to go the distance in the semi against Wendy Overton and Roy Emerson, 6-3, 3-6, 6-2.

Davidson, who earned $25,000 in 1973 prize money, knew his place alongside King, whose on-court earnings were $184,050. "She's the star—a total equal when we play," said O.K., who would never kick Billie Jean out of court.

"Mervyn Rose, who was coaching us both in 1967, suggested we play together then in the South African. We won and have played together since whenever we can." Their blend had amounted to seven other major titles (three Wimbledon, three U.S., one French), and they brought an 11-match winning streak to Dallas. Davidson won the U.S. title in 1966 with Donna Fales. He started 1967 by winning the Australian with Lesley Turner Bowrey. Then he ditched Lesley for Billie Jean to win at Roland Garros, Wimbledon and Forest Hills, thus completing a personal Grand Slam. The only other mixed Slam was accomplished in 1963 by Margaret Court and Ken Fletcher.

"We should win this," said Davidson. "We're the most experienced pair." So monstrous was that serpentine serve of his that left-handed Davidson went 24 games unbroken, never faced a break point and was skewered at deuce only twice. "Owen's second serve is worse than the first. There's more spin and kick to it," said Casals.

Rosie returned as well as could have been expected, but there was no way she and Marty could wrest his writhing serve from O.K. Ascending acrobatically for smashes, streaking and leaping for volleys and even scoring on a behind-the-back half-volley, The Rosebud emphasized her artistry at doubles. "Couldn't ask for a better partner," applauded Riessen, who has thrice won Forest Hills with Margaret Court. "The difference between Rosie and Margaret?" Riessen answered the question diplomatically. "Oh...about a foot."

"Mixed doubles," says Frank Froehling, "is get-the-woman. If you can. I try to intimidate the opposing woman, bomb my serve, poach whenever I get a chance, feed her plenty of topspin. I'm all over the court, and my partner tries to fill in the holes I leave."

His partner, Kristien Kemmer (they were finalists in the German mixed) said, "That's all right with me. I'm no Libber. The man's the boss out there."

"Of course," said Froehling, "there are women you can't intimidate—like Billie Jean and Rosie."

Davidson agreed, "There isn't a man in tennis who can do anything that worries Billie Jean. So we just play straight doubles. That's why she's so great to play with. I've played a lot of mixed where you have to play the entire court and tell the woman to get out of the way. You have fights. Not with Billie. You know she'll more than handle her half of the court. If we're in a situation where there's a ball down the middle and it's a backhand for both of us, she takes it. With my backhand, why shouldn't she? I'm not a total believer in female equality—but when I play with Billie, that's different. I'm a believer. I'm happy to share the check with her."

"Sorry, Wendy...Sorry, Wendy..." Roy Emerson kept saying, "Sorry, Wendy" as he practiced with Laver the day before the tournament began.

"What are you talking about?" Rod wanted to know.

"I'm just getting ready to be gentlemanly to my partner when I miss a shot."

"You never say 'Sorry, Rod' when you screw one up with me as your partner."

Emmo's tiger grin could be translated: "No, and you're not a fetching blonde."

"I was nervous, all right," said Wendy Overton after she and Emmo had beaten Valerie Ziegenfuss and Roger Taylor, 6-2, 6-3. "I had a crush on Roy when I was a little girl, and here I was on the court with my hero, one of the greatest players of alltime."

"You mean he was your mother's hero," interrupted Taylor.

"But Roy was so nice, and helpful. I lost my nerves," said Wendy.

Ziegenfuss frowned, "I thought he was a nice guy, too—until the first point."

If there was any doubt that gallantry would be out the window, Emerson dispelled it quickly by slicing an ace beyond Val's groping forehand on the opening point of the tournament.

"With this kind of money, nobody's gonna play patty-cake," said Casals.

"Not only that," said Billie Jean, "but it made me choke a couple of times in that tiebreaker against Durr and Drysdale. I was serving at match point (6-points-to-5) and Cliff blasted a backhand return past me. Then I served to Frankie and I really clutched. I nearly put the first serve in the seats. Somehow I got the second one in, and we lucked out the point when Cliff missed a volley. Yeah, I can choke—nobody's immune."

It was Taylor's idea, after he and Ziegenfuss lost so fast, "This ought to be best-of-five. I'm sure the women wouldn't mind." Gardner poled the chickies, finding them eager to try the men's distance, so it was agreed—a best-of-five final. "Now they can't say we don't work as long," chortled King.

Gardner was sorry "that someone like Roger comes all the way from England to play 40 minutes. It's worth it financially to him, but he feels a little cheated and so does the crowd if it's a brief match.

"Next year we may try a round robin like the Grand Prix Masters, or a double elimination."

My suggestion is VASSS round robin medal play to determine semi-finalists, then traditional knockout. Big Daddy VASSS, Jimmy Van Alen, produced a couple of the most exciting pro tourneys ever at Newport with his seldom-seen VASSS medal play format, which guarantees every team seven matches in a draw of eight. Each match is 31-point VASSS. Every point is important since your score, in trying to qualify for one of the semi-final spots, is the sum of the points you score for all rounds comparable to strokes in golf.

Talk to any marriage counselor and you'll learn that mixed doubles has caused more divorces than mothers-in-law. Still, as Donna Fales says, "Husbands and wives continue to try. If you're better than your husband (as ex-First Tenner Fales is), it can be very trying. But Gordon and I work it out...I think. The USLTA even held a national husband-and-wife mixed championship in 1967. One year of that was enough. You could hear the screams and growls all over Forest Hills."

The couple that plays together slays together?

The closest relatives Gardner could talk into his tournament happened to be the "greatest mixed team in Texas history" as the Richeys were introduced by the master of ceremonies. "I swore I'd never play mixed again after Nancy hit me over the head with her racket," said Cliff Richey of sister Nancy Gunter. "That was in the French years ago. I don't think it was intentional—I hope not. We both were going for the same lob, and we both swung...and Nancy got me.

"I swore off, but here we are again. But," said Cliff, "this is different. This has incredible appeal when you concentrate on mixed only, and put up this kind of money."

With the Texas crowd roaring them on, Nancy and Cliff nearly beat Hunt and Laver, slipping at last in the decisive tiebreaker, 7-points-to-2.

"Cliff," said Nancy, "we played one other time, recently. Remember?"

"Oh yeah, but barely. Fortunately. It was Paris again," said Cliff. "Last spring. We decided to try mixed again, but we were better prepared. We drank a bottle of wine just before we went on, and I never enjoyed a 6-0, 6-0 beating so much. Yeah, love and love. We got beat by a couple of Japanese, Sawamatsu and Kamiwazumi. Didn't mind at all."

Wine at the change games—or brandy-soaked sugar cubes in the style of Suzanne Lenglen—might settle uneasy or uncertain partners and bring about a state of mixed without fear.

I don't know if the Spalding International revealed all you wanted to know about mixed but were afraid to ask. Or whether it's time for Alex Comfort to publish an illustrated tome called "The Joy of Mixed"?

However, I do feel confident of this: because of what they got away with in Dallas—no raids, nobody arrested—more and more people are going to throw away their inhibitions and get into mixed doubles. With or without coaching from Masters and Johnson. ●

ARE COACHES DEAD WRONG?

Coaches once said this was a no-no. Rod Laver has just hit a forehand from open stance. Note Aussie grip.

Peter Schroeder

Dick Savitt bucked the Figure 8 backswing theory which was popular in his prime and went on to win Wimbledon. He has taken the racket straight back and makes this forehand with left foot forward instead of crossing it over.

by JULIUS HELDMAN

THEORIES of the proper way to play tennis are as impermanent as champions. A good idea is good only as long as it works and a champion remains the champion until he or she stops winning.

A style of playing cannot be "bad" if it works for a winner. Why tell Francoise Durr to change her oddly constructed backhand if it is her best stroke? (If some other woman tried it she might break her wrist.) The time to change a stroke is when it *doesn't* work; don't learn a new style simply because the "authorities" say your winning style is wrong.

Commonly accepted theories that are no longer commonly accepted are:

Teaching the closed stance on the forehand to beginners. Twenty years ago many pros were telling their pupils to step across with the left foot on the forehand, viz., step toward the alley. Today it would be hard to find a pro who doesn't teach stepping *forward* with the left foot, viz., toward the net. Potential power is lost if the weight moves sideways; weight transfer is automatic when the left foot steps forward.

Taking a Figure 8 backswing. A popular theory a generation ago was the semi-circular backswing on forehand and backhand and a wrap-around-the-neck follow-through on the forehand. A famous teaching pro in the East, as well as a very popular one on the West Coast, had passels of proteges who might have been much better, particularly on fast grass, if the wind-ups and follow-throughs had been shorter. The theory that a big backswing was necessary for power

was disproved by Dick Savitt, who took his racket straight back on the forehand and *always* prepared. Nothing is intrinsically wrong with a straight backswing, and a Figure 8 backswing is only for those who have plenty of time to hit the ball. Go out on grass or fast cement against an attacker who volleys deep to your baseline and then see whether you prefer the semi-circular wind-up.

Avoiding No Man's Land. The area just behind and just in front of the service line was considered out-of-bounds if you wanted to play smart tennis. For 10 years one player, Henri Cochet, defied that theory. He served, came in a few steps, volleyed, came in a few more steps, volleyed again and finally reached the net position. "Only Henri can do that," said the coaches. Net rushers were told to serve and run

California Photo Service

Ken Rosewall's Australian Grip is about half way between classic Eastern and the classic Continental grips.

Trapped behind the service line in No Man's land, John Newcombe readies for a half volley. It is a rare net rusher who can take a first volley as close as 6 feet from the net. Few can serve and come in that fast.

in as fast as they could so as to take the first volley from a position 6 feet from the net. Only Rafe Osuna could run in that fast. When net-rushing became predominant, most players started to take the first volley a foot inside the service line (smack in the middle of No Man's Land). The top players became superb half-volleyers—and the grass at Forest Hills during the U.S. Open is always scuffed worst in No Man's Land; the server stops 2 to 3 feet behind the service line to enable him to change direction, then takes his first volley 1 or 2 feet inside the service line.

Using the Eastern grip. Almost every American coach still teaches an Eastern grip on the forehand, albeit reluctantly allowing an intransigent junior with great talent to let his grip slide toward the Continental when the junior starts beating everyone in sight. Twenty or 30 years ago promising young champions with the "wrong" grip were urged to re-learn their forehands in order to have classi-

cal "Easterns." Eddie Moylan, who had a lovely Continental, was pressed to switch to a lovely Eastern. He did—and he made the First Ten—but he felt he would have been better off with his own natural style. Darlene Hard was one of the two best juniors in Southern California but Perry T. Jones, then the czar of tennis in that area, told her she would never go all the way unless she changed her natural Continental to an Eastern. She won the U.S. National Championships with her new grip, but the first stroke to crack when the pressure was on was her unnatural Eastern. Butch Buchholz won the Juniors with a Continental grip. He was a stubborn kid, never listened to his betters and refused to switch to the "right" stroke; he kept obstinately winning with a Continental. In the last 15 years, every top Australian but one has had a grip halfway between the Eastern and the Continental. Can anyone fault them because they do not conform to American standards?

Both of John Newcombe's feet are off the ground on this serve. It's legal, but look how far he is into court.

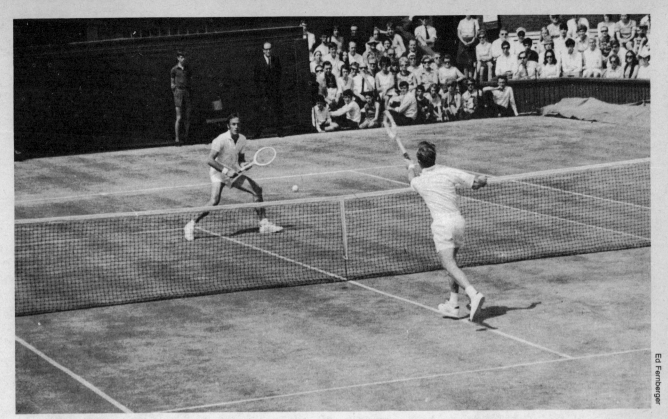

In the 1969 Wimbledon finals, Rod Laver has just hit a forehand stroke volley against John Newcombe. Laver has had great success with the shot. Don Budge, another famous stroke volleyer, took a full backswing on most high balls.

Keeping your feet on the ground on serve. When the footfault rule was changed a dozen years ago, players were no longer required to keep at least one foot on the ground before the ball was hit on serve. A few top players started to jump, hitting the ball while both feet were in the air. Many coaches felt the player would lose power if he wasn't anchored to the ground with at least one foot. But the top players were jumping and those on their way to the top also began to jump. The best a coach can now do is to advise acquiring a good, reliable serve before learning the jump.

Teaching the groundstrokes first. Five years ago almost every novice, whether through private lessons or at large clinics, was taught the forehand first. The volley was considered too advanced for beginners, possibly because the tyro was not able to prepare his way to net or because the forehand was considered more important than the volley. As a result, many non-athletes never could acquire a punch volley because their minds were grooved to groundstroke styles. In the last five years, thousands of men and women in their 30's, 40's and 50's took up tennis. Many older novices wanted to play doubles primarily, and therefore the volley was basic to becoming an adequate partner. Forty years ago it was not uncommon to see all four players on the baseline; today at least two are at net at all times, and in good doubles all four are frequently in. So why not teach the punch volley first? Once it is acquired, the player can then learn the groundstrokes required for baseline play.

Staying back on clay. The champions of the past generally believed that a great groundstroker would always beat a great volleyer. By the 1950s even the great groundstrokers realized the necessity for volleying on grass, and they began to attack just like their net-rushing cohorts. Although coaches agreed that good net-rushers had the edge on fast courts, they were almost unanimous in thinking one had to stay back on slow clay. Most of the great players thought so too—until a few started coming in. Yes, they got passed more often on clay but they also won more. The great clay court baseliners began to discover the benefits of *attacking on a slow surface,* and at this stage in the development of tennis a number of good

players are following serve in with regularity, although the old-time champions feel the odds are better if they play from the back court. Whereas 99 percent of tournament players only came in to net on clay occasionally 20 or 25 years ago (Barry MacKay, the exception, won the Italian Championships by following his serve in every time), more than 50 percent are attacking regularly today.

Punching all volleys. Everyone is taught a punch volley (taking the ball in front of the body with a short underspin jab) and is warned *never* to stroke a volley (taking a forehand drive swing on a high ball). Stroke volleys are too dangerous, say the coaches. Tell that to Don Budge, who always stroke-volleyed high balls, or to Rod Laver, who whacks every high ball with a stroke volley and scores an extremely high percentage of outright winners. The stroke volley has its use (on high balls), and a pro who tells a tournament player not to use it on high shots may be doing his pupil a disservice. In five years we may see the stroke volley as a part of every good player's repertoire.

The shibboleths of tennis exist only as long as they work. ●

NASTASE

Born to eccentricity, Ilie Nastase fits no pattern but his own.

by REX BELLAMY

THERE WERE mixed feelings at the end of the year when it became clear that, for the first time, Ilie Nastase had established himself—by a small but solid margin—as the best tennis player in the world. He had won the French and Italian championships, the Masters tournament, the Grand Prix series and $228,750. In terms of talent and achievement, personality and entertainment value, his supremacy is frankly recognized. But in terms of court conduct, few regard him as an ideal example for the aspiring young. In some ways he lacks the character of a natural leader.

The Muhammad Ali of tennis is an artist, a salesman for the game: but prone to excesses of showmanship. There is a hazy frontier between the delightful and the distasteful. Nastase's virtuosity is dazzling, his ebullience engaging. But his career has been blotted by incidents in which his attitude towards opponents, officials, spectators, and the game as a whole has fallen short of the courtesy we reasonably expect from the man at the top. Tennis is part of the entertainment industry. Its leading players have a responsibility to communicate pleasure. But they must be mindful of the boundaries of decent behavior.

When Nastase mischievously lopes to the net behind a half-pace, three-quarter length approach shot, defying his opponent to pass him, he reminds us of Ali dropping his arms to offer a deceptively inviting open target. Both are probably incapable of giving 100 per cent unless they fool around a little. "It's part of my game," says Nastase. "If I don't laugh on court, and do my gestures, it's not my game. I say to my wife 'If I don't get mad sometimes, I can't play.' It's like sitting at a table and watching the other guy eating. I don't enjoy it."

There is no harm in Nastase's tactical conceit, and no harm in a certain amount of clowning between games, or even between points. Indeed, the game would be less fun if all that went out of it. But it is inexcusable when Nastase mocks opponents or officials, bangs loose balls into the crowd, puts on an act between his opponent's first and second services, or does anything else to break the other man's concentration at crucial moments. Some players are more vulnerable than others. Tom Okker tends to be an intense and often irritable competitor. Twice in recent months (at London's Albert Hall and then in Boston) he reasonably objected when Nastase impishly pointed to the intended target area before hitting a smash. Okker argued that the pointing finger was a distraction to a player who should be watching the ball. And Okker was right.

On the other hand, Nastase and the equally exuberant Jimmy Connors gave the Albert Hall public some memorable comedy—in addition to highly skilled and dramatic tennis—in that same Dewar Cup tournament. A few conservatives were uneasy, but most of us accepted the match on the players' terms and enjoyed it as much as they did. Bantering asides punctuated the entire match, even its crises. In the third set Connors was serving at 3-5 and 30-love but was off target with a backhand down the line.

"I had to try that."

"Try again," suggested Nastase.

"Next time I might make it."

At 5-4 Nastase prepared to serve for the match. There was a respectful silence: but it could not quell Connors' appreciation of the drama.

"It's now or never, eh?"

Nastase won the first point: 15-love. "I think it's never for you."

And in the tiebreak Connors, two points to six down (match point), paused to admit: "I'm nervous…"

It was that kind of match from start to finish. And as long as Nastase and Connors keep the right balance between tennis and comedy, we shall look forward to many more like it. They give and take pleasure. Their enjoyment is infectious. But only a small minority of players can combine badinage with their best tennis—a mixture that demands an uncommon capacity for switching the concentration on and off. Connors seems to appreciate this more than Nastase, whose tendency to see himself as the star of the show sometimes leads him to forget the feelings of his fellow actors.

Lilly Wollerner

Richard Evans

TOP: Ilie Nastase, the imp, peeps over his sunglasses. He once appeared at Wimbledon as an ice lolly vendor. LEFT: On court Ilie's tennis is daring, spectacular and entertaining. BELOW: Dominique and Ilie enjoy a moment together in Stockholm.

Albert Evans

Of his famous court temperament, the 27-year-old Romanian says: "If I don't get mad sometimes, I can't play. It's like sitting at a table and watching the other guy eating. I don't enjoy it."

Nastase is a child of Nature, at the mercy of his moods. Many pretend to eccentricity. Nastase was born to it. He fits no pattern except his own. We must remember that the game's code of behavior sprang from an Anglo-Saxon tradition that is alien to many who play it. There is plenty of room for the fresh approach of a Nastase. If the man had more self-discipline, we might admire his conduct more but enjoy his tennis less.

He is a free spirit whose independence takes many forms (not the least of them the fact that it blossomed under a communist regime). He was tardy in joining the Association of Tennis Professionals. "Everybody was joined. Only myself and Kodes and a few guys. The first time, I didn't believe it would be strong enough. But after a year I joined, at Paris." He was also slow to accept the rigorous challenge of the World Championship Tennis tour, preferring the milder competitive climate of Bill Riordan's indoor circuit. "Two reasons. First of all, I agree with Bill to play his tournaments. Second, I was just married and take off a month and a half and was not prepared."

Nastase turned down a WCT offer of $100,000 a year for four years. The story of his later decision to join WCT is typical of his reluctance to commit himself, and his capacity for giving everything the stamp of theater. Last summer, on the Thursday of Wimbledon's first week, Nastase and his wife Dominique were invited to dinner by WCT's international director, John McDonald. But Nastase could not sign the agreement because he did not have it with him. So on Sunday morning (the deadline for WCT signings) McDonald went to the Nastases' London hotel. Dominique said she would get the agreement from Ilie. But the moment was not propitious: he had someone with him.

"That's it," thought McDonald. He walked slowly out of the hotel, got into his car, and turned into the stream of traffic. As it built up behind him, he glanced in the rear-view mirror and saw Ilie Nastase sitting in the back of a black Hillman Minx. It drew up alongside, and Nastase wound down the window. In his hand was the agreement. He passed it from the window of one moving car through the window of another. McDonald just had time to flip over the pages and make sure Nastase had signed. He had.

That was a dramatic weekend for Nastase. The previous day Alexander Mayer had beaten him at Wimbledon. Now he handed over his signed WCT agreement in the nick of time as two cars slowly nosed their way along Cromwell Road. Nastase also took his time considering the prospective merits of World Team Tennis. "Maybe it's a good idea. But it will take time to see how it's going. There are not enough matches (I don't think they have time). But it would be good to have like the Davis Cup. Or four singles and one women's singles."

Obviously he has more freedom than most east Europeans. "I have to play Davis Cup. That is the only thing. Otherwise I can play where I like." And what happens to the money? "I just want that people know I pay tax like in every country." The youngest of five children, he was born on July 19, 1946. His father, now retired, worked in a bank. He has three sisters and a brother, Constantin, who coaches at Pisa. "He played Davis Cup a few years ago, when Tiriac was young." That was in 1959, in fact, and Tiriac was already good enough to replace the elder Nastase in the Romanian team for the second round.

Until Nastase was 10, they lived in a house at the Progresul Club in Bucharest, scene of the controversial 1972 Davis Cup final. "But my parents never played and they never watch me. Not interested." He was seven or eight when he took up tennis. "Against a wall. Because I was not allowed to play. I began when I was 13. My first tournament, I win my group: 13-14. In 1959. My first new racket was English Slazenger. I remember well. 'All-White.' For winning 13-14. That was my prize money. I also have talent to play soccer. I was playing until 16 or 17. I try to play well—soccer and tennis. Then I switch from football to racket. The first time I left Romania was to Sofia, not far. I go with Tiriac and Marmureanu."

In 1966 Nastase made his Davis Cup debut and played his first Wimbledon. For a few years he was a kind of Trilby to Ion Tiriac's Svengali. His talent was obvious and gradually his boisterously bizarre personality began to emerge through his early inhibitions. But he was not widely respected as a competitor, except in doubles—in which Tiriac managed to harness the younger man's flair for the game. Tiriac provided the emotional and tactical cement in the partnership. He shared Nastase's liking for amateur dramatics on court. But Tiriac was more calculated about it. His behavior was directed by a strong character and sharp wits. When Nastase was playing singles, the massively brooding Tiriac was usually somewhere in the crowd, watching his compatriot with a quiet intensity that suggested a transfer of will.

Tiriac was friend and father-figure, mentor and interpreter, coach and model. He was the best player Romania had produced. Nastase eventually supplanted him in that role. For a while, Tiriac seemed to feed on Nastase's virtuosity and rumbustious zest, as if rejuvenated by it. On and off court, they were a lively and stimulating double act.

In 1969 they played their first Davis Cup tie on grass, beating Britain at Wimbledon to reach the challenge round for the first time. Two weeks later, Nastase marked his first appearance at Forest Hills by beating Stan Smith. In 1970 they won the French and Italian doubles championships—and Nastase became the first Romanian to appear on the list of Wimbledon champions when he shared the mixed with Rosemary Casals. In singles, he won the Italian title and was runner-up for the German (a bigger event then than it is now).

In 1971 Nastase was runner-up for the French championship. Then came the first proof that he could "win big" against the toughest opposition on a fast surface. That was in the Embassy tournament on a Nygrass carpet at Wembley in London. His victims included Roy Emerson, John Newcombe, and Rod Laver. "I am too good for these guys—too much talent," he told us after beating Newcombe. But he had mixed feelings about that run of success: because it was prolonging his separation from a new friend, an alarmingly attractive young lady called Dominique ("Niky") Grazia. "I want to go to Brussels," he said. "But I keep winning!"

The romance was still young. "I meet her at Forest Hills. She has younger sister, Nathalie, who like me at tennis. Mother promise that if Nathalie do well at school, she go to Forest Hills to watch. Mother and Niky come too. I play doubles with Tiriac. Three women watch and applaud like crazy. I ask friend if Dominique would like dinner. She say no, because she is already having dinner. Maybe second day. So I meet Dominique because of sister."

That was an important year for Nastase—the French final, Dominique, Wembley, and then a cherished win over Stan Smith on his way to the Masters title in Paris. In 1972 Smith beat him in a memorable Wimbledon final, but Nastase soon had the compensation of becoming United States champion. Of the major tournaments, Nastase thinks most often of Wimbledon. "I win Paris and Rome and Forest Hills. I don't think about them any more. But I think 1972 was the only chance to win Wimbledon. I don't know when I shall be so close. But maybe if I win Wimbledon, I don't win Forest Hills."

"I prefer to win Wimbledon, because for every player it is the best you can win. I prefer the clay courts, because I built my game on clay courts. But after playing so much on faster courts, I don't mind so much. I like England, because I have my fan club there and the people seem to like me so much. Also I like to play in France and Italy and the United States."

Dominique is half Belgian, half French. They had a civil wedding in Brussels followed by a religious wedding in Paris. There should have been a third, in Bucharest. "But we missed third, because we didn't have time. Must go honeymoon. And I can't do another wedding, because I get tired of being married. There are a lot of things to resist when you get married in Romania. You have to eat and drink a lot, to dance, to meet a lot of people. You really celebrate."

The Nastases have a rented apartment in Brussels and own a house in Bucharest ("and now, I hope, in the United States"). The new partnership is working well. "Niky is good for me. And she is my secretary."

Nastase's rise to international fame has inevitably earned him off-court benefits. "Just now I sign with Guy Laroche" (one of the leading Parisian couturiers). "He make special mode, personal mode. Suits. For the street. Not for tennis. Francois Cevert, racing driver, was model for him, also Jean-Claude Bouttier, boxer. Cevert die. I take place of Cevert. I am also professional representing Princess Hotel at Acapulco and Southampton, Bermuda. They are two the same. I make clinics and talk to people."

The future, after tennis? "I don't have time to think about this. And to be honest, I don't want to think about it. You have to have the help of money. Things would be much more nice, because with money you can do a lot of things. But now I am playing tennis." Here was another reminder that, though Nastase may be impulsive over little things, he thinks carefully before making the decisions that matter most. In the game of life, as in tennis, he has learned to discipline his natural disposition to play from the heart rather than the head. But a spirit of adventure and a taste for drama are deeply entrenched in his character.

Tennis will be richer if all of us can enjoy the sight and sound of him for a few more years. A rubbery athlete with an instinctive gift for improvization, he has astonishing speed or reflexes and footwork, a facile command of spin and touch and an abundance of shots. He knows how to play the percentages—but is never happier than when demonstrating that he is artist enough to defy them. And off court, we relish the confidence and wit with which he comperes his press conferences as if presiding at a talk show (again, a parallel with Ali). We may not entirely approve of the showman we call "Nasty." But we should certainly miss him. ●

The Intersexual Saga of Tennis

by BUD COLLINS

THE *Intersexual Saga of Tennis was a triangle involving Margaret Court, aging Bobby Riggs and Billie Jean King in 1973, and kept the world amused for half the year. First, Bobby–a quarter-century past his prime–challenged Court, and beat her. They played off the beaten court at Ramona, Calif. So then, King challenged Bobby, and beat him in the glare of a worldwide spotlight at the Astrodome where the largest crowd ever to watch tennis sat in person or eavesdropped via TV. Though a match that decided nothing, Riggs-King was undoubtedly the most compelling in the history of the game.*

Riggs ruining Mother's Day

A Dirty Old Man named Riggs is geritoling himself up to spoil Mother's Day for Margaret Court, which may be the meanest thing a guy has done since a Greek named Oedipus got carried away as mama's little helper.

But Margaret Court isn't Bobby Riggs' mother. She's younger, bigger, stronger, faster than this 55-year-old tennis hustler, who has set himself up as the Great Chauvinist Hope by challenging the world's No. 1 broad to a friendly little game—for $10,000.

Just a few friends in to observe, at San Diego Estates—plus the millions who'll be watching an international telecast, watching over Margaret's powerful right shoulder to see if she can shut up and shut off the little pest.

Boy and man, Robert Larimore Riggs—Wimbledon champ in 1939, US champ in 1939-41—has been scheming and scuffling, contriving this kind of come-on: where it looks like he's loaded himself with too much of a handicap. That's where the action begins, and Bobby always suggests there ought to be an amicable bet to keep the interest up.

Action is what Riggs lives for, like that Greek named Nick. Bobby will play anybody for money. Anybody. You…me…your mother-in-law…Stan Smith…Rod Laver. "We can set things up to make it interesting," says Bobby, who has handicapped himself by giving away huge point-spots; carrying fully-packed suitcase throughout a match; holding a dog on a leash.

"Riggs stories get exaggerated," he laughed over the phone. "It's not true that I played while holding a baby elephant on a rope. Even a baby elephant's too damn big. But I have tied myself to a poodle, which can make it tough to move. You can trip on that leash. It's even worse if the dog ain't housebroke.

"Now for you…uh," he mused, "I'll give you the two chairs. For a grand, Ok?"

What's the two chairs, Bobby?

"You can put two chairs anywhere in my court, and we'll play a match. Naturally, you hit the chairs, or maneuver me into them, I lose the points. I can't beat you, but it'll be fun."

No thanks, Bobby.

"Tell Laver I'll play him that way—only I put the chairs in his court," Riggs said.

Margaret Court, who has won more major titles than anybody to play the game—male or female—isn't betting with Riggs, though. Not money anyway. It will be a straight match. No gimmicks—except, obviously the whole thing is a gigantic promotional gimmick grabbing the imagination of us all involved in the perennial war of the sexes. All three TV networks fought to cop the program. CBS won.

Although it's being billed as "winner-take-all" for 10-grand, the Mother's Day Melee will mean much more to the women's movement in tennis. If Margaret loses, the money might not be enough consolation. "I'm not worried about it," she says, but—silly as it is—what she's betting may be the newly established prestige of women's tennis. This is what Bobby challenged: "I don't know why those dames are making big money, and complaining that they should get as much as the men. They're not as good. A broken down old guy like me can beat the best of them."

That started it. His verbal challenge went out along with I-dare-you telegrams to Court, Billie Jean King, Nancy Gunter and Chris Evert. Margaret accepted, saying, "I've beaten better men than Bobby in practice matches."

This isn't practice. Yet it isn't anything. Any really decent male player can beat the finest females at tennis. You could quickly name four or five guys in Boston who'd take Margaret apart: Paul Sullivan, Ned Weld, Jerry Cromwell, Ferdi Taygan, Chum Steele. There are several hundred across the country.

But the brashness of the aging con man in short pants—the fact that he was a "name"—has made it a classic of hype and ballyhoo, something like a big fight between boxers of contrasting styles. Probably the match itself won't compare with the buildup. Bobby loves it. His name is alive again, and he's giving the foe the kind of edge that makes talk and betting inevitable: Can Margaret, with physical and chronological superiority, outgun the crafty ancient?

Billie Jean King worries, "Our (the female pros) reputation is at stake, and I'm afraid Bobby will win. His nerves are too tough for Margaret, and Margaret wasn't too well at Sea Pines last week. Here's an old jerk, who dyes his hair, waddles like a duck, and has trouble seeing. Everybody knows the good men are better than the good women—but if a guy like Bobby can beat our best…well, that has to hurt us. We have nothing to gain. If Margaret beats an old guy, so what?"

When money's involved, look out for Riggs. He carries his own bookmaker (posing as a spectator) to lay on and lay off bets in the grandstand. Bobby made $100,000 betting on himself to win all three events (singles, doubles and mixed) at Wimbledon 34 years ago. "It was legal, with a bookie," he recalls. "I just let 100 pounds ride (worth about $500 then) at 3-to-1 for the singles, 6-to-1 for the doubles and 12-to-1 for the mixed. Of course if I lost in any of the three I lost my dough. Five hundred bucks was a lot of money in 1939... for an amateur tennis player," he laughs. So was 100 grand. "I've still got a bank account in England," he says.

Tennis isn't a betting sport in this country, but for one day, Riggs will change that. He'll have thousands going in side bets himself, the way he always has. He revels in that nervous atmosphere. It's new to Margaret.

People who've watched Riggs' action matches wonder, though, as Rod Laver puts it: "If Bobby has bet on Margaret and will go into the tank?"

Or maybe she'll rise to the bait magnificently. Maybe, as Rosie Casals hopes, "Margaret will run him to a coronary." So do Susan B. Anthony, Amelia Bloomer, Victoria Woodhull and the Libbers of Bobby's vintage who'll be looking down from that great court in the sky. Plus Margaret's contemporaries such as Gloria Steinem, Germaine Greer and Betty Friedan, who'll audit TV.

Porcine instincts have led me to put my money on Bobby, who has all angles, on court and off. But my heart's with Margaret. I mean, how can I cheer against a big mama on Mother's Day?

Bobby the wolf and Little Red Riding Hood

When he poses nude for the centerfold of Geriatrics Digest, what shade should Bobby Riggs dye his hair?

Will he accept an offer from Bertolucci to play the lead in a musical of "Last Tango in Paris"?

Can he maneuver himself into a best-of-three challenge from Linda Lovelace?

Is it time for him to begin peddling "You've Come a Long Way, Bobby!" bumper stickers?

Or marketing his "Oldie but Goodie" superiority complex vitamins for senile swingers?

Must tiny Bobby fight a duel with 6-foot-5 inch Barry Court for dishonoring—and devaluing—Barry's wife and meal ticket? And if so, will it be the Australian's choice of weapons: beer cans and boomerangs at 30 paces?

These are among the problems of sudden fame for Robert Larimore Riggs, who has come up with a new schtick: mugging young ladies with a wooden club in broad daylight—on international TV yet. Instead of being arrested, he is hailed as a defender of the faith in faded fathers.

That tells you what's happened to law and order. In the old days they'd have strung up this dirty old man for molesting an innocent who didn't know any better. Today he gets celebrity rating, and acclaim as the greatest sex symbol for the aged since Strom Thurmond.

Bobby never got this much attention when he was playing straight tennis. But papa's got a brand new bag. In fact he'd like to find one every week. If he could only pass, Riggs would make a million on the Virginia Slims circuit. No chance there. Judge Bookman of Houston, an official of the women's pro tour, says, "We won't accept Bobby in our tournaments. Not even in drag. The only way we'll let him enter is if he gets the operation and the silicone treatments."

Is that reverse discrimination?

But you're wrong if you think I'm gloating. Or pleased because I advised you to re-finance the house and put it on Bobby. True I'm dining out handsomely on numerous bets I collected, but I'm only just catching up. Remember me: I'm the guy who picked Dewey over Truman; Liston over Ali; Poland to win World War II; and Westmoreland over the Viet Cong.

Sure, Bobby gave a boost to the Social Security set. You had to admire his gall and ability, and put him up there in your pantheon alongside Ponzi, Billy Sol Estes, Willie Sutton, John Mitchell and the rest of the quick-fingered and flim-flamming. It was the old carny gig, and Bobby was playing the shell game with the rube from the Outback.

Yet only a sadist could have enjoyed watching. It was one of those things you have to see, like a bull fight or a geek eating broken glass. A spectacle, a happening, a public execution. But what was poor Margaret doing there? This wasn't her milieu and she found out quick. This wasn't Mrs. Muscle slugging out the less quick and strong on the lawn at tea-time while hushed worshippers watch appreciatively in a cathedral called Wimbledon. It was Little Red Riding Hood walking into the poolroom to test Wolf Bobby at 8-ball.

Even Wimbledon turned on her once, in 1971. They were tired of Margaret winning everything by then. When fresh-faced Evonne Goolagong appeared to captivate London, the hostility of the crowd—yes those mannered Limies—made her choke. It was quiet, subtle hostility, but the evil messages got to her then. England cried out for Goolagong, just as mankind prayed for Riggs. Anybody who witnessed Court's collapse marked her nerves as suspect in any confrontation at the climax of a publicity build-up.

So why did she stray? "Money," says Billie Jean King. "Margaret couldn't resist a guaranteed $10,000."

Could you, B.J.?

"I did," says Billie Jean, who appears next in line to try to vindicate womankind against St. Bobby, patron saint of dirty old men everywhere. Six weeks ago, amidst furious negotiations involving the three networks, Billie Jean said, "if I'm going to risk my reputation, it won't be for 10-grand." Her price was somewhere between $25,000 and $50,000, and the networks said no-thanks.

"I didn't think Margaret's nerves would hold up," King said, "but I didn't think she'd play so awful either. This hurts us. This is why I'm challenging Bobby. Somebody's got to shut him up, and show the public what's happening. I don't mean we can beat top men—but we can play well and fight. Margaret was awful. It wasn't a real indication of our tennis." B.J. at least has the style, combativeness and chutzpah to beat him.

As challenger, she wants men's rules (three of five sets), and her own court in Sea Pines, S.C. The resort she represents there will put up $10,000 for the winner. Of course there'll be added TV revenue, and the challenger. King, will want a big chunk of that.

So there may be another sideshow. Riggs has to hope so. He could become more famous than Bluebeard for pushing chickies around. And if he runs out of opponents, it's either silicone, or back to backgammon hustling.

Nuts, shekels in Astrodome

"I want you to shuffle off to Houston," said the boss.

"Houston?"

"That's right," he said. "The Astrodome..."

"Football game? Ali fighting again?"

"Nope. Tennis. Some old guy's playing a broad, and people are buying tickets. The honor of old guys and broads is supposed to be at stake..."

"Come off it, boss...you got to be kidding...a tennis game in the Astrodome?"

And that's how I wound up in the middle of a pecan grove on the outskirts of Houston, Texas. It seemed appropriate with all those nuts around that a tennis court had been built here only yesterday morning and carpenters were hammering away in the completion of grandstands as The Broad in question, Billie Jean King, skipped onto this court in her blue suede sneakers.

Promptly she beat up in succession Cynthia Doerner (6-0, 6-4) and Kristien Kemmer (6-0, 6-2). Only these weren't sparring partners, and this wasn't a hideaway in the wilds as the heavyweight champ of the tennis branch of the women's movement got ready for the champion of the dirty old men, Bobby Riggs.

It was the $30,000 Virginia Slims of Houston Tournament at the Net Set Club which is attached to a housing development, and Billie Jean was playing and winning her first two rounds—"be back Friday for the quarter-finals, after I get through with Bobby," she promised the promoter, Hugh Sweeney.

What was she doing out there on that steaming asphalt court playing real, live matches with all that alleged honor and genuine money at stake two nights later in the Dome? "Well, I committed myself to this tournament before I signed for Riggs," said Billie Jean, who could take away as much as $190,000 if she wins, and will settle for about $120,000 otherwise. "Besides I needed the work."

It seemed like Muhammad Ali taking on a couple of minor contenders for pocket money the week of a title fight. Not even Ali would do that. Suppose she broke a leg or pulled a muscle or had her head split open by an aggrieved opponent. "I'm not worried about my health now," said Billie Jean, who had gone groggy in her last two big matches, losing to Julie Heldman at Forest Hills and Chris Evert at Hilton Head, S.C., and had hurt her knee less than a month ago. "I'm stronger than ever."

That seems to be the King theme. "My vibes are good, and I feel like Helen Reddy singing, 'I Am Woman'." Which Ms. Reddy, who's appearing in Houston, may do in a serenade to Billie Jean prior to the match. It sounds like the sort of hype Bundini would pull for Ali.

As you can gather, the promotion evokes the heavyweight brouhahas of Ali in the Dome. I keep looking for Big Cat Williams or Buster Mathis to show up in the umpire's chair.

Larry King, watching his infrequent roommate put away two opponents in less than two hours, seems to have it in perspective: "Little and big," said Ms. King's Mr. King. "Little meaning, but big attention. Good for the game." Better for his bank account, since attorney King is also Billie Jean's agent.

"It's show biz, of course it is," said Billie Jean. "That's

Billie Jean tactfully holds down net, so that 55-year-old Bobby can easily clear it during publicity build-up for match.

what sports is today. But," she narrowed her blue eyes, "when the match starts the BS is over and Bobby better believe it. He isn't BS-ing me when it begins because that's when I start hitting shots. He better not try giving me flowers like he did Margaret Court. I told him I'm giving him a subscription to Ms. Magazine, and he didn't know what I was talking about. No awareness, that man. But I like him. He's made this match take off. I don't think he's the chauvinist he says he is. He talks so chauvinist that some of the chauvinists can't take him.

"He said he'd jump off a bridge if he loses. Well, man, I'll be out there selling tickets for the bridge-jumping. He says I can't take the pressure. Tell me this—has he ever played this big a money-pressure match?

"Who has the most to lose in this?" she paused for a moment. "Heck, he does. If I win, Bobby's through. Who'd pay to watch him against a top old guy? Pancho Gonzalez would kill him.

"Bobby needs us!"

So he does, the clever little piggy. Where would Bobby be without women, indeed? "I hope all his women keep him up for this," said BJ. "He'll need all the help he can get.

"He doesn't turn me on with those legs of his. I can be sexist, too. I know a couple of sportswriters with legs better than Bobby's." Bless you, dear.

I never heard Buster Mathis knock Ali's legs, but Billie Jean is starting to talk tougher than any of the fighters who've come into the Dome. "I can go the distance (best-of-five sets for the first time in her career) with any old guy even if he's in as good shape as Bobby."

That was all she had to say about Robert Larimore Riggs, the white, middle-aged, hard-of-hearing Muhammad Ali. "Now I'm going to practice against men, rest, and talk to nobody," said Billie Jean, leaving me where I belonged—in the middle of a pecan grove with the rest of the nuts.

Riggs serves pure schlock

Little Bobby Riggs was up past his bedtime, and his big brother, John Riggs, 63, was pouting and muttering, "Sure he was a fresh punk when he was a kid—but he wasn't this bad. Come on, Bobby, you got to get your rest. You got to take this thing seriously..."

Bobby Riggs, who has done more to advance the cause of womanhood than anybody since Jack the Ripper, was scrunched up in an easy chair in green-and-gold ski pajamas. His eager Koala bear face was dominated by an open mouth as he talked and gorged on vitamin capsules. You may have your daily glass of orange juice, but Riggs daily has 2000 oranges—"that's the equivalent in the amount of Vitamin C he takes," said his nutrition engineer, Rheo H. Blair, who lounged at Bobby's elbow, ingesting pills himself.

It was about one in the morning, and Bobby was feeling very good. Earlier in the evening, at his workout across the street from his motel, he'd lifted $1000 from a local banker named Sanders, a joyous holdup with racket—joyous for both. "These Texans are big sports all right. They come from all over to play me and lose. They love it. A hundred bucks is the minimum," said Bobby. Another contributor to the Riggs campaign fund was a Congressman, Rep. Bill Archer (R-Tex.). "He flew in from Washington just to play, paid his hundred, and flew off again with his button and his purple heart.

"They all want to be hustled by the Happy Hustler. When I beat them I give them a button that says 'I've Been Hustled by Bobby Riggs.' And a little purple heart pin."

Another of the hustled was Dr. Denton Cooley. "You know, the heart guy. He told me a man my age (55) shouldn't play singles. Then he examined me and said I've got the heart of a 40-year-old." A 40-year-old lion.

The phones were ringing. Lorne Kuhle—Riggs' top sparring partner was acting as a buffer. But Bobby was on two calls at once. And on, on, on continually in person. A masterful social juggler. "Yeah, Jim Welch...how are you

Pre-match publicity turned the contest into a confrontation between women's lib and male chauvinism.

Jim...how are things in Boston?" Bobby spoke into a phone. "Don't forget you're bringing down that 16-pound all-day sucker for me to give to Billie Jean. What a lollipop!" Riggs said to the candy manufacturer. "Just another surprise for her..."

The pill man, Rheo Blair, passed a plate containing 20-or-so capsules to Bobby. "Time for more," Blair said. "Bobby takes more than 500 a day, but some days he can't get down more than 300..."

Bobby grimaced and said in a low voice, "who the hell knows if they do any good...but it's psychological. He's got me believing they've rejuvenated me. And if you believe...but I think all these pill are giving me a glass stomach."

"It's the ortho-molecular approach of mega-doses," Blair was saying. "These pills, among other things give him the equivalent of six pounds of beef and two pounds of liver a day. Liver's very important for stamina. You know," said Blair, a wavy-haired, youthful Californian. "They did some tests on rats with these liver doses. They had two rats. One they gave the massive doses, and the other, nothing. Then they threw the rats in freezing water. Of course they died. But the one that took all the liver lasted for hours; the other was gone in a few minutes..."

Munching away like an experimental rodent himself, Bobby screeched, "but I'm not playing this match with Billie Jean in ice water, Rheo. This is a tennis match, not a swimming meet."

Supposedly it is a tennis match that Bobby will indulge in with Billie Jean King at the Astrodome, but it's become more than that. No matter how you feel about the young libber against the old libertine, Bobby has turned it into Schlock 'Round the Clock.

And reveling in every second of it. Riggs is no Walter Mitty. He was a great player once, the best in the world in 1946 when he took the pro tour away from Don Budge. But in those days he never sucked up as much glory as he wallows in now. No magazine covers. No TV, No universal celebrity. "I was big with people who followed tennis, but that was a minority. It was nothing like today, and I love it. Maybe I'm a gladiator against Women's Lib, but a lot of women love me. More than ever.

"But," he said, pleading celibacy during his last days of half-hearted training, "all I'm doing with my bosom buddies (as he calls his female friends) is shaking hands.

"Hey," he jumped up, "look at these costumes people want me to wear for the match." He began to model creations that had come in from designers across the country. One, baby blue with stars and "Bobby Riggs—Men's Libber" on the back, was decorated by probably the first codpiece to adorn a pair of tennis shorts.

"Look at this." He slipped on a T-shirt with cutouts, baring his breasts.

His white-haired big brother, John, snapped, "Take that off, Bobby, and don't wear it. It's nauseous in the extreme. Bobby was never this bad as a kid. Go to bed. You need your rest. Billie Jean's resting."

"But not sleeping," Bobby says. "She's got to be worrying about me. But, OK, John. My brother's had four heart attacks and I don't want to upset him."

Little Bobby Riggs finally did as he was told. The monologue ended momentarily, and he went to bed and dreams of sugar plum hustles danced in his head.

Wrinkled tiger tests the lady

The lady or the wrinkled tiger?

The goddess of the tennis auxiliary of Women's Lib or the sex god of the Geritol Generation?

Billie Jean or Bobby?

Who knows or who cares?

Apparently an awful lot of men and women across this Watergate-crashed country, who are debating and betting on the subject of Billie Jean in Wonderland against Mad Hatter Riggs. Curiouser and curiouser gets the spectacle which may be the best floated issue since the South Sea Bubble gang was watering stocks in 1711.

But your curiosity should be satisfied when through the looking glass of TV Billie Jean King and Robert Larimore Riggs—"born the same year as her father, 1918"—will perform in the living rooms of America.

Opposite them on another channel will be that other lovable couple, "Bonnie and Clyde," who had their own racket: robbing banks. It wasn't nearly as profitable, but it may have been more honorable than a fresh old man picking on a fresh-faced young woman. Or vice versa.

If you're silly-rich and curious, of course you're right here at the gates of the Astrodome, paying $100 a seat for the right to be close enough to sniff the athletes, who will have doused themselves in cosmetics they've endorsed. You can get in for $6, too, but those seats are as far away as East Boston. It will mostly be the more expensive seats swelling the crowd to as many as 35,000.

Never have so many people witnessed in person a game of tennis, if that's what is it.

"It's more, much more—the battle of the sexes," trumpeted Bobby Riggs for the 2,081,917th time. "Man against woman; sex against sex; an old one-foot-in-the-grave champion against the current Wimbledon champion. People can identify. Husbands argue with wives, bosses with secretaries. Everybody wants to bet." (The odds are 2½-1 Riggs, according to Jimmy-the-Greek Snyder who arrived from Las Vegas.) "It's great for the game—and it isn't bad for Riggs and King." Hardly: The winner will take at least $200,000, the loser half that amount.

Seldom has a champion been so overconfident as Riggs, the self-proclaimed monarch of women's tennis by virtue of his 6-2, 6-1 molesting of Margaret Court in May.

"Are you sure you can win, dad?" asked his 16-year-old son, Billy.

"Son, no broad is gonna beat me."

Regretfully, that's my feeling. Riggs in four sets is my sexist, piggy guess, but I wouldn't go into mourning if Billie Jean shoved the little con man's other foot into that grave he keeps citing. Could it be Miami Beach '64 all over again: the speed and youth of Billie Jean overcoming the fearsome, elder Riggs, as Muhammad Ali did Sonny Liston? The comparison isn't quite apt since Riggs in spirit out-Ali's Ali. "That man talks better'n Ali," said George Foreman, imported to present the winner's check.

"I'll tell you why I'll win," says Riggs. "She's a woman, and they just don't have the emotional stability. She'll choke just like Margaret Court did."

That infuriates King, who's been a big-match player. "That creep runs down women, that's why my feeling is like—hate. I like him for many things, but I hate him put-ting down women, not giving us credit as competitors."

"Please don't call me a creep," Bobby asked her at a joint press conference. "You don't mean it."

"Creep...that stands," said BJ.

Lorne Kuhle, Riggs' sparring partner, worried, "he's exhausting himself having a ball. Look at that..."

Riggs was leading his buxom cheerleaders in Riggs cheers at a Riggs pep rally in his hotel ballroom. He's been as accessible as a Combat Zone hooker, while Billie Jean has pretty much secluded herself—"psyching myself up."

Both are driven winners, and somewhere in the midst of a super-hype that would make P. T. Barnum weep in envy, they will play a tennis match to the hilt. Billie Jean is OK at Wimbledon. How will she be in Wonderland?

"If I lose, it's not the end. I know where I stand in women's tennis," she says. "If Bobby loses, he can go back to his booze and broads in Beverly Hills—but that's it in tennis."

"If I lose?" mused Riggs. "I guess I'll be marked the biggest talking bum of all time. I'll head for that bridge to jump off."

"Suicide Bridge in Pasadena?" somebody asked, remembering Bobby had mentioned the notorious structure.

"Hell, no," replied Riggs. "I'll go to Lake Havasu in Arizona and leap from London Bridge that they've put up there. It's about 10 feet. I've got too much money in the bank, and I'm having too much fun to go jumping off serious bridges."

Love at last sight . . .

Susan B. Anthony, Elizabeth Cady Stanton, Joan of Arc, Amelia Bloomer, Emmaline Pankhurst, Carrie Nation, Molly Pitcher and a lot of other bygone heroines must have been rocking on that great court in the sky when their spiritual descendant, Billie Jean King, landed on Bobby Riggs like a ton of mascara.

"How did Bobby play?" Billie Jean was answering questions following her emotionally uplifting 6-4, 6-3, 6-3 triumph over the Voice of Chauvinism in the tumult amidst the tumult created by 30,472 customers at the Astrodome. "Well," she giggled, "he played like a woman, Uh, like a lot of women I beat on our tour."

Billie Jean, a swooping volleyer who made Bobby a drooping follower, had never been accused of "playing like a woman" before Riggs began chiding her. Her attacking style is that of the leading male pros. Her competitive verve is second to none in any game. But Riggs had said that underneath it all she was "still a woman," which from his lips was a put-down. "She'll choke like they all do. No matter how good they are in their league, they can't even beat an old man like me with one foot in the grave."

As Billie Jean came on like thunder, Bobby Riggs was duck-waddling around the Astrodome with both feet in the grave, a guest of honor at Waterman's.

"Just one night—him or me—that's the kind of challenge I like," Billie had said. "If I have to play five sets, even though I never have, my psyche will drive me to do it."

Anything he could do, she could do better. Why not? She was 26 years younger. But most of us believed he could out-cute her, drive her nutty with lobs, and that his own time-tested competitiveness would break her down. The odds were 2½-to-1 on him for The Big Scrape-off (each had boasted "they'll have to scrape [the loser] off the Astrodome floor").

"Well, she never let me do what I wanted to do. She was all over me," sighed Bobby, who had only nice things to say as a loser. "I'd like a rematch, but that's up to Billie. She didn't beat me that bad."

Bad enough, as far as BJ was concerned, and it appears the Super Schlock of mixed singles is over. "I was upset with Margaret Court for accepting his challenge in the first place," said Billie Jean of Bobby's 6-2, 6-1 conquest of Court, the foremost female of this season. "We've got enough problems trying to build all women's sports without getting into something like this. But once Margaret had lost—and played so badly, nervously—in losing, I felt it was up to me to prove that we women pros can play a lot better than that. It wasn't Margaret's kind of scene—but I love this, all the noise and ballyhoo. I can handle it."

With the band playing, the dancing girls jiggling, the crowd screaming, Billie handled Bobby like a starlet hustling a sugar daddy, such as he proclaimed himself to be.

The hustler got hustled, muscled and bustled out of the joint. So inspired and invincible was she that Bobby was forced to say, "I guess the women are too tough for a 55-year-old."

She beamed and whispered, "he's OK."

They had both hustled the public and the media into producing unprecedented monies and headlines for tennis. "My dreams for tennis came true tonight," said Billie whose $100,000 purse put her over the 100-grand mark for the third successive year. "Everybody was watching. Everybody talked about it. That was a first for tennis. It was good from that viewpoint."

"I've said all that women are good for is the bedroom, but," Bobby smiled wanly, "Billie's pretty good elsewhere, too. She was great." Billie Jean smiled again, then went off to "celebrate with a couple of beers."

Early the next morning workmen were cleaning up the empty Astrodome. The Preposterous Panorama was over, the MCP's had gone home to nightcaps and nightmares, and the workmen were scraping something off the floor. It may have been Robert Larimore Riggs.

Pig and Riggs share sorrow

"What is the pig called?" somebody asked.

"Pig...just Pig," answered a tall young man who was holding Bobby Riggs' pig while it nuzzled and nibbled in a bowl of fried shrimp, declining the offer of a scotch and soda from a woman whose neckline plunged to the floor.

Pig was a gift to Riggs from Billie Jean King, before she turned little piggy Bobby into a boiled ham at the Astrodome. It was about 2 a.m. at the party following that phantasmagoria advertised as a tennis game, and Riggs and Pig were exchanging occasional soulful looks over the drink in Bobby's hands. Bobby, who said he'd had nothing to drink for a month but fruit juices, water, and protein elixir stirred by his nutritionist, Rheo Blair, was now going at the booze the way Chris Evert goes after a backhand—with both hands.

He deserved it. A blonde actress, Sandra Giles—one of Bobby's Bosom Buddies—was stroking his back, and other assortedly handsome females were sliding up for a kiss and a coo: "I still love you, Bobby..."

Pig munched on a slice of roast beef rare, and Bobby murmured, "Do you think anybody will want to talk to me now I'm a loser? I can't get over how quick Billie Jean was ...I hit balls past her, but she'd flick them back with unbelievable half-volleys...I wasn't my best...but no alibis...she made the action...she pushed me...sure I'd like a rematch..."

Across the penthouse barroom of the Astroworld Motel, Jackie Barnett, a show biz slicker from Hollywood who got it all started by promoting the Riggs conquest of Margaret Court, was saying, "Listen, there's a rematch clause." He sounded like a fight promoter, and there was nothing the atmosphere of King-Riggs resembled more than a heavyweight title fight. Except there's never been a fight duded up like this bout at which the principals arrived like empress and mandarin—she on a sedan chair borne by Central Casting-style Adonises, he in a rickshaw pulled by an array of chickies who can be described only as the greatest mass of breastworks since the fortification of Bunker Hill.

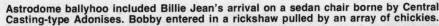

Astrodome ballyhoo included Billie Jean's arrival on a sedan chair borne by Central Casting-type Adonises. Bobby entered in a rickshaw pulled by an array of chickies.

"Oh, Bobby can have a rematch...it's in the contract," Jackie Barnett was assuring his listeners. Only Billie Jean won't have it. "It wouldn't be as big next time, but you could do it in Madison Square Garden," Barnett was fantasizing.

"No amount of money," Billie Jean said earlier when she looked in on the party briefly. "I proved what I had to prove. We women did enough for Bobby Riggs. He became a big man long after his day. A nice man, though. Maybe he can play better..."

Possibly Riggs can take his act out of the country for one more shot: A rematch with Margaret Court in a male chauvinist bastion called Australia.

"What was wrong with Bobby? Was he sick?" the diehards kept asking, unwilling to concede that Billie Jean—higher on emotion than you can get on pills—had played him off his duck-walking feet. "Do you suppose Bobby tanked—bet against himself?"

"No way," interjected an associate of Billie Jean's from Philadelphia. And he produced a $10,000 check decorated by Riggs' signature: The fruits of a wager with Bobby Riggs wouldn't say how much he'd lost. It was plenty, but he could afford it. "It still hurts, though," he said.

Not far from Riggs, Gracie Lichtenstein, a journalist who'd predicted Billie Jean's victory in the *New York Times,* was yipping, "we're rich!" She and the brilliant feminist writer, Nora Ephron, had just collected their women's lib communal bet from Bobby. They'd hustled the *Ms. Magazine* crowd and other friends to raise $500 to bet against $800 of Bobby's in a head-to-head gamble: The Movement against the monster. "It was a spirtual thing," Ephron had explained two days before when she arrived at Bobby's hotel room with the $500 in fives, tens and twenties.

"Money down the drain, Nora," Bobby had said whipping out eight hundred-dollar bills as his end, and giving the $1300 to a holder. "I know," Ephron said. "But we have to back Billie Jean. This came from a lot of people. A shrink put up $50."

"You mean a smart guy like a shrink, a guy with a psychiatric degree, would bet against me?" chortled Riggs.

"It was a she," Ephron said.

"You broads use she-shrinks?" he was amazed. "I'll be damned. You're really with the outfit."

But the outfit had beaten Riggs out of his money just as their avenging angel had beaten him out of his jock. Lichtenstein and Ephron were counting the money. "Thirteen hundred we made, Nora," Grace was ecstatic.

"Please, Grace," said Larry Merchant, whose new book, *"The National Football Lottery"* pertains to gambling. "You put up $500, so you only won $800. Not $1300."

"Thirteen hundred sounds better," she said.

Everything sounded better to Billie Jean's people, and tasted better. She'd taken the broads off the hook Margaret Court had left them dangling from. "So it was a circus, and so what?" said another writer, Neil Amdur. "But I think Billie Jean's win really did mean a lot to all women athletes. It was an inspiration. They don't play against men, but they get put down by men. Their games are good and interesting, and they play as hard, but they don't get much attention. Billie Jean has got to mean a lot to them."

Bobby was leaving the party, double-teamed by drinks and blondes. "Nice try, Bobby," people were saying and meaning it. "You made the show...You built it...it was

Billie Jean King holds her newly-won trophy high after beating Bobby Riggs in 3-straight sets. Billie Jean earned $100,000 in their winner-take-all "battle of the sexes."

your night as much as hers."

So it was. Bobby shook his dyed head in appreciation. "I gotta go jump off London Bridge into Lake Havasu..." You haven't heard the last of Riggs' ballyhoo.

"I wish I'd seen him in his prime," said an alleged blond writer from *Family Circle.*

"Hell," I said. "This is his prime. Who knew or cared who Bobby Riggs was in 1939 when he only won Wimbledon and 100-grand betting on himself to win? He's a magazine cover, a genuine piece of American Present and maybe Future Schlock. Maybe it tells you how sick our country is, but Bobby Riggs is a prime cultural hero." This is the kind of speeches I make at 3 a.m.

Pig wasn't listening. Pig didn't give a sow's ear about me, Bobby Riggs or Billie Jean King, maybe a sign of stability. Pig had become a item of Americana, too, a little red body on nationwide TV, acknowledged by Howard Cosell, applauded by 30,472 customers, framed by hundreds of cameras. Pig had even slept through all the noise of the occasion—the music, the cheers, the boos, the general tumult and ragtime. Very stable.

And now Pig was into the free shrimp, enjoying until that day when—like his master—Pig, too, would become a boiled ham. ●

The King vs. Riggs Story

by JEAN and CLIFF DRYSDALE

THE FIRST TIME *Jean Drysdale saw Bobby Riggs she was six-years-old. He was playing an exhibition match against Don Budge in Queenstown, South Africa. The next time was 22 years later in Newport where she played a mixed doubles exhibition with Bobby and Louise Brough. Queenstown must have been very little to him but he remembered. When Jean played against Billie Jean King in 1968 in Johannesburg (King won), Billie Jean was still vulnerable as a player. Jean said that if opponents could keep her away from the net and play her forehand they had a chance to win the point. King has no such weaknesses now. Her 6-4, 6-3, 6-3 victory over Bobby was a devastating exhibition of virtuosity. Cliff Drysdale, president of the Association of Tennis Professionals, had never seen Riggs play until Sept. 20, 1973, at Houston's Astrodome.*

Jean: Whatever happens tonight, Bobby is having his big moment. He's hustled the whole world.

Cliff: Of course everyone of these 30,000 and millions more watching TV enjoyed being hustled.

Jean: They think he's going to hustle Billie Jean. Is that it?

Cliff: It's everything that is dear to the hearts of the spectators. Big money. Big show. Team spirit (women-team against men-team). Crowd participation. Prize fight repartee. Gambling. It's remarkable to see.

Jean: Remember mixed doubles?

That was a Battle of the Sexes.

Cliff: Fortunately it's almost extinct.

Jean: Lovely game.

Cliff: The girls have proven that they can make it on their own even before Bobby Riggs. We're all delighted.

Jean: I'm afraid for Billie Jean. She's made of strong stuff but after the way Margaret played, anything can happen.

Cliff: I think Bobby's going to win anyway. He would even if they played with nobody watching. Billie Jean has to get in and attack to have a chance.

Jean: I think she has to mix it up a bit like she played against Chris Evert at Wimbledon.

Match Begins After Grand Entrance and Pig Ceremony.

Jean: I realize that it's good for tennis to have so many people but it's impossible to see the ball from here. Pass the binoculars.

Cliff: Billie Jean's made a good start. She's attacking all the time but playing the points. Bobby came in on the first point of the match on her serve. Then Billie Jean came in three points in a row. She's got Bobby running.

Jean: Bobby's hitting a lot of balls back now. Very soft stuff. It can wear you down if you're a girl. It all depends on whether Billie Jean can keep her game from being lowered to his standard.

Cliff: He's got no power! How can he be so mediocre? He's tried six cross-court passes off the backhand and Billie Jean's murdered all except one. He hasn't come in since the first point, not even on his own serve.

Four Games All in the First Set.

Cliff: I'm beginning to think that I'm going to lose my bets on Bobby. She is faster, hits harder and Bobby doesn't pass as well as I thought he could.

Jean: Do you think he's really trying? Perhaps he's playing some kind of hustling game.

Cliff: Hell no! He's trying as hard as he can.

Jean: He's not even moving. Look at that smash!

Cliff: Can't put them away. Bobby's passing shots are floaters. Billie Jean only has to keep volleying reasonably well to win.

Jean: I don't believe that after all this talking he'll go out like a frog in a frost. Perhaps his bosom friends are in the crowd making bets and Bobby will suddenly rise up and produce a stunning burst of brilliance to amaze us.

Cliff: No way! Technically Billie Jean has him grounded. She has a much wider variety of strokes off both sides. For instance she can chip the backhand approach, drop-shot exceptionally well, or come over it on a passing shot. He hits too softly and he's too slow.

First Set to Billie Jean.

Cliff: Bobby still seems to be composed. I suppose that's something. I wonder if he is always so sporting about acknowledging his opponent's good shots.

Jean: He's really behaving very well. He didn't bring flowers for Billie Jean.

Cliff: She's trying dropshots. She's starting to smell victory.

Jean: Bobby is running around his backhand and not doing anything with his forehand.

Cliff: He's tiring and he's not lost all his nervousness. Or he's tanking but I don't believe it. Billie Jean is concentrating very well. She claims not to choke and I believe that. Maybe I should start listening more closely to Billie Jean.

Jean: He's still running for the lobs. Unless Billie Jean throws it away now she can't lose.

Cliff: I can't see Bobby running like this for five sets.

Billie Jean Wins the Second Set.

Jean: Apart from the brass band and twirlers between games it's a very ordinary tennis match. Billie Jean is slowly but surely beating him down.

Cliff: On Sportface you have to come into the net like Billie Jean is doing. That's definitely in her favor. Bobby doesn't like to have to attack. He stayed back against Margaret.

Jean: It's not going to work against Billie Jean. She's too good a player. Billie Jean is playing like a man and Bobby like the girl.

Cliff: He's surely finished after this.

Jean: The trouble with a match like this is that someone not only loses but also loses face. I like to think that every player has their own particular value and losing a match is a matter of skill not of losing face. It's no fun to watch someone lose face.

Cliff: Bobby doesn't have anything to lose. He's 55 years old and he's having a last fling in tennis. Bless it, the whole thing started as a joke. If Bobby's smart he'll leave it at this.

Jean: But in the real world of tennis every player in the top 30 knows that on a given day they can all beat each other. There's no loss of face involved.

Cliff: Like Pattison beating Nastase, Amritraj beating Laver, Borg beating Ashe—that's true.

Two Games All in the Third Set.

Jean: I still have a feeling that there must be something of a hustle in the way Bobby's playing. If this is his best form he couldn't seriously have thought he would beat Billie Jean.

Cliff: No, this is no hustle. It's interesting to watch two players who have never played each other before but pretty soon you can work out how things are going to go.

Jean: Just proves that a better player will beat a worse player.

Cliff: If you analyze it Bobby really can only serve medium-to-soft slices. He has difficulty in getting under the ball to serve a topspin. He lacks a defensive forehand chip and he can't come over the ball on his backhand. He's having real difficulty in putting the ball away even overhead. Also they are both doing a lot of running which is hard work for a promising veteran.

Jean: You have to hand it to Billie Jean. She can do more with the tennis ball than any other woman I've seen. She sometimes makes a careless mistake but look at how many ways she can play points. She's been drilling Bobby's backhand and knocking off smashes but she can also rally from the baseline, pass him at net and drop-shot him.

Cliff: The only conceivable stage that might have changed the match was if Bobby had held his lead when he broke Billie Jean's service at 3-2 in the first set. Billie Jean might have lost confidence.

Jean: Bobby has doublefaulted. There goes a backhand into the net, it's over.

Cliff: What's that Greek fellow's name? Met him at University.

Jean: What Greek fellow?

Cliff: The one that creeps up behind you and hits you on the head. He just crept up on Bobby.

Jean: You mean Nemesis?

Cliff: That's it.

GROUNDSTROKE
VS
VOLLEY REFLEXES

by DON KLOTZ

FOR EFFECTIVE performance in tennis, physical and mental reactions must be the result of instantaneous responses to various situations encountered in match play. Conscious thought is essential for evaluation of the strategic aspects of match play, but it is totally inadequate to control body movements in fast action. These movements must be controlled by reflexes—natural or conditioned. Said one coach: "Under match play pressures, you don't think; you react."

Many of the fundamental mechanical responses employed in stroking the ball are instinctive and need only be refined through intense concentration and through repetition in practice and under the pressures of match play. However, some instinctive reactions are wrong and the proper responses must be introduced to the beginner at the earliest possible moment. If the undesirable instinctive response is reinforced by repetition and approval, the modification of that response at a later date will be an agonizing experience for both pupil and instructor. In some cases making the change will be so difficult and time-consuming that it won't be worth the effort. To have efficient and effective learning, only correct responses should be taught and carefully nurtured to the reflex stage, instinctive and conditioned.

Traditionally teachers have assumed that the full swing of the forehand drive must be *taught first* and in minute detail. Even before the beginner is allowed to hit a ball he/she must suffer through "racket back-weight on back foot-transfer weight-racket approaches ball-racket contacts ball-follow through" endless dry repetitions, by the numbers, and even to music. But it has been my observation that the instinctive response to an approaching ball by a beginner with a racket in his hand is a full swing regardless of whether the ball reaches him/her after bouncing or on the fly. It makes no difference whether he is asked to hit the ball a distance of 10 feet or the entire length of the court,

the response is the same—a full swing. Apparently it is purely instinctive, and if so it will not require teaching. Some instructors may desire a straight backswing, others an elliptical backswing and others a circular backswing. I accept whatever the pupil may take naturally.

While I have found that the full swing is natural without exception, I have never encountered a pupil who would use a short swing naturally. The full swing is a useful implement if the pupil is able to fully prepare for it and if he needs that much power. But he is also going to need a block or punch for the volley, a very short swing for the half volley, a block, punch or chip for return of power serves, fractional swings for activity in midcourt, and other fractional swings when he is out of position through his own misjudgment or because he is forced by his opponent. In short, he needs everything from a block to a full swing regardless of his level of ability. Since the fractional swings are not natural and the pupil must overcome the instinctive full swing, it is better to learn those shorter swings at the earliest possible moment. Practice on the full swing plus approval will only reinforce instinct and make the ultimate transition to shorter swings that much more agonizing for both pupil and instructor. Traditional though the practice may be, it is unsound and impractical learning psychology.

The solution is to introduce the volley FIRST, using the block or slight punch. Even with a toss to the pupil from about 15 feet he will answer with a swing, unless instructed not to do so—that old instinctive full swing. The most effective gimmick to prevent this swing reaction is to ask the pupil to catch the ball with his right (left) hand when it is tossed to him from not more than 10 feet. Whether he successfully catches the ball or not is unimportant. What is important is that he reaches out naturally with his hand to meet the ball. The reaching out to meet the ball I stress strongly. I have him toss the ball to me and I duplicate his catch for extra emphasis. Then I ask him to catch the ball with his racket just as he did with his hand. The toss is made from no more than 15 feet and is made underhand. If he attempts to swing at the ball we go back to catching it with his hand. Reach out to meet the ball. The pupil is always completely surprised that the ball bounces so far off his racket face with no or very little effort on his part. My usual comment will be, "You are surprised that the ball goes so far with so little effort, aren't you? You just made a perfect block volley."

Another gimmick that has worked well involves the use of some object as a target. It is placed just over the net from the pupil on the court, perhaps 6 to 8 feet from the net. The ball is tossed underhand from near the service line to the pupil at about head height. He is asked to "let the ball *bounce* off your racket onto the target." After one or two swings which hit the ball as far as the baseline, he will usually reduce his swing to near zero and actually let the ball bounce off his racket in a good block volley. We then go to waist high tosses to his right, watching for good footwork. We don't teach footwork unless we have to.

As soon as the pupil volleys acceptably from near the net, he goes back to just inside the service line. I now toss from near the net, perhaps 10 feet from it on my side. The chances are that the pupil will begin to swing on the volley at this new distance. If so, I check the tendency at once and we get back to block or punch. As soon as his form is acceptable we go to the next step. This next step, a tossed ball which reaches the pupil on the bounce, is performed at the same distance as the volley near the service line. Now the pupil will use a very short swing, hardly more than the punch volley. Longer swings are immediately discouraged. Once he acquires the feel of returning the ball to me with this short swing, I mix volleys and bouncing balls at random. If he handles the tossed balls well I begin a gentle rally with him, placing all shots to his forehand, hitting the balls in a slight arch and with a little backspin so that the ball does not reach him too quickly and sets up nicely to give him time to reach it and achieve good position. I will hit some balls short on purpose to draw him back to the net for volleys. All swings are kept short in this mid-court rallying.

I usually give one hour lessons. In that period most of my beginners will progress to the point of gentle rallies from near the service lines. Next we go to the backhand volley at the net and then move back to the service line just as we do with the forehand. Then the forehand and backhand strokes are intermixed, always bringing the pupil back to the net for volleys as a natural part of the rally.

As soon as my pupil is sustaining the rallies for two to four strokes, we move back another 10 feet to the middle of the back court, following the same plan of short swings on groundstrokes, a little longer than from the service line, with short shots to bring him back to the net for volleys. His swing will generally lengthen naturally as he moves away from the net. I have no set time schedule for progress away from the net. We go as fast as the pupil's abilities will allow.

A player without a good volley is missing half the fun of tennis and his opportunity to use strategy effectively is severely limited. Without the use of fractional swings he will make many more errors than if he had the ability to adjust the length of his swing to the to the situation on the court. He may never acquire confidence in these shorter swings unless they are taught early and well. ●

The joys . . .

YOU ARE a bank president or the owner of a fleet of oil tankers or a movie star. Perhaps you are a secretary or a sanitary engineer or a dental assistant. Maybe a young lawyer or associate professor or manager of a research lab. Whatever you are, assume you are a tremendous tennis enthusiast who would much rather consistently hit a great forehand down-the-line than make another $10 million or $1 million or $100.

In your fantasies, Rocket serves to you, your racket connects in the center and poor Rocket stands helpless as your ball sails past him and raises the chalk. Or you and Gorgo take on Smith and Lutz; there you are, a white flash streaking across the net to knock a ball clean through your gaping opponents. If you are female, Billie Jean asks you to "hit a few" and is astounded by your pick-up half-volley from the baseline and your smooth, hard strokes. But these are just your daydreams; in reality, you are at best "club level" and at worst "low club level." You would give anything to be good enough to make the WCT Circuit or, depending on your sex, the Women's Pro Tour. You would be ecstatic if your entry were ever accepted at Forest Hills and you could then shower next to Emmo or Muscles and exchange tennis banter with Roger Taylor or Arthur Ashe. You imagine yourself sitting in the Players' Section at Wimbledon; Fred Stolle asks you how you did against Haroon Rahim and you reply casually, "I lucked it out, 3, 4 and 4."

If you were only on the circuit, how happy life would be. You would get up at 10 A.M., have breakfast in your room, go for a work-out with Cox or Fairlie, grab a quick lunch at the club, play a match in the afternoon in front of 5,000 swooning females, have a leisurely dinner, play a doubles that night, then join Pilic or Kodes or perhaps a couple of girls for a few beers before going to your hotel room, which is in Milan, New York, Paris, Los Angeles or some other far-away spot. If you are female, the routine is almost the same except rich young executives are vying to take you to lunch or dinner, and whenever you ask for your key from the desk clerk, your box is full of mash notes.

The truth is quite different from your imaginative creations. After eight weeks on the circuit, between 10 and 20 percent of the men and the women are ready to throw in the towel. Player X has lost in 6 first rounds on the rough WCT

. . . and horrors of playing the circuit

Circuit. He still practices regularly and he still fantasizes hopefully, but depression has crept into his legs, he can't seem to hit the ball hard enough or sustain a rally and he continually fails to win the big points. Player Y has entered six WCT tournaments and has only won two matches, one of them against Player X. He thought he was going to have a tremendous year but he is now disgusted, discouraged and despondent. Player Z should be much happier: he has already won six matches and is a good "second rounder." He is the unhappiest of all. Last year he was among the Top Eight and this year, even though WCT is split into three groups, he is only in a tie for No. 15. He can't get his big serve going and he is no longer getting good depth on the volley. As a result he is now snapping at his wife, particularly when she tries to cheer him up.

As the tour enters the seventh week, the players at the top are feeling the grind. It is harder and harder to get "up" for a match. Player A, who is in a tie for second place, almost lost in the first round because he is mentally weary. Player B, at fourth place, is desperately afraid he may slip to fifth or sixth and therefore be out of the running for the $100,000 WC of T final. Player C has a bad knee. He was playing the best tennis of his life the first four weeks of the Tour, but now his knee swells up after every match and the last doctor he saw told him he needs an operation. Player D is playing superb doubles but his singles is wildly erratic. He is a bundle of nerves and could be beaten on a given night by almost anyone, with the possible exception of Player X. Player E has had the misfortune to meet one of the top players every week in the first or second round. He could probably beat 24 or 25 of the 32 players. Now he is on edge because he knows he can "kill" 15 players who are rated ahead of him and he never gets the chance to meet any of them. Player F is the victim of a "psych" job. He plays doubles with one of the top WCT players and they do very well, but if they ever do poorly, the top WCT player makes it clear to the gallery (and to the TV spectators) that Player F simply isn't holding up his end. Player F's singles (and personality) has taken a beating as a result. Player G is doing reasonably well—better than expected—but how long can it last since G is a "loner," can't or doesn't want to make friends with the other players and could not possibly latch on to a person of his own intellectual pursuits when he is only going to be in the city for one week. Player G's personality makes it impossible to be happy on a happy-go-lucky, fake-it, play-it-loose, athletic circuit. G basically belongs in Bloomsbury with Vanessa Bell and Virginia Woolf. Player H has reconciled himself to being, at best, a quarter-finalist, although a few years ago he was No. 1 in the world.

Meantime the world-famous Little Broads are playing their Virginia Slims Circuit. This is the roughest, toughest circuit in the world. Players who rank in the World's First Ten slip down suddenly and sadly to the Preliminary Flight. The Qualifying is so difficult that a dozen girls, by the end of the year, will either never or only once make it into the Preliminary ranks. But at least they are playing their confreres, players of comparable ability, and at least they have a second chance in the Consolation.

But each one suffers incredible disappointments. Player A goes through four great rounds of deuce sets or three sets to win the Consolation, then gets knocked off the next week in the first round of the Qualifying and the first round of the Consolation, Player B makes it into the Preliminaries only once, and then it is by double-default. Player C, who has worked so hard on her new forehand, finds herself slipping back into the old, bad habits. Player D has broken up with her boyfriend and her game has simultaneously broken up. Player E finds that the "rich young executives" who chase her around are neither rich, young nor executives. They are, sadly, callow youths with bad complexions who hope that E will get them a free ticket or a free lunch. Player F misses her mother. Nobody gives a damn about how she does except her mother, who is at home thousands of miles away.

None of the disappointed players, women and men, realize that they are in the top .01 percent of the world in tennis, that even if they "fail," they are successes to everyone else, that 20 percent of the current players will drop out and, if they are dedicated and can keep up their own morale, they will eventually make a higher level—and perhaps even the top Championship Flight.

So give it a go, players! You are the fulfillment of all our dreams. ●

01234!

THE NUMBERS RACKET

CERTAIN POSSIBLY psychological and environmental factors have been omitted in this analysis because of difficulties in predicting their occurrence and impact. For instance, if Ilya serves the first game and puts across a few fortuitous aces, he might get the mistaken notion that he is in control and become overconfident. Alternatively, Sasha, his opponent, may sense impending doom, see the twilight of his career, and begin quaking like an aspen, stroking the ball as though his arm were attached to a ratchet device. A slippery court may work more havoc on Ilya than Sasha, or Ilya might play far worse in the wind.

The strategy of this analysis is to assign a certain chance to a player's winning a point and extrapolate from this what his chances would be in a game or set. To predict the probability of winning a set with a score of 6-3 would involve considering all the possible ways to arrive at that score, assigning a probability to each, and then adding them up. This entails evaluating all the ways in which one can win a single game, which are numerous, since there is no limit on the number of deuces possible. To obtain the overall chance of winning the set, one adds up all the probabilities corresponding to the possible scores of 6-0, 6-1, 6-2, 6-3, 6-4, 7-5, 8-6, 9-7, etc. Again there is an infinity of terms involved, but fortunately the series converges in a respectable manner and can be handled with precision.

Theoretically the starting point of the analysis was the assumption of a percent chance on a point basis. This figure could be obtained, for example, by having the players engage for a session of 100 points with equal time spent serving and receiving. If Ilya wins 54 of the 100 points and Sasha only 46, then Ilya is given a rating of 54%. This does not appear to be a significant lead. But when translated into terms of games and sets, it is found to be important. Ilya will take 60% of the games and more than 75% of the sets. Reflection on past experience will assure any tennis buff that a little extra concentration or esprit de corps could easily make a difference of four percentage points. If Ilya had breakfasted on Grape Nut Flakes, foregone his morning snaps and so garnered 60% of the points, then the small gap between the players would have grown to a hiatus in terms of sets, with Ilya cornering 97% of them, leaving his frustrated opponent with a miserly 3 out of 100. Probably the result of a set would be a score of 6-1 for Ilya. But more than 600 sets would have to be played before Ilya's opponent could expect to win his revenge with an upset of 6-1 in his favor.

Suppose Ilya takes several lessons from the club pro on backhands and serves and so increases his lead to 70% on a point basis. Then he will win more than half the sets by 6-0 and will only allow the by now despairing Sasha one set out of 6300. To temporarily unseat Ilya with a 6-0 win, Sasha would probably have to play over a million sets, a rather arduous undertaking. If he had these overwhelming odds in mind, he might well invest in a few lessons himself.

Matters are complicated when reality encroaches on this simplistic scheme with the fact that one's chances are usually considerably enhanced when one is serving rather than receiving. The privilege of serving first in a match is usually coveted, with the implicit contention that the one who starts the show will have the better chance. Actually the set score will be influenced by who serves first, but not the chance of winning the set.

As an example, suppose Ilya has a mean slice serve and can win 70% of the points on his serve. However, his uncompromising antagonist, he finds, is lefthanded and delivers serves with unorthodox spin, making it difficult for Ilya, who consequently only wins 40% of these points. A reasonable observer might expect Ilya's chances to win a set much enhanced if he were to serve first. Yet, apart from such psychological influences as ego inflation, it will be of no advantage to Ilya to initiate the set. He should take 81% of the sets regardless of who serves first. However, the set score by which Ilya might win is very much influenced. If he serves first he will have a 31% chance to win 6-3, whereas if he receives first, his chances to attain this victory are reduced over three-fold. Receiving first would mean a most probable score of 6-4 instead of 6-3. In either case one service break is expected.

by R. I. SMITH-JOHANNSEN

If you average out Ilya's chances on a point by point basis to obtain a composite rating of 55% and then boldly predict the results of a set from this figure alone, you could hardly expect much precision. But as for his chances to take the set, remarkably, you would be off by less than a percentage point: 82% as opposed to the actual 81%. Yet the break-up in terms of set scores is considerably different. For instance, the predicted chance for a score of 6-0 would be nearly six times that observed. In general, when there is no difference between the chances of winning a point serving as compared with receiving, there is a smooth variation among the probabilities for the various scores. In the more complicated and realistic case, there is a "staggering" effect.

The Van Alen Simplified Scoring System or VASSS (where a player must earn at least 21 points and lead by 2 points to win) is subject to this same sort of analysis. If, instead of playing 21 points, a match consisted of only one point, then even an average player would have a small chance to defeat Laver in a single match. As the number of points in a set becomes larger, viz., 21 points or 31 points, the differences in abilities of opposing players become more exaggerated. Given two players of different abilities, no matter how slight the difference, there is a number sufficiently large to essentially insure the victory of the better player. The 21-point VASSS and the 31-point VASSS represents a compromise between the exaggeration desired and the time required for a match. The game-set schema is merely a combination of 4-point and 6-point VASSS.

For comparable players the game-set system is equiva-lent to about 41-point VASSS. For instance, giving our player Ilya a 60/40 advantage over his opponent, his chances to win a set were found to be 96.6%. If a 21-point VASSS were played his chances would be 90.9%, and 32-point VASSS would yield a 94.6% chance. A VASSS game of 40 points gives a 96.6%. But he would expect to play 53 points in both a game-set match and a 32-point VASSS match. So although both of these matches would require the same time, the game-set system would more efficiently exaggerate the differences between the players. Ilya would win 18 times as many matches as his opponent under 32-point VASSS but would acquire 28 times as many matches under game-set. The 40-point VASSS would allow the same exaggeration factor as game-set but would require an expected 66 points to play out.

Thus the game-set scoring is more efficient than VASSS. The contrast is not quite as sharp when the players are closer in ability.

The scoring system in tennis serves a useful purpose: to exaggerate differences between players. Understanding this gives an insight into why concentration can be so very important in leading to victory in a match and why frustration can lead to singularly dismal results. Efforts to improve your style, to smooth out your groundstrokes, to groove your serve can pay off many times over in success on the courts. It can work the other way, too. If your tennis friends concentrate a bit too much and reverse the situation, you can find yourself on the disappointing side of the charts. ●

POINT	GAME	SET	6-0	6-1	6-2	6-3	6-4	7-5	Most probable
50%	50	50	2	5	8	11	12	6	6-4
54	60	77	5	11	16	17	15	7	6-3
60	74	97	16	25	23	16	10	4	6-1
70	90	99.98	53	32	11	3	1	0-1	6-0

This table translates your chances of winning a single point into your chances of taking a game or set. It also gives your chances of prevailing over your opponent by a particular set score.

THE MOST COMMON FAULTS IN TENNIS

(And How to Cure Them)

THE LIMP WRIST. The good player hits groundstrokes and volleys with a firm wrist; the not-so-good player finds it difficult to maintain a relaxed arm and a tight, steady, immoveable wrist. As soon as a hard ball hits his racket, the weak player's wrist collapses—downward or backward. If you want to find out how difficult it is to hit a ball with a sagging, floppy wrist, try it deliberately: you lose all control and it is impossible to hit with power. Fortunately, you can practice the firm wrist motion any time, anywhere. Take an imaginary backswing on a groundstroke and watch your finish, making sure the arm is relaxed and the wrist firm.

The Stiff Elbow. The beginner tries so hard to keep his wrist firm that he freezes his arm from shoulder to fingers. Sometimes the rigidity extends down to his ankles, and as the ball approaches the knees are locked, the body paralyzed and the arm as stiff as a board. On the proper forehand, the elbow is bent on the backswing and the elbow continues to remain bent *through the hit*. Most of the bend disappears on the follow-through. Similarly, on the proper backhand the elbow is bent on the backswing, remains slightly bent on the hit and almost straightens by the end of the follow-through. See for yourself how "feel" of the ball disappears if you try to hit with the arm and racket in one straight, stiff line. Now tuck your elbow into your body as you start your backswing and keep your elbow slightly bent as you hit—but don't forget to follow through—and you will see immediately how much more control and "feel" you have. Think of yourself as a little package and keep yourself tucked together. When the arm stiffens, the package has come apart. Reminder: the elbow is bent but the racket is *parallel* to the ground (the racket head does not point down).

The Soldier Stance. You needn't be an Olympic sprinter to know you can't begin a race from a standing position. In tennis, the more your knees are bent, the easier it is to push off in any direction for a quick start. The soldier stands stifflegged, with feet together; the tennis player bends his knees while waiting for the ball and his feet are comfortably apart (12 inches to 18 inches). The soldier straightens his shoulders, throws out his chest and his back is rigid; the tennis player hunches his shoulders and bends slightly from the waist as he waits for the return. Stand in front of a mirror as though you were ready to march in a parade. It should be clear to you at once that this is an impossible position from which to hit a tennis ball. Now, still looking in the mirror, spread your feet 18 inches, flex your knees, bend slightly at the waist, let your shoulders droop, hold the racket with both hands in front of your body (the gripping hand is on the butt and the fingers of the other hand lightly support the racket throat) and bounce very gently to get the feeling of being on the balls of your feet rather than resting soggily on your heels. You look terribly unmilitary but you could now be mistaken for a tennis player.

The Groover. What do you do when your opponent chops a forehand to your backhand that skids or topspins a ball that bounces over your head or serves an American twist high to your backhand or slides one low to your wide forehand or sidespins, underspins or drop shots? Are you so grooved on medium-speed, non-spin shots that you cannot handle spit-ball, junk-ball or goof-ball artists? You can't get grooved to one type of shot only; you must always be ready for the unexpected spin, the change of pace, the net cord and even the mis-hit shot on the wood. When you are too grooved to one ball, you plant your feet. Then if the ball takes a crazy spin or a bad bounce you are sunk. You can't become a good player if you are grooved to return only a few basic shots, and the solution is to *understand* the various spins by playing a variety of opponents, particularly those with unorthodox shots, and to avoid committing yourself totally by planting your feet. Some spin clues: left-handed spin serves move *toward* the backhand side and should be handled with a very firm wrist before the ball bounces wide; chop forehands skid sideways and forward; heavy topspins bounce high and forward; sidespins when hit hard skid and have an extraordinary amount of sting on the racket; slice serves can pull you very wide on the forehand; underspins bounce low on the racket; slice serves can pull you very wide on the forehand; underspins bounce low and slow up; American twist serves bounce to the receiver's left and high but don't have much forward speed; and undercut, underhand spin serves bounce to the receiver's left and almost straight up, with very little forward motion. But saying is one thing and playing is another; now that you know, try to show, which means try it, you'll like it.

The Ankle Shot. Everyone is born lazy, but nowhere is it more apparent than in the Ankle Shot. Here the player, instead of *moving in* to take the ball at the top of the bounce, casually waits behind the baseline until the ball reaches *him.* By that time it has dropped to his ankles. Now think to yourself which is the easier shot—a ball taken at waist-height, well in front of you, bouncing somewhere between the service court and the baseline, where you can lean into it, or a ball that has dropped down to nothing, with you standing a foot behind the baseline trying to do something with it (such as a passing shot) as your tiger opponent stands on top of the net. On the latter shot, all you can do is scoop; on the former, you can give it a proper whop. When your opponent hits a short shot, this is your golden opportunity to force him. So get off your duff and don't let your meat loaf. MOVE FORWARD. Nowhere is this more true than on the volley. Why wait 8 feet behind the net while a ball drops so that you can foolishly pop up when, if you step in while the ball is at the top of its trajectory, you can hit down? You don't need a mirror for this demonstration; think about it for a few minutes and there can be only one conclusion.

The Alley Step. The good player's weight is moving forward on almost every shot to achieve power. Either he steps forward just before the hit on the forehand (a step toward the net with the left foot, with the weight leaning forward, just before the racket moves through) or, if he cannot step forward, he pivots with his shoulders, with the right shoulder coming forward on the forehand (and the left on the backhand). *The not-so-good player steps sideways rather than forward,* thus blocking all forward motion and thereby losing all power generated by weight transfer. The not-so-good player is hitting with arm and wrist only. This is the easiest concept of all to realize: if your weight moves sideways, how can the ball have fullest forward propulsion? But don't hit and step forward simultaneously; *lead* with the forward step and then hit, taking the ball well in front of you. So it's Step Forward-Hit in rapid succession, with the forward motion of the racket just a fraction of a second behind the forward step (then all weight is moving toward the net). Practice Step Forward-Hit over and over to get the rhythm. If you step forward *too* soon, you lose both balance and power.

The Leading Elbow. Beginners either stiff-arm their backhands or allow the elbow to lead the racket. There are two ways to correct the leading elbow. The first is to take the racket back with both hands (the side is to the net, the racket face perpendicular to the ground, both elbows bent and the right shoulder turned in). Then the player steps forward with the right foot (the shoulder is still turned in) and hits by throwing arm and racket forward and up as though aiming at the top of the opponent's fence. The *shoulder* is the pivot point, and the hit is as much from the shoulder as the arm. If the elbow still leads, try the second way: use the same approach but keep both hands on the racket all the way through (the two-handed backhand). Tucking the shoulder in, stepping forward and then hitting with both hands on the racket should make for a natural pivot. The left hand will bring the racket forward ahead of the elbow.

The Slasher. Beginners and intermediates, in the heat of play, take too large a swing on the volley. Instead of punching they slash. There is almost no backswing on the volley. The racket should never be taken farther back than the shoulder. The ball is punched, not stroked. Slashing is out, man.

El Toro. The Bull charges the Net as though he were going to tear it to pieces. He comes in so fast that he actually volleys while he is moving forward. His thought is to charge, whatever the cost in points, games and sets. The good net-rushers serve, come in, *stop* and then volley (or leap-volley). Not only is it difficult to volley on the run but, if the ball does not come directly to you, how can you move to the left or right while on the dead run? So serve, come in, stop, step and volley.

The Ass. A good approach shot is a *deep* ball, preferably one that catches the opponent moving the wrong way or forces him to run wide. Only donkeys would hit a short ball down the middle and follow it to net; their only hope is that the opponent will not look at the ball or will develop a case of nerves. When you do come to net, hit deep and with pace and to a corner, moving toward the side where you have hit the ball so you can cover the down-the-line (the opponent's crosscourt must be awfully sharp to catch you).

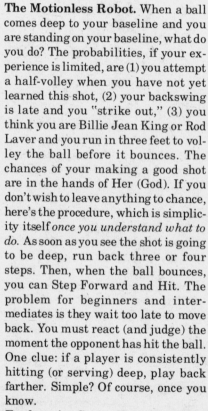

The Motionless Robot. When a ball comes deep to your baseline and you are standing on your baseline, what do you do? The probabilities, if your experience is limited, are (1) you attempt a half-volley when you have not yet learned this shot, (2) your backswing is late and you "strike out," (3) you think you are Billie Jean King or Rod Laver and you run in three feet to volley the ball before it bounces. The chances of your making a good shot are in the hands of Her (God). If you don't wish to leave anything to chance, here's the procedure, which is simplicity itself *once you understand what to do.* As soon as you see the shot is going to be deep, run back three or four steps. Then, when the ball bounces, you can Step Forward and Hit. The problem for beginners and intermediates is they wait too late to move back. You must react (and judge) the moment the opponent has hit the ball. One clue: if a player is consistently hitting (or serving) deep, play back farther. Simple? Of course, once you know.

Eyeless in Gaza. The top player watches the ball come off his opponent's racket and then makes his move; the not-so-good player watches his opponent. When the top player is at net and his opponent is serving, he watches the receiver's racket; the not-so-good player watches the receiver's face. When an opponent comes in against the top player, the latter sees only the ball; when an opponent comes in against a lesser player, the latter looks to see where the opponent is moving. Are you Eyeless in Gaza?

The Race Horse. Rushing is a fault common to quite a few good players as well as many who are not so good. The race horse is so eager that he has no time to stop, think and plan. Watch him as he gets ready to serve. He walks back to the baseline, turns, tosses up the ball and hits before he himself is ready. Was he going to serve deep to the backhand or a wide spin to the forehand or try a flat ball or change of pace? Does he know where his opponent is standing? Or does he serve every ball the same way because he is in too much of a hurry to think? The race horse also changes sides on the odd games as though he were heading for the finish line. No time to think about what went wrong in the first set—just rush, rush, and on a "bad" day he rushes himself out of the match. Be a race horse *when the ball is in play* and a thinker and analyzer when it is not.

The Double Backswing. Occasionally a player will take his arm back so early that when the ball finally reaches him, he takes a second backswing on top of the first. It is easily cured in a groundstroke: when the backswing is completed, tuck the elbow into your body so that you can actually feel it and then only permit yourself a forward motion. The movement of your elbow will warn you if you try a double backswing. Even more frequent is the double backswing on the volley: the player waits with the racket head up and in position for the volley, but when the ball comes the racket head flops back in a second backswing and the stroke is ruined. Take a look in the mirror to see what happens when you do it the wrong way: hold your racket head high and slightly in front of you as though waiting for a high forehand volley. Now let your wrist flop back. When it comes forward again for the hit, all you can do is slap at the ball. Now try it again but this time lift your left hand and put it behind your racket hand. You can't take a double backswing without hitting yourself.

The Late Wind-up. Every beginner and most intermediates will take too late a backswing against a hard ball or when they are forced to run or on a super-fast court. When you are playing a power player or are hitting on slick cement for the first time or are chasing a wide ball, *start your backswing early*. If you take your racket back *after* the ball bounces, you cannot possibly make contact with the ball in front of your body, which is the desired spot for contact. As a result, you will hook the ball behind you, and only if God smiles on you will your return go over the net. It will be luck, not skill, since if you hook behind you, your racket face cannot remain on the ball for more than a split second. On a fast court or against a power player, start your backswing as soon as your opponent has hit the ball and, if necessary, *shorten* the backswing. When you start for a wide ball, *start your backswing as you run* so that by the time you get there, your arm is already moving forward for the hit. N.B.: Shorten the backswing but don't shorten the follow-through.

The Overly Full Pivot. A follow-through should leave you in position to hit the next ball. As soon as you have finished one shot you must be ready for the next one. If you pivot so much that you have lost your balance, you can't possibly be ready for the next ball. The proper groundstroke follow-through ends, more or less, with the racket pointing toward the top of the opponent's fence and the body is still in balance. If you overpivot, your shoulder will be facing the alley (or even further), you have lost your balance and you must be late for the next shot if it comes back with any power. An easy way to test whether or not you are overpivoting is to see if you can bounce back *immediately* for the next shot, particularly if the ball is coming back a ton. Can you always bounce back into the Ready Position? Have you twisted yourself around so much that, with one small push, you would land on your nose? If so, practice your finish so that you *stop* when your racket points to the top of the opponent's fence.

The Low Bow. A good player constantly bounces, spreads his feet and bends his knees. The novice scarcely bends his legs at all, almost never stretches and bends from the waist as though he were bowing. This might appear courtly under other circumstances, but on a court to achieve good balance one must flex the knees and stretch rather than bow. Small bows are often taken by the novice server. He starts his toss by lowering the toss hand, and as he does so he bends forward from the waist, as though acknowledging the presence of his opponent. Sometimes the bow is deeper and even turns into a rocking motion as the toss hand makes a circular sweep. To prevent such bows, make sure your weight is on your back foot as you toss. Corrections are made by exaggerations so lower your right shoulder and raise the left as your toss arm goes up; it is then impossible to "bow."

Losing One's Head. An intermediate often rallies well, but the moment of truth is in competition. In the heat of match play, the inexperienced player will forget to finish his stroke, pat-ball his serve, look at the opponent instead of the ball, lose concentration, try shots he doesn't yet know, overhit or underhit and rush himself out of the game. The intermediate must plan before he plays—plan to move his feet, follow through on his strokes, hit deep shots in backcourt exchanges, watch only the ball when his opponent attacks, lob when in trouble and try, at all costs, to return every serve. The longer the point goes on, the more he must keep his head, hitting only the shots he knows will go in. This is self-discipline, and it is the key to winning tennis.

Hail and Farewell to the Softest Touch in Tennis

by BUD COLLINS

FINGERS FORTESCUE IS DEAD. "Deader than old balls," to quote one of his favorite expressions.

"Deader than a Santana stop-volley," to quote another.

As even net judges must, the revered C. Niles (Fingers) Fortescue has kept his appointment at Samarra. He has felt his last tickle of tennis ball against net cord, called his final "Not up!", marked his last scorecard. On Feb. 14, two days after his death, a tennis legend was buried beneath center court in the Forest Hills Stadium. "Some prefer Forest Lawn, but make mine Forest Hills where I spend my

happiest hours," Fingers had said. By special dispensation of the West Side Tennis Club's board of governors, and the borough council of Queens, Fortescue was allotted a plot where for decades he officiated at the net post—a model of duty, efficiency and probity. "By spring the place will be rolled flat," says Owen Sheridan, the groundsman. "There will be no indication of Mr. Fortescue's presence, no marker or anything. But we'll know he's there, and that's the way he wanted it."

Other imposing figures in the game have requested

Stadium interment, but only Fingers' wish has been granted. Such was the esteem for the man. "Any bad bounces they can blame on me," he once remarked to groundsman Sheridan after the West Side honored his written application for space in 1963. Charles Tucker, a spokesman for the club, said: "Mr. Fortescue left a bequest that will pay his dues forever. Thus we see no reason why he shouldn't use the court—as long as he stays out of sight."

Undoubtedly Fingers Fortescue will be the first net judge to be canonized by selection to the Tennis Hall of Fame at

Newport. Surely you have seen him at work, a distinctive individual always in evening clothes and top hat, hunched over the net post, ever at the alert to ferret out lets—the most overtly simple as well as the indistinguishably sly and clandestine. "He called a let a let—and let the groans fall where they may," extolled Bill Talbert when he learned of Fortescue's demise. "You couldn't intimidate Fingers, and you knew his eyes, ears and touch were superior to yours. When he said, 'Let!' you believed and seldom questioned. You were always glad to see him at the post for your match because you knew you were getting the best."

Fortescue was the Oliver Wendell Holmes of net judges, a man who so loved his work that he devoted a lifetime to hanging in there at the cord. He never umpired (a fear of heights kept him out of the chair) or performed as linesman. "I know my place," he would say, "and my limited role. I have studied netry, specialized in it. I'm monogamous, so to speak, married to the post and wish no other. I am comfortable and, I believe, competent, and wish to do only that which I do best. Perhaps I am less than adventurous in avoiding chair and lines, but I want nothing to distract from playing my small role to the utmost." Thus he, several times, refused nomination for the McGovern Award, sweetest prize in tennis officiating, saying: "It is a citation for all-around excellence. My proficiency is certainly isolated."

Although acquainted with Mr. Fortescue—nobody called him "Fingers" to his face—I didn't know him well. And it occurs to me that, if you have come to tournament spectating lately, you may not have seen him in operation, seated there like a concert cellist with that post between his legs, a look of rapturous concentration on his slim, handsome face. He was unable to work Forest Hills after 1967, his 92nd year, and had been failing since. At his death, in the master bedroom of the East Egg, Long Island, estate that once belonged to his friend, Jay Gatsby, Fingers was still clutching the tape of the net that hung across his bed.

"I knew he'd hold his own right to the end," said an admirer and friend of many years, Pancho Segura. "I first saw him at Seabright in 1944. The temperature over a hundred, and mucho humid, but Mr. Fortescue looks cool as a tequila sour in his tux and stovepipe hat. That man could catch lets that would escape any other human eye, ear or hand. Magnifico.

"And I remember he was on a match with me and Wayne Sabin—I think the first time he saw me play. I look over and he's got both hands on the net, with the scorecard in his teeth. Just for one point... and he wink at me: 'Senor Segura, two can play at two hands, you know.'

"Everybody thinks he's a sobersides, but I know he got a sense of humor."

So there, as his butler, Creighton, watched sadly, lay Fingers Fortescue, breathing his last with a slight smile on his face, one hand above the covers clinging to the net as though he were a straphanger making his last journey home. As, of course, he was.

Few knew of that net in his bedroom. There was no mention in the obits in the New York Times or the Wall Street Journal. Creighton told me about it, as directed by his master when he delivered a note from the deceased. "It was part of Mr. Fortescue's unceasing devotion to duty as a net judge," said the admirable Creighton. "The net was always there to practice on. Some people count sheep; Mr. Fortescue counted imaginary balls going over the net, and fell to sleep almost immediately.

"When Mrs. Fortescue, his wife, was alive, they would hold what he called 'match scrimmages' daily. He would close his eyes and she would attack the net with a feather: at irregular intervals she touched the tape softly with an ostrich plume. Unfailingly, at each touch, no matter how delicate, he would react with pronounced shouts of 'Let!' How sensitive his right hand was. After a half-hour of that, she would bounce a ball on the thick carpeting. Neither she nor I nor anyone else could hear the sound. Only Mr. Fortescue. Whenever she allowed the ball to bounce twice in succession, he would thunder—his eyes still closed, mind you—'Not up!'

"He drilled constantly to maintain his standards. The world," sighed Creighton, "has lost an artist." The world seldom realizes how much work and practice lies behind the art. Thus it was with Clarence Niles Fortescue, a rich man who wanted more than the pleasures of inherited wealth. He wanted to contribute to the game he loved, and he did so in unprecedented manner.

"Netry is not for everyone," he once told me. "It is a calling, a gift, and I am fortunate. Had I been born to less fortunate parents, I might well have become a pickpocket."

You may recall the night he stumped the panel of "What's My Line?"—even though Dorothy Kilgallen mused, "for some reason I see you as a man with his hand on the pulse of something or other. Are you a physician?"

Indeed, Florence Blanchard (the best known net judge of the present day, thanks to TV exposure) once said of Fortescue: "Dancing with him was an incredible experience. He could take your blood pressure merely by touching your back. I'll never forget the first time we waltzed, at James Barker Smith's Flamingo Hotel in Miami Beach. Mr. Fortescue cut in on me and my husband, and while we were gliding across the floor—he was a marvelous dancer—he muttered, '120 over 70, Flo. Quite good.'

"I had no idea what he was talking about until he explained that his fingers were so sensitive they could read blood pressure, pulse, and even give a cholesterol count. But he said he generally kept these things to himself for no one should practice medicine without a license."

Fingers' mother, Mrs. Giselda Frobisher Fortescue, always regretted that her son chose netry over gynecology, but conceded that he was probably destined for the former: "He was born holding the umbilical cord, you know."

Fortescue played down his skill. Nevertheless few possess the physical and mental coordination to make a profession of netry. Consider the action involved. First there is detecting the let, by ear, eye or digital sensation. Then you must react immediately, transmitting that detection with a loud, unmistakeable cry of "Let!" Simultaneously you raise the non-cord hand high in manual signal, all the while balancing scorecard and pencil on one knee. Try maintaining this alertness over five sets, perhaps several times in one day, without dropping pencil or card, without calling false lets or missing genuine ones. There are other responsibilities—observing sharply for double hits, double bounces, and toes and rackets surreptitiously touching the net. Also making certain, without embarrassing your partner, that the umpire is awake and has the correct score.

It isn't general knowledge that Fortescue went well beyond the call of duty by actually holding down both jobs—umpire and net judge—at the time to preserve the honor of his colleague, the celebrated Schuyler Pizzington. During Don Budge's 1938 run to the first Grand Slam, Fortescue and Pizzington were working Budge's semi-final triumph over Sidney Wood in the Stadium. Midway through the first set Pizzington passed away. You couldn't tell from the stands because Pizzington always looked and acted dead. Nor were Budge and Wood aware of it. I doubt they are today. But when Pizzington failed to utter a 15-30 call as promptly as he should have, Fingers whispered,

"Pizzer, wake up!" Usually that was enough to get Pizzington going again. Fortunately he wasn't a loud snorer. Yet even as he sought to rouse his comrade, Fortescue suspected the worst because there was no tell-tale snore, usually audible only to him at the foot of the chair.

Quickly and smoothly, so as not to attract attention, Fortescue grabbed Pizzington's ankle. With his sensitivity he realized at once the umpire had expired.

"The ultimate disgrace," thought Fortescue. "Death in the chair, spoiling the ritual, disturbing the players and spectators and—foulest of all—causing a breach in play while old Pizzer is carried off. Never," vowed Fortescue to himself. "Play is continuous. That is sacred." Whereupon, imitating Pizzington's voice as best he could—not too difficult if you've spent time on Martha's Vineyard, as Fortescue had, practicing duets with the foghorns—the resourceful Fingers continued to call the score.

Nobody knew the difference. Pizzington, slouched in the chair, had not been mortified by a human failing. When the match ended, Fingers motioned to a couple of his close friends on the lines, "I say, chaps, old Pizzer's had a touch of the sun. Let's help him off in a nice manner, shall we?" They got Pizzington to his car where his wife waited, as customary, in the driver's seat. "Drunk again," she sniffed. "Well, thanks, Mr. Fortescue." Two days later, Mrs. Pizzington, too, suspected the worst—and had it confirmed by the family physician.

Only through one of the linesmen who aided Fortescue in his mission of compassion did I learn that story. Certainly Fortescue would never have told it. Nor would he have told of any other demanding occasions to which he rose.

Certainly not of the time the impact of one of Mike Sangster's 140 mph serves on the tape broke three of Fingers' seismographic fingers. He carried on as though nothing had happened, in great pain. It was all part of the job.

Clark Graebner told me of another challenging situation. You remember that meek fellow Graebner who won all the sportsmanship awards and made it to the Forest Hills final in 1967? That was Fortescue's last match: Graebner and Jan Leschly in a desperate five-set semifinal which Clark won from two sets back. During a critical point near the end, Leschly swatted a ball that went long but on its way the ball was grazed by Graebner's racket. Only two people in that cauldron heard or knew: Graebner and Fortescue. A big, big point that was Clark's if he kept his mouth shut.

Was there any doubt that Graebner would refuse the point? "Mr. Fortescue was looking right at me," recalls Graebner. "It was only a quick glance, but those steely gray eyes revealed in a flash what the honor system was all about. Of course I told the umpire I touched the ball."

"I expected nothing less of Clark; there was no question what he'd do," said Fortescue later.

There were so many instances of his good influence on the game that even his mother decided Fingers wasn't a failure. At last she became reconciled to "my son the net judge. He was born to it. I'm glad we had the money to support him and his habit." Fingers' father, Stuyvesant Forbes Fortescue, the tissue king, was known as "The Toilet Paper Tiger."

In a conversation we had about her son many years ago, Mrs. Fortescue whispered, "I'm to blame for it all, perhaps, although it seemed to happen naturally. Once, when Niles was very young and couldn't walk, Mr. Fortescue and I took him with us to our tennis court. I put his little hands on the net cord and told him to hang there, where we could keep our eyes on him. He loved it. He giggled when the ball touched the tape and the tremor ran to his hand. It seemed almost a sensuous experience.

"I should have gotten him away from that net, but by the time I saw what was happening it was too late. One summer at Newport we had a box at The Casino. He saw the net judges at work—the famous one then was Colonel Hoppin in his boater—and Niles was hooked. That's all he wanted to do. He was a dutiful son. He went through the motions at Groton, Harvard and Oxford, but with no thought to the family business. Just planning to become a full-time volunteer net judge! What could I say to our friends? Yet I realize he does it with great style and distinction. And they say it is a unique contribution."

She related how, though a natural right-hander, he taught himself to write, eat, do all the essentials left-handed in order to save his right for the essential function—at the cord. Twice weekly an osteopath worked on his right hand which he kept sheltered in a silk and ermine muff while away from the net.

As I have said, nobody called him Fingers within his hearing. The nickname came from the acerbic typewriter of New York Herald Tribune columnist W.O. McGeehan in 1921, which I learned on opening the note from Fortescue, delivered posthumously by his man, Creighton. A thoroughly estimable human being, Fortescue—like all of us—had sinned. He had written me to unburden himself. From the envelope, along with his letter, came a xerox of a McGeehan column which began:

"Fingers Fortescue an official whose head was as stuffed as his shirt, held up not only the net yesterday at Forest Hills but also Bill Tilden. He saved Tilden with a homer's call favoring the American star when he was on the edge of extinction at the clever hands of Japan's Zenzo Shimizu in the opening Davis Cup match. Reprieved, Tilden went on...etc."

Next I read the letter from Fortescue:

Dear Mr. Collins:

Although I approve of neither you nor your work, you represent an outlet to the public which I now seek to utilize to acknowledge a transgression which haunted me for more than half a century. I was too proud to admit my guilt while I lived, but it must be entered into the record nonetheless. Yes, I wronged Zenzo Shimizu that afternoon at Forest Hills when the journalist McGeehan baptized me with the beastly sobriquet, Fingers.

It was the first match of the Challenge Round, as I'm sure you know, and this clever little man Shimizu was beating Tilden, 7-5, 6-4, 5-4. The gallery was in shock. Could Tilden lose? Would Japan, unheard of in tennis, take the great Cup to the Orient? Normally I could maintain strict impartiality, but in this case, to my discredit, I was as emotional as the rest, dreading the Yellow Peril. Only three years before I had served—alongside Jay Gatsby, I might add—with the A.E.F. in France. I'm afraid I looked at this match in terms of patriotism.

As Shimizu took the balls to serve at 40-30, match point, I was horrorstruck. What could I do for my country? He struck the ball perfectly and it shot down the center line for an ace. Tilden grimaced but began to stride forward to shake hands when I heard myself emit the scream of "Let!" The place was silent except for the enraged Shimizu's protests which I couldn't understand—and a peal of laughter from the gallery. I assumed later it was the sarcastic McGeehan, amused at what he described as "Fingers wrapping himself in the flag and discovering a non-existent let." Schuyler Pizzington, who was in the chair, whispered to me, "Are you sure, old boy?"

"Let," I repeated. Tilden shrugged his shoulders and returned to the baseline to receive. Shimizu kept bowing toward me in the polite Japanese way, all the time glaring and sobbing in Japanese. The translation of his remarks, I was told, amounted to: "You are the most despicable American since Benedict Arnold." Years later, when World War II ended, I learned that my name was on that list of Americans who were considered the most offensive to Japan and would be executed when the Japanese army occupied the United States. I would have deserved it.

Shimizu was useless thereafter. He double-faulted. Tilden won three straight for the set, and eventually the match in five. The dispirited Japanese lost, 5-0, and the Cup was safe. For a while I was proud to have saved it, but that feeling vanished, replaced by the proper one of guilt and regret. Although my reputation will suffer, and this disclosure may eliminate me as a candidate for the Hall of Fame, I feel it must be made public. Thank you for doing so. I suppose I shall hear Shimizu's words through an eternity in hell, and perhaps I shall have learned to speak Japanese so that I can get the full impact of their venom.

Sincerely,
C.N. Fortescue

So there it is—the revelation that Fingers Fortescue was not perfect after all. Who is? I don't think it tarnishes his name, do you? Who among us might not have done the same to poor Shimizu to preserve Tilden, then the idol of a nation?

The fact that Fingers is gone saddens me more than the news of his one slip. I doubt that we shall see his like again. I realize there are some who derided him as just another net fetishist. They will relish hearing of his frailty in robbing Shimizu.

After reading Fortescue's note, I wondered if I should print it. Would I only be gladdening the cynics? Would I be darkening a noble reputation and discouraging those who looked up to him and aspired to his high standards of netry, those he personally instructed in getting the proper grip on the net?

However, he had instructed me to print the truth, and I have.

Creighton, who knew the secret, said, "Mr. Fortescue intended to publish it all in his memoirs, entitled 'Nearer My Net to Thee.' But time ran out on him. He felt he could go easily to his reward if his confession appeared in print."

Creighton said a feeling of relief and peace came over Fortescue once he'd written the note.

"He passed away an untroubled man," said the butler. "As he departed, he was smiling. The same smile that lighted his face whenever he detected a particularly devilish let that would have eluded any lesser judge.

"I think," said Creighton, "he felt the touch of Big Daddy Death himself on that net over the bed because his very last words were:

"'Oh, it's you. Do you suppose we could play a let?'" ●

THINK OF THE BALL AS A CLOCK

by JULIE M. HELDMAN

WATCH THE BALL! A good player has to remind herself to do this every time her concentration wavers. A good coach says these three words so often that she could substitute half of every lesson with a recording of them. Boring, very boring, the same words all the time. However, there is a way to relieve some of the tedium of forcing intense concentration: think of the ball as a clock. As you look at a tennis ball, imagine that the top of it is high noon, and clockwise around visualize three, six and nine. Every shot you hit can be thought of in terms of what hour you make first contact on the clock and to what hour you follow through.

Watching the ball is one of the five absolute basics in every stroke. The other four are: 1) bend your knees, 2) get your racket ready early, 3) control your wrist (on volleys you should hold your wrist stiff, on the serve and overhead you must snap your wrist; and how you hold your wrist on your groundstrokes depends on what spin you are hitting) and 4) follow through properly. Watching the ball as a clock will help you concentrate on the hit and make sure that you follow through to the right place.

I learned this method originally from Don Prince, pro at the Menlo Circus Club in California, who was trying to teach me a serve 10 years ago. I did not then understand the mechanics of a slice serve. First, he adjusted my grip to a normal backhand grip, and then he told me to hit the ball between one and two o'clock. The first serve was not an ace, but I immediately visualized how to serve a slice.

For other spins on the serve, you must strike the clock at a different hour. The topspin serve, for righthanders, is hit from 10 to 12, and the American twist is hit from eight o'clock following through until 12. A completely flat serve is almost impossible to hit if you are under 6'3", but if you do try it, you must hit up at the ball face on, between six and 12, with a big wrist snap. If you are 9'4", snap down at 12 o'clock and all is well.

A completely flat stroke gives maximum power, but there is very little margin for error on a ball which does not have a downward arc or controlling spin. If you hit a flat

groundstroke with all your might, you must aim the ball no more than a few inches over the net. If you want to attempt a flat forehand, hit across from three to nine o'clock with a stiff wrist.

For a flat backhand, just reverse the clock, and hit from nine to three. The follow-through for a flat stroke is straight across the body. If you want to add a little sidespin control to a completely flat groundstroke, again hit across the clock—from three to nine for a forehand, and from nine to three for a backhand—but loosen up your wrist. You contact the ball slightly behind the wrist, thus imparting a little spin as you hit the side of the ball.

For classically controlled groundstrokes with power plus a bit of topspin, keep your wrist stiff during the entire stroke, and hit from four (forehand) or eight (backhand) up to 12. This makes the racket come slightly around and over the ball. Completing the follow-through, the player should be standing with the racket hand at eye level, his racket straight in front of him and pointing at the top of the middle fence post on his opponent's side of the court. If you want extra topspin and you want the ball to go crosscourt, loosen your wrist, hit around the outside of the ball more, and finish your stroke over the opposite shoulder (for a forehand hit from five to 10 and for a backhand hit from seven to two). If you want to hit a topspin lob or a dipping, down-the-line groundstroke, again use a loose wrist, and start at five for a forehand and seven for a backhand, but do not let the racket head go across the body. For a forehand, finish at one, and a backhand end at 11.

There are three kinds of groundstrokes hit with slice: one is for extra power to penetrate deep into the opponent's court, the second is for extra slice, which gives an exaggerated low bounce for a fast cement or grass court, and the third is a chip, which you hit when you want to keep the ball low as you come to the net and are moving forward at a ball waist high or above. To hit a slice you must hit down and across the ball. To get power, start high and finish with your racket pointing to where you want the ball to go (for a forehand two to nine, for a backhand 10 to three). To

achieve an exaggerated slice, hit from two to seven for the forehand or 10 to five for the backhand. A chip is a slice with a shortened wind-up, and is hit from two to eight on the forehand and from 10 to four on the backhand.

The volley is a punch. The only volley that has a wind-up and a follow-through is the put-away. The killer drive-volley frequently is used on a high easy ball, sometimes hit flat, but more often given added control with topspin on the forehand side and slice on the backhand. It is always best to hit the volley as far in front of the body as possible, and if the ball is waist high, it can be punched flat, at three and nine o'clock respectively for forehand and backhand. Many volleys are hit below waist height and so need to be lifted. There is no time for a wind-up on most volleys, so a topspin volley is nearly unknown. A volley is lifted by punching at four o'clock for the forehand, or eight o'clock for the backhand to give height and a little backspin. The volley is really a shortened chip, with almost no wind-up and follow-through. For extra backspin, punch the ball at five (forehand) or seven (backhand).

Here it is in chart form:

	Forehand	Backhand	Serve	Forehand Volley	Backhand Volley
Flat	3 to 9	9 to 3	6 to 12 or 12	3	9
Sidespin	3 to 9	9 to 3			
Topspin control	4 to 12	8 to 12	10 to 12		
Extra topspin	5 to 10	7 to 2	8 to 12		
Topspin lob	5 to 1	7 to 11			
Power slice	2 to 7	10 to 5	1 to 12	4	8
Extra slice	2 to 9	10 to 3	2 to 12	5	7
Chip	2 to 8	10 to 4			

HOW TO COMBAT THE JITTERS

by ED COLLINS

DO YOU GET ner…ner…nervous when you play? Many people are great ralliers but can't play. They get the jitters. Tennis is a difficult game to play when overly excited. Your body doesn't respond. Although your head knows what to do, your obstinate arms and legs won't listen. Experience builds confidence and confidence brings composure, but it takes a long time to develop these things.

Is it possible to force yourself to relax? Sure it is. A black belt in karate will tell you about conquering and controlling the physical with the mental. Basketball players force themselves to relax before shooting a free throw by bouncing the ball, taking a deep breath and shrugging their shoulders. Athletes in all sports have tricks to stay relaxed.

Here are some things you can do to relax and play up to your potential in tennis:

● **Don't serve the ball until you are ready.** Your opponent can't do anything until you serve the ball, so take your time. Get in the right frame of mind before starting the point. Calm yourself by bouncing the ball a few times before starting. Take a deep breath and *think* the ball to the target.

● **Relax your grip.** A "sawdust" grip is a major cause of tennis elbow and characteristic of a nervous game. Every time you serve, check your hand to make sure you are allowing the grip to "breathe." Wiggle your fingers to remind yourself. Do the same thing when you are returning serve. If it helps, you can pretend you are holding a parakeet— you don't want to squeeze it, but you don't want to let it get away. It is easy to remember to relax your grip before the

point starts, but what happens during the point? It's then that you tighten up like a vise. Some players develop an automatic reflex to combat this: they spin the racket in their hand. (One twist with the left hand at the racket throat helps keep the grip dry and the arm healthy.)

● **Relax your legs.** It is impossible to hit a ball if your arm is tight and equally impossible to move well if you are stiff in the knees. The sprinter knows that he has to be loose— and so does the tennis player. That is why he "bounces" between shots. After he hits the ball, he recovers his court position and bounces gracefully on the balls of his feet. This action reminds him to relax and helps his mobility.

● **Shrug your shoulders.** Before serving and returning serve, check to see if you are getting a little hyperkinetic. A good sign is the elevation of your shoulders. Relax yourself by sagging your shoulders and neck muscles. Think jello.

● **Say to yourself, "Get Nervous!"** It is difficult to tell yourself to relax. In doing so you confirm your feelings of nervousness, and that makes you more nervous. A psychiatrist might approach the problem differently, telling his excited patient: "Get nervous!" Try it when the score is four all in a Sudden Death tiebreaker.

● **Don't watch your opponent.** Many beginning and intermediate players become paranoid anticipating an opponent's next move. They have a breakdown when the opponent approaches deep to their backhand. They take their eyes off the ball to see where the opponent is and then miss the ball completely. ●

RAMONA: IT SANG OUT A DIFFERENT SONG OF LOVE

by NEIL AMDUR

MARGARET COURT never felt comfortable. Not when the match was first announced, as she fought to concentrate on other commitments, not when she arrived at the bizarre wilderness site she thought was San Diego, not when she walked on the court and curtsied quaintly after The Man presented her with a bouquet of roses for Mother's Day, 1973.

By contrast, the match was made in heaven for Robert Larrimore Riggs. It was, as a friend, Al Bunis, observed, "a reincarnation," an opportunity to bask in the sun again, after those dark, frustrating and forgotten years that tore at an ego which demanded constant feeding. When Bobby Riggs began beating the drums for "The Battle of the Sexes—The Match of the Century," as he called it, he was

doing more than sending out smoke signals to the Barona Indians who were encamped on a reservation a few topspin lobs from the San Vicente Country Club. What Riggs did was inflate the scope of HIS event to such preposterous tones that he knew he HAD to win to justify it as "The Greatest Hustle of All Time."

The best thing that could have happened to Riggs came when Billie Jean King, the queen of Women's Lob, told him to forget it. Since Billie Jean wasn't playing as well as she was capable of anyway at the time, Riggs carried his campaign to the top, where Mrs. Court was piling up tournament titles and prize money faster than her husband Barry could figure out ways to invest it.

The match was booked originally for late April, before a

No tennis event—and very few sports events ever—received as much coverage as the Court-Riggs encounter. Bobby beat Margaret 6-2, 6-1 as cameramen recorded every move each made. Margaret sadly reflects on the results.

final May 13 television date was agreed upon to slide in neatly on the CBS Sports Spectacular. When someone took the trouble to look at the calendar, and the words "Mother's Day" happened to be scribbled under that Sunday, it was another crosscourt passing shot for Riggs. How could a "55-year old player with one foot in the grave", as he liked to term it, beat a sweet, sincere woman with a 14-month old son on her one day of the year?

In another era, as it was a generation ago with other players, a match between a 55-year old man and a 30-year old woman might have been played on a lazy Sunday afternoon at The Piping Rock Club, watched by a dozen or so friends and relatives sipping Iced Tea Specials on the clubhouse veranda. But these are new times when women are struggling for identity, equality, a bit of an edge anywhere they can find it. When Bobby Riggs mouthed off that "women's tennis stinks" or that the women's place on a tennis court belonged in the doubles alley or in the box seats, his scorn became a battle cry for females everywhere: Margaret Court had to put this hustling dude in his place.

You have to admire Margaret. She may be the greatest women's tennis player in the world, but she is first and foremost a genuine woman. Watch her feeding her spirited son at breakfast or changing his diapers, and you can understand what a remarkable woman she is, especially when she can follow this routine and still beat the hell out of 99 44/100 per cent of her peers on a tennis court. Margaret Court also is a very private person. She would much prefer sipping a cold Foster's in a far corner of a room, with husband Barry at side, than standing in the center surrounded by reporters asking her for the umpteenth time, "Margaret, what are your real views on women's lib?"

Margaret Court is a liberated woman, as liberated as she could ever hope to be without going mad in these frivolous times. She does not need to go braless to exert her individuality or freedom, or talk tough with males by spouting four-letter words, because she has all the confidence she needs: she gets that confidence every day by walking out on a tennis court and proving to the world and to herself that she has achieved something that six million other women in this country would snap back their bras for—identity.

Margaret Court did not need a duel in the sun with Bobby Riggs as much as Bobby Riggs needed a match with a woman, any woman. Margaret had her security, even more so because Barry and Danny are with her almost every minute of every day to reaffirm the beauty of their world. How many women can have it all—a job they enjoy, a husband who digs the scene, a son who is going to be big enough and strong enough someday to do his thing, and genuine friends around the world who say, "Let's tip a few tonight for old times sake."

But underneath Margaret's quiet ways, pride can bounce like a drop shot, and pride is that part of a personality seldom seen in sports but always in focus. When Bobby Riggs, the 55-year old man with one foot in the grave, came calling, Margaret couldn't walk away. The money was inviting, the television exposure would be nice but, more than that, it was Margaret's competitive pride and curiosity that told her it might be worth a go, even though she knew that it was like holding hands with the devil.

Margaret never had a feel for the match from the first time she caught a glimpse of the San Diego Country Estates, or tried to find it.

If you're an Australian who merely travels around the United States, as Margaret does, when someone tells you "San Diego Country Estates," you have this vision of a wonderland development on the outskirts of a big city, or at the least a collection of condominiums in a fashionable suburb. It wasn't until Margaret and Barry tried to find the place, coming from San Francisco and a series of workouts, that they realized the site was 38 miles from nowhere, with the closest town something called "Ramona," as in the song. The difference is that this Ramona sang a stranger song of love—like you're on your way to getting hustled, pally. After all, wasn't "Wildcat Canyon," the two-lane access highway, famous as a spot where narcotics smugglers made their midnight aerial drops from Mexico?

This is not to suggest that the San Vicente Country Club or San Diego Country Estates lacked charm. In time, with its natural setting, it may become one of the great places to escape from future Watergates. But not a single home was on the property when the Courts arrived, which may explain why the development people were willing to cough up $5,000 as part of the $10,000 winner-take-all purse (Riggs contributed the other $5,000 as his challenge).

If Margaret felt as though she were stranded in the Australian outback, Riggs gave her little opportunity for privacy. He was everywhere, moving from courtside to the clubhouse and back to his hotel room, which was close enough to the Courts for him to bump into Barry wheeling Danny for a stroll along the highway.

Bobby Riggs has always been overlooked as a tennis player's tennis player. It is as though the mention of Riggs' name, in the company of Tilden, Budge, Kramer and others, would be an injustice. Part of the explanation for this pattern may be the sense of distrust some people hold toward Riggs as a person, because of the countless stories that have followed him around the circuit for the last four decades. The larger the legend in any athletic circle, the less likely there is for legitimate acceptance, and Riggs is near the top of the list in sports storytelling. Tucked off behind these exploits, told and retold over drinks at clubs from Long Island to La Costa, Riggs has the international titles that count—from Wimbledon to Forest Hills. It also must be remembered that Riggs entered the scene at an inopportune time—the War Years—when sports were being overshadowed by other national priorities. It took a .400 batting average by Ted Williams to shake the nation's fancy in 1941, but most sports stories between 1940 and 1945 lack the verve and excitement that followed in the Fifties and Sixties.

In pre-match workouts at San Vicente, Riggs gave the impression of a Senior who had either left his greatness in one of the 415 vitamin pills he kept saying he took each day, or that he was intentionally laying low. While Mrs. Court looked crisp and keen in all-out hits with Tony Trabert, the club pro, and Vicki Berner, a Virginia Slims player, Riggs was involved in a few routine $50 a set hustles with teaching pros who stayed by his side like Bundini Brown inflating Muhammad Ali's ego before a fight. Riggs looked so uninspiring that 18 of 24 newsmen on the scene for the match picked Mrs. Court in a pre-match poll. For the record, the six who saw something else in the wind were Bob Rowe of CBS-TV Sports, Will Grimsley of The Associated Press, Curry Kirkpatrick of Sports Illustrated, Dave Nightingale of The Chicago Daily News, Art Rogers of The Los Angeles Times and Al Bunis, who was filing in behalf of several Ohio papers while trying to put together a prize money circuit for Seniors.

The day of the match broke sunny and clear, after the morning fog in the neighboring Cuyamaca Mountains had burned off. It was, one cynic suggested, a perfect "mother's day," the sort of day to send the hustlers back where their two feet belonged. Riggs, however, refused to let this mood interfere with his motives. As late as two hours before his TV debut, the little man with the horn-rimmed glasses and styled hairdo was collaring Barry Court outside of Court's hotel room trying to convince Court that a rematch would be a natural, with even more money. Was Riggs nervous about losing or was it just another burst of energy? Probably a shred of both, since there was no way at the time Riggs could gauge what type of response Mrs. Court would produce during the match, and a hustler is only at his best once the door is open and he is free to move both feet for better position.

"Isn't he unbelievable?" Larry Krieger, Mrs. Court's attorney, said, watching the scene for a few moments before interceding to protect Barry from losing a baby carriage. "The guy hasn't even played one match, and he's trying to hustle another."

The scene around courtside was a combination of low Hollywood and high Forest Hills. Cadillacs and Rolls Royces rolled up the same dusty road with old trucks and campers, and the attire ranged from coats and ties to flimsy, fleshy two-piece something-or-others designed to light a TV director's fire.

Even before the first official coin toss was made to determine the first serve, the match was tossed about for the type of balls to be used and whether coaches would be allowed at courtside, á la Davis Cup. Why Riggs even needed a coach is a mystery, but Mrs. Court went along, although whatever Dennis Van der Meer told her throughout the match had best be kept out of future books on "how to play winning tennis."

Riggs won the toss. Instead of electing to receive serve, as many knowledgeable "Riggs Rooters" had thought he would to start the psyche phase of the match, Riggs decided to serve the first game.

The match may have been won in the first game. Riggs' first serve, to Mrs. Court's forehand, was so slow that you could have read the print on the ball. It was a pattern that he would keep throughout the match, with few exceptions, like the time he hammered successive aces at 30-all to take a 4-1 lead in the second set.

Margaret seemed as uncomfortable on the court, trying to resolve Riggs' soft-balling serves and offspeed ground strokes, as she was listening to his pre-match banter. Occasionally, as at 30-love in the opening game when she hammered a forehand return of service placement down the line off a dink first serve, there were flashes of the Grand Slam champion who had won 89 of her last 92 singles matches on the women's tour. But more often than not, the trend of the match was exemplified from Game Two in the opening set, when Margaret faulted three of her five first serves and lost the game at 15 as follows: she nets a backhand drive, after a backcourt rally of largely off-speed strokes, for 0-15; she attacks the net but drives her first overhead of the match into the net, off a short Riggs lob, for 0-30; she double-faults for 0-40; she plows a big first serve into Riggs' forehand, which he drives long for 15-40; and she overhits a forehand approach shot. GAME.

At no time did it ever seem as though Margaret could

Margaret, looking graceful in defeat, chose to come to net very seldom. Bobby beat her easily from the backcourt.

gain control of the match. When she finally held serve for 1-3, with a chance to get at Riggs' serve, he held serve at love. Two of Mrs. Court's three errors in the game came on service return errors from the backhand, which she rushed into and drove far behind the baseline, her nerves still unable to comprehend the pace and rhythm that Riggs was dictating. Serving at 1-4, Margaret's nerves went deeper into a hole when a helicopter landed on the golf course adjacent to the stadium court, bringing with it just the noise Margaret needed to lose feel of the ball striking that vibrant center of the racket on the serve.

Now it was Riggs serving for the set, and the Male Chauvinists in the capacity crowd of 3,500 were nudging their wives with glee, as though to say, "See, I told you so. You wouldn't listen."

Margaret made her last stand in the next two games. She broke Bobby's serve by reaching his backhand drop shot and pushing it down the line, into open court, for a winner. But she could not sustain her momentum, and Riggs broke back when Margaret made four more errors to lose serve. The first set lasted 28 minutes, and now the CBS people were beginning to worry whether they would have enough match left to fill their time slot.

The second set could have been worse; it could have been 6-0 instead of 6-1, although Margaret's best game of the match came for 1-all in the second set, when she uncorked two backhand volleys for winners and a forehand crosscourt placement. When she unwound a forehand placement down the line for love-15 on Riggs' serve in the third game, a shred of suspense entered. But Riggs returned to his offspeed sliced backhands and dink serves and won the next four points.

In retrospect, Riggs played almost perfectly. His dink serve, while slow, pulled Margaret so far to her right for the return, that she could never get comfortable or position herself in the backcourt. Instead of challenging Margaret with deep drives to the corners, where she thrives on crosscourt returns, Riggs hit the ball straight down the middle, right into her strokes, cramming her long arms to unwind for the off-speed return and kinking her footwork, which forced many unnatural returns and subsequent errors.

Much of Mrs. Court's game depends on a hitting groove, because of her size. Her toughest women's matches are against players like Rosemary Casals, Billie Jean King and Chris Evert, who can vary the speed and control of their shots and dictate some pace to Mrs. Court, instead of vice-versa. Someone suggested that Margaret would have been better off taking some practice hits with her husband Barry than Tony Trabert to find out how to adjust her rhythm to junk.

The difference between traditional strategy and coaching for a match against Riggs is that Bobby knows he wants to do what he must do to survive: as long as he is free to dictate this element into a match, he can continue to conquer. It is when he is forced into another game, as he is against Senior peers, that he becomes most vulnerable, which is precisely why many Seniors now enjoy taking him on.

In defeat, Mrs. Court evoked genuine sympathy from many followers, including men, who felt that she had been victimized in the bizarre tradition of the Great American Hustle. But it must be said that Mrs. Court is a professional who plays the game for a living, and thus subjects herself to whatever whims accompany the life of a pro, be it injury to mind or body. In this case, her fragility in the face of The Big Match once again surfaced, and it should be considered no disgrace that she lost: Arnold Palmer has blown matches on the 18th green, and quarterbacks have overthrown open receivers in the end zone because their hands suddenly tightened as they released the football.

If anything, Margaret Court's willingness to accept the challenge did as much for tennis as a sport as anything the game has seen in recent years. Forgetting who won or lost, the event itself merited mammoth coverage, as evidenced by the Monday morning pages of the country's biggest papers, The New York Times, Los Angeles Times and Washington Post.

May 13, 1973 will go down in tennis annals as more than just Bobby Riggs' return to the summit. The Riggs-Court match, coupled with the World Championship of Tennis Finals from Dallas, provided a blanket of coverage for a sport that once evoked scorn from television producers, who considered it a deathknell in the numbers game.

No more. The numbers are clearly in tennis' favor now, and Bobby Riggs and Margaret Court have done their share. For this, the sport should be thankful, even if it has helped Riggs put his feet and his mouth back on center court again. ●

Althea Gibson is Alive and Well...

by NEIL AMDUR

THE SONY PORTABLE, antennae pulled high, blared the beautiful soul sounds of WBLS-FM, as Althea Gibson moved to a chair in her office at the new Valley View Racquet Club in Northvale, N.J. She was sporting a handsome slacks outfit with a sleek vest and, for the moment, seemed far removed from the center court where her regal presence warmed the hearts of millions of tennis fans.

Outside her office, the antiseptic strains of Muzak, described by one of her friends as "morgue music," blended in with the Modern Suburban Tennis decor of the club, one of several to open in the area in the Boom of the last few years. On the six Grasstex courts, women's doubles teams in assorted shapes and sizes, all with the latest fashions in shoes, dresses and rackets, frolicked for their one-hour playtime.

"This is the position I should have been in when I was the world champion," Althea said, leaning back in her chair, comfortable as a program director with a five-year contract should be. "I've always said that an individual who devotes so much time to a sport should at least be able to make a living out of it."

In 1957 and 1958 Althea Gibson was the finest women's tennis player in the world. Some people believe she had no peers among the sport's great names in her prime. No one will ever really know, however, because much of her tournament time was spent as the Josh Gibson of women's tennis, playing in the more obscured American Tennis Associ-

ation the way Gibson labored as the Babe Ruth of the black baseball circuit.

In those days, the United States Lawn Tennis Association and its member clubs were not ready for black faces on their premises except in the kitchen or pushing backhands with a broom. By the time Althea Gibson made it to Forest Hills and Wimbledon, she knew she couldn't sustain a living as an "amateur"; so after blowing the world's big guns apart for a few years, she signed a professional contract in 1959 with Abe Saperstein, the big kahuna of the Harlem Globetrotters ("There was no incentive to remain an amateur," she recalls. "I couldn't eat trophies.").

No one ever bothered to ask Althea how much money she earned for her six-month tour of 100 cities with Karol Fageros. But when she came back home after the tour, she said she looked in her checking account and it "had over $100,000," which would have given her a decided head start over Billie Jean King as the first woman athlete to crack the six-figure category for earnings in a single year.

Don't get the idea that Althea was rolling in dough, as many people did during what she likes to refer to as her "Reign." Out of her earnings in those days, which frequently came to $900 a night depending on Globetrotters' success, Althea had to pay a manager *and* lawyer. "Women's tennis is better today," she said, discussing Then and Now. "During my Reign, Alice Marble and I were probably the only two who played aggressively, attacking con-

stantly. Today, women pros and many of the fine young amateurs are playing the net game. I always advocate an aggressive style because that's the way I grew up. Girls are playing progressively."

Even at her age, which you can check in any old USLTA Guide of the late Fifties, Althea still has the serve and volley. She played mixed doubles recently with Gar Mulloy at the U.S. Open Championships and traded shots with Billie Jean King and Rosemary Casals in a grand-opening exhibition at Valley View. Although she has not played singles in a major women's tournament for several years, she says she feels "fit enough" to make occasional tournament appearances, a la Richard Gonzalez.

It seems almost incredible that success off-the-court should finally come to Althea a decade after her Reign. But that is precisely what has happened; another indication of the rigid confines that existed in tennis, and still do to some extent. Valley View, situated in one of the country's typical white-bedroom suburbs, Bergen County, was the first club to approach her about a permanent job. Yes, the FIRST club, she says. She is doing commercials for Colgate Palmolive now. Fifteen years ago she was trying her luck with a series of one-shotters that everyone thought would open doors—a bit part in John Wayne's "The Horse Soldiers," an album for Dot Records, an autobiography. More often than not, the only doors that opened went the other way. In "The Horse Soldiers", which pops up periodically on those 4:30

Althea was given a ticker tape parade
by the mayor of New York City upon her
triumphant return from Wimbledon in 1957.

PM movies these days, Althea played "Lukey," a southern maid. She read the script and felt it was so degrading in its portrayal of the Southern black that she refused to accept the part until adjustments were made. They were. Only one tennis manufacturer, Harry C. Lee, even bothered to approach Althea about an affiliation when she was No. 1, she says, and the royalties for using the racket were so modest (less than $100 a month, she says) that Althea still is embarrassed about discussing the episode, particularly in view of the exclusive deals hammered out for today's top players.

The same situation prevailed when she joined the women's professional golf circuit. "I could call up and say, 'I'd like some clubs,'" she recalled. "Only one company stuck with me to provide equipment. Yet they would not sign me to a contract."

All of which makes Althea appreciate her role at Valley View, where she has a percentage of the operation, teaches and helps conduct a number of adult and children's clinics for that growing tennis population that is supposed to hit 15 million by 1980. "It was a case of being in the right place at the right time," she says of how she was selected for the job. Althea was practicing one day with Art Carrington at an indoor club in Westfield when Dr. Martin Sherer, the Valley View president, casually mentioned to Carrington that his club was looking for a pro.

"Why look any further?" Carrington told Sherer, pointing to Althea. "Here she is."

Althea lives in East Orange, N.J. with her husband of seven years, William Darben, an employment counselor. It is about a 45-minute drive to the club, but traffic generally is moving south toward New York City at that hour of the morning, so Althea has plenty of time to make 9 or 10 AM appointments.

There has always been a certain aura about watching Althea move among crowds. She has an overpowering presence about her, a sense of being that somehow manages to extract excitement or a commitment. It is evident among the novices who sip coffee in the lounge of the club and nod respectfully as Althea walks by. It is noticeable at any of her more public appearances.

Surprisingly, however, Althea will admit privately that she "held back a whole lot during my Reign." There were those frustrating times, she says, when she just wanted to shout "God-damn" in anger over a bad shot, poor serve or some other injustice. But she felt she had to be on good behavior, "on her P's and Q's" as she calls it, to fulfill the image that White Tennis America expected. Times have changed, however, and Althea no longer feels any embarrassment or timidity: the struggle is over, let the soul music play, like it or not.

"There are more opportunities for Afro-Americans in sports and tennis today," she said. "I use the word Afro-Americans because that's our heritage. I think the gate was opened when Jackie Robinson came into baseball and when I came into tennis. I don't like to say that to sound, you know what, but it's true."

Althea has great respect for today's champions—Mrs. King, Margaret Court, Nancy Gunter. "From my observation," she said, "Billie Jean has the type of game that is a winner's game. She has a good serve, volleys well and moves well. Also from what I observe, she's a thinker on a tennis court. Tennis to me is just like a chess game. You have to maneuver, you have to know your opponent's strengths and weaknesses. You have to know where to hit the ball when you're in a jam. It's a thinking game."

Another reason Althea is happy about her position at Valley View is that she hopes to be able to find potential players, black and white, for development—at least those not already signed up or commuting to the Port Washington Tennis Academy on Long Island. "I know there are plenty of young players who have the native ability and drive," she says. "That's what you need, drive and ability."

If Althea looks fit, it is because she has been training to keep her weight down. "During my Reign, I burned a lot of energy," she said. "I'd eat eggs, bacon, grits, milk, jelly and butter for breakfast and have big dinners. When I retired and stopped, I ate the same thing. I suppose it built up in the bloodstream because I discovered I had a high chloresterol count. Now I'm sticking to low fats."

It is hard to think of the all-time greats in women's tennis without including Mrs. William Darben. Anyone who watched her run through Louise Brough in straight sets at Forest Hills in 1957 and Darlene Hard the following year, or saw her dominate Wimbledon the same two seasons can appreciate her talents.

"I figured before my day was up, I'd get my due," she said, leaving her office to prepare for a lesson. "It's just the time span was too long. Some people have to wait longer for things than others. But I'm delighted I'm in this position now. It's what I always wanted." ●

Everything You Want to Know About Equipment

by JULIUS HELDMAN

WHAT DOES the L, M and H mean on a racket handle?

L means light, M means medium and H means heavy. As a rough guide, L corresponds to less than 13½ ounces *strung* weight, M between 13½ and 14 ounces strung weight, and H over 14 ounces. There is no recognized standard and so an L racket of one manufacturer need not be the same as an L from another maker or, for that matter, two made by the same company

may vary quite a bit but still both be labeled L or H or M. Strings weigh slightly less than ¾ of an ounce (⅝ for thin or tournament gut). All good tennis shops have sensitive scales, and the L, M or H marking should be used only as a rough screen if you want to duplicate the weight of a racket you have and like.

Will a cheap racket break quickly or warp? If not, why doesn't everyone buy a cheap racket?

Some cheap watches give excellent service, some cheap fishing rods are quite utilitarian and some cheap television sets are very satisfactory. Quality means both superior materials and workmanship, and the extra cost of an expensive racket is in the quality and also the quality control. A cheap racket may have the same wood or steel or aluminum as an expensive one, and it may indeed last as long, but the laminations are more carefully put together and cured in the higher priced wooden models or the welding or riveting or grommets have better workmanship in the more expensive metal rackets. The finishing, the trim and the grip cost extra, although the basic frame may be about the same in cheap and expensive models. Many manufacturers use their top-line unfinished frame rejects for their lower-priced models. If the frame is rejected for a meaningless wood blemish, there is no problem, but if the batch of glue was bad or the wood was not cured properly, you could be buying a lemon. So you pay for quality and quality control. Your chances are better, although there is never an absolute guarantee even with the most expensive merchandise. Some rackets are indeed more expensive to make than others, and they are the highest priced. Do you want a Cadillac or a Continental Mark IV or a Pinto or Volkswagen?

Why would anyone want a head-heavy or head-light racket? If I have a good volley, would such

a racket help or hurt me?

This question has been debated since the beginning of tennis. Some people say that unless the racket is evenly balanced, the racket head will swing through too fast (head-heavy) or will lag behind the wrist (head-light). Others say that the racket will do more work for you and will produce more momentum with an easy swing if it is very head-heavy. Gil Hunt, a First Tenner in the U.S. in the late 30's, used to fasten a thin strip of lead to the tip of the racket head and then used a swing only a foot or two long. The arguments used against this are that the head-heavy racket is harder to maneuver and tires the arm. If your arm can take it and it suits your timing, you probably *will* have a harder serve with a head-heavy racket. But fast-hand volleyers, who must move their rackets instantly, will probably go for a head-light (as well as a light) racket. My recommendation is to choose a racket that best satisfies the natural timing and wrist action of your most important stroke. For some that will be the serve and for others ground-strokes or volley.

Why do some players choose a wooden racket and some a steel or aluminum racket? How do I know which racket would be best for me? If I can't tell, then does it make any difference what I buy? Please make sense of this for me.

The reason is usually given as "feel," meaning the reaction when the racket and ball collide. This is a function of the stiffness of the frame and the gut tension as well. Forgetting the latter, the stiffer the frame, the more controllable the ball, viz., the less fast spring-back action of the frame to sling-shot the ball. Even before metal rackets, one could get whippy or stiff wood frames. Big servers liked whippy ones but most groundstrokers went for average or stiffer ones. Now metal rackets come in all degrees of springiness, even more whippy than the most flexible wood. My advice is to beg or borrow various types of bats to try before making an investment in a type which gives you fits because you cannot control your groundstrokes.

What weight rackets should children, women and men buy? What happens if you get a racket that is too light or too heavy?

The general ranges of strung weight are: children, 11-13 ounces; women,

12½-14 ounces; men 13-15 ounces. Today the top men players are using rackets about ½ an ounce lighter than they did in the 30's. If the racket is too light, you won't realize your full power potential but you can maneuver the bat easily. If the racket is too heavy, your arm gets tired and you may swing a trifle late. However, there are always exceptions. The late Maureen Connolly hit the heaviest ball in women's tennis during the era in which she played, but she used an extremely light racket. Don Budge, one of the all-time great players in tennis history and one of the hardest hitters, used and still uses a heavier racket than anyone else.

Can a player who hits two-handed on both sides use a racket with a very big handle?

There are so few players who hit two-handed on both sides, particularly in the tournament echelon, that it is impossible to make any dictum on the subject. The use of two hands would take off some of the strain and a larger handle could be used if it felt comfortable for the player. However, the handle would be too large for good "feel" on service.

How can you tell if a racket has too big or too small a handle?

The feel of a handle is the single most important factor in the suitability of a racket. The human hand is astonishingly sensitive to tiny variations in the circumference and shape of a handle. Racket handles average about 4⅝ inches in circumference, and many players can distinguish as little as two-hundredths of an inch variation. Not only that but they can "feel" a slightly different shape, which will

lead to a slightly different grip, resulting in a different opening of the racket face for a set wrist. Again, it is imperative to play with different handles, both size and shape, before selecting a racket. In the 1920s, handles of 5 inches to 5¼ inches circumference were the rage. Now men use 4⅝ to 4⅞; anything smaller or larger is uncommon. Women use 4⅜ to 4⅝ and children are down to 4 or 4¼ when such rackets can be found. The racket will turn in your hand too easily if the handle is too small or large. Very few players like round handles because they cannot home in on a secure, reproducible grip location.

How tightly should my racket be strung if I am a beginner; an intermediate; an advanced player; or a champion?

Beginners should not have tightly strung rackets because the gut wears out faster and the difference in stroke resulting is not yet important. Even though warping is far less of a problem than it was formerly, rackets occasionally still do warp and a tight string job is conducive to warping. As you improve and the reaction of the strings against the ball takes on more meaning and subtlety for you, you will probably want a tighter string job. However, there were some great players who insisted on "fish nets," viz., Australia's Sir Norman Brookes and John Bromwich. Most top players like their bats strung with thin gut up to 60 to 65 pounds tension. If the stringing is too tight ("board" tight), then all the resiliency of the gut is gone and it is near its snapping point. Some rackets have plastic grommets which yield a little when first strung, and the first string job on these bats will loosen substantially over the first week of use. Commonly, good players tend to believe a tight racket is most important on volley. Another important factor to consider is economics. The champions use thin gut and very tightly strung rackets, which means that the string jobs don't last as long, but then they are the professionals and the cost of restringing is necessary.

Do stringers still use trim and is it necessary?

Trim is unnecessary. It is just ornamentation—the mark of a certain type of craftsman.

What are the advantages and disadvantages of nylon, and who should use nylon in preference to gut?

There are two types of nylon, monofilament and braided (or twisted). Monofilament nylon is the cheapest and is waterproof. But it slowly stretches, losing its spring, and most importantly it can snap without warning at a place where its smooth surface has started to abrade or where there was a minute imperfection. Braided nylon is intermediate in cost, is waterproof and does not stretch as much. It simply does not have the liveliness of gut when strung tight (technically, it has a higher modulus). Nylon can abrade on a dusty clay court just as badly as gut. Gut is generally conceded to have the most attractive playing qualities, but it is expensive and frays and breaks when used in the rain. Hint: put talcum powder inside your racket cover and this will help to dry the gut after use. Beginners should use nylon, not tightly strung. Good players can stay with nylon but most prefer to change, often keeping one nylon-strung bat for play in a drizzle or on wet courts.

How do I tell good from bad gut? Is there such a thing as bad gut?

Stringers can tell good gut from bad so leave it to them. Bad gut is uneven in appearance, showing translucent "fat" patches and is soft and too stretchy. A reputable manufacturer will not sell "green" gut that is not properly cured.

If a string breaks a week after my racket is strung, can I get my money back? From whom?

If the string broke in the hole in the racket head because it wasn't smooth ("burned"), and if you bought your

racket from a reputable dealer or pro shop, you can probably get a new string job. Some may try to foist off a repair job on you. Stick with your local pro; he won't last if he doesn't treat his customers right. Patching a racket is never as satisfactory as a complete string job.

If my racket breaks (and I didn't throw or drop it), what recourse do I have?

If it is a quality racket and a good shop, you can usually get a replacement. The shop will work it out later with the manufacturer. The adjustment on the string job, which cannot be re-used, is a matter of negotiation. Don't be too tough on the shop; they have to make a living also.

Is there any difference between heavy duty and Tretorn balls? If so, what?

Heavy duty balls, which were introduced about four years ago, are balls with a cover which fluffs up higher than regular balls. The cover lasts longer on hard surfaces like concrete and coated asphalt. Heavy duty balls still have a pressurized core like the regular championship ball. Tretorns are one brand of "pressureless" ball, made with a soft core which does not hold gas pressure. The cover is the heavy duty type. Tretorns meet ILTF specs of size, weight and bounce, but they play as differently from regular balls as do nylon and gut. Heavy duty balls are often used by top players in preference to regular balls on concrete, asphalt or Laykold courts; the fuzz mats down or wears off too fast with regular balls. But on a slow, soft court, heavy duty balls fluff up and feel like lead, and so most top players prefer championship balls when they play on clay.

How long can I use balls before they go dead? What does dead mean?

Tretorn balls never go dead (lose their bounce) but they ultimately lose their fuzz and then do not have good playing qualities. Other balls can be used until their internal pressure decreases, meaning enough gas escapes from their core to the point where they bounce too low, or until the fuzz is worn off, whichever comes first. If the fuzz is smoothed down but not yet all gone, try putting a batch of balls in a washing machine and dryer. It will fluff them up again. Top tournament players use balls anywhere from two to four or five sets (less on concrete and asphalt, longer on clay or composition). Club players use balls anywhere from four sets to 10 sets, depending upon whether the surface is hard or soft. Beginners and Juniors use balls from eight sets on, to the point where all the fuzz is gone and the bounce is lost.

How long should a racket last me? How do I know when it is too old?

A racket will last until it goes soft in the head or warps. Good frames will last a long time, sometimes through three or four string jobs. Worn-out leather grips can easily be replaced. You will know when a racket is too old, just as you know when your car is too old.

How long should a string job last? Do some string jobs last years?

Tournament players with heavy spin serves, using thin gut and tightly strung rackets, will go through gut in 20 sets or less. But as the string is thicker and more loosely strung and as the spin is less, the gut lasts longer. If you don't play very much and if you don't have heavy spins, a fairly tight string job may last for a year. Yes, it does lose a little resiliency, and so if you are finicky or rich, get a restring.

Where should one buy equipment? How do you know if they are overcharging?

Comparative shopping or talking to the troops around the courts should solve the problem of knowing fair prices. However, it is good to back your local pro if you can and if he gives good service and stands behind his merchandise.

How can you tell a bad string job from a good one?

You can check average tension by sound if you strum the strings (the "ping" is high on a highly strung racket). If you look at the strings from along the handle, you can tell if they all have the same waviness, meaning they are all pulled to equal tightness. It is bad if they are not. After a few months, the sound of the strings will get lower, and when it gets too low you may want to get a new string job.

When you open a can of balls, can they ever be bad? How can you tell? Can balls go bad in a can and do they go bad in a box? Why are balls vacuum-packed and how does it help or hurt?

If the can does not hiss when opened, the balls will probably be dead because there was no pressure in the can. Balls are *not* vacuum-packed. They are pressure-packed; otherwise the pressure in their cores slowly escapes. Your shop should replace such a can; don't play with it. If the balls were not packed in a can, they must be fresh to be any good. I strongly recommend against buying open balls, unless they are the pressureless type, no matter how cheap.

How many rackets should I have?

The minimum is one, naturally, but most players who are past the intermediate level have two or more, and top tournament players generally have six or more. The reason: in case a string breaks, there is an immediate duplicate replacement.

How much should I expect to spend on equipment in the course of the year if I play three or four times a week, mostly doubles? My son plays seven days a week, including four to six hours on Saturday and Sunday. How much will it cost me for him and how does this break down?

You will probably buy a can of balls a week for your doubles game, which comes to about $75 a year. Then you will need two pairs of good tennis shoes at $20 to $30. The remainder will be on tennis clothes which will run $50 to $100 (you can get by for less if you are a thrifty shopper, but you will probably get hooked on an "impulse" sweater, fancy shorts, etc.). Rackets and strings will be $25 to $100 (more if you want). The total is $170 to $305, which is extremely inexpensive these days. Remember that court costs are not included. The three important

costs for a youngster are balls, shoes and racket. A boy who "hangs around" a lot may be able to pick up discarded balls or some generous adult may give him some, but he shouldn't wear out his welcome. Kids sometimes patch the toes of their tennis shoes with a tire patch. Shoes can be the biggest cost. If a boy is developing a good serve and playing on hard courts, he will wear them out every other week or so on the right toe. Spin serves also wear out gut or nylon. By adult standards, everyday tennis for two hours could cost $1,000 per year or more, but a dedicated boy or girl can hack it for $200.

Are color balls good and when should they be used?

Both the WCT and Virginia Slims Circuits are using yellow balls at least part of the time. They are particularly good on courts where there are lots of shadows and under artificial lights. White balls get gray on many courts, but the yellow balls retain their contrast to the court surface and backdrop. White balls are excellent on clay courts or two-toned cement.

How long should tennis shoes last?

California cement tournament players can go through the right toe of their shoe every week. The soles of the shoes, under the ball of the foot, might wear out first in two or three weeks if the hind foot isn't dragged on the serve. On clay the shoes should last twice as long; on grass, shoes are very long-lasting indeed. Players who slide on clay will wear through the soles surprisingly rapidly. Some even turn their feet over to stop and wear out the canvas or leather top.

What kinds of tennis shoes are there? Explain the differences and tell me which are the best.

The classical shoe is a low canvas shoe with rubber sole. The good ones have some kind of arch support and cushioning. The sole can be either smooth finished (for hard courts) or corrugated or pattern-molded for better gripping on clay or grass (or even hard courts). Basketball shoes, which come up above the ankles, are not used for tennis. They are too heavy and clumsy. Leather shoes have become very popular recently. The good ones feature cushioned sides as well as heels and are very comfortable and attractive, albeit expensive. Most are heavier than their canvas counterparts. There is no "best" in tennis

shoes and it is simple personal preference.

What are the best kinds of tennis socks—cotton, wool, nylon or orlon?

Thin cotton socks should be used only as an inside pair, with thick socks on the outside. If you wear one pair only, choose wool-nylon or thick orlon. Many good socks now are made with a thick bottom part only so that the rest is not as bulky. Pure wool is not recommended since the tendency to mat and shrink is always there. The modacrylics (orlon) and wool-nylon do not shrink.

What ancillary apparel and goods are vital for tennis?

A warm-up suit is vital in every country except the tropics. Sweaters are always necessary, both to stay warm ahead of time and to avoid getting a chill later. Racket covers are useful to keep the racket dry and the inside should be sprinkled with talcum powder, particularly after playing on a humid day or a wet court. Racket covers also help to identify rackets so that you will not switch inadvertently. A racket press used to be a must but it is much less important with laminated wood frames and of course they are not necessary with metal frames. A tennis bag is extremely useful and convenient if you change at the courts. A small towel is a good idea, but most people don't think to carry one. Absorbent wrist bands are a must for many players. Caps or hats, sweatbands and gloves are optional, depending upon the personal choice of the player. Tennis gloves were introduced relatively recently and have been adopted by some top players, viz., Cliff Drysdale. Some tournament players keep sawdust in their pockets, and this is a must for Fred Stolle and Manuel Santana. Many other players use rosin or a spray on hot, humid days.

Bryan Hamlin, a famous septuagenarian tournament player, appears on court with a case which holds the following: wrist bands (at least six), ankle brace, knee brace, elbow brace, ace bandage, adhesive tape, moleskin, scissors, gauze, antiseptic, band-aids, visor, cap, thermos of hot tea, thermos of orange juice, salt pills, glucose pills, an extra ball-holder to attach to his belt, a small towel to attach to his belt, a large towel, an extra sweater and two rackets. ●

A Better Way to Practice

by DON KLOTZ

THE OLDEST maxim in sports is "Practice as you expect to play in competition." Simple but sound. Practice patterns should be carefully planned to build in the player the conditioned reflexes on which he or she must depend in match play.

Traditionally in tennis up to 85% of practice time is spent on groundstrokes hit from the baseline. The players take the ball on the second or third bounce if necessary in order to maintain this behind-the-baseline position. While it is desirable to develop good groundstrokes and it is unquestionably fun to hit them, one must ask if the groundstrokes merit that much attention. A second pertinent question is how long can *anyone* work profitably on any one stroke? There is a real danger that after an optimum time for any one person, he will become careless and tend to break down the desirable mechanics that should be developed during the effective portion of the practice session.

Charting of tennis matches shows that the total strokes per point seldom average more than four. In televised matches this past season the average was 3.2 strokes per point. For simplicity take an average of four. The first stroke will always be a serve, the second stroke a return of service, and the third stroke will depend on whether the server remains on the baseline or goes to net. If he goes to net the third stroke will be a volley or half-volley and the fourth will be a passing shot or a lob. If he stays on the baseline the third and fourth strokes will likely be groundstrokes. This means 25% of the rally will consist of a service and 25% a return of service, or a total of 50% of all the strokes used in match play. The implications for the design of practice patterns are obvious. Traditional practice systems are inadequate to contend with the stroke situations faced in match play!

But aren't the return of service and the passing shot groundstrokes? Each one is, but a serve may come with all degrees of spin, slice, twist or topspin whereas the customary beginning stroke is hit flat or with very little topspin. The effective return of service also calls for a block, a chip or a slice return as well as a drive. A full swing will be very inadequate in returning some types of service.

The passing shot is a groundstroke but the psychological situation is vastly different from that encountered when rallying from the baseline. Many passing shots should be hit so that they will strike the court near the service line to make the net player volley up. This shallow return is just what *shouldn't* be hit if your opponent is on the baseline. The only effective way to learn to hit good passing shots is to place an opponent near the service line and then hit mostly shallow drives to right, left or at his feet. Baseline driving simply won't get the job done.

The only practical way to learn to serve and return service is to begin rallies with serves and returns of service. Here are some guiding points for implementing the plan:

1. Either player begins each rally with a serve rather than by hitting the ball out of his hand.

2. Serve from anywhere along the baseline. Do not necessarily go to a fixed spot as you do in match play.

3. Indicate to your opponent to which point you intend to serve, i.e., outside corner, inside corner or straight at him. In practice don't try to ace anyone but instead put the ball in play toward one of three targets so that the opponent will have a good opportunity to return the service. Select a convenient target for him. If he happens to be in the middle of the court, aim for one of the inside corners. If he is near the alley, aim for the outside corner.

4. Attempt to return all serves, in or out. A long serve is just as good for practice on return of service as a legal serve.

5. Hit the return of service directly back to the server or indicate where you intend to hit it so that he may go to that point and continue the rally.

6. Continue the rally after the return of service just as you would normally do.

7. Do not necessarily go to the standard receiving position each time. Take the return of service as may be convenient for you at the conclusion of the rally. The receiver can help the server with practice to the outside corners by staying directly behind those corners after retrieving balls near the sides of the court.

8. Do not serve into the net! Those shots benefit no one. A long serve is at least good practice for the receiver.

9. To repeat, either player may begin the rally with a serve just as now rallies are begun by either player hitting the ball out of the hand.

Beginning the rallies with a serve takes a little more time than hitting the ball out of the hand. However, it takes little skill to hit the ball out of the hand and not much more to return that first ball—two wasted strokes—so time is really saved by starting with a serve.

As one could logically expect, the quality of serve and return of service will improve dramatically, especially the return of service. As your confidence in the return of service increases, begin stepping inside the baseline to hit the ball, especially on the softer second serve. Go to meet the service, hitting it to either corner or back at the server's feet. Keep the return deep. If you have a decent volley, go to net and kill the weak return. *No player at any level of play should ever be allowed to get by with an easy second serve. And they won't if the return of service is allotted the practice time it deserves.* ●

Around the Tennis World with Bud Collins

Color & Commentary by America's Leading Tennis Writer and Telecaster

Stockton's stock soars

Young man on the way up is Dick Stockton. En-route to the 1974 Wimbledon semis he beat favorite Ilie Nastase in a match that gave the wives of both men the jitters.

LONDON—Like most young men, Dick Stockton traded in his parents on a wife, and he has asked mainly one thing of her: To die in silence "while I'm losing."

This is because Dick Stockton, the powerful 23-year-old American tennis pro who beat the No. 1 player of 1973, Ilie Nastase, at Wimbledon, has been running from a father who epitomized the Little League syndrome.

Stockton's old man screamed and fought with umpires, tournament officials and other parents. He even had a fist fight with Leonard Solomon, the father of Harold Solomon (a friend of Dick's), during a disputed junior match between Dick and Harold.

"He embarrassed Dick terribly," says Sue Stockton, a slim, engaging blonde from Dallas, who took over as the cheering section for Stockton, the No. 13 player of the U.S. "We didn't know if we should invite the Solomons to our

wedding because there was so much bad blood between the fathers. But Dick's father didn't come anyway... Dick has tried to get him to be not so intense, and I guess he was hurt."

In the ninth game of the fourth set, Stockton (who won, 5-7, 6-4, 6-3, 9-8) performed a fantastic serve-returning operation to cut up Nastase with four outright winners—three of them returns of first serves. That made it 5-4, and the match was his to serve out. "Dickie choked," said Sue. "It was all there—the biggest win of his life—and I could feel him shaking." The bad vibes reached her, and "I shook, too. We were both terrified." Everybody else was trembling. The weather was raw and drizzly.

Stockton, an All-America four straight years for Trinity (Tex.) University, conceded, "I choked all right." He double faulted twice, lost the game, and was in the grip of Nastase at set point two games later. His volleying—firm, imaginative and unfailing—held together and got him into the tie-breaker that he won, 7 points to 5. Stockton, who grew up on Long Island and was busing alone to distant kids' tournaments at age 7, had pulled himself together and Sue didn't have to pass away after all.

Sue feels, "I'm so competitive for him I'm glad I don't play. I wouldn't have enough competitiveness left over for myself. Maybe it's better that I don't know much about tennis."

That doesn't mean she isn't a valued partner. "I do the laundry—very vital," Sue laughed. "But I'm a bit cheap. Try to do everything in one 35-cent load. Sometimes I put my stuff in with his. In Orlando something of mine turned all his stuff pink. In New Orleans it was green. He dressed in secret. Dickie didn't want the guys to see his pink jocks."

Dominique Nastase, the smashing brunette Belgian, couldn't keep up with Sue Stockton. "I had to leave when Ilie was losing. It was too awful," she said. Dominique

Centre Court cries again

Dick Stockton

Wimbledon is a British shrine where the British hardly ever do well at the game they invented. When one—like Virginia Wade in 1974—nearly makes it, they hope and suffer.

LONDON—"It's only a game" and "the game's the thing" are phrases used by people who would like to minimize winning—and are probably losers themselves. They are most likely sensible people, and the English seem sensible folk, grooved at losing in games they invented. The English teach the rest of the world how to play—and how to lose—but just once in a while they pack all their well controlled emotions onto one of their own, like Virginia Wade, and decide, "it's jolly well time she won it for us."

It, of course, is Wimbledon, the shrine to a game called tennis that an Englishman patented a hundred years ago. The English worship each summer at Wimbledon, but they get a little tired of being submissive while God awards all the prizes to foreigners. English tennis players, like English heavyweights and pounds sterling, have a tendency to collapse at moments of great expectation.

But here was Virginia Wade out of Sittingbourne, Kent, who has spent nearly half of her 28 years looking forward to and regretting Wimbledon. Here she was right up there at the pinnacle of a career that has cloaked the island in frustration and agony.

Virginia had won four straight games from 0-2 in the final set and was now only two games away from beating a Russian named Morozova and entering the pearly gates of the championship round.

They were slashing and bashing at each other in a marvelous battle between handsome, aggressive women in Wimbledon's most sanctified chapel—Centre Court—where 14,000 faithful were jammed into pews and standing-room. Maybe they had a death wish because the winner was only going to be thrown in with the Little Machine, Chris Evert, who had ground up Kerry Melville, 6-2, 6-3. Evert with her 34th straight match win, seemed certain to become the first female to win the Italian, French and Wimbledon titles in succession since another 19-year-old American named Maureen Connolly two decades ago.

Nevertheless both ached to win. "I would be first Russian woman in final ever," beamed Olga Morozova, a dark-haired creature so witty and beguiling that you'd convert to communism in return for one of her smiles.

"Last year when Alex Metreveli was first Russian man in final they televised the match to Russia. I would like that to happen to me," said Olga the Volga Volleyer after she shattered the status quo and Billie Jean King.

Wade—slender, regal, athletic, intelligent, a person seemingly bred for the top—had won the US and Australian opens and numerous other titles. But she hadn't been close to a Wimbledon final, and Wimbledon is all that matters in her native island. Year after year she had "felt how much they all wanted me to win. It was so hard when you knew that it meant so much to everyone"—and she wilted before women who were practically strangers to their parents.

But now she was on her way to the title round that has been occupied by merely four Englishwomen (and no men) since World War II—or was she?

---

wasn't there when Ilie, the con man, grabbed an umbrella from a spectator and crouched beneath it to receive serve during the last set.

"I guess I could have served," said Stockton, "but I turned away until he settled down. I just wouldn't let him break my concentration. The last time I played Nastase, I led 6-1, 5-2, had seven match points and blew it. That was in the CBS Classic. You can see it on TV. If I'd blown this one it would have ruined me. I burned out at 12," grinned Stockton, who played his first tournament at 7. "I'm just making a comeback now, trying to regain my 12-year-old form. Until I won Atlanta over John Newcombe, I was afraid I was on a treadmill going nowhere."

Dick was going nowhere when he met Sue on the Trinity campus. "He had a broken leg, couldn't play tennis, so he had time for a date. He was like most tennis players. He sees the world, but sees nothing. Do you know that he was in college four years in San Antonio and never saw the Alamo? Sunday I insisted we visit the Tower of London. You have to see something."

Ken Rosewall, who's been around as long as the Tower gave his wife Wilma her usual "heart failure" during his rebounding victory over Roscoe Tanner. "I've been watching him for years," said Wilma, "but I'm always amazed." She was whispering. She'd lost her voice sitting in the rain, and regretted she had only one voice to give for her mate.

"Someday," sighed Sue Stockton, "a normal life. If I have kids I hope they aren't tennis players. I couldn't stand dying all over again with them. I hope my kids play the flute."

Virginia Wade

When Virginia won a point the applause was ferocious. Atypical cheers were even heard, and an occasional "Come on Ginny." Not cricket, old chap—but, in a country where nothing works any more, Virginia was working and winning.

An institution who had failed so often was succeeding. If she missed a serve the fidgety sucking in of 14,000 breaths sounded like the slurp of a giant whirlpool. Across a nation millions were empathizing with a lithe, high strung broad in an embroidered white dress who had been an honor student in mathematics at Sussex University. The country relaxed and rejoiced a little too soon. "All she has to do is get her serve in now," said one of the faithful who had become a believer.

It was but a ghastly illusion. The shrine became once again a horror chamber for pressure-ridden Virginia.

Russia's five-year plans in tennis haven't paid off, except with two players, Metreveli and Morozova "Other sports are more important," Olga says. Perhaps because Czar Nicholas was a tennis player. They shot him—but not just for his tennis.

"I lose a little bit confidence when Virginia win the first set 6-1," Morozova said. England's confidence soared. "The crowd helped me early—my luck was going terribly well" said Wade. "But later—with their oohs and ahs and gasps...I wish they'd relax as if they felt confidence in me. But of course they can't relax. It's a two-way thing—it transfers."

Olga began to come out with Stalingrad style. "After first set, you have to be fighter, run every point. I win the set, 7-5. Then Virginia four straight games to 4-2 in third, and I just decided I be fighter all the time."

Charge, charge, charge—Olga got "desperate" as Virginia saw it and rushed the net on every shot to plant her

volleying bombs. "I felt steamrollered by her pounding, pounding," Wade shook her head wanly.

Virginia had cried when it ended and she was barely withholding more tears, professionally trying to discuss how it happened. "The rain that held us up three hours, the bad court—it all hurt, but," she was quick to be sportingly English "it was the same for both."

It was no time to ask her if she'd choked on Wimbledon again. Olga had closed with a four-game surge for a 1-6, 7-5, 6-4 triumph that might win her a medal and a dacha at home—a raise surely and great acclaim.

"I'm destroyed," said a redheaded Englishwoman, tottering away. "I can't believe it. Poor Virginia. She tried so hard for us. The whole country was with her. Maybe it's too much to carry. I can't go through it again. Next time I come to Wimbledon I shall watch a couple of Hungarians or someone I don't care about. This hurts too much."

It was only a game and Virginia Wade and England would go on. But a little sadder and more disillusioned.

From India with love . . .

From India comes three-way brilliance, the Amritraj brothers—Vijay, Anand and Ashok.

BRETTON WOODS, N.H.—There are more Amritrajs than people in Bretton Woods, New Hampshire, according to the census figures which list the permanent population of this metropolis overrun by pine trees and Amritrajs as two (2). Those two, Mr. and Mrs. Dave Drummond, are suddenly outnumbered by the five exotic Amritrajs out of Madras, India, but nobody is complaining, "there goes the neighborhood."

The Amritrajs are just passing through, but they're so attractive and pleasant that any one of them would be elected mayor or head selectman if they were on the Drummonds' ballot. "Not postmaster, though," says Vijay Amritraj, well aware that's Dave Drummond's job.

An Amritraj, as you may realize, is a special species of Indian tennis player, and comes in three sizes: Vijay, 20, Anand, 22, and Ashok, 17. The other two Amritrajs are the folks—Maggie and Bob—who love their handsome sons dearly, but can't bear to watch them play tennis. If the Indian tennis public felt the same way, the grandstands of Calcutta, New Delhi and Madras would be deserted when these devastating dudes—sporting heroes of the subcontinent—went about their business. "Makes us too nervous to watch them. We can't stand to be within the sound of the score," confesses Maggie Amritraj, majestic in sari, a diamond piercing her nose.

Yet, if it weren't for her, a tennis player in school, and the one who decided a tennis court would be their home's foremost exterior decoration, the kids might not now travel at the upper level of the game. "She pushed us into it," says Vijay, the 1973 champion in the $50,000 Volvo International at the Mt. Washington Hotel. Vijay, the smooth and powerful 6-foot, 3-inch Madras Monsoon, ran everybody but postmaster Drummond out of town then—blasting Humphrey Hose, Jeff Austin, John Alexander, Rod Laver and Jimmy Connors in succession to elevate Amritraj to headlines celebrating his first major triumph. Vijay, shortly thereafter, again beat the Maestro of Mt. Washington,

Laver (the hotel's touring pro) at Forest Hills to gain the US Open quarterfinal.

Vijay, bothered by shoulder trouble earlier in the year, said, "my confidence needs some help"—it seems to be surging. After a nothing first set, Vijay struck down Pat Cornejo, 0-6, 6-3, 6-3. The baby brother, Ashok, who lost the Wimbledon junior final to Billy Martin, blew a match point in losing a first rounder to Mike Powers.

As he cascaded to the 1973 title, Vijay saved six match points—three of them against the great Laver. In stunning Izzy El Shafei in the first round, Anand cancelled a match point. These guys live more dangerously than an Indian who doesn't keep a pet mongoose.

Parents Robert and Mary Magdalene Amritraj aren't quite the folks-next-door. Particularly in India with its masses of desperately poor. He operates the Southern Railway, she directs a box manufacturing firm. Yet there is nothing haughty about them or their sons. They radiate good humor and friendliness.

There must be thousands of parents named Maggie and Bob, but how many of them come up with such distinctive names for their offspring as Anand, Vijay and Ashok? In Hindi that's Happiness, Victory and Wisdom, which is nearly as nifty as Faith, Hope and Charity. Or Shadrach, Meshach and Abednego. "Well," says Ashok, "in India Anand, Vijay and Ashok are very common names, but we realize they sound quite unusual wherever else we go."

Rod Laver says he'd never heard of the Amritrajs until Vijay sabotaged him here a year ago. "I'm aware, and ready now," Rod says, "but I was really amazed the way Vijay hit out on everything, even when he was in trouble. He's a marvelous prospect."

Laver is a little disturbed that he hadn't won his own tournament, an event that was launched in 1972. If he can get past the Amritrajs, Rod picks up $9,000, plus a Volvo, which he can keep in the trunk of the $21,000 Mercedes he won at the Alan King Classic, in addition to $35,000 prize money.

"I admire Laver so much," says Vijay. "I can't describe what it meant to beat him twice. I had Anand take a photo of the scoreboard after I beat Rod at Forest Hills."

However, that high couldn't approach the euphoria of Calcutta earlier in 1974 when Vijay and Anand carried India to a Davis Cup triumph over Australia, the champion nation. While papa agonized at home in Madras, bleeding internally like Madras cloth, Vijay and Anand won the monster doubles match over Col Dibley and John Alexander, 17-15, 6-8, 6-3, 16-18, 6-4, and then Vijay settled the 3-2 triumph by knocking off Bob Giltinan. Maggie, to her everlasting credit, gutted this one out, making herself watch. It was a national occasion— "and we play better when she does hang in with us," says Vijay.

"You can't imagine how mad the people went," Vijay glows. "To beat Australia! They carried us from the court. Thousands tried to get at us to pound our backs." Now India, in the semis, had a shot at the Cup facing Russia, with Italy and South Africa the other survivors. They could have been the first brothers to win the Davis Cup since Reg and Lawrie Doherty of England in 1903-04-05-06.

If it ever happens, Prime Minister Indira Ghandi will probably give Maggie and Bob's kids the nation-wide mongoose concessions—and of course Dave Drummond will present them with the key to city of Bretton Woods.

Heldman nudge dethrones King

One of the most incredible and controversial upsets at Forest Hills was defending champion Billie Jean King's fourth round surrender to Julie Heldman during their third set in 1973.

NEW YORK—The King was dead, and she knew it.

Billie Jean was "seeing stars" and "couldn't see the ball anymore" just before she declared herself ex-champion on a technical knockout by a triumvirate of Julie Heldman, respiratory infection and heat exhaustion.

For the sixth straight brutally torrid and sticky day, the US Open felt as though it was wrapped in a shroud of Harris tweed. Yet Billie Jean King looked minutes from a successful escape to the showers when she built her lead to 6-3, 4-1 against Julie Heldman, a shrewd, tough "thinking broad" (as Julie classified herself), but previously just another outclassed opponent.

What the crowd stacked around the clubhouse court at

Julie
Heldman

Forest Hills couldn't know was this: Nothing was left inside King, the woman who was later to test the Supreme Chauvinist, Bobby Riggs. They couldn't have dreamed that Billie Jean wasn't going to win her 15th straight match here, enroute to a third successive Open championship— and that within a half hour she would abruptly surrender after winning only one more game. They asked each other, "what happened?" and "where's she going?" as Billie Jean walked that woozy Last Mile to the women's changing room, a fallen, defaulting woman with the score now 3-6, 6-4, 4-1 against her.

Twice before at Forest Hills, the No. 1 player of the female world has caused a furor by packing it in and walking away pleading illness and shocking the traditionalists who say—coolly from the sidelines—that a champion must finish somehow. Suzanne Longlen defaulted to Molla Mallory in the first round in 1923. Helen Wills Moody forfeited the 1933 final in the third set to her bitter rival, Helen Jacobs. When Billie Jean won her first title in 1967, her final round foe, Ann Jones, was broken down with a bum leg, but Ann hobbled all the way.

"I wanted it any way I could get it," said Julie Heldman, a 27-year-old Stanford graduate, who knows the traditions, but appreciates the realities. "I thought it was a win that meant just as much to me, default or not. I played her into a surrender, didn't I? I'll take a win over B.J. any way I can get it."

Heldman, always at a disadvantage on grass, essentially a groundstroker, was nonetheless as determined as Casey

Everts play big role in Wightman Cup win

Jones in her gauzy, pink-billed engineer's cap, Her husky forehand was pushing Billie Jean around, but Billie Jean couldn't move much more after a harrowing 5-deuce game when Julie broke serve for 2-1 in the third. Billie Jean wasn't charging the net any more. She was sagging.

Julie said, "are you all right." A little psyche?

"I think I'm gonna faint," replied B.J.

"Sure you can go on?" Heldman asked.

"I've got to." King has never been short on guts.

They played two more games. It was 4-1 for Heldman. Her mother, Gladys Heldman of Houston, was smoking like mad on the clubhouse terrace. When Julie had trailed 1-4 in the second, her old lady kept saying, "dammit, I've been telling her to get the first serve in since she was eight."

Now Pancho Segura counseled Mama Heldman, "Julie's gonna win. All she has to do is put the ball over the net."

"I hope she doesn't clutch," said Mama. "She's so close, but B.J. is tough. Give me glucose, give me salt pills, give me a drink."

"You're not playing," said Segura.

"That's what you think."

On court, King was dawdling at the change game, trying to pull herself together like Joe Frazier in the corner after that first round with George Foreman. Her secretary, Marilyn Barnett—King must be the only athlete who brings her secretary along to the playground—handed the champion a towel.

"Is a minute up?" Heldman snapped at the umpire, Judy Lessing. "She only gets a minute to change courts." Julie knew the rules. The umpire nodded that Heldman was correct.

"If you want it that bad," Billie Jean sighed, "I quit."

To Julie Heldman, Billie Jean's rasping voice seemed as melodic as Renata Tebaldi singing "Un Bel Dio."

Julie put out her hand faster than Wyatt Earp. "I wasn't gonna debate. She said quit. That's it, I would have kicked her I wanted it so bad," said Julie. "I didn't want her to die on court" (in the locker room, maybe?). "But we're old enough to play by the rules. I'm no mean old woman, but I know the rules, and I called her on them."

Billie Jean recalled (after passing out to an hour's sleep in the dressing room), "I wanted to go once I tried to clear my head. But Julie pushed me on the 60-second rule, so I had to quit. I had a cold, an infection. I took penicillin injections. It wasn't just the heat. I've never quit in heat a lot worse than this in Australia." (She had defaulted once before, to Chris Evert, in 1971, in a match played too soon after surgery.)

Any time a champion quits, it creates a brouhaha. Remember Paul Pender and Sonny Liston giving up in their corners? The chauvinists will scream with glee. Jack Kramer, head of the men's union, said Billie Jean was "disgraceful" for pulling out. Still, when I consider what this extraordinary woman has done for her game and her sex—and that Con Edison was blowing gaskets all over town in that heat—I guess a dynamo named King can burn out, too.

The oldest team trophy in women's tennis is the Wightman Cup, dating from 1923. On the 50th anniversary, the two youngest women ever to play (and the first sisters), Chris and Jeannie Evert, led the U.S. to victory over Britain in Boston.

FIFTY YEARS ago Colette and Jimmy Evert were distinguished by their nonexistence. That was the year, 1923—a vintage year for bathtub gin—when an aging flapper, Hazel Hotchkiss Wightman, put the biggest Martini shaker in history into circulation: the Wightman Cup.

Eventually Colette and Jimmy Evert were born, got to-

Chris Evert

gether, and sired a couple of kids who provided the clinching points—as Hazel watched—for the US in the golden anniversary of the Wightman Cup war with Great Britain.

First came Chris Evert, devastating with both hands on the backhand, to win the last nine games from 3-3 in the first in beating gritty Englishwoman Veronica Burton, 6-3, 3-0. That sent the US to an insuperable 4-1 lead in the three-day, best-of-seven series at Longwood Cricket Club.

Then, after the British captain, Virginia Wade, had overpowered Patti Hogan, 6-2, 6-2, on came Jeannie Evert, 15, to accompany Hogan to a 6-2, 4-6, 8-6 doubles triumph over Lindsey Beaven and Lesley Charles. That made the final result 5-2. "I was scared," said the little sister, Jeannie, who served the match out on her second try, after failing at 5-4.

By appearing for the US, Jeannie broke sister Chris's record for precocity. Chris had been the youngest Wightman player ever at 16 in 1971. "I was scared I wouldn't live up to Chrissie," said Jeannie, the youngest pro in tennis. "There's a lot of pressure on me to do well, especially after all that Chrissie has won. My dad tells me I have to be myself, but that's hard. Everybody compares me to Chrissie."

Certainly Jeannie didn't quite measure up to Chrissie. After allowing Burton to surge back into the match on a three-game run from 0-3, Chris broke the Englishwoman down with a characteristic barrage of her deadly groundstrokes. She won going away.

Jeannie had to struggle in the exciting doubles. "I'm uncomfortable at the net," she said, "so I stay at the baseline." But from there she fires maddening lobs into the clouds and covers a lot of court, despite the shortness of the legs on her 5-2 frame. While Jeannie did that, Patti Hogan operated effectively at the net, crossing frequently to blast piercing volleys.

"I've heard about this Cup all my life," said Jeannie, a high school student barely bigger than the sterling Wightman vase. "Chris played for it, and I wanted to."

Said Colette Evert, mother of the first sister entry in the 50-year-old series, "everything that Chrissie does, Jeannie wants to do. They both want to win."

They were winners while 86-year-old Hazel Wightman nodded approvingly. There hasn't been anything to compare with the Evert mob in the half-century since Hazel furnished the Cup. It was a bad day for Britain when Colette caught Jimmy Evert's eye.

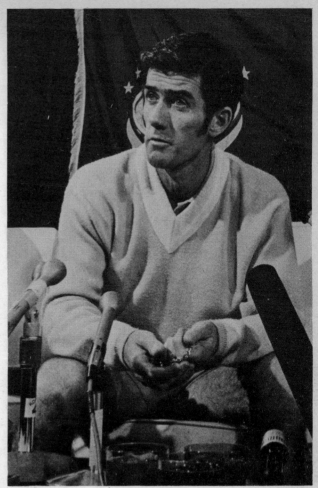

Ken Rosewall

Time waits for no man except, maybe, for Rosewall

The ageless one, Ken Rosewall, one of the game's landmarks, reminisces prior to his 1973 semifinal at the U.S. Open.

FOREST HILLS, N.Y.—When Ken Rosewall first showed his un-aging face in ghastly downtown Queens—at Forest Hills—John Newcombe was a second-grader in grammar school...Frank Sinatra was making a comeback chasing Ava Gardner...Elvis Presley's pelvis was merely a bone and had not yet become a global phenomenon...the most celebrated dog in the world was named Checkers (did his master bug Checkers' arfs and growls?)...and at the top of all the war charts was Korea.

It was 1952. "You could see the Empire State Building all the time. No smog," recalled that regal relic, Kenneth Robert Rosewall, who was gunning for two titles in the 1973 US Open as he edged up to Jack Benny's age. In the doubles final, Rosewall attempted to carry sagging Rod Laver to the only major title Laver has avoided: The US Doubles.

Rosewall also was in the singles semis against a 29-year-old man named Newcombe, a fellow resident of Sydney, who idolized Kenny the year Rosewall won his first US Singles, 1956.

Hank Aaron chased a dead man named Ruth. Kenny Rosewall, the Doomsday Stroking Machine, is pursuing a lively little man named Rosewall. The longevity records are his, a 19-year spread. First major titles: The Australian and French in 1953. Most recent: The US in 1970 and the Australian in 1972. He's been on top practically longer than Queen Victoria. If he can beat Newcombe, and then either Jan Kodes or Stan Smith, Rosewall will be the oldest champion in the tournament's history, two months short of 39.

Every game has geriatric freaks: Snead, Blanda, Johnny Green, Kaline, Gordie Howe. Rosewall is different. Every time he plays he has to do all the running by himself, miles

Newcombe juggernaut bests Kodes, captures crown

of it. All the shots must be made with his right arm, thousands of them.

"Ah, yes, I guess I'm exceptional," concedes Rosewall. From him that statement is tantamount to egotism and arrogance. But, of course, both qualities are foreign to him. "I'm resting more now between tournaments. It's been my life and...it goes on...maybe my wife doesn't like it so much...but that's pro sport, isn't it.

"I may have lasted this long because of my size (5-7, 137). I can curl up comfortably in an airplane seat. We spent a lot of our lives on planes. Not like when I started. No jets. Three days and two nights from Sydney to London.

"First time in America, 1952, we got $7-a-day spending money from our captain, Harry Hopman. We used to sell extra rackets to fans to make a few more shillings. But we never thought much about money," says Rosewall, who has made more than a million from playing since becoming a pro in 1956.

"That year Lew Hoad and I caused quite a stir here. On the same day (fourth round) Lew beat Art Larsen, the 1950 champion, and I beat Vic Seixas, the No. 1 American seed. We were 16, and we'd beaten the two best Americans." Hoad retired some time ago with a gimpy back. Over the last two decades, Rosewall has become as beloved at the Forest Hills stadium for his impeccable strokes as Mauger, the royal executioner, was for his stroke at the Tower of London in the old days. One of the prizes of yet another new generation, 19-year-old Vijay Amritraj, was "honored" to get the Rosewallian treatment in the quarters. "He told me, without saying a word that my serve must improve," said Amritraj, passed and pierced by innumerable of those magnificent returns.

Rosewall feels "the psychology of being a little man trying to beat bigger men may have pushed me this far. I've been trying to beat the bigger guys all my life." And he has. "But I think I'm more realistic now than I was, say, five years ago. I try hard, but when I don't win, it doesn't go so hard on me."

It's appropriate that he'll soon catch up with Jack Benny. But Rosewall will go beyond 39. I think he'll still be winning in 1984—and then we'll know who Big Brother really is.

Newcombe no longer idolizes. "Sometimes I'd like to kick the little bastard," says Newc who well remembers those stiletto backhands with which Rosewall liquidated him in the 1970 semis. "But, like everybody else I marvel at him. He's hard to play against because he has that sad little boy look and everybody is with him. At Wimbledon in the 1970 final when I beat him, the only people clapping for me were my wife and mother-in-law." Like hell. The mother-in-law, like all women Rosewall's age, was sneaking a clap for Kenny.

One of the greatest Forest Hills finals was John Newcombe's five-set triumph over Jan Kodes in 1973.

FOREST HILLS, N.Y.—Every once in a while John Newcombe gets drunk and tells himself, "put out or get out" of tennis. It's when he's been going bad, and the last time was in Rome after he'd lost to a Hungarian named Szoke.

Then he starts working hard "to get myself mentally and physically keen—and keep a personal commitment to myself to be No. 1. In my mind, I am, but I have to prove it to everybody else."

It's been a long time since the sinewy Australian looked as No. 1 as he did in a fourth and fifth set rush to strongarm the hurtling, hang-tough Czechoslovak Jan Kodes for the US Open championship.

Another record crowd (15,241) spilled over Forest Hills stadium and spent 2½ hours roaring and gasping at the extraordinary shotmaking in an extremely high-level final

John Newcombe

by a pair of quick, confident and determined acrobats in short pants. Winning shots were common, common errors, almost non-existent.

Although Newcombe won, 6-4, 1-6, 4-6, 6-2, 6-3 to collect the $25,000 first prize—and his first major title since Wimbledon in 1971—it was hard to believe that Kodes had lost. His returns of Newcombe's ripping serves on the grass were utterly fantastic, crackling liners, both backhand—Jan's forte—and forehand. Despite his continual moaning about grass—"it is for soccer not tennis"—Kodes came into tune on the lawn two years ago here when he sabotaged then No. 1 seed Newcombe in the first round, and proceeded to a final round defeat by Stan Smith. In July Kodes won Wimbledon, a feat downgraded because the tournament was diluted by the strike of leading pros.

Seldom, however, has a loser of Forest Hills put on such a high quality performance as Jan's, his lunges and leaps for scoring volleys dazzling Newcombe.

Yet never disheartening him. "I've been around too long to be dazzled," said Newc from behind his mustache. "I just had to go harder, like I did at Wimbledon '71 when Smith had me 2-1 in sets."

His ability to do that was the difference. The slugger caught up with the boxer in the last round. The bludgeon finally broke down the ballet dancer. Kodes, who had to go five hard sets in subduing Nikki Pilic in the quarters, and five harder ones—escaping a match point—to fell top seed Stan Smith at nightfall in the semis, shrugged, "I got mental tired at the end. Not physical; mental." ·

That was the toll Newcombe took as he kept hammering his serve. Twenty-three aces flashed from his aluminum racket, and his second serve was deep and well placed. Kodes put a mess of them away, but Newc still hammered like a mechanical man, grunting "Hunh!" as he threw himself into the ball, sounding like Joe Frazier issuing left hooks.

Newc has done nothing of account this year since winning the Australian Open in January. Seeded as high as 10th only on memories and kindness, John ackowledged that he got a tremendous lift from a fall at 2-5 with Kodes serving in the fourth set: a boom-sa-daisy forehand winner from flat on his bum.

He was up a break at the time, but ever in danger of being broken back by Jan's whirring returns. It was deuce. Kodes maneuvered Newc out of position in a rally and cracked a ball to the Aussie's right as Newc leaned left. He skidded, tried to change directions, sat down, but swung for a winner! That took Kodes to set point which Newc grabbed with a resounding backhand return.

"Now I was going," enthused the champ. "He had to press harder to serve well." In doing so, Kodes served shorter and safer—noticeably in the fourth game. A slight letdown, but it was enough to let Newc through for the break to 4-1. A slim opening for Newc as slim as his margin of superiority. "Too many lines he hit when I have him" sighed Kodes.

Margaret Court got another title, her sixth, with Virginia Wade, 3-6, 6-3, 7-5, over Billie Jean King and Rosie Casals. And Billie Jean came back for her third mixed title with O.K. Davidson, 6-4, 3-6, 7-6 over Court and Marty Riessen.

But nobody enjoyed their celebrational grog more than John Newcombe. If he wakes up squashy this morning, the headache will at least be a happy one.

Capitalist net grabs Soviet

Alex Metreveli

What is rarer than a Howard Johnson's in Moscow? A Russian tennis player on the American pro circuit—Alex Metreveli.

LA COSTA, CALIFORNIA—A chauffered limousine met his plane, his $50 room at La Costa Country Club was on the house, and the sun and the chickies beamed warmly on a rarity named Alex Metreveli—the only Russian playing a professional game in the United States.

"Not bad," said Metreveli, gazing around the super-capitalistic spa where he has appeared not to paint the town red, but to give the $50,000 Michelob Tennis Classic a touch of communistic class. "It's warm. Not crowded. That I like."

Nor did he mind the quick cement courts on which his foes would seem to have an edge, but where he purged Bob Lutz and O.K. Davidson to climb to the quarter-finals.

Maybe Metreveli was part of the wheat deal with Russia. The grain went there and he came here. Nobody will say, but he seems to enjoy making his bread here—"as long as I don't stay too much. I miss my home in Tbilisi, my wife and son. This tour is good. I get a three-week rest in the middle, and I go back. In May it's over and I return to play Davis Cup for Russia."

The quickest way to make him a mad Russian is to call Metreveli a Russian. "I am Georgian," insists Metreveli, a stern-looking 29-year-old citizen of Joe Stalin's hometown. Georgia, a Soviet Republic in the south, is one of the richer areas of Russia.

"There are more millionaires in Georgia than London," a Russian writer one told me. "Stalin made sure that his friends and people got the best deals and concessions."

Around the Tennis World with Bud Collins

Metreveli once wrote a letter to the Times of London asking that he be referred to as Georgian rather than Russian. But Olga Morozova, the leading female in Russian tennis, laughed. "Alex is just having fun. We are all Russians no matter where we live. But he is lucky to live in Tbilisi. The climate is mild, and it is not so big, so that everybody knows him. Everybody loves him. He can do anything. If a policeman gives him a ticket for speeding, then he sees it is Alex and tears it up," she said.

Another friend of Alex's said. "He can't pay for anything there. He is their hero, and lives in a beautiful home. Once in Baku, the people presented him with a solid gold one pound ball—which is worth several thousand dollars."

Metreveli is the best known Russian tennis player since Nicky Romanov (also called Czar Nicholas), who patted balls on his private court, presumably with Rasputin in the umpire's chair.

Tennis wasn't Lenin's favorite game—they shot the czar—but it has been the means for Metreveli to live a life beyond a czar's fantasies. Did the czar ever surf, and sip Foster's Lager in Australia...or gambol on the grass of Centre Court at Wimbledon...or spend a day in Agra partaking of the curry and the Taj Mahal?

Or eat at Howard Johnson's? Well, there are some drawbacks.

A game for patricians until the revolution, tennis pretty much resumed in Russia in 1922. But Metreveli is the only world class male to develop enough to hang in there with the pros. He beat Jimmy Connors, America's No. 1, on the way to the Wimbledon final a year ago, and currently lies third in WCT's Blue Division behind John Newcombe and Stan Smith. His prize money after four tournaments is $16,000, but Alex utters the stock line: "I am amateur." Nobody is an amateur at this level of sport, but it's a tiresome subject by this time.

His watchdog, jovial Siemon Beliz-Geiman, vice president of the Russian Tennis Federation, says, "His prize money goes to the Federation. We just keep enough for living expenses." Whatever, Master of Sport Metreveli is doing all right, a privileged Soviet citizen who travels everywhere on the strength of his good right arm.

He is the idol of "every tennis-playing Russian and sports fan, which means millions," says Beliz-Geiman. "We will develop other Metrevelis soon. We are concentrating more on tennis. We have 70,000 tournament players."

"It is good," says Metreveli, "to play the pro tour. I have improved much in the last year doing that. But I have my studies, too, at the University of Tbilisi. I am an aspirant for an assistant professorship in journalism, which I will receive in 1975. I have my undergraduate degree. I want to teach journalism."

Metreveli was a surprise starter on the pro tour a year ago. "We invited him aboard," says George Pharr of WCT, "but didn't expect he could accept. But after many unanswered cables, his federation contacted us with a yes. Apparently they want to showcase him as a hero and inspiration."

Bright, pleasant and fond of Texas—"warm place with friendly people"—Alex is sharp enough politically to say, "I am not interesting in politics." This, when asked about Solzhenitsyn. "I know about sports, not politics. I have not read him, but I think he wrote always too much about bad things of the country without saying about the good."

Blood, sweat and Aussies

Every year in Hartford the Aussies and Yanks battle for the World Cup, emblematic of the professional team championship. The Aussies, who revel in good times and good tennis, always come in lean and loose.

HARTFORD—Attila and his Huns are dressed in short pants and swinging tennis cudgels this week and are called Fred Stolle and his Aussies. The Aussies have invaded Hartford, a signal to the townsfolk to lock up their women, trophies and beer—but it's probably too late.

Before the weekend is over the Aussies will have overrun the American garrison, manned by such as Stan Smith and Arthur Ashe, carried off the World Cup and left the town's pubkeepers standing in line for refills at the breweries.

Aussies are a wild tribe from an island in the South Pacific who have made a reputation by beating up Americans—and everybody else—at tennis. And by gulping so much beer that their children are born with bent elbows—which helps them develop weirdly spinning serves. They don't stay too long in one place, seldom more than a week, but that place is never the same again.

"I think we can beat them," said Dennis Ralston, the US captain in the best-of-seven series at Trinity College. As boy, man, player, captain and coach, Ralston has been saying that about Aussies for nearly two decades, and a couple of times he's been right. "We'll hold them off," Denny promises, sounding like a Roman soldier the day the barbarians strolled in.

When the trumpet calls the Aussies to assemble for another concerted shot at the Yanks, which happens here every year, they come running from all over the world—Ken Rosewall in from Sydney, Rod Laver from Barcelona, John Newcombe from California, Tony Roche from Miami and the Old Hacker, Capt. Stolle, from Sydney. "We're getting older," says Stolle, 35, "but we still give good value. Put us up against the Yanks and we're kids again. Americans are our vitamins. We wash them down with beer. We love to beat them. They beat us once in a bloody while, and that's all right—once in a long bloody while. It's the best rivalry in international sport. We drink with them, but we beat their bloody brains in on the court.

"The money doesn't mean anything in this one. There's only one player who knows how much money is involved..."

Rosewall?

"Right. Old Muscles always knows the money," said John Newcombe. "In 1970, when the World Cup started, Stolle and I were the entire Aussie team. We played all the matches. Fred's too old now. But I tell you I'd default the two doubles, giving them a 2-0 lead, and then I'd like to play all the five singles."

"I think it's bloody time you went to bed, Newc," said Stolle to the No. 1 pro, looking at his watch. "Last year you played like a bloody old sheila (woman), and Smith and Marty Riessen both beat you. Rosewall took us off the hook."

Newc looked at his watch. All it showed was the date. How do you know what day it is, Newc?

"Well, if I'm in the final of a tournament…" he was showing a waitress his service motion, meaning bring another round, "if I'm in the final, I know it's Sunday. If I'm in the semis, I know it's Saturday. If I'm in the quarters, I know it's Wednesday or Thursday…"

But, suppose you get beat in the first round?

"Well, then, I go out and get so bloody drunk I don't care what day it is."

The waitress said to please sip with all haste because it was time to close. Newcombe closes more places than the sheriff. There is something about closing hour that brings out his best efforts.

"Closed Derek Sanderson's place, Daisy Buchanan's, with him the last time I was in Boston," Newc said.

Everybody thought you were dying. "I was," Newc said, recalling the semifinal of the Commercial Union Masters at Hynes Auditorium in December. He tore leg muscles at match point for himself against Tom Okker and had to surrender. "I knew the leg was going to go. It was tightening. I thought if I could just blast two more winners, I'd have the match, and I could get off the court and rest for the final against Nasty (Ilie Nastase) the next day. But the leg popped. I was so bloody mad. I wanted to play Nasty. The year's No. 1 ranking was on it. So about four doctors and Jock Semple, the trainer, packed me in ice and put me in to bed in the hotel. I was so bloody annoyed I couldn't lie there. I got up and hobbled down the street to Derek's, and we closed it up. Better not to die in bed."

Says one Aussie, "Nobody can play great tennis with a heavy head and no sleep like Newcombe. He'd leave Joe Namath for dead. He's so fit the grog doesn't bother him. Like all of us but Rosewall, Newc has to have a good time every so often."

"Keeps you sane in this bloody crazy, continent-hopping, competitive business of ours to let it all hang out now and again. I'll try to get a few hours sleep Thursday, Fred," Newcombe said to Stolle. "I don't play till Friday."

Newcombe and the other Aussies' periodic adventures in "relaxation," as he terms it, haven't eroded this remarkably sturdy mob (average age 33), whose collection of titles rivals the public library's.

"You better be ready," Stolle was heading for the sack.

"Don't worry, captain, I like to beat the Yanks, too," and Newcombe trundled off to dream of the great Aussie tribal rites: closing down saloons and American tennis teams.

Rosie baby, it ain't hay

SEA PINES, S.C.—Of course I am a sexist swine. My Mama raised me to like girls better than boys—although she probably didn't realize at the time that it might go out of style. So what better place for a bird watching foray than this wildlife sanctuary called Sea Pines on lovely, woodsy Hilton Head Island off the South Carolina coast?

The birds in their high style gamesplaying plumage—all drip-dry lace, buttons and bows, hot pants and cool decolletage—have alighted on the island for the richest tournament in women's tennis, the $100,000 Family Circle Cup, which would make anybody chirp and hustle. Particularly if you are that chickadee with chutzpah, Rosie Casals, who remembers "not so long ago when I didn't have $3.50 to enter kids tournaments in San Francisco.

"I never could afford a racket or balls or shoes," says the Rosebud, who slapped down the regal Englishwoman, Virginia Wade, 6-2, 6-3, to move to the semis, two wins away

Rosemary Casals

Around the Tennis World with Bud Collins

from the biggest bundle in her game, $30,000, which she won in 1973 by wiping out Billie Jean King and Nancy Gunter in succession. Also in the semis: Chris Evert, 6-2, 6-3 over Betty Stove; Evonne Goolagong, 6-3, 6-2 over Olga Morozova; Kerry Melville, 6-2, 6-3 over Karen Krantzcke. "Equipment companies gave me stuff," says Rosie, "because I was promising. That got me going. But I like money because I never had it. Money buys freedom to do what you want, go where you want—that's what I like about money.

"But, you take this $30,000 we're playing for. To me it's not tangible. Do you buy hamburgers or a beer with 30-grand? It's just a figure up there, but the numbers don't mean anything. What I'm trying to say is I play as hard for 30 bucks as I do for 30-grand."

Right on, Rosie. No athlete drives harder than the 5-foot-1 inch Rosebud, who was darting about the court as though she were one of the scarlet butterflies decorating her bodice. She isn't a beauty, yet Casals is winsome, a compelling woman—"the Liza Minelli of tennis," says Grace Lichtenstein in her fine new book on the female pros, "A Long Way, Baby."

The long way really started for her as a poor mite in San Francisco, haunting the public courts, making people notice her when she needed a stepladder and elevator shoes to peer over the net. I first saw her 10 years ago when she was 15. She hit the ball with so much verve and velocity that you knew here was a kid to make life uncomfortable for her elders—those who played and those who supervised.

She turned millions uncomfortable last September as a telecaster, putting His Piggishness, Bobby Riggs, in his place while her soul sister, Billie Jean King, put him down. Rosie was the only person ever to make Howard Cosell seem a good-mouth. "That made my name, one way or another. I was ABC's hatchetwoman. I did their dirty work. That was their game plan, for me to insult Riggs. It was show biz, and I don't regret it. But it wasn't the real me."

Hardly. Inside, Rosie is a great beauty.

"My mail was tremendous—about fifty-fifty for and against my act. But it makes me laugh when some women said I was unladylike. What does that mean? After the way Riggs knocked us (women's tennis) and Billie Jean?"

The long way began to get shorter in 1970 when Billie Jean and Rosie led the revolt of a few gritty players against the tennis establishment and helped launch the Virginia Slims circuit. "All we wanted was prize money that recognized our ability. The ratio was 10-to-1 favoring the men in most tournaments. So we split from them and got some $10,000 events going with Slims. But," her nut-brown eyes glowed, "I never thought it would come to a tournament for 100-grand in four years. I made $104,375 in 1973 and I was only fifth behind Margaret Court ($204,400), Billie Jean, Chris Evert and Evonne Goolagong." In the three years since the Slims gals went out on their own, Rosie made about $300,000.

It has meant a home in Sausalito, doing everything first class. "I like luxury. I won't pinch pennies anymore. How long do you live?" She is one of the few sporting figures who flies first class entirely. Lamar Hunt doesn't. It has also meant a few white hairs appearing amidst the black.

"Yeah, we've worked, Billie Jean and me. Played everywhere, all the time, promoted, made all the appearances, founded our union. I'm burnt out more than I should be at 25. We hustled to make tournaments like this possible. I hope Evert and Goolagong realize their responsibilities to the women's game. Because of us they'll get rich."

Hewitt, McMillan win WCT doubles

Doubles, the game most of us play, seldom gets much attention or prize money. But when lightly heralded South Africans Frew McMillan and Bob Hewitt won the professional championship of 1974 in Montreal they were noticed by TV watchers and collected $20,000 apiece.

MONTREAL—Put together a bad-tempered bald man and a guy with freaky strokes, who never takes off his cap, and what do you have? The professional doubles champions of the world is what you have—Bob Hewitt and Frew McMillan.

And they have 20-grand apiece following a brilliant 6-2, 6-7, 6-1, 6-2 victory over top-seeded Aussies John Newcombe and O.K. Davidson in the final of the World Championship Tennis playoffs at Richard Arena.

Hewitt and McMillan are names known mostly to tennis aficionados, but the string duet they play in doubles makes them seem a pair of concertmasters. Their reflexes and racketwork made them masters of the Aussies who had struck down the 1973 champs, Stan Smith and Bob Lutz.

"I guess I got stubborn," says McMillan, 31, whose weird repertory consists of two-fisted strokes, groundies and volleys. "I started out as a kid, unorthodox, and when people said I'd never be good, I was determined to prove I could." He is awfully good with his angled volleys and low returns.

His partner with shiny pate, Hewitt, 34, has one of the vilest tempers in sport. But he played so well, seldom missing a return or first serve or volley, that he growled only meekly a couple of times. "Missed four returns—that's four too many," Hewitt snorted.

With that kind of solid opposition, Newcombe and Davidson were pressed all the way. If there was a weak link against the South Africans, it was Davidson's serve: broken six times, he was just 50 percent on first serves, and double faulted eight times. Several were critical.

"My serve?" scowled downhearted Davidson, a lefty who accompanied Newcombe to the US Open title last year. "My serve was...whoops...I see there are ladies present..."

Newc and Davidson had led the Blue Group, McMillan and Hewitt the Red on the WCT tour. For the winners it was win No. 20 in their last 21 matches.

That—plus the heaviest paychecks of their long careers—was enough to make petulant Hewitt smile and McMillan remove his little white cap and bow to the crowd.

Love him tjender

Bjorn Borg

Teen Angel, Bjorn Borg, is a sex symbol hailed by women everywhere–but mobbed nowhere the way he is in London, at Wimbledon.

LONDON—Not since Mickey Rooney was leering his way through "Young Andy Hardy" has there been a teen-age sex symbol like Bjorn Borg, The Swedish Teen Angel. Well, maybe David Cassidy or Audie Murphy, Judy Garland or Little Orphan Annie. What about Wolfgang Amadeus Mozart? Strictly a child sex symbol.

However, the Borg Phenomenon appears confined to England where these seemingly staid natives dissolve in static when the 18-year-old Viking lands on their shore. "He is a national hero in Sweden and popular wherever he goes," says Borg's coach-and-baby-sitter, Lennart Bergelin, "but in London he is actually worshipped by the girls and women and mobbed wherever he goes. He cannot go anywhere without protection..."

Just then, exhibit A substantiating Bergelin's testimony nearly trampled us. A shrieking, clutching horde of schoolgirls enveloped tennis pro Borg as he came off Wimbledon's court 2, after beating Australian Ross Case, 3-6, 6-1, 8-6,

7-5. Wailing, trembling.

"I love him, I love him," murmured one. In their platform shoes, school blazers, ankle-length raincoats and strawberries-and-cream English complexions, they were finding nirvana merely by tiptoeing for a glimpse, or lining the driveway for hours waiting for his car to go by. Some were still there at dark, long after he'd been smuggled out of another entrance.

The bravest men in London are the Borg Patrol. The bobbies assigned by police inspector Ernest Hart to protect the callow quarter-millionaire on the tennis grounds. "Without them," smiles Borg, "I wouldn't be able to walk a step or hit a ball."

"It's much like guarding a pop star," says inspector Hart. "All the girls want to touch."

If, as writer, Grace Lichtenstein suggests, "tennis players are the newest pop stars"—then Bjorn's racket may become as celebrated an instrument as Elvis Presley's guitar. Certainly he plays it as provocatively, his strokes hard-rocking, belligerent, disrespectful of his elders. "Once Rod Laver was my idol," says Borg, "but no more. I can beat everybody now, so I have no more idols." And he can.

The male Goldilocks whose favorite author is Walt Disney, is a greater prodigy than the young Mickey Mouse or possibly even the young Ken Rosewall. Rosewall, still around, was the standard to measure precocity by. Ken won the Australian and French titles at 18 in 1953.

In this tougher era, Bjorn was world pro finalist to John Newcombe as well as Italian champ before he turned 18, and won the French title just after he turned.

"I am very tired from so much tennis," Bjorn said. "It has been almost every week for 11 months. I don't enjoy it so much for the moment, but," the boy's face hardened a shade, "I still want to win. I do not tire of winning. I will not be disappointed if I don't win Wimbledon this year. I have many years.

"All the girls cheering makes me stronger. They share in the victory and that is nice. Yes, they make it fun for me. And," he gratefully acknowledged the edge they provide, "they really do help. They bother my opponent and that is an advantage for me. I don't mind that."

It is Borg plus the female world against his opponent.

Wherever he plays the females form long queues to get in, and then jam standing-room sections to croon siren songs to their golden-maned lad below. The Borg chorus groans loud enough to be heard in Paris when he loses a point and erupts in shrill cheers that reach Stockholm when he wins one. Yesterday in a gloomy, misty scene seemingly from the mind of countryman Ingmar Bergman, Borg belted his way through the drizzle and out of trouble against Case, who served for the fourth set at 5-3. "I never get nervous," Borg smiled.

"I always win the important points—I don't know why." With his leap-shot two-fisted backhand and bolo-punch forehand, he swept Case aside in four straight games, and the chickies were ecstatic. It had been well worth standing hours in the rain to wait for his match to resume.

"Sweden gave the world Ingrid Bergman, Greta Garbo, Mai Britt, and many other sexy women," said the coach, Bergelin. "It's about time we contributed a sexy man."

But another Swedish player, Ingrid Bentzer, smiled sardonically and asked what was the use in being a sex symbol if it was too dangerous to go out and take advantage of it?

Around the Tennis World with Bud Collins

Mama's the big winner while Barry minds the baby

Barry Court

Margaret Court, the first to return to big-time tennis as a big winner from a maternity ward, was discussing life with baby and husband as she began her comeback in 1973. She won a record $204,400 that year. Another comeback began in 1975 after she took a year off to have a second child, Marika.

IF YOU ARE Barry Court, from a leading male chauvinist outpost called Australia, and you find yourself minding the baby while Mama makes the bank account—do you feel embarrassingly caught in a role switch?

"Ah, no," says Barry Court, a big ambidextrous guy handling baby Danny and a beer simultaneously. "My mates at home don't rubbish me. They think it's all quite natural in our case."

Well, it is a special case: You don't usually needle a rugged type like Barry. And who wouldn't keep the moveable home fires burning if Mama had stoked the bank account up by $67,850, just for playing tennis the first three months of 1973.

Mama, of course, is 30-year-old Margaret Smith Court, the most prolific winner of tennis championships ever to intimidate fuzzy ball with gut-strung club. Can you imagine this tall, incredibly strong and agile woman coming at you with a rolling pin? (I must stop entertaining these Male Chauvinist Piggy fantasies.)

"Barry has his own identity at home in Australia," Margaret was saying. The Courts were paying their first visit to the seaside retreat of Squantum, Mass., in the hope that Mighty Mama would grab six-grand more for winning the $25,000 Virginia Slims Indoor at the Boston Harbor Marina Tennis Center. She'd won 16 of her last tournaments—and 19 of 26 since depositing 13-month-old Danny on Barry's doorstep.

"Yes," Margaret went on, "Barry's known on his own at home. He's a world class yachtsman, and he's done well in business." He is not, then, Mr. Margaret Court? "Ah, No," she says, making it clear that her good natured roommate has been the settling influence on her, rather than the classic vice versa. "You know, nerves were my problem. I've played much better since getting married to him. And Danny has made it even better. I'm always thinking about Danny"—a 30-pound ruffian who pushes over pianos—"and that takes my mind off my game. Danny sleeps late like we do, and fits right in. He's no trouble traveling."

Billie Jean King observes the Court scene with amusement: "It's a real turnaround, especially by Australian standards. Margaret was the typical Australian girl, content to let the men do the talking, ready—we thought—to settle down as a housewife when she got married. She didn't want to be militant with some of us who got the pro tour rolling. But look at her—did you ever see a better example of Women's Lib? She's the breadwinner and Barry's the domestic. And she's come out of herself. She's become one of our top spokeswomen."

Barry doesn't exactly agree. "We just like being together, and I urged Marg to play as long as she wanted. Then we'll settle down. I rather like taking care of Danny a lot of the time. We get along."

"I never imagined playing this long," says Margaret. "But I'm lucky Barry is the way he is. I'm relaxed and feel I've still got three good years of tennis in me. And the money..." she grinned.

"Well, in 1970 when I won the Grand Slam (singles titles of Australia, France, Britain, US in one year) I made between $40,000 and $50,000 and thought that was the ceiling. Now, nearly $70,000 in three months! Ah, yes, I'd like to win the Slam again." And, she just might do that.

The kidnaped typewriter caper

Sometimes writing about tennis can be as competitive as playing it as reporter Mark Asher learned at the National Indoors of 1973.

JUST AS THOSE of the Good-murder Good-fire Real World School of Journalism will always revere the memory of reporter Ernie Pyle (killed in action, 1945), we of the toy department hail the name of sportswriter Mark Asher (clawed in action and thrown out of the joint as he defended his typewriter, Feb. 25, 1973).

There could be no way of 27-year-old Mark Asher of the *Washington Post* knowing that Sunday afternoon when he went to work that he'd be a near-martyr in an historic struggle for freedom of the press. After all he was at Wicomico Center in Salisbury, Md., covering the National Indoor Tennis finals. What could be more genteel?

That was until a segment of the crowd of 3000 turned on Asher as though they were Japanese Marines and he were Brian Donlevy manning the last machine gun on Wake Island. You see he was firing away at his .45 caliber Olivetti portable, trying to make his deadline (along with several other journalists in the press box near the court), and the tap-tap-tap of their literary labors was not poetry to the rabbit ears of celebrated moaners Clark Graebner and Ilie Nastase. Graebner and Nastase—engaged in a losing doubles job against Jurgen Fassbender and Juan Gisbert—have never been mistaken for noblemen on the court. Or even good sports. Their partnership is like putting Leo Durocher and Bobby Fischer together as allies. Part of the Graebner-Nastase charm is that they would have been shot at sunrise for their churlish behavior in the old days when tennis was ruled by a Victorian code.

Yet Graebner and Nastase invoked that code, insisting the typewriters interfered with their feeble concentration. They began bitching. "Give us a break," pleaded Graebner, who would be happier as an undertaker, but didn't mind accepting $58,000 in prize money as a pro in 1972.

The journalists kept typing, ignoring these juveniles, for the deadline is sacred, is it not? By this time a pro tennis player realizes that his only concern about typewriters should be: "Are they spelling my name right."

Think about the sanctity of a sportswriter's deadline for a moment: If we didn't meet deadlines, you'd have to read other areas of this newspaper...Chief Jock Nixon and Spiro would have no reading matter whatsoever...Could the world carry on without the sports page and all us correspondents out there defending posts as Mark Asher did, meeting deadlines?

Think about it.

But the good burghers of Salisbury didn't think. They began to glare at the press box and scream, "Shut up!"

Hadn't they heard of the first amendment?

"Incredible," said Asher, who'd just endured a season of taking down George Allen's quotes, suffering irreparable damage to his stomach. "Friday night Nastase took a dive in his match against Brian Gottfried, and even got fined for quitting. The crowd didn't get on him for not doing his job—but they attack us for doing ours."

Normally, in this day of pro tennis, the umpire instructs such complainers that workmen of the quill and court must coexist, and to get on with it. No announcement was made at Salisbury and the customers grew ugly. Finally one of them launched a banzai charge on Mark Asher. It was something Ted Williams dreamed of doing for years, not to mention Spiro.

Did the attacker say anything as dramatic as, "your typewriter or your life?"

No, this unidentified spectator grabbed Asher, drawing blood from the Postman's typing fingers. All two of them. (Like most of us Asher uses the Bible System of Typing: Seek and Ye Shall Find). "I had to get a tetanus shot after the ripping," confided the reporter. "When the guy grabbed my typewriter I was startled."

His assailant bolted for the door with the typewriter. Asher sprinted right behind knowing full well the injunction to all journalists on combat duty: the greatest sin is to lose your weapon.

"I was working—and suddenly here I am chasing this idiot, trying to get him arrested," says Asher. "But who do the cops grab? Me." And the police threw the journalist out.

"Peculiar," says Jim Clayton, an editor of the Post. "We haven't decided whether to sue. Lucky for Asher, another of our staff finished his story. There were no more complaints at that typing. Asher finally got his typewriter back."

"But," says the young reporter, whose hands are bandaged and whose veins bubble with anti-tetanus serum, "the ribbon was gone." Asher knows that not even his Post colleague, Jack Foisie, underwent such treatment covering Vietnam. But we of the toy department accept these hazards as part of the job. Just let the police reporters try covering a testy tennis tournament sometime.

Meanwhile, Mark Asher, defender of our faith, regrets that he had only one ribbon to give for his readers.

Smith downs Ashe, dons crown

For the first half of 1973 Stan Smith was clearly the best player in the world, proving it by winning the pro championship, the World Championship Tennis final, at Dallas.

DALLAS—Under the spreading money tree stands the Village Smithy of tennis: Stanley Roger Smith, a horse with a blacksmith's touch who picked up a $50,000 fee for hammering balls past Arthur Ashe in the World Championship of Tennis final.

Yet it was reach, not muscle, that snatched the final game at SMU's Moody Coliseum, a game that Ashe and the full house of 8451 were certain Arthur had won. Abruptly Ashe's charge was halted on two uproarious, disputed points—and Smith became the world pro champion in four sets, 6-3, 6-3, 4-6, 6-4.

Smith, lifting himself to $154,100 for the year, started blindingly, making hardly a mistake in winning the first two sets. For a moment, in the first game of the third, his

Stan Smith

Around the Tennis World with Bud Collins

serve collapsed, and Ashe slipped through for a break, the first time he exceeded 15 in a Smith service game. Arthur's whizzing groundstrokes began to click; he won the third and was breaking down Smith's control of the net to 4-5 in the fourth.

That game went to 40-15 for Ashe, and then his fling at the world crumpled as the crowd booed and hooted the officials.

Here's what happened. Arthur served the 40-15 point and Smith missed the return. Game? No, the side linesman indicated his view of the serve was blocked when Smith moved in front of him to make the return. Umpire Mike Blanchard asked the linesman at the other end of the court to make the call. Fault. So it was still 40-15, second serve and Ashe double faulted to 40-30.

Smith's tremendous reach then put Arthur into trouble he couldn't escape. Ashe slashed a volley, and the point and game again seemed ended. But Stanley, reaching like Plastic Man, scraped the ball off the court barely before it could bounce twice. His lunge turned it into a nifty lob, which Stan followed for a winning volley to deuce. Umpire Blanchard said 6-4. Smith had reached the ball in time. Ashe and the crowd couldn't believe it.

TV replays proved the umpire correct. Ashe then fought off one match point but succumbed to a pair of backhand volleys and the WCT title was Smith's.

'The french fries aren't bad, considering they're French'

Innocents abroad? Maybe not, but these American kids at the French Open of 1973 at Paris seem pretty provincial.

PARIS—A drizzly rain splattered the city where Marlon Brando and Maria Schneider played house without furniture, and made Bertolucci famous. Mist rose from the courts at Stade Roland Garros filtering through the chestnut trees and obscuring the Eiffel Tower so that the Americans in Paris to play tennis may as well have been in Des Moines, Indianapolis or Jackson, Miss.

It doesn't much matter to these affluent young vagabonds, whose lives seem so cosmopolitan—if you're reading their itineraries: Las Vegas one week, Paris the next, and Rome after that, and what does 18-year-old Chris Evert ask the moment she arrives in the City of Light for the first time? "Where's the McDonald's?"

"On the Champs-Elysees," answers another wordly citizen of Ft. Lauderdale, Brian Gottfried. "You can't miss it. The Big Macs aren't so big, and they cost more. The bread's a little stale, but the french fries aren't bad, considering they're French."

My God. The man, encountering genuine french fries after a lifetime of eating the cardboard imitations in America, thinks they're not bad. Chris Evert felt better.

Big Mac would watch over her in a town where Escoffier created chefs' dreams. She might not see Sainte Chapelle of Versailles, but McDonald's would satisfy her, architecturally.

"I'm still looking for a good pizza place," said Dick Stockton, a New Yorker who had come through nicely to the third round of the French Open. "So this is Paris? I'll take Pittsburgh. That's where I played my first tournament away from home when I was about 7. My parents put me on a bus and said, 'good luck.' I put myself on a jet to get here. I've heard it's a great place to eat, but a steak's a steak, right?"

"You have to see something. I can't understand you guys," said Tom Gorman. "I'm going to the Louvre and see the nudes. I think we're in the wrong racket. We should have been painters."

"Doesn't pay as well," said Gottfried, who had won $41,000 eight days before in Las Vegas.

"I played here three years before I saw anything but now I try to at least get to the Louvre," said Gorman. "How can you come to Paris and not see the Mona Lisa?"

"That's nothing," responded Stockton. "I went to college four years in San-Antonio (Trinity University) and never saw the Alamo."

If John Wayne knew that, he'd make his wife quit her tennis lessons.

"Well," beamed Paul Gerken, the rarest of tennis playing characters—a New Englander in the round of 16. "Well, I saw the Mona Lisa when I played here last year. That's about all I saw. Got beat in the qualifiers." Gerken, 23, a husky yellow haired resident of East Norwalk, Conn. said, "I also saw the Alamo." Gerken, like Stockton and Gottfried, was an All-America at Trinity. Americans are generally as much out of their element athletically as gastronomically here on the languid, spongy Parisian clay which is kinder to tenacious retrievers than torrid hitters.

"The court was dry, nearly as fast as cement when I beat Pat Proisy (a Frenchman who was runner-up a year ago). I guess," smiled Gorman, "they forgot to soak it down. They'll put firehoses on it if I play another Frenchman."

Gorman scouts the town for fine restaurants, wishes he spoke French, and yesterday bought a suit at Lanvin. He's an exception. Evonne Goolagong, making her fourth visit—she won the title in 1971—says she's learned two words of French and that's enough: "bien cuit." "That's 'well done'—for the steaks. But," she said, "they never do them well enough here." No French chef has heart to comply fully to the barbaric Australian custom of bien cuit.

Stockton concedes French bread is magnificent. He was eating a yard of it, packed with ham. "Really great," said Harold Solomon. "Eat it today and wear it tomorrow." Solomon, a little guy from Silver Springs, Md., who understands clay, was on his eighth ice cream bar. You know he's having a good year because these ordinary chocolate-covereds cost 70 cents apiece. Ah, Paris prices.

They wandered out of the players dining room to watch Stan Smith struggling against Erik Van Dillen. On the way they took a look at another Bertolucci—an Italian David Cupper tangoing madly against Andy Pattison to avoid his last day in Paris. Paolo Bertolucci, a pudgy Roman, looks like a pasta smuggler. Stockton figures he'll be the guy to ask next week about the wonders of Rome—like pizza.

74   TENNIS DIGEST

Mrs. Court has her day— to Chrissie's dismay

In one of the most extraordinary women's matches–a contrast in styles and ages–Mighty Mama, Margaret Court, rebounded to beat the teen terror, Chris Evert for the French title of 1973.

PARIS—Margaret Court was back in her own league, far from the clutches of that dirty old man, Bobby Riggs, and life was beautifully bearable again. It didn't start out that way, though, and for a long, anguishing time it looked like a fresh young thing named Evert was going to duplicate the wizardry of the ancient rogue, Riggs, and heap more gloom on Mama Court's household.

Christine Marie Evert, the schoolgirl from Ft. Lauderdale who was seven when Marvelous Mama first won this French Tennis Championship in 1962, recovered from a terrible, nervous start, escaped all kinds of trouble— including two set points—in taking the first set, and had a winning lead in the second. When Chris served for the match at 5-3, 9000 Parisians at Stade Roland Garros burbled happily, ready to salute a new champion, an extraordinary juvenile of 18.

"I got overconfident, if you can believe it, against Margaret Court," frowned Chris later, trying to explain why the title went instead, for a fifth time, to the phenomenal Australian, 6-7, 7-6, 6-4. "I'd beaten her three of four—and both times we'd played on clay. I thought I was there, and made four errors to lose the game. But I still had even better chances."

So she did. Two times the Little Icemaiden was within two points of winning—at deuce with Margaret serving at 4-5 in the second; at 5-4 in points in the second set tie-breaker with two serves of Court's to come. "I got tight there," Chris admitted. "So close, so near, and I tightened. Yeah, I did."

"At that point," recalled Court, "I thought I'd blown it. I couldn't get my mind off the first set"—when she'd led, 3-1, in games, and later 5-points-to-2 in the tie-breaker with two serves due her. Then Evert began to bang winners to ring up five straight points and the set on a resounding backhand return.

"But that Margaret—so tough," sighed Evert. "I didn't think she could guts it out with me all that time (2 hours, 17 minutes). Did you?"

Nobody did.

Would Margaret choke as she did against Riggs? The opportunities were there. "Once I thought I was clutching," Margaret said, "when I had a break point (2-2) in the second and hit four bad shots." But she got back with it. Her ability to attack Evert's second serve put just the extra pressure on Chris that was the slight difference. Margaret was a little too strong in body, mind and experience. She responded splendidly in the second set tie-breaker, from 4-points-to-5 by hustling in for a pair of winning volleys that struck lines. That's how close it was. Had those balls gone out, Evert would have won her first major championship.

"Line balls—Margaret deserved them," said Chris, whose day was doubly mournful. Her boyfriend, Jimmy

Margaret Court

Connors, (in cahoots with Ilie Nastase) lost the doubles final to Tom Okker and John Newcombe, 6-1, 3-6, 6-3, 5-7, 6-4.

The old tonic is to put an ocean between yourself and the man who breaks your heart. It worked for 30-year-old Margaret, who has "felt kind of funny since Riggs beat me." Her shot at the Grand Slam (singles titles of Australia, France, Britain and US) stays alive, half accomplished. And she returned to the court with Virginia Wade to win the doubles over Francoise Durr and Betty Stove, 6-2, 6-3. It was a $7000 day for Mama, putting her over 100-grand for the year. Her husband Barry Court rustled up a beer for her, and Margaret could smile again. Mother's Day had come three weeks late—but it had come.

Nasty Nastase an adventuresome sort

Ilie Nastase

Perhaps the most difficult championship to win is the French Open on the slow clay of Roland Garros in Paris. In 1973 Ilie Nastase hammered his way through it with style and ease.

PARIS—One fine morning in 1918 a young Frenchman named Roland Garros climbed into a winged packing crate known in those days as an airplane, coaxed the coughing thing into the sky and headed east in search of the Red

Baron or anybody else flying a German machine. All Roland found was immortality: He never came back, vanishing forever, becoming an instant war hero to the French, who were short on such types at the time.

French youth idolized Roland Garros in that time of foolhardy gallantry. Today, few can tell you who he was—although if he had taken the smart way out, veering his plane to the Riviera to sit out the first World War in disguise on a beach, schoolboys might still hail his name.

The name remains anyway, attached to the deteriorating, yet charming, tennis ground in the Bois de Boulogne where Ilie Nastase became the first Romanian to win the US Open in New York and he may well be the first to win Wimbledon in London. As such, Nastase is a national treasure of a small, little known country, and he was attended—following his 6-3, 6-3, 6-0 destruction of Yugoslav Nikki Pilic—by a retinue of Romanians that included the ambassador to France.

As the No. 1 export of the country formerly best known as the stomping ground of Dracula, Nastase won't spend much time at home. No money there. He won $16,000 by making the crowd of 7000 and Pilic gasp at the fluency and magic of his whipping backhand, and he hopes to surpass his 1972 season when he was the No. 1 capitalist in tennis with $176,000 in prize money. He's nearly at the 100-grand mark now.

"I just keep traveling. That is my life. I go back to Bucharest," he said, "to play a Davis Cup match against New Zealand after Wimbledon. Then to America, I go to America several times, finally to Boston in December for the last big one." (The Commercial Union Assurance $100,000 Grand Prix playoffs for the top eight men in the world) over the second half of the year. He got 100 Grand Prix points for his win yesterday, putting him in the lead. If he stays there, Ilie collects the $55,000 first place bonus.

"What kind of place is Boston in December?" he asked. "The wrong kind of place, unless you're playing for your kind of money. At least you'll get more sleep," I told him.

The 1972 Masters was in Barcelona. There they don't start to play until after dinner. Dinner is over at 11 p.m.

Nobody can quite figure Nastase out. "I am a little crazy," he says of himself. But brilliant on a tennis court. As Rod Laver fades, this is the man who should take over. Should—but his erratic artistry has never been able to overcome the meat-and-potatoes, hard work and straight arrow approach of Just Plain Stan Smith.

They are the arch-rivals for their world now, and Smith keeps saying, "I always think I can out-gut him in a big match." Which he did in the last Wimbledon and Davis Cup finals.

Nastase is the kind of guy who would have climbed aboard with Roland Garros for the hell of it. He drives his Ford 65 to 70 mph through downtown Bucharest, terrorizing pedestrians—until they recognize him. Then, shaking fists become salutes, and they act as though they'd be grateful to be run over by their own "Iliuta" (Little Ilie) himself. Bucharest is a town where only two kinds of people can get away with driving like madmen: High party officials in their black Mercedes sedans, and Nastase in his sports car.

Nastase's bad manners are famous across the world. He pouted, screamed, threatened officials while beating perfect gentleman Arthur Ashe at Forest Hills in 1972. "But he won the $25,000," says Jim Smith, a friend of Ashe,

"Arthur's gonna have to find out that gentlemen don't always get what they deserve. It's a new era in tennis."

Nastase, darkly handsome, has never been popular with his colleagues because he shows them up on the court, mimics their failings, hams it up for the crowd. "A champion is not supposed to do that," says a French journalist, "and Nastase is the first champion who has been so deplorable."

Pro Frank Froehling says, "There's one answer to that guy Nastase—the Graebner variation." Clark Graebner leaped the net and threatened to punch Nastase's sunburnt nose a year ago in London. Nastase not only stopped showing off, he stopped. "Graebner frightened me," he said, leaving the court and defaulting the match.

"You can't not like the guy even though he's so bad mannered," says Ashe. "Just call me nasty," says Nastase.

While the powerful British tennis press lectures the Romanian on deportment, trying to make him into the Victorian he can never be, British schoolgirls—those proper young things in their uniforms—form Nastase fan clubs.

Nastase sulks when things aren't going well. He admits throwing a match earlier in Salisbury, Md., because he was disgusted.

Other players wonder about his competitiveness because he ducked joining the big league WCT circuit to play easy tournaments elsewhere.

"I will play WCT. I want to be with the best" he says. "I'm going to be a better boy," he smirks.

Maybe. But he is a singular entertainer—"an unbelievable athlete," sighed Pilic, who won the first three games, and few points after that. Nasty talks to everybody as he plays, swears in Italian "because it is a beautiful language" and in English here "because the French understand Italian. Never in Romanian—it sounds bad to me."

While everybody of the old, narrow school which still governs tennis conduct, says "For shame, Nastase"—they secretly say thank God for Nastase. He is excitement. He sells tickets. He plays like a dream. He's a hero the game has been looking for, as appealingly nutty in his way as a kid named Roland Garros who would climb into a freezing packing crate to chase the Red Baron.

When in Rome—Scream!

Nobody has more fun at a tennis tournament than Italians, who scream and laugh and let it all hang out at Il Foro Italico in Rome, as they did on this day of the 1973 Italian Open.

ROME—When in Rome, do as the Romans do: Scream.

Scream your sunburnt head off for any Italian tennis player...Let your inhibitions hang out...Guzzle wine ...Munch splendid ice cream...Ogle signorinas in chic T-shirts...Yell "dai" (come on) at Di Matteo, Zugarelli, Panata and Bertolucci...and have yourself un ballo.

Nobody has more fun at tennis matches than Italians. Their carnival—the $134,000 Italian Open—is far removed spirtually from the cathedral of Wimbledon. Even though the setting, Il Foro Italico, is one of the most elegant in the sporting universe—a marble amphitheatre with a tiara of pines—the customers could be right out of Boston's Fenway Park bleachers. The English may have invented tennis, but the Italians humanized it.

That doesn't mean everybody enjoys. Ilie Nastase, the Bucharest hotdog who specializes in emoting for the gallery, was displeased when the gallery threw its affection to his opponent, Ezio Di Matteo, the fifth ranking Italian who had beaten Brian Gottfried. They were all for Di Matteo, and Nastase felt like a South Boston High football player performing in East Boston. One screamer in particular got on Nastase hard, jumping about, waving his arms and hollering, "dai, Ezio!" and "uccidilo!" (kill him). Nastase, who understands Italian, stopped playing and asked the guy why he was carrying on so. "I have bet 10,000 lire ($17) on Di Matteo," was the reasonable answer, and the chap kept on screaming.

Since Nastase won, 6-0, 6-3, it wasn't a good bet, although the price had been attractive. Rino (the Roman) Tommasi—this town's answer to Jimmy (the Greek) Snyder—had made Nastase a 6-to-1 favorito on his morning line that runs in the tournament program. It is surely

Nikki Pilic

Around the Tennis World with Bud Collins

the only tennis program that lists the odds for every match, a thoughtful service by editor Tommasi, the sport's leading handicapper. Says he, "no, gambling is not legal here, but don't you run the football and basketball point spreads in your newspapers?"

While the players themselves—increasingly like pros in every sport—seemed more interested in labor problems and conditions, the public concerned themselves with how the local boys were doing. The Jimmy Hoffa of the rug-beaters, union President Cliff Drysdale, was looking for solidarity from the Assn. of Tennis Pros on the matter of a Wimbledon walkout by the best players unless fellow laborer Nikki Pilic is reinstated.

Pilic was suspended for a month, costing him a Wimbledon payday, by the Yugoslav Federation for failing to play Davis Cup. The International Lawn Tennis Federation backed the Yugoslav establishment. "Can't impair Pilic's right to make a living over an internal squabble," Drysdale insisted justifiably. "We've got to stand so that Wimbledon allows him in." Meanwhile Mike Davies, Lamar Hunt's ambassador from WCT, was sizing up players for the pro circuit next year, revealing that the big league will expand (doesn't every sport, ready or not?) to three 32-man divisions.

But the customers weren't interested in that stuff. Five thousand of them gathered around the main court and raised their voices and arms in cheering Tonino Zugarelli (who had defeated Tom Gorman) from 1-3 down in the third to a 6-3, 5-7, 6-3 triumph over Welshman Gerald Battrick. "I don't mind the buggers," said Battrick of the screamers. "They make me more determined." But they made Zugarelli more determined, too. Despite the 90-degree heat, the crowd kept up a noisy banter for Italy's finest, Adriano Panatta. The weather and the fine clay court game of a Frenchman brought up in Algeria, Patrice Dominguez, got to sixth-seeded Panatta, though, as he dropped through a 6-4, 7-6 defeat.

Elsewhere on a side court, about a thousand loyalists packed the hillside and used their vocal cords to pull the Pasta Kid, chunky, heavy-legged Paolo Bertolucci, to a stunning victory over Roger Taylor, 4-6, 6-3, 7-5.

When he won Bertolucci raised his arms in a happy daze, and a mob of kids leaped the low fence to surround him and beat on him jubilantly. The same thing happened to Stan Smith Wednesday, which shows the enthusiasm isn't always partisan.

And at nightfall, Nastase was griping, "They aren't nice people here." He and his partner, Jimmy Connors, walked out of a doubles match in a huff, midway through the second set, defaulting to the French, Wanaro N'Godrella and Dominguez, because "the people are screaming terrible things at us. They call me Romanian bastard and they call Connors American bastard, and we aren't even playing against Italians. Why?" Connors was puzzled. He doesn't speak the language, but he took Nastase's word for it.

Maybe it's more fun if something is lost in the translation.

England hails Wimbledon's Wellington

Even Wimbledon isn't impervious to labor problems and strikes, as we learned in 1973 when most of the top men walked out. But an Englishman, Roger Taylor, bucked the union and played–and became a hero.

ONCE THEY'D FOUND enough bodies to replace the strikers, and the gates of Wimbledon opened for another year on schedule, the tournament looked like the unknown soldier's family reunion. The mystery guests signed in, and you wondered if their line was tennis. In some cases it was, but when you scanned the 128 names on the men's draw sheet you felt you'd dropped into downtown Tirana and were reading an Albanian phone book.

With 82 members of the union (the Assn. of Tennis Pros) sitting this one out in a dispute over the suspension of fellow laborer Nikki Pilic, you had such forgettable pairings as Buwalda vs. Iqbal, Pugaev vs. Ewert, Kronk vs. Hancock, Mignot vs. Pokorny, Bernasconi vs. Mitton and Lecher vs. Stock. Lecher, you should know, is not a dirty old man, but a nice looking young Australian refugee from a Melbourne garbage truck. While Stock is the greatest player in the history of Grundy Center, Iowa.

If few of the cast were as readily identifiable as the Man in the Iron Mask, there was one that was received like Nelson's returning from Trafalgar, or Wellington's arriving from Waterloo. It was the brooding Yorkshire countenance of a scab named Roger Taylor, who rode his heart in defiance of the union "I believe in."

At 5 yesterday afternoon, all of England stood and saluted this strikebreaker—14,000 customers in Centre Court and millions across the land having tea in front of the telly, including the inhabitants of his heavily Labor Party county, Yorkshire.

"We're sick of strikes in this country," said a man who'd slept in the line outside the gates to assure himself of a standing room place in Centre. "These aren't sportsmen who would strike Wimbledon, and when Taylor refuses to go along, why he's like an engineer who breaks a picket line at a station and drives an engine to take the commuters home."

"It hasn't been a happy week for me," said Taylor after he'd beaten Jean Haillet, 6-2, 6-3, 6-3. "I didn't know what to do. The boys in the union know I'm with them, but I just couldn't strike against this place, this tournament. They can go home. I live just a mile away. This is my country."

Even into Sunday night Roger was getting abusive calls from ATP members, demanding that he drop out.

"I answered the phone," said his wife, Frances, "and I still haven't told Roger some of it. Calls from people we know and thought were friends. It was awful."

Ilie Nastase, the tourney favorite, and Taylor were the only unionists to turn blackleg, as they'd say in labor circles here, and buck the boycott. Nastase, pleading he is the pawn of the Communist government of Romania, where they don't recognize strikes—and do want him urgently to win the title—seemed to have an out.

Taylor agonized. "I talked it over with my father, a union man in the steel mill," said Taylor. "I changed my mind a hundred times. It seemed easier to go with my friends in ATP, so I pulled out. Minutes after I did it I knew I was wrong, and I phoned up and told them to put me back in the draw. Since then the players have said some terrible things about me. They've threatened to cut me out of tournaments, and asked me to resign."

"You have to understand Roger," says a close friend. He comes from an unlikely background for tennis, a steel town (Sheffield) and he's pulled himself up a couple of classes, socially and athletically. He's No. 1 in Britain, a member of the All-England club (tourney host), has married well. Can he risk his gains by turning on his own public and walking out on a British institution?

"The other players should try to understand."

They don't. The union has behaved shamefully toward Taylor. They've made their point with the strike and should try to recognize that his decision to play was what his conscience dictated. Taylor has said he'll donate all his prize money to the ATP.

"I was pretty uptight when I walked onto the court. I've been thinking about everything but actually hitting the ball," Taylor said. Three years ago on the same Centre Court, Taylor put himself on every front page in the country by stopping Rod Laver's record Wimbledon streak at 31 matches. Today he's there again, as the man who wouldn't let down the side.

As Taylor and Haillet came into the court, they were attended by more photographers than Lord Lambton and Norma Levy, (leading figures in the current sex scandal). The Duke of Kent, in the Royal box, stood and led the applause, along with the Duchess (a Yorkshire chick from considerably different circumstances than Roger). Everybody else was up and cheering and clapping. Forty-seven seconds of it which is a lot of noise in this staid enclosure. "It felt good. For the first time I felt good," Roger said.

The scab was a hero. " 'e saved the bloody tournament, 'e and the Commie, Nasty," enthused a spectator. But did they? Wimbledon can probably stand alone as Britain did against Hitler. Despite the facelessness of the field, 22,603 customers showed (the second best opening day ever) and the spivs (scalpers) were doing good business.

As Stein might have penned (perhaps that old Brandeis fullback, Maury Stein): "A Wimbledon is a Wimbledon is a Wimbledon..."

Billie Jean King

King keeps tennis title; Kodes routs Metreveli

Wimbledon has known few champions more prolific than Billie Jean King, who won her fifth singles title there in 1973.

LONDON—An Old Lady, who doesn't yet have to live on her memories, Billie Jean King was having trouble living with one of them—named Chris Evert.

"I've never quite forgotten that beating she gave me in Fort Lauderdale a year ago, 6-1, 6-0. Nothing," winced Billie Jean at the thought of it. "Nothing like that ever happened to me. I really thought about that for two days before this match. I got psyched way up." The way she started out yesterday at Wimbledon—winning the first eight games on a loss of nine points—lets you know the militant Ms. King was trying to repay with interest. Eventually it was 6-0, 7-5 for the Long Beach woman who grew from tomboy to empress of tennis on a day when Centre Court was extremely unsafe for the pigtailed kid from Fort Lauderdale.

"This is the kind of memory I've wanted for a long time—a fifth Wimbledon championship," said King, who first showed up here as a teen-ager herself, winning the doubles at 17 in 1961, and has established herself as The Player of the post-Second World War era. Only Helen Wills and Suzanne Lenglen won more singles titles here. "Five, I wanted five," said Billie Jean, who ordinarily can't tell you what she's won. She keeps track of Wimbledon.

There were unpleasant memories of a much graver nature on the mind of Czechoslovak Jan Kodes before he took the court to beat the first Russian ever to grace a final, Alex Metreveli. Kodes could remember Soviet tanks grinding into Wenceslaus Square in his hometown of Prague five years ago, putting down thoughts of freedom among his people.

Metreveli served miserably during his 6-1, 9-8, 6-3 defeat, but he might have leaped into the match if he'd returned serve on set point against Kodes' serve at 4-5 in the second.

Kodes, who beat up Metreveli's second serve, moved in quickly to volley nimbly and adroitly. Kodes trailed 2-4 in the second set, battled to 8-8 and won the tiebreaker, 7-5. From there it was obvious he was on his way to the $12,700 first prize, emulating the achievement of Jaroslav Drobny, the other Czech victor in 1954.

Back on top of the world after a shaky six months when she was slowed by injuries and distracted by the political struggle within women's tennis, Billie Jean came on like the Wicked Witch of the West Coast against 18-year-old

Around the Tennis World with Bud Collins

Chris, rushing the juvenile lead into uncertainty and inadequacy.

Attacking devastatingly, probing with every spin known to racket, Billie Jean prevented Chris from getting set to make the booming groundstrokes with which she brought down No. 1 seed Margaret Court in the semis.

"I couldn't get started," lamented Chris. "When I thought I was getting into it in the second set" (coming from 0-2 to 5-4, including a run of 10 points), "well, Billie Jean just served and volleyed even better. She didn't make a mistake all afternoon." Maybe a couple.

Billie Jean, volleying with touch and thunder, lived at the net, winning a third of her points outright, hustling the kid into unaccustomed blunders for the others. She owns Centre Court. And she treated the kid like a trespasser.

"Long, long day, but I love this place—I'd play all night, too," said Billie Jean who was on court nearly five hours for 86 games in winning as well the doubles semis and final (with Rosie Casals) and a mixed doubles quarterfinal (with O. K. Davidson). It was her ninth Wimbledon doubles title (fifth with Casals), 6-1, 4-6, 7-5 over Betty Stove and Francoise Durr.

But Evert will be back. She hasn't done too badly, a semi-final and a final in her first two years.

Still Billie Jean is the empress, and don't be startled if she wins a couple of more. "I'd like to top Suzanne Lenglen (six titles), I guess I'm greedy," she laughed.

And now? "Bring on Bobby Riggs," challenged Billie Jean. "I've got some bad memories of what he did to all us women when he beat Margaret."

Jimmy Connors

Unseeded Connors invades Ashe country

Jimmy Connors, who strode to the top of the world for 1974 by winning Wimbledon and the U.S. Open, made his first impact a year before in Boston when, unseeded, he streaked to the U.S. Pro championship at 20.

BOSTON—Jimmy Connors came to town, and they all came tumbling down—Stan Smith, Dick Stockton, Cliff Richey, and finally Arthur Ashe—and, for one week anyway, the nerveless rag doll out of Belleville, Ill., was the boss of American tennis.

The US Pro Championships has been in a lefthanded groove for the last decade (five titles for Rod Laver and one for Tony Roche,) but this was a new kind of left-hander: an American, and the youngest ever at 20 to put the pro crown on his flappy brown coiffure.

"I never played so good in my life," said Connors after he outgunned Ashe in an extraordinary baselining performance, 6-3, 4-6, 6-4, 3-6, 6-2.

"I've played them all," Ashe said as he shook his head,

Arthur Ashe

"Laver, Rosewall, Okker... and I've never seen a guy keep hitting so hard and deep for so long. Jimmy never had a letup in nearly three hours. Sure, I won two sets, but he just kept pounding away. For one week anyway he was in a class by himself."

This is Arthur Ashe country and Longwood is the place where he won his first grade-A title, the National Amateur of 1968. Now at 30, he was "the old guy," in his words, "with this hungry kid nipping at my heels."

The devotion of the Ashe-ites and the excitement stirred by Connors' unseeded run through the New England Merchants National Bank's $60,000 bash sold the Cricket Club out by early afternoon. It was standing-and-lying room only as nearly 6000 witnesses scrunched onto every pew and into every cranny.

They were disappointed only by Ashe's fade in the fifth set, but elated by the verve and relentless nerve of the young dynamiter, who blasted away for the lines and corners either with his whippy forehand or his two fisted backhand. His style is different from Laver's. He prefers to stay back, but Jimmy displayed the Rocket's old let-er-rip outlook on life in a tennis court. He was a worthy southpaw successor in the winner's circle where he collected $12,000.

From that, the first expenditure went for champagne for his mother and friends in the clubhouse.

"Marvelous," said Gloria Connors, a trim blonde tennis pro who launched Jimmy's career 18 years ago. Marvelous it was. His groundstrokes so awed Ashe that the loser didn't attack enough, even though he had numerous chances on the second serve. Connors got away with poor first serving. Like Ken Rosewall he backed himself handsomely from the baseline in a match of long, enthralling rallies of zinging net skinners.

"I came in here knowing I had to lift myself to beat these guys," said Connors of the leading American pros. "When I beat Smith I was high and just stayed there."

He hit hard, harder and hardest. Always with accuracy and thought. Connors probably settled it against the ever-dangerous Ashe in the third game of the fifth. He'd broken Arthur for 2-0, and Arthur retaliated to 30-30. There Jimmy jammed him with a blistering first serve and got the game by hurling himself at the ball to make a full-bodied volley with all arms and legs flying.

That's the Connors style: throw everything into it, go for the money all the time. The money was his—the evening's big money, while Smith and Erik van Dillen split $2500 on a 4-6, 6-4, 7-5 win over Izzy El Shafei and Marty Riessen.

If Connors had gotten any higher, the bank president, Mark Wheeler, would have needed a helicopter to make the check presentation.

Confessions of an unabashed, male chauvinist ogler

There's more to tennis than watching the balls–for instance, watching the belles at the U.S. Pro Championships in Boston.

THIS IS AN unabashedly male chauvinist piggy column about why attendance is up at the US Pro Tennis championships at Longwood: It isn't the heat, it's the humanity sidling around in halters and shortest skirts and tightest jeans and skimpiest shorts and other lovely little outfits that would fully drape only Ms. Tom Thumb.

This is an unabashedly provincial column: Don't talk to me about the surf bunnies of the West Coast, the cycle chickies of the South, the polka dollies of Cleveland or the girl from Ipanema—because the New England girls of summer arrayed on the Cricket Club's bleachers are the fairest of them all.

The women come to watch the male tennis players, the men come to watch the women, and that's what makes the turnstiles go round. Every night the nearly 5000 seats have been sold out, and that's never happened at Longwood before.

Longwood has ever been the first resort of us sportsmen known as oglers, a smorgasbord for dirty old (and young) men. But this is a vintage year for The Girls of Longwood (okay Ms. Steinem, I mean the women of Longwood). There hasn't been such a comely crop, apparently, since 1900, when, though they wore white tents to their ankles, a British Davis Cupper, H. Roper Barrett, remarked: "The courts at Longwood are abominable, the balls are soft and motherly, the nets a disgrace—but the ladies are truly lovely to look upon."

So Barrett was an ankle man. That's the best you could do in those days. If he might return from that great Centre Court in the sky for just one afternoon at Longwood, H. Roper Barrett would at last feel fulfilled. A Victorian gentleman would watch this passing parade of centerfold candidates and sigh, "my ad!"

But, of course, if the Marquis de Sade were to reappear, he'd gasp, "your serve, mademoiselle—let 'er rip!"

If Ilie Nastase or Bjorn Borg were here, the female customers would be lined up all the way to Framingham Center, repeating the screams and quivers of their Wimbledon sisters. Nobody attracts better looking women than tennis players, and nobody has attracted more of them than the picturesque Romanian Nastase or the 17-year-old marble fawn from Sweden, Borg.

But they aren't here. Nevertheless, The Girls of Longwood seem perfectly willing to settle for the Zapata-like Marty Riessen (voted "sexiest" by the female pros); the cool, enigmatic Arthur Ashe; the intellectual Chopin-with-racket Jeff Borowiak; the collegiate Gunga Din, Haroon Rahim; the cotton candy topped King of King's Road, Ray Moore; the Bagel Twins, Harold Solomon and Eddie Dibbs; the smooth Latins, Jaime Fillol and Charlie Pasarrel; Chrissie's sweetie, Jimmy Connors; the towering Billy Graham, Stan Smith; the boy next door, Erik van Dillen; Mother Machree's boy, Tom Gorman; the poor woman's Omar Sharif, Ismail El Shafei, and the boy next door (if you live next door to Popeye the Sailor), Nails Carmichael.

It is a cast for which we sexists can be grateful, because it brings out the finest in halters. At Longwood everyday, male heads are swiveling left and right in the classic movement—watching not the balls but the belles. You don't think men would pay good, hard cash to watch other men play tennis, do you?

But put the Girls of Longwood in the stands, and the oglers will follow after, and yeah verily the stands will be full and the coffers overflowing—along with the T-shirts.

At Fenway Park if one exceptional lovely walks in, 15 guys fight for the press box binoculars. At Longwood, even a guy with wide-screen eyeballs can't capture the scene.

"Why you're a horrid sex-object oriented gawker," scolded Marji Wellington, who caught me swiveling and ogling madly. "Watch the tennis!"

"Why?" I wondered. "Tennis is only a game. Ogling is The Game, and if Gloria and Germaine and Bella and Betty don't like it, they can show up in burnooses."

Around the Tennis World with Bud Collins

Say hello to Mrs. Wightman

One of the illustrious names in the game is Wightman— Hazel Hotchkiss Wightman: triple champ in 1909-10-11; donor of the Wightman Cup in 1923; and still perky at the Cup's 50th anniversary battle in 1973.

I'M STILL A LITTLE embarrassed about the time I first met Hazel Wightman—but she has forgiven me, she says, so I guess it's all right.

This was a long time ago—I think the Everly Brothers' "Wake Up Little Suzy" was big that summer—and I was covering the Massachusetts Women's tennis do at Longwood Cricket Club. Somebody said, "you ought to meet Mrs. Wightman. She's running the tournament…" And before I could suitably gear my dialogue for a brush with immortality, I'd been led to a hand shake with this small, white-haired lady with pale-but-competitive blue eyes.

"Uh…gee," came my smooth Midwestern rube response, "I thought you were dead, ma'am." Not by a long shot.

"Hazel Wightman hasn't been dead for years," according to that razor-tongued clothing designer, Ted Tinling, who was rebuked by her a couple of decades ago for daring to attach a brightly colored hem to a tennis dress worn by an Englishwoman in a Wightman Cup match. "She used to think she was Queen Canute, holding back the tide," says Tinling. "But Mrs. Wightman is having a renaissance. She's come right along with the times."

That would not be a revelation to the friends of Lady Tennis, who marvel as she dwells in the present and future. Yet there was a time, I guess, when she felt herself to be a guardian of All That Is Right in tennis. It is recalled that Hazel once chased one of the top players in the world to the dressing room and ordered her to get rid of a pair of flesh-toned panties. "I don't object to these changes in dress,

Hazel Wightman (r) with Chris Evert (l).

really, as long as they're in good taste," says Mrs. Wightie, as she's called most of the time. "But I've always felt that a player has to concentrate, and you can't concentrate if people are staring at you for something odd you're wearing."

It is only fair to report that Hazel, a girl out of the Golden West in 1909, attracted plenty of the wrong kind of stares herself for something she was not wearing at the Philadelphia Cricket Club. Her father had sent her from Berkeley East at age 22 to play the National Women's Championships. Though she conformed by trussing herself in corset and dress that touched her sneakers, Hazel had them aghast because she bared her…elbows!

Yes, she came to play in a short-sleeved dress her mother made—"long sleeves were just too constricting; I could run pretty well in the long skirt"—and Philadelphians excused her only because nobody obviously knew any better Out West. And because she knocked the bustles off the opposition, winning the singles, doubles and mixed doubles. She would repeat that feat in 1910 and 1911—nobody has won the nine titles in three years since—en route to a record 45 US championships in various categories, the last in 1954 in senior (over 40) doubles when, apparently, she was over 40.

I suppose I hadn't been prepared for Hazel's presence on this planet, that day we were introduced, because these old, revered trophies-bearing-names always seem to be memorials, like the Davis Cup, the Stanley Cup, the Walker Cup. You don't connect them with somebody still hanging in there, even swinging a tennis racket at 86, continuing to give pointers to youngsters in her garage.

So Hazel lives. Does she ever. And it's a pleasant touch that her club, Longwood, has brought the 50th anniversary Wightman Cup matches to town: a three-day best-of-seven match series. She didn't set out to start an enduring Anglo-American rivalry when in 1923 she presented a silver vase to the US Lawn Tennis Association. "It wasn't supposed to be called the Wightman Cup," she says. "I've grown accustomed to that, although I didn't approve at first. I had hoped the women of the world could have a competition similar to the Davis Cup (launched in 1900 by another Longwood member, Dwight Davis, and now involving more than 50 countries). I gave the cup to the USLTA with that thought in mind, and understood it would be called the Women's International Lawn Tennis Challenge Trophy.

"In 1923 a British women's team was sent to the American tournaments, and Julian Myrick of the USLTA thought it would be nice to have an American team play them for the Cup in the new stadium at the West Side Tennis Club, Forest Hills. That was the first. I captained the team and Eleanor Goss and I won a doubles. I had hoped the competition would expand, but the British liked the idea of America and Britain, and that's the way it's stayed. I'm pleased there's another Cup now (the Federation Cup) that brings in all countries like the Davis Cup."

Although Britain's female tennis players have an international record about as strong as Britain's heavyweight prizefighters—they are attractive, well-spoken good losers—the event has been an artistic success. The US leads 37-7, and because of the format the British cannot lose worse than 7-0 this time. But everybody enjoys. That, to Hazel Wightman, is what tennis is all about.

She accepts that all the contestants, including the No. 1 ticket seller 18-year-old Christine Marie Evert—making her Boston debut—are professionals. "I just hope the money doesn't get in the way of their enjoying the game. I wouldn't have taken money, and there were offers," says Hazel.

She is an amateur at heart: a lover of the game. But she is up-to-date Hazel, too. She'll hit out the first ball for the matches with 1923 vintage racket, a bit of show biz which should delight the photographers but probably would have been vetoed by the 1923 Hazel. I suspect, too, she'll be wearing a short-sleeved dress, showing the elbows that had Philadelphia whispering in 1909.

Living to 86 isn't that great an accomplishment, but making it this far with an abiding interest in life and people, and continuing to be a dear friend to a multitude is a neat trick. It is very nice to have you around for this 50th, Hazel. The strings in your 1923 racket may be dead, but I'm happy to report you ain't.

More to life than tennis

An unusually thoughtful athlete is Argentinian Guillermo Vilas, who came from nowhere to become one of the leading men of 1974.

MAJOR Richard Castillo of the US Army went to war a few years ago in Vietnam and hasn't been heard of since. MIA: Missing in action. Guillermo Vilas, a kid out of Argentina who plays tennis for a living, never met Major Castillo—and will never forget him. Encircling the left wrist of Vilas—the wrist that has sent the tennis world into a Vilas spin—is a steel bracelet inscribed with Castillo's name and serial number. "I read about these bracelets and how you can help the POW families by buying them," says Vilas. "So I buy two of them." On his right wrist is Lt. Joseph Mobley ("He has come back, thank God.")

"Sometimes when I am playing tennis, and it is very hot...I am playing badly, getting beat, maybe, and I think it is hard...I look at these names," Vilas nods at his wrists, "and I know I don't have it bad. Others have it worse."

Perspective, rare perspective. Guillermo Vilas is 22. He won six tournaments and more than $25,000 in 1974. But those are merely numbers for sports pages. In his head, where it counts, Vilas has it all in perspective, wouldn't you say?

"Life is a theater, and we all have roles. I like to play tennis. Each day," says Vilas, "is different. But if we all play tennis, who writes the newspapers? A lawyer is more important than the person who picks up papers, but if everybody is a lawyer, who picks up papers?"

This is not quite a conversation out of Rod Laver, who is happy in the Australian mystique: Hit the hell out of the ball; work harder than the next guy; get to the ball and the beer faster than your neighbor. Yet Vilas, with his awesome topspin, and capacity for work has a lot of Laverian lefthandedness in his style, if not his psyche.

Vilas sits beside a club swimming pool. His jeans are blue, his shoes brown wooden clogs, his hair a brunette mane, his eyes amber, and his mood questioning. Now the Young Bull of the Pampas is quoting a Spanish poet, Machado: "It is hard for me to translate, but this is close—

there is no road...the walker makes the road as he walks and when he looks back (as on past wins) he stops going ahead.

"I want to go ahead, to do the best I can, but that is my only goal—to do my best. I don't think of being No. 1. I do not look at the mountain top as I climb, just the next step. When I was down 1-4 to Eddie Dibbs at Louisville (the semis of a tourney Vilas won), it would be easy to say I'm too far behind, to look up and think it's impossible. The only thing to do is play the next point as well as possible...and the next...and..."

Vilas, a lonely child on a country estate, was brought by his father to the seaside resort of Mar del Plata to learn tennis "so that I would meet other children. Make friends. But you have few friends, really, and it is better to be alone than to travel in bad company." Today he is a boffo celebrity in Argentina, interviewed daily over the phone by the country's newspapers, trailed by Argentinian cameramen. The President, Isabelita Peron, received him when he came home following the US Open. The government pays his air fares.

He says he is influenced by listening to tapes of J. Krishnamurti, an Indian mystic. "With life rushing by, Krishnamurti asks you to stop and think...to ask why ...why...why. He does not want followers, but people who will question, who will not accept what they hear or read just because they see or hear it. I am becoming famous, so my words mean more to people...but that's silly. Why should anybody be considered an expert on many things because he is in one field? I am born a Catholic, but because I am studying other religions now I am more a Catholic. It is good to be one thing if you know about other things.

"You learn from all things, from good people and bad. My grandfather would say thank you for my enemies and friends—from friends I get help and learn to get ahead...from enemies I learn the way I don't want to go. A wonderful man.

"I got very tired in Indianapolis," Vilas returned to tennis, commenting on the one tourney in a six week stretch in which he didn't grace the final. "I was playing and winning every day. It was too much. Then my body adjusted, and I feel very strong again." His friends will be happy about that, his rivals depressed.

Throughout the summer circuit Vilas astounded the crowds by asking linesmen to correct calls against his foes whenever he thought the officials were wrong. He did so several times in the Louisville final with $16,000 at stake when he beat Jaime Fillol. This seemed as unreal as Carl Yastrzemski refusing to accept a base hit on a drive down the line that he thought was foul. "But," says Vilas, "in tennis you are alone. The opponent is your friend, too, as well as opponent, and you are having fun together. You wouldn't want to see him cheated. First you are sportsman, then professional athlete. You play for the game, then the money."

This is not the sporting philosophy for 1975. But it is Guillermo Vilas, the Young Bull of the Pampas, who says, "sometimes it is bad to be famous and not to have to stand in lines, because in lines you meet the people"...who quotes poetry, discusses religion, stomps his opponents...and who realizes no loss, however painful, on a tennis court can compare with the loss sustained by Major Richard Castillo and the people of Major Richard Castillo, MIA. ●

Why Your Volley Isn't Improving

by GLADYS M. HELDMAN

IF YOU HAVE been practicing your net game for the last three months and you see little or no improvement, there has to be a weakness in the stroke itself. First, make sure you know exactly what you are supposed to do. If you try to hit a forehand volley directly in front of your body rather than to your side, or if you keep volleying on the dead run as you charge to net, or if your wrist is floppy so that the ball moves your racket instead of your racket moving the ball, all the practice in the world won't improve your net game. Check your own volley against the list below; it will make you a better analyst of the game and your practice sessions will be of more value.

• **The feet are apart and the knees are bent.** It isn't possible to hit any shot well if your feet are together. Low volleys will be your nemesis if you don't bend your knees: when you stand straightlegged to hit a ball below knee-level, your racket head must drop and all control is lost. Get down to all low volleys so that wrist and racket head can be on the same level.

• **Never hit a volley on the dead run.** The intermediate typically serves and dashes headlong to net, volleying in the middle of his sprint. The good player serves, moves in quickly, stops, then moves (or, if necessary, leaps) to the left or the right for the volley. It is as difficult to volley on the dead run as it is to serve on the dead run.

• **Punch the volley or, in a quick exchange, block it.** Inexperienced players get overly excited on a high volley and swing wildly, sacrificing control and accuracy to achieve what they hope will be a power shot. If the novice is asked to hit the high volley deep to his opponent's backhand, he will find the only way to do so is by shortening his wild stroke to a punch. Unlike the groundstroke, the volley wind-up begins well in front of the body. On the forehand side, the palm of the hand is approximately a foot in front and a foot to the right of the body (on wide volleys where the player has to stretch, the palm is a full arm's length from

Stan Smith sometimes has trouble getting down to low volleys, but he is in good shape here as he starts to punch this forehand volley down-the-line. There is no backswing on this shot. The racket face is opened as required to provide necessary under-spin and lift.

John Newcombe is a masterful volleyer because he sticks to fundamentals, always blocking or punching them. This back-hand volley, blocked with enough underspin to lift it over the net, is carefully placed down-the-line.

the body). The racket head is on the same plane as the palm. In other words, the wrist isn't broken back so far that the racket head trails, and the racket head only leads the palm when one is volleying crosscourt.

The entire volley punch is only one foot long as compared to the tremendous full-bodied arc on the groundstroke. The volley finish ends with the arm almost fully extended and the racket head and palm still on the same plane when volleying down the line (on forehand crosscourts, the racket head will lead the palm). The backhand volley has the identical motion: palm and racket head start together, a foot in front and a foot to the left of the body, although the racket head will lead slightly on crosscourts. At the finish, the arm has almost straightened. The racket head and palm are on the same plane for the down-the-line but the racket head leads on the crosscourt.

If there is no time to react against a hard ball, the start is the same but racket and palm move forward only a few inches at the hit (a block). Blocks utilize the power of the opponent and can be controlled well because the action is so short (the longer the action, the more chance the player has to err). All hard balls can be blocked back, but soft shots must be punched if the volleyer wants power.

• **Don't hit a backhand volley with an Eastern forehand grip.** Most good players volley on both sides with a Continental grip, which is almost as far over as an Eastern backhand. Beginners almost always are taught to volley with the same grips as they use on groundstrokes: the Eastern forehand and the Eastern backhand. In fast exchanges, the beginner will sometimes be trapped on the backhand side with a forehand grip. This can jolt his elbow and it makes for an awkward stroke, particularly when the beginner points his elbow up and tries to hit his backhand with the same racket face that he uses on the forehand.

To avoid this possibility, those volleyers who switch from Eastern forehand to Eastern backhand should wait with

Virginia Wade, reaching to hit a low forehand volley crosscourt, opens her racket face for lift and brings the racket head forward, slightly ahead of the palm of her hand.

Rod Laver gets down well to a shoestring backhand volley. His front foot is planted because good players hit volleys from a stationary position whenever possible, though their weight is moving forward. The stroke will be little more than a block.

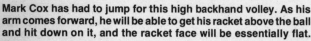

Mark Cox has had to jump for this high backhand volley. As his arm comes forward, he will be able to get his racket above the ball and hit down on it, and the racket face will be essentially flat.

Billie Jean King leaps to intercept a forehand volley, arm and racket stretched out but racket head still above the wrist. Though she is fully extended, Billie Jean is still in control of the shot and is blocking it down-the-line.

the *backhand grip.* Then, if the volleyer is trapped on the forehand side with a backhand grip, he will get an inkling of how it feels to hit a forehand volley Continental-style. At first his volleys will shoot so wide crosscourt that they sail beyond the alley. Later he will learn to flatten (lay back) his wrist. He will still find it difficult, but a lot of practice on punching forehand volleys with a backhand grip will show him the way.

• **Pretend every ball is coming right at you.** If you are continually late on the volley or if you generally back up in a fast exchange, your eyes, your racket and your feet are not "ready." When you stand at net and your partner is serving, do not watch the receiver's face; keep your eyes glued to his racket. As soon as contact is made, follow the ball and be ready for the move. In a fast volley exchange, don't look at the opponent's racket; look at the ball. You can't be ready if you don't hold your racket in front of you, if you are not bouncy on your toes so that you can push off in any direction and if your knees aren't bent. Flexed knees help in getting a fast start and in getting down quickly for a low shot. When you wait with your racket in front of you, don't point your racket way over to the left since this will make you late on all forehand volleys. Generally the racket is pointed a few inches to the left in the most natural position (pointing it straight in front of you is a bit awkward).

• **Step forward for extra punch.** You won't always have time to take a forward step, but whenever you can, step toward the net with your left foot on a forehand volley

and with your right foot on a backhand volley. The step comes a second before the hit so that your weight is already moving forward. On wide volleys, it is preferable (but not always possible) to move sideways and forward, and again the intermediate should make every effort to take the step with the left foot on the forehand side and the right foot on the backhand side. On very wide volleys, this is not possible.

• **Wait for slow balls.** Overeagerness on soft, high shots ruins more volleys than any other factor. The anxious intermediate who wants to kill the high, easy shot comes apart at the seams: he takes a stroke instead of a punch; after he has the racket in the punch position, he pulls it back in a second and bigger backswing because he has too much time; or he forgets to be a small, tight package and, just as though the string holding the package suddenly snaps, he flails at the ball wildly and without control. Wait for the slow ball; you have all the time in the world to watch it, step forward and punch.

• **Place your volleys.** You must see the ball well in front of you to place it. Flatten your wrist for the down-the-line and see your racket meet the ball. Turn your racket head slightly forward for the crosscourt and again see the ball in flight and see it as your racket makes contact. Never look at the opponent to discover where he is, or at the spot on the court where you want to hit; you are playing the ball and you cannot possibly play it if you don't look at it.

• **Open your racket face on low volleys.** The lower the

volley, the more your racket face must open if the ball is to clear the net. It must be open as the punch starts and at the finish as well. The bevel of the racket face does not have to change; it starts tilted and ends tilted. If your volley shoots high up, you have opened the racket face far too much. A little practice will show you just how much to tilt it to make the ball rise above net level.

• **Hit with a downward motion on high volleys.** When the ball is at shoulder height, you can hit with a downward punch for more power. However, if you close the racket face too much, your volley will go short. The aim of most volleys is depth (to hit as close to the baseline as possible). The arm motion is down: the wrist starts at slightly above head-level on a high volley and ends at shoulder-level or, frequently, at waist-level. The racket face is flat on a high volley, slightly tilted on a waist-high volley and tilted at a big angle on low volleys.

• **Learn to leap.** Beginners will only hit volleys that come directly at them, intermediates will move several steps to the right or the left, advanced players will cross over quickly to cut off a high ball and tournament players will leap, often with both feet off the ground, to prevent a ball from passing them. The first leap is the hardest. When it looks as though a ball is going by you, leap with your racket stretched out. The pleasure you will get in cutting off a passing shot is one of the greatest thrills of competition. It's the start of your being an effective net player.

• **Don't try a trick volley until you have mastered the punch and the block volley.** The basic volleys are the punch and the block. When you can hit deep, place well and control your shots on high, medium and low balls, you are ready to try drive volleys and drop volleys—but not until then. The drive volley is hit like a groundstroke and your timing must be good because the swing is so long. It is most commonly used from mid-court against a high ball. Often a player standing on the baseline will see that his opponent has hit a high, deep shot. Instead of waiting for it to bounce, the player moves in and may drive volley the ball at shoulder height. Drop volleys are the last to be learned. Just as the racket makes contact, the wrist turns delicately and the racket face opens and slides under and across the ball, with the follow-through moving into the body instead of moving forward. It is the least essential shot in the game, so don't worry about it until you reach high tournament level.

• **Position yourself on court in relation to your volleying ability.** A beginner will volley almost exclusively in doubles since he has not yet learned the approach shots to come to net. He should stand much closer to his alley than to the center service line. If he is quick, he should stand five feet from the net to give himself every opportunity of putting the ball away. If he or she has slow reflexes, the position is halfway between the net and the service line *or wherever the player will be able to move forward without fear*. A beginner should never volley with his weight going backwards (fear of being hit causes him to move his rear end backwards with the hit), so it is better for him to play a little closer to the service line while timidity remains. Intermediates can stand halfway between the alley and the center service line in doubles and halfway between the net and the center service line. Tournament players who know what they are doing can move a step toward the center service line to put the pressure on the receiver since a good volleyer can usually leap to cover his alley. In *singles*, beginners should only come to net when forced to do so by a short shot. Intermediates and advanced players will come in more often depending on the depth and pace of their approach shots. Always, in singles, the player will take his position to the right of the center line when he has hit to the backhand corner and to the left of the center line when he has hit to the forehand corner.   ●

Rosie Casals steps forward to punch a low forehand volley. The racket head and palm of her hand are in the same plane, with the wrist broken back sufficiently to place the volley down-the-line.

Ilie Nastase is executing a carefully placed forehand volley, choosing to get down to the ball and block it even though he could opt for a harder shot.

The Imaginative Player

EDWARD and Bob are tournament players with pretty much the same tennis history. Edward has the more forcing strokes but Bob is the better player; Edward loses to John, Steve and Bill while Bob beats John, Steve and Bill. In their formative years everyone picked Edward to be the better player because his forehand was deadlier, his backhand was every bit as good, he volleyed with more sting and his first serve was much stronger and better formed than Bob's. Bob had one thing going for him: imagination.

Edward has one style of play; Bob

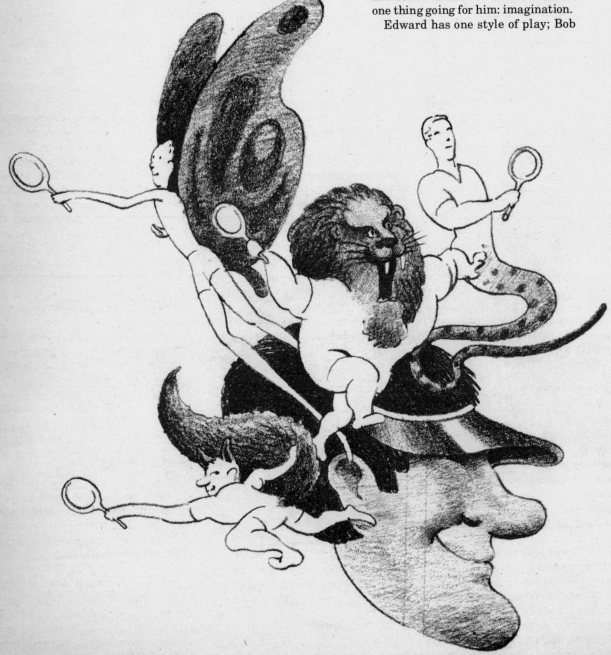

has a dozen. Edward plays the same on grass, cement and clay; Bob changes his game with the surface and the opponent. Edward has a "thing" about the wind; Bob eats it up. Edward has a big, fairly consistent first serve and a good spin second serve; Bob's serve has less pace but far more variety. A good player gets grooved against Edward's big, attacking game; the same good player has a harder time getting grooved to Bob's shots since they are designed to ungroove the opponent.

Here's what Bob does:

He quickly finds out if the opponent can handle a wide, spin serve to the forehand in the forehand court or a serve into the body. He serves deep to the backhand as his "safety" and, although he doesn't have a really tough, flat serve, he throws in one occasionally to keep the receiver off balance. By varying his toss he gets more and different spins; he tosses to his right for a heavy spin to the forehand, in front of him for a deep, topspin serve to the backhand and over his head for a "kick" or American twist to the backhand. He never serves doubles because his philosophy is never to "give" points. Although his second serve is not superb, it is never short. He thinks before he serves as to the amount of spin and the spot where he will place it. In the backhand court he regularly pulls his opponent wide on the backhand, then tosses in a deep one on the center service line; he has traded in power for accuracy and spin control, and his deceptively easy serve is continually disturbing the receiver's rhythm.

Bob has no one way of receiving serve. He stands two feet behind the baseline, on the baseline or two feet inside depending on the surface, whether or not his opponent is attacking, the speed and /or spin of the serve and the depth and/or accuracy of the second serve. If the court is slow, the serve is not coming in, and the delivery is hard but not wide, he will stand two or three feet behind the baseline and "throw" back big serves all day long. He stands on the baseline and takes a much shorter stroke to return a fast serve when the opponent is coming in. Here his return is often a

"block" (a drive with a very short backswing): it comes back fast and hard at the server who must volley it at or behind the service line. On heavy spin serves he will try to stand *inside* the baseline to cut off the angle. On short second serves he runs around his backhand and goes for a forceful forehand to a corner. If the short second serve is accurately placed wide of his backhand, he *drives* (not slices) his backhand well in front of him, more often than not down-the-line deep to the forehand corner, but occasionally crosscourt so his opponent can never outguess him. He is murderous only on short serves since he is never one to let an opportunity go by. He does not "murder" deep serves; he drives them, blocks them, dinks them, chips them and lobs them, in the process of which he discovers what his opponent likes least.

Bob has the basic topspin drives on forehand and backhand. Additionally he can sidespin his forehand and slice (or underspin) his backhand. He uses the chip with moderation, mostly so he can throw in an unexpected drop shot using the same chip action. He lobs defensively (deep to the middle) when he is way out of position and he lobs offensively with excellent disguise as his "third" passing shot.* The sidespin forehand is not his basic weapon but a bit of change-of-pace artistry. He uses the slice backhand on many low shots, as an approach shot and for variety in backcourt exchanges. His lobs do not have the tremendous topspin that he wishes he had but he does hide them well and often catches the net man cold. On slow clay he will hit balls that clear the net by 15 feet since this gives him excellent depth.

Bob is not as athletic as Edward and doesn't leap as well at net, but he comes to net often and always imaginatively. He makes up for a certain lack of athletic talent by his knowledge of the court and his opponent: if the opponent scarcely ever lobs, he closes in more; if the opponent keeps trying the down-the-line, Bob "antici-

---

*The three passing shots are: down-the-line, crosscourt and over the head.

pates"; if the opponent can only slice his backhand, Bob keeps boring in on deep forehands down-the-line. Bob doesn't hit his overhead very hard but he compensates by deadly accuracy, which is better than speed. As a Junior he practiced hitting a dozen overheads a day for two years and the practice has paid off.

The theory behind Bob's play is the Four Tennis Commandments: *Know Thyself, Know Thy Surface, Know Thy Court* and *Know Thy Opponent.* By knowing himself he never tries a shot he can't make, viz., a desperation winner off a wide shot when a lob will be the safer return. As a result he is no Rod Laver but neither is he Joe Schlunck. Bob knows his surface, playing steadily on clay, using his spin repertoire on Sportface, attacking on grass, wrong-footing his opponent on a slippery court, lobbing under the lights or into the sun, and playing the altitude, the wind and even the heat for all he can. Bob also knows his court dimensions much better than his opponent does—the necessity for depth on serve, for angles on passing shots, for serves down the center to cut down the opponent's angles, for approach shots down-the-line to limit the degree of the angle, for pulling the opponent wide to open up his court, for lobbing deep down the center to close up his own court, for dinks to make the net man volley up and deep drives to make the baseliner return short. Most important, Bob knows his opponent and feeds him everything he dislikes—junk balls, bloopers, chips, a barrage of wide shots to the backhand, serves in the body, deep shots to bring him in and lobs to chase him back.

Regretfully, Bob is not the best player in the world because he lacks one really powerful shot to force the big hitters. But he is much, much better than players with much, much more ability. He also has a lot more fun.

You can, too, if you use your imaginative powers. God gave you legs to run on, an arm to hit with and a head for thinking. You've been using your legs and arms; start using your head. Otherwise it may atrophy. ●

How I Won the Singapore Open

by BOB GOLTON

"WHY GO to Singapore?"

"Well, to win the Singapore Open!"

When I'd say that my friends at Golden Gate Park courts would look at me quizzically, then drop the subject. I was playing the Northern California "B" circuit—more than a dozen weekend tournaments that stretch over the summer—and at the time my chances were as good as anyone's. Dropping out would leave me with insufficient data for next year's rankings.

So why pass up a summer of good tennis for the unknown? I wasn't even sure there was a Singapore Open. When the federal government notified me that I could go there on a short grant, I had read through the last two years of foreign tournament results only to find one Singapore tournament mentioned. Was it open? Had it already been played? And none of the travel brochures even mentioned tennis. Although discouraged, I was still determined to play tennis in Singapore.

The trip, sponsored by the U.S. Office of Education, was for 20 teachers who teach a large number of Chinese-American students. I qualified because I teach math at Galileo High in San Francisco. The government paid the roundtrip and gave us each $650 for expenses from June 25 to August 25.

The 27-hour flight was gruelling and the two-day stay in Hong Kong en route wasn't much fun, except later I was glad to have a comparison. Hong Kong was dirty, hectic and not very friendly on the face of it. Singapore was the opposite.

My first day in Singapore was a Saturday. I grabbed my rackets at noon and took a bus from the hotel to Farrer Park nearby. Across a spacious soccer field was a super tennis complex with 20 courts. Most were clay and a half-dozen were red and green hard courts, like the ones I left at Golden Gate Park. Beautiful. But positively deserted. Even the backboards were locked up. The caretaker mumbled something like, sure, people played the game, but not all the time. And, yes, players would be there the next morning.

So was I. The courts were nearly full. I only had an hour, but I wasn't there five minutes before Jimmy Tan walked

up and invited me to play. Jimmy is a slender 5-5 and about 50. He introduced me to half a dozen people by name, followed by their company affiliation. We played some doubles, complete with ballboys.

I later found out Jimmy Tan rented all the courts every Saturday and Sunday morning for his business friends and paid the ballboys $2 Singapore an hour. (U.S. $1 equals S$2.30.) I had walked in, a perfect stranger, and was at once treated with gracious hospitality. For my entire two months that pattern was the rule, not the exception. Even now I am amazed at the opportunities that are automatically extended because someone is simply a tennis player. That was more important than my being a teacher in a place where education is king.

I played with the group a few more times over the next two weeks. The reason there was tennis activity on Sunday morning and not Saturday, for example, is because the common work week in Singapore is 44 hours. That means nine to one on Saturday. And nobody plays between 11 and two because it's too hot. The average temperature is 80 degrees and the humidity is fierce—annual rainfall: 99

inches. You never try to play a match without a spare dry shirt.

The city of 2.2 million is 75 per cent Chinese and 13 per cent Malay, the Malaysian peninsula being north three-quarters of a mile across the Strait of Johore while to Singapore's south is Indonesia. Some eight percent are Indian and the rest European, a catch-all distinction that caught me. Inscriptions on public monuments appear in no less than four languages.

Tennis is certainly not for everyone there. It's too expensive. There is no free public instruction or play. (But there is in school, and as a student goes up the academic ladder all his school expenses are paid by the government.) Court rentals are S$1.50 an hour, lessons from S$10 to S$16. Although Fred Perry apparel is half as expensive as in the U.S. and a cheaper local "Alligator" brand keeps Lacoste off the shelves, rackets cost the same and balls slightly more.

After some weeks I found that a Singapore Open did exist. Singapore has six tournaments a year and half are open to outsiders. The National Hardcourts Open was soon to be played, but entries had closed far in advance, in fact, the day I had arrived. I was told I could get in if someone didn't show. As my luck would have it, the day before the tournament, Singapore's national team left to play Cambodia—there. Five seeds dropped out. I asked a local teaching pro who used to compete how he thought I'd fare. He said, "the quarters."

Now, there are a couple of small things that distinguish Singapore tennis from other brands. There's hardly a warmup. Players usually hit a ball or two and say they're ready. Also, they don't take any practice serves. Since the serve is my mainstay, I never could get used to using the first few games as a driving range. In tournaments you aren't assigned a playing time or a court, but rather a number. You become, say, the fifteenth match of the day which means you've got to hang around waiting. It's inconvenient but that way I got to meet about everyone there.

I had a bye in the round of 64, then played a 17-year-old whose father had built him a lighted court and sends him to play in Australia during December and January when school is out. We later became friends and I played at his home several times. When I told him I might write an account of my sojourn, he was anxious that his name not be used. Kidnapping used to be big business in Singapore and people still fear it. His home had a towering electric fence around it and a night watchman.

The kid hit nice, though erratic, strokes. I thought I might have my hands full. He won the first game and I the next 12. In the afternoon I beat an Indian love and one and people started touting me as the best bet. I think it was that match when I glanced up at the searing sun and silently proclaimed the courts hadn't been built on a north-south plane. Then I realized I was only 80 miles from the equator.

The next day I had an easy time, too. I lost six games getting into the finals. The city's two newspapers had reporters there to interview me.

The day of the finals it rained torrents, certainly enough to wipe out any tournament I've ever played in. Yet, the courts were dry in an hour. That's how hot it was and I had to play singles and doubles semis in the morning. In the afternoon, Hassan, a teaching pro, and his pupil, Rai, acquaintances I had met some days before, showed up with a camera to form my personal cheering section among some 80 spectators seated on rented chairs. I was so happy I didn't even mind that he coached me during the match.

Incidentally, there's a very strong link between tennis teacher and pupil. I can only guess that it has root in the master-novice relationship of the martial arts which are very big in Singapore. Rai says Hassan tells him what to eat, how late to stay up before a tournament and "how to conduct yourself with a woman."

I didn't need advice in the finals. I needed endurance. To my shock the match was to be three out of five. My opponent was Carl Knudson, a lanky South African who is reported to have once played Wimbledon.

It was a close match, but I was up for it. I served well enough in the first set to close it out with a tiebreaker. The next two sets were close, too, but I had the edge and won them 6-4, 6-3. I walked off the court and immediately got leg cramps. I wasn't too lively in losing the doubles afterwards, ending an 11-set day.

Because I had achieved such an emotional high, I never played a match in Singapore thereafter where I really cared if I won or lost, which was just as well. I was invited

every place in the city to play and kept meeting more and more people, many of whom I would see casually on the streets, too. A social life blossomed. I played at two of the best private clubs and on grass for the first time. I was invited to work out with the national team when it returned from Cambodia, and I did so from time to time.

All the team members are wealthy by Singapore standards, except the best player, Sharin Osman, the only Malay on the team. Sharin is Singapore's tennis success story. He started as a ballboy, watched closely and worked hard to develop orthodox strokes. Still, it's a bleak future, for there's no money in tennis, just subsidy. And once you become an instructor you cannot compete.

Perhaps this reality and the emphasis on education explain why there aren't any young players coming up. With one exception, all the best are in their 30s, like Margaret Loh, a vivacious mother of three and the number four ranking woman player. She's also a doctor and married to a MD who teaches at the university. Margaret only comes out of "retirement" to play tennis regularly when it is the season for national team competition. Like all players, she gets a leave of absence from her job.

I noticed at once that the tournament played all the men's matches first then put the women on in the hottest part of the day. I asked Margaret about women's lib, since the arrangement was patently unfair. She rationalized that men played better and had a bigger draw, so it was only natural. Women having a secondary role seemed the "comfortable" way in Singapore, she said.

The only youngster who showed great promise was Lim Phi Lan, a 19-year-old girl with quite a good game who is close to tops among women. As for the boys, they seem to lack desire and mental discipline. They spend so much time studying they only play three times a week. You watch them practice and guess by their stroke quality they will win, and then they just get killed. They can't seem to hit overheads and they refuse to lob.

Tennis clubs are very inexpensive by U.S. standards and have open membership, excellent courts and first-rate facilities. An initiation fee runs about S$250 and monthly dues S$15 or so.

In the older section of town, near the water, is the Singapore Cricket Club. Before I knew about it, I was walking across a vast, adjacent lawn one night, idly noting a profusion of neckers sprawled thereon. I glanced down for some reason only to find, lo, I was net-rushing! I had just crossed a service line and was on my first grass court.

Nearby is the famous Raffles Hotel, named after Sir Stamford Raffles who brought the island under British control in 1824 because of its potential as a port. Now Singapore is independent and ranks as the world's fourth largest port. The Raffles is also where Kipling and Maugham wrote many stories and it has been visited by such luminaries as Elizabeth Taylor and Haile Selassie, on separate occasions.

In the Raffles' magnificent courtyard with palm trees surrounding a pleasant lawn, you might have drinks, a complete quail dinner and cherries jubilee. The price for two with tip will be about $14 American.

On the flight back I reflected on the fact I had hardly seen any of the places tourists are supposed to see. Nevertheless, I had come to win the Singapore Open, did it, and all the while an incredible piece of the world unfolded for me. ●

"I'M READY"

Nick Bollettieri Explains the Difference Between Stroking and Playing

by MARCIA AMES KEY

I STOOD at the baseline, motionless as death. Tears fell softly down my cheeks. I cast my eyes about in all directions, disbelieving. In two quick sets I had been wiped off the court by a female systems engineer whose backhand drive had the impact of a peanut butter sandwich.

How could it have happened? I had rallied for months. My forehand cleared the net with crushing regularity. My volley had a message. I lobbed crosscourt and the ball dropped in. A week at the Hopman-Bollettieri Tennis Camp the summer before had given me a basic arsenal of strokes. I had learned to "coil, uncoil and freeze!" on my goundstrokes; to "scratch, catch and hit!" on the overhead; to spring, punch and flick. Outdoors under the burning sun, on clay, I had learned to "step into the ball"; indoors, on carpet, I had learned to "move it!" I was ready.

But something had gone awry. In a ghostly flashback, I saw it all happening again. I moved in close to the net. The computer expert angled the ball past me for a winner. I stayed back on the baseline. She dropped it over the net. For my every action she had a reaction—a better one. In desperation I sent up a magnificent lob that landed two inches from the baseline, traveling toward heaven. She plucked it out of the sky as carefully as though it were a butterfly, then sent it crashing back into the clay at my feet. In what seemed like seconds it was all over. I felt as if I had been data processed.

Right there on the baseline, with a sickening sensation in my stomach, I made a momentous discovery. I wasn't out there in the hot sun in order to experience the exhilaration of executing beautiful shots or to look at the scenery or to lose a few pounds. I was out there for one purpose—to win. Strokes were the means but winning was the end, and there was evidently some vast, mysterious distance between polished strokes and winning tennis. It was essential to know how to hit the ball, but with every stroke it was the why, when and where you hit it that made the difference. Forehands, backhands, lobs, volleys and overheads were merely isolated phenomena until you learned to "put them all together" as part of a pattern. Every shot had to be hit for a definite purpose—not only in the right way, but at the right moment and to the right spot—where she wasn't.

At four o'clock in the afternoon, on a clay court in Queens, the awful truth stared me in the face. I had strokes but no strategy. I wanted to win and I didn't know how.

That established, back I went to tennis camp and the reassuring calm of the neat, green courts; the hundreds of white-clad fanatics moving tirelessly in pursuit of the perfect stroke. I was still unstrung by my devastating defeat, and on a rainy evening halfway through the week, I cornered Nick Bollettieri on the indoor courts in Amherst.

"Nick," I said, "these drills we do at

"In two quick sets I had been wiped off the court by a female systems engineer."

tennis camp are fabulous conditioners, and all the practice on our strokes is simply great. But I seem to be the one person who doesn't know how to put them all together." I gazed down, sheepishly, at my new sneakers, almost afraid to admit the truth. "I don't know how to play a game."

Nick eyed me warily and I hurried on. "Oh, I know that there isn't any formula and that tennis isn't cut and dried, but aren't there general tactics that might help an intermediate player, any rules of thumb?"

"I thought you'd never ask," he said. "Maybe I can give you a little help."

On the court, two instructors were exchanging a series of deep, resounding forehands and backhands. The rhythm was as comforting as background music. We sat down and I pulled out my notebook.

"Let's call this Intermediate Women's Singles, just to pin it down," Nick said. "But first, let me tell you that playing is your best teacher. Get out and play every chance you get. You're ready."

"I did last week—a systems engineer," I answered through clenched teeth. "It was a disaster. She was everywhere. I got my racket back early, met the ball in front of me, stepped into it, hit through the ball and finished in perfect position..."

"And your opponent?"

She hit late on every shot. Her form was terrible. She had this look of crazed determination on her face and her racket was flailing somewhere around her thigh. She won both sets."

He laughed. "Go on."

"From what I can remember, my first serve was good and deep, to her forehand."

"And?"

"She returned it with a short crosscourt that hit the net and dropped—on my side."

"Let's stop right there," said Nick. "Your serve should be to her backhand."

"Always?"

"Nothing is always. I'd say usually.

Your second serve must be to her backhand, and you should learn to put some spin on it. Try to keep all your serves deep; otherwise you lose all advantage in serving. Serve to her forehand only when you think she doesn't expect it."

"Her first serve to me in the forehand court went right past me down the center line. It wasn't all that fast, but..."

"It had the element of surprise?"

"Uh-huh."

"Where were you standing to receive?" he asked.

"Right where the baseline meets the sideline."

"You should have expected her serve to come to your backhand. If you are standing over that far, you can't get to it all that easily. Stand in a foot or two from the sideline. And be on the balls of your feet, ready..."

"I know—ready to 'move it'."

"Right. On her first serve, unless it is weak, your main object should be to keep the ball in play. Get it back; that's primary. Later on, when you find you can do a little more, try to hit to one of the corners—deep. Move in a foot or two on her second serve. She will then have to be more careful, and your moving in may worry her enough to serve short or pop up or even double-fault. If she puts more spin on her second serve, you are in a better

position, anyway, before the ball spins away from you."

I was making notes, rapidly, all over the page. "Serve to backhand—usually"..."Move in on second serve"..."Be ready"..."Return serve deep to corner"...

"How would you describe your opponent's game?" Nick asked.

"Deadly."

"I mean what were her weaknesses?"

I thought about that for the first time. "Her backhand, I guess. Also, she stayed around the baseline a lot. As a matter of fact, I don't think she ever did come to the net."

"Then hit most of your shots to her backhand," Nick said. "She will either have to hit relatively weak backhands or run a long way around in order to hit relatively strong forehands."

"Why didn't I think of that when I was playing?"

"Do you know how to break up a baseliner's game?"

"Get her off that baseline, somehow. Bring her to the net."

"Sure. It's where she doesn't want to be. Where were you hitting your shots when she was on the baseline?"

"Back—when I was lucky."

"If you were hitting them down the center, you were putting them right on her racket," Nick said. "Never let a baseliner stand in the center of the court for long; it is exactly where she wants to be. Every ball you hit should make her move. So try to hit away from the center on every shot, but give yourself a margin for error. Don't hit for the sidelines until you have confidence in going for the lines. In this particular case, you should keep moving her wide on her backhand until she either makes a short return or is pulled over so far that you can hit wide to her forehand. Then she will have to run like the devil to get to that forehand, and she will never make the same forcing shot that she can hit on the forehand when she doesn't have to move."

"I guess I was making it rather easy for her."

On the far court two tow-headed youngsters about ten years old were warming up. I wasn't sure they needed it.

"Use your warm-up period," said Nick, "to spot your opponent's strengths and weaknesses. Did you? Hit her a variety of shots. For example, try a few high shots to her backhand. That's usually a tough shot for an intermediate. Hit some short ones, too. See how she comes in. Then, when you see that she likes to stay on the baseline, mix in a few shallow shots to keep her moving up and back. Your warm-up should tip you off to her weaknesses and give you some idea about the kind of game she likes to play best. Of course some players blast every shot in the warm-up, then soften up 50 to 80% when they play. The warm-up doesn't always tell everything, but it can give you clues. The first two games will give you a better idea of how she likes to play."

"Then what do I do?"

"Don't let her play that game unless it helps you play your best game. For example, if your best shot is your forehand crosscourt and you play your forehand down-the-line badly, you have to play the crosscourt often, even if it is to your opponent's strength."

"I guess volleying is the best part of my game," I said, "but I don't have a strong serve and I don't know how to get up to net. It's tough when you have to keep volleying from the baseline!"

He laughed. "Don't think about trying to come in after your serve yet," he said. "And never try to come in on a ball hit deep to you. But keep your eyes open for a ball that lands halfway between the service line and the baseline. Hit it deep to the corner, then come in as quickly as possible. That's the time to attack, if you think you can. Try to take your first volley somewhere near the service line."

"I did that a couple of times but I was coming in so fast that I hit it on the run and knocked it through the fence."

"Stop before you hit. Try to hit down the line, if you can manage it; after you hit, move in closer to net. Then you should be in a position to put the return away."

"At an angle."

"Right."

"What if she lobs over my head? Even after all our practice on overheads, I find it difficult to move back fast enough."

"You must be ready for the lob when you come to net," said Nick. "Side-step back and hit your overhead, if you can, or just get back there somehow and keep the ball in play. After you hit your overhead, move back to net and favor the side you have hit the ball to."

By doing so, you will probably force your opponent into making a weaker return and you will also be in position to volley for a winner. How many of us hit an overhead and think it's all over? We stand there, frozen in self-admiration, and watch the ball limp back over the net for the point."

I knew the feeling.

"Let's see what you could do if things were reversed. If your opponent were rushing the net…"

"Well, I could try to hit it past her. That's what she kept doing to me."

"Pass her," he corrected. "Or, if she came in slowly and found herself in the middle of the court (No Man's Land) you could hit the ball at her feet.

"I could look down the road of the future and see hundreds and hundreds of defeats stacked end to end."

But if she rushed in fast, like a fullback charging the line, lob over her head. It's terribly difficult for anyone to change directions."

"This is wonderful, Nick. When I played last week, I had no tactics, no plan at all. Now at least you have given me a few ideas about what I ought to be trying to do. When I was out there on the court, all I could think about was keeping the ball in play."

"That's not bad for a start," he said. "Concentrate first on getting the ball back; on steadiness. Let her make some of the errors. Later on add depth, placement and, eventually, power."

I closed my notebook. "There's so much to it. I'll never be able to remember it all."

"You don't have to," Nick said. "Now, if I were you, I'd throw away all those notes and go out and play. There's an exception to everything I told you. Get out and play every chance you get. You're ready! There are all kinds of things to learn about when and where to hit and not to hit certain strokes, but the place you will learn them is on the court. You can go on improving your strokes forever. We all have to. Look at us at tennis camp. But after you have played for a while, you will begin to get some idea about your own weaknesses; then you should try to take a few lessons on those particular aspects of your game."

I was picking up my racket and sweater to leave when Nick caught me by the arm. "Here's the most important thing. It isn't enough to be ready with strokes and strategy. If you really want to play tennis you have to be ready to be beaten, hundreds of times if necessary, in order to learn."

I stared. "You mean I have to go through the crucible of defeat?"

"I guess you could call it that."

"And every time I do…"

"You will learn something from it; something that will help you the next time."

I thought back to that ignominious lacing I had taken on the court a week ago, and all of a sudden it didn't seem so bad anymore. It was almost laughable. I could look down the road of the future and see hundreds and hundreds of defeats, stacked end to end. There were so many things to look foward to—upsets by red-cheeked schoolgirls and field hockey instructors; trouncings by public relations secretaries and dieticians; routs by senators' wives, boning up for Pro-Celebrity tournaments—each one giving me new knowledge and ammunition for an even more important defeat. And someday, who knew, perhaps a good, clean whipping by a bona fide tennis player.

We stepped out of the bubble. The rain had stopped. Tomorrow would be a good day.

"Thanks, Nick," I said. "I'm going to work on my strokes all this week. But on the week-end, when I go home, I'm going back to that court in Queens…"

He laughed. "Good luck!"

I walked away into the starry night, repeating carefully to myself, "Strokes and strategy aren't enough. You have to have the willingness to be defeated, over and over again, in order to learn…"

But about 20 feet from the bubble I stopped in my tracks. Defeated? Again? Never! I had already thrown down the gauntlet: "Systems engineers of the world, look out! I'm ready!"

●

POACHING

by JULIUS HELDMAN

POACHING, a doubles maneuver, is the invasion of your partner's side of the court when you are at net to cut off a ball. The object of the poach is to end the point at once with a put-away volley since if the poacher does not put away the ball, he and his partner find themselves on the same side of the court and can easily be passed. But poaching has another objective—to put pressure on the opponents and to force them to hit at a sharp angle to avoid the leaping poacher's racket.

If you, the netman, are rooted in one spot and never poach, you give the receiver an edge by allowing him a larger area for his return without fear of having the return cut off. If you poach consistently, the receiver is going to make a lot of points down your alley. So you must poach— occasionally and, I think, inconsistently. Within this broad framework there are many factors.

The first is your own bent. Are you aggressive? Fast? Nimble? Big? Then you should poach relatively frequently.

Are you slow? Tentative? Do you have a weak volley? Then you should poach only on occasion but you may get some good surprise value and, hence, some unexpected points.

Most players poach better on their forehand side—for one thing, their reach is better—and so if you are right-handed you should poach more when your partner is serving in the deuce court. But this is not universally true. One player I know poaches much more, and better, on the back-hand side. He has more confidence there and starts a step faster. So confidence is an extremely important factor.

If your partner's serve is weak, it is difficult even to stand at net, much less attempt to poach. The opponents will be hitting returns that are hard, low and accurate, which means poaching is extremely difficult unless you have "quick hands." Still, you must try it sometime, although

seldom. If it is good, you will be able to leap about more and intercept more returns.

In more advanced play, you and your partner should mutually agree on general tactics in serving to each of your opponents. Barring obvious weaknesses, serves should be to the backhand because most backhand returns tend to be underspun more, they are slower than forehands and they have less disguise. This gives you more of a chance to poach successfully. When your partner knows you are going to poach, he is ready to cover the unexpected lob over your head.

You don't have to be a great poacher to "fake" and "double-fake." A step or a hop just as the opponent is about to hit may tempt him to return down your alley, opponents are aware that you may fake a movement, a double-fake can be a successful poach and will keep the opposition always uncertain about your movements.

Here are some basic rules on poaching:

• When you go for a poach, go for the winner.

• Poaching must always be aggressive and never defensive.

• The easiest poach, obviously, is off a high ball and the most difficult, obviously, is off a hard, wide one.

• Even if you poach badly, poach occasionally so that the opponents are forced to try more difficult shots.

• When your partner poaches, be ready to cover a lob over his head.

• Keep track of the number of successful poaches you make, counting as "successful" a poach movement that forces the opponent into error. If you are not making more than 50 per cent successfully, cut your poaching down to the minimum.

• You can poach not only when your partner is serving but when your partner is returning. ●

Tom Gorman- A Wee Bit O'Irish

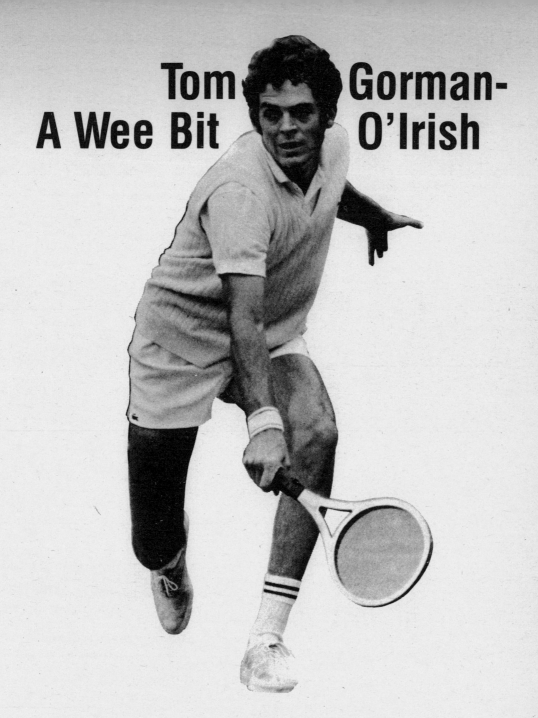

by REX BELLAMY

WHEN AN American takes a bite of Danish and washes it down with a sip of Irish, the flavor has to be interesting. That is the pedigree of Thomas Warner Gorman, a tennis player who has popped into the world's Top 10 like a cork coming out of a bottle. Warner is his mother's family name. But Tom's Danish grandmother was a Larsen and his father's Irish grandfather was an O'Shaughnessy. To spice this exotic dish, Tom has sisters called Shaughn (no prizes for guessing where that label came from) and Celia—which is also the name of a character in Shakespeare's "As You Like It."

We seem to be moving in that strange half-world between fact and fantasy (appropriately, because that is a feeling we often get when Tom Gorman's droll wit is in full flow, but only his eyes are smiling). Let us explore the area further

by insisting that the man has to be related to Arthur O'Shaughnessy, a poet responsible for those famous lines "We are the music makers, and we are the dreamers of dreams" (which seems to sum up the way Tom Gorman blithely dances through life). That same O'Shaughnessy, by the way, produced books of poetry including "An Epic of Women" and "Lays of France." That can't mean what I think it means. But it does sound as though Arthur lived a little (he died at 37).

One fact to hang on to is that Tom Gorman's Irish connection is three generations back. No matter. The blood sometimes takes that long to regain its strength—and a drop of Irish is still authentic, even when watered down. Gorman is as Irish as you can get without being Irish. He looks the part: and his articulately extrovert character, exuding

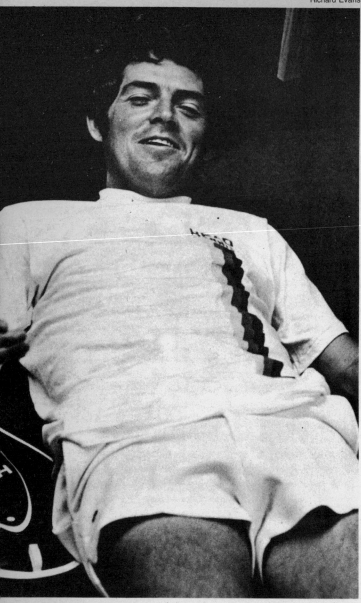

Gorman, known for his wit and easy approach to life, once turned to the fans at London's Royal Albert Hall after a furious rally, and coolly asked "Did the Beatles really play here?"

laughter and goodwill, has all the best qualities of the breed.

His gear proudly flaunts a shamrock (as a result of a long personal association with a Seattle-based clothing company, he endorses a line known as the "Tom Gorman Tennis Trail"). Even his tennis is Irish—bold, quick-witted, imaginative, bubbling with ideas and backed by the courage to try anything. Mark Cox (they have something in common in that both took up full-time tennis at 23 after graduating in economics) has been on the other side of the net often enough to appreciate Gorman's game: "His tennis is rather like his personality. All the time he's coming up with tricks—like half-volleying a ball behind him and charging to the net. He's good for the game because he always looks as though he's enjoying it, even if he isn't. And he must be one of the most amicable fellows on the tour."

A dashing d'Artagnan of the courts, intelligent, witty and amiable, Tom is also a handsome and immensely personable bachelor. He may be new to the Top 10. But not in the pop charts. When he plays in London, fans are always asking questions about him. At the Albert Hall last November, one teenager burst into tears when I told her Gorman had flown home that afternoon. The trouble with great sportsmen like Tom Gorman is that they can be taken for granted. When he played Nastase once at Wembley, the Romanian behaved perfectly and observers were quick to make the point that he was a nice guy at heart. True. But my wife put forward the equally valid view that players like Gorman, who behave well *all* the time, are seldom given as much credit as petulant players who happen to be in a good mood. Gorman used to fret about the impression he gave—the attitude that he just went out on court to have a good time. "When I was 17, 18, 19, I would come off court and people would make comments like 'It didn't seem as if you were really trying.' But I was trying as hard as I could. It's just that I wasn't a racket-thrower or a yeller. But for a time it worried me. So I tried to get very stern out there. Even drop a racket. But it was so out of character. I didn't feel right about it. I don't have the temperament for outbursts. It isn't natural."

Anger is often no more than a weakling's reaction to the adversity that puts every man's character to the test. Gorman's parents set him on the right road, in this respect as in others. They were interested in sport for the children, he says, "basically as a background of learning fair play and things like that. They never really stressed the win factor. Just to do things as well as we could. As many things as possible. They were not overly pushing. They gave us freedom of choice and said 'Do it as best you can.'

"I was born and raised at Seattle. I've spent all my years there, except for a couple of years when I was three and four (my parents have never told me where we were then...). I played some tennis while I was growing up, and was runner-up in the 15-and-under city championship." But his early competitive experience was with his twin sisters, four years older. "They were enough incentive while I was nine, 10, 11. They were beating me all the time. The rivalry kept me going.

"But I was more interested in baseball when I was younger. My dream was to be playing in the World Series for the New York Yankees, who were world champions at the time. Basketball was my second favorite sport. But all of a sudden I stopped growing. In two short years I went from giant to midget. I also played a lot of soccer. The

Catholic school system didn't play American football. They played English soccer up to 13 or 14. I was left-footed and outside-right (or was it right-footed and outside-left?). I played soccer in the fall, then a lot of basketball in the winter and baseball in the spring."

That notorious back injury dates from Seattle University. "It was just a pick-up game, intra-mural. Everybody was showing off to the new freshmen at college that they were former all-American football players (and of course none of us was). I can't remember whether I fell or tripped over a blade of grass. But it stiffened up and for two months or so I had a lot of problems. I was having cortisone and got temporary relief, but it didn't seem to do much good. But after about four months I recovered and could actually play tennis. That continued for four or five years. Sometimes it was stiff and sore, but never to the point where I had to quit or default. The first really bad recurrence was against Laver." (At Wimbledon in 1971, Gorman beat Laver in straight sets in a quarter-final but did his back so much harm that he could not give Stan Smith much of a match in the next round.) In December of the following year Smith was again on the opposite side of the net, during a semi-final of the Masters tournament in Barcelona, when Gorman quit after reaching match point. His back had gone again, and he knew it would be impossible to give the customers and the sponsors a decent final later the same day. For a sportsman like Gorman, there was only one solution.

Gorman has been ranked for eight successive years: at 31, 24, 12, 14, 6, 4, 2 and 4 again. Born on Jan. 19, 1946, he is 5-11, 165 pounds. He left college in 1968 and for a year, including a trip to Australia, he was backed by the Seattle Tennis Club. The pattern in those days, he reminds us, was for a youngster to play for a year or two after getting through college, and then go back to graduate school and become a stockbroker. The other possibilities were "shamateur" or, for the select few, professional tennis. "But open tennis put another 10 years on your tennis life. I wasn't that well ranked in the juniors. The only reason I got into some tournaments in the men's circuit, when I was 20, was a rule that each USLTA section was allowed at least one player on the circuit."

Gorman's timing was perfect. He graduated in the first year of open tennis. He became a professional and in March, 1969, earned his first prize money—$150 in Mexico City. I happened to see his first tournament in England, at Guildford two months later. This was his first experience on England's inimitable loose-top courts and he was beaten by the 15-year-old Stephen Warboys. But, in the same year, Gorman reached the last 16 of the Wimbledon and United States championships. During the Dewar Cup tournament at London's Albert Hall he asked a question that is now part of the Gorman legend—because it was utterly true to his nature as a man whose detached appreciation of peripheral absurdities can pop up through the most dramatic competitive crises.

That was quite a match, anyway. He was playing Gerald Battrick. They were both charging about the court like demented hares, and kept rebounding from the stop netting. Gorman sometimes seemed to be in three different places at once—and doing exciting things in all of them. The match was long, close, thrilling. After one particularly hot rally Gorman clung to the back netting, stared at the crowd and coolly asked them: "Did the Beatles really play here?"

"I've always been amazed," he told me recently, "that

rock groups play at the Albert Hall. It doesn't seem the place for rock groups. It's not the most obvious place for a tennis tournament either, come to think of it."

It was in the final of that tournament that Gorman (he had a match point before John Alexander beat him) became the first man to achieve an unlikely "double"—losing matches on both sides of the Atlantic without losing a service game on either occasion. But that, of course, was in the early days of the tiebreaker. And the early days of Tom Gorman. If memory is telling the truth, he still had a habit of running round his backhand volley so that he could take it on the forehand. But he no longer has anything to hide.

Tom Okker, who is noted for frivolously terse asides, reckons Gorman has never been the same since he fell on his head. That refers to another 1970 incident, which occurred after Gorman had set out on a double date. "I was mugged by five guys, and had stitches in my head. I was on my way to pick up a date. As I was driving a by familiar and popular tavern close to Seattle University, I saw a friend's car and went in to pick him up. My timing couldn't have been worse. Because as I opened the door these guys were just coming out after robbing the tavern. They dragged me inside, hit me over the head and ripped my wallet out (only because I couldn't unbutton the back pocket—I was pretty nervous...got the elbow...choked like crazy...). But I made it to the game—pro basketball."

The same year, 1970, produced the first Tom Gorman and Erik Van Dillen show, a mixture of crosstalk and slapstick that has since enlivened the eve of every Davis Cup challenge round or final. The United States was about to play Germany at Cleveland. "Erik and I were the rookies on the team. We'd believe anything those guys told us. We were so impressed by everything. The second day of training these guys (Pasarell, Lutz, Ashe, and Smith) told us it was a policy that the rookies put on a skit. We said 'Sure' and got together. We both enjoyed the Johnny Carson show and that's what we modelled our thing after. The first year we had about 12 people there—just the team and trainer and captain, and Fred Stolle, the German coach." But since then there have been three more shows, creating an increasingly popular tradition.

In 1971, Gorman took a set from Laver in the Italian championships, then beat him at Queen's Club (London) and Wimbledon. In 1972 he reached the semi-finals at Forest Hills and in the Masters (when he retired at match point) and played singles in the Davis Cup final against Romania in Bucharest. In 1973 he beat Jan Kodes on his way to the French semi-finals, reached the last 16 at Forest Hills, defeated Riessen, Smith, Okker and Borg in successive matches to win the Stockholm Open, played singles in the Davis Cup final against Australia and then beat Nastase in the Masters.

Gorman is no machine. He has often found it difficult to keep himself "up" throughout a tournament. But Davis Cup experience has done a lot for him in terms of mental preparation and concentration, and has undoubtedly helped to lift him into the Top 10. He has been making a conscious effort to use his opponent's game to try to improve his own. He cited his personal role in the last Davis Cup final as an illustration.

"I'm talking about playing a better player. The example is Laver. He went absolutely bananas in the fourth and fifth sets. But the situation and the opponent had raised my game higher than it had been for a while. Okay, we lost. I don't feel that I will ever play two guys in a row who will play that well. I may look back on Laver and Newcombe as the most difficult opponents I have played, knowing that I was also playing at a higher standard. But for me it was a real confidence booster in that I saw a higher level of play in my own game. I look back on the Davis Cup as helping me to accomplish something in striving to become more proficient. A practical example was beating Nastase in the Masters."

World Team Tennis? "I've had very brief talks with the Oakland team. The most beautiful area in the United States—the San Francisco Bay area. But to me, the other factors are much stronger. There's a real need to preserve the European circuit. And WTT might mean that I couldn't play Paris. I've had a lot of good fortune in the French" (doubles final in 1971, doubles semi-finals in 1972 and singles semi-finals in 1973). "Overall, I've had pretty good luck there. I've always made it through to the Friday of the final week, so I had a chance to enjoy it. I like the atmosphere, the feeling the place gives you. I've made money in Paris—and for the players it's one of the most expensive cities. If you're there for two weeks it can run you close to $700, depending what you do and how you live. I've enjoyed it more than others, because I could afford it."

He likes Rome, too. "I can't even afford a *pensione*. But I love it, and I'll go back. It's the only place I don't need to hold my pants up, because the food's so great. I can't hit a ball there, but I like the scenes. 1972...Chanfreau and Di Matteo on a side court, with the police holding back the crowd...They had to bring down a whole row of policemen because the fans started running out on the court to get Chanfreau...But after the match it's fine. And taking a set from Laver in 1971, the first time I'd played him, was almost like winning a match. A boost to the morale."

The political scene? "We'd all like to see a little more harmony, or at least some result from our boycott at Wimbledon. I realize you're working with a lot of different groups, in probably the most international of sports. But for the players to stay together and do what they did at Wimbledon was kind of shocking to everybody. I would like something positive to come out of that. We're working on it—involvement with tournaments, setting up our own circuit. I'd like to see it go faster."

Tom Gorman has certainly been around since he popped out of the Pacific Northwest five years ago. A man's basic talent is a gift of Nature. What he does with it is his own concern. Gorman is no Laver, no Nastase. But he has made the most of what he has. The best of the European tennis magazines, *Tennis de France,* picked him as their first 1974 study in that analytical monthly feature, *guide des champions*. They described him as one of the most spectacular players in the game. They referred to the "extraordinary" reflexes that permit him to play difficult shots in awkward situations; to his eagerness to get to the net and exploit his "exceptional" volleying. They contrasted his alert liveliness with the ruffled hair that suggests he has just got out of bed. And even in the 8th arrondissement of Paris—quite a step from Seattle—they appreciate his personal qualities as one of *"les plus aimables"* champions of the international circuit.   ●

Olga the Volga Volleyer

by BUD COLLINS

IN THE MATTER of Russian heroines, I used to muse fondly on Lara hibernating with Dr. Zhivago...Ninotchka discovering silk stockings in Paris...Natasha tending Bolkonsky's war wounds...Madame Ranievskaya trying to save the old cherry orchard...Nastasia mooning for Prince Myshkin...Rosa Kleb planning some special treat for James Bond...Anna Karenina trying to derail an express train with her body. Lovely characters all, but could any of them zing-along with the Volga Volleyer, Olga Morozova Rubanov?

The last female champion of czarist Russia was the all-time Wimbledon title winner, Elizabeth "Bunny" Ryan in 1914. Bunny won a total of 19 doubles and mixed doubles crowns, then caught the last train out of Russia before the war sealed the borders. Olga Morozova (who goes by her maiden name with the compliments of her fellow rent-payer, husband Viktor Rubanov) is the latest in the line of succession that was interrupted after Bunny Ryan caught her train. Tennis was considered a capitalistic exercise during the years immediately following the revolution, and not until 1959 did Russia venture into the international spirit of the game by sending a party of players to Wimbledon. Three years later Russia came into the Davis Cup.

Olga Morozova is the best of the Russian exports. She is the only Russian ever to receive a World Ranking (she is No. 10), the only one to win a title at Wimbledon (the Junior Singles in 1965) and the only one to reach the quarter-finals of the U.S. Open (she nearly beat Chris Evert there in 1972. She was Wimbledon singles finalist in 1974 and mixed doubles finalist with Alex Metreveli in 1968 and 1970, high points of achievement for Russians in their brief history as tennis carpetbaggers. In 1973, she and the delightful teen-ager, Marina Kroshina of the Kiev Kroshinas, became the first Russians to smuggle a U.S.

Championship out of America when they won the USLTA Indoor Doubles at Hingham, Mass., over Aussies Janet Young and Evonne Goolagong.

"We need more regular play on a pro circuit," said Olga at Hingham. "This is the first time we play indoors outside of Russia. Our courts at home are fast Swedish plastic. This court (a Uni-Turf carpet) is slow."

Until Olga smiles, her face seems a plain, almost stern Slavic countenance. On court, her black hair in no-nonsense pigtails, she is deadly serious, charging the net as though she were a student of an earlier era intent on throwing a bomb at the Czar to liberate Mother Russia. But the smile changes everything. The dimples appear, the teeth are good, the eyes warm and suddenly she is a woman handsome of visage, figure and wit.

Olga and Viktor Rubanov were married a couple of years ago. ("He said if you want my name, okay, but if you want to keep your own, that's okay, too.") While Olga is on tour, electrical engineer Rubanov holds down the apartment in central Moscow, cooking his own meals and watching sports on TV. "What can he cook? Scrambled eggs and coffee. I think he misses my borscht."

Morozova will remain Morozova "for a few more years until I start to have babies. Then I will be Rubanov and settle down." In the interim, please get that pronunciation right, accent on the second syllable: More-OH-zo-vah, not MORO-ZO-vah. (Her partners are called KRO-shina and Ru-BAN-ov.)

At the age of 10 Olga watched some kids on her block in Moscow batting a tennis ball against a wall. She tried it and liked it. Her parents, who are engineers, sent her to a neighborhood club for lessons. At 15 she was made a Master

Rocky Weldon

Olga Morozova is an aggressive all-court player who is at her best on a fast or low-bouncing court where the premium is on serve and volley. She will even take net on return of serve.

of Sport and was tabbed as a future Russian champion, a kid who might be one of the better exports since caviar. "I went to Moscow University in physical education, but there was always enough time off for tournaments. The dean was also a tennis player!" East or West, it doesn't hurt a student to be a jock.

Olga hopes to teach physical education, particularly tennis, when she is through playing, and her degree and Master of Sport rating will assure that she is well paid.

Olga's prize money goes to the Russian Federation. "We are amateurs," she states. Nobody is an amateur, but it is a tiresome argument by now. But I do believe that the cash is the least of her concerns. "The life is so good in tennis," she says. "Because of tennis I learn to speak a little English. I meet the people from everywhere. Our group, we are the United Nations, something like, anyway." She nodded around the lounge at the German Ebbinghaus, the Dutch Schaar, the Colombian Fernandez, the Italian Nasuelli, the English Mappin, the Japanese Sawamatsu, the Czech Neumannova, the American "Irish Mafia" Hogan and Walsh, the Australian Goolagong, the Indonesian Sugiarto.

It is the old sporting story. "We all get along together. It is good to know we can. Tennis brings us together." But Olga winces when you mention Federation Cup. "Yes, I would like to play, but..." The USSR political stand against South Africa keeps the Russians out.

Travel is a leading benefit of tennis, probably dearer to a Russian than the rest of us who can move about more freely. Olga and Marina, unlike the others on the USLTA indoor circuit, were accompanied by a...uh...watchdog is the way an American would describe the companion or companions of Russian celebrities abroad. In this case he was Eugen Korbut, tall, genial vice-president of the Russian Federation. Accompanying Alex Metreveli on tour with WCT's Rosewall Division is another Federation official, jovial Siemon Belitz-Geiman, once a champion of his country in the parochial days when nobody outside was aware of what was going on inside Soviet tennis.

"My trip to Australia was very wonderful," recalls Olga, "because I came back to Moscow black from the sun in mid-winter, and everybody at home is pale. Very nice, dah-link." We're all snobs about tans, aren't we?

"But this American trip is the most exciting because we are going to see more than New York, where I have been before. Here in Boston I know is the home of Phil Esposito, the great hockey player for the Bruins. And the home of your revolution. I love hockey. I saw one of the Canada-Russia games at the stadium in Moscow, the rest on TV. Sometimes I cannot get my husband away from all the games on TV."

While tennis takes you to a lot of splendid places, it mostly, as Evonne Goolagong laments, exposes you "to the court and the hotel. You don't see much else." Thus it was with Morozova and Kroshina, who couldn't get away from Hingham long enough to see the great Esposito or the Revolutionary battlegrounds at Lexington and Concord.

There are also places not so splendid. Given your choice between Siberia and Akron (the second stop on the USLTA tour), you would reasonably choose Siberia. But Olga and Marina were good sports about it, and that stopover did give them a glimpse into the Heartland.

Naturally, everywhere they went the Russians were special curiosities. Even after these many years of Soviet-American games-playing hostilities, Russian athletes aren't all that commonplace to Americans, and Metreveli, Kroshina and Morozova are the first of their kind to be let loose outside of Manhattan and Queens. Olga conceded that she could become as celebrated in the U.S. as at home. "Oh, people know me in Moscow, of course, but it is a huge city. They don't stop me on the street much. There are too many faces. But for Alex Metreveli it is very different in Tblisi.

"Everybody knows him. It is a smaller city. They love him and he can do anything he wants. If he gets a traffic ticket, the policeman says, 'Forget it, dah-link.' But Moscow is not the same, even for him. Once he got a ticket there and he was just like anybody else." Maybe you have to be named Brezhnev to fix a summons in Olga's town.

She is amused by the recent Metrevelian stir in England and the U.S. about his nationality. Alex insisted to reporters that he was not Russian but Georgian, conceding he is a citizen of the USSR. "Oh my dear, he is Russian all right. We are Russian, but I think he likes to have some fun with the press. You are from Massachusetts, but you are an American. You are also a Massachu...uh...whatever you say, but you are an American. He is a Georgian, but Georgia is part of Russia and he is a Russian. Oh well."

Although brought up on slow clay, Olga prefers quicker surfaces. Indeed, her two renowned near-misses of 1972, against Goolagong and Evert, were on grass where her strong serve and aggressiveness are point and bread-winners. What happened at Wimbledon (fourth round) when she served to No. 1 seed Evonne for the match at 5-4 in the third? Or at Forest Hills (quarter-finals) when she came from 2-5 in the third to catch No. 3 seed Chris and serve for the match at 6-5, only to lose nine of the last 10 points? Olga shrugs. "It is a game..." She shakes her head and pats her blue-jeaned thighs. "Things happen in games."

That is why we play them, to see what will happen, to work up a sweat while these things are happening. If they happen badly, you've had your healthful sweat. There's no percentage in brooding.

"I like to win, but what I have done is not bad, dah-link. I like to play Evonne and the 'little machine' (Evert) some more and see what I do."

It will be pleasant to see more of what Morozova can do. When an athlete blends charm with skill, you like to have her hanging around, upgrading the games-playing mob. As the current ruler of All the Russians, Morozova is doing even better than her legendary namesake, Saint Olga, a competitive 10th century chickie who bossed Kiev after her husband, Prince Igor, died.

Prince Igor's comments on his Olga's cooking are not recorded. Whether she whipped up saintly borscht, we'll probably never know. But Viktor Rubanov will put his Olga's borscht up against anybody's. It is, I am assured, a heroic broth made by a heroic broad. But borscht, alas, won't win Wimbledon or Forest Hills. That's done with the backhand, not the back burner, and I don't know that our Russian heroine will ever do it. I can only hope.

Still, can you imagine how they'd react at the Kremlin if Comrade Olga became champion of the world? Why, they'd give her one of the domes of St. Basil's, a lifetime pass to Lenin's Tomb and maybe...maybe...her very own cherry orchard, each tree with a no-cut contract. Madame Ranievskaya should have had it so good. ●

A TENNIS DICTIONARY

by LANCE TINGAY

THE RECENT growth of tennis has brought the need for an authoritative definition of the many technical terms used in the game. Even among long standing devotees there is often misuse of what is in fact a precise language. For instance, let me quote from a description of the 1939 Wimbledon Championships which states "Riggs went on to win his semi-final in straight sets." The misunderstanding is absurd. Whoever heard of Riggs winning a straight set?

Ace. A service delivered before the receiver is ready, or a fault, delivered at so high a speed that the line judge freezes to an astonished silence.

Advantage. A term used in scoring to indicate that the previous point was won by one's opponent with an outrageous fluke.

All England Club. The venue for a British tournament where the Association of Tennis Professionals charges its members an entry fee of $10,000.

Amateur. A term, since 1968, confined to Russian professionals employed by their Ministry of Sport; prior to that year it also meant a professional whose earnings were paid into a secret numbered bank account in Switzerland.

Ambidextrous. This refers to a player who has so consistently run round his backhand that it has disappeared entirely.

American tournament. A method of playing a tournament based on the fallacious assumption that all players are born free and equal.

Backhand. A method of hitting the ball in which, in the case of a right-handed player, the body is poised on the right foot or, in the case of Francoise Durr, on the right knee.

Ball. A spheroid object with a mind of its own.

Bonne Bell Cup. A marksmanship award given to Chris Evert for shooting kangaroos.

Boycott. Captain Boycott, whose name gave origin to this term, was an Irishman. His sister settled in Croatia and married a man called Pilic.

Cannon ball. A dangerous missile fatal to the receiver if he fails to dodge it.

Center Court. A place where tennis players are judged and often found wanting.

Champion. A player with an income exceeding $100,000 a year.

Championship. A tournament with a strong sense of grandeur.

Circuit player. One who has to look in his passport to find out where his home is.

Clay court. In Europe a clay court is a hard court which in the U.S. is a cement court which isn't a clay court and a clay court is different from a hard court (Europe) anyway. This is why England still sticks to grass since everyone knows what that is.

Committee. An official body comprised of club members with a liking for wearing big badges and giving players the runaround.

Covered courts. In America these are indoor courts. In Britain they hardly exist.

Davis Cup. An international men's team competition in which about 50 nations annually compete to decide whether Australia or the United States is the best.

Deuce. A catchword designed to annoy Jimmy Van Alen.

Dink shot. The outcome of a shotgun marriage between a fast drive and a drop shot.

Double fault. A service ace with a negative sign in front of it.

Double-handed. A method of playing the forehand and backhand with the same stroke.

Doubles. A method of playing tennis by which the natural antipathy between the different sides of the net is furthered by mutual antagonism on each side of it.

Draw. The method of arranging matches in a tournament in order that every player may bore his friends with the greatest hard luck story of all time.

Drive. Driving licenses are mandatory and may be obtained from three authorities, (1) the ILTF, (2) the ATP, or (3) the WTT.

Drive-volley. A method of driving without a license.

Drop shot. A ball that having crossed the net changes its mind and tries to get back over it.

Expenses. Up to 1968 this was an authorized unauthorized professional fee to amateurs. Payment is now made only to officials of sufficient importance to justify their transportation costs to be entertained by sponsors.

Fault. A service born out of wedlock.

Federation Cup. The outcome of a union between the Davis and Wightman Cups.

Fifteen. The value of the first point in a game after adding sales tax of 1,400 percent.

Foot-Fault. A Romanian cry of triumph when a visiting Davis Cup player is serving on an important point.

Forehand. The left-hander's secret weapon from the backhand court.

Forest Hills. An area in Queens, New York, adjacent to the Long Island Railroad and under the flight path common to both La Guardia and Kennedy airports, where search is made for the lost secret of growing grass.

Foro Italico. A tennis venue in Rome where the linesmen have a choice between sacrificing a visiting player or being put to death by the crowd.

Game. That which is hunted by tennis players.

Grand Prix. A method of fairly distributing prize money, so arranged that those players who have earned most get more.

Hard Court. This depends whether you are American or British. All players, whether American or British, find the court hard if they fall down, unless it is a grass court after a rainstorm.

ILTF, The Institute for Lawn Tennis Folly.

Indoor court. A court where you cannot lob into the sun.

King's Cup. A trophy never won by Bobby Riggs.

Laver, Rod. Archimides said, "Give me a lever and I will move the world." He added, "Give me Laver and it will no longer Budge."

Lob. A shot played on the assumption that what goes up must come down.

Love. A pointless emotion in tennis.

Line ball. A shot, hit by an Italian in Italy or by a Romanian in Romania, that falls within three inches out of court.

Linesman. An official blinded by a sense of his own importance.

LTA. An institution where the unpaid legislate for the overpaid.

Mixed doubles. Where the set is taken by the pair first getting to sex games.

Nastase, Ilie. The number three seed in a championship where King Feisal of Arabia was first, Henry Ford second and John D. Rockefeller fourth.

Net. Twine woven into reticulated interstices that is irresistibly attractive to the ball.

Official. A man, and sometimes a woman, whose function is to reconcile the unreasonable demands of players with the impossible demands of sponsors. A line official is one who thinks he knows a good shot when he sees one, unlike players who think they should be shot for a bad one.

Open tennis. A condition of complete freedom for players to compete anywhere they like subject only to conditions laid down by ATP, ILTF, WTPA, WTT, WCT, USLTA, SALTU and the Supreme Court.

Open tournament. A tournament from which players in good standing with the ILTF may withdraw to maintain good standing with ATP.

Out in the country. The courts at Wimbledon where matches are played in secret.

Overhead. Unless carefully watched an expensive way of hitting the ball.

Passing Shot. Like the passing bell rung out at a funeral, this marks the death agonies of a volleyer.

Plate events. A system whereby one is consoled for being beaten by a good player by being beaten by a bad player.

Point. The 48th part of a one-sided match.

Prize money. The dollar receipts by which Romania balances its budget.

Professional. One who has dedicated his skill at the game to the benefit of the public and his banker.

Qualifier. A good player who has quarrelled with the referee.

Racket. Frame and gut conspiring together to thwart an honest endeavor to hit the ball over the net into court.

Receiver. He has to take what the server gives him, hopefully from a double fault.

Referee. A one-man peace-keeping force who arbitrates on all disputes between players and line officials by ordering a let to be played. He is unarmed and given police protection in South America, Italy and Romania.

Round robin. A method of playing a tournament whereby one is able to lose not only to a rival competitor but to all other competitors.

Seeding. A method of separating players in a draw so that those with high incomes do not put their earnings at risk until they meet players with comparable incomes.

Selector. An official who would know a good player if (1) he had time to watch him play or (2) he was at college with his father.

Senior. In Europe he is called a veteran because of his experience in many a battle. The senior knows what he should do and knows he cannot do it. The younger player lives in hope.

Server. The natural enemy of the foot-fault judge.

Service. For most the dictionary definition applies. It is work done for the benefit of others—in tennis for the receiver.

Set. A scoring term meaning that one's opponent has won at least two dozen points.

Silenzio, per favore. A phrase used by Italian umpires, meaning "It's not my fault if the Italian player has won the last point."

Singles. A single player is unmarried. A singles player may be wed or unwed but is without dependents on court.

Smash. A profitable way of cutting down overheads.

Sponsor. An individual or business with sufficient income or profits to make it worthwhile making a tax deductible contribution to the income of tennis players.

Stade Roland Garros. A concrete edifice in Paris celebrating France's tenure of the Davis Cup. The courts there are softer than the seats.

Stop volley. A volley whereby the ball, usually badly bruised by hitting the frame of the racket, decides to die on the other side of the net.

Straight sets. A method of winning by which one's opponent drives one round the bend.

Sur la ligne. A cry used by French crowds to tell the linesman that the ball, hit by a French player, was not more than a foot out of court.

Ten minutes rest. A rest period varying between 20 and 30 minutes.

Thirty. The value of two points plus sales tax. Also the amount to which 15 may be added to make 40.

Tiebreaker. A scoring system designed to favor the lucky rather than the skilled player with more stamina, since the latter might make the audience feel tired. In the American "sudden death" nine-point system, a player can go right through the match without dropping a single point on his own service and yet lose, which serves him right.

Tournament. Originally a sporting event where knights in armor tried to knock each other off horses; the winner was rewarded with the hand of a fair maiden. In tennis tournaments the knights no longer wear armor, nor ride horses, and the fair maiden is too busy playing in a Virginia Slims event.

Tramlines. That part of a doubles court which may be used for real estate development while playing singles.

Umpire. The unseeing who calls the score to the unbelieving.

Volley. A method of hitting the ball

at the earliest possible moment with the greatest possibility of error.

WCT. Welsh Commercial Talent, a Texan concern controlled by Mike Davies with assistance from Lamar Hunt.

Well played. A British ejaculation, meaning "Blast your eyes, how lucky can you be!"

Wightman Cup. Another marksmanship trophy gained by Chris Evert for shooting down British players.

Wimbledon. A tournament in southwest London where Nicki Pilic used to play.

WTT. World Tennis Trouble.

Underarm service. A delivery made (1) with a dislocated shoulder or (2) while wearing a hat.

Yards out. A line ball hit by the other side.

Yours. A phrase used in doubles meaning, variously, "I've twisted my ankle," "I've got sun stroke," "Why do you have to put up such a short lob?" or "You got me in this mess, you get me out of it." ●

The compiler acknowledges the assistance of B. Collins, Professor of Linguistic Studies at the Boston University of Unnatural Sciences; of N. Amdur, Reader in Semantics at the New York Institute of Subway Education; of W. ApGrimsley, Reader in Welsh and Obscurantist Dialect at Columbia; of M. Asher, Professor of Divinity at Watergate University, and of the staff of the Lamar Hunt Institute of Gross Arts and Top Spin Research, Dallas, Texas.

No Second Bounces

by DON KLOTZ

TWO fundamentals of tennis are sustained concentration and good position for the stroke. Concentration involves watching the ball until it is almost to your racket, over and back again as long as the rally lasts. Which comes first, the egg or the hen? In tennis, concentration is the egg, the chick and the hen. Without it, forget all the rest.

The elements of good position are: feet apart, knees bent, sidewise, the racket taken part way back as the ball approaches. It is interesting that even beginners, when asked to pose for the forehand, will almost exactly duplicate this position without instruction. The mechanics of the human body are such that a player can hardly miss hitting the ball over the net and into the court if he can assume good position for each stroke. Poor position sharply reduces accuracy, power and consistency.

In match play there can be no second bounces. Logically, then, in practice take the ball on the first bounce or on the volley unless it is completely out of reach. Go to the ball, don't let it take a second, third or fourth bounce. Do not end a rally if the ball goes out of bounds. A drive that lands out is just as good for practice as one that lands in.

Don't anchor yourself behind the baseline. Move forward to the ball rather than reaching for it. Reaching is almost certain to result in a weak error into the net or, at best, an ineffective return.

Another reason for playing shots that are out of bounds is to strive for sustained concentration. Few players can sustain their stroking for more than two or three shots. Poor concentration is the basic cause of this inconsistency. Mental endurance is as important as physical endurance.

If you have bad practice habits, you will have to overcome a strong tendency to continue in that pattern even though the logic is obvious. At first you may be disappointed because you will find that your ability to get into good position is worse than you had imagined. But, you will now be conscious of good vs. bad position, not to mention lapses of concentration. However, there will be a steady improvement in both position and concentration if you bear down hard. As a consequence your percentage of forcing returns will pick up remarkably. Paralleling this improvement will be increased self-confidence, the golden asset that can raise your entire game.

And are you beginning your practice rallies with serves and returns of service? These two strokes make up more than 10 percent of competitive tennis. ●

Marty Norman

BIOGRAPHY OF A BACKHAND

by ROY JOHNSON

YOU'VE GOT TO understand that I was desperate. I would normally be a little skeptical of anyone who offered to sell me a new backhand. But, well, I haven't got a backhand. Never have. All I have is a half-decent forehand. And I'd just been wiped out 6-1, 6-0 in the first round of the monthly club tournament by a real hack whose strategy was to just lay the ball on my backhand and take the net. Believe me, I was in some kind of depression as I left the club and stumbled out to the parking lot.

This guy must have seen me playing, because he seemed to be waiting just for me. Strange looking duck. He had a long overcoat on, which struck me a little funny since the temperature was in the 90s. As I approached my car, he sauntered over and said, "Hey, buddy! Like to buy something guaranteed to help your game?"

I thought he was kidding. "Man, I'd buy a sack of rattlesnakes if I thought they would help this game of mine. Don't happen to have a used backhand, do you?" I laughed at my joke, but he didn't crack a smile.

"No, I don't have a used backhand, but I can let you have a new one pretty reasonable."

"A *new* backhand? You have a new backhand for sale?" I

knew he had to be kidding.

"That's right. Got one right here, direct from the factory. Never been opened." With that he pulled a package, about the size of a shoebox, out from under his coat. It was wrapped in brown paper. Now I'm nobody's dummy. I know you don't just go out and buy a new backhand...or even an old, used one. You get a backhand only after years of agony, taking lessons, practicing, cursing, sweating, bashing a dozen or so rackets into oblivion. And then maybe, just maybe, you might have developed, among other things, some semblance of a backhand.

"Now wait a minute," I said, scarcely keeping the derision out of my voice. "You don't really expect me to believe you've got a...backhand in that box?"

This seemed to irritate him. "Look, if you don't want it, just say so. I ain't got all day."

Well, he seemed so serious about the whole thing that I figured just out of courtesy I ought to hear him out. "Hey, no offense intended. How much you want for it?"

"Twenty bucks, cash."

"Twenty bucks cash. Man, that's a little steep, isn't it? Any guarantee on the thing?"

"Absolutely! You install this backhand per the instructions that come right here in the box, and she's unconditionally guaranteed."

"No kidding!" I looked at the box. Hard to believe. But then what if this guy really did have something? The things they're doing with science and all these days...

"Would you consider 15 bucks for it?" I asked. No use letting him get away with 20 if I could bargain him down a little.

With that he tucked the package under his arm and started to walk off.

"Hey, wait a minute," I yelled, leaping after him. "All right, already! Twenty bucks. Okay." I dug for my billfold. "Here, 20 bucks."

He took the money and handed over the box. "You're making a good buy," he said, turning to go. "Just follow the instructions. All you need to know is right there in the box." With that, he strode off down the parking lot, jumped into a beat-up Edsel and sped away.

I stood here for a long moment, open-mouthed. Then I looked at the package in my hands. It was light. I shook it. "Good grief," I thought. "Do you suppose I bought an empty box?" Panic came over me, and I ripped open the brown paper wrapper and opened the lid. Inside the box was an instruction sheet titled, "Installation of Your New Multi-Purpose Backhand." Underneath the paper I found a small, sealed cellophane bag with what looked like a red leather band in it.

Eagerly I read the instructions:
Congratulations! You have just bought the finest backhand made. This is a professional-type backhand, guaranteed to give you hundreds of both topspin and underspin backhands.

My hands started to tremble.
The installation and use of your new backhand is very simple. Just remove the red band from the cellophane bag, put it around your racket handle, about one inch above the top of the grip, and clip it tight. You are now ready to play.

I dropped the box on the pavement and tore the cellophane package open, put the band on the handle, about an inch above the leather and clipped it in place. Then I removed the racket cover and took a few practice swings. I got a feeling I never had before in my life. The racket was alive, pulling my shoulders back further than I ever turned them before. Then the racket seemed to pull itself down, sweeping forward and through the hitting area, finishing in a nice, high follow-through.

I was almost in a state of frenzy as I picked up the box and my racket cover and raced back into the club looking for someone to hit with me. I finally ran across our pro, Arnold Stanger, picking up practice balls on the teaching court. "Arnold... Arnold!" I had to wait to catch my breath. "Arnold, I've got to hit a few backhands. Okay?"

"Sorry, Roy," he grunted. "Maybe tomorrow."

"Arnold, *please*! Look, I'll take a lesson. A backhand lesson."

Arnold shrugged his shoulders. "It's your money."

He picked up a handful of balls, walked to the baseline, and banged a sizzler at my backhand. What followed can only be described as a mystical, almost sensuous experience. Arnold hit me every kind of shot he could; blazing hard drives, high floaters, short little dinks—all to my backhand. And I drove every one of them past him, crosscourt or down-the-line, *wherever* and *however* I wanted.

After about five minutes, Arnold, who hadn't said a word the whole time, walked to the net and motioned me in. "What in hell have you done to your backhand?" he asked. The incredulous tremor in his voice was worth all the money I had ever paid him for lessons.

"Oh, I just bought a new one," I said rather nonchalantly.

"You *bought* a new backhand? You mean you've been taking lessons from somebody else, right?" There was a definite tone of irritation.

"Honest, Arnold. I haven't had any lessons. I bought a new backhand from some guy out in the parking lot. Here," I pointed to the handle, "see this little red band? That's it. That's my new backhand."

Disgusted, he stomped off the court.

For the next 12 months I was truly in tennis heaven. My new backhand quickly raised me from a low "C" player to a high "A." I won the club championship. I beat Arnold four times. And it got to be the club joke about the red band on my racket.

Then about a year later, I was seeded second in our city tournament. In the second round, I was paired against an obnoxious klutz from another club whom we all called "The Hotdogger" because he pounded every shot, was bowlegged and always wore tennis shoes with no socks.

As we were getting set to go out on court, he casually turned to me and said, "Say, I have something to show you, Roy. See this?" He pointed to his racket handle. There, about an inch up from the leather, was a *blue* band.

I felt myself choke just a little. "Where...where did you get that?" I squeaked.

The Hotdogger laughed. "Oh, I think it was that same guy who sold you your backhand. Of course, this," he said, fingering the blue band, "is not just a backhand. It's a combination forehand and backhand. Latest thing out, you know."

"You kidding me? You're putting me on, right?" I looked at him for some sign it was all a joke.

His laugh had a malicious tone. "Put you on? Not on your life." He pointed to my red band. "You have an outdated backhand, my friend."

We went on court and started to warm up. I have never seen anybody hit such awesome groundstrokes in my life. Every shot caught the baseline going a hundred miles an hour. For the first time in a year my backhand began to sputter, and then it finally died. All I could see was The Hotdogger swinging that racket with the blue band on the handle. And all I had was an old, outdated red-band backhand.

Needless to say, he wiped me out, love and love. After the match I went out and hit on the backboard, but it was gone. The backhand was gone.

It never came back. I lapsed into my old "C" backhand. For a while I searched desperately for the guy who sold it to me. I even broke down and asked The Hotdogger if he knew where I could find him. He just laughed. "Hey, if I'd known you wanted a new backhand I'd have given you mine. I threw that blue band away right after I beat you."

There was a strange look of satisfaction on his face as he walked away, chuckling. Now why would a guy throw away a brand-new combination forehand-backhand...? ●

TENNIS CAMPS COME OF AGE

TWENTY YEARS AGO no one had heard of a camp devoted to teaching tennis to kids. Ten years ago there were perhaps three or four tennis camps. Today? The listing at this writing, as complete as we could make it, has 61 camps with major tennis programs (and a few may have slipped by us).

The first tennis camp was the famous Hoxie Tennis House, started by Jean and Jerry Hoxie in the Detroit suburb of Hamtramck, almost 20 years ago. The Hoxies had been teaching kids for 10 years, literally taking over public courts for their pupils, when *World Tennis* publisher Gladys Heldman called to see if daughters Julie M. and Carrie could come to Hamtramck to play for several weeks. The Heldman kids were the first paying customers.

At times 95 percent of the Hoxie campers were on scholarships, and sliding rates (up to $150 a week) were worked out for the rest. Jean Hoxie was known for her "open the door—shut the door" forehand instruction and requirements that students work out on a backboard before going on a court. A student who double faulted in a match risked being told to serve underhand.

Hoxie ex's such as Julie Heldman, Peaches Bartkowicz, Ray Senkowski (who now has a camp of his own), June Stock, Jerry Dubie, Pacho Castillo, Ken Angyl, Bessie Stockard, Elaine Lewicki and Phyllis Saganski regularly earned national junior titles. The camp used public courts and the large Hoxie home, with apartments in a high rise building next door taking care of the overflow. Mrs. Hoxie died several years ago, but the camp continues at Midland, Mich.

The increase in tennis camp popularity is typified by the growth of Don Budge's tennis camp. In 1963 Budge and his wife opened their camp, one of the earliest. "That first season we had 17 campers, two staff members and three courts," Mrs. Budge remembers. Now, a decade later, with the aid of a staff of 25, the Budges handle 300 campers on 21 courts—nine of which they personally built to increase the facilities at the school they take over during the summer.

"We bought 12 dozen used tennis balls for that 1963 session," Don recalls. This year they will purchase 22 gross of new yellow balls.

"A camper will hit close to 2,000 balls a day," says Tennis America's guiding light, Dennis Van der Meer, another successful camp operator.

Neil Chase owns and operates the second oldest of the tennis camps. As a teacher in Westtown, Pa., and a friend of Bill Talbert and Tony Trabert, he arranged for the Westtown School to be used during the summer months for

Left—A typical tennis camp has outstanding physical facilities. These are the eight courts of the Fairfield Tennis Camp. Above—At Don Kerbis' camp all campers must stop at the chinning bars on the way into the dining hall for meals.

by CANDACE MAYERON

a tennis camp. "That first year, 1958," says Chase, "we had only 23 campers. Kids would stand on their individual courts and call to each other 'Come play on my court'!" Chase camps now boast over 3,000 graduates from 47 states and many foreign countries. Another early camp was Stan Singer's Irish Tennis Camp. Singer now has a camp in Monaco.

With so many camps to choose from, it no longer is just a matter of picking the one closest to your home. Other exotic camps such as Andy Stern's Club Mayrhofen in Austria and Summertime Adventure in Chamonix (at the foot of Mount Blanc in France) offer foreign travel and skiing as well as a tennis program. Frank Sedgman's Tennis Camp of Australia takes advantage of the rich Down Under tennis tradition. Many U.S. camps offer a wide variety of activities and some concentrate on tennis to the exclusion of almost every other sport.

Camps where tennis is the main activity are usually located on school campuses. Excellent tennis facilities are usually available at schools, with most having at least a dozen courts. Campers live in dormitories, and as the regular kitchen staff builds the campers up, the tennis instructors wear them down. Usually the swimming pools and gymnasiums are at the disposal of campers. Camps may

offer horseback riding, swimming, sailing, volleyball, basketball, hiking, golf, water skiing, canoeing, softball, archery, languages, drama, extensive arts programs, bowling, riflery, photography and special tutoring in school subjects.

Many camps have an association with the name stars of the current circuit or recent past. Some of these camps feature visits by the associated stars, while others are run by and supervised by the big name pros. Among those with full-time supervision and instruction by their "name" teachers are: Welby Van Horn Camp; Tut Bartzen's Texas Tennis Camp; Don Budge Camp; Tony Trabert Camp; John Newcombe Camp; Lakeway World of Tennis (Cliff and Jean Drysdale); Don Kerbis Camp; Cliff Buchholz Camp; Ron Holmberg Camp; and Sabin-Mulloy (Wayne Sabin).

"Stars" running camps work as hard, if not harder, than any of their counselors. Daily, Budge introduces the "stroke of the day." He demonstrates it, talks about it, answers any questions; then he moves from court to court pointing out errors, correcting faults, re-explaining and praising a good shot.

Trabert's method is much the same: "I believe there are about six basics to any stroke and those are the things I talk about. I'll mentally run down the list while I'm demonstrating the stroke. If a kid hits the stroke pretty well, I'll have him come out and demonstrate it."

The tennis programs stress: technique, strategy, rules, sportsmanship, physical conditioning, proper care of equipment and a history of the game.

Methods and daily routines actually vary little from camp to camp. Most camps offer a ratio of one instructor for every four or five campers. An average of five hours per day is spent on demonstrations, exercises, drills, lectures and competitive play.

A typical daily schedule might look like:

  7:15 Rise and Shine
  7:30 Breakfast
  8:00 Room clean-up
  8:45 Exercise and jogging
  9:15 Tennis instruction
 11:15 Cold drink break
 11:30 Tennis instruction
 12:45 Lunch
  1:30 Rest period
  2:15 Tennis instruction
  4:30 Swim or open tennis period
  5:30 Back to dorms
  6:15 Dinner
  6:45 Instant replay analysis
  8:30 Planned evening activities
  9:45 In dorms
 10:30 Lights out

"Some parents are concerned we might overtax their children," says Trabert. "They don't realize much of the time is spent in lectures, or by the kid picking up balls for his fellow campers. We want the kids to have fun; we don't want to work them to death. But those that can handle more time on the courts get it. Even with all the physical exercise, some of the kids aren't as tired at the end of the day as we'd like them to be, and sometimes the little buggers try to sneak out."

Campers are usually divided into groups according to their ability and experience. "Each camper is challenged to progress at his own pace through a series of individualized tests," says Mrs. William Ramey, a popular and successful tennis camp director for many years. Mrs. Ramey, whose six camps are located in the Midwest, believes in good competition to supplement the drills and tests.

Methods of instruction are much the same for children as for adults. The real difference is in the amount of time spent daily on drills and instruction. William Kaiser, president of National Tennis Schools, says, "Children are more adaptable physically, but less likely to retain the reasoning. To groove their strokes you really need a minimum of two weeks. Adults want tennis 24 hours a day, and a six-day program is usually all they can physically handle."

Dennis Van der Meer records each new student on videotape the first day of camp, so that he can go over their strokes in detail at a later time. Van der Meer's teaching aids also include a 10-foot net for students to get the feeling of height and depth on the serve and a stringless racquet to give the feeling of hitting through the ball.

The counselors-instructors at most camps are usually college students, sometimes working on their own games, but more often than not anticipating the future when they might want full-time jobs as tennis pros. Trabert points out that a "name" camp does more than just add glamour. "The best counselors are drawn to our camps, because a recommendation from me or Budge is worth a lot." Mrs. Budge agrees. "Our counselors are all-round athletes, usually college physical education majors. We want, and get, the real squares—the Eagle Scouts and Sunday school teachers. They're a marvelous bunch of guys."

All is not hard work at a tennis camp. Almost every camp stages some kind of talent show, holds dances and shows films. Movies are usually tennis films, ranging from training sequences, showing techniques and tactics, to championship matches. Budge shows slow motion films of the tennis greats of a bygone era: Vines, Perry and Donald Budge.

The purpose of the camps is to give the boys and girls a fun summer through tennis. Although there is some opportunity for tournament play, camps on the whole are not trying to turn out future Wimbledon winners. (However, Dr. Alex Mayer's star pupil, son Sandy, or Neil Chase's ex-pupil, Dick Stockton, may achieve that title. Frank Brennan's one-time student, Billie Jean King, already has.)

Most camps finish up sessions with intra-camp tournaments. These might be round-robins or eliminations. "I call ours the Choke Open," says one director. "That's when all the old bad habits resurface—follow-throughs are nonexistent, wrists flip-flop, and the crying, hair-pulling and racket-tossing begins." Another camp holds a camp championship and a camper-counselor doubles tournament. Some camps have camper-parent matches on the last day of the session. Trophies are given out for "Most Improved Player," "Most Improved Forehand (Backhand) (Serve)," "Best Dressed" (a trophy given for neatness and tidyness, not largest wardrobe!).

At the end of the session, the camper will return home healthy, happy, with a new confidence in his tennis, and, maybe the ability to lick the Old Man. ●

A Classic Doubles Point

by JULIUS HELDMAN

THIS IS A classic doubles point, played on clay. It is early in a match (note the alleys are still brushed and there are no slide marks yet). John Newcombe is serving, Tony Roche is at net, Marty Riessen is receiving and Tom Okker is at the net near the service line. Tom never looks ready but he is; his reactions are incredibly fast. He is always on the move, taking small steps continuously.

This is a second serve in the right court, with everybody in text-book position. Note that Newcombe is half-way between the center marker and the alley. The serve is to Riessen's backhand. He takes the ball on his baseline and chips diagonally back to Newk, who is advancing behind his delivery. Actually the stroke is a little longer than a chip and perhaps flatter, but in any event it is not a long drive.

Roche, the netman, has one of the world's great backhand volleys and is always alert for a poach, but apparently he has not attempted a kill this time even though Newk takes the ball near the center line on his backhand. Newk's first (backhand) volley is hit while he is still moving forward, back to the receiver and well away from Okker, who in turn is alert to intercept any ball within leaping reach.

Riessen moves sideways and falls back as he returns the ball. It is a lob. Newk prepares himself for the smash. The lob comes down in midcourt and Newk does not let it bounce. Here is the guessing game. Okker chooses to stand in rather close, just on the baseline. This is typical of the lightning quick reflex player. Riessen is farther back, hoping to run down any ball to his side or deep center. He knows that Newk likes to hit wide (to Marty's forehand) but cannot move too far over because then the center would be open. Newk chooses the angle, hitting wide to Marty's forehand.

But was it in? In the last two frames, there may be the beginning of a hassle as both Newk and Roche look at the sidelinesman while Okker starts to stride over in that direction. Riessen remains impassive. ●

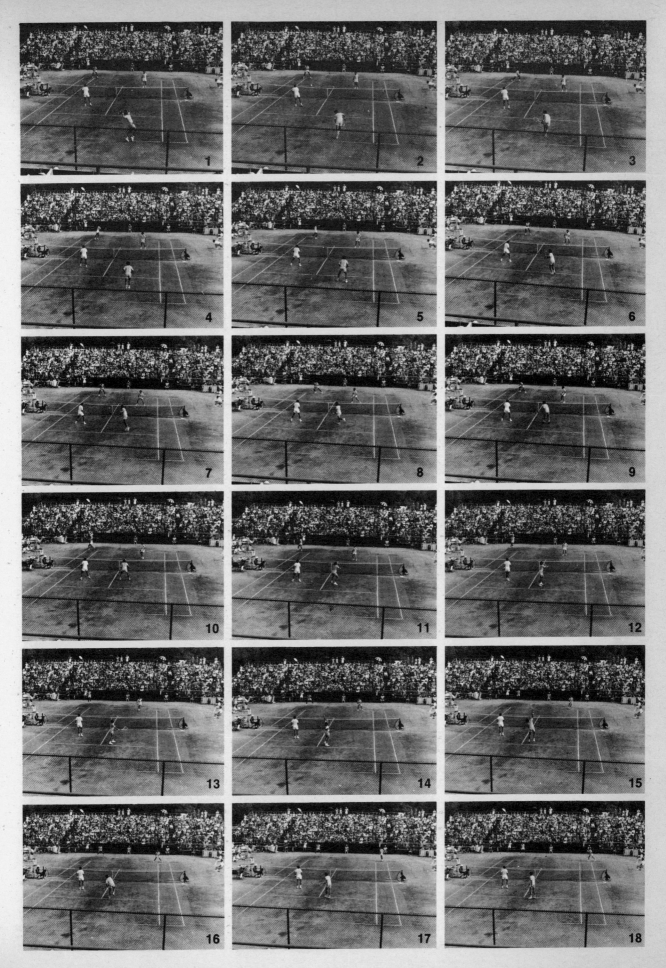

Tennis Etiquette

by GLADYS M. HELDMAN

IF THE PLAYERS on the next court are having a long rally, can you walk (or run) in the back of their court to pick up a ball that has rolled there?

Not if they are in the middle of a point. If they are warming up and haven't started to play, yes. Do unto others, etc.

Is it bad manners to beat someone 6-0, 6-0
No. It's bad manners to gloat after your victory.

* * *

If I see that a ball I hit landed on the line, may I correct my opponent's call if he said it was out?

Not unless he asks you to call the ball for him. The player has the right to call all balls on his side of the court. He cannot call any balls on your side unless you ask him.

* * *

Who should buy the balls when you play doubles? How is it arranged?

It's like "who buys the drinks" when four of you sit down at a table. Occasionally someone will say, "I have a new can. Let's use mine." (It's your turn next time.) Sometimes you "split" the balls, buying a can at the tennis shop and each paying his share. It's never bad manners to say "Let's split it four ways" unless you are by far the worst in the group and are lucky to be in the game at all. Adults should not expect children to have the same size wallet, and so the adults generally split the cost. Since balls are usable again, the player who bought the balls gets to keep them.

* * *

If I only plan to hit for five or 10 minutes and therefore don't want to waste $3 on new balls, can I ask to borrow someone's used balls?

That's like asking to borrow someone's sandwich.

* * *

Why is it considered bad manners to dispute a call? Suppose your opponent is cheating? Are you expected to accept bad calls?

If it's a tournament, you have the right to ask for an umpire, although none may be available. If that's the case, you might ask another player (but not a relative or best friend) if he will help on line-calling. If it's not a tournament match, you can either have a terrible hassle or simply decide never to play the person again. Players who would never deliberately make a bad call can sometimes make an honest mistake, so don't lose your temper over one call. In one famous tournament match at the Berkeley Tennis Club, a player was the victim of repeated bad calls. She waited until her opponent served. The ball was two feet in. She caught it and yelled "Fault" as an act of reprisal.

* * *

Can I ask a much better player to hit with me?

Yes, if you are married to him. Let the better players ask you; you ask those of your own level or those not as good.

* * *

I'm the worst player at our courts. I can't find anyone my own level or below. Now what's the solution?

Use the backboard or a rebound net, practice your serve and look eager. If this fails, encourage an uncoordinated neighbor or friend to take up the game and play with you. Above all, remain confident; you are bound to find someone worse than you.

* * *

Why is it impolite to return a first serve that is out? I have seen plenty of tournament players do it.

In tournaments, you should return every close serve (even if you think it is out) because the linesman may call it good. Returning an obviously "out" ball is an irritation to the server: he may think you played it as good or it may destroy his rhythm for the second serve. Everyone at some time returns a close "out" serve, but usually the player immediately calls, "Out. Sorry." The time to practice your return of serve is not against "out" balls.

* * *

I got exhausted in a match and thought I'd faint if I didn't stop for five minutes. My opponent told me there was no rest period at the end of a set and that I'd have to default if I couldn't continue. Isn't that terribly rude?

No. It's the rule. If players could take a rest whenever they felt like it, tournament play would be chaotic. Tennis is a game of stamina as well as skill.

* * *

It's obviously bad to throw a racket or hit a ball over the fence in a fit of pique, but must one play without any expression at all as though one were an inanimate doll? Must all matches be contested in absolute silence?

This is up to the player. Self-remonstrating after missing a crucial set-up is natural, but continual groans are a pain to everyone—the opponent, the players on the next court, bystanders, the pro giving a lesson five courts away, etc. Some players think that if they groan every time they miss, anyone watching will believe that normally the player wouldn't miss that shot. If Margaret Court doesn't groan when she is beaten by a lesser player in the second round, why are you groaning?

* * *

If you are not sure a ball is out, can you ask your opponent to play the point over?

If you can't see the ball out, you have to play it as good.

* * *

What is a court hog?

A player who occupies the court for more than one hour when others are waiting to play. He cannot justify holding the court for himself because the players waiting are mere beginners. Everyone is entitled to equal court time, no matter how well or how badly they play.

If there is a tremendous disturbance near your court just as you are about to hit your shot, can you ask to play a let?

Only if the disturbance is actually on your court. An airplane flying overhead, a baby screaming near your sideline or a dog barking is no reason for a let—unless the airplane, the baby or the dog are inside the boundaries of your court. If it's your baby or your dog, your opponent has the option of taking a let; you don't.

* * *

What do you do when an opponent wants to warm-up seemingly forever before starting play?

In major tournaments there is sometimes a specific time limit on the warm-up period. In local tournaments where there are no umpires, you can drop a gentle (or tough) hint, depending on your personality, that five minutes have gone by and you would like to get started. If the opponent remains obstinate, stop running for balls so you don't exhaust yourself.

* * *

How do you tell a player who shouts "Oh, no!" when his forehand or overhead lands on your side too softly, that his noises are disturbing you?

If he shouts during a point, the point is automatically yours. That's the rule. Tell him next time you will have to take the point.

* * *

What do you do about an opponent who constantly makes conversation after every point?

Tell him: "I may win the match but you have already won the conversation, seven paragraphs to none."

* * *

I went over to our local courts to watch a tournament and spotted an old friend whom I hadn't seen in years. I waited until he and his opponent changed courts on the odd game, then said, "Hi, Bob!" He glared at me and didn't answer. Remember, I didn't do this during a point but at the end of a game. Was this so terrible?

Never engage a player in conversation, even to say hello, until the match is over. He is trying to block out all outside distractions whereas you are insisting that he acknowledge your presence and greet you in the middle of a contest of skill and concentration.

* * *

I was walking by Court 1 at our club while a game was in progress. I did not walk onto or behind the court but simply on the pathway to the side of it, a good 10 feet from the court. One of the players turned to me and shouted: "Sit down!" Who was wrong?

If it was a match, you should have waited until the point was over. If the players were only practicing, then the one who shouted at you must think he is Stan Smith or John Newcombe, although neither of the latter would have made such a remark.

* * *

I had brought a can of balls over to the courts and, while attempting to take off the lid, I broke it. So I asked the guy in the pro shop if he could open the can for me. He glared at me and sullenly opened it. I certainly won't give him any of my business from now on. Am I right?

It sounds as though you never gave him any of your business in the past. If you buy a ham sandwich at one coffee shop, don't go around the corner to another shop and ask for free mustard. Patronize the pro shop at your courts and the pro will always open your ball can with a smile.

Do you have to wear all-white on a tennis court?

Not unless the courts have a rule requiring white only. The only rule on all courts is to wear proper tennis shoes so that the court surface is not damaged. Many top players wear colored shirts (and sometimes matching shorts), and the Virginia Slims Women Pros wear pastel tennis dresses.

* * *

I have just moved to a new city and would like to join a tennis club. How do I go about it?

Almost all indoor tennis clubs are open to anyone upon payment of the membership fee. Phone an indoor club in your city and ask for information about joining. Outdoor tennis clubs are often primarily social: one member has to propose you, another must second you and a membership board passes on you. Additionally, you have to be invited to join. If no one invites you, don't invite yourself: you wouldn't ask yourself to someone else's house for dinner. You can play at the public courts (open to all) or get a group together and form your own club or join an indoor club if there is one in the city.

* * *

I sometimes play at a friend's court. He is terribly bossy and is always arranging the foursome. "Okay, John, you're in the next set. You play with Bill, etc." Is there anything we can do about it?

No. It's his court.

* * *

There's a fellow I have played pretty often and I have never lost a set to him. However, he tells everyone we are about even. What can I do?

Next time you are in a group together, pay him a compliment, viz.: "You're improving so much that sooner or later you are bound to win a set."

One of the fellows in our regular doubles always plays with a cigar in his mouth. Isn't this a distraction?

Not on the court. Only in the shower.

* * *

A woman we play with regularly always arrives five or 10 minutes late and we only have the court for one hour. What should we do?

You have plenty of options: a) ask her to be prompt, b) get another fourth and play the first set without her, c) warm-up without her and start the set as soon as she arrives, d) arrange for your group to arrive 10 minutes after your tardy "regular" e) draw up a petition or f) accept her idiosyncrasy because you really want her to be the fourth. ●

The Poet Laureate

by LINDA TIMMS

THERE IS A curious office in Britain known as the Poet Laureateship, the holder of which receives a stipend as an officer of the Royal Household, and who was originally supposed to produce odes, elegies and the like on appropriate national or royal events. The first official holder, in the seventeenth century, was Dryden, and in between some much less illustrious incumbents have been Wordsworth and Tennyson. The significance of the subject today is that the newly appointed Laureate, John Betjeman, is not only by far the most popular of English poets—his Collected Works have already sold 230,000 copies—but he is, to my knowledge, the only poet to have glorified the female tennis player.

Betjeman's chief claim to immortality in the tennis world must rest on "A Subaltern's Love Song." This eulogizes a certain Miss J. Hunter Dunn (perfectly designated as her name would appear on the referee's draw sheet) whose outstanding attribute is that she soundly beats the male narrator in a "strenuous singles" in a club tournament—obviously the literary inspiration of Women's Lob. The beauty of Betjeman's attitude is that not only, unlike the Stan Smiths of today, does the hero not mind defeat at the hands of his Home Counties Billie Jean; he positively revels in it:

"Love thirty, love forty, oh! weakness of joy" and

"I am weak from your loveliness, Joan Hunter Dunn." Indeed, his oncourt humiliation elicits an offcourt proposal of marriage, prompted by the appeal of her "strongly adorable tennis-girl's hand." This is idyllic middle class Britain's tennis club-land at its idealized best. But Betjeman shows his genuine appreciation of the girl as a player when he writes:

"With carefullest carelessness, gaily you won." Such comment is worthy not of a romantic but of an expert.

The other poem which deals explicitly with the female tennis player is "The Olympic Girl," which turns on a striking change of metaphor. First Betjeman describes the sort of girl he likes to see, a kind of Christine Truman/Margaret Court figure who "smiles down from her great height at me" and "stands in strong athletic pose". He wishes he were her racket—one of the only objects "fit to claim her look"—when he would be "swished into the sunlit air," and he promises: "For you I will do brilliant things." But then suddenly, when the match is over, he becomes not the racket but the discarded ball:

"Little, alas, to you I mean,

For I am bald and old and green."

This idea of the tennis girl as Amazon persists in another poem, "Pot Pourri from a Surrey Garden," in which Pam, the "great big mountainous sports girl" is "whizzing them over the net, full of the strength of five" with a "wonderful backhand drive" too strong even for her "old Malvernian brother." And again, in "North Coast Recollections," the female player triumphs over her mixed doubles opponent, this time by perhaps more traditional means: "Demon Sex,

That tulip figure in white cotton dress

Bare legs, wide eyes and so tip-tilted nose

Quite overset him."

Such words were written long before women's tennis came fully to be appreciated for the unique attraction that it is, and it is to be hoped that Betjeman has not said his last word on the subject. Even though the Queen herself is known not to be a tennis enthusiast, surely any future British success at Wimbledon must be recorded as a matter of duty. Should Virginia Wade ever perform the miracle, he already has the perfect line: "Fair tigress of the tennis courts."

Betjeman's phenomenal popularity, combined with his poetic vision of sport, make him a tennis publicist not to be ignored. Paradoxically, his greatest evocation of the sheer joy of playing superlative tennis comes in a poem on golf, where he writes of "A glorious, sailing, bounding drive

That made me glad I was alive."

That, to me, is a backhand pass down the line straight into the corner, the sort of which Evonne Goolagong said so charmingly at Torquay, "I hit one and it went in, so I thought I'd try a few more." It was a remark that Betjeman would have appreciated. But you don't have to be a Goolagong to experience that joy. Indeed, the virtue of Betjeman as a tennis poet is that, if he reflects a somewhat old-fashioned, restricted, even snobbish sports world, at least it is an amateur world in the best and most literal sense of the word. His Miss Hunter Dunns, though they might turn up their pretty noses at prize money they could afford not to need, do really love the game. I hope that as Poet Laureate John Betjeman will spend many fruitful hours in the Royal Box at Wimbledon. ●

A Centennial Primer:

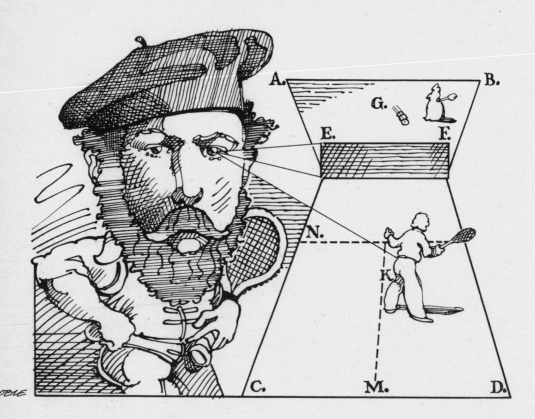

L. NOBLE

ONE DECEMBER afternoon in 1873, Major Walter Clopton Wingfield—known as "Clops" to his cronies—was moping around his castle in Wales, out of sorts and under foot. "I say, Clops," said his wife, Alice, "why don't you run outside and play?"

Was that how it all started? Apparently so...

"Play what, Alice? What"

"A game, silly."

"I don't know any games. I was trained as a soldier," said Major Wingfield.

"Well, make up a game then. Any child can do that. Don't be sticky about it, Clops."

"Sticky? Sticky... hmmm... old girl, you may have something there. Perhaps a game called Sphairistike, what? Lovely name for a game. Greeks had the name for it—now if I could only think what the hell game they had in mind. Something to do with a ball..."

"Yes, yes, Clops. Follow the bouncing ball and all that sort of thing. Just go out and run around the garden for a while. Clear your head. Do you a world of good. Remember we're going away for the weekend to the Naylor-Lelands."

"Drat. Nearly forgot about that, Alice. Must we go? Always such a dull time there. Same old absurd party games. Charades. Kick-the-decanter. Spin the jeroboam."

"Yes, we're going. We always go, you know, Clops. So think up a good game and perchance we can break the monotony with it. Something the women can play with the men—but nothing naughty."

A little later she looked out to the courtyard to see the major and his valet, Jacob Faltz, a German immigrant, swatting away at a ball with a couple of beaters that the servants used to clean rugs. They'd strung a rope between two trees, and were trying to knock the ball back and forth above the rope.

Faltz swung at the ball clumsily and hit it below the level of the rope. "One more, Faltz," cried the major. The valet tried again and failed. "That's double, Faltz. My point," chortled Wingfield.

Could Jacob Faltz, who gave good service in every other respect as valet, have imagined that his shortcomings as Clops Wingfield's opponent would be incorporated into the language of a new, eventually universal game? On his tombstone in the Confucian Cemetery of Mingo Junction, Ohio, where he ended his days, is this inscription:

Jacob Maximilian Faltz
1843-1932
"To double fault is human –
to forgive oneself is unlikely"

The Way It Really Was

by BUD COLLINS

(Faltz checked out by guzzling a double-hemlock milk shake following his last double fault, on match point in the Ashtabula Senior Doubles.)

Clops was excited when they stopped playing and came back into the drawing room. "By George, I've got it, Alice! Sphairistike. It's court tennis outdoors on a lawn, of course. We'll use court tennis rackets or perhaps have a different shape made up. A rubber ball will be necessary, as will proper netting and a marked off court in the shape of an hourglass. What a fertile brain I have. A first, by thunder. I've invented a game that will sweep the world. I'm the Alexander Graham Bell of sport, I tell you..."

"Take it easy, Clops." Alice hadn't seen him so enthused since the Christmas two years before when she gave him his own yo-yo. "That telephone of Bell's hasn't been patented yet, you know. Besides, dear, didn't Major Gem do this very same thing on the lawn at Edgbaston back in '58?"

"Gem? That pasty chap? Perhaps, perhaps, Alice, but they didn't have a name for it. They didn't patent it. Wait and see. We'll try it at the houseparty at Nantclwyd Hall, and everybody will be wild for it."

For once, Clops Wingfield was right. "Jolly good," applauded the host, Thomas Naylor-Leland after he and his hung-over guests had a go at the major's game a few mornings later. "Clears the cobwebs, what? Although I must say I'm a bit humbled by what you call Double Faltz. Too much pressure, I suppose. I say, Clops, what do you call this diversion?"

"Sphairistike, old boy. Catchy, wouldn't you say?"

"Like pellagra. Odd name..."

"Greek. Classical. Olympian."

"I see, Clops. Don't want anything too intelligible—it's not for the masses, after all."

"Certainly not. It is a game for the gentry."

"No tiebreakers or simplified scoring, Clops?"

"Are you mad? You've seen this game. You realize it is perfection, don't you?"

"I agree," said the host, who was too winded to debate. "This is, I believe, a historic occasion. Shall we all drink to Pops Clops, the Big Daddy of very-thicky!"

"Sphairistike, if you please, Naylor-Leland."

"Right you are. Three cheers for hairy-what!"

"Sphairistike, for God's sake."

Alice nudged Clops, "Don't make an issue of it."

"It looks like tennis to me," Jacob Faltz whispered to Mrs. Wingfield's maid, Winifred, who replied, "I'm 55-years-old with one foot in the grave, but I'll bet I could beat any of the men I saw here today. I don't think men are sta-ble enough to play this game. I'd give you a handicap, Jacob. I'll push the baby carriage and I'll still beat you."

"This," hissed Faltz, "is a gentleman's game. No one will ever wager on it."

Riding back to the castle, Wingfield glowed. "We'll make a fortune once I've patented Sphairistike, Alice. This is the game for a lifetime. Truly the game of the 70s. Just needs a little commercial push. Do you think we could get Queen Victoria to play in a celebrity mixed doubles?"

Mrs. Wingfield was not as optimistic. "Don't count your aces until they're served, Clops. Who really wants to chase a little white ball around? Not anyone completely sane, certainly. It's a nice catharsis for you and Faltz, to go out in the garden and run about. Better than a cold shower, possibly. But I wouldn't take it seriously if I were you. You may sell it in Greece, but Sphairistike is strictly from Hungary if you ask me. Nobody ever got rich from a game, pet."

(This was before the coming of Laver, Rosewall, Ashe and Smith.)

Both Clops and his wife were correct. He did patent and promote, and the game quickly became a success in Britain. But as tennis. There was little money in it for him. Sports' devotees weren't ready for a Greek revival. Sphairistike caught on nowhere but on the isle of Lesbos where the World Sphairistike Championship is played annually Sept. 30 between four and five p.m., and is usually won by Herodotus Faltz, a descendant of the Wingfield servant. Wingfield's rules were changed, the equipment and his hourglass court altered. His patent didn't mean a thing.

However, it is the centennial of Wingfield's patent that we are celebrating, the 100th anniversary of lawn tennis nee Sphairistike.

"This game will go a long way, baby," Clops told his wife that fateful day when he and Faltz brandished rugbeaters in the courtyard. The rest, as we say, is history.

Jacob Faltz, who outlived his master by two decades and was present at the opening of the Forest Hills Stadium in 1923, used to say, "The major was a man of genius, but truthfully, it was an idea whose time had come. When he mentioned playing a game to me, you might say we put our heads together and thought it up jointly. He overruled me on only one item: the net. For me, a net took all the fun and friendliness out of the game. It was like building walls between people. On my own court at Mingo Junction we never use a net. You'd be surprised what that does for your serve and strokes."

Faltz felt, and I'm sure you'll concur, that tennis would be no more popular than Latvian blintzes if Henry Jones and

Mary Outerbridge hadn't lived. Without knowing it—in fact entirely by accident—Outerbridge and Jones were two of the greatest missionaries to be associated with any sport.

From this distance of about a century, Henry Jones looks heroic. Actually he was doubly disreputable: a sportswriter *and* a croquet player as well.

An outrageous combination of evils. You remember that chorus of the famous song memorializing him:...*save the bones for Henry Jones 'cause Henry don't eat no meat?* It was literally true. Like a dog, he did chew on bones, and that unseemly habit led to the establishment of tennis at Wimbledon.

In 1868, at a time when croquet was the opiate of the masters in London, Henry Jones and four other men founded the All England Croquet Club on a green patch in the London suburb of Wimbledon. It was the scene of many vicious battles of mallet and ball, tense struggles to penetrate enigmatic and inscrutable wickets. The most memorable, and explosive, was for the All England title of 1875 in which Henry Jones was up against the imperious Duke of Norfolk. The Duke, 73, was called (not to his face) "Old Ironballs," a salute to his awesome clout that sent an opponent's ball flying prodigious distances when struck by his own.

Throughout a long, nervous afternoon, during which neither man spoke to the other, they played neck and neck. At times the silent combat was so furious that several members of the gallery woke up. At last it appeared the Duke was within a stroke of triumph. He had been a finalist in 37 successive major finals without winning. Now...now he was poised over his ball...about to conclude all the frustration...it was lined up...he began to swing when—

"Crack, snapple, glop!" Henry Jones was chewing on a pheasant bone. Not much of a noise, really, but in that setting it was thunderous.

It was too late for the Duke to halt his swing, which jerked at the sound. His ball dribbled wide of the mark, and Jones was in position to win it all.

"Gad, man!" the Duke screamed. His face was as purple as Rosie Casals' dress that enraged Wimbledon in 1972. "You are a cad, the lowest of the low. You're as low as...as," the Duke foamed, "you're as low as a tennis player.

"If you have any honor at all, you will accept my challenge at once. Toe-to-toe with mallets until one of us is bludgeoned to eternity!"

Henry Jones, experienced journalist who had been castigated by the best of them, merely bowed. "My turn, your lordship." And he went on to win the game and championship.

No duels for him, thank you. As he chomped on his victory T-bone, having fed the steak to his cat, Jones thought about the Duke's ultimate insult, equating him with a tennis player. "Why not?" he wondered. "Might as well keep Old Ironballs in a serene mood." The next day he proposed that an area of the young club be given over to the new game of lawn tennis.

Two years later, J.W. Walsh, one of Jones' colleagues in forming the club, suggested that they hold a tennis tournament for all-comers. That tournament became Wimbledon, and the club subsequently lengthened its name to the present All England Lawn Tennis and Croquet Club.

Jones took up the game himself, and his disconcerting manners got him into trouble again. Fatal trouble, it would seem. In the final of the club "B" singles, against the Count of Palermo, a Sicilian nobleman who summered in London to satisfy his passion for tea and tennis, Jones was again near defeat. But, at a break point against the Sicilian, Jones refreshed himself by gnawing on a rib.

It was like breaking the sound barrier. Unnerved, the Count emulated Jacob Faltz. He couldn't hit another ball squarely. But he didn't screech or blubber. Instead of shaking hands with the triumphant Jones, the Count kissed him on the cheek, saying, "You are very heavy-handed, Jones. It might be well for you to be heavy-footed, too."

A week later Henry Jones was found in the Thames, wearing concrete sneakers.

Henry Jones had served the purpose for which he was undoubtedly born for, as anyone in England will tell you, Wimbledon is the result of divine intervention.

Maybe the same is true of Mary Ewing Outerbridge of Staten Island, a pretty young thing responsible for introducing tennis to the United States one hundred years ago. Her saintly act was more unintentional than Jones'. It happened only because, as her mother later said, "Mary can't resist anything in a uniform. Including the milkman."

In this instance, at least, the uniform was more acceptable than most, belonging to Capt. Malcolm Congreve Dalcolm IX, of the British army, the same army that gave us Clops Wingfield, although not the same outfit. Capt. Dalcolm was with the garrison in Bermuda, one of the early strongholds of Wingfield's game, and he was a mad convert to tennis. For Capt. Dalcolm the army had been only an interim bit. He felt a call from on high, and planned to enter a seminary to study for the priesthood when his enlistment was up. But his first swing with racket was profound: like so many others he sensed he could find salvation through tennis.

Humming *A Mighty Forehand Has Our God,* Dalcolm smote all before him with his racket and won the Bermuda championship. It was about that time the Outerbridge girl arrived for college week. In those days college week in Bermuda wasn't quite what it is now. Mary was the lone visitor. As such she was extremely popular with the soldiers. All pursued her, but it was Capt. Dalcolm whom she pursued.

She threw herself at him, and got nowhere. "My strength is as the strength of 10 because my heart is pure," he responded.

"Please see me—love me," she pleaded. "Tonight. Any night. Anywhere."

"All my action is on the court, " said Capt. Dalcolm, on an entirely different wave length. "Dear girl, I'm sorry, but I have no time. The one spot in my schedule where I might possibly fit you in is a seven to eight a.m. court. What grip do you use?"

"Wait'll you try to get loose..."

But it was all tennis. Mary hated it, separated by the net from Malcolm. "The only place I ever was where love meant you weren't scoring," she recalled afterwards. Nevertheless, Malcolm developed a genuine fondness for her. They played every morning, and when the day came for her to leave Bermuda, he volunteered to see her to the boat. They were a handsome couple on the dock.

"Will you kiss me goodbye?" Mary asked.

"I will do much more because I feel very close to you," he said. "I must do for you something I've never considered doing for anyone else—"

"Gee," Mary was suddenly nervous, "there are a lot of people around."

"Hang the people. I don't care who sees what I'm giving you." With that he lifted a huge package from the carriage. "Here, Mary, I am giving you life itself."

"What in the world is it?" She felt dazed.

"A complete tennis set—rackets, balls, nets, instructions, rules," Malcolm beamed, directing a porter to take it along with the Outerbridge luggage.

"Yuk!" Mary slapped him.

"Marvelous stroke, Mary. Your forehand has come along."

"I can't stand tennis, Malcolm. It's pointless."

"Only if you stay at love."

"You monster. You lead me on, and then you give me this junk."

Malcolm did not flinch. "Mary, I see you as a woman of rare drive, the sort to spread the gospel of tennis in America. Take this equipment and plant the seed. Through tennis you will find peace. Believe me..."

Mary ran up the gangplank muttering, "What a jerk!"

On the voyage to New York she tried to forget Capt. Dalcolm and tennis. She was reasonably successful until she moved through customs with her belongings.

An inspector questioned, "What are these nets? You got a commercial fishing license, miss? Strange gear you got here. Never had anything like this come through the port."

"Keep it, I don't want it," she said.

"Can't do that, miss, but we'll have to impound it until we can determine what it is and the amount of duty."

Weeks later a notice arrived at the Outerbridge home. Customs was satisfied that her imports were harmless, and she could pick them up. "You go," she told one of her brothers, Emilius. "It's a present for you and Eugenius. I can't stand to see it." The Outerbridge brothers marked off the first American court on the grounds of the Staten Island Cricket and Baseball Club, while Mary warned her friends, "Never trust a Limey who asks you to come over to his place to play tennis. That's exactly what he wants to do."

Clops Wingfield, Jacob Faltz, Henry Jones, Mary Outerbridge—those are among the names to remember. You will hear tributes to other pioneers, and any number of glorified tales about the origins and advances of tennis. But I felt my account should stick to the essential history and disregard folklore.

Much is made, for example, of a guy named P.F. Hadow, winner of the second Wimbledon in 1878. He has long been considered the patron saint of hackers as the inventor of the lob. Since his were the first lobs ever seen at Wimbledon, propagandists of the All England Club, such as Henry Jones, have cited Hadow as the progenitor.

Not so. The primal lob was launched in 1876 by Leviticus Schallau (great-grandfather of the current No. 11 female of the U.S., Mona Schallau). Not only was he the avant garde lobber, but Leviticus Schallau never used another stroke, mainly because he learned tennis and played it all his life on America's first indoor court—a silo in Marengo, Iowa.

But enough debunking. Let Hadow have the honor. The first hundred years have been good fun, so why should I spoil the legends with the facts?　●

THE AXIOMS OF TENNIS

by COLIN MacARTHUR

MANY TENNIS PROS *try to get results by merely telling the student what to do without a reason or how to do it. There is nothing inevitable about keeping your eye on the ball just because you've been told to do so. Starting with this all-important eye-on-the-ball business, let's look at the axioms of tennis, the reasons and the methods to obtain the desired effect.*

Axiom I: Keep your eye on the ball.

Always keep your eye on the oncoming ball so that you will contact it at dead center of your racket and achieve maximum control in directing the ball for placements and maximum power in hitting the ball. In addition, keeping your eye on the ball will, by automatically controlling your footwork, help you get into the best position relative to the ball for proper execution of the stroke.

To keep your eye on the ball, watch it as it comes off your opponent's racket. Watch it hit the strings of your own racket. Then, for one full second, (except during a close exchange at the net), fasten your eye on the contact point, actually watching the spot where you hit the ball before letting yourself look up at your receding ball. Constantly doing these three things will automatically cause you to watch the ball longer and more consistently. You should remember that watching-the-ball-long-enough-and-doing-it-constantly is, unlike many other requirements of the game, not something mechanical that can ever be relegated to the subconscious. It must always be held foremost in the conscious mind, even by the champion.

Axiom II: Feet apart; get your weight forward.

Always assume a good waiting position so that your weight, when distributed as needed for maximum balance, will be in the most relaxed, most "ready" state prior to action.

With feet well apart—comfortably far apart—bend your knees but not your torso. This will automatically cause your weight to move forward off your heels and onto the balls of your feet, where you want it. Your straight torso will allow you to retain better balance.

Axiom III: Get your racket back as quickly and smoothly as possible by pivoting.

Synchronizing body-pivot and arm-movement, you should always get your racket back as quickly as possible so you won't have to rush or jerk during the forward stroke. Taking the racket back as smoothly as possible can establish and maintain necessary rhythm for good stroking. The quick and smooth backswing of your arm-and-racket (as one unit), with the synchronized pivoting of your body, will help still further by acting to automatically pull back your body weight, thus insuring the correct distribution of your weight for the start of your forward swing.

Hold your racket in front of you (not too far out) so that it points at the net. Allow your hitting arm to relax at your side so that your elbow rests on, or close to, your hip. Then, as you step in an across-the-body direction, allowing the back foot to pivot, your step which is both sideways and forward will automatically cause your hip to turn. This turning of your hip will cause your hitting arm and racket to go back. This is the faster, easy-to-copy Rosewall method vs. the time-consuming and more tiring loop of a Laver. The former method employs the body much more than the arm as though the arm were an integral part of the body and the arm's very movement dependent upon the turning of the hip. Who in the world, except a Laver or an Okker, has fast enough reflexes to constantly employ the looping backswing or even a modification of this and still get the racket back in time? Yet our beginners and our intermediates are attempting it by the thousands, God help them. (Or maybe we should.)

Axiom IV: Keep your wrist locked.

If you're a beginner or an intermediate or, in many cases,

Synchronizing body-pivot and arm-movement results in a smooth, fast method of getting the racket back.

A locked wrist helps put crispness into groundstrokes and volleys. Racket face stays perpendicular to ground.

Natural follow-through insures "hitting through" the ball, imparting topspin and power to your shot.

even a tournament player, you should always keep your wrist locked for both groundstrokes and volleys. Then you will be less apt to upset your timing of the hit, you will put more authority (crispness) into each hit, and you will find that, since body-weight transfers more readily through a firm, locked wrist, much more of your weight will go into each shot.

Throughout the backswing and the forward swing, during contact with the ball and, finally, in the follow-through, keep your racket face at a right angle to the ground. At the same time, after making sure your elbow is tucked well into your body, keep your racket in line with your hitting arm just as though it were an extension of the arm. Constant observance of these two rules will automatically cause your wrist to be locked and stay locked.

Axiom V: Get your body weight into the shot.
Always transfer your weight so that, as you hit each shot, your forward-moving weight, and not your less dependable arm, will be what produces the power and smoothness for the shot. Arm gyrations are more wearing on your energy than are "body leanings."

As your racket makes the backswing (with the turning of the hip), let your weight rest (for an instant) on the back foot (back knee well-bent) and, at the same time, extend—really stretch—your left arm (if you are a right-hander) out in front of you so it's pointing a little to your right. This is the moment of the completed backswing. Now both arms should be about in line with one another. Next, as you bring your racket forward to meet the ball, a further stretching forward of your left arm will automatically cause you to pull your body weight into the shot. (Incidentally, as an added bonus, your left arm, when extended, will help you retain better balance and will automatically cause you to rotate both shoulders instead of only your right shoulder. Finally, your extended left arm, revolving slower than your right arm, will be at a point close to your racket at the end of your follow-through and will allow you to quickly take the weight of the racket in your left hand, relieving the strained muscles of your right hand and wrist.)

Axiom VI: Be sure to follow through.
Once you have hit the ball, if you always allow your racket to continue under its own momentum by never checking it in its forward and upward path, you will automatically impart to the ball a greater degree of topspin, putting the ball into the desired arc for better control and placement. By allowing your racket to continue on its natural path for the follow-through you will be "hitting through" the ball, putting more power into your shot.

Pick a spot such as the top corner of the fence (good for the forehand drive), then, after contacting the ball, allow your racket to move forward and upward so that the racket head traces a straight trajectory that ends at your own head level and also ends pointing at your pre-selected spot on the fence. This movement of your racket, when accompanied by your straightening hitting-arm, will cause you to follow-through as you should. A good follow-through is essential for pace, spin and control. At completion of the stroke, if you freeze like a statue it will allow you to check yourself for straightness, racket angle and racket direction. This visual check will help you to judge and correct your own errors and expedite your own progress. ●

Tips On Winning Matches

IF YOU HAVE equal or better stroke equipment than your opponent and if you are as fast on your feet, why do you lose? Assuming that you have the same stamina and can hit every shot approximately as well but you still get beaten, your weakness is match play. If your strokes are worse and you beat so-called "better" players, then you *are* a winner and you could probably write this article better than I.

Player A on the WCT Tour says he is hitting the ball extremely well but cannot win a match. He often takes the first set but he almost never wins the second and third. His problem is that, when the situation gets critical, he tightens up and plays Dumb Tennis. He starts to drop shot, not because it is the proper shot but because he has choked. He goes for the winner three times in a row and is suddenly down 0-40. He comes in on Rosewall's backhand. His first serve hasn't gone in on his last two service games, and he isn't even aware of his zero percentage. He has lost his groove because he feels the pressure and has consequently lost his head.

Regaining one's composure is achieved by players in many different ways. Billie Jean King stares at the ball so that she will watch only it and not her opponent. Pancho Gonzales shouts and blows off steam. Ken Rosewall hangs his head—and thinks. Margaret Court towels off deliberately on the odd games, regaining her poise and composure. Player X looks up at his wife for confidence, Player Y at his teammate, Player Z at his coach. Each is trying to achieve that equilibrium that will prevent him or her from pressing, blowing or forgetting to think. Analyze and work out a winning strategy.

The ideas below may help you when you are losing a match that you could win. Some are for mental stability, some to regain lost control and some to establish a battle plan.

The Tournament Player

• Never "count the crowd." That's the promoter's job. Your eyes and attention should be on the court.

• Look at the ball, not your opponent. Watch the ball as it

leaves your opponent's fingers on the service toss and see it come over the net. You will find that you prepare your stroke far more unhurriedly and, as a result, you will be less pressed. Watch the ball in every exchange; when your opponent comes to net, you see only the ball and you will be far cooler on a passing shot or lob.

• If you find yourself nervous at a critical point, play the ball (its spins and its pace) rather than the opponent. Never let the ball play you (it means you are not getting ready soon enough) and never let your opponent play you (it means you are thinking about the opposition, which is a distraction, rather than the action of the ball).

• If you are getting wiped off the court and are not even in the match, calm down and collect your thoughts at the change-over. Take the full 60 seconds allotted on the odd games to analyze what is happening. Are you getting to the ball too late? If his backhand is coming in a ton, is there any way of breaking up his timing with chips or loopers? Are you lobbing often enough or high enough? Are all your first serves going in and are you thinking about direction and spin on each of your serves? Can you change the pace of the match by slices or sidespins or topspins? What spins or what tactics is he using? When he comes to net, are you always going for the down-the-line or always for the crosscourt? Is he mixing up his serves and can you antici- pate them? If he is hitting very hard, can you shorten your backswing? Are you half-volleying too many balls, which means you are constantly trapped by deep balls? Will you have a better chance if you play back one step farther? Will a forehand sidespin return of serve offer him any problems? Are you trying drop shots when you are too far back? Have you forgotten to try drop shots when the right opportunity presents itself? Does he have you on a yo-yo and can you get off by changing your pattern of play? If your timing is bad, is it because you are not moving your feet or are taking your backswing too late or are not watching the ball or are thinking about the point you lost two games ago or because you think the crowd is against you? Are you concentrating like mad on every point? If your strokes are off, can you go back to fundamentals, eliminating all the extras, to get back your "feel?"

The Intermediate (Slugger)

Although the above should be read by intermediates and beginners, the latter have problems that are very different. Mr. Intermediate loses a "friendly" match to Ms. Inter- mediate, and he cannot understand it because he knows he is the better player. But is he? He thinks he is because he can hit such a hard ball that she almost never returns it. His problem: his hard balls seldom go in, and when they do they are without accurate direction.

Mr. Intermediate's problem is ball control. His motion is so swift on the stroke that he must connect at exactly the right fraction of a second or the ball will career wildly into the fence or the bottom of the net. He is concentrating so much on power that he has forgotten balance and footwork. The wrist quickly turns over in all his strokes; he does not know how to keep the wrist flat and motionless through at least 12 inches (preferably longer) of the hit. When the wrist approaches the ball in steady fashion (without turn-

ing over), the face of the racket will "stay" on the ball for a good 12 inches. Then, if Mr. "I" should mis-time the ball, the wrist still has not turned and he can make a good shot.

Before Mr. "I" makes winners, he has to get the ball back regularly, with proper depth and proper direction. Why hit a ball hard when you don't know where the hell it is going?

Mr. "I's" strategy must be different from that of the tour- nament player. It is not recommended that he try drop shots or side spins because he still does not have ball control on basic drives. However, he, too, can learn winning tennis, and many of the shots suggested to the tournament player will be applicable to him. He, too, must watch only the ball, play the ball rather than the opponent and attempt to in- terpret what the opponent's ball is doing. The difference is in his riposte.

Mr. "I," like the tournament player, should try to get ready early, consider the value of the lob and, in his own way, change pace or direction *while still looking only at the ball*. Mr. "I" double faults a lot ("Here, opponent, I want you to have this point"), throws in cannon-ball serves that almost never go in and pats or pushes in his second serve. Mr. "I" has the big return of serve—whop, boom, zoom ("Out!"). He must temper his passion for hitting winners with the thought that this causes him to lose to losers. Basi- cally he must learn to keep the racket face on the ball for as long as possible, to acquire some steadiness and to learn direction and then sharp angle. He is a player without finesse. He loses his cool constantly; even when he has the set-up, he gives it such an enormous wallop that it could land anywhere. His thoughts should be as follows:

• Losers serve double-faults.

• Losers have cannon-ball first serves and pat-ball sec- ond serves.

• Winners will only miss two or three returns of serve a set against other intermediates.

• Winners can consistently play the opponent's back- hand.

• Champions *never* miss a set-up (they need not neces- sarily hit the ball 125 mph).

• Losers come to net without adequate preparation (or adequate overheads).

• Winners in the intermediate level can hit forehand crosscourts and backhand crosscourts all day long; they only try the down-the-line when the return is short or when they absolutely know the down-the-line will go in.

• Winners play percentage tennis, making the most of their own strengths and the most of their opponent's weak- nesses. If the winner has a weak backhand he plays it only as a steady shot; if the winner gets a short shot to his back- hand that he can run around, he takes it on his forehand.

• Winners keep track of their own losers, not their win- ners. A real winner knows how many backhand returns of serve he has missed after a match. There won't be very many because, if his backhand return is failing him, he will lob or loop or even kick the ball back in.

• Winners know that even if they miss two or three vol- leys in a row, it is still not necessary to stay in the backcourt every point. However, after losing three games by coming in and getting passed, the winner will change his strategy.

• The winner would rather win than look good; the loser would rather hit hard than win.

The Intermediate (Pooper)

Ms. Intermediate depends solely on steadiness and perhaps some depth to win for her. She is at a level where she can acquire some additional skills, particularly ball control and a little more power. While Mr. "I" is knocking balls all over the arena, Ms. "I" is pooping them in the air. This in itself is good strategy against most other intermediates. If she can also run down balls well, she will win many matches. But she will win many more if she can retain her steadiness while adding to her game a drop shot, a punch volley, the angle shots and a reasonably hard putaway shot on a set-up (a short, high ball).

The Beginner

Winning strategy for beginners is also possible, even though they are still learning form, footwork and balance. They still can work on concentration and watching the ball. They should read the above tactics for advanced and intermediate players so that they will know the direction in which they are heading. Because they are still working on strokes, their guidelines are slightly different. Their "strategy" takes second place to improving their form, but it is never too early to think about tactics. Their basics are:

• Watch the ball and prepare early.
• Take the proper backswing and follow-through.
• Maintain balance.
• Keep the strings of the racket on the ball as long as possible.
• Hit the ball in *front* of the body whenever possible.
• Use the crosscourt as your basic shot. If your crosscourts are going wide, aim toward the center of the court.
• Allow a 10 foot margin in hitting the ball over the net so it will go deep (if you skim the net, the ball will go short).
• Make adjustments in timing to compensate for errors, viz.,if your forehands are going wide to *your* right (the opponent's backhand), you are hitting too late, and if your forehands are going wide to your left (the opponent's forehand), you are hitting too early.
• If the opponent hits a deep shot, step or run back at once so that you will still hit the ball at waist-level. (If you don't step back, you will have to half-volley the shot and your chances of error are extreme.)
• If your balls are sailing (hitting the fence), either your wrist has stopped at the moment of impact or you have opened the face of the racket so that it is tilted skyward. If your balls are hitting the net, make sure you get under the ball and your follow-through ends high.
• As soon as you have acquired some ball control, hit to your opponent's weakness, which will generally be his or her backhand. Sometimes, however, it is better to play your own strength than your opponent's weakness: if you have a very good forehand crosscourt, playing this shot (even if it is to your opponent's strength) may be your best ploy.
• Winning factors are steadiness, depth and control. Steadiness means always returning the ball, depth means the area close to the baseline (two or three feet) and control means the ability to put the ball deep to the backhand or to the forehand. After you have accomplished the first, work on the second and then the third. ●

Improving Your Tennis Brain

by JULIE M. HELDMAN

WHAT KIND of tennis book do you want? A pretty book on the coffee table for guests to flip through casually? A simplified teaching manual which tells you where to stand but doesn't explain why? If your answer is yes, don't read this review because I am writing about the books of C.M. (Jimmy) Jones, which are difficult and challenge your thinking. They can't be easy because tennis is a complex sport, and Mr. Jones wants to teach everyone to be a great player.

Professor Jones is really giving a course in "The Complete Champion," starting his students with the basics of stroke production and tactics, taking them through training, practice programs and studies of the psychological make-up of champions, and then showing them how to come through under pressure.

Jimmy Jones passionately believes in the theories he has evolved for the scientific instruction of tennis. Although he never received proper coaching and guidance, he became one of England's top players in the 1930s, representing his country in Davis Cup after Fred Perry turned pro. He developed his theories as a player, then expanded them by watching others in big matches. He supplemented his observations with numerous studies undertaken in conjunction with his magazine, *Lawn Tennis* (formerly known as *British Lawn Tennis*).

OK, you say, this guy has a lot of theories. What has he done which should make me want to read his book? For a start, he took a struggling young girl named Angela Buxton who had just lost badly in the first round of Bournemouth and guided her to the singles finals at Wimbledon three years later. He has been the friendly uncle of all players who come to England, eager to advise anyone who asks him to fix a stroke or to develop tactics to beat an opponent who has a difficult style. Jimmy does not believe in obvious answers unless they win tennis matches. He believes in adapting the style you have evolved on the practice court to the crisis at hand. "Never change a winning game" is an adage which falls apart when your lead starts to erode as your opponent creeps up from 2-5 down. "Wrong theory,"

says Jimmy. "Intensify a winning game." After you have reached a winning position, use the same tactics you did before but double your efforts. If you are attacking, concentrate on taking the ball after the bounce. If you are defending, make sure you give your opponent nothing to hit.

If you are playing well but serving badly and your opponent keeps coming to net against you, don't try to serve harder. Instead direct your serve toward the alleys so that if your opponent has enough guts to come in, he or she will have to leave a lot of open court. This must be a good tactic: Bobby Riggs used it against Margaret Court. If you are hitting good passing shots and your opponent has such a great reach that he seems to have glue on his strings, hit right at the opponent. If your opponent can lob you to death, what do you do? Stand on the baseline lobbing back? Hit overheads after the ball has bounced? No, says the Professor. Take advantage of your knowledge of geometry. Move forward, take the ball on the fly and move to the net. You will give yourself a better angle to hit the ball, give your opponent less time and you will break his rhythm.

Jimmy gave inspired advice to a friend in England a few years back. Gerald Oakley was playing a top Englishman who was slow to warm up but strong and accurate once he found his rhythm. The Professor told Oakley to abandon his natural attacking game and instead use soft ball tactics during the first set to mix up the opponent. No matter what the outcome of that set, Oakley was told to attack at full force for the rest of the match. Oakley won 9-7, 6-2, 6-1 against an opponent he had never previously beaten.

Jimmy's first two books, *Tennis: How to Become a Champion* and *Match-Winning Tennis,* constantly give me new enthusiasm to go on the court and try some improvement. I carry them with me on the Virginia Slims Pro Tour. From his pages, and from the Professor, I have learned how to practice properly. If you want to improve, don't stand in one spot on the practice court, bashing forehands at an equally motionless opponent. The best way to learn is to have short spurts of deep concentration. Tennis is a game of motion; you should learn to hit strokes as you are moving

towards the ball. Practice "chess board" or "pattern" tennis. If you want to learn to come in down the line on your forehand, have two people standing on the other side of the court feeding you forehands. To one you hit sharp crosscourt and to the other you hit down the line, following the ball to the net. Do this five or ten minutes at most before changing.

Through careful reading you will fill your day with a new kind of challenge that may make you a champion. Watch your opponent carefully. Figure out how many forehands go crosscourt and how many down the line. Where does he or she hit the overhead and when does he or she dropshot? Once you know, you can choose your tactics. You have to be fit to use the tactical ploys Mr. Jones describes. He even tells you the best exercises to get into shape. And what to do to play better doubles, how to have the right attitude and how to take care of your equipment.

C. M. Jones' newest book, *Improving Your Tennis,* is for the younger player who wants to learn the game and then improve his strokes. Each chapter has check points at the end so you can discover what you are doing wrong. In the chapter on serve there is a check list of eight items to go through when your serve is going into the net and another seven if you are hitting too long. There are drawings of how to hit the ball and drawings covered with huge circles and X-marks of how not to hit. it. As always, Mr. Jones is intrigued with "the intangibles," and in this book he devotes a chapter to the attitudes of players. Did you know that almost all top players like being nervous before a big match? That when someone hits a great shot against Pancho Gonzalez, he acknowledges to himself that it was good and then determines that he will hit a better one the next point?

Read these books if you want to learn the game of tennis—or even if you want to know what is happening when you watch tennis on TV. Don't be scared off by the scientific details and don't skim. Learn not only "how to" but "why to." ●

Mike and Flo— Hero and Heroine Of the Highchair.

by BUD COLLINS

THE VOICE AND THE VISE. You'd know them anywhere, from the sound and the sight…the timbre and the touch…the gravel and the grip…co-piloting a match in the chair and at the post…roommates…courtmates…playmates…helpmates: Mike and Flo. Winslow Blanchard II and Marie Florence Hermine Letendre Blanchard. Could you operate a tennis tournament without them? Maybe…but not as well.

But in the beginning were the words—like "fifteen-thirty"—spoken by The Voice from on high, from the pinnacle, the green highchair, the seat of judgment for the court crier. And at first, decibels were more in demand than wisdom or presence: "They wanted guys with loud voices," says Mike Blanchard, who is in his fifth decade of umpiring. "This was in '31 or '32 that I got started. Longwood Cricket Club in Boston, the National Doubles. It was before they used microphones, and they wanted somebody that could be heard all over the place. Dave Niles, the referee and a top umpire in his day, said, 'You've got the kind of voice we need. You can see. Why don't you help us out?' I was a tennis nut, no more than I am today, and I took my vacation and worked Longwood. Started out like everybody else, on a line, on a very outside court." At the time Blanchard was a paint salesman for Sherwin-Williams (the same company, I understand, that supplies Bobby Riggs' hair coloring). Eventually he became the best-known umpire in the business, through longevity and television, the voice so distinctive and identifiable, flowing from your screen—deep, slight rasp, authoritative yet understanding: "…Advantage Newcombe." The best umpire? Perhaps. Perhaps not. Certainly a cardinal if not the pope. There are numerous superior umpires (though not enough to go around), but in going around, and being thoroughly professional in an essentially amateur avocation, Mike works most and is esteemed highest by the players.

He is The Voice.

After The Voice came The Vise. "Hardly knew a thing about tennis until I met Mike 27 years ago. I'd never even," laughs Flo, the best-known net judge, "picked up a racket. I was 30 before I got onto a court." Yet she became a teaching pro, attained a national ranking among the seniors, was a quarter-finalist in the maturebroads' Nationals twice. Only a *Kamikaze* serves to her backhand more than once. Her hands—ambidextrous, she grasps the net cord with either—have been seen (via television) by millions, the most famous on the tube since the cameras focused on the nefarious mitts of racketeer (no pun) Frank Costello during the Senate hearings on organized crime in 1951.

Florence's hands are sexier than Frank's, and more just. But she does go about her business with the sensitivity of a hired strangler. Detecting the tick of ball on tape, the slightest brush of fuzz against cord, she reputedly has the finest digital perception since the exhalted Hall of Fame net judge C. Niles (Fingers) Fortescue (see "Hail and Farewell to the Softest Touch in Tennis " elsewhere in this book), one of her preceptors.

Unlike the late Mr. Fortescue, Flo doesn't confine herself to the post and the cord. Also, due to TV, she sits as the most celebrated female umpire, but, like Mike, she pays her dues in relative obscurity on the lines as well. She and Mike worked face-to-face a few months ago in the cathedral, Centre Court Wimbledon, at opposite ends of a sideline. That is as far as a woman can go in her field. Although Mike was granted a chair in Centre for the Izzy El Shafei-Jurgen Fassbender second rounder (the third American in a quarter-century to be accorded such divine trust), the best Florence, or any other woman, can hope for is a line. No net cord. Heavens, no chair! "We are not quite ready for a woman in those positions on Centre," referee Mike Gibson consoled Ms. Blanchard.

Absurd, assuredly. Still, she was not miffed. "I'm not a women's libber," says Flo during a peppy morning doubles, prior to working the First National Bank Classic at Louisville. "I'd just as soon my male partner served looking into the sun and played the backhand court."

"But I am for treating them just like men," says Mike, butting into the conversation—and the point—and ungallantly drop-shotting Flo to break her serve.

Florence learned a long time ago that she'd be better off slaving over a hot tennis court than a hot stove if she wanted to see much of her husband. Love me, love my dodge—that was the outlook of Mike Blanchard, who quit working and got into tennis as fast as he could find a way to make a living therein. The way was as a sporting goods rep with Wilson, then Spalding, making the tournament rounds, dealing and officiating…next as a teaching pro at the Paradise Valley Country Club at Scottsdale, Arizona…now with Wilson again as roving ambassador of helpful goodwill, along with aide de court Flo, calling lines, scores, refereeing (at the U.S. Open among other outposts), befriending the athletes, soothing brouhahas, remarkably calm and agreeable through the long days and nights.

At 67 Blanchard is still a high-grade hacker, issuing a bitchy sliced serve from his right armpit, warmed by the memory of cold winter evenings within the Longwood Covered Courts where he and Lois Felix won the National Indoor Mixed Doubles title of 1954. "Of course I made the draw for that tournament, and selected the best woman for

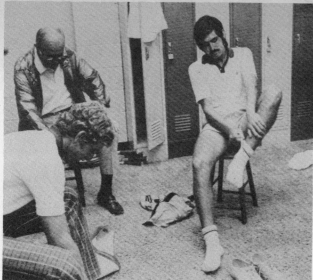

Russ Adams

Herbert S. Workman

RIGHT: The Voice, Mike Blanchard, is in the chair while wife Flo, The Vise, calls on the most sensitive hands since Fingers Fortescue as net judge. ABOVE: Mike talks with Mexico's Raul Ramirez, right, after a court incident at the National Clay Courts in which Ilie Nastase was defaulted for cussing an umpire during a match with Ramirez. Blanchard's excellent relationship with the players helps make him one of the international circuit's most respected officials. Brian Gottfried is in the left foreground.

my partner," Mike grins. He may not be able to count past 40, but he's no dummy. Flo is more at ease in the role of dummy: an exceptional bridge player, she is merely 21 red points away from the big league classification of Life Master. Bridge used to be a big game on the tennis circuit; now it's backgammon. "That's understandable," she says. "Two people, and you've got a game. You need four for bridge. On all the plane trips, backgammon is a simple proposition."

They prefer to drive between tournaments if practical. It's a little more civilized and relaxed than flying, from which the glamour and chic flew long ago. Travel... travel...travel...over the years the Blanchards have put in more time on the road than Henry Kissinger or Kenny Rosewall. They sit in a Ramada room amidst open suitcases, expense account data, tennis clothing, newspapers. It is get-away day in Louisville—next stop Indianapolis for the National Clay. Only a two-hour drive, one of the simpler movements.

"The thing is," Mike is saying, "I'd be doing this even if I were a millionaire. I'd still be going to tournaments, umpiring, watching, helping out. I like to be around tennis, the players. Some things I don't like as much as I used to—the splitting up of the men and women, for instance. I enjoy watching the women as much as the men." (Mike isn't deprived of women since he is on Virginia Slims and USLTA payrolls as well as Wilson, and serves time on the women's circuit.) "But I liked it better when everybody was together. It was more like a family. But the thing is, I'm a tennis nut, a hopeless tennis nut."

"Boy," grins his pert, auburn-haired Flo, "is he ever hopeless. Any kind of tennis. We'll go up to the Wentworth," (a summer resort hotel at Portsmouth, N.H.) "and I'll find Mike on the porch watching the seniors. Not

just the good seniors like (Chauncey) Steele, (Don) Manchester or (Bill) Power, but any seniors. The real hackers. He just can't get enough tennis."

That, of course, is lucky for tennis. Rod Laver says, "One trouble with our game is that by and large the people umpiring and calling the lines do it maybe once a year, when a tournament comes to their town. They try, but they're amateurs put briefly into a professional situation, and something is always going wrong. But you see Mike and Flo—they've been working my matches since I first came away to America in 1956, when I was a junior—and you know they know what they're doing. Sure, they make mistakes. Everybody does. But you know they're in the game like we are on a regular basis, and that you're getting the best, not just a part-time effort. A big tournament without them around seems strange."

Laver is easy to get along with. He seldom queries a call. Others—Ilie Nastase, Bob Hewitt, Patti Hogan to name three—can be, shall we say, more difficult. But the Blanchards seem to be soothing balm on them. "Oh, Ilie acts up when I'm in the chair. That's his nature. But I can usually calm him down," says Mike. "Not that awful time at Salisbury last year though, at the National Indoor Open when he tanked against Brian Gottfried. He was provoked about a call.He was hitting serves and returns at linesmen. Totally lost his head. He was heavily fined. But Ilie can be a very sweet guy. In '72, after he beat Arthur Ashe in five sets to win the Open at Forest Hills, he was very cooperative about going right back on court to play mixed, even though he thought he'd done enough for the day.

"The worst blowup I ever had was from a normally placid guy, the Swede, Sven Davidson, at Forest Hills. I'd say this was '57, a semi-final against Mal Anderson. Anyway it was the year a rule change by the ILTF had just gone through concerning an umpire's judgment on a linesman changing a call—whether there should be a let.

"The Aussie sliced a serve wide to Davidson's forehand, one that was way out of his reach. A fault was called, and then the linesman switched his call to good. Normally— before that new rule—you would have played a let. But the rule said that in a case like this, if in the umpire's judgment the receiver had no chance to play the ball, then it was an ace. So I called the point for Anderson. Davidson went wild. 'Let! It must be a let!' he kept screaming. This was a very tight match, and he obviously felt he'd been wronged, that I'd made a mistake. I tried to explain that it was a recent ruling, and that we'd posted it in the dressing room. But he kept raving. Sven prided himself on knowing the rules, and surely they wouldn't make such a change without notifying the players personally.

"It took a long time to get him settled down, but I don't think he could accept it, particularly since he lost the match. Of course, few players, if any, know the rules thoroughly."

I've respected Mike Blanchard for years; but it was another decision, on a serve, that made me aware how sharp he is. It involved one of the great gamesmen, Gardnar Mulloy, during the 1957 National Doubles at Longwood. Mulloy,then 43, and Patty, 33, had the month before been the oldest winners of the Wimbledon doubles, but here they were being hassled by a couple of kids, Mike Franks and Mike Green. When Franks received serve in the right court, Green jiggled at the net, and kept edging toward the center line, hoping to distract the server. Mulloy didn't like it. "You're crowding me boy, stop it," Gar advised Green once when they changed courts.

"I knew something was going to happen," Blanchard laughs. "Mulloy is going to serve, and Green keeps moving around, practically at the center of the court."

"Cut it out!" I recall Mulloy shouting at Green, who would not desist.

Then—Pow! Right in the kisser! as Jackie Gleason used to threaten. Incredibly, Mulloy served a shot that caught Green between his blinking eyes.

Unblinking, Blanchard in the chair rumbled, "Service ace..." before uttering the score.

Ace? Indeed. Extraordinary spleen and accuracy had earned Mulloy an ace because Green's head interfered with the flight of the ball, even though, had he been alert enough to duck, the ball would have sailed long and well wide of the service court. Blanchard knew the rule, responded immediately, remarking today, "I've never seen it before or since. That was losing the point the hard way for Green, but he behaved after that."

"Mulloy," says Blanchard, "was involved in so many incidents. I was in the chair on the grandstand court at Forest Hills when he psyched Kenny Rosewall out of a match. I believe it was Rosewall's first trip to the United States, and it was the semis." (Correct, 1952.) "Mulloy must have seemed pretty ancient to Rosewall, but he never stopped to rest on the change games. It was five sets, and he kept right on walking, saying to Rosewall, 'Come on, kid, can't you take it? Let's go.' That finally got to Kenny.

"Then there was a time in Florida—I wasn't there— when Mulloy's opponent in an early round was footfaulting. Mulloy called for the referee, who poohpoohed it, saying 'Come on, Gar, we don't call foot-faults this early.' So what does Mulloy do? His next serve, he stands on the service line, saying if foot-faults are allowed he might as well join in. They got the message fast, and a foot-fault judge was sent to Mulloy's court."

You can tell, as Mike talks, he's fond of the geezer, Gar. But then, he likes most of the players and the feeling is reciprocated. "Yes, you'd like to see a certain guy or gal win a match you're on. You have favorites, but it doesn't affect your judgment. It can't. You're doing your job, they're doing theirs. Of course," Mike laughs, "you root for the person who wins the first set. When you do so many matches, you tend to want some quickies. But you know your rooting doesn't do a damn bit of good, and again, it doesn't affect your discipline. After all, you have as much pride in your work as the players.

"Some long matches are beauties and you get caught up in them.

"Like the Laver-Rosewall five-set WCT Final of 1972. This was a championship watched by more people than any before, and many think it was the greatest of all-time, with Kenny winning by two points. You'll never see one better. It was a pleasure to work it."

Flo seconds him, then scowls, "But some matches aren't a pleasure. Like that one you assigned me to at the Buckeye Open outside of Columbus a couple of years ago. I suspect you and Bill Macassin (the assistant referee) set me up, wanting to see what would happen. It was a doubles— Pancho Gonzalez and Jimmy Connors against Bob Hewitt and Andy Pattison—which, as you can see, had possibilities of not being too placid. Hewitt and Gonzalez were growling at each other all the way, and finally when Pancho had his back turned, between points, Hewitt tapped a ball at him that hit him. Nothing serious, except that they were both ready to explode. Much X-rated language. I thought this was it, so I summoned up my strongest, deepest voice—'Gentlemen (and I was using the word loosely), shall we play tennis?' They both looked up at me surprised, and they were lambs the rest of the way."

Flo cites Gonzalez as "one of those players who can blow up without letting it affect his game. Billie Jean (King) is another. She'll make an awful fuss over a call, but it's show.

She gets right back to business. But Patti Hogan or Nastase can be wrecked by a call, unable sometimes to overcome temper. By being around these kids all the time, you gain their confidence, and you can sort of give them a look and a couple of words and get them back in the right mood.

"But it works both ways. You'll get a piercing look from one you know well, and that lets you know you've blown one."

"Well," says Mike, "we all blow calls. We're not machines. Someday we'll be replaced by machines."

Mike was easily replaced at school, he remembers, when his family settled in Boston after living in the Midwest. He has the poise and aplomb of a Bostonian who went to all the right schools, though the accent isn't there (no "thutty-fawty"). "Well, I was thrown out of a couple of the right schools, Chauncy Hall and Brown & Nichols. One reason or another. So I never got to college, or even out of prep school. I went to work selling paint. And I was playing any tournament I could find in New England."

Currently the Blanchards are caught up in The Great Ball War. They work only where Wilson balls are used, which, until recently, was nearly universal in the U.S. But Spalding cut in on the market by contracting with the Association of Tennis Pros and the Women's Tennis Association for their events. "Wilson has always been a leader in the field. When I started out, old L.B. Icely, who headed the firm, came up with the idea of autograph-model rackets. Ellsworth Vines, Eleanor Tenant, then Alice Marble were the first. They were a tremendous hit. Other companies followed. Now the competition is heavier than ever with so much money being spent on equipment. You can't blame Spalding for making a new, big effort." No one is more conversant than they on the chaotic subject of tennis politics. But the Blanchards are above it. Thankfully, and unlike so many frantic people on the circuit, they don't regard the politics as something on par with the Middle East or the quality of life in South America.

The quality of life on the circuit has changed considerably. "It's a business, not a game any more," says Mike, not bitterly. "You recognize that and it's still fun. Not as much fun as in the Thirties and Forties when there was a party every night, and very few were playing the game for a living. Frank Shields would show up in time for his matches at Newport still wearing his tuxedo. The tennis, obviously, is better now. Many more good players. Back when I started, if it was a clay court tournament you knew Frankie Parker would win. On a fast surface it would be Don Budge. The game was too formful. Not now. With all the talent and travel and money pressure there's a different winner every week. That's good for the game."

Also good for the game are the Ad Couple, Flo and Mike. That was apparent long ago. Never more apparent, maybe, than at Forest Hills when Mike was assigned to umpire the matches of the Pole, Jadwiga Jedrzejowska, who was runner-up to Pauline Betz in 1942. "I was the only one who could pronounce her name," Mike grins. "I think it was yen-jay-hoffska. I was nervous as hell about it. I'd practice it over and over before I went to the court. But I was never more nervous than on Centre Court in July. They have a different style in England. You don't repeat the linesmen's calls...you have to keep on your toes."

Flo and Mike will stay on their toes, and hang on as long as they can climb the highchair or clutch the cord. "It's a vacation, really, but I suppose we'll retire someday to our place at the Wickenburg (Ariz.) Inn and Tennis Ranch," says Flo.

Mike repeats, "Like I said, we'll be made obsolete by a machine. If you can get a man to the moon, you can come up with a machine to call the lines, maybe even umpire. I hope I'm around to watch when some player blows his stack over a call, but there's nobody to gripe at...and somebody in the audience yells, 'Tell it to the machine, buster!'" ●

"Are you sure we have to try to hit the balls *through* the net?"

by JULIUS HELDMAN

A NEW LOOK AT THE FOREHAND

THE CLASSICAL tennis instruction books always started out with what was considered the basic stroke of the game—the forehand—and taught the Eastern grip as the only proper grip, or at least the preferred grip. The description was "shaking hands with the racket" and the illustration was like the sketch in Figure 1. There followed a discussion of how far from the end of the handle to hold the racket (the grip in Fig. 1 is slightly "choked", i.e., the butt of the palm is not at the end of the handle) and how much to spread the fingers (the slight spread shown in Fig. 1 is average for good players, providing some assistance in keeping a firm wrist compared with the grip with all fingers together).

I have always had trouble with the concept of "shaking hands with the racket." There are differences in hand-shaking styles. When beginners are told to shake hands, some grip the racket with the Eastern grip but just as many choose Australian or Continental, which I am coming to. My own hand-shaking style is pretty close to the Continental grip. And what do you do about people who have a dead fish handshake?

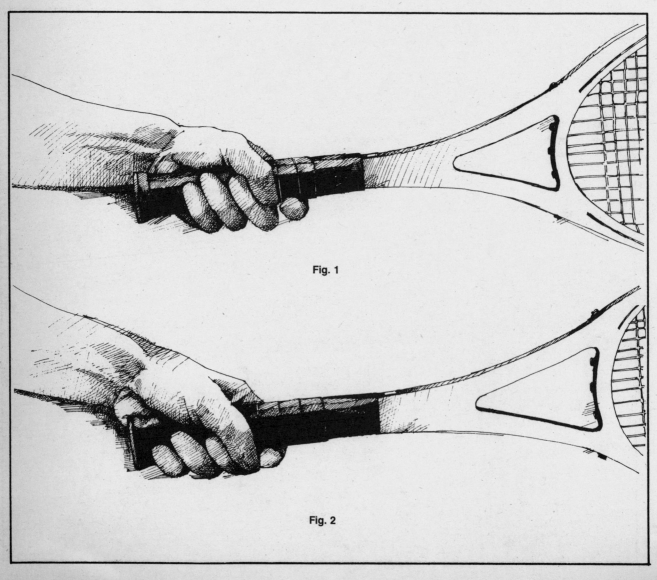

Fig. 1

Fig. 2

The least ambiguous description of the Eastern grip refers to placement of the butt of the palm. Put it against the wide back side of the handle (which is in a plane parallel to the racket face), grasp the handle as shown in Fig. 1, and you have the Eastern grip.

Tennis teaching and theories change. There is a school of thought today which holds that the forehand has to be learned somewhere along the line. With the very large number of good players who are now using a grip which is clearly not "Eastern", it's tough to rationalize a dogmatic insistence on it. There is even less to be said for changing an existing grip over to the strict Eastern. The un-learning and re-learning processes are doubly difficult and rarely if ever justified. What I want to do here is describe the grip and stroke which a great number of good players develop naturally, many with little or no instruction. If you have a forehand anywhere like it in grip and action, don't let anybody talk you into trying to change.

There are various names to describe the in-between forehand grip so many players use. It came to full recognition with the post-war (WW II) influx of Australians, al-most all of whom used it or some close variant, so let's call it the Australian grip. It is illustrated in Figure 2. The butt of the palm is on the narrow diagonal plane of the handle, one-eighth of a turn from the wide back face. It is comfortable and secure for many players, perhaps because in this position the "V" between thumb and forefinger is on the top of the handle (if you use a normal-size handle). No two players will grip the racket exactly alike, but any grip between the Eastern and Continental qualifies as Australian, or modified Eastern, or modified Continental—the same thing, really.

If the butt of the palm is on the top handle plane, the grip is Continental. This is the grip which can be used for all strokes and is probably the best for all except the forehand. Some Australian grips verge on the Continental, and I wouldn't change anybody who developed this style naturally, but the full Continental has limitations on high forehand drives, which the medium Australian overcomes.

By now you have realized that the grip sketches are those of a left-handed player. There are a number of good left-handed Aussies, and southpaws should have some instruc-

Fig. 3

Fig. 4

Fig. 5

Fig. 6

Fig. 7

tion aimed at them, too. If you want to use the illustrations for right-handed instruction, hold them up to a mirror.

Nothing is sacred about the exact details of any feature of the forehand shown in Figures 3 through 7, but taken as a whole they illustrate sound, clean, Australian forehand style. Actually, the stroke is a little more economical in its production than some of the full free-swinging Aussie wallops and is therefore probably more suitable as an example.

Begin with the ready position (Fig. 3). The racket is cradled, legs are spread, knees flexed, back slightly bent, weight on balls of feet, eyes on ball. As the flight of the ball is sighted, motion begins as in Fig. 4. The left shoulder comes back (opposite for right-handers) and the hip pivots as well, the weight shifts to the back foot and the backswing starts. Don't let anybody kid you; practically no one draws the racket back straight. Most players raise the racket head and many bend the elbow, holding the racket close to the body on the high backswing. I personally like the close-in backswing, which gives a feeling of control and also seems to be good for balance.

For a big swing, the racket continues back and up. For a normal, controlled swing, the racket is held as in Fig. 4 until it is ready to start forward as in Fig. 5. Other things happen at the same time. The right foot has stepped forward toward the ball and the racket head is coming down and forward as the elbow starts to straighten. But the shoulders and hips have not yet pivoted and the body weight has not yet come all the way forward.

Just before the ball is hit, Fig. 6, the shoulders are almost parallel to the net again, the hips have also started to pivot and the body weight is forward. This pivot and weight shift is responsible for the easy power of the stroke. At the same time, the elbow has straightened so that the shot will be hit with arm fully extended. The position of the wrist hardly changes during the stroke. This statement is fine for teaching, but in real tennis situations it is almost always necessary to make some wrist adjustment for direction control; also, wrist snap can give extra power at the expense of accuracy. The actual hit should be in front of the body, about parallel with the front foot, if the situation allows it.

Comparison of Fig. 6 with the follow-through, Fig. 7, indicates the easy, natural topspin which is imparted by swinging upward and just slightly turning the racket face over. The follow-through is fuller and freer than the backswing. If you restrict your follow-through, you may develop a jerky action with decreased power.

The preceding descriptions, except for the Australian grip rather than the Eastern, could easily have come from one of the standard teaching texts. The stroke is in fact a closed-stance rallying stroke from the baseline. There is a case to be made for the open-stance forehand, hit with both feet facing the baseline. When a lefty is moved to his left, he can save a step by ending on his left foot, *not* crossing over with his right, and swinging with an open stance. Fully one-third of the forehands hit in today's tournament game are open stance, illustrated in Fig. 8.

Finally, what happens when a low ball comes your way? Fig. 9 shows what to do. Bend, bend, bend more than you think you should, and especially spread your legs, wide, wide, wide and reach forward to hit the ball. Again, this is excellent advice for teaching a rallying stroke, and very pretty too, but forget that "splits" action if you are going to run forward to attack behind your shot. The concerted hit-and-run-to-net is a different, more advanced technique.●

Fig. 8

Fig. 9

A Century of Tennis

THE YEAR 1974 was the centennial of tennis (properly known as lawn tennis to distinguish it from the parent, real tennis or court tennis, an indoor racket, ball and net game dating to the middle ages). Although tennis had been played outdoors in Britain at several locations in the late 1860's and early 1870's, it was given the consequential push in 1874 by an Englishman, Major Walter Wingfield, who took out a patent on the game under the name Sphairistike (Greek for ball game). The name didn't catch on, but the game—as lawn tennis—did, and is now universal.

During a century of tennis, these are the significant happenings:

1874
Major Wingfield patents an outdoor game called Sphairistike, which, with a few changes in rules and court dimensions, will become lawn tennis, or simply, tennis. Mary Outerbridge of Staten Island, New York, having watched British soldiers playing the game in Bermuda, brings equipment home, introducing tennis to the U.S.

1875
A portion of the grounds of the All-England Croquet Club (founded in 1868) is set aside for tennis courts. Eventually the club will change its name to All-England Lawn Tennis and Croquet Club and become the most influential in the game as the site of the Wimbledon championships.

1876
America's first tennis club, the New Orleans Lawn Tennis Club is founded.

1877
Rules are pretty much standardized, and will remain essentially unchanged. The first Wimbledon championship is played, in July, and Spencer Gore is champion.

1879
May Langrishe wins the Irish title in Dublin, the first national event for women.

1880
The first tournament of note in America is staged at the Staten Island Cricket and Baseball Club, won by Englishman O.E. Woodhouse.

1881
Leading clubs in America form the U.S. National Lawn Tennis Association (later the National is dropped) to adopt uniform rules and govern the game in this country. A national championship tournament is played at Newport, R.I., won by Bostonian Dick Sears, a Harvard student, who will win every title through 1887, a record of seven straight never equalled.

1883
Philadelphians C.M. and S.J. Clarke, brothers, are first Americans to play Wimbledon. A women's tournament begins at Wimbledon, won by Maud Watson.

1887
Ellen Hansell wins the first U.S. women's singles championship, at Philadelphia.

1898
Leo Ware wins the first national indoor singles title in New York.

1900
Longwood Cricket Club in Boston is scene of first Davis Cup match, U.S. turning back the invaders from the British Isles, 3-0. Cup donor Dwight Davis, Malcolm Whitman and Holcombe Ward are U.S. team.

1903
Britain beats U.S., 4-1 at Longwood and Davis Cup leaves the country for first time. H. L. Doherty of British team is first alien to win U.S. singles.

1906
Californian May Sutton is the first American to win Wimbledon.

1907
Australasia (Norman Brookes of Australia and Tony Wilding of New Zealand) take the Davis Cup Down Under for the first time, ending 4-year British reign, 3-2, in London.

1908
First American expeditionary force to Australia (Beals Wright and Fred Alexander) in search of Davis Cup fails, losing 3-2 to Brookes and Wilding, at Melbourne. "At least we saw some kangaroos," says Alexander.

1909
Hazel Hotchkiss (later Mrs. Wightman) comes East from Berkeley to scandalize Philadelphia by winning the U.S. title in short-sleeved dress. Elbows are not to be seen, but she gets away with it, beginning a career decorated by a record 45 U.S. titles in various events.

1911
Bill Larned wins his fifth straight U.S. title and seventh altogether, equalling Dick Sears' total.

1912
The Californian Comet, Maurice McLoughlin smashes the East's monopoly on the men's title by winning at Newport. Britain breaks the Australasians' hold on the Davis Cup, then loses it to the Americans in 1913.

1913
A world-wide governing body, the International Lawn Tennis Federation, is formed.

1914
Elizabeth Ryan, an American, wins the first of her record 19 Wimbledon titles, all in doubles and mixed. On the eve of World War I, Brookes and Wilding regain the cup from the U.S., 3-2, at New York.

1915
After 34 years at Newport's Casino the national men's championships is moved to the West Side Tennis Club in the Forest Hills section of New York, the present location. Molla Bjurstedt (later Mrs. Mallory) wins the first of her record eight U.S. singles titles.

1918
Vinnie Richards, 15, allied with Bill Tilden, is the youngest to win a major title, the U.S. doubles.

1919
Suzanne Lenglen of France, perhaps the greatest female player, bursts onto the scene to take the first of a record five straight Wimbledon singles.

1920
Bill Tilden and Billy Johnston voyage to Australia to recapture the Davis Cup, 5-0, and start a 7-year streak of U.S. superiority, the longest hold on the cup by any nation. Tilden lifts the U.S. title from Johnston and settles in as the most dominant figure the game has known. It is his first of six straight titles and seven in all, equalling the record total of Dick Sears and Bill Larned.

1923

The inaugural Wightman Cup match between British and American women opens the 14,000 seat stadium at Forest Hills, the largest tennis arena in this country. Donor Hazel Hotchkiss Wightman plays doubles and captains the U.S. women to a 7-0 victory.

1926

Henri Cochet snaps Bill Tilden's Forest Hills winning streak at six titles and 42 matches in the quarters, heralding an era of French supremacy by becoming the first European to wear the U.S. crown. Professional tennis begins as Suzanne Lenglen, Mary K. Brown, Vinnie Richards, Howard Kinsey, Harvey Snodgrass and Paul Feret sign contracts with promoter C. C. Pyle, and begin American tour of one-nighters.

1927

Henri Cochet makes the most remarkable comeback in a major tournament, from 1-5 in the third set to topple Bill Tilden in Wimbledon semi-final, 2-6, 4-6, 7-5, 6-4, 6-3 and continues to win title over compatriot Jean Borotra. Young Californian Helen Wills, 21, wins the first of her record eight Wimbledon singles. After two futile shots at the U.S. in Davis Cup Finals, France's "Four Musketeers" (Cochet, Borotra, Rene Lacoste and Jacques Brugnon) finally seize the Cup, 3-2 at Philadelphia as Cochet beats Billy Johnston in decisive match. America's 7-year reign is over. Vinnie Richards wins the first U.S. Pro title over Howard Kinsey.

1928

For the first time a Davis Cup final is played in Europe, on clay, and France repels the U.S., 4-1, after the event survives an international crisis in the form of Bill Tilden's suspension by the USLTA on grounds of professionalism. The French are furious, and U.S. ambassador to France, Myron Herrick, tells USLTA that Tilden must play to preserve Franco-American harmony. Bill plays, winning only U.S. point.

1929

Billie Tapscott, a South African, shocks Wimbledon by appearing bare-legged. She is not, however, sent to the Tower, and stockings will soon be passé.

1930

Bill Tilden decides to take his money above the table and turns pro.

1933

Englishman Fred Perry arrives as the dominant player and a 4-year British era begins with a 3-2 victory over France in the Davis Cup, ending a 6-year French mastery. The international rivalry of the two Californian Helens—Wills and Jacobs—takes a new turn, toward Helen Jacobs, as she wins the U.S. title at Forest Hills over the usually superior Wills. Bunny Austin liberates the male leg, wearing shorts at Wimbledon where long trousers have ruled since the beginning.

1937

Fred Perry has turned pro, and the U.S. regains the Davis Cup, riding Don Budge to victory.

1938

Don Budge wins the Australian, French, British (Wimbledon) and U.S. singles in one year, an accomplishment to become celebrated as the first Grand Slam.

1939

With Budge now a pro, the U.S. loses the Davis Cup to Australia, 3-2 at the outbreak of World War II. Aussies Jack Bromwich and Adrian Quist are the only team ever to rebound from a 0-2 deficit in the final.

1946

Peace brings prosperity to U.S. tennis, as the team of Jack Kramer and Ted Schroeder recapture the Davis Cup in Melbourne, 5-0.

1947

Jack Kramer wins Wimbledon, beginning the most successful run of American titles, there, five.

1949

Pancho Gonzalez makes one of the memorable comebacks of Forest Hills to beat Ted Schroeder in the longest U.S. final, 16-18, 2-6, 6-1, 6-2, 6-4.

1950

Frank Sedgman's rise restores Australia in the Davis Cup, he and Ken McGregor grabbing the big bowl from the U.S.

1951

Maureen Connolly, at 16, is the youngest U.S. singles champ. Aussies Ken McGregor and Frank Sedgman score the only Grand Slam in doubles.

1952

Frank Sedgman takes Wimbledon, then the U.S. title to found an Aussie dynasty at Forest Hills.

1953

The first female Grand Slam is completed by Maureen Connolly.

1954

Newport's Casino becomes the site of the U.S. Tennis Hall of Fame. Three men who will later be enshrined at Newport—Capt. Bill Talbert and players Tony Trabert and Vic Seixas—stun the largest crowds to watch tennis, 25,578, at Sydney by winning back the Davis Cup, 3-2.

1955

Tony Trabert turns pro after the U.S. loses the Davis Cup to Australia, and begins a head-to-head tour against Pancho Gonzalez.

1956

Pancho Gonzalez completes a triumphant pro tour against Tony Trabert, the first of seven in which he will overpower the best of the amateurs entering the pro game. Ken Rosewall, who will be next for Pancho, wrecks a Grand Slam for countryman Lew Hoad by beating Lew in Forest Hills final.

1957

Althea Gibson, who has broken the color bar earlier in major tournament play in the U.S., becomes the first black champion by winning Forest Hills, adding that prize to her Wimbledon title. Americans Gar Mulloy, 43, and Budge Patty, 33, are the oldest team to win the Wimbledon doubles.

1958

The U.S. reaches long distance to regain the Davis Cup, recruiting Peruvian Alex Olmedo for the team. Olmedo, whose homeland is without a team, has refined his game at the University of Southern California. He leads 3-2 victory over the Aussies.

1960

After 20 successive U.S.-Aussie Davis Cup finals, the party is broken up by Italy with a 3-2 semi-final round decision over U.S. The Aussies easily keep the Cup, 4-1 over Italy, the first European nation in final since France nearly 30 years before. Southern Cal undergrads Denny Ralston, 18, and Rafe Osuna, 20, are the youngest team to take Wimbledon doubles.

1962

Aussie Rod Laver follows Don Budge's path over a Grand Slam. Mexico beats U.S., 3-2, in Davis Cup preliminary round, the first loss for the U.S. to another country in the Americas.

1963

Chuck McKinley momentarily pierces Aussie superiority by winning Wimbledon, with Denny Ralston, snatches Davis Cup from Down Under, 3-2. Federation Cup, world-wide team competition for women in spirit of

Davis Cup, commences with 2-1 U.S. victory over Australia in final, Billie Jean King and Darlene Hard the top Americans.

1967
U.S., shut out of Davis Cup final every year since losing the Cup back to Aussies in 1964, hits bottom on 3-2 loss at Ecuador, one of the most incredible sports upsets. Stock of pro tennis soars as Dave Dixon and Lamar Hunt form World Championship Tennis and George MacCall forms National Tennis League and begin signing leading amateurs for their promotions.

1968
Agitation for open tennis, eternal but ever thwarted by amateur authorities, grows markedly as the best amateurs —Roy Emerson, John Newcombe, Tony Roche, Roger Taylor, Nikki Pilic, Cliff Drysdale—begin pro careers. Never had so much quality been drained from the amateur game at once, and the British, backing a Wimbledon decision, opt for open tennis. The ILTF agrees, and the first open is played at Bournemouth in April, the British Hard Courts. Englishman Mark Cox is first amateur to beat a pro, downing Pancho Gonzalez and Roy Emerson in successive matches, but Ken Rosewall takes title over Rod Laver in all-pro final, Laver wins the first open Wimbledon over Roche, but amateur Arthur Ashe bombs through the first U.S. Open at Forest Hills, then leads the U.S. to Davis Cup triumph at Adelaide.

1969
With all the Grand Slam tourneys open for the first time, Rod Laver sails around his second Slam. Romania is first communist nation to reach Davis Cup final, losing 5-0 to U.S.

1970
Margaret Court makes the second female Grand Slam. Ken Rosewall wins U.S. Open, 14 years after his first Forest Hills success. West Germany attains Davis Cup final first time, is beaten, 5-0 by U.S. But Aussies John Newcombe and Fred Stolle fell the U.S. Davis Cup team, 5-2 in a new Australia-U.S. competition called World Cup. First significant rules change of the 20th century takes place in U.S. where the Sudden Death tie-breaker, conceived by scoring reformer James Van Alen, is installed at Forest Hills to conclude deuce sets at 6-games-all. Most tourneys will adopt tie-breakers.

1971
Rod Laver sets financial records with $292,717 in prize money, becoming the first tennis player to win over $1 million. But Ken Rosewall jolts Laver to take $50,000 prize in world pro singles final, a new event. Billie Jean King wins the National Clay Court title, becoming first woman to have won national titles on all four surfaces— grass, clay, cement and indoors. She continues to take another Open at Forest Hills, and amass $117,000 in prize money, a female high. Frank (Spider Man) Froehling beats Ion Tiriac in key match as U.S. repels Romania, 3-2 in Davis Cup.

1972
Ken Rosewall wins Australian Open, an event he first won in 1953—the 19 year spread is unprecedented. Then he shocks Rod Laver again in the world pro singles final. Stan Smith wins Wimbledon, the first American male champ there in eight years, and Billie Jean King regains title she held in 1966-67-68. Teen-age sensation Chris Evert, 17, goes all way to semis in first Wimbledon try. Chris wins both her singles as U.S. turns back Britain, 5-2, in Wightman Cup. Ilie Nastase is first Romanian to win U.S. Open, and Billie Jean King conquers at Forest Hills for a third time. Another new trophy, the Bell Cup, is the prize for an annual team match between Australian and U.S. women, taken by Aussies, 5-2. Playing a Davis Cup final on European clay for first time in years, the U.S. scrapes by Romania, 3-2 at Bucharest on dominant performance by Stan Smith.

1973
Margaret Court and Ilie Nastase are dominant figures, but the most attention goes to 55-year-old Bobby Riggs, the Wimbledon champ of 1939. He challenges Court to a match, beats her, setting the stage for the most ballyhood confrontation in the history of the game: against Billie Jean King, Sept. 20. A record tennis crowd at the Houston Astrodome, 30,472, watch King uphold womanhood with a 6-4, 6-3, 6-3 victory in "Battle of Sexes." Men's new union, the Assn. of Tennis Pros, boycotts Wimbledon in dispute over ILTF suspension of Nikki Pilic. Non-union man Jan Kodes wins title in diluted field. King beats Chris Evert for women's prize. Australia sweeps the Cups as Rod Laver makes comeback to lead 5-0 Australian romp

over U.S. in Davis Cup final, ending American streak at five years and 17 matches. Aussies also win World Cup over U.S. men and Federation and Bell Cups in female competition. John Newcombe and Court win at Forest Hills, she adding this to her Australian and French titles. Nastase, who wins 15 tournaments including French and Italian, beats Newcombe, then Tom Okker in Commercial Union Masters at close of year to claim No. 1 ranking.

1974
Chris Evert, Jimmy Connors and Bjorn Borg are the bright stars. She wins Italian, French and Wimbledon titles at 19, the first woman to do so since another teen-ager, Maureen Connolly in 1953. Connors has best season since Rod Laver's Grand Slam of 1969, winning Australian, Wimbledon and U.S. Opens along with U.S. Indoor and Clay titles at 22. Borg, at 18, is youngest winner of Italian, French and U.S. Pro crowns. Story of the year is Lovebird Double: Evert-Connors romance and engagement, but it breaks up after Forest Hills where she is upset after 56 straight wins by Evonne Goolagong, title going to Billie Jean King. Julie Heldman leads U.S. women to upset of Australia in Bell Cup, and they in turn are upset by Virginia Wade and Britain in Wightman Cup. Australia retains World Cup over U.S., but fades to India in early round of Davis Cup. Politics darkens Davis Cup, India defaulting final to South Africa as protest against apartheid. U.S. has been jolted early by Colombia. South Africa becomes fifth nation to win Davis Cup, first newcomer to break through since France became fourth in 1927, joining U.S., Australia, Britain and France in select circle. Radical concept, World Team Tennis, begins shakily and with great financial losses with 16 city franchises and male-female teams in U.S. Denver wins title over Philadelphia, whose player-coach Billie Jean King is first woman to boss male pros. Guillermo Vilas, practically unknown six months before, is surprise meteor, finishing as hottest player in world to win Commercial Union Masters over Ilie Nastase, earns $266,210, second only to Connors' $285,490. Evert breaks Margaret Court's female financial record ($204,400 for 1973) by winning $239,000. ●

Analyzing an Opponent

by GLADYS M. HELDMAN

MR. D has been watching the tournaments at Forest Hills for 10 years. He is dedicated to the proposition that tennis is a serious business; his notebooks are crammed with data on each match. He can tell you that Player A served five aces and 11 double faults, made seven overhead winners, 16 volley placements and volleyed nine times into the net. He also has data on the number of successful forehand passing shots, the number of erring backhand passing shots and how many drop shots were winners. Unfortunately Mr. D cannot tell you if Player A has an underspin backhand or a topspin forehand, at what points in the match he served to the forehand, whether or not his approach shots were short, how deep his volleys were and if he tried more crosscourt passing shots than down the line.

Mr. D is so busy transcribing an analysis of his points that he overlooks analyzing the style of Player A. Player X, who is going to meet Player A in the next round, would only get minimum help from Mr. D's prolific notes. Here is what Player X would like to know:

• Does Player A serve with topspin, slice or very little spin at all and does he alternate the spins? Can you tell by looking at the toss what spin he will use?

• Are most of his serves to the backhand and when does he serve to the forehand? On 30-0? On 40-15? In a five-set match, did Player A serve only three times to the forehand in the forehand court but 15 serves to the forehand in the backhand court?

• If Player A is a lefty, does he spin the serve out from the backhand, saving up his "forehand into the body" serves when he is down 0-30 or 15-40?

• Is it easier to stand in on Player A's serve so as to return it before it spins wide, or is it better to stand back a foot or two because the serve is so deep and has so much pace?

• Is Player A's second serve a little short? If so, can one step around it and wallop a forehand?

• Does Player A put more spin on his second serve or just less power?

• Was his serve relatively weak in the first game and did he start hitting it with much more power thereafter? Did he weaken on serve slightly in the fifth set and did his second serve go shorter then? If his serve did weaken, did more serves go to the opponent's forehand?

• When Player A comes in on serve, where does he takes his first volley? Is he usually just inside the service line for it? If he has to half-volley this shot, does he hit it down the middle and is it generally deep? If he volleys the first return, is it mostly to the backhand or mostly to the center or does he vary it?

• How close does Player A come in for the second volley? Is he "crowding the net" and would he be a sucker for a good lob?

• How good are Player A's low volleys on the forehand and backhand? Does he have a tendency to return the ball on low backhand volleys? Are his low forehand volleys hit with so much underspin that they bounce up?

• Does Player A have a preference for a side on his backhand volleys? Does he alternate hitting down the line and crosscourt and does he favor one side more? Does he get good angle on his volleys or does he shoot for depth? Are the volleys hard or just deep and well-placed or (worst of all for the opponent) hard, deep and well-placed? When, if ever, does he try the sharp angle volley?

• How does Player A handle his overheads? Does he leap very well? Does he go for "the big one" and make a fair percent of errors? Does he place them to the obvious opening or do they normally go wide to the backhand? Will he always run back for an overhead that hits the baseline and, when he does, will he try a screaming winner or a lob or a reasonably low groundstroke down the line or crosscourt? Does he alternate or stick to one pattern?

• Is it extremely difficult to pass Player A when he comes in behind serve and is it better to hit low to Player A's feet and then try to pass him on the second return?

• Did Player A win many of his points because his opponent's passing shots netted or went wide? How many times in a service game did Player A win the point because his opponent tried too good a passing shot and did not succeed in getting the ball in court? How many times did Player A win the point on the first volley? On the second volley? Without having to volley at all?

• Was Player A's overhead as good in the fifth set as it was in the first? Was it as hard or as accurate?

• Does Player A have a better forehand or backhand volley? When he has to leap for the volley, is one side better than the other?

• How does Player A return serve? Does he always stand on the baseline or just inside or one foot back? Is his forehand return a chip or a drive? On short second serves, does Player A run around the ball and clout it with his forehand or does he continue to chip? How does he return a high serve to his backhand? Is his backhand return a short chip, a large slice or a full topspin drive? Or does he vary them? Can he handle a serve into his body? When served very wide to his forehand in the forehand court, did he always go for the forehand down the line or did he ever lob?

• Were Player A's returns of serve generally dinks or angles or were they medium-paced or did he occasionally or often go for the big passing shot?

• Did Player A make a lot of forcing shots off second serves? Did he ever come into net behind returns of second serves?

• Would Player A's return of serve be characterized as erratic and very hard or dipping and consistent or medium hard and well placed or a combination thereof? Did he show any patterns on returns of serve?

• Is there a difference between Player A's return after a deep ball and after a short ball on the backhand side? Does he show a trend to lob off a very deep ball or will he hit a topspin drive crosscourt? On short balls when his opponent is at net, does he always go for the down the line or does he vary the shot? When the opponent is at net and Player A gets a deep ball to his backhand, does he topspin when he is going crosscourt and underspin when he is going down the line?

• What kind of forehand does Player A have? Does it have a little or a lot of topspin? Does he ever sidespin when he hits down the line? If he has a lot of topspin, does he use the lob aggressively and does it have good disguise? Is he so proud of his forehand that he only lobs when in deep trouble? When the opponent is at net, will Player A run around a ball slightly to the left of center and take it on his forehand? Does he have a pattern of going crosscourt then or does he vary, sometimes hitting directly at the net man (particularly on short balls) and sometimes lobbing?

• Are there any weaknesses in Player A's passing shots? Is there too much underspin on the backhand? Does he try too big a shot with the resulting number of errors when he

is pressed? Does he lob so seldom that the opponent can close in much more for the volley?

• Does Player A handle spin well? Does he prefer pace to spin? Does Player A handle pace well, using the opponent's speed to make an excellent return? Does Player A cover court well, running down balls that seem impossible. Does he anticipate deep shots and what is his riposte to a drop shot: does he drop shot back, angle the ball or drive deep to a corner?

• What happens when Player A is involved in a long baseline exchange? Does he come in on the first short ball? Does he get impatient and come in on a ball that is relatively deep? If the opponent is hitting high and deep, will Player A come in and hit the ball on the volley? In the deep baseline exchange, are most of his shots crosscourt? How good is his depth? Is he hitting with just medium pace (his opponent does not have to run that fast to get to the ball) or is he really moving the opponent around? Does he vary his spins in a long exchange?

• How good are Player A's approach shots? Do all his forehand approach shots go down the line and are they chipped or hit with topspin or sidespin? Do they go very deep? Does he ever hit a forehand approach shot crosscourt? Is the backhand approach shot generally hit with underspin and does he go down the line always? Does Player A ever hit an approach shot deep down the center?

• Does Player A use his head or does he play in a rigid pattern? Can his rhythm be broken with change of pace and spins? Are there any weaknesses in his backcourt or net game? Does he ever get sloppy in preparation? After he plays a loose game, does he get right back in the groove or is he slightly more erratic for the next few games? Does a bad call affect him for several games or does he take it in stride? Do gusts of wind affect his game adversely: does he misjudge overheads or hit too short when the wind is against him? At what point in the match, if any, did he suffer a let-down?

• Does A play better against an attacking or a retrieving game? Does he start pressing (overhitting) when the barrage is heavy? Does he get impatient when every ball comes back? How consistent is A and how much does he attack?

• Do A's shots feel heavy on the racket (does he use sidespin)? Has he any peculiarities of style such as a stroke volley or an enormous topspin forehand which always appears to be going out but generally goes in?

The analyst sits behind the baseline whenever he can. He generally watches the serves of both players for several games, then concentrates *on the receiver*. The reactions of the receiver tell him the pace, direction, depth and spin of the serve. He sees whether the receiver takes a large, medium or no backswing and to what part of the court the server volleys. Thereafter the viewer switches from watching the general play to watching one player. In particular when the play is very fast (serve, return and volley), he concentrates on the receiver; when the rallies are longer, he watches the point. There is no definitive rule for watching except *to think of what you want to watch* so that your analysis of the player can be relatively complete.

No one day reveals a player's strengths and weaknesses: the worst judgments are always made by someone basing his analysis on one match only. Then one would think that Bobby Riggs was "15" above any woman champion and that Margaret Court had no forehand, serve or net game. ●

Married Doubles
or
You Take the Backhand, Mr. Hyde

by MARLENE FANTA SHYER

WHAT TRANSFORMS a husband capable of wit in the living room, charm in the dining room and patience in the bedroom into a surly, cantankerous, black-browed horror on the tennis court? Show me one husband capable of sustained good humor towards his wife lasting more than three consecutive games and I'll show you either Norman Vincent Peale or Billy Graham. Other men, capable of boundless benevolence towards any partner not related to them by marriage, grow fangs when a spouse doublefaults. These are the same men who accept all manner of incompetence in other partners—who smile benign smiles at beginners, victims of bursitis, $5 rackets and Ace bandages, and say things like "Good try" when Partner slams a groundstroke into his own shoe and "Was I in your way?" when hit in the ear with Partner's second serve.

Witness, for example, Vera and Victor, the embodiment of Love Story off court, now side by side for a friendly game with Lorna and Lou. They arrive as Mr. and Mrs. Congeniality, addressing each other as Honey or Hon and exchanging friendly banter a mile a minute during the warm-up.

Now the game begins. Lou serves to Vera, putting on as much spin as a gentleman can put in a serve to a lady. Vera hits the ball with the edge of her racket and the ball zigs straight up and zags down to her feet. Victor, the Good Sport Husband, says, "She ought to have her racket rewooded, ha ha," and prepares to accept Lou's next serve. Vera laughs politely.

Lou serves to Victor with the intention of lopping off Victor's head with the ball. Victor retaliates by sending the ball zapping into the horizon. Vera says, "Jonathan Livingston Seagull." Victor does not laugh politely.

Lou serves again to Vera, who effectively returns the ball, but the ball is intercepted by Lorna, who slams it at Victor, who hits the ball into the net. Victor, says to Vera, "Don't hit at the net man, remember?" to which Vera says, "Do you think I *intended* to hit at the net man?" to which Victor says nothing. This nothing is, however, a malevolent nothing. It implies that he thinks Vera intended to hit at the net man. It accuses Vera of aiming directly for the net man and the net man's racket. It accuses Vera of being a Baddie on purpose.

In the meantime, Victor is returning Lou's serve, hitting it neatly back at Lou's feet. But good old Lou is on and he gets it back, right to Vera's backhand. Vera manages to blump the ball back and Lou crashes it back at Victor. The ball sails past Victor's nose. Victor smiles with his Good Sport Husband smile and says, "Aim crosscourt, Vera."

Vera thought Victor would congratulate her for getting it across in the first place and here he is, telling her to aim crosscourt. As she is pondering how to aim a last-second blump of a backhand crosscourt she misses Lou's next serve and loses the game. Victor says, "You've got to keep your eye on the ball, Vera." Little fires are burning under his white shirt. Gone forever is the Hon and Honey form of address.

"I will try," Vera says, very sweetly. She will save the snappy, well-worded comeback for later, at home, where there are acoustical ceiling tiles.

Vera does not double-fault; she does not dare! However, she does not hold her serve. Lorna places two alley shots that sail past Victor, who is busy poaching at the net. He really blames Vera for forcing him to poach, but keeps smiling and saying things to Lorna like "Nice," and "Good shot!" The Good Sport Husband smile never leaves his face, but his remarks to Vera are made principally with eyebrows. Little moans can be heard emanating from his dry throat. Poison is in the air.

As they change sides when the score is four-one, war hangs over the net. The *guerre a mort* atmosphere makes smiling difficult. Victor wishes to cut a hole in Vera. Instead Victor says, "Getting humid, isn't it?" Vera agrees that it is indeed getting very humid. She is now a nervous wreck, capable of hitting the balls into the Pro's group lesson or into the coke machine. When the score is 5-2 and Victor tells her to step back, move into the ball, turn her body, keep her feet on the ground and swing earlier, she vows never to set foot on a court with him again. She wishes they would install acoustical tile here on the courts so she can say what she thinks of him right *now*.

But!

The Tennis God now chooses to smile upon Vera and Victor; their luck changes in the second set. Friendship is slowly restored. Victory is therapy. With each gain in score, warmth creeps up on Victor. A two game lead puts a Jekyll bloom on Hyde.

The second set finds Lorna and Lou becoming progressively more silent. Lou is smiling on the outside, squalling on the inside. Mutterings are heard, and bitter little laughs come flying across the net.

Familiar, so familiar. But not hopeless. One day they are going to do away with those superfluous line judges and put marriage counselors in those chairs around the court.

It can't be too soon. ●

ON PLAYING TENNIS FOR YOUR COUNTRY

"Why are you playing this Bonne Bell Cup thing?" asked Rosie...

by JULIE M. HELDMAN

SITTING IN THE locker room at Forest Hills, waiting for her match to go on court, Rosie Casals looked at me quizzically.

"Why are you playing this Bonne Bell Cup thing?" she asked, looking at me as if I had really lost my mind. "How can you play this match when they are only putting up $30,000 prize money?"

Sneakily, I asked in reply, "Can you tell me that playing for Detroit is any better than playing for the USA? I know you don't want to represent the USLTA, and you think that Bonne Bell should be putting up $50,000, as much prize money as each of the sponsors of the women's tournaments this fall, but I don't have the same qualms about the match." I was thinking that $2,000 per player for the losing team and $4,000 per player for the winning team was not bad.

You probably noticed that I did not really answer her question. Because the answer is very complicated, I had to think for a long time to organize my feelings, but here they are now:

I am proud to represent the United States in tennis. It is an honor for a professional athlete to be recognized as the best in her country at whatever she does, and to attempt to prove it in competition against the best from other countries. In international play, I am on the court as a respresentative of the tennis players of my country. I do not represent the USLTA, although that body is in charge of promoting the event. I do not represent the politics of the U.S. government, or of the Wall Street bankers who control the finances or of the big companies who control everything. And I do not represent the United States only on condition that big money is offered, although I do not play for free when people are paying to watch me.

Most arguments boil down to a difference in faith, semantics or priorities. Obviously whether or not you represent your country in tennis is mostly a matter of priorities. The U.S. lost a Davis Cup tie to Colombia this year because few of the top American players were available. Arthur Ashe and Stan Smith had prior commitments to play exhibitions, but if Dennis Ralston had thought the match against Colombia important enough, Ashe and Smith would have changed the exhibitions, if at all possible. They are really eager to play for their country. On the other hand, the top four

U.S. women were not available in 1974 for any match representing their country. In a parallel situation to the Davis Cup, Chris Evert and Billie Jean King had scheduled a very lucrative exhibition during the Wightman Cup tie. The difference is that Evert and King did so knowing that they were in conflict with the match against England. The Wightman Cup is no longer important enough for them to want to change the date of their exhibition.

U.S. women tennis players have three chances every year to represent their country: the Wightman Cup, the Federation Cup and the Bonne Bell Cup. The Wightman Cup is played between the U.S. and Great Britain, and has been going since 1923. In amateur days, being named to the Wightman Cup team was an honor on a par with winning Wimbledon. The esteem associated with the cup has become devalued recently, because no one on Britain's team, except Virginia Wade, is in the top 30 in the world. Although the Wightman Cup has been revitalized with $30,000 in prize money, I do not think it should continue as a full international event, but instead should become a trophy for international 18 or 21-and-under competition between the U.S. and Britain.

The Federation Cup, started in 1963, is an attempt at a Davis Cup for women held in one week. Although it is a good concept, usually well executed, it has never developed much prestige. Like the Davis Cup, there is no prize money, although each country pays its players' expenses, sometimes generously.

The Bonne Bell Cup, a competition between the top two countries in women's tennis, the U.S. and Australia, just finished its third tie. The Bell Cup, with $30,000 up for grabs in 1973 and 1974, was the first international women's team event to put up big prize money.

This year Billie Jean King, Chris Evert, Rosemary Casals and Nancy Gunter have not been available for any of these competitions. All but Chris Evert were playing World Team Tennis, and so were contracted to play for their teams during Fed Cup, although they, as Evonne Goolagong did, could have written into their WTT contracts that they would be free for international events.

Chris Evert was not available for Fed Cup because she was resting for the Italian Championships and a long tough struggle on the European circuit in the spring. Each woman had different reasons for being unavailable for Bonne Bell and Wightman Cup. Nancy Gunter does not like team matches. Rosie Casals had a major disappointment in 1970 when, because of tennis politics, she was not named to the Wightman Cup team. For that slight and because of many other fights with the USLTA, she does not want to represent the association again. Chris Evert was resting the week after Forest Hills, which was also the week of the Bonne Bell Cup. Further, she had an exhibition scheduled during Wightman Cup.

Billie Jean King has won everything and has achieved all her own goals. Her new goals are to boost the Women's Tennis Association and to bring bigger prize money to the women's game. She has said she will play Bonne Bell Cup or Wightman Cup if a percentage of the gate goes to the WTA and if the cup competitions have the same prize money as other tournaments on the WTA major tour. If any one of the top four would consistently play in matches representing their country, the Cups would take on a different aura. The problem? A new goal.

And the new goal is money. In the United States you are not important unless you make a lot of money. Women's tennis became a major attraction when the crowds saw that the players' purses were bulging. Only after they saw green did they realize how good the women's game is to watch. Billie Jean King struck the right note in the American chord when she made a big deal about being the first female athlete to make more than $100,000 in a year.

The men have benefited from the tennis boom by attracting top athletes from other sports. Unfortunately, the successful women players must still prove themselves, because they are the first female athletes to be accepted in our society. Women tennis players cannot easily play for just the joy of doing their best and making good money. They have to contend with dozens of people who come up to them, asking why they are not married and "by the way, can you support yourself running around playing tennis?" After the 50th person asks these innocuous-sounding questions, even the most reticent players want to wear a sign on their chests with last year's earnings emblazoned in neon lights.

If an athlete is making very little or no money, her first goal must be to increase her earnings. Once she is doing very well, she has time to turn her mind to additional goals, which is what the top women players should do. After all, what will all those dollars be worth if we have a big recession?

The first goal should be to insure the future of women's tennis. The women can do this by having more tournaments with less prize money in each one. Next year from January to April, 32 women will compete for $75,000 each week on the Virginia Slims tour, for which my bank manager and I are eternally grateful. Another 64 women will compete for $7,000 every week on the feed-in Mini Tour. This discrepancy means a select few make a lot of money, and the rest, among whom there are many good players, must struggle or stay home. What kind of incentive is this for young female athletes?

Lest you think I am some kind of turncoat from the women's movement, let me assure you that I believe in equal pay, and I believe that the women should get the same prize money as the men at Wimbledon and Forest Hills, where we draw the crowds. Where I differ from many militant women professional tennis players is that I think their emphasis on money is too strong. Instead, we should emphasize pride of performance in our chosen field.

Our pride should include making the women's game exciting to spectators and interesting to galleries all over the world. The men have achieved interest throughout the world largely through the Davis Cup. This men's international competition has always been far more important than the women's events because it has been going for much longer on a big scale and because it has been well supported by the players. If the women players want to be as important as the men, we should make our international competitions vibrant. We should make them professional competitions where the sport and the players—not the flag or the money— are revered.

That, Rosie, is why I played the Bonne Bell Cup. ●

Teaching Youngsters to Serve

by ED COLLINS

CLEO, age 8, is learning to serve. She is having her share of problems because she cannot yet throw properly. She does not understand how her older brother can do it so easily when she is having such a tough time. But her brother spent several years learning how to serve before he was ever introduced to tennis. By throwing rocks in the canyon and playing Little League, he came into tennis with a good idea as to what serving was all about.

Cleo will have to start from scratch. First she must throw correctly and then she can take on the serve. Learning to throw is a prerequisite to the serve. Young boys get the idea through their peers but girls never seem to experience the need or pressure to acquire it.

This pictorial sequence depicts how to teach youngsters the throwing motion. ●

The left foot is forward, the ball held in front of the body at waist height and both hands are on the ball.

The left hand lets go of the ball and the right hand and arm start to swing back naturally.

As the arm comes back, the coach helps Cleo, age 8, to bend the elbow and to bring the forearm up.

The elbow bends further so that the ball is now almost touching the back.

The ball is released when the arm is straight and slightly in front of the body.

The follow-through is natural, bringing the weight and right shoulder forward.

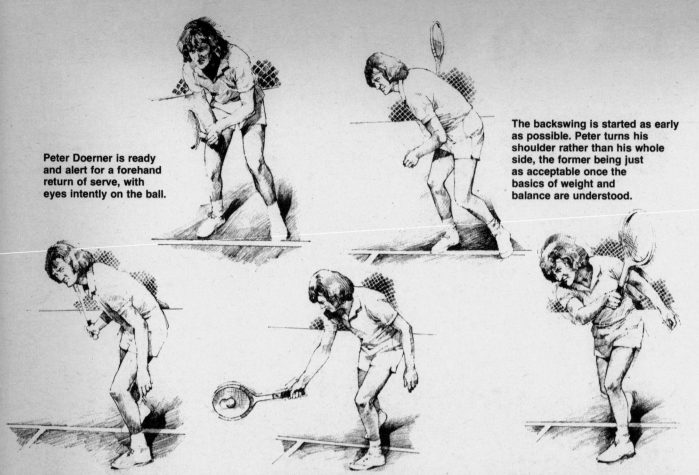

Peter Doerner is ready and alert for a forehand return of serve, with eyes intently on the ball.

The backswing is started as early as possible. Peter turns his shoulder rather than his whole side, the former being just as acceptable once the basics of weight and balance are understood.

Peter turns on the balls of his feet and brings his left foot forward, starting to shift his weight from back to front.

The weight is on the front foot and then he hits the ball: weight forward, THEN hit. The eyes never leave the ball.

The follow-through is determined largely by necessity to maintain good balance. Peter's follow-through is longer than most.

Concentration, Early Preparation and Balance

THE THREE fundamentals, besides mechanics, that are necessary to any tennis player's success are:

CONCENTRATION. Tom Brown, a former Wimbledon finalist, was asked: "What one factor contributed most to improving your game?" Without hesitation Brown replied:

"When I learned to concentrate. During one match I realized I had broken concentration, so I began to count the number of times my mind wandered during that match. Before I was through I had broken concentration over 20 times. When I learned to cut the number down to two or less, I was playing in the First Ten of the U.S."

You might ask, "What do you mean by breaking concentration?" Here are a few examples: hearing what people are talking about in the spectator area, watching someone in the stands, brooding over a bad call instead of putting it out of your mind when you go back to serve or return serve, failure to keep the score of the game, set and match in mind, not playing for the score and failure to watch the ball because of outside distractions.

I was practicing with Bill Tilden at Skokie in the summer of 1924. I said to Bill: "That North Shore train noise drives me nuts." "What train?" replied Tilden.

In 1918 A. McCray of Hollister took me to the Berkeley Tennis Club while he played with "Little Bill" Johnston, Peck Griffin and Ray Casey. Little Bill came up to me at noon and said: "Fritz, why don't you go in and shower?" I asked him why and he replied, "You are going through the motions, not hustling or trying to get in position to hit the ball, and you are learning bad habits. You would be better off to go out there for 20 minutes, concentrate and do your best, rather than do what you are doing now."

Another suggestion came from famous coach Pop Fuller, who told me, "Fritz, you don't concentrate very well. I am going to tell you what I have told the two Helens (Helen Wills and Helen Jacobs): every time the ball hits the court, you are to say 'bounce' to yourself; every time you or your opponent hit the ball, you are to say 'hit.' Be sure to say it exactly the same time the ball bounces or when the ball is hit. To do this takes 100 percent concentration and all nervousness will disappear."

EARLY PREPARATION. It sounds easy, but unless you have trained it is doubtful if you will be

Look at this sequence and spot the difference. Do you know what's wrong?

This is the same stroke but looser throughout. Peter is just going through the motions and he isn't hustling.

Less attention to fundamentals leads to sloppy play, and as a result the player picks up bad habits.

The knees are not bent, the backswing is higher because there is no crouch and there is little weight transfer.

Not until the follow-through has the weight shifted forward, and by that time it is too late.

by FRED A. EARLE, Jr.

lucky enough to be prepared early for each stroke. Do you always turn sideways except for your head (the eyes should be watching the ball) before the ball gets on your side of the net? Years ago, when I was fortunate enough to have world-famous Junior players on my Modesto J.C. teams, the local boys could not even rally with these outstanding players. Two weeks of training in early preparation made it possible for the locals to rally and practice successfully against superior players, thereby building up their egos and their games.

Are you starting on the balls of your feet as you turn sideways or are you starting flatfooted? The only time your heel should touch is in stopping and in anchoring your foot as you hit the ball. On return of serve do you have your racket back behind the an-

ticipated height you expect the ball to bounce before the ball crosses the net on your side? Are you standing up like a tall tree or are your knees flexed with the weight on the balls of your feet? Are your feet crossed when your opponent is about to come forward with his racket? Don't handicap yourself in the ability to prepare early for the next stroke.

BALANCE. If you have balance as a result of a correct start and a good finish of your stroke, then all you need is concentration on the ball. You can then hit it at the proper time, in the center of the racket, and you will end up with a good shot most of the time. By balance I mean: shifting your weight from your back foot to your front foot a fraction of a second before you start your forward swing, and finishing with 90 percent of your

weight flat on your front foot and with both feet in contact with the court whenever possible so you may recover rapidly for the next stroke. You cannot have balance on your backhand if your head is tilted. Misjudging a ball may cause you to bend from the waist rather than bend from the knees, thereby losing balance. Too big a follow through will find you off balance and unprepared for the next shot. Use your free arm and move your feet to aid in your balance. There are many times in advanced tennis when you cannot hit the ball from a set position, but if you have good body balance you will have a pretty good chance of returning the ball.

The three fundamentals of concentration, early preparation and balance are a necessity for good match play. ●

Sketches, Hodges Soileau

The Reminiscences of Rod Laver

by ROD LAVER

THERE AREN'T MANY of us left, the old boys who remember what pro tennis was like in the days before 1968 when the game suddenly got up-to-date—and started going out of sight financially—with the approval of opens. Now the bright youngsters like Jimmy Connors, Dick Stockton, Bjorn Borg and Guillermo Vilas come into the game knowing the financial side is secure if they can play well.

But in 1963 when I turned pro there was no such feeling whatsoever. Amateur—or so-called amateur—tennis was the recognized game, and those few of us who wanted to earn our money above-board were outcasts who played the world on one-night stands in unbelievable conditions. It was both agony and fun, but nothing like it exists any more. And I think those of us who endured it—myself, Ken Rosewall, Pancho Gonzalez, Pancho Segura, Andres Gimeno, Butch Buchholz, Luis Ayala, Barry MacKay, Mike Davies, Lew Hoad and a few others—sort of glory in the bizarre experiences that are gone forever. Now all the tournaments are big-money affairs, out and out professional, and that's good. That's what we worked and hoped for—and never expected to see. In 1963 when Ken Rosewall beat me in the final of the U.S. Pro Championship at Forest Hills, we got each other's handshake, and nothing more. The promoter didn't draw enough at the gate to pay us. That wasn't the only time we played for nothing. Times were really unsure, but we believed in the game, and we loved playing.

I wonder if the kids today would have the persistence to do that. The next year the New England Merchants National Bank in Boston picked up sponsorship of the U.S. Pro and that was the act that started the pro game turning around and toward better times and open tennis, though we couldn't realize it at the time. The bank put up $10,000 total prize money. That was only a few years ago, 1964, but it seemed like a million bucks then. Consider that in 1971, I set a single season record of $292,717 in prize money, and that in 1974 Connors came close to breaking it with $285,490. Obviously one of the players will break it soon. Why, Chris Evert set the women's fiscal mark of $238,585 in 1974, and a few years ago there weren't even any female pros...or that much money in the entire men's game! When we fled phony amateurism for honest professionalism we never expected to play at such places as Wimbledon again. We were swept under the rug and away from respectability, but thankfully open tennis in '68 changed all that. We were welcomed back to Wimbledon and all the other great locations, and tennis began booming.

Considering the incredible success of Wimbledon, the men like Herman David, who run the place, emerged as extremely principled blokes in their determination to stage an open Wimbledon in 1968 in opposition to the wishes of the International Lawn Tennis Federation. Wimbledon sells out regardless of the quality of the tennis. The British love it and the game so much they'd turn out to watch Ma and Pa Kettle play mixed doubles against the champions of Spearfish, South Dakota.

But Wimbledon stood for the best, and insisted on being the best in more than name. Only the prestige of Wimbledon could break the status quo and force open tennis into existence in 1968. I really never thought I'd see it in my day as a player, and I was resigned to exclusion.

Our professional game was bumbling along, the money was fairly good, and though we were always discussing and arguing open tennis, we weren't expecting it. There was no point in moaning about our exclusion; we'd chosen our way of life. We'd had the prestige part of tennis as amateurs. Now we were away from it but able to earn a decent living anyway.

So we bounced around on our one-nighters. We traveled to remote places like Khartoum, La Paz, and Reston, Virginia. There was never any time off to adjust to the changes in time zones after a long flight. That's still a problem, combatting the punchiness you feel after flying, say, from New York to London. I've found that taking a brisk workout as soon as possible after I land—instead of going directly to bed—helps clear the fuzziness quicker. Either a practice session or a run. This could apply to anybody.

We'd play occasional eight and 12-man tournaments in the summer in the U.S. Reston, a suburb of Washington, D.C., doesn't sound remote, but when we played there in 1965 they were just building the place. Our tournament was part of the promotion for this brand-new city, and everything was disorganized. You needed a guide to find the court. The area was so dusty we thought we were coming down with silicosis, and there were no dressing rooms. We dressed in our cars and showered some other time.

I thought about a lot of these times in my ragtag life when we heard that we'd be going back to Wimbledon like pardoned men. The time in Khartoum in 1965 when they'd been having serious rioting and there were soldiers and machine guns everywhere. We were scared to death, and we'd gone there for $1000—to be split among four of us. We'd go anywhere for almost anything in those days. Because of the trouble there had been no newspapers or radio, no way of publicizing the matches. But the promoter wasn't giving up. He and a couple of his friends got on the phone and started calling people. It started a chain reaction, and there were about 1000 people there for the matches. We couldn't believe it. We started in the late afternoon on grass courts and played until dark at six. Then everybody walked to a nearby cement court that was lighted and we resumed and played until the bug curfew. After a while the lights attracted so many insects that it was impossible to go on, and that's where the matches ended. The crowd realized this was a natural conclusion, and went away quietly and happy, having enjoyed some good tennis.

La Paz was interesting, but I don't want to go back. Not to play tennis. In that altitude—something like 12,000 feet—the balls fly like pigeons and if you play hard you're liable to get a nosebleed. We played a four-man tournament, and first prize was a $600 watch. I laugh when I think how we killed ourselves to win a watch, blood streaming down our faces and the balls zooming everywhere.

Nobody but the spectators knew we were in Bolivia playing on top of a mountain. Personal pride pushed us, that's all. Everywhere. I tried as hard at La Paz and amidst all those bugs in Khartoum as I ever did at Wimbledon or Paris. They may have amounted to nothing more than exhibitions, but I seldom saw a pro give less than his best

unless he was sick or injured. I'm certain I never saw anybody tank a match, or take it easy to make the other guy feel better. There were occasions, against the weaker players—we called them the donkeys—that I could practice certain shots, try to work on my weaknesses. That was possible and helpful—and could get me beat once in a while.

One of the things I experimented with was lobbing through the rafters. This isn't a tactic you'll find in any tennis text, and it may never come in handy again with the game growing up for us pros. But in the gypsy days, when we played in all sorts of odd buildings, low beams weren't infrequent, and you had to be able to adjust. I soon found out in pro tennis that you were dead without a good lob—by far the most underrated shot in the game. And you had to be able to lob over and through the rafters many nights. Pancho Segura was the leading practicioner of rafter-lobbing. His lobs always found their way through mazes of rafters and beams. I got pretty good at it and one night in Utica I beat Gimeno with a beaut that wandered among the girders as though directed by radar.

You had to be able to laugh it off, even when you didn't get paid or when the conditions were so ridiculous that a rhinoceros wouldn't have gone onto the court. The word was around about tennis pros: "Put up the money and they'll play barefoot on broken glass."

It was absolutely true. Gypsies don't make demands regarding playing conditions. We'd play if we suspected the money wasn't forthcoming. You can look at a crowd—or a noncrowd—and guess what's happening. But we liked to play tennis. It never seemed like a chore to me.

Maybe I thought about the perfect grass, the adulation and the limousines at Wimbledon as I inspected an armory in Utica for openings in the ceiling supports. But that was my life then.

These hardships we pros shared made us proud of our skills and perserverance. They were good for us. I think they helped our games, made us more determined. The five-year exile from Wimbledon and the rest of the places at the top made me appreciate open tennis more than the younger players who've moved right into it as a matter of course. They never had to risk their necks playing in a crummy ice rink like the one in Altringham, England, where Hoad and I almost broke our necks on the slick portable floor. Condensation dripped from the ceiling making the footing horrible. Neither one of us could do much. They should have taken up the flooring and given us skates. The score went to 20-20 and I did the splits going for a shot. Snap! I felt something go. A tendon? No—my jockstrap. With a face that matched my hair I called time and trotted to the dressing room for a replacement. "Emergency," I blurted to the umpire as the spectators guffawed. We had to quit at 27-27, the longest set I ever played, because we could hardly stand.

And there was another English rink in Nottingham where Frank Sedgman hit more passing shots by me than I'd ever seen. I was passing him pretty well, too. We suddenly got the idea the court might be too big. It was—a yard wider than regulation, and two feet longer. Somebody painted the lines wrong, and there was nothing to do but settle down at the baseline. No use rushing the net with all that extra room to cover.

The first pro match I played in the U.S., at Boston Garden, didn't do anything to help my state of mind. Instead of spreading the canvas court on the basketball floor, or the ice, as is the practice in large arenas, they put it on a rough floor of planking that covered the ice. Another mistake. You might as well ask Minnesota Fats to shoot pool on a lumpy table.

That was the beginning of my first winter in America—my first real winter. I'd seen snow only once before, briefly during a tournament in New York the previous winter. This winter of 1963 there was to be no escaping it. One hopeful aspect of my pro debut in America was that I was playing big Barry MacKay. It was nice to get away from a menu of Hoad and Rosewall. It was like taking my head out of the cement mixer for a night, but I soon found out Barry could be worse on a court like that. He had one of the biggest serves going, and trying to return it on that bumpy court was like trying to swat jackrabbits with a broom. "Jesus," I thought, "so this is the pro tennis tour?"

Another beating. It took me a long time to get even, and by the time I did I was just pleased to be alive. That U.S. tour was 60 matches in 80 days. It seemed like around the world in 80 days. There were six of us—Rosewall, Gimeno, MacKay, Luis Ayala, Butch Buchholz, and me—and a couple of station wagons. We were on the run every minute, grabbing hotdogs, getting to bed about three every morning, driving, driving, driving.

One night in upper New York State, cold as a witch's mitt, snow all over the roads, we were on our way to Albany. The road was like grease. As we slid and swerved, I said to myself, "What am I doing here?"

The money was all right, but what was I doing freezing and skidding on my way to Albany when I could have been getting on nicely as an amateur, playing in Jamaica that week.

Of course, everybody has his doubts about his job once in a while. As I began to play better, I felt better. I wound up the tour second to Rosewall, and I collected more than $50,000 for the year, so I was sure I'd make my guarantee.

It was $110,000 over three years, although the word "guarantee" is a bit dreamy. All through 1962 the pros were after me to sign on with them. There weren't promoters backing the operation as Lamar Hunt does now. The players themselves were trying to hold pro tennis together, and they weren't doing very well—but how could they? They were trying to play and do everything else too.

They all talked to me about turning pro, but mostly Hoad and Rosewall, since they knew me better than the rest. They started with a $75,000 offer for three years, and I said to come back after Forest Hills. Then I'd won my first Slam, and they knew they had to go higher: $85,000. I decided I wanted six figures, and finally we settled on $110,000. This was after I'd turned down a separate offer from Pancho Gonzales of a $50,000 minimum and $100,000 maximum for a one year head-to-head tour. Pancho and I would have cut up the gate, and no doubt I could have made the maximum with the old champion coming out of retirement to face the Grand-Slammer. He had the biggest name, but I didn't know how I could face my Aussie friends if I did that, and I wasn't too keen on Pancho. I felt surer of a long-term contract with men I knew.

It was all on trust, actually, this figure of $110,000. There was nothing in escrow, no millionaire or experienced promoter to back it up. I was to get 25 percent of the gate on nights I won and 20 percent otherwise. Hoad and Rosewall pledged themselves to make up the difference if I didn't reach $110,000 in three years. They didn't have to, I'm glad to say, because I made $150,000 my first three years. I'm sure Lew and Kenny would have tried, but it was still a pretty shaky contract, and I doubt I'd have held them to it.

A financial gamble, maybe, but I wanted to get off on my own, and not have to haggle with every tournament as I did as an amateur. Even though I had earned a nice living as an amateur, I just wasn't a man to bargain and haggle over expense money like some of the fellows. I'm sure that several not as good as I extracted more money, and good luck to them. The most I ever asked for—and got—was $1000 to play the National Indoors in New York in 1962. I thought I was being exorbitant, and purposely so, because I didn't want to leave home in February. When they complied, I reluctantly made the trip, and saw snow for the first time.

I hope it doesn't sound egotistical to say that in addition to trying to secure my own future, I was doing something for the future of professional tennis as well. The boys were desperate to get me. They needed new blood badly, a new face, the amateur with the big reputation. They hadn't signed one in a long time. Their most recent converts had been Ayala, who wasn't a big name, and MacKay, Alex Olmedo, Buchholz, and Gimeno, who were just beginning to make names when they signed pro contracts. No top star had turned pro in three years. Gonzales hung out in one of his innumerable retirements, and the last tremendous name to sign on had been Hoad in 1957. They really needed me if there was going to be any kind of pro tennis at all, and that's why they were willing to give me such a large cut of the action. I'll admit that 25 percent of zero isn't always rewarding, but many nights the take was all right.

After five years like that, I could take any kind of playing conditions. Butch Buchholz, who'd been an outcast longer than I, felt the same. At the beginning of 1968 when Lamar Hunt began a badly organized tour with rookies Roger Taylor, John Newcombe, Tony Roche, and Niki Pilic, almost everybody was miserable but Butch, the old hand.

"As long as the building doesn't blow up, nothing can shake me," Butch said. "I'm a veteran of the Texas death march. My first year as a pro, 1961, somebody—and it must have been a fugitive from the Texas Rangers—scheduled us throughout the state on a tour that meant about five hundred miles a day driving. We were in towns that nobody has heard of yet, playing the worst buildings and courts, for short money. Every night I wanted to quit and go home, try to get reinstated as an amateur. I was only twenty. But I was a pro and I stuck it out. These kids now don't know what a tough tour is like."

They are less likely to know, and perhaps the opportunity is gone—if opportunity is the word. As the game booms a complete circuit of opens in the leading cities has sprouted and the sport is becoming genuinely a big league one. I guess I'll never play Nottingham again, or Khartoum, or Accra, or La Paz. The kids who miss out on this seasoning just can't know the sensation of deliverance running through us old pros when we walked through the Doherty Gate into Wimbledon again on June 24, 1968, a part of the act once more. Newcombe, Roche, Pilic, Taylor, had never been away. They were amateurs in 1967, pros in 1968. They couldn't know the elation of being recognized as respectable men again. ●

The Tanner Serve

by JULIUS HELDMAN

ROSCOE TANNER has the hardest left-handed serve since John Doeg,* who won the U.S. Nationals in 1930 on a serve and prayer. Doeg served 32 aces in his semi-final match against Bill Tilden. Tanner whistles aces past opponents on grass, and slower surfaces too, with similar frequency. He does not have the variation, the change of spin and speed from the same wind-up that characterized southpaw Neale Fraser's delivery in his great year of 1960. But Roscoe makes up for his lack of sophisticated finesse (a questionable virtue anyway) by sheer blinding speed on all first serves, and his second serves are almost as hard. This speed comes out of a fast concerted wind-up which fires the serve before the opponent knows what has happened.

The fast wind-up and concerted action are necessarily associated with a low toss. The toss must indeed be high enough so that the server is stretched out to full height when he hits the ball, but anything higher than such a toss means that the ball is hit while it is descending after reaching its peak. It is then moving, rather than dead still as if it is hit at the exact zenith. If the toss is high, there must be a timing pause at some stage of the wind-up. With the concerted action there is less chance for timing error, and the server hits a dead still ball. The only danger in the minimum toss is if it is actually too low, and in this case the server

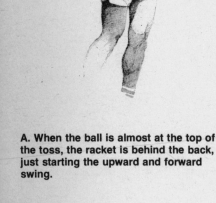

A. When the ball is almost at the top of the toss, the racket is behind the back, just starting the upward and forward swing.

B. The ball is motionless at the top of the toss. The arm is almost straight up but the racket head lags behind.

C. The racket head is now brought forward faster than the arm through wrist rotation. The left leg swings forward.

*Jimmy Connors might dispute this statement.

D. The racket head leads the arm after the hit, indicating the rapid acceleration of the head when the ball is struck.

E. The left leg is now in court and the racket head is rotated downward to Tanner's left while the arm starts down.

does not use his full height and usually develops a cramped, hurried swing as well. Tanner has mastered the toss perfectly, although he occasionally has a small tendency toward low toss and cramped swing. Bill Tilden was the first great exponent and master of the minimum toss, and his fine serve was as much due to fast concerted action as it was to speed.

Another advantage of the minimum toss is timing and weight transfer. One of the commonest problems on serve, from beginner to champion, is the premature swinging through of the right leg and shoulder (left for lefties) on the serve. When this happens the server loses power and tends to pull at the ball, which is now behind his head. But with the minimum toss and no-pause concerted action serve, there is less likelihood of swinging the body through too soon. Tanner's weight transfer timing is excellent and he achieves maximum power with it.

Roscoe does not always swing his left foot forward as he swats the ball. On his bullet first serve he springs up at the ball before his left foot crosses over, and his momentum carries him forward into court about as much as if he had deliberately swung his left leg forward in the manner of almost all net rushers. On his second serve, which has a little overspin for control, he does swing his left leg over, but not too soon.

The last factor which is vital in producing speed on serve is racket head velocity at impact—the necessary momentum transfer to the ball. And no matter how fast or hard the arm swings, the racket head will move faster if the wrist rotates forward at impact. Wrist snap adds substantially to the speed of the serve and is necessary to the development of any good serve. Roscoe develops full wrist action, the result of which is a racket head which moves farther and faster than the arm during the critical part of the serve.

Tanner's serve is excellent because all the factors fit together. It takes strength, stamina and confidence, all of which Roscoe has, to make this style effective throughout a match. Few players are as gifted as he, and therefore others must hit the ball less hard, with sufficient spin to control it. It is a rare player who can get the first block-buster in. ●

F. This view of Tanner's serve does not reveal the racket (behind his back) but shows the forward lean for a forward toss.

G. This drawing shows Tanner launching himself at the ball, all extended in an upward and forward line into the court.

Trigger Your Concentration

THE OLD conundrum over which comes first, the egg or the hen, has only one answer in tennis. Concentration, intense and sustained, is at once the egg, the chick *and* the hen. Without a high level of concentration all the mechanics and strategy of the game become strictly secondary.

Concentration on what? On the ball, its speed, direction and spin so that we can achieve perfect position for stroking the ball when it arrives in our end of the court. The more often we can attain perfect position the more effective we can be with consistency, accuracy and power. These qualities add up to a much higher percentage of winning tennis. Without sustained concentration that percentage will drop off sharply.

For the fully rounded game, concentration on the ball must be supplemented by an alert analysis of the opponent's strength, weaknesses, mental and psychological reactions and a sense of the total strategical situation as the match develops.

By "triggering" concentration I mean the use of a key concept from which intense concentration will immediately follow. The most effective trigger I have been able to find is this: never assume that the ball will be hit to you in practice. Rather, assume that it may be hit anywhere and that you will have to go to the ball.

Rallies should not end when the ball may be hit out of bounds—not if it can be reached. In striving for sustained concentration, keep the ball in play as long as possible in practice. A ball that lands out of bounds is just as good for practice as one which strikes within the court, so why pass up an opportunity to stroke it?

Illustration A shows the stance of a player who is not concentrating intently at the moment the ball is to be put into play by her opponent. Note that her weight is on her heels. Knees straight. The racket is close to her body.

I asked Janet if she was expecting the ball to be hit directly to her. She thought a moment and then replied a bit sheepishly, "Yes, I guess I was."

"Now," I suggested, "assume that Mike will not hit the ball to you. Rather, assume that he may hit it anywhere in the court!"

"Oh!" she exclaimed, and unconsciously took the stance shown in Illustration B. Note the slight crouch,

feet apart, racket out away from the body. She is watching Mike's every move, ready to go to the ball no matter where it may land, in the court or out. This position of alertness was not described to her. She assumed it naturally, an instinctive reaction. Try it—I

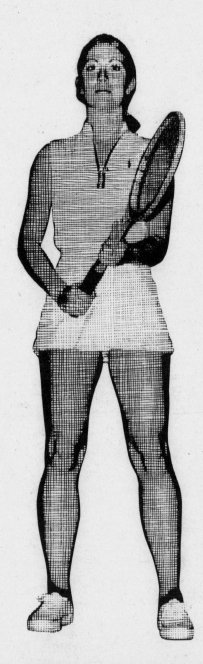

ILLUSTRATION A—Janet has her weight on her heels, her knees are straight and she can't respond immediately.

by DON KLOTZ

think you will find yourself doing exactly as Janet did.

Does this "trigger" immediately transform a player's concentration from "wandering" to sustained? Hardly! Old habits are not to be overcome that easily. You will find it necessary to remind yourself at the beginning of every rally that you must not expect the ball will be hit to you, that you may have to go anywhere to receive it. If you begin the rally, do not allow yourself to "just hit the ball over the net" in the general direction of your opponent, but place it carefully to his forehand or backhand. Allow yourself no lazy concentration once the ball is to be put into play. Your future as a tennis player will depend directly upon your ability to concentrate intently and to sustain that concentration as long as the rally may last.

Frequently I am asked, "Coach, why did I hit the ball on the wood? Is it my grip—my swing—my—???" This error is due almost 100 percent to a violation of one phase of concentration: failure to watch the ball long enough. It is nearly impossible to watch the ball right up to the strings, but if the eyes do not follow the ball long enough, those off-center hits will spell disaster no matter how highly skilled you may be.

As I observe players of all degrees of ability, I see so few who average more than two strokes each per rally. There just doesn't seem to be a conscious effort to develop either stroke consistency or concentration endurance. The ability to sustain concentration is a must if stroke consistency is to be achieved. And both are just as important as muscular endurance in the development of a winning game.

The two fundamental causes of short rallies are failure to sustain intense concentration and over-hitting. Over-hitting is trying to hit the ball with too much power or attempting to place the ball too close to the lines. No player can ever achieve his potential without control over these two weaknesses.

The next time you go out to practice, try reminding yourself at the beginning of every rally, "I have no idea where the ball may go! Watch it!" You will see a difference in your ability to get to the ball in excellent stroking position. And with that result will come a growing confidence in your ability to play the game well. Confidence is the name of the winning game.

P.S. You are beginning most of your rallies with a serve and return of service, aren't you? Over 50 percent of the game consists of these two strokes. Why neglect them? ●

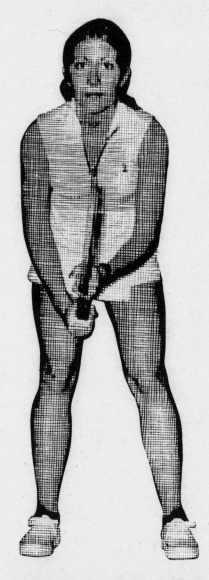

ILLUSTRATION B—When told to prepare herself for any shot by her opponent, she automatically assumed correct stance.

HOW TO PRACTICE:
Plan Your Workouts

by GLADYS M. HELDMAN

THE NUMBER of hours one practices does not necessarily determine the rate of improvement. Hitting the ball as hard as one can straight down the center and taking the ball on the second bounce is not an effective practice pattern. The courts are crowded with athletic youngsters who think the essence of the game is banging the ball with all one's might and that if they bang it long enough and hard enough, one day all their shots will go in. There are also masses of adult beginners who practice four to six hours a week and who improve at an extremely slow rate because they neglect to practice footwork, stroke control, depth and placement.

Most top players have developed excellent practice patterns. These are designed to speed up footwork and reflexes, work the kinks out of strokes, develop more accuracy and control against heavy pace and spins, build up stamina, acquire more power, touch and/or spins and to achieve instinctive reactions to the opposition's patterns. Top players do not stand flat-footed when they are practicing. They never stroll casually around the court picking up balls after a rally. (They run.) They don't lose concentration because they are "only warming up." Above all, they don't practice with anyone who isn't serious about practicing. The worst kind of warm-up opponent is an indifferent one—a wild slugger, a bored competitor, an unenthusiastic foot-dragger, someone who wants to play instead of practice and who then gives it less than 100 percent when the set begins.

Practice sessions, depending upon the stage of one's development or whether there is a particular stroke or footwork problem, vary enormously, but all have these factors in common:

- Concentration must be complete; an hour of hard practice is worth five hours of foot-dragging.
- The player is never flat on his heels. He bounces, jumps, hops and runs full-out.
- After a ball is netted, another ball is put into play immediately. There is no pause between rallies (and certainly no conversation).
- All shots are taken on the first bounce.
- From the moment the player steps on the court, each shot has a purpose—the first few hits to warm up the arms and legs and to get one's timing and thereafter to work on a particular phase of the game, viz., crosscourts, return of serve, lobs, volleys, overheads, serves, backhand approach shots, drop shots, forehands, down-the-lines, etc.

The better players practice patterns that are impossible for beginners, viz., drop shots and lobs or "one at net and two on the baseline." Novices will waste a lot of time practicing serves and returns of serve: many serves will be netted and the receiver will sometimes have to wait six or eight shots for a serve to come over the net. Each level requires a different kind of pattern—one that will result in hitting the maximum number of balls to achieve the greatest amount of improvement. Beginners, for example, will get much more out of a practice session if they work with a basket of used balls rather than the three new balls that top players use.

Patterns for Beginners

Most novices tire quickly. At the end of five minutes they are often down to a slow crawl. At this point it is better to stop for a moment and get one's breath than to drag around limply. Novices are notoriously as slow as snails and they cannot advance into the intermediate category until they have learned to run to pick up every ball. The most important pattern for the beginner, therefore, is to pick up his feet, move fast, run, hop, bounce and skip. Walking to pick up a ball is *verboten*.

Some practice patterns for beginners are:

- Both players stand on the service line, each holding several balls and with several others in pockets. One starts the rally. The target here is control, not power—to keep the rally alive, not to put the ball away. The ball must be hit inside the service line so the opponent can return it. The emphasis is on seeing the ball at all times, taking a backswing early, hitting the ball in front of the body and following through.
- After the players can maintain a rally of 10 shots without missing, they move back so they are now half-way between the service line and the baseline. Again the object is control, not power, and to keep the ball in play. The player does not stand still while he waits for the return; he bounces and hops.
- One player stands at net while the other stands a little behind the service line. The net man volleys his return while the opponent hits forehands and backhands. Neither player should forget the objective, which is steadiness and returning the ball directly to the opponent. After five minutes reverse positions, the net man moving back and his opponent coming in to volley.

- When both players are consistent enough, rallying starts from the baseline. However, if there is too much loss of control and if the players are wildly spraying balls all over the fence, they move back in four steps each so that the rallies will be longer.
- The players move to the *same side* of the court and each *separately* practices serves, with one serving into the forehand and the other into the backhand court. This is another reason to have a full basket of balls since far too much time is wasted if one has to pick them up constantly.
- When the players are able to rally from the baseline and to get a sufficient number of serves in to make it worthwhile, they play a practice set. The aim is not to put the ball away for a winner but to get it back over the net. Since this is a practice set and not a match, all efforts are concentrated into keeping the ball in play. Each player tries to see the ball early, move quickly, take an early backswing and hit a full stroke. As soon as one player hits the ball, the other player starts moving. After each point is over, the balls are picked up *quickly*. If the players tire badly, they rest for one minute, then continue at full speed.

Patterns for Intermediates

An intermediate is defined as a player who seldom double-faults, has a reasonable forehand which he can hit at will crosscourt and usually at will down-the-line, an unreasonable backhand (but he gets a good percentage in unless pressed) and some experience at net although the volley is not precise and the overhead slightly shaky. Intermediates have experience: they do not desire to play with beginners and prefer not to play with other intermediates. Among the shots they have not yet acquired are: a half-volley, a drop shot, a drop volley, a topspin lob, a deep slice serve to the backhand, a sidespin forehand that they can alternate with a topspin forehand, a backhand slice that they can alternate with a topspin (they have one or the other—not both) and a penetrating approach shot. Intermediates can whack balls away for placements; their problem is they make far too many errors and, on too many occasions, the opponent gets the ball back. Intermediates know an enormous amount about the game since 90 percent of the players today are beginners, but they quickly find out what they don't know when they come up against an advanced player or when they talk tennis to the tournament players. The best thing an intermediate player can do since he has come this far, is to work like hell on his game for a year in order to get to the advanced stage.

The intermediate who is keen to take the big jump to a higher class must, first, recognize his own weaknesses and, second, sublimate his desire to stick with what he has (the big bash forehand volley taken on the dead run, or the "cannon ball" first serve that lands four feet out, or the poorly constructed backhand that has no chance of becoming first class) in order to develop a stronger game. Each intermediate has a style of his own—attacker, defender, basher, unorthodox retriever—but he must learn to round out his game, play percentages, acquire accuracy and move twice as fast as he ever thought possible. His practice sessions are going to be extremely rewarding because he will no longer try to show the practice opponent how hard he can hit, but how well he moves, sees, concentrates and con-

trols. His patterns are designed to improve strokes and footwork, and if one or either are bad, a series of lessons are in order so that he knows what to work on. Assuming he takes these lessons, his practice patterns would be somewhat like this.

- For the first few minutes he hits forehands and backhands down the center to get his timing and warm up his arm. He bounces, hops, stretches and takes a full swing.
- For 15 minutes he hits forehands. He concentrates on seeing the ball well so that he can take it in front of him. He remembers what his pro has told him about the swing. For the first five minutes he hits forehand crosscourts and for the next 10 minutes forehands down-the-line. He is interested only in depth (hitting the ball as close to the baseline as possible). He tries to groove the down-the-line, and gradually he feels the difference in the positioning of his shoulders and feet and the point at which he takes the ball: the down-the-line requires slightly quicker timing and so is more difficult to execute against a hard, deep shot.
- During the next 15 minutes he endeavors to do the same on his backhand—crosscourts (the more natural shot) and down-the-lines. Pretty soon he will realize that the timing on forehand and backhand is a fraction of a second different. Therefore, when he has a great day on his backhand, his usually reliable forehand may go off. This sense of timing is only acquired by practice. It is like rubbing your stomach with one hand and patting your head with the other at the same time (two different kinds of timing are required). Once you get it, you understand the two different rhythms.
- Now one player takes the net for 10 minutes and the other the baseline. The net man tries to volley deep down the center from both forehand and backhand side. Every fifth or eighth or tenth ball, a lob is thrown up and the net man works on his overhead. If he starts with simple, short set-ups, he develops a rhythm and confidence. Gradually the lobs are made more difficult—higher and deeper—but basically his aim is to acquire an extremely consistent overhead on short set-ups. After 10 minutes the positions are reversed and the net man now tries to hit low, hard shots down the center, alternating occasionally with a lob. Now he is trying to keep the ball low (not to go for depth) since this is the kind of shot he will hit in match play when his opponent comes to net.
- Intermediate players have good returns of serve so serves and returns can be practiced. One player serves 40 balls while the other returns, but this is more than just serving into a rectangle or returning the ball haphazardly. The server hits 20 serves in the forehand court—10 to the opponent's forehand and 10 to the backhand. Meanwhile the receiver returns five down-the-line and five crosscourt, then five down-the-line and five crosscourt. No longer is the server (or the receiver) just hitting; each serve and each return has a purpose. The intermediate has now grown two inches in stature; he is learning placement on serve and return of serve. Serves and returns are also practiced in the backhand court. Depth as well as placement counts: a serve deep down the center is about to be acquired by the intermediate.
- The last phase of the session is a practice set or two. Everything the intermediate has practiced he now tries in this set—deep crosscourts off deep shots and sharp

down-the-lines off short balls, service placements to the backhand and return of serve deep to the backhand or wide to the forehand. On short balls the intermediate clears the net well (to get depth) and follows in behind the shot to make his volley. The intermediate begins to realize that to get depth, he must clear the net by five to 10 feet. However, when his opponent comes in, he lowers his trajectory (to make the net man volley low) or raises it by lobbing.

Patterns for Advanced Players

It is not a bad idea for the advanced player to read about the practice sessions for intermediates. He is not so advanced that he no longer has any intermediate weaknesses. A realization of his own weaknesses is the panacea to his problems. How good is his down-the-line or with what depth does he hit his second serve?

The advanced player has many more shots than an intermediate and he reads his opponent far better. He moves in the second he knows his opponent has drop shotted. He runs around his backhand to clout a forehand return of second serve. His backhand is both consistent and accurate (often it is his best stroke). If he doesn't volley well, he compensates with an extremely strong baseline game; if his groundstrokes are unsteady, his volleying is impressive. He does not bang a shot to impress the gallery. He thinks on the court and very often he reacts instinctively, which is one step better than thinking.

The advanced player's practice sessions are far more strenuous than those of the intermediate because he misses fewer balls and he both starts and runs faster. Depending upon how advanced he is, here is what he can practice:

- First there are the usual crosscourt and down-the-line drills. Now these are alternated with occasional drop shots: the player runs in to get the drop shot and his opponent lobs deep. After 10 or 15 drop shot-lob patterns, a player begins to round into mid-season form. It is strenuous since the player must hit the 15th as well as he did the first. Another excellent pattern is down-the-line alternated with an occasional *sharp* crosscourt (one that goes short and wide). The receiver runs wide for the ball and goes down the line deep, following the shot to net. No ball is ever taken on the second bounce.
- One of the best patterns for advanced players is the approach shot off the short ball and the sharp crosscourt volley. Both players hit from the baseline until one player accidentally hits a short ball. The other player (A) then approaches net with a down-the-line deep to the baseline—sidespin is used on the forehand and underspin on the backhand. Player B tries a low passing shot and Player A responds with a sharp crosscourt volley. This pattern is practiced off all short balls for at least 15 minutes. It grooves approach shots and makes the crosscourt volley automatic.
- Both players now stand two steps inside the service line and volley at each other, gradually increasing the pace. After a few minutes one player takes two steps in while the second player (B) remains in the same position. Player A has to speed up his reflexes on the volley while Player B has to do more half-volleying. The positions are then reversed.
- Serves and returns of serve are practiced for 10 minutes or more. The first player hits 40 serves but a maximum of

two in a row to each court (the second ball is his second serve). In other words, each player is practicing not just his first but his second serve, and if he "double-faults" or serves too short, he is instantly aware of it. In turn, the receiver is "up" for the second serve and is ready to pounce on it if it lacks spin or is short.
- If either player has a weakness, this shot is practiced for the next 10 minutes.
- For the finale, they play one or two practice sets, working on approach shots after short balls, crosscourt volleys, lobs, overheads and passing shots. The whole pattern is one of intense concentration; how does one improve if one is lackadaisical?

Patterns for Tournament Players

The tournament player will use the practice format for advanced players with additions of his own. He may jog two to five miles a day, finishing in the stretch with a sprint, or he may jump rope, do pushups or any other gymnastic exercise designed to strengthen his leg, arm, stomach and wrist muscles. Additionally, he will practice longer and harder than the advanced player. Conditioning, accuracy, timing, touch, power and speed of foot are the factors that distinguish him from his lesser tennis brothers, and any easing of the program will affect his game adversely.

The category "tournament player" encompasses a vast group of champions—the junior star, the Satellite Circuit player, the College No. 1, the Davis or Wightman Cupper and the top Wimbledon and Forest Hills competitors. The club or parks champion is on the lowest level, followed by the city winner. Thereafter, in the national and international level, the heights a player reaches depends on how good he is on his worst day and whom he can beat through fight alone when his strokes have failed him or his timing is off. A great player may lose on occasion to a lesser one but never to a terrible player. The more he keeps himself in top condition through regular practice, the less chance of losing to a player ranked many notices below.

Some tournament players have few ambitions. They are happy to distinguish themselves in their own city or state and do not want to make a professional career out of tennis. Others like to reach the top or near top but they are bored with practice and semi-resigned to their fate as "permanent qualifiers." The ambitious and eager who cannot seem to get enough tennis are the most likely to improve—with two provisos. First, their practice patterns must be designed to take the wrinkles out of weaknesses such as a serve with no bite or a shaky overhead or an inability to leap for the volley; and second, they must have the nerves to go with the heart, and this they can only work out through coming back just as fiercely and eagerly after each loss.

The tournament player will use the same practice patterns as the advanced player, but added to these are conditioning exercises and long hours of work (often with a coach) to iron out the weaknesses. The patterns are simply practiced for longer periods of time (three hours a day instead of one or two) and are mixed in daily with several practice sets in singles and doubles. Additionally, he plays between 15 and 30 tournaments a year. If done with total concentration, the prognostication is: steady improvement and a much wider experience of match play, which means a better chance to win.

The Key to Good Footwork

by DENNIS Van der MEER

A POOR PLAYER tends to use a variety of strokes to accommodate the different ways a tennis ball can bounce. Unfortunately he neglects his footwork.

When the ball crowds him, a poor player will use his "digger-outer"; when the ball is out of his reach he uses his "telescopic shot"; and then he invents a hundred more innovative ways to return the ball, all without moving his feet.

The good player tries to use one grooved stroke by making his feet adjust for every variety of bounce. Only in an emergency will he deviate from his grooved technique. Good footwork can be practiced by drawing small circles on the ground and numbering them. First practice your forehand. Call out the numbers at random to yourself and see how quickly you can shuffle, run, back pedal, glide or step towards the spot you have called out. As soon as your right foot hits the spot, balance yourself, step in with your left foot and play a perfect shadow stroke. Reverse the sequence of footwork for the backhand.

This type of exercise will reduce the number of "emergency shots" you will have to play and by using the same strokes more often it will truly become grooved. ●

The key to proper body placement is the right foot, which should be in place at the start of the stroke. Practice all the ways of getting it in position. The model: California's Susan Mehmedbasich.

As soon as your right foot hits the spot, balance and step in with your left foot.

The finish of a perfect shadow stroke, with the good balance associated with foot and body placement.

TENNIS TEST
Rating for Beginners and Intermediates

Test yourself to see what level of player you are (answers at the end of quiz). If your score is 39 consider yourself an advanced player.

Scoring

1. If the first set is 6-4, do you change sides for the first game of the second set?
   A. Yes   B. No
2. In Sudden Death (the 9 point tiebreaker), do you have to win the tiebreaker by two points?
   A. Yes   B. No
3. Do women ever play the best of 5 sets in tournament play?
   A. Yes   B. No
4. When does Wimbledon use tiebreakers?
   A. At 6-all   B. At 8-all   C. At 10-all
   D. At 8-all except no tiebreaker is used in the final set

Stroke Terminology

1. If an opponent lobs you, your return is called what?
   A. Overhand   B. Underhand   C. Overhead
   D. Smash   E. Overhand or Overhead
   F. Overhead or Smash
2. What is a half-volley?
   A. A volley that lands inside the service line
   B. A volley that is angled to a corner
   C. A pick-up shot hit just as the ball is rising from the ground.
   D. A very high volley
3. The term "not up" means which of the following?
   A. The ball bounced twice before the player hit it
   B. The player's racket hit the ground before it hit the ball
   C. The player missed the ball completely
   D. The ball hit the net before the player hit it
4. A "let" is:
   A. Any ball that touches the net
   B. A first serve that ticks the net and lands in the proper service court
   C. A first or second serve that ticks the net and lands in the proper service court
   D. A second serve that ticks the net and lands in the proper service court
   E. The replaying of a point because of outside interference or a long delay
   F. A combination of C and E

Rules

1. Is it illegal to serve by letting the ball drop below waist level and then hitting it with an underhand swing?
   A. Yes   B. No
2. If you are playing indoors and your lob hits one of the overhead lights, what happens:
   A. You play the point over
   B. You lose the point
   C. You win the point
   D. The point is replayed but you only get one serve
3. When a footfault is called on a player it is because:
   A. He stepped on the line on first serve
   B. Although neither foot touched the line, one foot swung over the line before the ball was hit
   C. He stepped on the line on second serve
   D. He stepped on the line on either first or second serve
   E. Both feet were off the ground when the serve was hit
   F. One foot was off the ground when the serve was hit
4. If just an edge of the ball touches the outside edge of the baseline, the umpire rules it as:
   A. Out   B. Good   C. Replay the point

Courtesy

1. When a ball from your court rolls into the next court where a point is in progress, what should you do:
   A. Wait until the point is over
   B. Politely ask for your ball back
   C. Retrieve it quickly yourself if the ball is not in their actual playing area
   D. Call "replay" to them and then ask for the ball
2. If you hit a shot in your opponent's court and you are positive your shot was good, what do you do:
   A. Tell him your shot was good
   B. Ask him to replay the point
   C. Say that you think the ball was good but he should call it any way he wants to
   D. If he asks you how it was, tell him it was good
3. Toward the end of a long, tough match played under overpowering heat, which of the following can you do if you are thoroughly exhausted:

A. Request a 5-minute intermission
B. Take 60-seconds on each odd-game change-over to refresh yourself
C. Leave the court area, as long as it is for less than three minutes, to get water and/or salt pills
D. Ask your opponent if he would agree to a specified rest period, knowing that if he doesn't the match must continue

4. If your opponent hits a shot and you are not sure how it is, what do you do:
A. Call it out
B. Play the point as good
C. Ask to replay the point
D. Return the ball and if your shot is out, ask to replay the point

History

1. Which players have won the Grand Slam (the Wimbledon, French, Australian and U.S. Singles titles all in the same year):
A. No one
B. Jack Kramer
C. Billie Jean King
D. Don Budge, Maureen Connolly, Rod Laver and Margaret Court
E. Bill Tilden and Helen Wills

2. Which of these British women won the Wimbledon singles:
A. Virginia Wade
B. Angela Mortimer
C. Angela Buxton
D. Kay Stammers Menzies

3. Who were the "Four Musketeers":
A. Darmon, Barthes, Goven and Jauffret
B. Borotra, Brugnon, Lacoste and Cochet
C. Lenglen, Mathieu, Durr and Chanfreau
D. Aramis, Porthos, Pietrangeli and Panatta

4. Where was the first U.S. National Championships played:
A. The West Side Tennis Club in Forest Hills
B. The Merion Cricket Club, Haverford, Pa.
C. The Meadow Club, Southampton, L.I.
D. The Longwood Cricket Club, Chestnut Hills, Mass.
E. The Newport Casino, Newport, R.I.
F. Madison Square Garden

Tactics

1. At which of the following times should you drop shot:
A. When your opponent is in midcourt and you are on the baseline
B. When you are exhausted and want to end the point quickly
C. When you are fairly close to the net and your opponent is on the baseline

2. Which of the following shots is good for returning serve in doubles:
A. A high crosscourt floater
B. A short lob to the net man
C. A "dinker" at the server's feet
D. A drop shot

3. When is it most important to use underspin on the backhand drive:
A. To pick up the low, short ball and hit it down the line

B. To hit a deep, hard baseline crosscourt
C. To pass the net man

4. If your opponent is at net, do you have a better chance of passing him if he hits a ball that:
A. Bounces on the baseline
B. Bounces on the service line

Techniques

1. On the wind-up of the service action, should the racket at one point drop behind your head and practically scratch your back?
A. Yes   B. No

2. What grip do good players usually use on the volley?
A. Eastern   B. Western   C. Continental

3. When hitting a low ball, what is the best approach:
A. Bend from the waist
B. Drop your racket head to ball level
C. Bend your knees

4. How do you get the most control and power on a forehand, assuming you are a right-hander:
A. By stepping toward the net with your left foot just before the hit and meeting the ball in front of your body with a motionless wrist
B. By stepping with your left foot toward the alley and hitting the ball at your side
C. By hitting the ball at your side and coming across the ball with a lot of wrist snap

Spins

1. How do you underspin a backhand?
A. By starting with your racket head at a point below ball level and following through high
B. By tilting your racket backwards so that the face is slightly open to the sky
C. By turning your wrist over as you hit.

2. In serving an American twist, where would you toss the ball:
A. To your right
B. Slightly in front of you
C. To your left and slightly behind you

3. If your opponent is a lefty who hits a slice serve to your forehand, where would it move after the bounce assuming you are right-handed:
A. It would move into your body
B. It would move far toward your right
C. It would drop quickly and move toward your right

4. What kind of spin would make a ball rebound very high with forehand motion:
A. Underspin   B. Sidespin   C. Overspin

Attacking

1. When you serve and come to net, what should be your approach to the first volley:
A. Hit it on the run
B. Run forward, stop, volley the ball, then move forward another few steps
C. Run forward, stop, volley, then wait to see where your opponent is going to hit

2. If you hit a forehand down the line to your opponent's backhand and you come to net, where should you stand to anticipate his return:
A. On the center service line, halfway between the service line and the net
B. Several feet to the right of the center service line
C. Three feet from the alley line

3. What would be the best attack in men's tennis against a high floating ball:
   A. Half-volley it immediately after the bounce
   B. Move back, letting it drop to waist level, and then step in and hit it
   C. Move in and take the ball as a high volley

Doubles
1. If you played the forehand court in the first set, can you switch in the second set and play the backhand
   A. Yes   B. No
2. If your partner is lobbed but has a very bad overhead, what would you do:
   A. Call out "hit"
   B. Tell him to bounce it and hit the ball as a groundstroke

   C. Say nothing
3. If you are at net and your partner is in the backcourt and if a lob comes over your head and your partner runs for it, what would you do:
   A. Crouch down below net level
   B. Quickly run to the other side of the net
   C. Do nothing
4. If you have been poaching at net and suddenly have been passed in your alley, what would your plan be:
   A. Guard the alley thereafter
   B. Stop poaching
   C. Feint as though you were going to poach in the hopes of luring the opponent into trying another alley shot

THE ANSWERS

How To Score Your Test
Advanced player with excellent knowledge
of the game 37-39
Advanced player who could use more
information about rules or history 32-36
High intermediate player or, possibly,
advanced player who tests badly 29-31
Intermediate 26-28
Beginner .... 25 or less

Scoring
1. B. You stay on the same side for one game. If the score of the first set were 6-3, you would change sides for one game only. So it's "stay for one" (when the first set score is an even number) or "change for one" (when the first set score is an odd number). Or "stay on the even, change on the odd."
2. B. At 4-points all in the 9-point tiebreaker, one point gives either party a set. Hence the name "Sudden Death."
3. B
4. D

Stroke Terminology
1. F. The word "overhand" is in disuse.
2. C
3. A
4. F

Rules
1. B
2. B
3. D
4. B. Any ball that touches any part of the line is good.

Courtesy
1. A. Never go into a neighboring court while a point is in progress.
2. D. You cannot volunteer a call on your opponent's side unless he asks you.
3. B. The 60-second rest is allowed on odd games and need not be requested.

4. B. When in doubt, you must play the point as good.

History
1. D
2. B
3. B
4. E

Tactics
1. C. Dropshots are most effective when you are closer to net and your opponent is far from it.
2. C. A dinker is a low, dipping shot which forces the opponent to hit up to you.
3. A. Underspin makes the ball rise up and takes some speed off it and so it is not an effective passing shot.
4. B

Techniques
1. A
2. C. By using the Continental, one does not have to change grips for forehand or backhand.
3. C
4. A. You lose power if your weight is moving sideways rather than forward and you lose control if the wrist is not firm.

Spins
1. B. The description given in A is of a topspin.
2. C. The American twist finishes past the right leg rather than across the left leg as in topspin, slice or flat serves.
3. A
4. C

Attacking
1. B. You must come to a stop when hitting the volley but you must also move in after the first volley has been hit.
2. B. The angle of the opponent's return will generally be between your right alley (for a down the line return) and your center service line. He has to hit a very sharp, short crosscourt to pass you, and this is not an easy shot.
3. C

Doubles
1. A
2. C
3. B. If you don't cross to the other side, you and your partner will be in the "I" formation.
4. C

Bill Cosby is one of the most popular players on the celebrity circuit. The pros enjoy being his straight men on the court.

Photo by Richard Evans

CELEBRITY TENNIS

Show Biz On The Court

by CANDACE MAYERON

"WHAT YOU MEAN, I can't step over red line?" demanded Ion Tiriac, long accustomed to stepping on anything he damn well pleases. The red line—laid across the regular service line, explained tournament host James Franciscus, was an attempt to equalize the disparity between the professionals and their amateur doubles partners, to keep the tennis pros from rushing the net and blasting the amateurs on the other side off the face of the earth. The "earth" in this case was the court at the pro-celebrity

tournament in conjunction with WCT's Green Group Kemper International at Palm Desert, Calif. The 16 "amateurs," including Neil Simon, Harvey Korman, Burt Bacharach, George Peppard and Rod Steiger, were paired with 16 professionals. And there was prize money at stake.

Celebrity tennis, in case you've been living in Mongolia, is when your favorite movie/television/recording performer (and a few you have never heard of) venture onto a tennis court with a playing professional as a partner, for what can sometimes be described as a set of tennis.

But wait. Laugh out of the other side of your mouth. Celebrity tennis is rapidly becoming serious business to more than just the stars involved.

Southern California has always had an abundance of sunshine, stars and tennis courts. It was only a matter of time until someone thought to put them all together and capitalize on the mixture.

Of course celebrities have been playing tennis since the advent of sound on film. Ex-boxer Errol Flynn

was one of the best. Kate Hepburn could wield a racket (remember in *Pat and Mike* when she gave Gussie Moran quite a bit of trouble?) But celebrity tennis didn't get organized until 1970 when Tommy Cook, the Sol Hurok of tennis-playing celebs, organized a tournament at La Costa. He brought in 72 celebrities, including Clint Eastwood, Charlton Heston and Robert Wagner, and was able to entice a large paying crowd to watch them play doubles without the security of a script.

Since that time, celebrity tennis has changed its format many times to fit many different needs. While there are variations, celebrities either stage their own tournaments with singles and doubles events, or they form doubles teams with a regular touring professional and hold their matches along with a men's or women's pro tournament.

At the Franciscus tournament prize money was given to the pro on the winning pro-celebrity team. The 16 teams, composed of first round losers in the singles and their celebrity partners, were divided into four round robins of four teams each to determine who advanced to a playoff.

The prize money gave a lot of pros a chance at a large purse. The $5,000 first prize was as large as Roscoe Tanner's runner-up purse in the main event. Indeed, it was Antonio Munoz, low man in the Green Group standings, who eventually won the celebrity tournament (paired with Bill Cosby) and took home the largest purse of his life.

The presence of movie stars drastically changes the atmosphere of a tennis tournament, making it like a rollicking side show. Everyone is congenial and friendly, as the crowd follows favorites around. To many people, seeing a movie star—and telling cousin Nellie in Topeka about it—seems to rank right up there with walking on the moon. One feels less self-conscious star gazing at a tennis tournament than on a Beverly Hills boulevard. Little old ladies with blue hair giggle over Burt Bacharach's bare knees. Businessmen who daily make million dollar decisions shyly ask for autographs for their "sons." Encouraged to root and cheer, fans maintain a running patter with their favorites. An excited fan shouts at Franciscus, "Hey Jim, I never saw you run so fast." "You never will again!" he throws back. It's all noisy and loose.

The whole purpose of all this fun and frolic is to raise money for charity. It seems as if all celebrity tennis tournaments are played for the benefit of some charity, and depending on the size of the event, the charity can expect to garner anywhere from several thousand dollars to almost $100,000. At La Costa this year with WCT's Blue Group, the celebrities raised $10,000 for the Motion Picture and Television Relief Fund. Last year the Children's Asthma Research Institute and Hospital made over $80,000 from a Liza Minnelli concert and tennis tournament at Toronto's Maple Leaf Gardens. That was arranged by Tommy Cook.

Cook got his start as a sometime Hollywood actor, but had more talent on court than on screen. He became the most sought after tennis teacher to the stars, counting among his pupils Dyan Cannon, Dino Martin Jr., Claudine Longet, Ruth Buzzi and many others. He finally formed a company (Limelight International) and began packaging celebrity tennis tournaments. By his own estimate, Cook has raised between three and four million dollars for charities through tennis. He also made some nice fees for Limelight.

Actually, the celebrity tennis itself is not the money maker. The crowds do not exactly break down the gates to make it to the 10 a.m. matches. What it does is help lure the big money sponsors like Michelob and Kemper into the game. Television commentator Jim Simpson says, "We usually have to televise the celebrity tennis and then join the men's singles in progress. The sponsors want the celebrities to get the air time. They feel—right or wrong—that the audience would rather see Johnny Carson playing bad tennis than Stan Smith playing good tennis."

Sponsors are choosy about the charities they support. They must be accredited, with good IRS credentials. Charities with national affiliations are preferred for their greater publicity value.

A sponsor is absolutely essential if the charity is to make any real money, for expenses can cut into as much as 50 percent of the gross. While the stars are never paid for their "appearances," all their expenses are paid—their air fares, food and lodging. The sponsor also picks up the tab for setting up the seating, which can amount to considerable money. There are other miscellaneous expenses that, if not picked up by a sponsor, must be paid off the top: parking attendants, the fee to the celebrity tournament organizer (usually 1% percent of the gross), security guards, free food and drinks for V.I.P.s, decorations, office expenses, etc.

"The name of the game," says Cook, "is trade-out. We don't like to pay for anything if we absolutely don't have to." The sponsor gets a trade-out in publicity, starting with his name above the title. His banners are displayed at the courts and at the usual dinner show. Even the balls used—an average of two to three gross per tournament—are arranged on a complimentary basis.

Hotel accommodations may be paid for by the sponsor, or more frequently, arranged for on a trade-out basis. The hotel has the right to take publicity pictures of the celebrities and gets a full page ad in the program. The hotel will make additional money from the liquor for the cocktail parties, and their street bars do a booming business from celebrity hounds.

The biggest expense is transportation. Federal regulations prohibit airlines from giving free seats. If an airline wanted to be a sponsor, it would have to donate the money directly to the charity; the charity would then use that money to buy airline tickets.

Expenses are offset by a large dinner show or concert usually held the Saturday night of the tournament. "Seldom do we put on just a celebrity tennis tournament without the concert," says one charity director, "because there's just not enough money to be made." The dinner show, where each star does an impromptu 10 or 15 minutes of his or her Vegas act, enables the charity to sell the high priced patron tickets. The patron tickets entitle the holder to the best seats at the tournament, entrance to the private cocktail parties where they can rub shoulders with the stars and a table at the dinner show or seats at the concert. Patron tickets sell for $100 and up, depending on what the charity thinks it can get, and sometimes the tickets are sold only in blocks of eight starting at $1,000.

For the stars, celebrity tennis means a weekend of fun, comraderie and tennis—all expenses paid. Limousines transport them from the airport to the hotel and to and from the tournament. Arriving at their hotels they find welcoming fruit baskets, liquor and little gifts—tennis balls, perfume, tennis accessories. At one recent tournament each celebrity was given a new graphite racket (retail value: $175) with his name engraved on the handle.

Playing in these tournaments has become so popular with stars that they now have annual tournaments of their own. La Costa's tournament is named after Ross Martin, and there's the Claudine Longet tournament in Denver, the Bill Cosby in Los Angeles, the Clint Eastwood in Pebble Beach, the Merv Griffin tournament in Kansas City (Merv has an uncle, Clarence Griffin in tennis' Hall of Fame), the Charlton Heston in Fort Lauderdale, and the James Franciscus in Palm Desert.

One celebrity who annually headlines his own tournament says, "It's a real ego trip for me. I get a tennis tournament named after me, the publicity and the prestige of lending my name to a worthwhile charity. And I get great personal satisfaction from having other celebrities coming to play in *my* tournament."

Make no mistake, the celebrities take both their tennis and these tournaments very seriously. What they lack in skill and savvy they make up for in zeal. Often more celebrities will request to be a part of a tournament than can be accommodated. Every movie star worth his weight in Guccis is playing the game; however, a band of hardy regulars play most of the tournaments: Ross Martin, Ron (Tarzan) Ely, Dan Rowan, Franciscus, Cosby, Ed Ames, Bacharach, Peppard, David Hartman, Steiger, Griffin, Heston, Glen Campbell, the Bridges (Lloyd and son Beau) and Robert Stack. "We seem to have formed our own road company," says Macdonald Carey.

Other celebrities besides motion picture stars play tennis. Sports figures like O. J. Simpson, Gail Goodrich, Jerry West and Jim Brown cut quite a swath on the courts. High fashion designer Oleg Cassini never misses the Alan King Tennis Classic in Las Vegas. The Robert Kennedy Memorial Tournament at Forest Hills, held just prior to the U.S. Open, attracts all the tennis-playing political figures: Senators Javits, Weicker, Kennedy, Sargent Shriver, Eunice Shriver and columnist Art Buchwald. ("The Kennedys all play very well, very aggressively," says Cook. "Ethel plays much better than Teddy.")

Dino (of Dino, Desi & Billy) Martin, Jr., son of Dean Martin, is easily the best of the Hollywood singles players. Seldom is he even allowed to compete with the other celebrities because his tennis is so far beyond theirs. A few years ago he travelled to Europe and entered some major open events. (He played Rosewall first round at Bristol and lost 6-0, 6-0.)

Aside from Dino, there are a half dozen other good celebrity players. One rule of thumb is that the less a celebrity works at his own career, the better he is likely to be on the court. Thus John Beradino, Bernie Kopell, John Lupton and Chris Connelly all have strong games, while Clint Eastwood and Gene Hackman can

barely hit the ball. Although busy, Burt Bacharach often takes the time to work with Pancho Segura. "The problem with Burt," says George Plimpton, himself a swinger, "is that he has been told countless times to bend his knees and he has taken this lesson quite literally. He crouches around the court, tucked into an egg-shaped form, and only springs out of his fetal position to sweep the ball into the net."

Ross Martin takes the game so seriously he makes Cliff Richey look loose. A competitor on and off the court, Martin has used tennis to keep in shape after being hospitalized some years ago. If matches were won on the basis of desire and dedication, Martin would win every match in a walk.

Johnny Carson is a relative newcomer to the celebrity circuit, but in his first tournament he made it to the semi-finals. Between points he will joke with the crowd, but once the ball is put into play his body stiffens from concentration (or fear), and his lips pull back over his teeth in a snarl designed to throw terror into the heart of his opponent.

Charlton Heston was honored by the players at last year's WCT playoffs in Dallas. He has been touting tennis long before it became the fashionable thing to do.

A favorite with the ladies is Glen Campbell. Golf is still his main hobby, and although he can't play tennis very well ("I just learned how to hit, I haven't learned to aim!"), he always steps onto the court spiffily dressed.

Alan King loves the game and promotes it every chance he gets, but he simply cannot play it. "Jews have no backhands," he says. "Two thousand years of persecution and all that built-up aggression is going to come out in a good, stiff forehand. The only good backhand I ever ran into was my mother's. She used it across my mouth."

The celebrities are very knowledgeable about the skills of the professionals they will be partnered with. To a man, they want to play with pros who will try the hardest to win and not ease up when serving to the opponent. Cliff Richey (natch), Denny Ralston, Roy Emerson and John Newcombe are among the favorites. Burt Bacharach would rather play with Segura than with Angie Dickinson. The least sought after pro partner is Stan Smith

who makes no secret of his dislike for celebrity tennis.

"Yeah," says Cliff Richey, "I like to play celebrity tennis if I'm in the right frame of mind. It may sound crazy, but I find I enjoy it more if I try to win. Oh, I don't really suffer if I don't win. It's like playing mixed doubles with my sister."

Denny Ralston says he enjoys playing with someone who doesn't get upset if he misses a few shots, "like Eastwood. We have a good time. Mostly I like celebrity tennis because guys like Heston and Franciscus did a lot for pro tennis in the early days, and I feel it's a way to pay them back."

The favorite performer with the spectators (and therefore, with the promoters) is Bill Cosby. He does not shed his humor with his warmups, prancing onto the court, dressed in baggy shorts and black power red-green-black striped socks with matching wrist bands. He understands the crowd is not there to admire his volleys or groundstrokes. He constantly jokes with the spectators, the other players, the linesmen. His serve lands five inches out of the service box, the lineman calls a fault and Cosby calls him a liar. The umpire refers to him as a "dark horse" and Coz calls for the referee. He engages in mock battles with the opposing celebrity at the net. "Are you sure you didn't give me the busboy?" he wails when his partner, Munoz, misses a shot. The crowd eats it up.

And lo and behold, amid all the clowning, it soon becomes evident the guy can play tennis. It figures. Cosby was a good college athlete and five weeks a year he does nothing but train with a coach, and at one time had a coach traveling with him. His backyard boasts both a clay court and probably the only grass court in Los Angeles. And he is adding a second grass court. "Got to let one rest and be fertilized while I'm using the other."

Celebrity tennis is, at its worst, exceedingly dull and sloppy. At its best it is highly entertaining. But never is it instructive, never can it be considered an art form, and fans should not approach it that way. One cannot admire the grace of Rod Steiger the way one admires the grace of Laver or Nastase. Clint Eastwood hasn't the balance of Rosewall. Johnny Carson hasn't Tom Okker's speed, but he's funnier. ●

Denver Cooks Ol' Mother Freedom's Goose

by Mike Lupica

Racquets were a picture of brotherly and sisterly love after winning first WTT championship. From left, trainer Willie Williams, Jeff Austin, Francoise Durr, Bud Fisher, Kris Kemmer, Pam Austin, series hero Andy Pattison and Stephanie Johnson.

AND SO World Team Tennis, the sport's Coney Island, ended its first—and some have said last—season like a party where the liquor ran out two hours early. It ended where it began, in Philadelphia, except that 7,000 fewer fans showed up for the finals than for the opener. Had the final series between the Philadelphia Freedoms and the Denver Racquets gone one more night like it could have, the tennis match would have been the first half of a double header with a box lacrosse game. Follow all that? Of course you don't. But remember, this is Team Tennis we're talking about.

Yet the league that ushered us into a brave new world of fans cheering double faults, loudly discussing female anatomy and questioning the ancestry of umpires—all on the same point—stumbled to the conclusion of an inaugural first season best summed up by Boston Lobster coach Ion Tiriac when he said "At least no one got pregnant." To the best of anyone's knowledge, no one did; although there were bad calls and blind linesmen, forfeits and fines, romances and rowdies. Through it all, WTT survived. Somehow.

The league that also brought us the coeducational locker room finished up on the 54th anniversary of the Nineteenth Amendment, which gave U.S. women the right to vote. WTT had followed this to its logical conclusion by giving them the right to coach, but the significance of all this was obviously lost on Ol' Mother Freedom herself, Billie Jean King. Coach King blew a chance to celebrate the Birth of Lib by blowing a championship that her Freedoms were supposed to win. Not only the championship, but the Teflon Cup that went with it.

The Teflon Cup?

Nope, it was the underdog Racquets who won the frying pan...er, cup. With the cookware really at stake, a team coached by a faith healer's patient and owned by a Wolfman Jack look-a-like, scrambled the Freedoms. Led by the winner of the Smirnoff Cup (awarded the league's MVP in the playoffs, honest folks), Andy Pattison, Denver won the best-of-three series from a Philadelphia team that had only lost five times during the regular season. Nobody was sure how much money this meant to the Racquet players, but as far as the Teflon prizes were concerned, it was strictly pots and pans on the line.

The story of the Philadelphia defeat was, well, the story of Buster and Billie. The unhappy ending was a natural; all the characters died in the end.

Ol' Mother Freedom began the final series in Denver by losing the first set of the night to Francoise Durr. She spent the rest of the night complaining about the randy, raucous Denver crowd. Billie Jean spends a lot of time saying how she loves the crowd to let it all hang out, but on the opening night of the finals, she got all hung up on a hostile arena.

"There was no way we could concentrate with them all over us all the time," she said afterward. No way. The Racquets got ahead early and went one-up with a 27-21 victory; they had let it all hang out, too.

Two nights later, in Philly, Player King had Durr 4-0 in the first set. But then Francoise and her ugly bag of strokes sneaked back. King eventually held on to win the set 6-4, but had she won it 6-2 like she should have, neither Coach King nor the rest of her team would have had to bad mouth young Buster Mottram after they lost.

Mottram had been held out of the series opener because of an alleged illness. In Philadelphia, he claimed to still be suffering from a temperature of 104 degrees, but apparently Lad Buster has a way of turning up with 24 hour viruses within two or three minutes of an important match. King started him against Pattison in the second match, and he was trailing Andy 0-3 (having won one point) when he was yanked and replaced with Brian Fairlie. Fairlie, coming in cold and having to serve immediately, promptly lost the next three games (winning three points in the process). This is what is known as coaching strategy, tennis fans.

"I asked Fiery (Fred Stolle) what he thought," said King, barely disguising her contempt at the press conference. "He said that if I didn't get Mottram out of there, he was going to lose the

set at love. So I pulled him."

So much for the official line. In the locker room, Ol' Mother Freedom said her boy wonder had "no guts." Fairlie, thrown into an impossible situation against the hot Pattison, called his teammate "gutless." And Stolle, who usually has bad words to say only about a bartender who closes a bar on him, concurred.

"The kid just lacks guts," Stolle said flatly. "None of what you blokes call intestinal fortitude. He has all the equipment to be a great player, but he never will be." The Freedoms, as it is plain to see, are just loaded with brotherly and sisterly love. The scene a couple of nights earlier in Denver emphasized this.

King went out to argue a line call late in the match. In the middle of a rather heated discussion with the umpire, she yelled for Stolle to come out and back her up. "The call was correct, Billie," Fred said. "The ball was out." Coach King then yelled for Fred to do something that no girl in Wahroonga (where he lives in Australia) told him to do. Coach and captain just glared at each other.

On the other side of the net, things were all sunshine, lollipops and roses, as you would expect them to be with any group coached by Tony Roche, that world famous star of the faith-healer's operating room. Roche has himself a solid, if relatively starless, team. Durr, Pattison, Kris Kemmer and Roche himself are all competent workmen/women, but truly the most colorful member of the organization is the man who owns it, Bud Fisher.

Fisher, who is also part owner of the ABA Denver Nuggets, really does look like Wolfman Jack. He also wears electric blue jump suits that look like they are made of double knit lamé. One of the great diamond wearers and cigaret smokers of our time, Fisher was running around hugging anyone who looked friendly after his team had won WTT's historic first Teflon. In the middle of his enthusiastic glad handing, he was letting out happy screams in a voice that he puts to good use back in Denver as a part-time auctioneer. He sells furniture and real estate, too. Up until Team Tennis, he made money.

"So what if we lost more money than we thought," he rasped later. "Man, we are the *champions.*"

It was the coach of the champions,

Philly coach King had her eyes on the Teflon Cup, but all she found was frustration against Francoise, feisty crowds in Denver and fractious Freedoms everywhere.

Roche, who put a lock on that championship with his 6-4 mixed doubles win with Kemmer in the final set of the last night (Denver led 22-20 going into the set). Roche had defended all year long his decision to go with Pattison in singles and himself in two doubles matches, and on that last night he looked like a genius.

He told Kemmer before the set, "Fred is going to hit the ball as hard as he can at you every chance he gets. You'll just have to hang in there because there is going to be one shot that you'll hit that is going to make all the difference." It never did come down to one Kemmer shot because tennis' beautiful blonde hit so many good ones. She first served crisply, and Roche had plenty of easy volleys to put away. Thus, Denver ended up clinching the title in an event considered one of Philly's strongest (with Stolle and Julie Anthony).

"I guess I'm one of the guys now," Kemmer giggled afterward.

"The only thing I can compare it to," the classy Roche said at the press conference, applying a huge icepack to The Elbow, "is a Davis Cup win when you've had a group of people working together towards one goal."

Roche was asked if he had indulged in some of the champagne that Fisher provided. "Beer will be enough for me," he grinned. "Where I come from, that's considered champagne."

Indeed, it was a beer party that Roche said got his team going after a low start that was supposed to be a Rocky Mountain high. Denver had been picked in the preseason to win their division, but began by losing eight of their first 10 matches. It was then that Roche decided to take the team out for a few Coors (they were in Los Angeles at the time). He told them to relax and have some fun. They bought it, and it brought them the championship.

It is a fact that no one seemed concerned about what the monetary reward for winning was going to be. Supposedly, the players were to receive some complicated division of the gate receipts; if they do it that way, then Roche, Pattison, Durr and Company will each get about $2.65. But remember, this is Team Tennis we're talking about.

And if we are talking Team Tennis here, we must take a look at a somewhat shaky future. Despite the fact that 16 teams were too many to start with, there is no talk of cutting loose some of the weaker franchises. The truth, though, is that most of the smiling new money that came into the league with such high hopes a year ago is foundering. Ray Ciccolo, the owner of the Boston Lobsters, seemingly one of WTT's more solvent franchises, is looking to sell all or part of his operation. He blames his $300,000-plus losses this year on advertising and promotional expenses that far exceeded his greatest expectations. And Ciccolo hasn't got one of the higher priced rosters in the league.

One member of the Minnesota Buckskins, one of the league's attendance leaders, said that the owners are having a contest to see who loses the least money because no one is going to make any. Bob Love, general manager of the Detroit Loves (no connection, it could be dangerous in Detroit), when asked about the future of his team, said: "How are we doing? We're like every other team in WTT. We're for sale and if nobody buys us, then there isn't going to be any team next year."

Things are probably not that bleak, even though there could be as many as 10 new ownerships in the league in 1975. So World Team Tennis may have failed slightly in Year One, but the life signs still look pretty strong. ●

ASHE IN SOUTH AFRICA

by RICHARD EVANS

MIDWAY through his arduous and fascinating 12 days in South Africa late in 1973, Arthur Ashe commented to Alan Paton, author of *Cry, the Beloved Country,* that so many things he had seen and heard seemed odd and contradictory. Eyes twinkling over his half moon glasses, Paton replied, "The whole world thinks we are odd. I suppose they are right. There is not much that adds up down here."

Given that the Vorster regime practices the most inhuman, degrading and unjust form of government in the *free* world, that is certainly true. South Africa is a mass of contradictions; a daily kaleidoscope of conflicting incidents and situations that defy explanation and blow logic sky high.

A genuine affection and respect exists in most homes between the white family and its black servants. Yet that affection seems to stop at the back door. For there is only passing concern for other blacks who are harassed—sometimes brutally—by the police if they are caught in white neighborhoods after 10 PM without correct papers. Whites will tell you such actions are necessary because there are so many burglaries.

We met scores of English-speaking whites who are sincerely embarrassed and deeply troubled by apartheid—both from a practical and moral point of view. But few seem capable or willing to actually do anything about it. That there are no easy answers is obvious, but an attitude of inert concern is not going to produce any answers at all.

Yet to say that nothing is being done would be wrong. There has been a re-cent wage increase for black laborers; all kinds of petty apartheid laws are suddenly being overlooked and not only Arthur Ashe but black South African players showered and changed next to Cliff Drysdale at Ellis Park. Progress? Certainly, but as former South African Davis Cup player Gordon Forbes said, "We are running in front of a tidal wave of pressure from the world at large. It is just a question of whether we can reach the shore of sanity and reason before we are engulfed."

Forbes, a man of considerable wit and humanity, views the problem philosophically. But for most whites who voiced their concern to me over and over again, questioning me on what I thought would happen and on what I felt about South Africa, there seemed to be one underlying sentiment running through all their questions—fear.

The openness with which so many people admitted the problem and acknowledged their fear surprised me. But then the trip, for me, was full of surprises: the opulence of the homes in the northern Johannesburg suburbs; the insidious efficiency of the apartheid system (uniformed police are conspicuous only by their scarcity). But then, for those few who try to buck the system, the proximity of an agent from BOSS (Bureau of State Security) is a daily part of life.

I was surprised at how incredibly charming, friendly and hospitable everyone was to us—and I mean everyone, white, black and colored. I was amazed to be able to walk around Soweto, the blacks-only township of

Arthur Ashe rates 18-year-old Shepherd Mojanaga, right, one of the most promising Africans he hit with during his visit. ▶

A passerby watches as Arthur Ashe conducts a clinic in Soweto, a ghetto of more than a million blacks near Johannesburg. Ashe was admitted into South Africa after agreeing he would not indulge in overt political activities during the trip.

one million people 15 miles from Johannesburg, without receiving a single hostile stare or unpleasant remark. The surprise was compounded when a resident of Soweto confirmed for me what I had always assumed, that there is a deep hatred and resentment of whites in general in the black community. Then why did it not show? Out of politeness to someone they suspected might have been with Ashe's party (it was the same when I went off for a walk on my own), or because, as Ashe so aptly puts it, of 100 years of Pavlovian conditioning?

I was surprised that, in such a rich nation enjoying the benefit of cheap labor, there is so much inefficiency. The postal service is reputed to be awful; calling or trying to find a taxi is an hour-long operation and what passes for a telephone system is a joke. (As an expert on bad phone systems, South Africa's is the worst I have encountered anywhere.)

But most of all, I was surprised at how so many decent and intelligent people could have remained apparently oblivious to the injustice of the system under which they were living for so long.

Time and again I got the impression that it has only been in the last two or three years that people have become aware of any problem. One example: a white schoolmaster—a man of sensitivity and intelligence—told me that only one year ago he had visited Soweto for the first time in his life. "I saw the house our maid lived in," he said.

"As soon as I did, I was acutely embarrassed because the previous Christmas we had given her an electric iron. She had seemed thrilled with it. It was only when I saw her house several months later that I realized it had no electricity. It seems incredible now, but the thought had simply never occurred to us."

If a new awareness is beginning to infiltrate the white community, there is the firm impression that it is only as a result of outside pressure, of world opinion. Even that would not have been sufficient to make South Africans take a deeper and more realistic look at their society had not that pressure materialized into something more tangible such as the sports boycott. More than anything it was South Africa's expulsion from the world's sports arenas that brought about the first hint of change. And ultimately it brought Arthur Ashe to South Africa.

It was because Ashe is so much more than just another athlete that it took him so long to get there. Tennis players Evonne Goolagong, Bill N'Godrella and Bonnie Logan, golfer Lee Elder and a black French rugby player had all preceded him as the Pretoria government tested the waters of progress with a cautious toe. The Nationalist leaders knew they would be in it up to their ears as soon as they let Ashe loose in their country no matter what kind of advance assurances that he would not indulge in overt political activities during his visit.

After several high level discussions at the South African Embassy in Washington, such assurances were given. Neither before nor during his trip would Ashe indulge in any inflammatory criticism of South Africa or its politics.

It was a price Ashe was prepared to pay. He had no illusions about the possible effects of his visit. He knew that he was wielding a double-edged sword that could cut as deeply into the wall of apartheid as it could dull the ferocity of world opinion. He knew the Vorster government would use his presence to feign a new liberalized attitude. "That is a risk I have to take," Ashe said. "I have to see for myself first hand whether there is anything I can contribute. One has to put emotion aside and be practical. There is not going to be a revolution in South Africa in the foreseeable future, so the only alternative is to work at changing things step by step."

That was Ashe's attitude when our party, consisting of Donald Dell and his wife Carole, Frank Deford of *Sports Illustrated* and myself, boarded the BOAC 747 at London. Sitting in the top deck lounge somewhere over the Sahara, we put Arthur through a trial press conference. "You once said you'd like to see a bomb dropped on Johannesburg, Mr. Ashe, so why are you here?" In fact, the real press conference that took place a few hours after our arrival at Ellis Park was surprisingly devoid of tough questions. The few awkward ones Arthur did receive were fielded with a dexterity and confidence that was to grow impressively in the following days.

The gentle tone of the reporters' questions was symptomatic of everyone's reaction to Ashe's presence. There was no doubt that promoter Owen Williams and Blen Franklin, the president of the South African Lawn Tennis Union, were sincerely and genuinely pleased to see Ashe standing on South African soil. They had, after all, worked hard enough to get him there. But I also got the strong impression from scores of people that Ashe was a very welcome guest in the white community—an impression that was enhanced ten days later when 90 percent of the entire crowd, not just the non-white section, loudly and unashamedly rooted for Arthur when he played Jimmy Connors in the final. Ashe never once ran into a direct apartheid problem. He had dinner in two restaurants in Johannesburg and stayed in hotels in Durban and Capetown and no one so much as raised an eyebrow. However, I suspect that both restaurants were warned in advance as to who was coming to dinner.

Ironically, it was the blacks and colored who instigated the only confrontation and conflict that Ashe faced during his entire stay. An Asian berated him in front of a small crowd of people at Ellis Park one afternoon because the stands were not totally integrated as Arthur had suggested they would be in an article he wrote for the London *Sunday Times*. Ashe admitted he had been too rigid in defining "totally integrated," but pointed out that box seats had been sold to blacks; that non-whites were sitting in areas previously reserved for whites only and that the strict segregation law was not being enforced. "It is true that

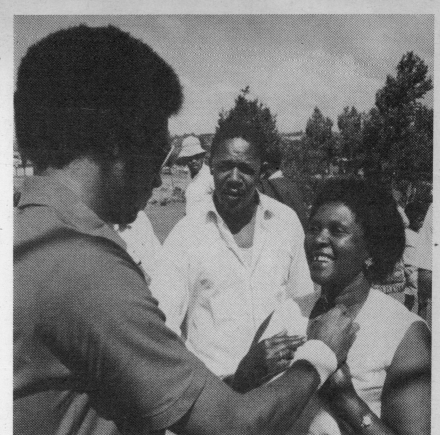

Ashe obliges a new South African fan with an autograph—on her chest. Militant blacks opposed Arthur's visit, feeling that he was being used by the government without gaining meaningful concessions in struggle against apartheid.

tickets are still printed with sections marked white and non-white," Ashe said. "But I cannot change the law. What we can do is try to dilute it so that eventually nobody bothers to enforce it any more."

This remark encompassed the basic thesis of the message Ashe spread whenever he met, talked and argued with members of the non-white community—which was often. Be practical, be realistic. Change what you can, when you can, how you can. Ashe knew that this line of thinking would enrage the hard-line militants, but he braced himself to ride the storm and never attempted to side-step the criticism he received. With enormous patience and fortitude he faced it on numerous occasions, allowing himself to be used as a punching-bag for pent-up frustrations.

His willingness to undergo this painful ordeal was never better illustrated than the night he met with some 50 black journalists at the U.S. Information Service offices in Johannesburg. He began by asking the one question he posed many times, "Does it help your struggle for me to come

here or would you rather I stayed away?" Some of the editors and writers present in the smoky room said they were glad he had come; that it was an inspiration to see him play and beat whites at Ellis Park; that it enabled them to laugh at the system that maintains integration of the races causing friction and strife.

But an equally large number stood up and made impassioned speeches offering the opposing view, "Your presence here simply creates an illusion," one journalist said. "When you leave nothing will have changed. Black tennis players will have to go back to their third rate courts and facilities in Soweto. If you stayed away, the isolation of the white sportsmen would be so terrible they would be forced to change completely. Please do not come back."

The meeting went on for hours. Ashe, still dressed in his warm-up trousers and sweater, stood before the emotional gathering, often saying nothing for long periods. When he did speak, Arthur stuck to his argument that if he did not come someone else would. No one could control all the black athletes in the world. (By the end of his visit, American boxer Bob Foster helped prove that point by saying openly he was there for a $200,000 purse and that the black Africans' problems were no concern of his.)

It was an enlightening, stirring and fascinating session and when it was over, Ashe was deeply moved. "I feel so helpless," he said as we left. But perhaps the most poignant aspect of the whole occasion was the fact that the man who had been responsible for arranging the meeting—a colored journalist and poet named Don Mattera—had, just that morning, been banned by the government. "Banning" in South Africa means a person is deprived of the right to pursue his profession. In Mattera's case it means, for the next five years, none of his work can be published or broadcast. He cannot meet anywhere, at any time, with more than one other individual. To support his wife and five children he will now have to take a menial job that will be an insult to his intellect.

Mattera had met Ashe the day before at Ellis Park as a free man. Twenty-four hours later he was forced to greet us on the street outside the USIS offices with an agent from BOSS lurking a few feet away. He could not attend the meeting he had arranged. For the next five years he will exist as a non-person in South African society. Appalled at the plight of this still cheerful and charming man, one was forced to derive what bitter satisfaction one could from the fact that the inane bureaucratic machine had mindlessly churned out his banning order with such exquisite lack of timing. If the banning order had been delayed for 10 more days, the incident— just one of many to befall those who voice opinions that displease the government—would have passed unnoticed by the outside world.

His work may not be printed in South Africa, but it will be published abroad. He is a poet of talent and insight. Unlike most people, it did not take Don Mattera long to discover what Arthur Ashe is all about. The first verse of his poem *Anguished Spirit—Ashe,* reads:

"I listened deeply when you
   spoke
   About the step-by-step
   evolution

Of a gradual harvest
Tendered by the rains of·
   tolerance
And patience.
Your yourthful face,
A mask,
Hiding a pining, anguished
   spirit,
And I loved you brother—
Not for your quiet philosophy
But for the rage in your soul,
Trained to be rebuked or
   summoned..."

A few nights later Ashe ran into more criticism at a reception given by USIS cultural affairs officer John Burns. Clad in flowing African robes, six members of two of the most militant student groups—the South African Student Organisation and the Black People's Convention— surrounded Ashe in a corner of the living room and, after a long, heated discussion, told him bluntly, "You're a tool of the government." For the only time on the whole tour, Arthur nearly lost his temper, just managing to control himself.

"You're letting your emotions cloud your thinking," he told the students clustered about him. "Do you think Zulu chief Buthelezi feels any different from you? Do you think he likes carrying around a pass book or being called a *kaffir?* Do you think he enjoys hearing the government preach independence of the Zulu homelands while knowing they are being denied their full ancestral acreage? Do you think he likes hearing Mrs. Betsie Vervoerd say Africans smell bad? Yet he does what he can, when he can, within the system. He tries to communicate because, in any conflict, the longer you stay away from the conference table, the bloodier the eventual confrontation."

The students took his point but still felt he should not have come. But there were many others who held the opposite view and he met them all during his stay.

He met most of the black and colored tennis leaders such as Reggie Ngcobo; in Durban he chatted with Archbishop Hurley and cricketer Barry Richards, the great batsman; at Stellenbosch University outside Capetown—the hotbed of Nationalist thinking—he rapped for two hours with three graduate students and one Afrikaner

professor of anthropology and came away greatly stimulated by the exchange. Also in Capetown he was shown black and white babies lying side by side at Christian Barnard's Red Cross Children's Hospital, and then he learned more of the progress being made in South African medicine when he dined with the famous heart surgeon that night. At the same dinner party he listened quietly to the views of the ultra-liberal leader of the Progressive Party, Colin Eglin. The following morning he made a last minute dash to Pretoria for a second meeting with Dr. Piet Koornhof, the minister of sport. Ashe knew that the meeting was vital to the whole success of his trip. He felt he had kept his end of the bargain and now he wanted to know what Dr. Koornhof was prepared to do to ensure that progress did not come to an abrupt end as soon as he climbed aboard the plane home. The meeting was private, but I believe the minister did give assurances—if not outright promises—that there would be further and immediate relaxation of the apartheid laws in sport.

For the time being Ashe is prepared to take him at his word. Being an intelligent and, in Afrikaner terms, an enlightened man, Dr. Koornhof must realize that Ashe is now a far better known and far more esteemed figure in South Africa than he was before his arrival. Arthur bent over backwards to be reasonable in the hope that, by taking a positive line, he will stimulate positive results.

Ashe wants to see blacks and Asians playing on the Sugar Circuit; he wants to set up a foundation to ensure that facilities in Soweto—where there are only 20 courts, mostly in deplorable condition—are dramatically improved; he wants to see white South African players take more time and trouble to coach the non-white players; he wants progress on all fronts, all the time—not just for 12 days at Ellis Park.

If there are signs that this is happening, then I believe Ashe will return to South Africa. But if everything grinds to a halt as soon as the world spotlight turns away from the troubled republic, then Dr. Koornhof had better listen well to the words of Don Mattera when he talks of the rage in Ashe's soul, trained to be rebuked ...or summoned. ●

Checkpoints For Intermediate Players

by GLADYS M. HELDMAN

THE intermediate player can direct the ball to the forehand or backhand side at will. He has reasonably consistent groundstrokes but hits better off one wing, usually his forehand. His high volley is better than his low volley. He is much better on short overheads than deep ones. He is an intermediate rather than an advanced player because a) spins or change of pace bother him, b) he doesn't yet anticipate well, c) he has not mastered the half-volley, d) his own shots have no disguise, e) his strategy is limited to hitting to the backhand, f) he overhits set-ups, g) he frequently comes to net on a weak shot, h) his passing shots are inconsistent, i) in a baseline exchange he tries for a winner off a deep shot and he fails to maintain depth himself, j) he has not yet developed a consistent, forceful serve and k) he often "presses" or jerks when he tries to hit hard. His objective is to raise himself to the "advanced player" category; if he watches the checkpoints, he will reach that objective very quickly.

Spins and Change of Pace

A heavy topspin shot jumps forward and bounces high. Heavy underspin causes the ball to slow up and bounce low. When playing against an opponent with a big topspin forehand and a heavy underspin backhand, the intermediate must move *back* for the forehand and *up* for the backhand. By moving back, the intermediate no longer has to drive a ball that is shoulder height or above; he takes the ball instead slightly above waist-level, and because he has jumped or hopped or skipped backwards to get ready, he can step forward just before the hit. (Advanced players—not intermediates—often take such balls on the rise.) When the intermediate returns an underspin backhand, he moves forward, keeps his wrist stiff and bends his knees. In handling underspin the racket must be held firmly so that he moves the ball rather than having the ball move his racket. An opponent will frequently come to net on a forehand sidespin down the line. This ball moves to the intermediate's left and can feel "heavy" on the racket.

A right-handed slice serve moves to the receiver's right and a left-handed slice serve moves to the receiver's left. A right-handed slice serve to the forehand in the forehand court will move the receiver into the alley or beyond, whereas a left-handed slice serve to the forehand in the forehand court will move into the receiver's body. The receiver will find the closer in he stands, the less the effect of the slice: he can take the wide slice to the forehand before it has a chance to pull him really wide.

Change of pace and change of spin can "ungroove" an intermediate unless he is mentally prepared. He must be ready for high loops to the baseline, backhand crosscourt slices that pull him short and wide, hard sidespin forehands down the line, drop shots, teasing lobs, sharp angles and deep balls with no pace. The intermediate must be on his toes, bouncing and ready for a drive or a loop. He watches the ball come off his opponent's racket and he is ready to hop back and then step in on the big topspin, to run wide and take his wind-up as he runs, to handle a hard, deep shot by blocking it, to manufacture his own pace by stepping toward the ball just before the hit, and to run up for the shot that is hit with backspin.

Anticipation

An intermediate can get some weird ideas about anticipating, viz., watch the opponent's feet/eyes/head/hands. There are two ways to anticipate well: watch the ball come off the opponent's racket and remember where the opponent has been hitting his previous shots. Many players will hit all backhands crosscourt except on a short shot when they may go down the line. Some players will invariably hit forehand passing shots down the line and many more will forget to lob a net-rusher. Watching the ball only and never watching the opponent enables the player to start a fraction of a second early.

The Half-volley

The half-volley is a ball which is hit when it is only a few inches off the ground. Anyone who comes to net will have to half-volley frequently. It is not difficult when one learns the timing; it is simply a ground stroke hit with a smaller backswing and smaller follow-through. It should be hit one to two feet in front of the body. There are four rules to remember: watch the ball, don't try to hit it hard, stay down to the shot and never hit it on the dead run.

Disguise

The intermediate regularly signals when he is going to drop shot or lob: he changes his wind-up and thereby gives away his strategy. The reason he changes the wind-up is because he shovels rather than drives his lob (with a little practice, he can acquire a perfectly disguised lob which will catch the net man cold). His drop shot is merely a "dump" shot that falls reasonably short but has no backspin. Several hours of practicing coming under the ball at the last minute with an open racket face and an extremely short follow-through will help him to acquire this useful change of pace shot. On groundstrokes the intermediate positions himself in two different ways—one for the crosscourt and one for the down the line. If he took his backswing early and *held it,* he would "hide" his shot until the moment of impact.

Strategy

The intermediate has not yet experimented with side-spin, heavy topspin, backspin and angles. He has learned to serve to the backhand and to play to the opponent's weaker side. He does not yet know how to lure a baseliner to net or how to make winners wide to the opponent's strength or how to keep the attacker from crowding the net. First he can learn several serves. By tossing the ball to his right, he can develop a heavy slice that will trouble most inter-mediates. Next he can acquire a forehand sidespin coming-in shot by letting the racket come across his body on the follow-through at slightly above waistlevel.If he has a topspin backhand drive, he can easily learn underspin by opening the face of his racket and following through at slightly above waist-level. If he has an underspin backhand drive, he can work on developing topspin by keeping the racket face perpendicular to the ground and following through high (the racket head points to the top of the opponent's fence). By using underspins, topspins and sidespins, the opponent can be maneuvered with deep shots to the corner, wide and sharp angles to the opponent's service line, loops, lobs, drives, drop shots and dinks. The "don'ts" of strategy: don't drop shot from the baseline, don't hit short and straight down the middle deliberately, don't give away all your shots by failing to use disguise, don't hit to the opponent's strength unless you hit wide to his strength, don't let your opponent get grooved by hitting all shots with the same pace, don't come to net on a short ball to the opponent, and don't try shots you have not yet learned, viz., lob-volleys or drop volleys.

Set-ups

A set-up is a high, short ball that can be put away for a winner. For tournament players, set-ups are high, soft serves, high volleys, short overheads and high balls that bounce near the service line. An intermediate cannot al-ways put away what are set-ups to advanced players, but his goal should be to make near-winners or forcing shots out of "easy" balls. The worst mistake he can make is to hit the ball into the net or outside the court boundaries. There-fore precision is the key. A high, short ball is a set-up be-cause a) the receiver can hit down on the ball and b) the opponent has less time to reach the ball because the re-ceiver is standing close in. The choices on a set-up are: a deep shot to the corner, a sharp, wide crosscourt or a trick shot such as an extreme angle almost parallel to the net or an angled drop shot with backspin. The intermediate

should first learn the "deep to the corner," which is the safest shot. As he gets more secure in approaching this shot, he adds more pace so that his riposte is a putaway.

Approach Shots

When the intermediate comes to net, his approach shot must be deep. If it is short and high, only a very weak or nervous opponent will fail to pass him. He can come in on sidespin (forehand), underspin (backhand) or topspin (either side), but his depth must be good. Naturally the harder he hits his approach shot or the more bite to his spin, the more difficult it will be for the opponent to pass him. However, he must hit with control: the first rule of the ap-proach shot is that it must go in.

Passing Shots

There are four passing shots—down the line, crosscourt, straight at the net man's body and over the head. The more disguise to a passing shot, the more chance for a clean win-ner. Passing shots need not be hard: they can be hidden lobs or crosscourt dinks. The intermediate too often hits the passing shot with all his might, and for every winner he makes, he has racked up four or five losers. Disguise, preci-sion and change of rhythm/shot/direction/pace are much more successful than wild slugging.

Deep Shots

The most important factor in a baseline duel is depth. The ball must clear the net by three to six feet since low skimmers fall short. If the intermediate hits short, his op-ponent has the edge. If the opponent hits with great depth, the intermediate often fails to be prepared and either tries a half-volley from the baseline or returns short. Inter-mediates should play two to three feet behind the baseline against opponents who consistently hit with depth. The deeper the shot, the more topspin the intermediate should use to return the ball. Consistent depth generally elicits short balls. The worst time in a rally to try for a winner is off a deep shot; the best time is off a short one.

The Serve

Practice is what makes for improvement, but practicing a bad shot (one that can never be forceful) only grooves a bad habit. There is little point in practicing a serve that lacks pace. It may be caused by a bad toss, poor weight transfer, too many wiggles or frills, or failure to snap the wrist or to follow through with shoulder and arm. If the serve has no sting, discard it and start again from scratch with the help of a good pro. Once you have a good foundation, the more you practice, the better the serve will become. A consistent, forceful serve is one of the most important factors in win-ning tennis.

Hitting Hard

Good players get power without jerking or pressing; their power comes from transferring their weight forward just before the moment of impact. They look silky smooth and relaxed, but their shots have sting and pace. The in-termediate tries for power by moving arm, shoulder and/or wrist vigorously. The result is a jerky motion and uncon-trolled power: mixed doubles partners are hit, balls wildly spray the court and errors multiply. "Step-hit," not "bam-bam," brings controlled power. ●

WHERE HAVE YOU AND YOUR GAME GONE, WHITNEY?

by BUD COLLINS

A SMALL CARD arrived in the mail recently proclaiming that another hero has feet of clay after all: Whitney R. Reed had wed.

Whitney always was impetuous, a delight of an improviser—and so if he was going to be rash enough to rush into marriage at the formative age of 40, well, we expect the unexpected of him, don't we? Since Whitney always gave us the feeling of knowing something that nobody else knew, this impulsive act may make you wonder if there isn't actually something good to be said for marriage.

The announcement engraved on the 3-by-4 inch card brought back, if not a flood, at least a trickle of Reed memories which made me regret that *his day* antedated the broadening TV coverage of tennis. It is the sporting public's loss that only a relatively few people who wandered by the places he played witnessed Whitney galumping about like some gouty ape while flicking incredible half-volleys for winners, along with a variety of other touch shots. He would shake that blonde mane, seemingly trying to clear away the fuzz of a night that ended only moments before, realize he was in the wrong place on court but somehow bunnyhop in the proper direction and stick out his racket to angle another winner.

I recall him disdaining an elevator as a dreadfully commonplace vehicle, instead transporting himself up to and over rooftops like a cat burglar to attend a penthouse party in Boston's Back Bay. Jack Frost (with whom Whitney formed a Laurel and Hardy style doubles team) remarked one afternoon during the National Doubles at Longwood: "I may have to go on alone today. Whitney has found another momentary partner, and I think romance will take precedence over tennis this afternoon." But Whitney showed up eventually, as did a rainstorm which he insisted on playing through, to the annoyance of his and Frost's less agile opponents.

"Whitney is the guru," explained Frost after the two of them had treated a clubhouse gathering—the downpour having vacated the other courts—to a variety of weird and winning shots. "Whitney says that rainwater is pure and healthful, and we benefit from exposure to it," continued Frost.

"Yeah," postulated Reed, who had greatly enjoyed swinging in the rain.

In spirit and appetites, Whitney was Namathian. For one year, 1961, he was No. 1. From No. 8 in the rankings to No. 1, to No. 6, and thence to oblivion as far as major tennis was concerned. Where did he go? "I think he's got a paper route," somebody would say, quoting a Reed line that often answered the perennial question put to the professional amateurs of that era. As in the usual tournament-party-banter: "...but what do you do for a living, Mr. Reed?"

"Oh, I've got a paper route."

Maybe he did. It would have surprised no one to see Whitney pedaling up the walk, tossing the Chronicle through a second story window onto the customer's bed—he had that kind of accuracy—and, if this was a friendly customer, flipping a bottle of gin up there, too, because you need something to get that morning orange juice down.

Whitney didn't take it too seriously when he was ranked No. 1 in the United States. Admittedly the cast he headed wasn't easy to get serious about. He got to the top startlingly by reaching the quarters at Forest Hills in 1961, a rare elevation for an American at that time. But his memorable accomplishment was a defeat, the next year in third round, by Rafe Osuna. It was five delicious sets of cat-and-mouse maneuvering by men with the dexterity of successful dips. At the end the mouse was barely out-reflexed 10-8 by an Osuna at the peak of his powers. Reed was seen at Forest Hills only once thereafter, losing a first rounder to another fading eminence named Donald Dell.

Reed and Dell had been Davis Cup teammates in 1961, during the loss to Italy, and Whitney gave it one more try. That may have finished him, according to the 1962 captain, Bob Kelleher. "We had a very rigorous training program and Whit, to my astonishment and pleasure, went along with it," said Kelleher. "But whereas training should help a player, it seemed to hurt Whit. His system wasn't geared to conditioning and he didn't play very well."

Indeed, it may have taken Whitney a decade to recover from all that running and sleep and long hours of physical hardening that Kelleher was peddling. However, apparently, he was ready to face the rigors of marriage, and I know you join me in wishing him and the former Claudia Evans all the best in Alameda, California.

This wasn't intended as a "remembrances of Whitney" article, but his name, mailed to me from out of the past, under the cover of an 11-cent stamp, started me thinking about the incredible distance from his day to this. Not in years. Only a dozen have passed, and a scattering of his rivals are still around and making a buck—Laver, Froehling, Emerson, Pietrangeli.

Yet eons have elapsed, spiritually and conceptually, since Reed fluttered Westward and off the international whirligig, and never again will an insouciant soul as he be able to scramble uninhibitedly to the top. Even in an off year. There's something sad about that, and I don't mean the passing of an amateur spirit, whatever that was. Reed was no more an amateur than anyone else who traveled the tournament circuit of their time, although the rewards weren't as glittering as those of today. The amount to be haggled for beneath that well known table was insignifi-

Reed was very much an individualist on court, even in doubles. He teamed with Donald Dell in 1961 when they were teammates on the Davis Cup team. Reed was ranked No. 1 in the U.S. that year.

cant compared to the millions now. But they were free agents and freer spirts.

As we plunge into the mid-70's tennis has become a hard, cold business—just like any other sport—and that good old cause called greed will lead the male participants to flog themselves beyond sensible limits. In a way they will have to. That's how the new system has been laid out for them in this most ambitious of years for the game: for starters, play the 11 World Championship Tennis tournaments squeezed into four months, plus possibly the three extra special events...then the European circuit...followed by British grass, topped by Wimbledon...back to America for the summer and early autumn...and if there's anything left, the Dewar Circuit in Britain...finishing up with December and early January in Australia. It is understood that there will be time off to do the laundry. Unless you happen to be playing Davis Cup.

Well, they shoot horses, don't they, so we mustn't be astonished when tennis players break down in droves and beg to be delivered from their misery.

In trying to put the fractured world of tennis back together again, the International Lawn Tennis Federation and WCT have sought to make everybody in the administrations of both sides happy, at the physical and emotional expense of the players. Not the financial expense, though, for there will be a lot of rich cripples hobbling on the courts about three-quarters of the way the season. The WCT requirement that its 64 entrants take part in every one of the 11 singles and doubles tournaments is too tough—and shortsighted as well since it will diminish the athletes' efficiency and, if continued, their careers. And the ILTF stipu-

lation that the players enter the so-called traditional championships as well as a specified number of Grand Prix tournaments is just as thoughtless.

You don't hear the players—or not many of them—complaining now because the scent of gold is overpowering. But I think you will detect moans around the world by the end of the season, if not before.

Will the moans do any good? Who knows? In every major sport today the players are overplayed—baseball, basketball, football, hockey in the U.S., soccer in Britain and Europe. The seasons are too long and the standard of play suffers. Injuries increase. But the players are so well compensated that few have the temerity, or sense, to speak up about their well being and the harm done themselves and their game. Those who do are told to check their bank statements and cautioned that they've never had it so good. If everybody is worn out and competing at a common level of fatigue, the contests stay close and exciting don't they?

That seems to be the way of sport in the 1970s: dilute the product and it doesn't matter because the customers still show up at the box office and the free-loaders hang in there at teleside.

Only in golf, without team demands over the course of expanded schedules, and lacking the tournament requirements of tennis, are the competitors free agents the way tennis players used to be. Golfers, once they have attained a certain professional standard, may enter as many tournaments as they please, or refrain. Since they are no less human than other pros, golfers, too, overdo. But they have the choice that is being taken away from the men in tennis.

I suspect that at the close of this most back-blitzing and

elbow-eroding season, choruses of screams will issue from the union, the Association of Tennis Players, and that playing demands from WCT and the ILTF will be negotiated down. In fact, within a year, as the union strengthens, WCT and the ILTF probably won't have much to say about what a player does or does not. Ideally the ATP will grow to the status of the PGA (Professional Golf Association), and WCT and the ILTF will adjust to their reasonable roles as promoter of tournaments and administrator of amateur tennis respectively,

With the pro game burgeoning, the ILTF is bound to fail—as it should—in attempting to control male and female professionals. Having somehow survived the dullness, spitefulness and stupidity of the tennis war of 1970-71 (WCT vs. ILTF), I wish to say very little about the next, which is loaded with the same iniquities: ILTF vs. the Women's International Tennis Federation.

But I will say this to the USLTA and ILTF, neither of whom has done much to further the growth of female pro tennis: come on, you guys, quit acting like the chauvinist porkers we suspect you to be, react sensibly to the handwriting on the backstop and let the chickies alone. Since chivalry is as out of date as the ILTF, you fellows should be familiar with it, and able to apply it here, recognizing that the chickies are in business, and doing it a lot better than you could or would. Ban is a deodorant, not a tactic applicable to major tennis today, so why stink out the game by applying a futile ban on the women as you did on the men? Amateur tennis, men, that's your racket. Please return to it while you can do so graciously–before you're pushed. You have no business in tennis business, except to oversee the national championships of your respective countries.

Enough for the ILTF, for whom a paragraph is more than too much. Nice guys, most of them, but totally out of touch with the realities of today's professional sport.

I have wandered a long way from Whitney Reed and 1961 just as tennis has. In Whitney's day there was no indoor circuit. Today, following those pioneers named Riordan and Fernberger, the inside jobs have become the big league. The place to make their mark for Whitney and colleagues was on grass. Today grass is deader than George McGovern, although Wimbledon will presumably continue functioning as a magnificent museum of sporting horticulture. The players are unionized; they will be demonstrating for higher Davis Cup pay; their faces are on television and some of them have actually become known; they need tax accountants. In Whitney's day nobody paid taxes on those expenses.

We can't go back; nobody wants to go back. But are we having as much fun as Whitney had? Whitney knew you couldn't eat trophies. You had to make something out of it. But he realized it was just a game, too, and he enjoyed the hell out of it.

Would anybody play in a downpour now, just for fun? (I doubt that Reed and Frost were getting more than lunch chits at that National Doubles.) Is it going to be fun much longer on this unceasing week-after-week grind for higher and higher stakes? Or will there always be a few guys like Reed who manage to get their kicks in sunshine or under a leaky roof? We'll find out. Maybe, Whitney, you got out at the right time. You might not recognize your game anymore. As happened in all games, the businessmen have taken over tennis. •

Whitney had little or no regard for footwork or body placement. He could and would hit low balls while leaping up and backwards. His wrist control, eye coordination and instinct for spins were marvelous. This backhand slice from the baseline looks like a short volley action—or drop shot.

ALL ABOUT THE TWO-HANDED BACKHAND

What are the advantages of the two-handed backhand?

It overcomes problems of a weak wrist and it offers both precision and disguise to a shot. The two wrists reinforce each other so that they hold firm even when meeting a hard or deep shot. This wrist solidity leads to precision. Backhand errors arise from a wrist so weak that it cannot hold firm against a hard impact, and also from a wrist which moves slightly as the ball is hit even if it is not a hard or deep shot. The two-handed shot has built-in extra control from the solidity which comes from the reinforcement. Disguise is also inherent in the shot. Changing the direction of a two-handed drive is simply accomplished either by hitting the ball a little earlier, or later, or by swiveling both wrists in unison (but still mutually reinforced) to advance or retard the racket head. This action makes it virtually impossible to anticipate the direction of the return.

Who specifically would be helped by using a two-handed backhand?

Beginners who lead with their elbow, letting the racket head drag behind the arm, will find that the two-handed grip assists the racket in coming through at the same time as the arm. Beginners or intermediates who time the backhand badly, letting the weight fall backwards the moment they hit the ball, will find the two-handed shot will help bring the body weight forward since the shoulders pivot automatically when both hands are on the racket.

What are the disadvantages of the two-handed backhand?

The lack of reach is a clear disadvantage. Cliff Drysdale and Jimmy Connors both let go of the racket with the other hand when they have to reach far out, sideways or forward. On low, short balls, underspin is the best method of lifting and controlling the ball, and this is the one action that is most difficult with two hands on the racket.

What famous players have had a two-handed backhand?

The first famous two-handed backhand was that of Vivian McGrath, an

Harold Solomon puts a lot of overspin on his two-handed backhand. The pronounced topspin and built-in disguise make his somewhat cramped backhand difficult to play net against unless he is forced hard, wide and deep.

Chris Evert has a trained, precise, controlled swing on her two-hander. The follow-through is always stopped where the racket head points in the direction of the ball's flight. On this shot the racket face is slightly more open than usual.

by JULIUS HELDMAN

Australian Davis Cupper who played in the early 30's. Then came John Bromwich, a left-handed Australian. Today there are Cliff Drysdale, Jimmy Connors, Roscoe Tanner, Harold Solomon, Chris and Jeanne Evert, Laurie and Carrie Fleming, Bjorn Borg and a number of young Floridians. Perhaps because of Evert and Connors, two-handed backhands are a current fad among young players.

Should the right hand use the Eastern forehand grip or should it be turned back slightly as it is for a one-handed backhand?

One should shift to a backhand grip. In the one-handed backhand, the problem of using an Eastern forehand grip is the enormous wrist strength required. However, when one grips the backhand with two hands, the help from the left hand alleviates the problem and it is therefore *possible* to use an Eastern forehand grip. But what happens if the player has to reach out wide and use a one-handed grip? If the player ever wants to change to a one-handed grip later, he should certainly use a proper backhand grip. The left hand, which grips the handle above the right, should probably be Eastern

Frew McMillan is unusual in three related respects: he hits two-handed on both sides, he doesn't shift his hands so he hits cross-handed on his left side and he does these things on volleys as well as groundstrokes. He is an amazing sharp-angle volleyer, gaining his control and disguise from his double wrist brace. This is a cross-handed volley.

The trained Evert backhand is hit with elbows comfortably bent, straight backswing, short swing, flat (no spin—racket face vertical) and firm wrists. This example is actually a bit cramped, because grass bounces often require some adjustment, but Chris handles it precisely.

Cliff Drysdale is hitting one of his favorite shots, a two-hander on the run, moving forward, with his close-in-to-body style and short, high follow-through apparent. Cliff puts a lot of topspin and double wrist snap on this shot, which is impossible to guess.

since this gives most support to holding the racket head firm.

Does the left hand dominate the stroke so that, in essence, it is tantamount to a two-handed forehand for a left-handed player?

No, because the left arm is usually so cramped. It is possible, of course, to develop the strokes so that the left arm dominates, but this generally does not happen. Rod Laver plays golf with right-handed clubs and Roy Emerson and Ken Rosewall with left-handed clubs, in effect taking advantage of their stronger arm on the backhand stroke.

Should the follow-through be a long one or should it be brought up quickly and over the right shoulder?

Any unnatural stretch should be avoided. It is better to keep the follow-through on the short side to avoid being off balance for the next shot. If you take a full wallop, as Drysdale sometimes does, the racket will wind around your neck or close to it. But notice Chris Evert's follow-through ends with the racket pointing in the direction of the ball, which is excellent for control.

Should the right arm be bent or extended on the volley?

A two-handed backhand volley is not recommended except for put-away high stroke volleys. It is awkward and hard on your balance to volley with your right arm extended. On the one-handed volley, the right arm is still bent at the elbow unless you have to reach very wide.

How does the two-handed backhand differ in style from the one-handed backhand?

Both can run the gamut, but two-handers can be hit more in front of the

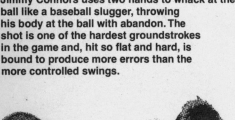

Jimmy Connors uses two hands to whack at the ball like a baseball slugger, throwing his body at the ball with abandon. The shot is one of the hardest groundstrokes in the game and, hit so flat and hard, is bound to produce more errors than the more controlled swings.

Drysdale's wind-up (backswing) has lots of interesting features: semi-open stance, low racket head, right arm against body and left arm bent at elbow. This will be a topspin drive, racket ending high and over Cliff's right shoulder.

Young John Bromwich pointed his racket head to the sky (corresponding to both wrists cocked) and completely baffled his opponents. No one could guess the direction of his stroke, which he could change at the last instant by simply turning his wrists to move the racket head forward or back.

body with more of an open stance, and two-handers find particular problems in trying underspin. But it is generally true that the two-hander would look like a good one-hander if the left hand let go before the ball was hit. Some players develop this style consciously, particularly if they want to use underspin.

Should you hit a two-handed backhand in front of or by your side?

It is preferable to hit the ball in front of the body. Whenever you take the ball early, you give the opponent a fraction of a second less time to prepare. More power is also achieved by hitting the ball in front of rather than by the side.

Is the two-handed backhand as powerful as the one-handed?

It certainly can be. McGrath, Drysdale, and Connors are good examples. Bromwich and Evert have more control than speed, but the speed is certainly adequate.

Is it as consistent?

Yes. The most erratic one-handers are those who would probably benefit most by going to two hands.

Can you underspin or drive as easily with a two-handed backhand?

You can certainly drive, flat or topspin, as easily with a two-handed backhand. Underspin is more difficult because the left arm has to move down and stop short. It works reasonably well on drop shots but the motion develops so little power that it is hard to hit deep balls with lots of underspin with the two-hander. But who needs it if you can achieve accuracy without so much underspin?

Do any two-handed players volley with two hands?

They all drive-volley high, close-in set-ups with two hands. Chris Evert mainly volleys with two hands but the others all have one-handed backhand volleys or volleys in which the left hand comes off the racket before the volley is hit.

If you eventually decide to go to one hand, does it involve a great change in timing and in style?

It need not, but it gets more difficult as time goes on to make the change easily. It is recommended that the one-handed volley be used as soon as the wrist is strong enough. ●

Bjorn Borg's two-hander is hit farther from his body than any of the others. It is basically a classical one-handed shot with the left hand used as a brace for the right wrist.

Bromwich played soft, low, controlled, teasing shots until he got his opening when he would rifle bullet winners with the same short backswing. Brom, a lefty, was another two-handed volleyer.

Meet Alex Mayer, the player who turned down $42,000 so he could play college tennis— then quit the team.

by MIKE LUPICA

YOU CAN ALWAYS spot the tennis playing member of the Brushed Denim Generation moving cool and kind of slow like through almost any hotel lobby in the world: he's the jean machine wearing the Gucci loafers and the Pulsar press-button watch, carrying fourteen rackets, one leather bag with his name on the side and one beautiful girl. And he's holding hands with his agent.

There is no more touching or typical scene in the tennis world these days, in fact, than a player and his agent gazing longingly into each other's eyes over a drink in a dimly lit Ramada bar as each gently fondles a new endorsement contract. A player would sooner be without his four-speed brush dryer in the wind at Vegas or his eight-track cassette in television-less South Africa than go anywhere—or do anything—without his trusty 10 percenter in this tennis time of plenty.

On the sensible advice of the McCormackDellRiordanHambuechenScotts who now overrun the sport, the professional tennis player now saves receipts, lodges chambermaid tips, records cab rides and flies coach with the best of the expense account magicians. He grabs big deductible checks with more quickness than he's ever shown lunging for a volley at the net. He is careful, careful, careful.

Alex (Call me Sandy but I really like Alex) Mayer is careful, careful, careful. A Stanford graduate and former NCAA tennis champ who began his career in World Team Tennis after the 1974 Wimbledon break, Mayer is represented by both Yalie Gene Scott and a California firm called Professional Finance Coordinators as he moves cautiously into the pros; in addition, Mayer negotiated his own contract with the WTT's New York Sets. A pre-law major at Stanford, Mayer looks to be taking few chances as

he sets out on his way up the tennis organization.

In fact, Alex Mayer is so careful, careful, careful that he followed the lead of some alumni of another California firm—this one called the J. Walter Thompson Company—while this story was being prepared. He *tape recorded* our interviews. Every one of them. Each morning during the Wimbledon fortnight, we would sit down to breakfast in the dining room of the Gloucester Hotel; Mayer would pull out his cassette and I my modest little notebook, and we would begin. I found myself deleting my own expletives and inaudibling all over the place. I was worried that if I set my bowl of Rice Krispies too close to the microphone, we might have a missing 18 minutes of tape.

Yet for all this seeming prissiness, Alex Mayer had a very un-careful, un-businesslike 1974. He turned down a lot of big bucks during the winter season to maintain his amateur ranking and the chance to win a second consecutive NCAA championship for both himself and his team.

And then Alex Mayer went back to Stanford and quit that team.

* * *

"What did I think when the kid told me he was staying an amateur and didn't want the prize money," Wily Bill Riordan, who runs the US Independent Jimmy Connors Indoor Circuit, was saying during Wimbledon. "They have an expression for it over here. I thought the kid had gone 'round the bend'."

Riordan was referring to the fact that Mayer played the Connors circuit last winter, won three tournaments, over $40,000 in prize money (he also finished second to Connors in the Schick Grand Prix points race), and turned it all down to go back to Stanford, finish his final quarter, play on

Alex Mayer feels life on the tennis circuit is "a great way to stay immature and youthful...You can say what you want and do what you want. It's not really the real world." From left, at a 1967 junior tournament, Alex, his father and brother Gene.

Dick Gould's team and lay more foundation for the winning tradition, even dynasty, that he had hoped to establish when he went out there in the first place.

"You gotta have a great deal of respect for the kid," Riordan continued, hyping Mayer in the hope that Alex will return to the independent tour the next winter. "Here's a guy who had the character and integrity to stand up for what he thought was right. How many people are there like that in the sports world? What can you say about a guy who gives up $40,000 for what he believes in?"

The entire matter was not nearly that complicated, nor that grandiose, as far as Mayer was concerned. He is a blunt person, precise in his language—indeed sometimes *too* precise—and he seems to take a certain pride in his outspoken candor.

"Don't make any big moralistic or idealistic thing out of this," Mayer was saying one afternoon in Towson, Md., on his way to a victory over Clark Graebner in the finals of the Riordan tournament there. By this time, Mayer was playing well, and had already begun to hear variations in B flat of the character-and-integrity composition.

"I just happen to like college and the people I've been associated with there. I like to screw around with them, party with them, drink with them. I've got plenty of time to make money playing tennis, but I'm never going to be in a college-type situation again."

At Wimbledon, after the fact, after the quitting and the prying by West Coast reporters for the "real reason" and the mystery that really still surrounds his decision despite his explanation, Mayer was still talking positively about his decision to attend Stanford and his career there.

"Tennis-wise," he said, "I'm very glad I decided to go to college. As far as the academics were concerned, I never got as much out of it as I would have liked to. I studied hard and did classwork but I never did the extra stuff or delved into one area. That's not to say that I didn't have a good time or learn a lot, but I played a lot of tennis."

Gould had recruited Mayer at some junior tournaments and at a Junior Davis Cup camp of his that Mayer attended. At that time, he had already induced people like Roscoe Tanner and Rick Fisher to go to Stanford and as Mayer says now: "Maybe we can win the NCAAs, that's the kind of feeling we had then. We might win Stanford's first one in a long time. And it wouldn't be like it is at USC or UCLA where it's just a factory."

According to Mayer, when he returned to school in the spring his disenchantment was almost immediate.

"It started from the fact that the coach had over-recruited," Mayer says. "We had this year about 12 guys competing for six spots during the regular season and four spots in the NCAAs. They were all first class players, and they all had first class egos. It was a very shattering thing to the ones who didn't make the dual match spots, not to mention the NCAA spots.

"Also, when I started on the team a few years ago, the guys on the team were all really close, just a friendship thing. We were together all the time. When we screwed around, we screwed around together. I got a fondness from it that I had no right to expect from any tennis team situation. When I went out on the winter circuit, I got away from that and lost friends that had graduated.

"I came back and found an unnaturally tense situation.

Everybody wanted to play and most wouldn't. I saw a team packed with talent. But I didn't feel comfortable. I felt I had gotten maybe as much out of tennis as I had a right to expect. I felt almost guilty about taking up a spot from someone who could probably reap more benefits from it than I could. Maybe I had just passed out of that phase of my life. I left without any hard feelings, none on my part. And I'm glad they won it, just for my own peace of mind."

Stanford, under the congenial, buddy coaching of Gould, did win it again, with John Whitlinger (No. 4 on the team when the season started—with Mayer) winning both the singles and the doubles. In the singles final, he beat teammate Chico Hagey. Mayer is quick to point out that Hagey wasn't even on the team at the beginning of the year, yet ended up in the finals.

The fact that his decision to quit, in retrospect, cost him $40,000 seems to matter not at all to Mayer. He seems to prefer to attack all problems involving choice in a tough, straight-ahead fashion; once he has made his choice, it is behind him, a dead issue, not worth his worry quotient. He tells of the time when he was 11 years old, right after he had made it to the finals of the national 16-and-unders, when he decided to quit tennis altogether. He told his father, tennis teacher Alexander Mayer, that he would work at the elder Mayer's summer instructional camp, but that he was through with the game.

"Basically," he says, "I really did quit in my mind. I just wasn't that happy with the way I was on the court. I wasn't comfortable and I wasn't thinking very well. Working that camp was the best and the worst thing I ever did. I gradually started hitting a little every day, and within three or four weeks I really started liking it again. Midway through the summer, I was raring to go." Like the decision to quit Stanford, following the decision to remain an amateur, he made the decision to quit, then the one to resume, with little regret or looking back.

"I had made my peace with my maker about the money question a couple of years ago," he says. "I never questioned the worth of the team as compared to the money. I felt that I had gotten a lot out of the team in terms of unity and friendship. So I never worried about the money. But when you've come to expect a rapport, and then it's gone, you start to think that maybe it's an unbalanced situation. Maybe you're giving up a little bit more than you're getting. Up until then, I felt I was getting something at least equivalent to the money I was giving up."

* * *

Alex Mayer was two years old, he says, when his father started training him to be a tennis player. "It was never to make me a champion, or anything like that," Mayer maintains. "It was just that I was always really close to my father, and my father was a pro."

Alexander Mayer, Sr., is probably the single most vital person in shaping the character and attitudes of his son. In many ways, the story of the father surpasses that of the son, at least in its dramatic scope and breadth. He was born in a small city on the border of Hungary and Yugoslavia which has been shuttled back and forth between the two countries ever since. In the curious ways and means of Eastern Europe, at one time the elder Mayer described himself as a Yugoslav citizen of Hungarian nationality.

As a young man, he played tennis for both Yugoslavia and Hungary; he was a good doubles player, never ranking more than No. 4 in Hungary as a singles player.

During World War II, he was in Hungary when that country was taken over by the Germans. The Germans then called the Hungarian army back into service and Mayer was sent to officer's training school. On an eventual mission, he surrendered to the Americans, and after the war ended up in an American prisoner of war camp, where he spent nine months.

He came to the United States in 1951. Just before the war had broken out, he had gotten his law degree in Hungary, but that proved insufficient for the practice of law in this country. So he spent varying lengths of time working as an elevator operator and at the YMCA in Manhattan. Eventually, he began helping build tennis courts, and soon began to teach. He teaches today in New Jersey, and his summer camp at Mt. Freedom, N.J.—where his son decided that he did want to be a tennis player—is one of the most successful on the East Coast.

"I received really good training from my father," his son says. "Both in the mechanics of tennis and in my own mental training. He's very practical and a realist and he always lets me know when I get out of line.

"I think I look at my tennis successes a lot through what I think are his eyes. When I'm playing well, *he's* really happy. When I'm not, *he's* really down. I'm not sure he realizes the effect he's had on my game."

Indeed. When Mayer came back to Wimbledon in 1974, it was as a celebrity from the Energy Crisis Wimbledon a year prior, when the Nikki Pilic Affair kept most of the top pros in the world away—with the exception, the press and public thought, of Ilie Nastase, regarded at that point in time (after victories in the Italian and French Opens) as the best player in the world. In a Round of 16 match on the first Saturday, Alex Mayer, fresh (and tired) from his victory in the NCAAs over Raul Ramirez, beat Nastase. His father flew over to London the next day.

In 1974, with all the best players back to the land of Strawberries-and-Cream Forever, the scenario was reversed. Mayer was beaten in three sets by Rolf Thung in the second round on the same day that he had beaten Nastase in 1973. The next morning in the hotel lobby he shook his head and grinned wryly.

"How do you call up your father and tell him you just lost to someone he never heard of?" he asked.

Mayer's game, when all its slashing parts are fit together in a working order, is one based on surprising power, great quickness and a gambling style of play, particularly at the net. A small, basically baseline player as a child, he's an attacker now, and the credit, he says, goes to his father.

"My father is a much better gambler and a shrewder person than I am," he says. "He has literally taught me how to gamble in tennis. Like he'll tell me, 'I don't want to ever see you within a foot of the middle of the net when you come in to volley.' He means that he wants me to gamble, anticipate, go one way or the other and *know* where the ball is going."

Despite his reputation for difficulty in dealings with the press and despite what some feel is a tendency towards officiousness on the tennis court, Mayer seems these days always to know where the ball is going—and not just on the tennis court. In fact, he may truly be one of those rare people who may be too bright ever to be a championship caliber performer.

"The tennis world," he says, "is a great way to stay immature and youthful. Off the court, this whole way of life doesn't provide very much mind challenging or shocking stuff. You travel in a circle where social restrictions don't exist. You can say what you want and do what you want. It's not really the real world. In this situation you're not going to have many nervous breakdowns."

"It's not an easy way of life at all as I see it," he continues. "Three weeks is about all I can take of living out of a suitcase. I'm just gonna have to learn how much I can take of this as a pro and then pace myself. Just about everybody I know is playing too much tennis."

"I got my WCT invitation," he grinned one day before Thung became one of Wimbledon's annual un-Thung heroes. "It was pages and pages of rules. There will be a fine if you wear white…a fine if you don't wear the same color shirt as your doubles partner…a fine if you obstruct the normal interview process after a match. You can play six, seven or eight tournaments, but if you choose six tournaments, they tell you what six and tell you when you can rest."

"It is," said Alex Mayer, "corporate tennis."

The Riordan-Mayer mutual admiration society really is, by the way, a duet. Now, Riordan was talking about Mayer's character and integrity, right?

"I'm really glad Riordan's circuit is around," Mayer says. "I'm really glad Riordan's around, to tell you the truth. He has the guts to say a lot of things I really think need saying."

* * *

"I usually try to act on major things pretty slowly," Alex Mayer, Stanford grad and tennis playing man, says. "Right now, I have a difficult time handling the idea of a pro tennis career. There's so many different options in terms of how you want to conduct your own career. There are three winter circuits, then team tennis or Grand Prix tournaments or the smaller European tournaments. You have the rest option in the fall or the Far East circuit. Then when you're talking about the unions, there's ITPA (Riordan's organization for his independents), ATP or non-alignment.

"Any of these organizations will then label you as a renegade or a corporate entity. It's unfortunate that you just can't play tennis anymore. I just don't see that I can play 35 tournaments a year and be sane, or play that well."

Mayer is turning professional at what old eyes would surely call the fattest time in the game's history. So people find it hard to handle his sometimes stinging indictments of his sport, his way of life, his less serious fellow players. One writer, after hearing of Mayer's decision to leave the Stanford team, raised the question of whether or not "Sandy finally needs a psychiatrist."

But I wonder how much any of these people—myself included—really understand about having a tennis racket from memory's boundaries on, playing every day, catching buses on the weekends so courts could be found on Long Island. I wonder how much we understand about a kid of 11 or 12 and even older having to deal with the pressures— self-imposed and otherwise—of junior tournaments. Then high school matches and college matches, then Connors and Nastase and the others ad infinitum.

Alex Mayer is a tennis player who has developed his game to this point without cold-storaging his brain. That makes some people nervous. But then, that always has. ●

The Return of Serve in Singles

by GLADYS M. HELDMAN

THE EASIEST way to judge whether your return of serve needs improvement is to count the number of return-of-serve errors you make in the course of a set. Unless the serve is tremendously good or the server an excellent volleyer, you should not make more than one or two return-of-serve errors per set. You are probably making six or eight or even 12, except against players who are much weaker than you. When you play against someone much worse, your return-of-serve errors may dwindle to two or three; when you are up against someone much better, they rise to the phenomenal number of eight or ten (not counting pop-ups to the net man). The reasons you return badly against a good player are: (1) he or she has a better serve than what you are used to and (2) he or she pressures you so much if you don't make a forcing return that you try to hit too good a shot.

The return of serve should be reasonably forcing as well as consistent. If the serve is weak, the return of serve should dominate the point either through an outright winner or a shot that has the server stretching or puts him out of position. If the serve is strong, your ability to make a good return is really tested: if you can only pop up (hit a high, short floater) or whack the ball mindlessly, hoping it will go in, your problem may be caused by one or more factors, each of which adversely affects return of serve. You

Grand Slam winner Don Budge's ready position will allow him to make the fastest possible reaction to any serve: his feet are comfortably apart and his left hand cradles the throat of the racket. Don prefers to await serve with a forehand grip and stands inside the baseline against spin serves. ▶

may be waiting stiff-legged or off balance or with your racket dangling or pointed too far to the left. You may be standing too close to the baseline or too far to your left to protect your backhand. Perhaps you only see the ball when it is too late or you wind up after the ball has bounced or you cut short your follow-through.

Here is a quick way to find out your return-of-serve weaknesses. Take the test to learn the theory, then go out on the court and put your knowledge into practice.

RETURN OF SERVE TEST (SINGLES ONLY)

Score one point for every correct answer. You are a sharp analyst and should have a good return of serve if you score 26-30. You may have a fine return of serve but you are either lazy at analysis or careless if you score 20-25. Anything below 20 indicates inexperience in competition *or* lack of understanding in tennis techniques.

The Ready Position

1. When waiting to return serve, should you bend from the waist or from the knees?
2. Should your racket point straight in front of you or should it point slightly to the right or left?
3. Should your feet be touching or a few inches apart or 12 to 18 inches apart?
4. Does the left hand play any part in the Ready Position and, if it does, should it be on the handle or the throat?
5. Does it matter if you wait with a forehand grip or a backhand grip?

Where to stand to receive

1. When receiving in the forehand court, should you stand halfway between the alley and the center service line, almost by the alley or three feet to the left of the alley?
2. Is it better to stand three feet behind the baseline or just inside the baseline against a spin serve?
3. Should you stand in on a hard serve to take it on the rise or should you move three feet back and take it at the top of the bounce or just as it is beginning to drop?
4. When receiving second serves, should you *always* move in one or two steps?
5. If a serve is short, should you generally try to hit it with your forehand, even if it means running around your backhand, or is this a function of whether your forehand or backhand is stronger?

Concentration on returns

1. Should you watch the whole motion of the server or should you concentrate only on toss and follow the ball?
2. If you follow the ball in flight, should you be able to see it bounce or should you just guess as to where it will bounce?
3. Should you be able to hear spin as well as see it?
4. Should your body be relaxed or tensed for the return?
5. Is it possible to make a really good return of serve if your opponent serves before you are ready?

The drive return of serve

1. Should you pivot your shoulders and hips on a forehand return of serve?
2. If you are driving a return of serve, should the follow-through be as big as in a regular groundstroke?
3. If your opponent serves a wide ball to your forehand in the forehand court, and you decide to drive the return, should you hit a deep crosscourt, a deep down-the-line, a deep one down the center or any one of the three?
4. Is it better to drive a return of serve down the line or crosscourt or should you mix them up?
5. Should the drive return of serve be taken by your side or in front of you?

Blocks and chips

1. Should a block return of serve be used against an American twist serve, a spin serve, a hard serve or any of the three?
2. Which would you use, a block or a chip, when you plan to follow your return of serve to net?
3. On a block return of serve, do you take a small or a big wind-up and a small or a big follow-through?
4. Would you ever block a short, low serve?
5. Against a cannonball serve, where you are standing three feet behind the baseline, would it be better to block or chip or can you do either?

Return of spin serves

1. Will a right-handed slice serve to your forehand in the forehand court move to your alley or into your body?
2. Will a right-handed American twist serve to your backhand move you wide on your backhand or will it break into your body?
3. Will a left-handed slice serve to your forehand move you wide on your forehand or will it break into your body?
4. Does a good American twist serve bounce higher or much lower than a regular spin serve?
5. Will an underhand serve hit with a lot of spin bounce to your right or your left?

THE ANSWERS

Ready Position

1. Most good players crouch down, bending from the knees and from the waist.
2. Generally the racket points slightly to the left since it is unnatural to break the wrist and point the racket straight ahead. However, if you put down "straight ahead," score your answer as correct since a number of tournament players hold the racket that way.

3. The feet are 12 to 18 inches apart.
4. The fingers of the left hand cradle the throat of the racket, thus aiding in a quick shift of grip. Many players keep the left hand on the racket as they start the backhand wind-up; the left hand moves up toward the handle and releases its grip either early or midway in the wind-up.
5. This is an individual choice. Some wait with the forehand grip and some with the backhand.

Where to stand to receive
1. Almost by the alley. If you don't stand way over, you will be aced on the forehand side in the forehand court and on the backhand side in the backhand court.
2. Inside the baseline against spin. The farther back you stand, the more the spin can pull you wide.
3. If it is a hard serve, it is better to move back at least three feet. C.M. Jones of England, who has coached many players, states that even the champions return big serves just as they are beginning to drop rather than at the top of the bounce. Only a player with a great eye and amazing reflexes would try to take a hard serve on the rise; the percentages are against successful returns when the receiver stands close in.
4. Not *always*. Some players hit their second serves as hard as their first. However, the receiver has a psychological edge when he moves in a step or two to return second serve.
5. The player with the big forehand should run around a short serve to go for a winner or a forcing shot off return of serve. It puts tremendous pressure on the server to hit the backhand line on serve. John Newcombe received this way in the ATP tournament final at Tucson against Arthur Ashe's second serve, which isn't exactly weak. Other players are so confident of hitting winners or forcing shot returns of serve off the backhand that they never run around the ball. Unless a player's forehand is shaky, it is a good idea to take the optional ball as a forcing forehand because it presses the server to try for more pace, depth and accuracy and results in more service errors.

Concentration on returns
1. Most players find it impossible to watch the whole service action and still concentrate on the toss and the flight of the ball. Unless you are one of the rare ones, try only to watch the toss and then to follow the ball in the air.
2. Your chances of a good return go way up if you can see the ball bounce. All your efforts should be concentrated into seeing the bounce; otherwise you are a dead duck.
3. Near-sighted players hear spin. Experienced players who see very well depend on their eyes, but many believe they hear spin also. All good, nearsighted players can hear when a ball is hit off center and can recognize

with their ears the sound of a spin serve as against the sound of an almost flat serve.
4. Relaxed. When the body is tense, it fights the ball: the legs are too rigid for easy, quick moves and the arm too stiff to swing forward freely.
5. If you are lucky. This serves to point out how important concentration is in receiving. You must be in the Ready Position, all extraneous noises (and thoughts) must be blocked out and your eyes must be focused on the ball as the toss begins. A "quick serve" catches you before your mind, body and eyes are ready.

The drive return of serve
1. The shoulders and hips pivot *on the wind-up* so that they face the net. Beginners sometimes swivel their hips and shoulders as they hit. A good cure is to concentrate on keeping the side to the net while still allowing the weight to come forward.
2. Yes. If you stop the follow-through in the middle, you are not letting the racket do the work.
3. All three have their place. The down-the-line or the crosscourt can be outright winners if hit hard; a return deep to the center allows the receiver to get back into position.
4. Mix them up; never let the server get grooved.
5. All shots, including the drive return of serve, should be hit in front of the body.

Blocks and Chips
1. Blocks are best against hard serves. They utilize the power of the hard serve in making a hard return.
2. A chip shot. It slows the ball down and the receiver can move behind it to a postion at net. Blocks are *not* approach shots.
3. A very small wind-up and follow-through. A block is like a flat volley.
4. No. Short, low serves should be stroked (with topspin to make the ball rise over the net) or chipped (if the player is following the return to net).
5. Block the cannonball serve and it will go back hard. If you chip the return from a position three feet behind the baseline, it slows up the ball and gives the advantage to the server. However, Pancho Gonzalez did use the chip return to great advantage, angling it so the server had to both stretch and volley a low, dipping ball.

Return of spin serves
1. It will move to your alley.
2. It will move you wide on your backhand.
3. It will break into your body.
4. Much higher.
5. A slice forehand underspin (sidespin) serve will bounce to the receiver's left. It is conceivable that someone like Bobby Riggs might hit a slice *backhand* underspin serve, and then it would bounce to the receiver's right. ●

MOON-BALLING: TENNIS ON THE MOON

by E. K. HAMMOND, Sr.

NOW THAT Americans have gamboled on the moon and are planning orbiting space stations for shuttling to and from the moon, one can contemplate the possiblity of a tennis game on our nearest celestial body. Certainly there would be spooky differences due to three established facts—the absence of an air envelope, reduced gravitational pull, and a different court surface. There is no simple solution to these problems. Of course one would take along oxygen, but this creates new problems. Furthermore, the balls are still out there in a vacuum, behaving altogether differently from what you expect on Earth. After many moons *you* may be able to adjust to the one-sixth gravitational pull, but are the balls able to adjust? After all, they are little celestial spheres in their own right—in a void of space—affected and controlled by the same physical laws as their larger cousins throughout the cosmos.

And how can you correct the playing surface of deep, dry dust? Not by growing grass nor by wetting and rolling as we do in the Southland; there is neither the water nor the clay, which is a deteriorated state of sedimentary rock, of which the waterless moon has none. That last statement also rules out a cement surface, for the main component of concrete is limestone formed in ancient bodies of water. An asphalt base cannot be used for two reasons. In the first place, there is none on the moon inasmuch as such compounds are animal and plant residues of a bygone era. Furthermore, such a surface laid down at dawn

would soon become a sea of oil in the intense solar heat. So, for the time being, we go ahead as planned for the first moon match—dust or no dust, gravity or no gravity, air or no air.

First comes the proper dress and equipment. Forget about shorts or other abbreviated costumes. In their place take a space suit with all of its accoutrements—helmet, oxygen tank, heavy shoes, telephone, etc. Telephone? Yes, telephone! Be very careful in selecting the balls for they may promptly explode in your face in the vacuum up there. Your best choice would be pressureless balls. Even so, those with sea-level pressure might balloon up to basketball size when they first pop out of the can on the moon.* So, be prepared for this phenomenon; otherwise, you may suffer a heart attack before you hit ball one.

Take your heaviest racket. You will be surprised to discover that it is very light up there—less than half the weight of a badminton racket down here—actually about two ounces. You may ask, "Is this the racket with which I must hit that basketball?" Yes, provided you do not strike too hard. Remember this basketball weighs only a small fraction of an ounce, that there is no air resistance to slow it down, and that once it is slammed to the ground there is insufficient gravity to prevent it from bouncing a hundred feet high, coming

---

*If the outer covering of the "pressureless" balls is sufficiently porous (permeable to gas), then the air inside can escape without expanding the ball temporarily.

to rest in some distant crater.

By this time you must be worrying about being loaded down with gear—helmet, shoes and oxygen tank. No problem with weight. If you and your gear weigh 330 pounds here, you would weigh only 55 pounds on a moon court. Imagine how fast you could run, weighing so little and with no air resistance to hold you back! You would have the same strong muscles to propel you forward at frightening speed with strides of 30 feet each. Reckless? Yes. A fall on a sharp rock could tear your space suit so that you would have to forfeit the match.

In spinning the racket to decide choice of serve or court you are surprised that in such quietness you did not hear it hit the ground. You did not hear it because it did not make any noise; it did not make any noise because there is no air to carry sound. You have also discovered by now that you cannot hear each other talk (no air about you to carry the vibrations). So you use the built-in telephones you brought along. In keeping score and otherwise communicating during the match, either you use the telephone or resort to sign language which you have sometimes used on Earth during noisy traffic hours.

During the warm-up you may be surprised that various spins on the ball which were the foundation of your usual good game on Earth have absolutely no effect on the ball in its trajectory on the moon. All balls, whether hit with topspin, backspin, sidespin or slice, travel the same blunt parabolic path of the flat ball. There is no wind

to rush them forward or hold them back or blow them sideways off the court, no air resistance to curve the various types of spins, nothing but a very weak gravity which eventually pulls the balls down. Now you think that spins are out and all balls must be hit flat and easy. You soon discover that, while spins do not affect the trajectory in flight, they do affect the bounces essentially the same as on Earth. A spinning ball will "grab" the surface and ricochet in the direction of the spin.

During this warm-up period in dead silence you discover that you are seriously handicapped by not being able to hear the "ping" of your racket against the balls nor the thud of bounces. You are now operating on only one cylinder, vision, whereas you have grown accustomed on Earth to visual and auditory aids. You are probably surprised to discover that your good game was so dependent upon the sounds of racket against balls and balls against the court. It is also disturbing to see your opponent dashing about the court as noiselessly as a specter from the tomb. You may even begin to wonder if you will arrive at the proper hitting position in time to return the balls inasmuch as you can hear no sounds of your own running.

When it comes your time to serve you will be amazed to see the ball in your usual toss rise 20 feet above your head before it begins its slow descent. There you are in your usual serving stance, ready to start the forward swing, and the ball is floating straight down like a feather, still 15 feet above your head. Then you remember that objects do not fall fast in only one-sixth G. You try a different ball and it behaves the same way. As an experiment you pick up a large rock in one hand and a fluffy piece of lint from a new tennis ball and drop them simultaneously from the same height. You are enchanted to note that they fall with the same speed. Then you recall that in a vacuum there is no air resistance, and that gravitational pull alone accounts for their equal rates of descent. Your opponent is now trying desperately to reach you by telephone to inquire into your unusual behavior. Moon madness, maybe? At first you are inarticulate, stuttering and jabbering excitedly. Now he races to you, convinced that it is moon madness. You recover your composure in time to

think, "This is a tennis match, the first one that is really and truly out of this world, and I am not going to blow it by telling my opponent everything I know."

So you blink your eyes, swallow hard, smile and say, "Thanks, pal, I'm OK, now."

You now try some practice serves by gently tossing the ball and delaying your backswing to allow for the slow fall. But something is in the way of your "back-scratcher" backswing. It is the oxygen container. You must now delay the swing more than ever because the racket cannot travel as far as usual. You soon discover that with this shorter swing you are able to deliver as hard a serve as is necessary. You deduce that three factors demand a rather easy serve: no air resistance to slow it down, no topspin to bring it down, and only one sixth normal gravity to bring the ball down into the service court. These three scientific facts add up to a mandatory slow and easy serve, unless the net is lowered at least a foot.

You recall that your opponent never practices his serve during the warm-up and does not know the significance of what you have just discovered. You win the toss and elect to choose a court rather than serve. You are hoping that your opponent's bevy of surprises in his serving will so upset him that he will lose the match. This will pay him back for the humiliating defeat he handed you at Wimbledon.

Because of the poor bounces on the dusty surface the match soon becomes a volleying duel. Even then, many successful returns must be caressed gently to prevent their sailing beyond the court boundaries. This is the inevitable result of no air resistance, ineffectiveness of topspin and one-sixth G. Each time your opponent serves, you can hear his muted expressions of "Well I'll be damned! What the hell?"

A conference of physicists, meteorologists and tennis professionals would, as a result of this match, probably make five recommendations for the first moon tournament:

1. Increase all long-axis court dimensions. This would eliminate the necessity of lowering the net and would allow all balls to be struck with greater impact without so much hazard of their going out of bounds.
2. Design balls with a vacuum, sealed

in a vacuum container, to be opened only on the moon.
3. Increase the height of the court fence.
4. Design a portable, stable, smooth court surface to place on the deep, dry dust.
5. Provide umpires with high-powered binoculars to follow the high lobs and bounces.

Such a committee would also most likely make the following pertinent observations:

Both high and low temperatures pose not only problems but definite threats to life. The complete absence of an air envelope means that the solar heat warms the moon surface very rapidly soon after dawn. For the same reason, the heat escapes very rapidly after dark. This becomes especially significant in view of the moon day being a fortnight long. This allows a terrific build up of heat over a two week duration of sun, sun, sun—no air to filter it and no clouds for shade. Likewise the nights are two weeks long and the devastating heat of a fortnight's duration quickly escapes, allowing frightfully frigid temperatures.

It is recommended that matches be scheduled only for the relatively early morning hours, probably the second or third Earth day (after the frigid cold has been expelled and before the temperature rises too high). This would mean only one or two matches per lunar month. It is suggested therefore that each player take something, dominoes or dames, to wile away the long nights.

Do not schedule any long, leisurely walks during dawn or dusk. There is no twilight on the moon, no subtle dusk or dawn, simply because there is no air to diffuse the light just before dark or sunrise. "The sun comes up like thunder" on this airless hunk of rock, and light just as quickly disappears at sunset, save for probably a little Earth shine.

If you are pressed for a short breathing spell during play, it is ethical to throw up a 400-foot high lob which will require several seconds to fall back down.

Now that I have analyzed the situation, I am convinced that our closest heavenly body would be better for honeymooning than for any other sport. ●

THE TOPSPIN FOREHAND

Bob Kreiss, the 1971 Wimbledon Junior Champ, hits a closed stance forehand. The racket on the backswing is between waist and shoulder level (above hit level).

Just before the hit, the racket is below knee level or, more important, below ball level, which is the basic concept in topspin. Bob's wrist is laid back.

The racket head comes up and forward, but in this case there is absolutely no wrist roll.

The follow-through ends well above the shoulder level: the racket brushed the ball upwards.

by GUY COGNEN

THE FOREHAND drive is an arch weapon of aggressive tennis. Most of the attacking strokes come from this wing; therefore a good player must possess a hard, safe and dependable forehand. A forehand can be hit four ways—with sidespin, without spin at all (flat), with underspin or with topspin. The sidespin forehand is used by only one or two "name" players as a basic stroke and it is mainly for down-the-line shots. Players such as Marty Riessen will use sidespin often for the down-the-line. The flat forehand is difficult to control in fast play; it must be hit perfectly since gravity rather than spin is what brings it into court. These days underspins are generally "chips" which resemble long volleys and which are used mainly by players as approach shots (to get them to a net position). In most cases these chips are down-the-line to the opponent's backhand. The topspin forehand is the best because the ball is controlled by spin and it can be hit hard and still land in court, it allows great margin of safety and it is an attacking shot.

The topspin drive can carry great pace. As the ball bounces, the topspin causes the ball to shoot forward and to bounce faster and higher. As it clears the net the ball dips, forcing the net man to volley up.

A flat ball does not turn in the air in the course of its flight. The sidespin ball rotates sideways, the underspin or chip ball rotates toward the hitter even though it is moving forward (this is why it slows up on the bounce) and the topspin ball rotates away from the hitter toward the opponent's fence.

There are two ways to impart topspin to the ball. The swing is started slightly below the flight of the ball and the follow-through ends high above shoulder level. Rod Laver and Lew Hoad use wrist roll, which means the racket face turns over the ball at the moment of impact. This second style is not easy to master and it will never be as secure as the locked wrist shot. The topspin forehand is fairly easy to learn since all one must do is brush the racket face upward as well as forward as it meets the ball. The easiest way, of course, is to start low (on the backswing) and finish high (on the follow-through).

If you have a natural sidespin or a natural chip, don't discard it. However, if your sidespin and chip only go down the line, you will be a much better and sounder player if you can add a topspin forehand to your repertoire. If you only have flat shots, you should be able to learn a topspin in less than an hour, and it will come in handy on those days when your flat forehand is sailing out or netting. ●

Richard Evans

A Pilgrimage to Barellan— Where A Goolagong Grew Amidst the Wheat

by BUD COLLINS

THE NEXT TIME you're in Barellan, drop by Barry Tubb's butcher shop. You can't miss it, unless you're a fast walker—in which case you might miss the entire town. It's the only butcher shop in town, and maybe the only one in the world fronted by a stained glass door labeled:

BILLIARDS
E.J. Reid Prop

E. J. Reid's three-table pool hall went out of business in 1949, a couple of years before E. F. Goolagong moved into this village she would celebrate by playing a different ball game, called tennis. The Tubb brothers replaced cues with cutlets and eight-balls with T-bones, but they didn't replace the door with Reid's name on it. The colored glass was pretty and unusual, distinctive in a dry, dusty place not overrun with distinction.

Besides, everybody knew the meat market had taken over. The Tubbs didn't have to advertise. There aren't any secrets in Barellan. "Everybody knows what everybody else is up to, which is one reason you want to get away," says Evonne Goolagong. She goes back a couple of times a year, for two or three days, to visit her family. Then Evonne closes the door on her old world and returns to her present one, a universe that stretches as far as jets can reach, and counts her as one of its better known citizens.

But I didn't invite you into Barry Tubb's to gaze upon the lamb chops, handsome as they may be. Hanging on a shabby green wall is the prize exhibit: a huge, fading photograph of Barellan's Great Moment, captioned "January 2, 1932, wheat carting. 116 teams, over 600 horses. 13,000 bags delivered in one day, an Australasian record."

"What a day that was," says whiskery 82-year-old Chris Campbell. "Horses and wagons as far as you could see. A man climbed up on the railroad semaphore to take that picture."

It is a picture of horses and wagons and bags of wheat lined up from the tallest structures in Barellan—the silos where Evonne Goolagong later nervelessly skipped on planks 90 feet above the ground in search of pigeons. The line extends into the distance.

"Barellan," says Barry Tubb, the butcher, "will never have another day like that. Town's going down. Cities are taking over, and the young people won't stay. We got about 450 people here now. The wheat's still good, and the sheep, but machines cut down on the people you need. Young people don't want this kind of place. There's nothing for them to do."

Great Moment II for Barellan, of course, was July, 1971, when the girl from Bendee Street beat Margaret Court to win Wimbledon. Red Dicker, who has lived in Barellan longer than anybody else—"hatched here in 1901"—sips his beer amidst the grimy, hardworking *cockies* (grain and sheep farmers) who gather at the social center, the War Memorial Club. "We were all here," he points to the TV set, "at about two in the morning to watch her win. She's our girl. She deserves everything. Never gone *flash* (conceited), Evonne. It was something to see one of your own in London on the TV winning the world championship.

Resembling a scene of the old West, Barellan's Yapunyah Street is dominated by the Commercial Hotel, left.

Evonne at nine, a school sprint champion. The Goolagong
family, she says, was treated "no different to anyone else."

"Have another beer. I'm *shouting* (buying), Yank..."

I said I would, thanks. Country beer in Australia is a wondrous elixir. I've known only two Aussies who committed the treasonous act of admitting they don't like beer: Bob Hewitt and Evonne Goolagong. Bob was deported to South Africa. Evonne was forgiven, only because she is Evonne, one of the country's most agreeable exports.

Barellan. Barellan, Narrandera Shire, New South Wales, Australia. Late in October I decided to make a pilgrimage to the least likely spawning ground of a tennis champion, and I wound up 400 lonely miles west of Sydney, strolling down Yapunyah Street, the Champs Elysees of Barellan. It could also be the principal boulevard of any number of westerns you've seen. You walk beneath the tin marquees that shelter the sidewalk from the sun, toward the balconied Commercial Hotel, and you half expect somebody to draw on you. "Barellan could pass for Dodge City, couldn't it?" laughs Evonne. "If the cars weren't parked along here."

A middle-aged woman nods, "Gu-dye, Eee-von, owzit gun?" Translation: Good day, Evonne (heavy on the E, accent on the first syllable), how's it going?

"Where you going next?" asks the woman.

"South Africa."

"People nice there?"

"Quite nice."

"Have you been to Ireland?"

"Yes, to Dublin."

"I hear it's gorgeous. One trip to Ireland would do me, but I'll never get there. Well, good luck, Evonne. It's nice to see you."

"Country people are nice, friendly. Notice," says Evonne, "how slow they talk? Everything is slower here. After a couple of days it's time to go for me. Too slow now. It's nice country. What we call the inner country. Everybody writes that I'm from the Outback, but that's not true. That's out farther. I'm a *bushie* all right, a country girl, but this isn't the Outback."

It's out farther than most people would want to go. A few streets are paved. The majority aren't. Yarran Street, where the Goolagong family now resides—three of the eight kids are still at home with their parents—is a red dirt lane. Dust much of the time, mud when it rains. Summer paints the town red with dust.

"It was a good place to grow up. We were poor," says Evonne, "but what did that matter? Maybe we didn't have bicycles or some things other people had. But there was enough to eat, and so much for kids to do. Fishing, swimming, climbing up in those wheat silos to look for pigeons. I wouldn't go up that high now. I'd be scared to death, but you don't notice when you're a kid. Plenty of room to play; a big family. It was good.

"Then there was the tennis."

And the myth, the tale that Evonne started in primitive circumstances, on a bumpy, unkempt court. Not so. The Barellan War Memorial Tennis Club, a few yards from the now uninhabited shack that was her first home, is trim, neat, equipped with four well-tended and lighted clay courts. The clubhouse, a small brick building, is bordered by roses as lovely as those at Wimbledon. Few small cities in the United States have tennis clubs as attractive. I doubt that any locale in the world of 500 or so residents can come close to matching the BWMTC. Yearly dues: four dollars!

The reason for the club was the man behind Evonne. Bill

Evonne is very much at home at net hitting a backhand volley, perhaps her favorite shot. Her arm is straight and wrist firm and cocked so the racket is at a right angle to the arm.

Kurtzman, a retired grazier who died in 1973 at 78, raised money to start the club in 1956. He noticed Evonne hanging around when her older sister and brother played, and encouraged her. It was Kurtzman who made arrangements for pro Vic Edwards to undertake the tutelage of Evonne, and for her to eventually move into the Edwards household in Sydney where she became genuinely one of the family. Without Kurtzman and Edwards, Evonne knows, she'd still be in the bush, probably raising a family. "It was very lucky."

Vic Edwards is a thoroughly strong guy. I've never seen a man of 65 stand up so well to the beating he gives himself: smoking 60 cigarettes daily; going beer-for-beer against some of the best country drinkers; working long and sleeping little. Svengali...Prof. Henry Higgins...surrogate father...take your pick. Vic Edwards is a little of each, but mostly himself: an original. He has organized perhaps the largest tennis-teaching program in existence, his instructors dealing with 4,000 pupils a week at various centers. Yet his heart is "still in the scrubs" much of the time, where he spent his youth on huge stations as a *jackeroo,* learning the business of raising great numbers of cattle and sheep. "That's where I wanted to make my life, but the big opportunity never came along," says Vic. "So I went into the tennis coaching business with my father (Herbert Edwards), who was the first pro in Australia."

While working alongside Aboriginal hands on the long cattle drives, Edwards developed the belief that Australia's dark people could be raised to equality through education, concern and attention. He saw a challenge in the Aboriginal girl from Barellan, "a challenge to cultivate that talent, to help her rise as high as she could."

His rugged youth prepared Edwards to shrug off prob-

American titles (National Indoor, 1973). I really thought I had the Australian in 1971 when I led Margaret 5-2 in the third, but I cramped. She was smart. She moved me all over when I was in trouble and won five straight games."

Vic was happily surprised when Evonne undercut his prognostication by three years at Wimbledon. Uneasily, though, he wondered whether the unexpected victory in her second shot at the Big W hadn't diminished incentive. "Yes. I worried about that for a while. I don't know, candidly, if she'll ever overcome the 'walkabout'—the lapses of concentration when she loses interest. But her Wimbledons of 1972 and '73 weren't disappointments. Hardly. Losing to Billie Jean King both years, in the final and the semis, a great player with so much more experience. Beating Chris Evert in the Italian final, on clay, was making great progress. She was only a point or so away from beating Margaret (Court) in the 1973 Forest Hills final. And she did well against Billie Jean in 1974.

"Evonne is coming along as I planned and hoped, but we have to be careful that she gets enough rest and isn't over-taxed in tennis and outside activities. That's why I'm protective. That's why she won't play everywhere they want her—why she won't play indoors in the States this winter—and why she won't accept all the financial opportunities. Everybody needs time to re-charge, time for other things..."

"I like to get away from tennis, not even hear a word about it," says Evonne. She was on her way to the Queensland beaches for a holiday with her pal and foster sister, Jenifer Edwards. "Jenifer can't stand tennis. If you mention it, she leaves. She's good for me."

Vic resumes, "I think my conservative approach is a lot like that of Jimmy Evert, Chrissie's father. Jimmy and I have talked a lot about this together. We have to protect these girls. I had nothing against Virginia Slims or Billie Jean and the other pros when we refused to join their circuit. We were criticized then, but it was simply that I didn't want Evonne to overdo. As long as I have anything to say about it, she won't overdo."

Because of his philosophy, it was assumed that Edwards would turn World Team Tennis down flat. Stunningly, he and Evonne both signed with the Pittsburgh Triangles, Vic as general manager and adviser to the coach. "The money is tremendous, and as long as she can play the major events, too, Wimbledon and the French—to which WTT has agreed—we're happy."

It was understood that Evonne could withdraw if the 1974 season wasn't to her liking. With Billie Jean, Margaret, Evonne and Kerry Melville all signed up, and Chrissie on the verge, it was doubtful that the International Lawn Tennis Federation and their national associations would have the nerve—or stupidity—to ban WTT recruits from the tournament mainstream.

Far from any mainstreams are the trickles for which Barellan (Aboriginal for meeting of the water) was named: Sandy Creek, Mirool Creek and Colinroobie Runner. Most of the time they're nearly dried up; more beer than water flows in Barellan. Still, the streams are there, and it's fascinating that Evonne Goolagong has gone from one confluence of three rivers to another: from Barellan and its anonymous streams to Pittsburgh and its mighty Monongahela, Allegheny and Ohio.

"So that," said Evonne, "is why the team is called the

lems and criticism later. "Nothing they can say about my handling of Evonne can hurt me," he says convincingly. "She and I know we've done the right things." You believe him. Evonne and Vic have a deep belief in each other, and the kind of love that exists between him and his five daughters. Add his peppery, jovial wife, Eva, and you have "Vic Edwards' harem," he roars. "Someday I'll get away from them. I don't know how one man has survived." The public Edwards is frequently brusque, gruff, stern, his deeply lined face contributing to the picture of a hard man. But he has a good, dry sense of humor and a warmth the rappers don't suspect.

"I've been very protective of Evonne, but I don't think over-protective." Many would disagree with his close supervision, considering that she's a 22-year-old woman. "It's no different to what I'd be with any daughter of mine." Obviously Vic hasn't sheltered them into spinsterhood: four of the five are married; he and Eva have 13 grandchildren. "Any woman as famous as Evonne, and moving around the world as she does, needs management. I'm the manager, with help from the Mark McCormack firm (International Management Inc.) in the States. She couldn't do everything for herself. Her job is to play."

Goolagong readily agrees.

"Just this one more year," sighs Edwards. Both he and Evonne are keenly aware that when she got aboard the world circuit in 1970 Edwards predicted, "She'll be the best in 1974. She'll win Wimbledon and be No. 1."

Evonne says, "I know he feels this will be my year, and I'd like that very much. I'd like to make a Grand Slam, but first of all I'd like to win the Australian Championship. I haven't won the title of my country yet, although I've won France and Wimbledon (both 1971) and Italy (1973) and one of the

Sheep raiser Bill Kurtzman built Barellan's neat tennis club and encouraged Evonne when she began hanging around the courts. Kurtzman later made arrangements for her move to Sydney.

Arthur Cole

Vic Edwards, left, with daughter Jenifer and Evonne. A former jackeroo, his tennis program now reaches 4,000 pupils a week. Evonne has become a sixth daughter to Edwards and his wife.

Triangles?" Right. Will there be a Barellan Triangles in World Team Tennis one day? I'll defer judgment until I see whether WTT can survive.

As the only Aboriginal family in town, the Goolagongs were "treated no different to anyone else," recalls Evonne. "Our house was small and crowded and not very nice, but there was plenty of room to play outdoors, and lots to do. I played all the games, including rugby and cricket with the boys.

"But I always wanted to go to Sydney. I knew I couldn't do anything in tennis unless I did. My parents urged me to go." Evonne has purchased a better home for the family, and seen to painting and refurbishing of the dwelling, a one-story *fibro* (fiberboard) with corrugated iron roof, typical of that part of the country. Her father, Ken Goolagong, lean and withdrawn, worked as a sheep-shearer until his death in 1974. "He did his 200," is the tribute of the men in the barroom at the War Memorial Club. If you can strip the beige wool from 200 sheep a day with your electric clippers, you're doing a good job in Barellan.

It is a place of toil and tedium and flies, an area as flat as Holland, covered by vast stands of grain and tinged purple by a weed called Patterson's Curse. When infrequent rain washes away the drabness, bringing a coat of green that eases the eyes, it is remembered well. They can recite the years of good rains and bad droughts, quoting rainfall statistics as surly as Superstat Rino Tommasi spiels Wimbledon and Davis Cup years and figures. The talk is constantly of crops and the fight against Nature. Evonne Goolagong is a treasured product, but not a major concern, not nearly so important as the wheat. "Will the rust hurt the wheat?" is a more gripping topic than, "Will Evonne improve her second serve?"

Old Chris Campbell peers into his beer, "It's a gamble. The wheat's not ours until it's in the silo." Apparently Nature saves too many match points, and sometimes steals the match.

Those cement silos are the architectural masterpieces of Barellan. When the harvest is good, and they're full, everybody is happier than the day Evonne won Wimbledon. They rise high above the fields, visible for miles, like six ancient towers. Up the ladders, up above Barellan, young Evonne climbed, nimbly crossing the broad cylinders on skimpy boards, snatching at pigeons that lived below the roof.

"A marvelous view up there," she says. "You can see way beyond Barellan."

She is still climbing above and beyond her origins, hoping not to slip and fall, grasping for Barellan's Great Moment III that may come in the new year as divined by her wizard.

"But if I don't do these things," says Evonne, "I won't cry. I love tennis, but tennis isn't that serious." Hardly as serious as beer is to the hardy, friendly men who come in hot and tired from the fields and the sheep pens of Barellan. Another Wimbledon couldn't possibly taste any better to her than their daily grog does to them.

The taste is in the playing, a joyous feeling Evonne transmits to those who watch her. Maybe she will have another Wimbledon. Possibly she will have a Slam. But I can't be sure it matters very much in Barellan until Barry Tubb puts her picture up on the wall of his butcher shop, next to that really Great Moment, the wheat carting of 1932. ●

Rocky Weldon

How to Adapt to New Surfaces

by GLADYS M. HELDMAN

A PLAYER who has learned his tennis on one set of courts, viz., clay, has enormous difficulty switching to another surface, viz., concrete. He loses his rhythm, times the ball late and feels jerky, uncoordinated and frustrated. Even the top players, who "find" their timing after hitting three or four balls on a new surface, have problems in adjusting their whole game from a slow court where sliding is possible and the bounces are uneven (clay); to a fast surface where the ball often skids, the bounce is much lower and unreliable (grass); to a medium surface where there are no bad bounces, it is impossible to slide and spins are only moderately effective (Laykold or Plexipave).

Adapting to a new surface requires a change in rhythm and style of play. And you can adjust your game only if you know what is going to happen when the ball comes to you with topspin, sidespin and underspin; how high it will bounce on a deep, high ball, how low on an underspin and how fast on a hard ball (will it "jump" at you or slow down more than you anticipate?); whether the footing is secure when you change directions; how wide a crosscourt undercut backhand will veer; how deep and high a heavy topspin groundstroke will come at you; whether it is possible to run down almost any shot if your reflexes are quick enough and your feet fast enough; and if even a medium volley can be a winner or if hard volleys are "gettable." If this analysis sounds too technical don't let it frighten you off; there is a method of adjusting to new surfaces for every level of the game.

Top players make the fastest adjustment. Hitting a few balls gives them the general "feel" of the court. The significant adjustment for them is in style of play: attacking more on a fast surface; waiting for openings and playing more consistently on a slow surface; utilizing more spins on courts where spin is most effective; compensating for bad bounces when the court is rough; drop shotting more frequently when the ball "dies" on the court, etc. Beginners and intermediates make the slowest adjustment since their timing is thrown off by switching from a fast to a slow court or vice versa. Often it will take a full week for a novice to adjust to an entirely new surface. His biggest problem is to control his frustration and to analyze why he has mis-hit so many balls and how he can make the correction.

Beginners and Intermediates

John Smith has been playing for a few months on a Sportface or Sporteze carpet, which is medium-speed. He is going to play on clay (slow) for the first time.

John finds he has lost his "feel." Sometimes the ball bounces into his body and he cramps his arm so that he can't take a full, free swing. Often his timing is so bad that he has to stretch forward to hit the ball; even then he barely gets it before it bounces a second time. He often misjudges what looks like an easy shot and hits it while bending double from the waist. He feels awkward, helpless and angry at himself for being so unathletic and inept.

Since John's experience has been limited to one surface only, he is going to have a hard time grooving his timing to a surface that is only a little bit slower but where the bounce is uneven. These thoughts will help him adjust much faster:

• He must take a slower backswing. The entire backswing, not just one segment of it, is slowed down slightly. If he takes his regular backswing, he may have to come to a complete halt just before the moment of impact. This makes the swing jerky instead of flowing.

• He must move *forward* for every ball. If he does not move forward, the ball will start to drop faster than he has anticipated, and then he will be forced to bend or lean forward in order to hit it before it bounces a second time. Sometimes he will have to move a good two steps forward so that he can hit the ball at waist-level; if he only moves one step forward, he may make contact at ankle-level.

• He can never plant his feet because the ball may take a bad bounce. Clay is never perfectly smooth, and if the ball hits a bad or rough spot, it may bounce into or away from John. If he has planted his feet, then he has to twist his torso and cramp his arm into his body or extend the arm so straight and stiff that he loses all control. John has to be bouncy, on his toes, ready to hop sideways in either direction depending on the crazy bounce of the ball.

• John has to have a happy outlook. As soon as he gets discouraged, frustration goes into his feet (they refuse to move) and his right arm (it moves, sluggishly, almost reluctantly). He must regard changing to a new surface as a challenge which will take work and enthusiasm and which will help him become a far better player.

If John moves from clay (slow) to cement* (fast), his frustration will be even worse unless he has prepared himself for the necessary changes in stroke and timing. Now the ball will be coming at him so fast that half the time he will be late; instead of hitting the ball in front of him, he will often "hook" it slightly behind his body. He has no timing; his backhands go into the left alley and his forehands into the right alley, a sure indication that he is taking the ball late.

Instead of taking a full, free backswing, he must *shorten the entire swing and start it earlier*. Instead of a semicircular wind-up, he cuts off the preliminaries and takes the racket straight back. He starts his forward swing *at once*. He should try to hit crosscourt exclusively. Even then, he will find that his shots will never go in the crosscourt alley (in the left alley for a forehand, in the right alley for a backhand). When the shot goes into the wide crosscourt alley, the player is taking the ball too soon.

To make a quicker adjustment, John should prepare his mind, which in turn will prepare his eyes, arms and legs. These ideas will be helpful if John is a positive thinker:

• Adjustment to fast courts is never easy. John must face the challenge happily since a pessimistic attitude will adversely affect his eyes, arms and legs. The mind is the transmitter of thoughts; an arm or a leg never operates independently.

• The ball is going to come twice as fast as expected. John has to face that he will often be late, but occasionally he will hit the ball well in front of him. And, if he continues to try to speed up his reactions, he will hit more and more balls in front of him.

• John has to shorten his backswing and should start the forward swing *before* he thinks he should. Surprisingly, John will seldom if ever take the ball too early.

• The eyes must work with more concentration and faster than ever before. John has to train himself to see the ball come off his opponent's racket (he can no longer wait with his feet planted until the ball has crossed the net). He then has to move in the direction the ball is going and should try to get there well ahead of the ball. His efforts should be geared to getting there too *early*, and it will frequently turn out that he has reached the spot just in time.

Advanced Players

Many advanced players have similar, but not as pronounced, adjustment problems with a new surface as do intermediates. Even though the advanced player has more experience, a change of surface can be quite traumatic to his timing. Players who cannot make an immediate adjustment should give careful reading to the suggestions for less advanced players.

Fast Court Attack and Defense

Once the advanced player has acquired the timing for a slower or faster surface, he must adjust his style of play. On fast surfaces: he cannot afford a weak second serve; he must take advantage of every short, high ball by either putting the ball away or hitting it deep and coming to net; his passing shots must be harder, lower, more disguised, more angled since his opponent can more easily put away the volley; his defense must be clever and designed to keep the opponent guessing since the aggressor always has the advantage when the court is fast; and he must step up his pace slightly (never to the point of pressing) because the court favors the harder hitter.

There are two kinds of fast courts—one with perfect bounce (cement) and one with an unpredictable bounce because the surface is not perfectly even (grass). A third type of fast court, wood, is so rare today that it is scarcely worth more than a mention; spin is incredibly effective on boards—a left-handed slice serve to the forehand jumps into the body, an underspin backhand moves wide and low after the bounce and a heavy topspin forehand "takes off" with a high forward bounce.

Grass and cement, particularly cement that has been finished with a glass-like patina (no rough troweling to slow it down), are much faster than most carpets, compositions, asphalts and acrylic-painted surfaces such as Laykold or Plexipave. However, even though grass and cement are noted for their speed, a slow, high ball will not have more appreciable speed on grass and cement than it does on clay, asphalt or acrylic surface. Therefore two push-ball artists or retrievers paired against each other will not find the pace of cement or grass any different from that of clay or Har-Tru.

A ball hit on grass ordinarily has a low bounce, a ball hit on bad grass often takes a bad bounce and a ball hit on wet grass frequently does not bounce at all. One can never position oneself firmly on grass since the bounce is never totally predictable. The knees must bend far more than on any other surface; the worse the grass, the more the knees must bend.

Underspins on grass "take off" with a sideward motion and must be handled with an extremely stiff wrist since the ball is skidding sideways from the racket. For the player who is not yet secure, an underspin backhand crosscourt should be returned crosscourt, because the ball is moving to the left of the receiver and, at worst, the leftward spin will bring it slightly more to center. He will have worse luck if he tries to hit it down-the-line, because the leftward spin will carry it into the opponent's alley.

Sidespins are also extremely effective because there is forward as well as sideways motion after the bounce and, moreover, the ball feels "heavy" on the receiver's racket. A forehand down-the-line sidespin will come to the receiver's backhand and move forward as well as to the left. This is best handled with a very stiff wrist and with a crosscourt return to counteract the sideward bounce: the ball is moving to the left and so a down-the-line return may go into the alley, whereas a crosscourt will, at worst, go toward center.

Spins are effective on fast cement but underspin will slow up the ball appreciably, so topspin and sidespin are the preferred shots. Obviously underspin must often be used on low, short balls and on many backhand approach shots, but the hard topspin backhand on a fast court is more aggressive and is hard for the opponent to reach. Heavy topspin on the forehand is extremely useful because of its forward motion: even if the shot goes short (a few feet beyond the service line), the forward motion is so great and the bounce so

---

*The word "cement" stands for "Portland cement concrete." It is the most common surface in California where the courts are usually very fast. However, "cement" can be very slow if it is heavily troweled to make the surface rough.

high on cement that the average opponent cannot come in but must play the ball from the baseline. A deep, heavy topspin forehand often forces the opponent to a position six feet behind the baseline.

There are three spots from which to return serve on a fast court: three to six feet behind the baseline against a very hard serve; on or in the area of the baseline for a heavy spin serve (in order to hit it before the spin has pulled the ball wide); and two feet or more inside the baseline against short second serves. The short second serve presents the receiver with his opportunity to step around the ball and smack a forehand down-the-line (usually) or sharp crosscourt (occasionally).

Slow Court Attack and Defense

The slower the court, the easier it is to return any ball. A great player can on occasion run down a ball that has gone past him or chase an angled overhead into the next court and retrieve it before the second bounce. Patience and speed of foot is the name of the game on very slow courts, although there is still opportunity for attack.

On slow courts the slugger is at his worst, the retriever at his best and the clever, heady "chess player" can more easily use his bag of tricks.

The net rusher has to have a superb serve if he is to follow it to net regularly. (Today more and more top men players with big serves are coming in behind serve on clay or Har-Tru and doing better than they would if they stayed back.) If the serve is not superb, the net rusher will find himself ruefully staring at a steady stream of passing shots. More often he will have to work his way to net by forcing a short shot from his opponent, then hitting it with both depth and pace to a corner. If the opponent retrieves it, the net rusher may have to leap high to smash a sky-ball lob. Overheads are harder to put away on slow courts, and very few bounce-overheads smashed from behind the baseline are outright winners. The net rusher must therefore be patient because he can be driven back from the net by high lobs and his short volleys become set-ups to the passing shot artist. He must wait for the short balls or, when he can, volley the high ball and come in behind it.

The consistent player has a field day. If he is fast, he can throw back hundreds of balls. If he hits deep as well, he is going to be extremely tough for all but the very best players. If he is accurate on passing shots when pulled wide and can also put away a short ball, then he is going to win almost every clay court tournament. His name is Guillermo Vilas. Her name is Chris Evert. The only players capable of beating consistent passing shot artists such as Vilas and Evert on slow courts are aggressive players who are almost as consistent (Connors and Borg for example, among the men, Court and Goolagong among the women).

The "chess player" also does extremely well on a slow court. This player relies on change of pace and change of spin to create openings. A backhand is sliced down-the-line, then mixed with a harder backhand crosscourt, a high looping forehand, a drop shot, a forceful down-the-line forehand, a delicate lob, a deep-down-the-line, and even an underhand serve with tremendous spin. The aims are to keep the opponent off balance, to disguise what is coming next, to prevent rhythm by mixing up loops with drives, with spins, with angles.

The advanced player who comes from a fast court to clay must "think clay," i.e., getting back many more balls, primarily, and going for fewer outright winners if the percentages are proving fatal. He need not stop aggressive tactics but he cannot afford unnecessary errors. He may be able to create openings (short returns) with a big topspin forehand, which is always an effective shot on clay. If he drop shots well, he may rely on a drop shot-lob-drop shot pattern to exhaust and wear down the opposition.

If he is lobbed, he may not go for the overhead winner, particularly if he is much closer to the baseline than the service line. When he gets a short lob, he will always go for the winner (which is often an angled overhead), since he will never have a better opportunity. If he knows how to slide, he slides into wide balls. He "thinks" clay which means the emphasis is on consistency, depth, retrieving, creating openings and taking advantage of openings when they present themselves.

Medium-Paced Courts and Maverick Surfaces

Clay, Har-Tru and a number of other composition surfaces are slow. Grass, cement and wood are fast. Asphalt, acrylic paints, carpets—surfaces neither fast nor slow, lie somewhere in between. Here the adjustment is mostly for spin. As an example, Laykold and Sportface play almost identically except for the way the surface takes spin: underspins are more accentuated on Sportface and will pull the player wider.

Carpets also vary, with Sporteze (or Sportface) faster than Supreme Court, and Supreme Court accentuating spins much more than Sporteze. A player who does not understand spins will experience extreme frustration his first time on Supreme Court. Bolltex (another carpet) is easy to turn and run on; Uni-Turf is more difficult when you want to change directions; one can slide on Har-Tru or other sandy-topped surfaces, but a player can break his ankle if he tries to slide on a carpet or a hard surface.

When coming off a fast court to a medium court, the player has more time to hit the ball but he must remember that he has to move *toward the ball*. Read the paragraphs in this article with regard to changing from a fast court to a slow one. The same applies in the change from fast to medium, with the additional factor of learning to recognize what happens to the bounce after spin shots are hit.

Maverick courts are the most confusing to intermediates. Tennis Quick, a popular European surface, is extremely slow and has its own peculiar bounce on drop shots and underspins. Le Club in Fort Lauderdale has two courts which behave like no other courts. A combination of forehand topspins and backhand underspins is guaranteed to drive an intermediate player up the fence—until he gets used to them.

Carpets that were installed a few years ago when some carpets were then in the experimental stage will play a prominent role in bringing the visitor's game down 30 points. A maverick court gives a bounce off a spin that is comparable to no other on a "name brand" court. When you play on a maverick surface, give yourself *at least a week* to learn to react to the challenging bounces. You will adjust faster if your mood is happy, if you never plant your feet and instead keep hopping, and if you watch the ball like a hawk so that you can improvise at the last minute. Watch that bounce so that you can be the perfect All-Surface Player. ●

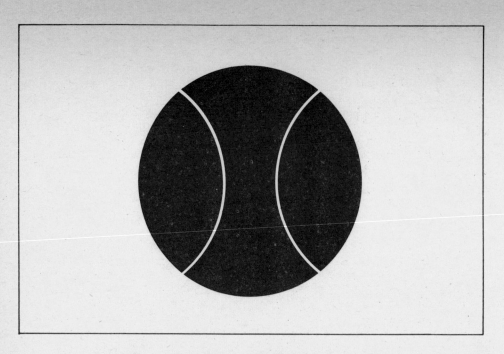

Japan, Land of the Rising Tennis Boom

by JEAN DRYSDALE

THEY SAY Japan's tennis boom began when the Crown Prince met Princess Michiko at the Karuizawa Tennis Club. For the first time in 2,000 years of Japanese royal history, a prince married a commoner. It was not only a romance but a tennis romance and it captured the imagination. Perhaps it also set the stage for the successful promotions of the WCT, Virginia Slims and open tournaments. Names like Billie Jean, John Newcombe, "Kenny Losewall," and "Miss Jiggens" (Valerie Ziegenfuss) have become famous overnight it seems.

The real tennis boom is predicted to arrive in two years time exactly and I have no doubt that it will be the most efficient tennis boom that has ever happened. Throughout the year, delegations of Japanese promotors and organizers have been visiting the United States and making careful notes about club facilities, equipment, courts, and recruiting players for tournaments and clinics. John and Angie Newcombe were there in February, Tony Roche was having a clinic near Mount Fuji while Cliff and I were busy in Tokyo and Karuizawa, and Ken Rosewall was there in November.

Meanwhile, there is a remarkable situation in Japan. Firstly, two different kinds of tennis are being played at the same time. Secondly, there are only eight registered teaching pros in a country of 100 million people. "Soft tennis" is a traditional game and is taught at all schools. At the moment three million people play soft tennis and a mere million play "hard tennis." On the whole "hard tennis" players look with indulgence on "soft tennis"—it's not so expensive (e.g. balls can be used until they fall apart or perish), it's not as difficult, it's amateur, and it's not international.

At the first clinic it was very puzzling to discover that many of the players classed as "beginners" had extreme Western forehands, wild swooping swings, perfect timing and footwork and peculiar services—all well-grooved. One such "beginner" hit 10 forehands straight over the back fence with no trouble at all.

"Ah!" said the local instructor wisely. "Soft tennis player."

So we went to watch a "soft tennis" tournament. Rackets are shaped like antique tennis rackets and strung by hand and the balls are soft rubber. The Western grip is used for all strokes—forehand, backhand, serve and volley—all hit on the same side of the racket with terrific topspin. Only doubles is played. All four players run onto the court, bow to the umpire (who bows back) and hit two strokes to warm up. After that, pandemonium breaks loose. The accepted thing is that players and spectators should make as much noise as possible, especially during points. As the server hits the ball they all begin to chant to encourage themselves and distract their opponents. The sight and sound of 30 soft tennis matches played at the same time is like walking into a tennis tournament gone mad! ("So much for all our arguments about concentration," said Cliff. "It's a good thing nobody knows about soft tennis in the States. Don't tell anyone.")

It is, nevertheless, great fun. Players batter the ball so hard that it practically disappears from view during rallies. But it is not a game of touch and control, which is why we had some trouble converting soft tennis players to tennis.

Isao Watanabe,—"Call me Izzy. Japanese names difficult for English"—after being the top player in Japan and travelling the world circuit, turned pro last April to form the first Japanese pro association which includes his brother, Stetomu, ("Call him Tom") and Kimiyo Hatanaka, both international players. They are the nucleus of the new association and they have a very busy time.

Izzy handles three two-hour clinics a day for six days a week at the Seijoh Club in Tokyo, among other things.

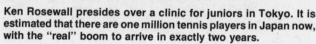

Ken Rosewall presides over a clinic for juniors in Tokyo. It is estimated that there are one million tennis players in Japan now, with the "real" boom to arrive in exactly two years.

Cliff Drysdale, left, and Izzy Watanabe teaching at the resort town of Karuizawa. Lessons begin with bowing by both students and instructors. Izzy heads a new teaching pro group.

"Tennis boom," he explains. "I teach 400 players a week."

Izzy took off a week (of relaxation) to help us with translation and some gentle nine-to-five work. It was a pleasure to watch him in action. He has an immense love of tennis and pride in his work. Happiness and instruction exude in a mixture of English and Japanese: "Okay! Backhando—Ich —Ni—San—HAI—One—Two—Slee."

We taught tennis and we learned a great deal about courtesy and enthusiasm. Each day we began by lining up on court for introductions and a hearty bow.

At times there were 20 players, two assistant instructors acting as ball machines, two coaches and an interpreter all on one court. This would have been a pro's nightmare anywhere but Japan. But there is no such thing as boredom or tiredness. One laughs at such things.

Each player runs eagerly onto the court, bows to the instructor, (who bows back) and the first stroke begins. Ten forehands—"Your follow-through is too low. You must end the stroke up here not down there. Thank you. Thank you." Everyone bows again. There are no tantrums, no balls hit, or rackets thrown in anger. Yet, there was also no lack of competitive spirit. The players tried so hard that they pulled muscles and sprained ankles going after impossible shots. Japan has not yet produced a player in the Top Ten of the world. On the other hand, Japan has not yet had a tennis boom as it is having now. In 1974, for the first time, two Japanese players joined the big pro circuits. Kazuko Sawamatsu on Virginia Slims and Jun Kamiwazumi on the WCT tour. They have a long way to go in those cauldrons of sweat, nerves, tiebreaks and flying missiles, but it's the first step.

Izzy's smile does not fade through the hottest of days after the rest of us have collapsed into after-images of forehands and backhands. In the evenings we discussed "Philosophy of Tennis" (which translated means, what is

going on between the ILTF, WCT, ATP, WITF, and WTT, and first of all what do all those things mean) and "Instruction of Champions."

"Is it possible for people who are not very tall to become tennis champions?"

"Of course it's possible. Look at Kenny Rosewall."

"Hai. Kenny Losewall."

A walk down the main street of Karuizawa with Izzy is like tripping after the Pied Piper. Friendly greetings are shouted from every doorway, people stop to chat.

"Everybody knows me," he explains. "My brother Stetomu (call him Tom) is King in Karuizawa but I am Clown Plince." We were introduced ("Cliff Dlysdale— fourth best plo in the world last year") and signed autographs, and Izzy tossed off snippets of information over his shoulder. "People come for tennis and golf; 300 tennis courts in Karuizawa; biggest golf course in the east, 72 holes. Ha! Shall we have ice cleams? Best ice cleams in the world."

Dear Izzy. As a well-travelled tennis player he is conscious of the differences in culture and was concerned about Cliff's head throughout the tour. "Mind the loof!" he said at every doorway, adding as explanation, "Japanese style loof."

The Japanese must be the kindest, pleasantest and most courteous people we have ever met. Each day was a dizzying experience. We marvelled at Bullet trains, and earthquakes, and Kobi beef, and three different alphabets and the violence of thunderstorms. We went from smoggy heat in Tokyo past fields of rice and lotus flowers and mulberries to the misty mountains of Karuizawa. We worked together with many people, discovering anew that tennis is a way of communicating in itself and that tennis players, whoever they are, have a bond together. It is a happy thought. ●

A TOURNAMENT POINT
Okker-Riessen vs. Newcombe-Roche

by JULIUS HELDMAN

THERE IS a lot of interesting clay court doubles play in this point. It is still going on as the special sequence camera runs out of film. The lob takes up a lot of time—and sequence shots—and on slow clay you will see a lot of high lobs, even with the best doubles players in the world. These four are surely among them.

Tom Okker is serving, his partner Marty Riessen is at net, John Newcombe is receiving in the right court and his partner, lefty Tony Roche, is waiting inside the service line.

The action starts with Okker following in behind his serve, which is somewhat towards the center service line. Okker's serve has enough spin so that it doesn't "hurt" Newk on clay. He chooses to wait for the ball inside the baseline and also moves toward the center of the court to take the ball on his forehand. His forehand return is cramped, and he finishes the stroke practically at the center of the baseline. Okker, now on the service line, moves over to intercept Newk's crosscourt forehand and responds with a low crosscourt forehand volley back to Newk's open court.

Newk, moving to his right to reach the volley, ends up on his right leg, with a completely open stance, as he starts his forehand response. Many players hit clay forehands this way rather than with a closed stance. Part of the reason is footing; there is less tendency to slip after running for a shot and more precision in a controlled slide. More and more teachers are becoming tolerant to, if not actively advocating, open stance forehands. Newk can hit both kinds, open and closed, equally well.

In this case, however, there is another object—disguise. See if you can guess what shot Newk will choose. Don't cheat by looking ahead. He takes the shot with practically no backswing and he lobs down the line, ending in a rather awkward pose. But it is an excellent lob and Riessen is forced to turn and run for the baseline. Newk's shot was an offensive lob, no underspin, in effect a forehand drive with trajectory just over Marty's head so that Riessen has no chance to leap back to take it in the air and has to relinquish the net to Newk and Roche.

As Marty runs back, Okker merely turns and watches while Newk advances to the service line. Why isn't Okker also running back or Newk moving in closer? The answer is that all the contestants know Marty will throw up a very high lob. Okker will have plenty of time to retreat to the baseline, and Roche and Newcombe will await the lob near mid-court. And that is what happened. Marty's sky ball gives everyone a chance to regain position. Okker is perhaps a bit lazy in his retreat, but he ultimately makes the baseline without losing sight of the ball, which is on Newcombe's side.

John is poised to take it on the fly, but a high lob coming straight down in long mid-court is not easy to handle and he finally elects to let it bounce. When he does choose the bounce shot, he immediately hops back behind the baseline. Meanwhile Tony is doing what every doubles partner must do: he crouches down, with bent knees, to get below the level of John's overhead if it is hit in Tony's direction. This crouch is a must if your partner is hitting an overhead behind you. In this case, John's smash is indeed over Tony's head, back to Okker.

Now the action gets interesting again as the sequence camera runs out of film. Because Newk is so far back, Tom is going to attack his forehand return, which he can do on slow clay even though Newk has hit a hard overhead. Riessen, anticipating Okker's action, has started for the net before Tom hits the ball. ●

Ed Fernberger

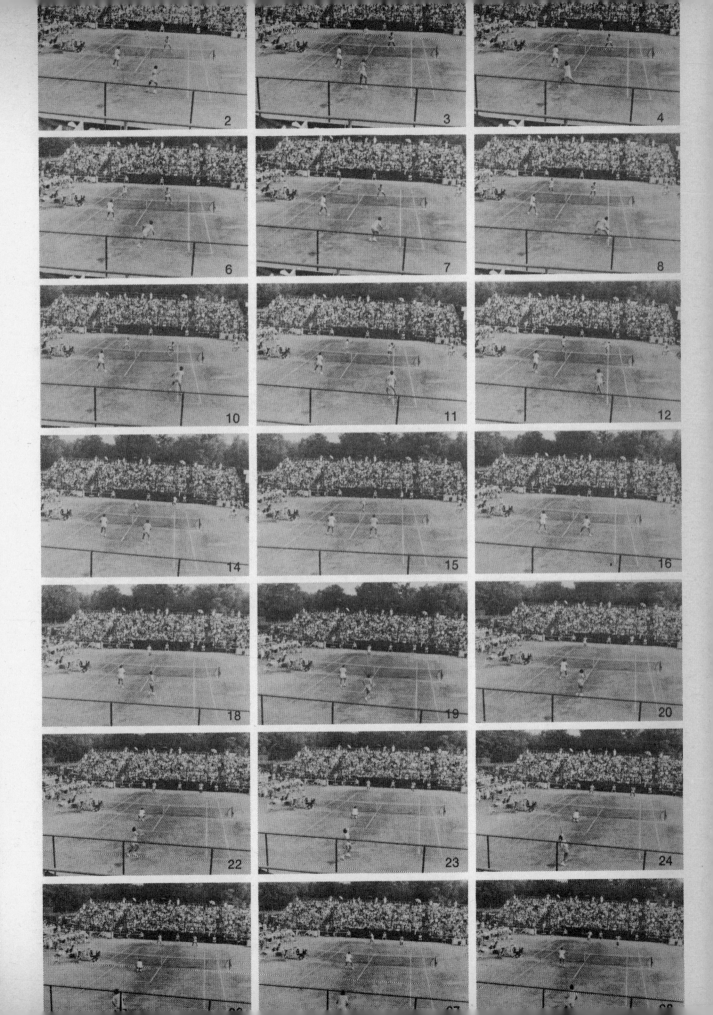

THE REAL DURR

by REX BELLAMY

FRANCOISE DURR is very special. Her character and her tennis are rich in contrast and paradox. Far from giving us a clue about the real Durr, superficial impressions can be totally misleading. To take the tennis first, her outrageously inimitable technique clouds the tactical virtues of a game that has much to teach the aspiring young. In addition to all the usual difficulties of playing tennis, she invented a few of her own—an extraordinary grip, a sliced backhand that tends to take her down on one knee and a service that suggests she is afraid of hurting the ball. She is blatantly a self-made player. Watching coaches sometimes fear she could put them out of business by destroying every convention about stroke production. Yet she is effectively unorthodox, getting remarkably good results from apparently poor material—like a gifted actress making a bad script sound like a work of genius.

The important thing about her tennis is where she puts the ball, not the way she does it. That ball is controlled by sharp wits and unyielding concentration, which override her technical eccentricities and to some extent exploit them (her game is inevitably difficult to read). She is always thinking—and she thinks fast. She applies pressure by brain power rather than violence, teasing her opponents rather than bullying them. She is shrewd and painstaking, experienced and tough. Her tennis is a reminder that a player's level of performance is as much a measure of effort (mental and physical) as it is a measure of talent. She is, in short, a far better player than the casual spectator may think she is. We can only speculate how good she might have been had her early grooming been sounder. But she would certainly have been less interesting.

Effectively unorthodox,
Francoise plays tennis
like a gifted actress
making a bad script
sound like a
work of genius

All this has long been evident to those familiar with Frankie's game. But her character, the private Durr, is more elusive. She is exceptional in that her court personality is a distorted reflection of her true nature. Even on court, her restless impatience between points is at variance with the way she plays them. In appearance and manner, she is so French as to be almost a caricature. But the stamping and the "body talk," the squealing and the snarling (plus that wonderfully expressive shrug) suggest—wrongly—that her emotions all lie on the surface and have no depth to them. The reverse is closer to the truth. She has the tenderness that Europeans, perhaps more than Americans, expect from women. Her kindness and droll Gallic wit are legendary. She inspires lasting affection in those who know her.

Yet there are qualities common to the tennis player and the woman: the hard, practical, no-nonsense shrewdness, the warmth and wit, the craving for patterned order in a society that demands improvization. She took up the guitar because she could not travel with a piano: because there is music in her and, one way or another, she has to express it.

Frankie has homes in Paris (in the 15th arrondissement, handy for the Eiffel Tower and Roland Garros), New York (on 59th, between First and Second) and, when last we met, she was acquiring a third in Denver. As Oscar Wilde observed, three addresses always inspire confidence. "I found New York antipathetic the first two years. I just have one idea—to leave as quick as I could. But I was engaged to a New Yorker and he give me a different angle of New York. Not like a tourist see New York. And I have a lot of friends." She also has an airedale called Topspin, purchased from a pet shop on 14th, who has learned to commute between Paris and the States and to walk on court toting one of Mlle. Durr's rackets. "I find it very nice when I lose a match and go back and she is there, wagging her tail and happy to see me."

Frankie has long been a much-travelled world citizen. She speaks a special brand of fluent and sometimes fiery English. "I can also get by in Italian and Spanish—I can understand what's going on." But she knows no Dutch, even after three years as a chum of Betty Stove's. When the blood is running warm, she can let loose a torrent of French that arouses alarmed conjecture. But, not often. "If Olga (Morozova) go and swear in Russian, nobody understand. So sometimes I prefer to say the bad word in English, so that everyone can tell what I say. If I say something in French, everyone think what I say is bad—when people don't understand a language, they always think it is dirty when you talk. But sometimes it is not."

This bundle of fun was delivered to the world by Madame Delphine Durr on Christmas Day, 1942. That was in Algiers, though Frankie spent most of her childhood in Oran. Many of her relatives are still there, maintaining a link that spans four generations. The family originally moved to Algeria because they tired of Alsace-Lorraine's role as a political tennis ball bouncing between France and Germany. Her father was in the French Air Force. "After going through the war he died in a plane crash in 1946, flying from Marseilles to Paris."

Oran was Frankie's home from 1946 until 1962. Then came the move to Paris ("the troubles were getting so bad in Algeria"). Her mother had property in Algeria and was heavily involved in running tennis tournaments. ("She was a good player.") Nowadays Madame Durr is a familiar and popular figure in French tennis, spending the winters as secretary to the Racing Club de France and the springs and summers organizing tournaments in the South of France or Switzerland—or visiting her children. Frankie has a sister, Janine, a medical doctor, and a brother, Jacques, who is older ("He played good tennis—even now he would give me a good practice").

The family belonged to a tennis club and played most Sundays. But Frankie was more interested in swinging about on the gymnastics apparatus in the nursery, or cycling or playing handball with the boys. At school she played basketball and enjoyed running a lot. Sprinting. "When I was 13 my mother said 'Why don't you play in a tournament?' I say I can't play. So she put me in anyway. I don't know how to play, but I reach the semi-final. I was running around. My only stroke was a forehand.

"After that, I thought it was a nice game to play. But in a club they only let adults play. At night I play with my mother or brother, or practice against a wall. I never had a coach until I was 18 or 19 (still in Algeria). So I picked up what was a good way, to me. I won the Algerian junior championship at 17. So I was sent to Paris to play for the French national junior championship, and reached the final. I lost to Chantal Langanay. She was putting everything back. She was like Chris—bing and bong...bing and bong...

"On the way to the final I beat the French junior champion, Evelyn Firmin. So they said, 'She must be pretty good,' and they sent me to an international junior competition, at Aix-les-Bains. Simone Mathieu, the captain of the French women's team, had never heard of me. I beat Francesca Gordigiani. She led by one set and 5-2, and I won. Lea Pericoli was watching. She said, 'You don't have too much tennis, but you have a good head and good legs.' I was still running a lot, to avoid my backhand. I didn't have a good backhand until I was 18 or 19. I was trying to hit it a lot more, but I was not feeling comfortable. But the coach told me to put my right foot in front if I want to hit my backhand, and that has helped me a lot."

That backhand has become one of the inimitable features of an inimitable woman. Always something of an original, Frankie Durr has been one of the central figures in many of the innovations of recent years. From 1968 to 1970 she was part of George Mac-Call's contract professional group, the National Tennis League. In 1971 she joined the Gladys Heldman "rebels" who inspired a revolution in the women's game. In 1974 she joined Denver of World Team Tennis.

Her long and distinguished competitive record first approached the peaks in 1965 when she reached the last eight of the Australian, French and United States championships. A year later she was in the Italian semifinals. And in 1967 she was French and German champion and reached the last four at Forest Hills. In 1969 she again advanced to the Italian semi-finals and in 1970 she did the same at Wimbledon. In 1972 and 1973 she was again in the French semi-finals. She was the first Frenchwoman since the war to reach the last four at Wimbledon and Forest Hills.

Her doubles record is even more impressive. In 1965 she and Janine Lieffrig captured the heart of Wimbledon with the infectious enthusiasm with which they beat the top seeds, Margaret Smith and Lesley Turner (as they were then), on their way to the final. From 1967 to 1971 she was French champion for five successive years, three times with Gail Sherriff (later Chanfreau) and twice with Ann Jones. In 1969 she also won the Italian and South African titles with Jones and the United States championship with Darlene Hard, who had emerged from retirement to find out what the modern game was all about. In 1972 Frankie was again U.S. champion, this time with Betty Stove.

That is a startling record when you look at the game with which Frankie achieved it. One of her outstanding memories, of course, is the 1967 tournament at Roland Garros, where she gave France their first women's singles championship since Nelly Landry (French by marriage) in 1948 and their first French-born winner since Simone Mathieu in 1939. The top three seeds, champions of Wimbledon (Billie Jean King), France (Mrs. Jones), and the United States (Maria Bueno), were all beaten in the quarters on the same day.

Frankie won 5-7, 6-1, 6-4 against Bueno ("She was such a beautiful player—I used to watch her play, and not watch the ball at all. But when I beat somebody once, I know I can beat them again"). She defeated Kerry Melville in a semi-final and Lesley Turner, now Mrs. Bowrey, in a final that spanned an hour and 35 minutes of a hot Sunday afternoon on the center court. In the mind's eye I still see Frankie then—already a familiar figure in sunglasses, with her hair tied back in a bright ribbon.

That win over Maria Bueno is one she particularly treasures. Another, a real "pressure" win, came at Philadelphia in February, 1971, when she came through 6-2, 5-7, 7-6 against King, who had won her previous 28 singles matches. Each had three match points and even the watching male competitors (not easily impressed by women's tennis) got excited. "Beating Billie Jean in that tie-breaker was the match that gave me the most satisfaction. When she is good, she is so good. She is the one I most enjoy watching—and also for

Fred M. Hublitz

Frankie is an accomplished volleyer. Though she relies mainly on placement, she can swat high backhand volleys as hard as necessary, even with her legendary grip. Her backhand grip is like an Eastern forehand, but with forefinger up the handle.

what she has been doing for women's tennis. But the most difficult to beat would be Evert and Court. Evert really make me mad. She's got the same game as me, but much better. I have the feeling that I have my head against a wall all the time, without getting any place. Court is very powerful. She overpower me a lot."

And favorite tournaments? "I really enjoy Wimbledon because it's for the players—and that's nice. I like the tournament in San Francisco as well. It's very well run. And the French (I feel at home and I like Paris, such a beautiful city). Hamburg was a very nice tournament. After Wimbledon, to me it was the best run. I hate Forest Hills. It's like a circus."

Frankie has so much experience and balanced good sense that she is always instructive company. Let us hear her off-the-cuff views on some topical issues...

On doubles—"I think doubles is underrated. The public enjoy doubles much better than singles. It's the game people play most of the time at the club. Also it's more quick, more exciting, not so boring. It's more relaxed, too. Not so much pressure (I don't know if it's because there is not so much money involved). More and more people will decide to put on only a doubles event. At the mixed doubles tournament in Dallas, there were great matches all the time."

On America's advance at Europe's expense—"It's a shame that most of the tennis is now in America (the big money is here, let's face it), because tennis started in Europe—and if we don't do anything about it, it will die. Not so much for the men. But the women don't have anything to play in Europe. It's always been a difficult situation in Europe for women if they want to make a name and earn a living. Sportswomen are not so well considered as they are here (though in England women are very well considered, maybe because we have so much more coverage). I think it will come. But it will take time."

On World Team Tennis—"Since I have been in the beginning of every change in tennis, I decide to go to WTT. If I was young, maybe I won't, because people don't consider WTT that well. But I am nearly at the end of my career. It doesn't matter if I get banned. The concept is good—especially in America, where they really support the team for the city."

On the Women's Tennis Association—"The players should run their own profession. At the moment it might be difficult because we are so new and don't have the authority and money and contracts to do it. But we are making some great improvements. The satellite tour has been going very well. That's a good idea. I think sometimes women are not professional enough. They don't realize that if you are not good enough, you should go to practice and come back when you are ready. Tennis has been an easy way of life. In a way we should cut that down and make it a profession and have some kind of criteria. If you get through, it mean you have some kind of potential. The women at the top deserve the best. And you really have to prove yourself. The semi-finalists in every satellite tournament get a chance for two weeks on the major tour and if they do well they can stay a lot longer. And the bottom part of the championship will go down if they don't do well. That was good thinking."

On separate circuits for men and women—"At the beginning I was a lot against it. But if we always stay with the men we won't get the popularity we get by ourselves and will always be in the shadow of the men. Now the public say, 'We enjoy the women better, because they play the way we play.' The public identify much better with a woman than with a man and I think that's why we have been so successful. They learn a lot more, watching the women play. Maybe for the big tournament we should be together. But for most of the tour we should be by ourselves, to get more publicity and recognition."

On the indoor circuit—"Playing indoors is a lot easier (it's harder work to play outside). The conditions are better. The carpet is very good for the girls. Not too fast and not too slow. And you can bring the public. If you want to make a popular sport, it have to be indoors. Because you can never depend on the weather. People won't come (outside) if it's a dodgy day. We have to be indoors. And a lot of people will have a better chance to go to a sport arena than to a country club."

On prize money—"Four years ago we thought $10,000 was fantastic. Now that's the first prize in one tournament. And that's in four years."

On colored clothing—"The colors are really nice, especially when you will be on TV. When I look, on a Sunday, I know about tennis and who's playing. But people who don't they can have someone to look for—blue shirt, or red shirt...Outside, it's good. Pale colors are nice. Like to go to a skating rink or something, if women wear white it will not look so good. At Wimbledon I find something dull, and I realize it is because everybody is wearing white. A shoe producer should make a nicer shoe. At the moment they have blue. But they should have red or pink or something, to match the dress."

On the sudden death tiebreak—"At the beginning I was not too happy. But now we know what's important in a tiebreaker. I think the public enjoy a nine-point tiebreaker, and we get used to it like anything else. We have been playing the 12-point, but it can be very long sometimes, and that kills something for the public."

The nature of all these opinions tells us something else about Frankie Durr. She is not by instinct a revolutionary. But she examines the evidence for and against change with open-minded good sense, weighing the value of what may be gained against the value of what may be lost.

One last question. The future? "The money is too good to retire when you are not already going down the drain. I am going to be a touring pro. Team tennis for two years. Then I might be resident pro at North Palm Beach. Jack Nicklaus' company is building a tennis club there." Oran...Paris... New York...Denver...maybe North Palm Beach...there can be no knowing where Frankie Durr will turn up next with her mind-boggling backhand and racket-toting dog. But one thing is for sure, her arrival, anywhere, will always be good news. Because she brings a little of Christmas Day with her. ●

"What's Wrong With My Backhand?"

by PANCHO SEGURA

ALMOST ALL players are stronger on one side than the other. In general, beginners and intermediates are better on the forehand and advanced or tournament players feel more confident on the backhand. There are many exceptions (I was always a "forehand" player and so were Jack Kramer, Jaroslav Drobny and Beverly Baker Fleitz), but it is rare to see a relatively inexperienced player with a better, more consistent backhand than forehand. The reasons: timing and strokes.

Timing

There is a fraction of a second difference in the timing of a forehand and a backhand. Therefore when you are having a good backhand day, the forehand often goes "off." Once you realize the two strokes are timed differently, half the battle is over. It's like knowing a spin shot will bounce differently: the awareness gives you a new perception and helps you recognize the strange bounces of spins. The different timing of forehands and backhands will be more pronounced if you hit your forehand well in front of you and your backhand by your side. Ideally, particularly for those with an Eastern grip, the ball should be hit as far in front of you as possible: you attack the ball instead of having the ball attack you.

The Grip

The Eastern backhand grip is achieved by turning the hand slightly to the left as shown in Illustration 1. If you've been cheating by using a forehand grip on the backhand, you can get rid of the old habit quickly by practicing the backhand grip while you are sitting around the house or walking onto the court or waiting for the return in a rally. Note that the fingers are slightly separated and the thumb extends naturally around the handle. There are some players who keep the fingers together (a "hammer" grip) or who stick the thumb straight up the handle, but more good players today hold the racket as in Illustration 1.

Start Low, Finish High

The basic backhand is the topspin drive. Once you have learned it, you can easily add a backhand slice (also called "underspin") to your repertoire. It is much more difficult to start with a slice and then learn to drive. Topspin is imparted to the ball by starting low on the backswing and finishing high on the follow-through. If you started at waist-level and finished at waist-level, with the racket face perpendicular to the ground, there would be no spin on the ball at all (a "flat" shot). The ball would sail in an absolutely straight line until it hit the net or until gravity brought it down.

Although you start low, the racket head does not drop, viz., point downward. On a low ball you bend your

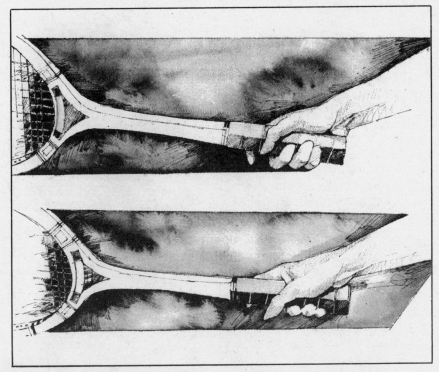

TOP. For the Eastern forehand grip, hold the racket head perpendicular to the ground and "shake hands" with the handle. Use an ordinary handshake.

BELOW. For the backhand grip, let the "V" between thumb and forefinger move to the left so that it is practically on top of the handle.

knees; you *don't* drop the racket head. The racket head is perpendicular to the ground. If the racket face were open (tilted slightly skyward), you would be undercutting the ball. Later, after you perfect the drive, you can always learn to underspin.

Shoulder, Elbow and Wrist

The ball is hit with a combination of shoulder and arm. If you look at Illustration 2 you will see the shoulder is turned in, the arm is held close to the body and the elbow is bent comfortably. The racket is at waist-level and is almost a straight extension of the elbow-hand line. If the elbow-hand-racket line pointed upward at the start, then you would either have to make a semi-circular swing to get the racket at waist-level or you would undercut the ball too heavily. Note: As a player becomes totally confident in his backhand drive, he often adds a semi-circular backswing for rhythm or because other good players do so.

If you start from this backswing position (Position 1) and end with a follow-through position (Position 4), *nothing can go wrong with the actual hit.* It means 1) the shoulder has acted as a pivot for the arm, 2) the wrist has not flicked or snapped forward and 3) the elbow has not led the racket head. How to go from Position 2 to Position 4 is the easiest of all: think that you are throwing your arm and racket to the top of the opponent's fence. Throw it freely and naturally. If you go wrong, you will see it at once in the follow-through, viz., you will have lost your balance (you have followed through too far) or your elbow will be jutting out (you forgot to throw your arm and racket freely). Remember that the shoulder is the pivot and that you are actually throwing arm and racket from Position 2 to Position 4.

The wrist is practically motionless. The fingers grip the racket tightly and the wrist is firm, while the arm and shoulder do the work. Don't let the wrist bend backward and then slap forward for then you must time the hit to a fraction of a second. Instead the firm wrist enables you to compensate for a badly-timed shot since you have substantial margin for error.

Footwork

The side is to the net when you hit a backhand but your right foot steps

1 Take the racket back with both hands. The shoulder turns in, the feet are apart and the knees are slightly flexed.

2 The right foot has stepped forward and now, with the shoulder acting as pivot, the elbow-wrist-racket come through as one.

Illustrations, Hodges Soileau

3 The ball is taken well in front of the body. The most common backhand error is taking the ball late (behind the body).

4 The natural follow-through, without losing balance, brings the racket head upward, pointing to the opponent's fence.

WRONG. The feet are not spread, the knees not flexed and the bend is from the waist.

WRONG. The elbow led and the racket head trailed, the ball was caught late, the weight is on the rear foot and the head is tilted to the side.

forward (toward the net) rather than sideways (toward the alley) just before the hit. The timing is: 1) shoulder turns in to bring elbow-arm-racket back, 2) right foot steps forward and, at the same time, 3) the shoulder begins its forward swing to "throw" arm-racket at the opponent's fence. In other words, the weight has moved forward (with the right foot) with the shoulder-arm-racket following immediately thereafter.

Balance

In order to achieve good balance, the feet should be comfortably apart and the knees flexed so that the center of gravity is low (close to the ground) and you can push off or spring forward and/or sideways for a backhand. If you stood stiff-legged, with the feet close together, there would be no way to get power ("weight") into the shot and you would be totally dependent on shoulder and arm. By stepping forward, your whole weight leans into the shot to give natural power to a smooth and easy stroke. Be bouncy on your toes, with knees bent, and push off with your right foot to move toward your left.

Hit In Front

Often a hard shot or a deep volley will catch you before you can step forward to meet the ball. Then you play it defensively, catching it late, with your weight moving backwards, because the ball has attacked you instead of you attacking the ball. If you are playing a hard-hitter or deep-volleyer, your safest ploy is to play several feet behind the baseline so that you can step forward and meet the ball six inches to one foot in front of you. If you catch the ball at your side, you practically have to twist your whole body around to hit the ball crosscourt (unless you slice the ball). If you catch the ball slightly behind you, you need a Laver wrist to return it aggressively. When you take the ball in front, it is easy to guide it crosscourt.

The Most Common Errors

• **The Courtly Bow.** Instead of bending from the knees, you bend from the waist. The power goes downward—with your head.
• **The Erring Elbow.** The elbow juts upward, distorting the stroke, which now resembles a lefthander's writing posture.

• **The Cocked Head.** The head is tilted sideways so that only one eye can focus on the ball.
• **The Tin Soldier.** The stiff knees make it impossible to stretch forward or sideways without losing balance.
• **The Reverse Twist.** Instead of stepping forward, the body leans backward. This means 150 pounds or so of body weight is moving away from the ball. Often in the process of tilting backwards, the right leg kicks up so that all coordination between body and racket is gone.

Some hints to prevent the common errors: keep your legs springy; hold your elbow in, guiding it back as the stroke starts with two hands; watch the ball with both eyes and hold your head naturally; stay on your toes with feet comfortably spread apart; and if a deep ball comes to you, spring back quickly so that you can step forward before the hit.

When your timing leaves you, or, particularly, when you cannot control the jutting elbow or hit freely with a good follow-through, the easiest remedy is the two-handed shot. By hitting with two hands you will automatically turn in your shoulder on the backswing, the chances of the elbow leading become much lower and the follow-through automatically brings your weight into the ball.

If you still have problems in hitting a backhand without awkwardness, there are three possible reasons: 1) you are letting the ball drop before you hit it. Try to take it on the top of the bounce by moving toward it. 2) You are playing against someone who is hitting too hard for you. Try your luck against a softer hitter and see if your timing gets better. 3) The spins of your opponent are confusing you, causing you to be too late or too early or to take the ball too close or too far away from you. Analyze what the opponent's ball is doing after it bounces. Is it skidding sideways or jumping towards you or bouncing lower or higher than you expected?

If you switch to a faster surface or play against tougher competition, take your backswing earlier or even shorten the backswing slightly. When you are up against tougher competition, don't try to hit the ball harder but try instead to get ready earlier and to use your opponent's speed by taking the ball well in front of you.

Keep a stiff upper wrist! ●

THE ASHE FOREHAND

by JULIUS HELDMAN

Photographs, Arthur Cole

ARTHUR ASHE is hitting on an English "hard court" (usually a pebbly clay). He has a graceful, distinctive style which is often imitated because of his popularity but which has some features that teaching pros would not wish others to emulate. It is a fluent, powerful stroke but hit too "loosely" to suit some purists.

As Arthur moves toward the ball (large in the foreground) in Frame 1, he has already started to draw his racket back. At this stage others might still have their left hand on the throat of the racket or would have just removed it, but Arthur does not cradle his racket much, if at all, between shots. If the ball crosses to his forehand, as here, he moves toward it with his right arm at his side and the wrist cocked so that the racket head is high. His grip is one-eighth turn from the backhand and is close to the "Continental."

As the ball approaches, Arthur moves into position, taking his racket head back by moving his right shoulder back (compare Frames 3, 4 and 5). His steps are carefully spaced so that as he and the ball reach each other, his left leg has crossed over in front of his right and is moving forward—the pushoff is from his right leg—to produce the weight or power on his shot. Note that at all times on the backswing and early forward swing, the racket head is cocked up sharply and is at least as high as Arthur's head. Arthur's backswing is always high.

The forward swing starts in Frame 11. The front foot is just coming down, transferring the weight forward. The racket head is just starting to come down, coincident with the forward swing. It will ultimately have to come down to ball level, of course, which will be just above the knee. Arthur is taking this shot as part of a baseline rally, choosing not to move in on the attack and therefore letting the ball drop well past the top of the bounce.

Another point to watch is Arthur's left arm. At the beginning it was rather tight against his body, instead of cradling the racket. As he winds up, the left arm naturally swings over to Arthur's right for balance; as the forward swing starts, the arm again naturally swings back to counterbalance the forward swing.

In Frame 14 Arthur is close to hitting the ball. His stance and knee-bend are excellent. Note that his back is straight. Many pros recommend bending from the knees only, not the back, if possible. Now the racket head is laid back by wrist movement; it is no longer high. The right arm is straight, although many power hitters prefer to hit with a slight elbow bend. The shoulder and hips have started to pivot.

Frame 15, the hit, illustrates clearly the relative positions of all parts of the body and racket: arms, shoulder, legs, knees. The wrist is in a natural, firm position on this stroke; on other forehands, Arthur often uses much more wrist roll than in this shot. Arthur is hitting with topspin; in this case he will apply the overspin by pulling the racket up on the follow-through rather than by turning his wrist over.

The shot is taken close to the right sideline. From the angle of the racket at and just after the hit, it is apparent that the stroke will be crosscourt. The remainder of the frames illustrate Arthur's follow-through, with his racket head ending up very high. The high-low-high of his forehand is certainly very characteristic. In the last frame, Ashe is just starting to pull his racket back. It looks as though he is watching his stroke without preparing for the next one. That's fine if it's a winner or an error, but otherwise he should be moving back to center.

WE REMEMBER YOU, BILLIE JEAN

by BUD COLLINS

"I REMEMBER YOU..." as the song goes.

"You're the girl who made Bobby turn to glue..." as a new refrain should go.

But that's the fate of aged thoroughbreds and war horses, isn't it? Glue. So Riggs shouldn't feel too bad, considering that no spavined nag has ever been rendered in such extravagantly romantic circumstances. And considering Bobby's finding that there's life after Death-at-the-Astrodome. And also considering that Robert Larimore Riggs, in deep-freezing Mighty Mama Court and then goading Billie Jean Moffitt King into the rectangular ring for The Big Gig, really brought tennis out of the closet.

Sure, I remember you, Billie Jean, but on Sept. 20, 1973, the rest of the world said "Howdy-Do, B.J." You were discovered by the masses and so was your game.

"Hey, didja see that broad Billie Jean whack the ball last night?" people all over the world were asking each other the next day.

"Yeah. I never knew what the score was or how the hell you keep it, but she win it big over the old guy, din't she?"

It was as though a new game and a new person had descended on Earth from Betelgeuse or somewhere. Tennis and Billie Jean aren't new to you and me, of course. You've been reading and I've been writing about her for years, more than a decade. If you aren't a tennis degenerate, then why are you reading this book? The tennis boom in America has been on for several years, but the Billie Jean and Bobby caper turned it totally public. Americans who didn't know John Newcombe from fig newtons had an opinion on Billie Jean and her conquest. "We got to the non-tennis populace," says Billie Jean, "and that was a first. There's no telling the long-range impact. That's what I'm proud of...more than the win itself...what the match did for tennis."

Suddenly a tennis player had nearly as much celebrity as the man who has been the world's No. 1 athlete for several years: Muhammad Ali. I suspect it was much the same in the other countries where the telecast was received, but I can speak only for the United States. "In 1939, when I was Wimbledon champion, and in 1946, when I was the best player in the world, the pro champ after beating (Don) Budge," Riggs mused, "I didn't get much attention. Tennis people knew me, but how many people followed tennis?

"Today," he was beaming as he shoveled in 24 vitamin pills, about one-fifteenth of his daily intake while in "training." "Today everybody knows me." To know him is to love him, according to Bobby's Bosom Buddies, his groupies who constitute the greatest breastworks since the fortification of Bunker Hill.

Bobby, the hustling gambler who made $108,000 betting on himself during his triple crown spree at Wimbledon in 1939, must have been pleased that bookmakers in America were handling tennis for the first time when he and Billie Jean went to the Sportface mat. That, perhaps more than anything, tells you that everybody in the U.S. was turned on. "Little kids in school were betting dimes and quarters," Billie enthuses.

In putting Billie Jean in the same sentence with Muhammad Ali, it's interesting to note that both are nonconformists with a cause—cherished either for or despite their rebelliousness. Also interesting that Odessa Clay and Betty Moffitt sure didn't raise their darlings to raise all that fuss; Cassius-Muhammad about the treatment of

Theiner Hoover

Fourteen-year-old Billie Jean wears a tennis dress at the Los Angeles Tennis Club. Three years earlier she was not allowed in a group photo there because she wore shorts.

Opposite Page:
Bill and Betty Moffitt flank their daughter, the champ. In 1955 Billie Jean's parents told her she could swim, golf or play tennis—but no more football.

the Essex County Club at Manchester, Mass., one of those beautiful and doomed tournaments (The Ladies Invitation) permeated by sea air; old money; private school inflections; summering ambassadors and magnates; sloppy-rich costumes of khaki, Madras, straw and smudgysneakers; tea-and-cake in the players' lounge; gin-and-tonics in the venerable paneled bar; sailboat rides; lobster cookouts; private boxes beneath majestic trees and flowing awnings; greenbacks beneath the antique table for a favored few.

Her first trip East for the late, great-in-the-rankings grass court circuit. "I never thought I'd still be playing when tennis got away from that stuff, but the game had to get ahead. Oh, I had a good time. I was uncomfortable with all those rich people, but they were nice to us."

"Let them eat cake," was one of the cries—and B.J. ate. Cake, ice cream, candy bars. She was sweet, but not exactly svelte, 16. "I gained 25 pounds that summer. Nobody knew me when I got home to Long Beach." Imagine how she'd have looked if she hadn't been hell-bent-for-perfection on the tennis court every day? Miss Gorilla Monsoon?

An ice cream junkie she was then, and for several years. "Psst, hey little girl, want a fix—pure, mainline, rich, creamy vanilla? Better than Acapulco Gold."

Nevertheless, I recognized a diamond in the fluff: a champion-to-be. Was I a genius? Was James Wilson Marshall on Jan. 24, 1848, when he found gold at Sutter's Mill, precipitating the California Gold Rush? Mercy, no. He just came across it, like I found Billie Jean merely by keeping my eyes open.

Anybody would have recognized, if anybody had been there. A few people lazed in the early afternoon sun as Billie Jean took on the No. 1 American of that year, Darlene Hard. Not many of the general public were inclined to drive 30 miles north of Boston and then try to find a secluded, selective club just to watch some women play tennis. That was Billie Jean's knock against tournament tennis-as-it-was: "It's the property of a handful of members of stuffy clubs, and tennis is too good a game to be confined that way."

I was there because it was my job as a reporter. Not that it was an onerous assignment. Essex was one of those vanished joys, a casualty of big-money tennis, a week on the seashore amidst the pines to get well from covering baseball at Fenway Park and basketball and hockey in ghastly Boston Garden.

So there was Billie Jean, all zippety-zazz, getting her jollies with volleys that flew beyond Darlene Hard's reach. After losing the first set, Billie Jean won the second in a matter of minutes—and six games. She'd blitzed Darlene in an incredible display of hitting and *lese majeste*. True, Darlene recovered in the third set to chastize Chub ("as I was called by the kids at home"). But right there, you would have said to yourself, is the next headbreaker and head woman. I know you would have.

Not quite a year later, her first title—Wimbledon Doubles with Karen Hantze. I was lucky to be there, sent to London to cover the Paul Pender-Terry Downes middleweight championship fight, my plane arriving a few hours before Billie Jean and Karen knocked over Aussies Jan Lehane and Margaret Smith. A milestone in that it was the first Centre Court final of 16 for Margaret and 22 for Billie Jean—and the introductory confrontation of the women who would be 1-2 right up to and including the pre-

Ed Fernberger

Billie Jean and Larry King were in college when they married in 1965. Now she credits him with much of her success in tennis and many of her women's lib feelings.

blacks; Billie Jean about the treatment of women. "There's a lot of similarities in the ways blacks and women are put down," says Billie Jean, "and sports is one of the places we can both make it—on performance."

I said to her, "You're as dynamite as any athlete in America right now. You can't touch Muhammad Ali elsewhere in the world, but in America...wow."

"When you're up," replied B.J., the only tennis player with a traveling secretary-buffer (Marilyn Barnett), "it's nice. Nice for me...nice for the women's game...nice for the game of tennis...but you don't stay up long. I've been down, too."

Down how far? Down like everybody's been down, where the only people who noticed you were your parents.

I noticed when you were down there. I remember you when you were Moffitt the fubsy moppet. August of 1960, at sent. The unseeded teen-agers, Billie Jean and Karen, made a jubilant run through No. 1 Sandra Reynolds-Renee Schuurman, Nos. 4 Sally Moore-Lesley Turner, and finally Nos. 3 Smith-Lehane. Sixteen Wimbledon championships have been added to that one by B.J., landing her two behind the all-time winner Elizabeth (Bunny) Ryan, all of whose prizes were in doubles and mixed.

Impulsively, since I hardly knew either one, I asked Billie Jean and Karen if I could put them on my expense account for a celebrational dinner. They accepted, and we had a fine, giggly time. I thought champagne was in order, but they said no-thanks, they didn't drink. They didn't need bubbly to get giggly.

I hope I can play Wimbledon for a few more years. That's special," says Billie Jean. "You know I don't pay any attention to records, but since you brought it up, I would like to win three more titles and take the record away from Miss Ryan. That would be something.

"But I'll be less and less into tournaments now that I'm the player-coach of Philadelphia in World Team Tennis. I'll play some of the Slims tour, because I feel a strong debt of gratitude for what Virginia Slims has done for women's tennis. But I'm going to concentrate on WTT. I know team tennis is going to work, it's a way of getting to a broad public with the team concept in modern arenas. I'm kind of burnt out on the tournament system. Maybe I've been doing the same kind of thing for too long." Billie Jean was making these remarks during the Phoenix stopover the first week in October. Her 30th birthday was little more than a month away.

"I'm feeling generally burnt out, emotionally and physically. It was a struggle getting the WTA (Women's Tennis Association, the new players union) off the ground, but I think that's in good hands now with our executive director, Marty Carmichael. The Riggs thing was a lot of pressure, and I've been injured a lot this year. All in all I'm looking forward to a new kind of challenge at Philadelphia—making our team work.

"I'm anxious for us to sign Fred Stolle because he's such a good doubles player, and the mixed doubles is going to be important to every result. We're going to have to trade for another strong woman and maybe another strong man if we can't sign Cliff Drysdale and Brian Fairlie. I'm pretty sure we'll get Brian. But our top women draft picks, after me, are Laura Rossouw, Tory Fretz and Laurie Fleming. Laurie is promising, but young. I think we need more strength there."

So here is Billie Jean—the champion, the feminist, the labor leader—in a new role: Coach King. She sounds like a baseball manager or football coach discussing prospects. Like Bill Russell, when he coached the Boston Celtics to a professional basketball title because he had Bill Russell as center, she can't be too unhappy about having Billie Jean King on her roster. She alone would make Philly a favorite.

"She might as well do it—she's done everything else," says Jerry Cromwell. Jerry remembers Billie Jean well because he was Bobby Riggs' predecessor: a male impaled on her racket. "I guess I was 11," is Cromwell's recollection of their duel in a sunny Long Beach park. "It was the final of a kids' tournament that boys and girls could play in together. Yeah, she beat me. She's about seven months older than I. We were good friends, but I still didn't feel very good about that beating. After that I got stronger, and she never could

Billie Jean and Karen Hantze won the Wimbledon doubles in 1961, defeating Margaret Smith and Jan Lehane in the finals. King now has won a total of 17 Wimbledon titles including five singles.

do it again. We practiced a lot together. In high school I walked her to school at Long Beach Poly. It was four miles. She walked it purposely, one of the things she did to combat her weight problem then. And she wanted company. So I went along."

"I'd forgotten that," Billie Jean smiled, on hearing of Cromwell's reminiscence. "Yeah, I did beat him. I should've remembered that for the Riggs propaganda—that I'd beaten a nationally ranked man."

Not precisely. Cromwell, a handsome economics consultant in Cambridge, Mass., did rise as high as No. 17 in 1965 when he was playing seriously, before he decided it was more important for him to pursue a PhD than a fuzzy ball. But that was years after his ego-pricking experience with Billie Jean.

That was shortly after she'd asked her old man—Bill Moffitt, the Long Beach fireman—"What's tennis?" Millions of Americans were asking the same question before Sept. 20, 1973 when Billie Jean showed them—and Bobby.

"It came up at the dinner table in 1955, this discussion of tennis," says Billie Jean, whose career as the fastest, hardest-nosed halfback on West 36th Street had ended tearfully when she was cut from the team by her mother. Betty Moffitt had enough of B.J. scrimmaging with the boys on the pavement, and yanked her into the house. She wasn't rearing a daughter for the Rams. "Mom kept me inside when the game started, and I was pretty bitter," Billie Jean recalls. The boys B.J. was running through and over probably applauded Mrs. Moffitt as Mother of the Year.

"I was a darned good softball player. Every year I played shortstop on my dad's team at the firemen's picnic, and I was on a women's team. Third base and shortstop. I hit good, and I liked the game, but the girls were older and a little tough. My folks didn't think that was much better than football."

Bill Moffitt, a singular sporting sire who fathered both a major league pitcher (25-year-old son Randy Moffitt of the San Francisco Giants) and a world tennis champ, thinks, "Billie Jean has such great hand-eye coordination and gets down so well on those volleys because of all the time she spent fielding ground balls before she got into tennis. But, as much as I love baseball, and competition, we were looking for something a little more feminine for Billie Jean. She was competitive, that was obvious, and I was very pleased about that, but softball..."

"So," resumes Billie Jean, "we were talking about things for me to play because it was agreed I wasn't going to stay in softball. My dad said there were three good outlets for girls—golf, swimming and tennis.

"Golf just didn't appeal to me. Too slow with all that walking and not much action. I couldn't see spending all day in a swimming pool, which is what you did if you were going to compete.

"'What's tennis?' I said. I had an idea, of course, but I really didn't know. I said I'd try it, but first I had to earn the racket. That's the way my folks are, and I sure owe them a lot. I did baby-sitting, ran errands, mowed the lawn, and put the money in a jar. I think my folks sneaked a little money in there for me, too. When I had $6 I bought a weird maroon racket with a grip that felt velvet-ish. I went down to the park and tried it out, and after the first day I was excited. I told my mother I was going to be the best player in the world, although at the time I wouldn't have known

what you were talking about if you'd mentioned Wimbledon or Forest Hills.

"Long Beach had a tennis instructor named Clyde Walker, and he started me and Jerry Cromwell out. He'd be at a different neighborhood park every day, and you'd get instruction when he came to your park. Jerry and I followed him around so we were at a different park with Clyde every day. Clyde died of cancer in 1961, just after Karen and I won the Wimbledon doubles. His wife says he made himself stay alive long enough to see how I did in my first Wimbledon. That really got to me. I'm glad I could win for him."

Susan Williams and Ann Savitowski—wherever you are, Billie Jean remembers you. "First match I ever played was against Susan Williams. She beat me, 6-0, 6-0. That didn't discourage me." Obviously.

"The first three-set match I played was against Ann Savitowski. We were one set apiece, and I thought it was all over, a tie. I didn't even know about best-of-three sets. She told me we had to keep playing, so we did. For a long time. Ann won the third, 11-9, and I was a dead little girl that night."

That was unusual. Her dad says, "Billie Jean had so much energy that when she came home from the courts, she'd pound a ball against a redwood fence in the back yard. She drove the neighbors crazy with the noise." When the fence collapsed before its time, under her assault, Bill Moffitt put up a cinderblock wall.

"Once I got into tennis my folks were great, even though they liked other sports better," says B.J. "They wore out a couple of cars driving me to tournaments. But they had a hard time watching. They'd get too nervous. My mother couldn't watch at all then. She'd wander off and knit, and then send Randy to the court to find out the score every so often. My dad would watch for a while and then get too excited. He's very competitive."

Jerry Cromwell says, "I used to think Mr. Moffitt was going to swallow his cigar during Billie Jean's matches. He'd really grind away on it. And she'd be talking to herself, urging herself on. They're quite a pair. But I always noticed in the toughest matches, the ones that meant the most, she'd be very quiet and within herself, concentrating unbelievably like she did against Chris Evert at Wimbledon and against Riggs."

How then did the All-American Tomboy from Richard Nixon Country become today's right-on radical, member of the Movement, co-defender, with Gloria Steinem, Germain Greer et al, of the faith in women's equality?

"The radicalization of Billie Jean King?" she probes with a smile. "That's the fashionable way of saying it, isn't it? Well, I don't think I've been radicalized. I've just become aware. That's the term I prefer: awareness.

"A couple of men had a lot to do with it, pro and con: Larry (B.J.'s infrequent roommate, Larry King) and Perry Jones (the absolute monarch of Southern California tennis, now dead).

"I first encountered Mr. Jones when I was 11, playing my first Southern California sectional tournament at the L.A. Tennis Club. (This was 1955, the year the ranking of Billie Jean began: No. 9 in the Southern California 13s.) They were taking group pictures, and Mr. Jones pointed to me, 'Not you. You can't be in a picture because you're not dressed properly.'

"I was wearing my usual outfit, white shorts and a white

"When you're up it's nice. Nice for me...Nice for the women's game...Nice for the game of tennis...But you don't stay up long..."

T-shirt, but I found out that Mr. Jones expected you to wear a tennis dress. That turned me inside out. The experience didn't make me bitter, but I found out that these people were more concerned with what you wore than how you played. And that men were making the decisions about what women should do—"

Just as they still do at Wimbledon, telling Rosie Casals she couldn't wear her little purple dress in 1972?

"Right. Right-on," says Billie Jean. "You have to conform to what men expect of you, but that's what we're trying to change. And we will change it. The 11-year-olds playing tennis are a lot more aware than I was at that age, probably more aware than I was five years ago. If the men who run tennis think I'm radical, wait till they have to deal with the kids coming up. But radical is the wrong word. Women just want a fair shake, like we finally got at Forest Hills with the equal prize money.

"But there's still a long way to go."

There certainly is, when you consider that the International Lawn Tennis Federation, an all-male bastion, continues to assert significant control over female tennis. And when you realize how shameful the ILTF conduct has been toward women: a virtual rape of the unrepresented. Financially, the ILTF's four-year-old Grand Prix scheme is loaded shockingly in the men's favor, and the finale—the Masters playoff —once again is for men only. Even more unconscionable is the fact that the Virginia Slims women—though peace was made some months ago—are still being punished. Although they may enter Grand Prix events, the Slimsies are excluded from the standings and do not share in the bonus pool payoffs based on performance. This seems illicit to me, and I'm astonished that Commer-cial Union Assurance, the Grand Prix sponsor and generally a good influence in the game, goes along with this bit of ILTF tyranny.

"Larry told me it would be this way," says Billie Jean of the man she married in 1965, while they were students at Los Angeles State. "He warned me that men would fight us all along the line, particularly where money is concerned. He's had a lot to do with my lib feelings. In some areas he's more women's lib than I am. I never imagined I'd be playing tennis at 30. I assumed I'd be settled down with a family, living the so-called normal life. I know my mother and father wonder about this. They'd like some grandchildren. These are the child-bearing years, but Larry and I have made the decision not to have a family yet. It's not an easy decision, but Larry has always stressed I should make the most of my talent, which happens to be as a tennis player. If it weren't for Larry, I wouldn't have become a world champion."

This may sound strange to those who view the Kings' marriage as odd, disjointed and on the brink of dissolution. "I hear the rumors, too, about me and Larry. It's our business. We're not together much, but we know where our heads are. We have our own closeness. What is supposedly normal for some people may not be normal for us. What is 'normal' any more? We got married too soon. In those days when you went together for a while, you were expected to make a move of some kind. We were touched by Puritanism like almost everybody else. Sometimes Larry kids me, 'Let's get divorced and live together.' We're not defending or advocating our style. But we know each other, and know what we have and how much we mean to each other. We enjoy each other when we can..."

It is theirs to work out. The only part of Billie Jean that belongs to us is her performance on the tennis court, and what a treasured belonging that is. For most, the memory of Billie Jean will be as the Joan of Arc of the Astrodome, swinging a gut-strung mace in Bobby's unbelieving face. Throughout her life people will tell her, "I saw you at your greatest, against Riggs."

However, I like my lionesses outside of the circus. While I wouldn't have missed whatever-it-was that happened in Houston—and I appreciate the tremendous pressures built up artificially by Riggs' "Battle of the Sexes" battlecry—I'll take struggles over slaughters. I'd rather remember Billie Jean as she was in beating Ann Jones in a Wimbledon semi of 1968 (4-6, 7-5, 6-2, after Jones led 4-2 and 3-5 in the second and served for victory at 5-4). Or beating Margaret Court in the Forest Hills semi of 1972 (6-4, 6-4). Or stopping Chris Evert in the Forest Hills semi of 1971 (6-3, 6-2). Or beating Chris Truman in 1963 on sweltering clay at the Cleveland Skating Club in the longest Wightman Cup match (19-17, 6-4). Or overcoming Rosie Casals in a magnificent *pas de deux* for the 1968 National Indoor title (6-3, 9-7), when Hazel Wightman remarked, "I don't think I've ever seen two women play better tennis." Or losing that glorious 1970 Wimbledon final to Margaret Court (14-12, 11-9, both women hurt yet striking out at each other with unbelievable verve and thunder).

I have many other memories of Billie Jean, and aspirations for her. When I told her, after she won the National Clay in 1971, that she had become the only woman to rule the four U.S. surfaces (grass, clay, cement, indoor), B.J. said, "God, isn't that just like a sportswriter to come up with something like that? Nice to know about it, but I'll probably forget it. I can't keep track, and I don't try."

I'd like to see her make an unprecedented American Slam—winning on all four surfaces in one year—as well as the Grand Slam. I'd also be pleased if she and Rosie Casals were the first women to make a doubles Grand Slam, emulating the 1951 accomplishment of Frank Sedgman and Ken McGregor. It's unlikely she'll even try. But it is within Billie Jean's reach to occupy the No. 1 American ranking longer than anyone else.

I'd like to see her do all these things simply because I feel they would be fitting achievements for a person I consider the foremost achiever in the history of the game, quite possibly the most important player to take up a tennis cudgel. I'm not arguing that she's a better player than were Suzanne Lenglen, Maureen Connolly, Alice Marble, Pauline Betz, Margaret Court—or who did you have in mind? I don't know, although I suspect her best would overcome their best. (We know it for a fact in regard to Court.)

What I'm saying is that no man or woman in tennis has made such an extraordinary triple thrust as Billie Jean in advancing herself, women and the game as a whole. Bill Tilden was a personality of the greatest magnitude, but later revelations of his homosexuality may have diminished the game severely in the public eye. I happen to think so. Regardless of the controversy often enveloping her ("How can you glorify this woman who has had an abortion?" is the sort of letter I frequently receive concerning Ms. King. But these are different times, and perhaps now Tilden's aberration would receive sympathy today)—and possibly because of it—Billie Jean carries tennis upward and onward.

Her evident zest in her work, her skill, her candor and her nerve win us over: the fireman's daughter shows us that tennis can be Everyman's game—or should I say Everyperson's, so as not to offend the *Ms. Magazine* crowd? Only Billie Jean could have beaten Riggs in that cauldron of pressure (even though I believe several of the women are capable of it). And only Billie Jean could have made female pro tennis take off when the Slimsies set out in 1970. She had the game, the presence and the mouth to stand up to the Establishment. True, numerous of the male pros resent her, curse the fact that she earns more than they, feel she should shut up and get lost in a nursery. Yet the most enlightened of them must realize that every move she makes puts more money in their pockets because tennis gets bigger for everybody as her stature increases.

By this time, you may have divined that I'm bullish on Billie Jean Moffitt King, and always have been. Right. Not that I'm unaware of her flaws and inconsistencies. All professionals are guilty of unprofessionalism and so is she. Jack Kramer apparently will never forgive her for walking out (along with Casals) on his Pacific Southwest final of 1971. That is getting to be a bit ancient history, and you'd think Jack would genuflect toward Long Beach every time he considers that Billie Jean is around calling attention to and enriching his business. That default remains a blot.

Inconsistency? Heavens, she was really off base in a pre-Riggs press conference, though few picked her up on it, the press being the general sporting press since a tennis press as such is not yet upon us in America. (It's building though, and will eventually be as formidable as England's.)

She went on about how sorry she was to miss the St. Louis Virginia Slims event, but that (following her Forest Hills illness/collapse/surrender against Julie Heldman) her doctor had ordered a rest. So she went to Hilton Head. And what did she do there besides rest? Nobody asked, but a few of us knew: she played another tournament, an unpublicized taped event for ABC, to be shown nationally during the winter.

Where, she asked, had the press gotten all these stories about her bad health prior to Riggs? Hypoglycemia etc. She had only to look across the room to Larry King, who had been giving those medical reports by phone from Hilton Head.

So, goddesses are flawed. We know that. She talks too much. What public figure doesn't? God knows the ILTF-USLTA males still trying to run the game are worthy of censure. Still, she too frequently knocks without knowing all the facts, and therefore sometimes unfairly. She is human, and I guess this humanity is what we may remember longer than the backhand volleys. We—not Robert Larimore Riggs.

"She's quite a girl...uh...woman. Great, great," says Riggs. Yes, Bobby can be gracious. "She did it when she had to. She made the shots. I wasn't ready for a Billie Jean like that."

Neither was Perry Jones. Nor the USLTA and the ILTF. Nor the country club types who owned the game, and such as Maria Bueno and Margaret Court who couldn't believe this pudgy kid in the glittery spectacles would shove them from the top. Nor 11-year-old Jerry Cromwell for that matter.

They could also gang up in a chorus to sing:

"We *remember you...and we're still trying to forget.*" ●

HOW TO PRACTICE

by DENNIS Van der MEER

THIS WINTER I paid a visit to several indoor tennis clubs. The amount of tennis activity was prolific but, sad to say, the level of tennis was horrific. I soon discovered why. Since the cost of indoor tennis is relatively high, many players sign up for just an hour a week. Since they have only 60 minutes every 7 days, they refuse to devote any precious minutes to a proper warm-up and stroke practice.

The once-a-week player starts off with a quick slap at a few balls, has two practice serves and begins his match. He plays until his time is up. Quite possibly he may not hit a single overhead during the match. Comes the next week, and at a tense 4-5, 30-40 score he finds himself in a situation where he has to play an overhead. His first overhead in two weeks! There is no way he is going to make the shot. Combine this with the other occasional strokes which also are never practiced and you have the reason for the unpredictable kind of tennis played.

The solution is to go through every stroke at least once a week. Here is a routine used by Tennis America pupils.

1. Practice one minute of forehand volleys. Your practice partner plays easy groundstrokes so that you can think about getting ready, getting set, holding the racket out in front, bending for the low shots, recovering and, above all, keeping the ball in play.

2. After one minute switch roles and give your partner some forehand volleys.

3. One minute backhand volleys.

4. Switch roles.

5. Practice one minute predictable alternate volleys. The groundstroker now has to direct the ball well.

6. Switch roles.

7. Practice one minute overheads with easy hits. Just meet the ball dead center. The lobber runs down the smash and tries to keep one ball alive.

8. Switch roles.

9. Combine the three strokes. Again predictably practice a forehand volley, followed by an overhead, followed by a backhand. Try to keep the ball in play.

10. Switch roles.

11. Serve easy serves, predictably to your partner's forehand. He practices his return.

12. Switch roles.

13. Serve easy serves to your partner's backhand. He practices backhand returns.

14. Switch roles.

15. For the 15th minute, keep one ball in play, concentrate on early preparation, stroke the ball and go for depth.

Now spend the remaining 45 minutes playing your match and you will be pleasantly surprised at the improved level of play. ●

Billie Jean King, five times Wimbledon Champion, and Bill Maze, National 16 Champion, go through their practice routine.

Billie Jean plays a forehand volley (top), anticipates an overhead (above) and immediately prepares for a backhand volley.

The two players try to keep one ball in play. After a minute they switch, with Billie Jean setting up the strokes.

LESSONS FROM THE MASTER

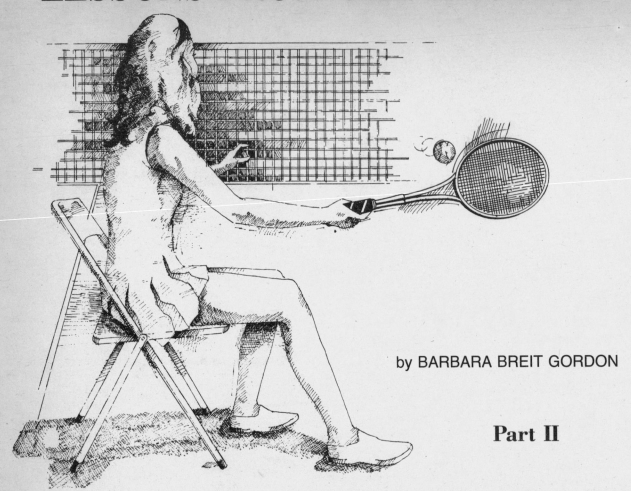

by BARBARA BREIT GORDON

Part II

Introduction

THE late Mercer Beasley had a number of extraordinary protégés over three decades. He did not play tennis himself. His pupils idolized him but there were some players who talked strokes to "Beas" who could not understand what his contributions to tennis knowledge were. In the 1950's he was teaching his protégés a chop return which outsiders thought was passé; it is the chip return used so frequently today against big serves or by the incoming receiver. He taught students to think. His loyal champions included Frank Parker, Ellsworth Vines, Doris Hart and the author. He was once called a Svengali who "managed" the match from the bleachers with hand-signals and ESP (see the British newspapers when Vines played at Wimbledon). Did he know anything? Was he a fraud or a master? Hot ideas or hot air?

Barbara Breit Gordon, the author, was a former Beasley pupil. "Beas" travelled with her on the circuit and she had her best year ever. When she switched to another coach who was also a great player, she lost interest and soon dropped out of the competitive game. For "Teacher" in this article, substitute "Mercer Beasley".

This second installment is a continuation of lessons begun in the first edition of TENNIS DIGEST.

Lesson 21—Meet Miss Twinkle-Toes

Teacher: I want to tie together some concepts we have been working on. You have been jumping rope so that you are moving faster; you are *recovering* in time and you are *planning ahead*. Now I want you to react sooner and pivot (get your racket back) faster.

Carol: I can see that by becoming quicker I am more in command of the point, of the shot, and this is going to help me get the edge on my opponent.

Teacher: Let's discuss being "weightless."

Carol: Being weightless? I thought I could only lose weight by going to some distant planet or the moon.

Teacher: Do you ski?

Carol: Poorly. What has skiing to do

with this?

Teacher: Did your ski instructor ever mention being weightless on the turns? Dropping down, bending the knees, enables you to maneuver your skis around on the turns.

Carol: I don't use skis on the court, in case you haven't noticed.

Teacher: Sometimes you move as though you do. I want you to learn to bounce. I know you have watched the outstanding lady players.

Carol: Those aren't ladies. They're tigers.

Teacher: Haven't you observed how they are always bouncing, knees bending, keeping their feet in action, while their feet barely leave the ground?

Carol: Yes, but what does that do?

Teacher: It speeds up your feet so you can start moving sooner—as soon as you perceive where the ball is going. Secondly, if you time the "bounce" right, it makes you weightless so that you can start your pivot sooner as well as increase the speed of the pivot.

Carol: I'm still lost. I can understand how this "bouncing" speeds up my feet. But the weightless part? And what do you mean by "timing the bounce right"?

Teacher: Bear with me. Let's go into weightless. Are you agreed that when you drop from a standing position to a bent-knee, slightly crouched stance that you are weightless during the time you are dropping?

Carol: Yes, but....

Teacher: If you are bouncing (remember, just barely off the ground) on the balls of your feet after you *recover*, watching your opponent hit, planning your shot, etc., you are keeping your concentration and momentum going. Time the bouncing so just as her racket comes forward to hit the ball you are springing up into another "bounce." As you start to land onto the balls of your feet and go into the bent-knee, slightly-crouched position, the ball has travelled about 5 feet from her racket. At this point you know whether the ball is coming to your forehand side or backhand side and you are also weightless. So it becomes an easy matter to pivot. Remember the balls of your feet are on the ground, knees are bent and you immediately, without pause, go into a speedy pivot.

Carol: Sounds like this would take a little work and precise timing.

Teacher: It takes some work, like anything else, but the rewards are well worth it. One thing that helps is to say, out loud, while you are learning to do this, "fore" or "back" as soon as you see where the ball is coming.

Carol: How high is the "bounce"?

Teacher: Very low to the ground. You don't want to look like a jumping jack.

Carol: I don't recall too many men doing this "bouncing" routine.

Teacher: Most men do the "drop." Think back to how the good men players get ready for a service return. First they bend a little, then straighten up, then just as their opponent serves they "drop" and pivot immediately. In other words, they too are weightless when pivoting. When we worked on running up to the net, we had you do a "hopscotch" step. The men do that too, only just for the merest fraction of a second. Again they are weightless so they can improve reaction time. So men use the same principle, but women seem to find the "bouncing" helps them attain the feeling better.

Carol: Let me sum up:

(1) Bounce continuously to speed up reaction time, both for the pivot and the running.

(2) Time the bounce so that you are springing up as the opponent brings the racket forward to hit.

(3) This makes you weightless at the point in time where you can perceive if the ball is coming to the forehand or backhand side.

(4) Being weightless enables you to go into an immediate and quick pivot.

Teacher: Good going. Learn this and I'll no longer accuse you of playing tennis with skis on your feet.

Lesson 22—"Check Your Bubble-Gum"

Carol: Coach, I'm going to turn the tables on you. I've got a teaching gimmick which helps on all strokes.

Teacher: Intriguing. How does it help you?

Carol: It insures that I shift my weight when I hit the ball.

Teacher: I'll play the role of student. Why is it so important to shift weight on a shot?

Carol: When I lean back, my shots pop up. So the first reason is it makes for a more level shot. The second reason is it enables me to put more force behind the ball. And the third is that shifting the weight permits me to "carry the ball on the strings" which gives me ball control.

Teacher: You're going to put me out of business. Tell me more about this teaching gimmick. Does it help you on groundstrokes and volleys?

Carol: Yes, and serve too. I was working with this kid on his groundstrokes last week and he kept leaning back. I tried the FCC (Freeze-Check-Correct) routine. He froze on the follow-through and I made him check to see if he had the proper form, which he didn't. He was always tilted back. I tried different ideas such as "keep your front shoulder down," "lean into the ball" and "shift your weight." He couldn't relate to any of them. All of a sudden it hit me. On the next stroke, when he "froze" on the follow-through, I told him to spit out his bubble-gum. It hit him on his tummy. I told him, "your bubble-gum should land 3 inches to 4 inches in front of your front foot, about 3 inches closer to the net than your stepping foot."

Teacher: It's a pretty graphic illustration. Did he get it?

Carol: Did he! Within five shots he was leaning into his backhand. We tried it on the forehand and had the same success. On every stroke, when he held the follow-through, he corrected his ending position and made sure the "Bubble Gum" would land in front of his front foot. If the gum hit his shoe he was not leaning forward enough.

Teacher: Didn't the gum get a little soiled?

Carol: We switched to imaginary "Bubble Gum." It helped me too. I went out with my doubles partner and rallied. I tried concentrating on it on both groundstrokes and volleys. Every shot was better. The gimmick enabled me to be in charge of my groundstrokes and it kept me leaning into each volley instead of pulling back as I sometimes do.

Teacher: Great. Let me try it. Yes, it is amazingly easy to visualize if the "Bubble Gum" is in the proper place, 3 inches to 4 inches in front of my front foot. I'm going to serve a few. It works on serve, too.

Carol: Who says teachers don't keep learning?

Teacher: I'm going to incorporate this into my teaching. Thanks for the lesson.

Carol: I need help on my service. I never believed I could lose a match because I wasn't serving well. Now I know. Do you have any check points for me?

Teacher: You already know some of them.

Carol: I know my toss isn't too good, but other than that, what should I correct?

Teacher: Hold it. Drop everything. Call a policeman. How important do you think the service toss is to the success of the serve?

Carol: I know it's important, but aren't there other things to work on also?

Teacher: You're missing the crucial message. You can have no consistent service, no consistent accuracy, no consistent power without a consistently good service toss. There are other things to work on, but only after you understand and learn a good toss. There's no point in going one iota further until this information seeps in. Think about it.

Carol: I'm thinking, I'm thinking. You mean there are no shortcuts, no ways to avoid hard work when learning a good service?

Teacher: No. It starts with the accuracy of the toss. Tell me, what is the biggest difference between the service and all the other tennis shots?

Carol: You hit it over your head.

Lesson 23—Everything Begins with the Service Toss

Carol: Following your advice to "Hit only the good tosses" has been tremendously helpful on service. I made a few observations regarding the effect of the toss on my serve.

Teacher: How's that?

Carol: If I toss the ball too far in front of me the ball goes into the net. That is, if I don't compensate. Conversely, if I toss the ball too far in back of me the serve goes high and long.

Teacher: The compensation factor is important. For instance, some people, when throwing too far behind them, will put spin on the ball.

Carol: When can I learn spin?

Teacher: Patience, one step at a time. What other observations did you make?

Carol: I realize I don't make too many good tosses. I'm not really sure where the toss should be and how high. I would also like to learn how to be more accurate on the toss.

Teacher: Line up sideways to the net as you do when you serve, holding your regular grip. Now, swing the racket as you would normally for your basic service without using a ball. Swing the racket comfortably, shifting weight. This time stop your racket up in the air, at the exact spot you would like to make contact with the ball—where it feels most comfortable and where you feel the most power. See where the SPOT is and how far to the side in relationship to your body. See how high it is.

Carol: That's higher than I thought.

Teacher: You have a tendency, as do many players, to hit a "poopy" service because you don't reach *up* for the ball. This should help. Get a mental picture of the "SPOT."

Carol: Poopy service?

Teacher: I hope I've insulted you enough to motivate you. Sometimes, when you serve, I hope you don't tell anyone who your teacher is.

Carol: Thanks a lot.

Teacher: The point is to toss the ball to the SPOT because that is the easiest place to swing, *not* to swing at any old toss. This causes errors.

Carol: I see the SPOT. Now how do I execute the toss successfully?

Teacher: The thumb and the first two fingers hold the ball you're going to toss. The fourth and little fingers hold the second one. Hold the tossing ball near the finger tips. Assuming the side to net position, start your hand low, palm upwards, keeping your arm straight. Lift your arm up and forward to just under that SPOT and release your fingers away from the ball. The ball should continue to float upward. It has been moving upward within the hand. Ideally, the tossed ball should have no spin on it and it should land right back into your upstretched (that's a combination of up and out-

stretched) hand.

Carol: Do I leave my arm up then?

Teacher: Yes, until you are ready to hit the ball. Make like the Statue of Liberty. This keeps you erect, which enables you to reach up high to hit the ball.

Carol: It looks like I have to shift my weight forward to get my tossing hand under the SPOT.

Teacher: Correct. The important thought here is to keep your left knee slightly bent. For that matter, both knees should be bent.

Carol: When should I release the ball?

Teacher: When your hand reaches the top of your head. This is approximate.

Carol: Let me try a few. Hmmmm. Start low, you said. I'm used to starting high with my left arm and racket.

Teacher: It's not wrong, but while you are learning a good toss let's simplify it. By starting high you are tossing from a low position, merely flicking the ball up with your wrist. To be accurate on a toss it is much easier to release the ball from head height (where the tossed ball only has to travel a little more than a racket's length) than to release the ball from waist height.

Carol: That makes sense. How do I co-ordinate this with the racket and arm?

Teacher: Start both hands low and close together, pointing towards the net. You are still sideways. As you lean towards the net, shifting your weight from the back foot onto the left foot, bring your left hand forward and upward. Simultaneously the right hand is bringing the racket downward and upward. Hands separate about the time the right arm is passing by your navel. At the time your left hand is releasing the ball, the right arm is at approximately the same height. Your arms will look like a modified "U" when you are releasing the ball.

Carol: I'm going to have to work on this. It feels like that co-ordination exercise of rubbing your tummy and patting your forehead.

Teacher: Some people call this service toss and racket-back the "Scissors" motion. Do 100 of these a day for a week, releasing the ball and seeing if it will land back into your hand. By sighting the ball with your left hand you can learn to tell if it will land back into your palm.

Carol: I have my work "cut" out for me with this "Scissors" motion. To sum up: 1. Start with weight back, arms low. 2. Shift forward, bringing left arm and right arm back. 3. Release ball at head height, arms resembling a "U." 4. Knees bent. 5. Toss should land back into hand.

Teacher: That is a very good summation.

Carol: What About...

Teacher: Next week, next week.

Lesson 24—Oh! the Complications of the Service Swing

Teacher: Did you practice 100 service tosses a day?

Carol: Yes, and the accuracy of my toss has improved. I can tell when the toss is high enough and when it is in the proper "SPOT." Now I'd like to work on the service swing.

Teacher: You have already started by learning the proper way to toss so you have part of it assimilated already. Use the forehand grip while learning the basic swing.

Carol: Is there another grip?

Teacher: Yes. As you become more proficient you will learn the Continental grip, which is toward the backhand grip. The main advantage of this grip is that you will be able to impart spin on the ball.

Carol: I'm not ready to contemplate that right now.

Teacher: Assume your waiting stance for the serve. Your weight is on the back foot, your side is to the net and your hands are low. Let's call this position Zero, also known as 0. Shift your weight and toss the ball so that you are in the modified "U" position.

Carol: You mean the Scissors motion which I worked on last week?

Teacher: Right. Let's call the weight shift and toss No. 1. Now, staying sideways, as the ball leaves your left hand and continues upward, let your right arm "bend" at the elbow so that the racket head is pointing down towards the small of your back, the racket edge sort of perpendicular to your back, your right elbow about shoulder high. We'll call this No. 2.

Carol: Is this correct?

Teacher: Almost, but don't thrust your shoulders back and make sure the heel of your hand is still holding onto the handle. If you let the racket head drop down by letting loose with your grip, you are cheating.

Carol: Feels a little like throwing a ball overhead.

Teacher: Right! It is almost the same motion. For No. 3, let your right arm come out of the bend by reaching forward and upward to full extension in time to connect with the ball at the "peak" of the toss (when the ball has stopped going up and before it has started descending).

Carol: There isn't enough time to do all this and still meet the ball at the "peak."

Teacher: While you're learning, toss your ball extra high and don't worry about meeting it at the peak. You need the extra time right now, for your swing will be slower because it is more studied.

Carol: All right, here goes. It feels a little awkward as I reach up for the ball.

Teacher: While you are reaching forward and up, let your shoulders and hips rotate towards the net.

Carol: That feels better. Is the follow-through next?

Teacher: You're a step ahead of me. No. 4 is the follow-through. Let your racket continue going forward and down towards the left side of your body and finishing there.

Carol: On the left side of my body? I thought the right side.

Teacher: That explains your sore shoulder and your sore shin. Now, on your follow-through, all your weight will be on your front foot, leaning forward, your shoulders are level and your eyes are up looking at the contact point. Your right foot should be back.

Carol: Can't I bring my right foot forward? I thought that gives more power.

Teacher: If you have a perfectly co-ordinated serve, yes, that is true. But if you are merely forcing yourself to fall forward or are chasing a bad toss, it leaves you off-balance. Without balance, there is no control. Unless you are going to charge net, stepping over the line leaves you in "no-man's land" and you will just have to back up immediately.

Carol: You mean I can have a powerful service without stepping over the baseline?

Teacher: Absolutely. Watch. Now how much difference was there in the two?

Carol: Not much, barely perceptible.

Teacher: But by stepping over the line, if my intention is *not* to run to net, I have to hurry or I will be caught moving backwards.

Carol: Very interesting. I've got a lot of information to digest. Let me sum up:

0—Waiting stance, weight back, arms low, sideways to net

1—Weight shift forward, arms separate and toss ball (scissors)

2—Ball travels up from toss, right arm bends at elbow, sideways

3—Arm straightens and reaches up to meet ball as shoulders turn

4—Follow-through on left side, weight forward, balance.

Lesson 25—How to Have Spin Serves and Influence People

Carol: I'm still working on my service, and although it is coming along nicely, I don't seem to be getting any zap on it. There must be more to this, like spin and wrist snap.

Teacher: Let's talk today about ball rotation and one method of achieving it. We will also discuss various spin serves. Next lesson we will go into the use of the wrist.

Carol: At last!

Teacher: What do you mean, "at last"? You weren't ready until now.

Carol: That's what I like about you. You always keep me humble.

Teacher: The ball can move across the net with no rotation at all. This is called "flat." It is pretty difficult to hit a perfectly flat ball. The ball can also spin sideways, in an easterly or towards-the-right direction. The reverse is also possible but not too practical for righthanders. Remember, I am referring to the service. Name another rotation.

Carol: A forward rolling motion, topspin, like I hit on my forehand and backhand drives. But I'm still not sure how to do all this.

Teacher: Patience. Don't forget, if you knew all this already I'd be out of a job. There's one more type of spin that you could impart on a service.

Carol: A chop? Backspin, where the ball appears to be rotating back towards you.

Teacher: Right.

Carol: But when would you use that?

Teacher: Most people wouldn't use it on purpose, unless they had problems with their shoulder. It makes the ball skid and stop, but it is difficult to control. Now let's try some of these spin serves out. Toss the ball *above* your head, *not* in front of you where you usually toss it. Now hit it. Trust me, have faith.

Carol: It feels weird. See! Look what happened. The ball sailed out, as you told me would happen if I hit a service toss too far behind me.

Teacher: Do it again. This time turn your head and arm in slightly so that the racket face is more vertical, more closed, rather than open. And hit the ball as usual. Let me make an aside. We are going to have you learn a new service grip next week. This method of turning your racket face is strictly for demonstration purposes.

Carol: Okay, but I still don't like it. Hmmmm. That ball went over the net high but still landed in. It had more zap, too. It also had a different sound. It feels different. Let me do it again. What's happening here?

Teacher: You'll find out in just a moment. Swing now without a ball. Notice that there are two distinctly different parts to the swing. And you could be connecting with a ball when you are doing either part. There is the "up-swing" when you are extending your arm upwards. This is when you are straightening out your arm. The second part is when you are coming down on the ball. Your arm is straight and the racket head and arm are coming down. Now do the service again. Toss the ball above your head (which we call behind us because it is "behind" the normal hitting zone, farther away from the net than the normal tossing area). What do you notice?

Carol: By tossing the ball above my head, I am hitting the ball on the "up-swing," and this is imparting topspin to the ball, which is keeping the ball from sailing out—if I keep my racket head vertical and not open.

Teacher: Very good. Right now, by virtue of WHERE you toss the ball, you can impart some spin. Tell me, what are the characteristics and advantages of topspin on the serve?

Carol: The topspin serve goes over the net fairly high but still lands in the court. The speed of the swing goes into the rotation of the ball so that when the ball hits the court it shoots off towards the back fence in a hopping action.

Teacher: Now where did you read that?

Carol: Just for that insult I'm going to go one step farther. I've figured out this lesson's message. I'm going to toss the ball way in front and hit it. By doing this I am demonstrating that I am connecting with the ball on the "downswing" of the serve, when my arm has reached full extension. This makes the ball go more or less flat, hard and slightly down. If I were to toss the ball any more in front, the ball would go into the net.

Teacher: And how would you describe the action of the flat service?

Carol: It is harder, faster and bounces lower. It goes over the net with less clearance—too little margin for error, actually, so I would say the disadvantage of this flat service is that too many would go into the net and out.

Teacher: Fantastic. Now toss the ball way to the right of your normal tossing spot. What do you notice?

Carol: I'm really curving around the ball. I have to or I can't keep the ball in the court. That is the slice serve, right?

Teacher: Right. It is the sidespin we mentioned. Notice how the slice serve really curves to your left and to the receiver's right. The advantages are many: to pull the receiver off the court, to hit to his forehand, to serve into him and as a surprise.

Carol: Great! This was an exciting lesson. Let's re-cap here.

Teacher: Today you learned about spins on the service or ball rotation. You learned to impart spin by virtue of where you tossed the ball in relation to your body. This determined whether or not you would hit the ball on the "upswing," the "extension" of the arm, or on the "downswing" or on a curving arc.

Carol: Which means, translated:

For topspin: Toss the ball behind me, above my head, which makes me hit the ball on the "upswing."

For flat: Toss the ball in the normal hitting zone, slightly in front, which makes me hit the ball on the "downswing" with a straight arm.

For slice: Toss the ball more to my right, which makes me hit the ball on a curving arc.

Teacher: Terrific! Next lesson we will go into the use of the wrist.

Lesson 26—Put Wrist Snap in Your Serve

Carol: I'm getting the feel of spin on my serve. Today you said we were going to go into the wrist action.

Teacher: That means you are going to start using a Continental grip, spreading the fingers apart.

Carol: Oh, no! I tried that once and lost all control of the ball. Why is it necessary?

Teacher: I'll reply by having you go through a progression now. Put your racket down, and with your hand simulate the different service swings. Start by tossing up an imaginary ball and shadow swing a topspin serve.

Carol: I will pretend to toss the ball above my head and I will swing up, hitting on the "extension." What is this doing?

Teacher: I'll ignore that for just a moment. Speed up the momentum of your hand. And not just by speeding up your arm.

Carol: Hmmm. How do I do that? Oh, I see. I let my hand go up and forward and over.

Teacher: In other words, a wrist snap. For greater wrist snap, cock the hand back as you come out of the "loop" and then, just as you begin to make contact with the ball, flip up and forward and over. In effect, simulate the action that the racket head will make.

Carol: Let me try it with a racket and then I can understand more of what you are saying. For topspin, I hit the ball on the "upswing."

Teacher: Correct. For increased topspin, let your wrist snap your racket head (while vertical, while on edge) up and then arc over, letting the wrist break forward and over, as you hit on the "upswing."

Carol: I've got it. But it feels like I can't bring the racket head over far enough. My wrist action is impeded by the butt of the racket handle.

Teacher: Now try your Continental grip.

Carol: I see what you mean! Now there is full wrist action and rotation. And, therefore, greater spin, I presume.

Teacher: Right. Now remember, the greater spin, the more control. Topspin on your service enables you to arc it high (5 feet) over the net and still have the ball land in with ZAP! But you have to create momentum in your racket head and follow-through; otherwise the ball will sail out from lack of spin or just die in the net. You HAVE to swing HARD on a spin service. The power goes into the ball rotation. And you have to use wrist to give you this extra amount of spin.

Carol: Let me try it with a ball. This really feels weird. My orientation is way off. I don't feel I'm getting as much topspin as I should.

Teacher: I have to mention another factor here. To get more topspin you have to exaggerate the upswing. And here is where we have to discuss how the racket head and shaft come out of the loop. On an exaggerated topspin service, toss the ball a little behind you and a little to your left. The racket head will come out of the loop near your left wing bone and the racket shaft will be slightly parallel to the ground. As you brush up towards the ball, your wrist action as you hit will be one of coming from lower left to upper right on the ball. This, of course, will make the racket head strike the ball from lower left to upper right, which puts more topspin on the ball.

Carol: Very interesting. So there are three factors to imparting spin: (1) where the ball is tossed, which affects (2) how the racket head and shaft

Texas' Daryl Gralka employs a true Continental grip. The fleshy part of the palm extends beyond the butt of the racket handle. The forefinger is extended.

The topspin serve is used for control; the ball arcs high over the net and still lands in court. Toss is a bit behind and to the left; ball is hit on the upswing.

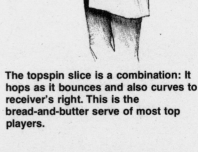

On the slice serve, toss is to the server's right. The wrist action is one of curving around the ball on the right.

Sketches, Hodges Soileau

The flat serve is potentially the hardest but most difficult to control. Ball is tossed in front of body, racket shaft is vertical, wrist action is forward and over.

The topspin slice is a combination: It hops as it bounces and also curves to receiver's right. This is the bread-and-butter serve of most top players.

come out of the loop, and (3) wrist action.

Teacher: Correct. Let's talk about the slice service now. (1) The toss is to the right, (2) the racket head will come out of the loop around on the right side of the body, and (3) the wrist action will be one of curving around the ball on the right.

Carol: And on the flat service I will: (1) toss the ball in front (2) the racket head will come out of the loop straight up, with the racket shaft coming up vertically, and (3) my wrist action will be forward and over, with the racket face going straight over.

Teacher: There is one more possibility here. The topspin slice service. This is a combination serve. It is very effective for it not only hops as it bounces; it also curves to the receiver's right. You achieve this serve by coming around the ball as you brush up. You would toss the ball above your head but a little more to your right than on a topspin.

Carol: I find this all fascinating and understand it intellectually, but I don't see how I'll ever get used to it.

Teacher: The first part has been to understand the theory of ball rotation on the service. You now see the reason for the Continental grip and how you impart these spins—by where you toss the ball, how the racket head and shaft come out of the loop, and the use of wrist snap. The second is practice!

Carol: Agreed, but I'm not looking forward to it.

Teacher: I want you to spend one week practicing only the slice serve when you play. The next week topspin serves only. The third week hit flat serves. And the fourth week use the topspin slice. Naturally you will be rallying, too. But *no* matches.

Carol: No matches?

Teacher: The fifth week, see if you can call your serves. Try mixing them up. One flat, one topspin, one topspin slice and then a plain slice.

Carol: In match play, when would I use what serve?

Teacher: The flat and the slice should be first serves for they have less margin for error—less arc over the net. The topspin and topspin slice should be second serves for there is

more forward rolling spin for control.

Carol: Couldn't I use the topspin serves for first serves too?

Teacher: Sure, and it's smart to do so. You put more pressure on your opponent by getting more first serves in.

Carol: What do you mean, no matches?

Teacher: Under stress you will revert back to your poopy serve. If you really want to make the break and move on to a good serve, make it easy on yourself.

Carol: How long will it take me to master these serves?

Teacher: Count on 6 months and you won't be far off.

Carol: You mean I can't play matches for 6 months?

Teacher: I'd like you to refrain from match play for 2 months, but don't expect to have full confidence in your new serves for 6. Think of these months as a small investment of time. You're going to play tennis for another 40 years, so what difference is 2 to 6 months going to make?

Carol: I don't really like how that sounds, but I'll accept it, Coach.

Lesson 27—Rushing Net on Your Serve is Tricky

Teacher: I feel you are now ready to serve and run to net. You weren't before, but now your service is harder, has more spin and it is more accurate and consistent. Additionally, you have been working on your jumping rope so you are moving faster, and you know how to move up to the net in stages.

Carol: Am I going to play the attacking game?

Teacher: Right. Does that appeal to you?

Carol: It does, but the last time I tried it I got zapped.

Teacher: It's one of those areas where you have to know what you are doing. Let's start now. What kind of a service do you feel would be the most advantageous to follow to net?

Carol: The hard, flat one.

Teacher: Why?

Carol: Because I would most likely get a weak return.

Teacher: But it would come back faster and that would give you less time to get close to the net.

Carol: Yes.

Teacher: Also, isn't there less margin for error on a flat, hard serve?

Carol: Yes. Now I see why I was getting killed. I should use a service that will give me time to get up and that will have good margin for error. I should also elicit a weak return. For all those prerequisites I would need a topspin or topspin slice.

Teacher: Right. Now where would you place it?

Carol: To their backhand normally, because for most people it is their more defensive shot. Or I could put it right at them.

Teacher: Good. Now here comes the tricky part. You are going to toss the ball farther in front of you so that you are crossing over the line with your right foot after you hit.

Carol: Wait a minute. You said there were two reasons I shouldn't step over the line on my service. You told me it was due to chasing a bad service toss and it brought me into "no-man's land" where I would have to back up in a hurry so I wouldn't be late on the next shot.

Teacher: What you said is valid, except when you are going to rush the net. Then there is a purpose for crossing over the line. It is to get a head-start. It gives you almost three feet into the court, thereby enabling you to get closer to net.

Carol: That's another reason why I was not successful previously in serving and running up. How will I be able to serve my topspin or topspin slice

Volleying from a stationary position, as Daryl Gralka does here, is relatively easy: Continental grip, wrist firm, racket head high, left foot steps toward the net.

The stationary backhand volley is almost a mirror image of the forehand. It is also hit with a Continental (or backhand) grip, and again wrist is firm and racket head high whenever possible.

When Daryl comes in behind serve, she takes three or four steps, hops, then stretches, leaps or lunges. She must stop before she hits in order to be able to change directions.

After hitting a spin serve, which gives the player time to get in and get set for the volley, the movements are: three or four steps, a hop to be able to change directions, and then a leap or stretch as needed.

Sketches: Hodges Soileau

service if I toss the ball that far in front of me?

Teacher: You will have to lean way forward so that your body, head and arm are in the same relationship to your toss as before, when you did not cross over the line. It's not easy. Here, try some.

Carol: It feels awkward at first. I can see I really have to pinpoint where I want the toss. But this is great. I'm going to like this after I practice.

Teacher: Yes, practice! A lot—about 100 a day for a couple of weeks. Don't do them all at once since it's quite strenuous.

Carol: How many steps should I take into the court?

Teacher: Take at least three steps. Remember, your right foot crossing into the court is one step. Your last step is your "hop-scotch" step, where both feet land on the ground at the same time.

Carol: I remember the "hopscotch" step. It enables me to be weightless at the moment my opponent hits. Therefore I can change my direction smoothly and quickly.

Teacher: Obviously, the closer you can get to the service line before their return comes, the better. But the over-riding rule is "Stop just before they hit." So the first "home-base" or "resting spot" is behind the service line. Now what?

Carol: As soon as I see where the return is coming, I will move in to meet the ball, putting my first volley—the mid-court volley—deep to their baseline, most likely to their backhand. By trying for an angle shot from mid-court, I would be attempting a low-percentage shot, which means I would hit more out or in the net than I would make. When I get closer to the net I can go for the angles.

Teacher: I can see you remember your lesson on "How to Move Up to Net." Let's continue. What are you going to do after you've hit the first volley deep?

Carol: I'll move in closer to the net, to the next "home base," again pausing with a "hop-scotch" step just as they are about to hit. When I see where it is coming I will move in and cut it off or run back for the lob. Which reminds me: I want to work on my overhead.

Teacher: We will very soon. You forgot to mention that you will put yourself, after you hit, into the "Center of the Possible Returns."

Carol: That comes so naturally to me that as I move up to net I automatically move a little bit to the down-the-line side.

Teacher: Let me add a few other items. First, run up only after your first service. The second serve is weaker. Second, "Serve and Go!" Don't wait to see if your service is in. Then it is too late. Assume your service is good. Third, don't feel you have to run in behind your service on every point. It's a strenuous maneuver. It's good to utilize the element of surprise. Mix it up and save some energy too.

Carol: I'm glad to hear that. Even though I've been skipping rope, I'm not in that good shape.

Teacher: Here are the checkpoints for today's lesson. When you want to serve and run up to net:
(1) Use a topspin or topspin slice serve to the backhand; (2) Toss the ball out in front farther than normal, leaning forward and bringing your right foot over the line; (3) Keep the same "body-toss" relationship as on your normal topspin or topspin slice service; (4) Come in on first service only; (5) Don't wait to see if your service is in. Move! (6) Get in as close to the service line as possible before the opponent hits, ending with a "hopscotch" step.

Lesson 28—The Secret of Returning a Fast Serve

Carol: Serving and running to net has improved my game enormously. I'm playing aggressively now. However, it's made me conscious of a big problem—my service return on hard, strong serves.

Teacher: The more you learn, the more you'll find out how much you don't know. I don't want to make you feel bad, but returning a fast serve is the easiest shot in the game.

Carol: Thanks.

Teacher: But it's one of the hardest techniques to learn. I'm convinced it is the Puritan ethic in our culture that makes this shot so difficult: nothing that easy can be right. The mind can't accept it.

Carol: Enough of this. What's the secret?

Teacher: First, make sure you are standing in the proper spot to receive service, namely, on the baseline and in the corner.

Carol: Why?

Teacher: You receive on or inside the baseline so that you can cut off the angle of the service and save running to the ball. The farther back you wait, the wider the ball can go. Conversely, the closer you wait, the fewer steps you need take—maybe none or only one.

Carol: I can see that, but why in the corner?

Teacher: Again, to cut down on steps. Remember the concept of the "Center of the Possible Returns?"

Carol: Of course. I should always place myself so that I equalize the territory I have to cover on either side. But this is against a good server, one who can place the ball well.

Teacher: Right. I'm also assuming you don't have a particularly weak side that you are trying to protect. Now let me serve to you. I'll start off serving softly.

Carol: These serves are easy.

There's enough time to get ready.

Teacher: Here are some hard, fast ones.

Carol: See what I mean? I'm so late! There's no way to get my racket back and still meet the ball on time.

Teacher: No, there isn't.

Carol: Then what should I do? Not take a backswing?

Teacher: Right. No backswing.

Carol: No backswing? But then I won't have enough power.

Teacher: Yes, you will, only you'll use your opponent's speed and power. Let him do the hard work.

Carol: I don't understand.

Teacher: See what I mean about the secret being a difficult concept to accept?

Carol: Yes. Let's go over this again, please.

Teacher: There is no time to get the racket back on a fast service. Therefore there is speed and power for YOU to use. Since you don't need the speed and power that a backswing gives you, don't take one. By not taking a backswing and merely meeting the ball ("blocking" it), you are saving all the time a pivot, racket back and swing would use. In other words, you do not have to react as quickly. Use the time you have saved to judge the direction of the ball. The net result is that the service return becomes easy.

Carol: Fascinating. You mean I just put my hand and racket forward to meet the ball, almost like a volley?

Teacher: Yes. It's better to take a step into the shot if you can. Think of the move as that of a fencer except that you put the side of the sword towards the net, not the tip.

Carol: This is great. I can take my time now in reacting.

Teacher: That's the secret. Another way to think of it is to imagine you are going to catch the serve with a baseball glove.

Carol: I like that. Let me return some more fast serves now.

Teacher: Very good, Carol. One other thought. In order to place the ball more accurately, add a short follow-through.

Carol: I'll try it. It's so easy. I just stick the racket out, intercept the ball and guide it with that little stroke.

Teacher: There's another advantage to this return. You are, in effect, just "dumping" the ball back. This gives your opponent nothing to hit. The ball has no pace on it for him to use. It just dies and he has to generate the speed.

Carol: I see. How about the placement of my service return against a net rusher? Where should I put it?

Teacher: You answer that. What did you find was the most difficult shot to handle when you served and ran to net last week?

Carol: The return at my feet. Yes, of course. The answer to my question is short and low, at his feet.

Teacher: If he stays back, you want to keep the ball deep so you don't give him an opportunity to come up.

Carol: I'll do the recapping: (1) stand on the baseline and in the corner when returning service against a strong server; (2) on a fast serve, take your time in judging where the ball is coming and simply block the return without a backswing; (3) to place the ball, add a follow-through to the spot you want; (4) against a net rusher, dump the ball at his feet.

Teacher: I'll add a No. 5—recover. That means get 5 feet behind the baseline and in the "Center of Possible Returns" before he hits the next shot. Of course, if the opportunity presents itself, you also have the option of moving to net.

Carol: I liked this lesson. Now I see what you meant about the hard serve being so easy to return.

Lesson 29—The Net Rusher's Plea: "Please Don't Lob."

Carol: I need help on my overhead.

Teacher: I'm not surprised. The overhead is the most difficult shot to time. It's the first shot of the professionals that goes off when they haven't played for a while.

Carol: Why? It's basically a serve, isn't it?

Teacher: The answer is "Yes, BUT." On the serve you can be set; there is no moving or footwork. You can wait for a perfect toss, which is a set-up. On an overhead, you have to take the shot your opponent gives you. You not only have to worry about meeting the ball in front of you and in the right alignment to the body but you also have to be concerned with the height at which you meet the ball. To do this you must move quickly (more often than not, moving back) to connect with the ball before it is past you or over you.

Carol: Can I hang my head now?

Teacher: This is by way of explaining why the overhead is so difficult. The swing isn't the hard part; it's the positioning of your body to the ball in time. I'm glad you are in shape. If you weren't, all you could attempt to smash would be the very easy, slow lobs.

Carol: Now I feel better. What should I do when I am at net and get a lob?

Teacher: Let's discuss three things. *First,* sight the ball with your left hand, pointing your left index finger at the ball. Let this left hand simulate the feeling you have after you have tossed a ball for your serve. Use this hand as an aid for guiding you in moving, for you want to position yourself so that the ball, when you hit it, is in the same relative position to you as on your service. Remember to watch the ball, seeing your left hand only peripherally. In other words, think "service." Move so that the ball is lined up to your left hand, a racket length above it. *Second,* put your right arm up, taking your racket up to the "halfswing" position as in the service. Pick your racket up as though you were lifting a hammer and let it drop down low behind your back in the "back-scratching" stance.

Carol: Why not take a full swing?

Teacher: You don't need that much power on an overhead to make a putaway; it takes longer to bring your racket back with a full swing; it makes timing the ball that much more difficult; and it's hard for the feet to move as long as you are swinging the racket back. So it means a slow start.

Carol: You've convinced me. What is the *third* thing to do on the smash?

Teacher: Bring your right foot back, towards the baseline, enabling you to turn sideways.

Carol: Couldn't I bring my left foot forward to the net and get the same effect?

Teacher: Yes, but that would bring you closer to the net. By stepping back, you are now two steps back from the net. On the overhead, the hardest thing is moving back for a high ball, not moving up.

Carol: I see. If the lob is that easy, there is still plenty of time to move up and kill it. However, if it is a high, deep shot, those two steps will probably save the point for me.

Teacher: You've got it. I want you to try some shadow-practice. Do your overhead pivots, remembering the three things. *Both arms up and right foot back.* The left hand sights and the right arm is up above the shoulder.

Carol: Even though it feels strange, I can see it is going to help. What about moving to the ball?

Teacher: Assume your overhead "ready" position again, *both arms up, right foot back.* Start sliding back towards the baseline, using a two-step motion.

Carol: This feels very slow. Why couldn't I just back up, running backwards?

Teacher: That's a great way to fall and injure yourself. There is a proper way to run. For the moment, consider this. As you practice this "two-step" motion you will speed up. If you react quickly enough, remembering the three basics, you will be able to recover most lobs with this footwork. Remember, watch the racket face as well as the ball as your opponent brings the racket forward. This already gives you a tip-off as to what he is going to do with the ball.

Carol: I guess this is part of the secret of anticipation: watching my opponent's racket as well as the ball. Then I can react sooner. But what do I do if it is a deep lob that I *must* run back for?

Teacher: Run. Turn your body towards the baseline and run. Sometimes you can turn your head over your shoulder and watch the ball as you run; other times you estimate where the ball is going and just take off.

Carol: What do I do with a lob that comes fast and just high enough to get over my head and lands right on the baseline?

Teacher: Say "Good shot." Some shots are too good. Let's talk about placement for a moment. In general, place the ball to the backhand corner. Again, as in the volley, the closer you can get to the net, the more you can go for an angled shot, probably to the forehand side. Don't get too fancy on an overhead. A firm, well-placed hit is all you need, aimed to a corner. On a defensive, late overhead, hit it easy, deep to the backhand.

Carol: I want to ask you about the swing. Is it a service motion essentially?

Teacher: Yes. However, you may have to stretch more and hit from an off-balance position. You may also have to leap if the ball is too high or if it gets behind you.

Carol: I've seen players jump. They shift their weight from the right foot, leaping up and turning towards the net, all the while reaching up with the right arm and racket to meet the ball. After the hit, they land on the left foot. It's fantastic. I'm looking forward to mastering it. But for now I'll settle for returning easier lobs with an overhead.

Teacher: Want to try to sum up?

Carol: Here goes: (1) Both arms up and right foot back; (2) Sight ball with the left hand; (3) To move, slide back sideways, using the two-step. Advanced players turn and run back; (4) Think "serve"; (5) Meet the ball in front and high; (6) Watch the ball, not the court.

Teacher: You mentioned one point that I neglected. You're right: watch the ball. Good lesson, Carol.

Lesson 30—Why Not Lob?

Teacher: Working on your overhead last week reminded me we should pay some attention to your lob. The lob is the most neglected shot in tennis. Many players are afraid to lob because they don't want to be called dinkers. Actually, one mark of the outstanding player is the judicious and frequent use of the lob.

Carol: I lob sometimes.

Teacher: Let's change "sometimes" to often. When do you lob?

Carol: When I am out of position and need time to get back. You saved me a lot of points by teaching me that.

Teacher: I am glad that you lob when you are out of position. That is an extremely important time to lob. Do you know other important lobbing situations? I can think of six others.

Carol: Six? Well, I would lob over the net man's head.

Teacher: Okay. That's an obvious one, although many players do try to slug the ball past the net man. Go on.

Carol: Oh, I don't know. Help me. What are they?

Teacher: We've talked about lobbing to give you time to get back into position. There are two other situations when you need to gain time. Try lobbing to catch your breath when you are winded and as a ploy for an approach shot.

Carol: You mean to lob when I come up to net?

Teacher: Yes, it not only gives you the time to get up, it also draws a weak return.

Carol: That will help me beat Steady Stella. She always hits the ball deep and never gives me an opportunity to get to the net. By the way, I just recognized another time to lob. What about lobbing to stroke weaknesses of opponents such as when they have difficulty handling a deep, high ball. For instance, I hate high balls to my backhand.

Teacher: Correct. How about a sneaky, dirty reason? Lob because the sun is in their eyes.

Carol: I like that. I've got one more, now that you've started my thinking process. Lobbing is a great way to change pace to break up an opponent's rhythm.

Teacher: Absolutely. The hard hitters can't stand a slow ball. It really shakes them up. That makes seven times to lob. Lobs fall into two categories, offensive and defensive.

Carol: By defensive you must mean those times you lob out of desperation, such as when you're late and leaning back and it is all you can do.

Teacher: When you have no choice, when you are not in command of the shot, when the ball is pushing you around, when the ball isn't in your proper hitting zone and when you are off balance and late it is time for a defensive lob. The defensive lob is usually an undercut shot, giving the ball backspin. Big things to concentrate on when in that situation are: get it high, deep and to your opponent's backhand.

Carol: I try that shot frequently. I even lob defensively when I don't intend to. How is the offensive lob different?

Teacher: To begin with, it is a shot hit deliberately. You will have to meet it in your most advantageous hitting zone—in front and to the side. Then, the ball will have topspin, a forward rolling rotation, as it leaves your racket.

Carol: We've talked about topspin. It enables you to hit the ball hard and the spin makes the ball drop into the court.

Teacher: How deep would you like the lob to land?

Carol: As deep as possible. Near the baseline.

Teacher: Where would the apex of the lob have to be then?

Carol: I would guess that the highest part of the lob would have to be above the net.

Teacher: Wrong. Since the ball has more force right after you hit it, the flight pattern of the lob is this—it will go forward as well as up, overcoming gravity, until it runs out of steam and then it will fall down in an almost perpendicular manner. That means straight down and not forward and down.

Carol: If I aimed the apex above the net the lob would land shallow, so I have to aim the apex of the lob some-where inside the service line. Right?

Teacher: Right. This is the reason most people lob short. They figure the apex is above the net, which is wrong.

Carol: When I lob the ball goes long. Why?

Teacher: You have to slow down the swing. You've been hitting the lob with the same speed you have been using on your drives.

Carol: When I slow down, the ball barely makes it over the net. Now that I know about the apex I should be able to get more depth.

Teacher: That's right. But you also have to have a follow-through for control of spin, depth and placement. Let's spend some time discussing the execution of the lob. You don't want to "telegraph" your intentions, so when you pivot and take your racket back it should look the same as it does on a drive. However, as you come forward to connect with the ball, open the racket face up about 45 degrees hitting the underside of the ball and lifting the ball up. It is almost like you are lifting a tray. Pretend that you have some cups on your strings and you have to keep the racket strings horizontal or they will fall off. End your follow-through with your arm above your head and in front, with the racket face extremely open.

Carol: This lifting motion is certainly different from what I have been doing. I have to concentrate on getting under the ball.

Teacher: A side benefit of that is that you will be watching the ball.

Carol: They're going out, so I'm going to slow down.

Teacher: Cradle the shot. Gentle. Remember, this is a touch shot. You can't just slug it. Swing slow-motion and follow-through. Adjust the apex accordingly. If the lob still lands out, aim a little lower and make sure you are imparting topspin to the ball.

Carol: I'm going to work on the offensive lobs.

Teacher: You now have more options on what to do with the ball. This means your opponent cannot take you for granted. He can't be sure of what you are going to do.

Sitting on a chair helps Carol "get low" and "stay low," two of the keys to returning low, short balls.

Lesson 31—Avoiding Elephant Killers

Teacher: I'd like you to work on a new shot, Carol. It's often overlooked because it seems so easy but it's not a set-up and most people blow it.

Carol: I'm intrigued. What is it?

Teacher: The low, short ball. Not the one that makes you scramble and dive but the shot that brings you in closer to the service line and is lower than the height of the net.

Carol: Oh, that shot! I'm always missing it. Either it lands in the net or sails way out. I call them elephant killers. I can't figure out how to handle them.

Teacher: This shot can be turned from a loser into a good approach shot. The solution is to "Get low, swing low and stay low."

Carol: Will you elaborate?

Teacher: Let me explain the difficulty players have in handling this shot. Since you are close to the net and the ball is lower than it, it makes the net very high in proportion to the baseline. You have a shorter distance than normal to get the ball over the net and still make it land inside the court. You not only have to get the ball *up* but you also have to get it to come *down* immediately. If you look at the flight path of this shot, it becomes obvious there is little margin for error.

Carol: You said "Get low, swing low and stay low." What does it mean and how does it help?

Teacher: "Get low": bend your knees and get your fanny down. "Swing low": swing as parallel to the ground as possible. Don't swing up. You will swing up anyway, but by *trying* to swing low you will obtain the correct amount of topspin. "Stay low": keep your body in the same position as when you started. Don't pop up. This flattens out the trajectory of the ball's flight. The shot not only clears the net but lands in as

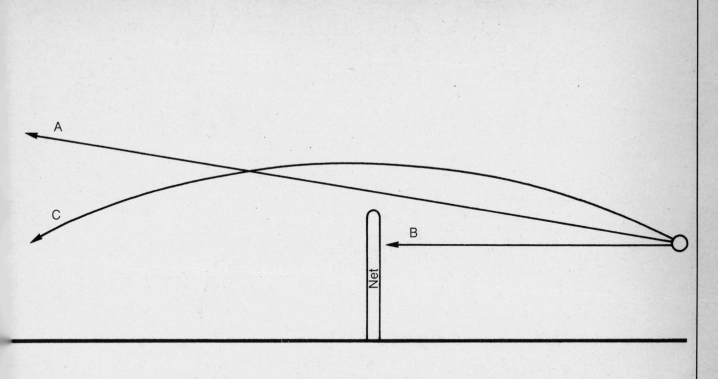

A

C

Net

B

This diagram shows the small margin for error in returning a low, short ball. A is the "elephant killer" shot. B is too low and hits the net. C is the desired trajectory.

well, due to the topspin you have imparted.

Carol: That sounds very clear. How hard should I hit it?

Teacher: Hit the ball with medium speed; it is not a "kill" shot. Where should you go after you have hit it?

Carol: I'll move up and split-step just before my opponent hits the next shot.

Teacher: Don't wait to see if your ball lands in. Assume it will and move! Where should you look when you are hitting this shot?

Carol: At the same place I should always look: at the ball, not the court.

Where should I place it?

Teacher: Deep to the baseline, generally to the backhand. Don't go for the angles. It's a low-percentage shot.

Carol: That's right, I remember. Whenever I am near the mid-court area I should aim deep. Only when I am extremely close to the net should I go for the angles. I'm anxious to try it. Hit me some. See, the same old wild shots.

Teacher: Sit on this chair and I'll feed you some balls.

Carol: What will this do?

Teacher: By sitting down you make sure you will do two of the three items

on the list, namely, "get low and stay low." Now you only have to concentrate on "swinging low."

Carol: I'm dubious but willing. Hey, it works. I'm amazed. The ball goes over and still lands in. It's almost an easy shot.

Teacher: Now remove the chair. Here are some more balls. You can do it.

Carol: This is great. I've just turned a weakness into a strength. I'm going to remember this tip. On low, short balls, "Get low, swing low, and stay low." Thanks, Coach.

Lesson 32—Taking the Terror Out of Topspin

Carol: I've been playing people lately who use a lot of spin on their shots. I find it confusing because I can't judge the bounce.

Teacher: Shots with an extreme amount of spin are tricky. Let's confine our lesson to the extreme topspin shots.

Carol: How do I know if a shot is going to have topspin?

Teacher: You are already familiar with some of this, but today we will go into greater detail. When imparting topspin, your opponent will start the racket head forward motion from way under the ball and will follow through way up and high, almost in a 90 degree path. On the topspin serve, the player then snaps his wrist and racket head over the ball on the follow-through. On groundstrokes, he might roll the racket over at the completion of the shot.

Carol: I see. It is an extreme version of regular topspin, the "low-to-high" swing. Next question: what are the characteristics of an extreme topspin shot in the air and off the bounce?

Teacher: It has forward rotation, which means the ball is rotating towards you as it comes through the air. As soon as it has reached the peak in its trajectory, it will drop quickly. Topspin also causes the ball to move faster on the rebound. Normally the angle of incidence equals the angle of reflection, which means the angle off the court (at the bounce) is the same as that into the bounce. Spin is one factor that changes this. Topspin makes the ball have a lower angle of rebound and therefore a longer bounce. The ball will travel a greater distance before it bounces a second time.

Carol: If topspin rebounds at a smaller angle of reflection, why do so many topspin shots (especially serves) bounce up high, at shoulder level?

Teacher: The ball has arched over the net extremely high and is descending in an almost vertical angle, with a great amount of spin. Therefore, when it bounces, the lesser angle of reflection is still quite great, and there is still a lot of speed and spin on the ball

to shoot it forward and up high. Topspin shots bounce higher than expected.

Carol: So the amount of rebound depends upon several factors: the force of the ball, the amount of spin, the height at which it arched over the net and the type of court surface.

Teacher: Right. Also the way it arched over the net. Was it straight? Over the net, up and over the net or straight down over the net?

Carol: My third question is crucial. How will the ball come off my racket?

Teacher: Extreme topspin will have a tendency to rebound "up" off your racket.

Carol: That's what I wanted to know. Now I have something I can use.

Teacher: Amazingly, an opponent's topspin comes off your racket with underspin. The ball keeps its same rotation after striking your racket, but it changes direction and becomes underspin.

Carol: I'm hanging in there. Now let's get into the implications of this information. Let's get it down to something practical. I don't want to be thinking "angle of incidence is greater than angle of reflection on topspin" when I'm playing.

Teacher: First, you need a little more background. You can reduce the effect of extreme topspin by hitting the ball more forcefully. Whatever way you decide to handle the shot (block, chop, punch, drive), hold your racket firmly and keep it solid as you swing. This enables you to neutralize the spin. If you have a loose grip, *their* spin becomes a dominating factor.

Carol: So to minimize the effect of their topspin (or spin in general), I should be strong in my hit. I think I'm beginning to understand the theory. I'm glad I discovered that topspin bounds "up" off my racket. Now I can compensate for that action. Let's discuss returning an extreme topspin drive.

Teacher: You have two choices, based upon either the kind of spin you desire to impart or need to impart if you are in a defensive position. The

two choices are, I'm sure, no great surprise to you: topspin or chop (underspin). Remember to allow for the "up" action of the ball regardless of your choice. You can drive it back with topspin—you have enough force from your backswing and follow-through to change the rotary direction of their ball as well as its linear direction. It is usually easier to drive back a low ball because you are coming from low-to-high. If the ball bounces up high, it is easy to chip it back, particularly on the backhand side. This way you would be using their spin. Remember, their topspin becomes your underspin. But don't put too much backspin on the ball or you will lose control.

Carol: That's a lot to digest, but it's coming. I think we've covered my next question. How should I return the topspin serve, an extreme kicker?

Teacher: Well?

Carol: I could do what the pros do: just block it back or hit it with a minimum amount of underspin since the shot catches me up high.

Teacher: Yes, the chip shot. It's prevalent against today's topspin service. Now you can understand some of the reasons why. Now, how would you handle a topspin shot when you are at the net?

Carol: I would volley it back with a modicum of chop, but allowing for the upward bound of their shot. I must remember to move in on the ball and catch it as high as possible since their topspin will descend quickly and I don't want to be volleying from below the height of the net.

Teacher: Very good. I know this lesson has been like an extreme topspin shot from your opponent: heavy.

Carol: But valuable and revealing. Let me sum up the main points of this lesson.

1. Watch my opponent's stroke to determine the kind of spin he is imparting to the ball. Topspin is imparted from an extreme upward swing.

2. A topspin ball from my opponent rolls towards me in its flight and descends quickly after it reaches the peak of its arc.

3. Upon bouncing, a topspin ball will: (a) rebound at a lower angle, (b) bounce faster off the rebound, (c) have a long bounce and (d) bounce higher off the bounce than expected.

4. The amount of rebound off the court depends upon several factors: (a) the type of court surface, (b) the amount of force applied to the ball, (c) the amount of topspin on the ball, (d) the linear trajectory of the ball and (e) the height of the ball as it passed over the net.

5. A topspin ball will rebound "up" off my racket.

6. To reduce the effectiveness of topspin, I should hold the racket firmly and stroke with force.

7. The easiest way to handle high bouncers on the backhand side is to chip them. On my forehand side, I can block or chip them back.

8. On the low bouncing topspin groundstrokes, I will use my drive.

9. When volleying a topspin shot, I will hold my racket firmly and apply a moderate chop.

The author wishes to thank Gene Barr for sharing his knowledge of physics.

DEFINITIONS

UNDERSPIN, BACKSPIN, CHOP and *CHIP* are used interchangeably: *fairly short strokes which can be used as approach shots.*

DRIVE: a groundstroke, usually with topspin, although it might have sidespin on it.

HIGH BOUNCER: a ball that bounces shoulder-high or higher.

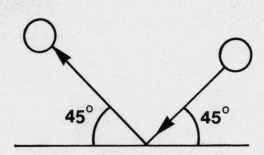

The angle of reflection equals the angle of incidence if there is no spin on the ball.

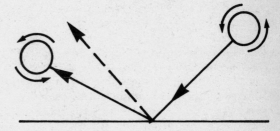

The angle of the rebound decreases when there is topspin on the ball.

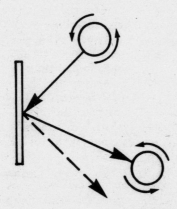

Topspin will rebound off the racket with more "up" than expected, whether the ball comes from above (left) or below (right). Topspin rebounds off the racket as backspin.

Lesson 33—How to Handle Underspin

Carol: It helped me to know how to handle my opponent's extreme topspin shots. You know what I want to work on today?

Teacher: Yes, the underspin shots, also known as backspin, chop and chip.

Carol: What is slice?

Teacher: It is a long stroke with backspin or sidespin, although others differ slighty in their definitions. On the service, it refers to sidespin. More on sidespins later. Let's get back to backspin. Can you recognize when a shot is going to be a chop?

Carol: Yes. My opponent swings with a "high-to-low" motion. When there is going to be extreme backspin on the ball, he starts from way above the height of the ball, ends up way below and may even bring his hand and racket face to a horizontal plane under the ball on the follow-through.

Teacher: Right. Now, regarding the flight characteristics of the underspin shot:

1. As the ball comes towards you in its flight, it is rotating away from you. The top of the ball is going away from you and the bottom of the ball is rotating towards you.

2. Due to the laws of physics, a backspin ball will rise: it tends to "hang" in the air longer. It reminds me of a paper glider: the air currents get under it and make it nose up.

Carol: I made an observation regarding backspin shots. They don't go as fast through the air for the amount of force applied to them.

Teacher: That's true because the spin fights its forward (linear) momentum. The ball is going foward but the ball is rotating backwards.

Carol: You said a backspin ball will rise. Then how come some backspin approach shots come over the net in a downward trajectory?

Teacher: If one chops the ball above net height, one can counter the "rising" action of a chop shot. The lower the ball when one chops it, the more marked will be the tendency for a backspin ball to rise.

Carol: What does backspin do to the bounce off the court?

Teacher: You remember, from our last lesson on topspin, that normally a ball will bounce off the court at the same angle it came into the bounce: the angle of reflection equals the angle of incidence.

Carol: And spin is one factor that can change this. Based upon what I learned, I have figured out that an underspin ball bounces at a greater angle of reflection and has a shorter bounce. It will not travel very far forward before it bounces twice. Also, it slows down on its bounce.

Teacher: Which means you have to get closer to the bounce of a chopped shot or it will bounce twice before you can get to it.

Carol: Yes. It's also the reason backspin is so effective for a drop shot.

Teacher: Let's talk a little more about the rebound. Just like on topspin shots, the amount of rebound on a chop shot depends: on the court surface, the power with which the shot was hit, the amount of backspin on the ball, the linear trajectory of the ball and the height at which the ball crossed the net. The last two are obviously influenced by the height at which the ball was hit. Also, a backspin shot will hug the ground after the bounce, which means it will tend to bounce lower than expected.*

Carol: I hope I don't have to do all that thinking everytime my opponent hits a ball.

Teacher: Of course not. I'm just giving you background information here. You will learn by trial and error, on an unconscious level, what kind of bounce to expect.

Carol: Thank goodness! Since topspin rebounds off my racket *up*, backspin must rebound *down*.

Teacher: Correct. Always allow for

---

*While physical laws (angle of reflection, magnus effect, etc.) point to the fact that an underspin ball will bounce to a greater height than a topspin shot, the practical result (at least on concrete courts) is that most backspin shots will rebound much lower than a student expects.

the down action of an underspin shot.

Carol: That is what I neglected to do in my last match. She chopped shots to me at net. As I volleyed, the ball went down into the net. I should have aimed my returns higher.

Teacher: True. Also, move in on it. Remember the ball is probably rising. Catch it at a point higher than the net, if possible, and hit it with moderate chop. This brings to mind another point. You can reduce the effectiveness of your opponent's spin by waiting, and this idea of postponing your hit works extremely well on an underspin shot. A chop shot has its greatest spin in the air. When it bounces, its rotary action is greatly reduced. That's why the ball slows on its bounce. And if you can wait until after the ball has reached its peak after the bounce, its spin is usually negligible.

Carol: So what you are saying is that a chopped ball is most difficult to return in the air on a volley.

Teacher: Correct. Hold your racket firmly and volley with force. That also counters the effect of the underspin.

Carol: How would I return a chopped shot that bounces?

Teacher: Consider waiting until the spin is off the ball and then drive it back. If you have decided not to wait until its spin is reduced, return it with topspin also, but allow for the downward action of the backspin on your racket. In both instances, get closer to the bounce point than normal.

Carol: I shouldn't hit it with too much topspin, though. An opponent's underspin becomes topspin after hitting my racket. If I put too much spin on it, the ball will spin off, probably into the net.

Teacher: Wait until the backspin is off the ball, then chip it back. If there is still some backspin left on the shot when you hit, allow for "down" action and hit it flatter.

Carol: I feel I'm ready to go out and handle the club spin artist. Let's re-cap here:

1. Watch your opponent's swing to anticipate the kind of spin. Underspin is imparted from a sharply downward

and under-the-ball motion.

2. An underspin shot from my opponent rotates away from me as it comes toward me. It tends to rise and "hang" in the air.

3. Upon bouncing, the underspin shot will: (a) rebound at a greater angle, (b) have a slower bounce off the rebound (c) have a shorter bounce and (d) bounce lower than expected.

4. On an underspin shot, the amount of rebound off the court depends upon several factors: (a) the type of court surface, (b) the amount of force applied to the ball, (c) the amount of backspin on the ball, (d) the linear trajectory of the ball and (e) the height at which the ball came over the net.

5. When returning an extreme underspin shot, get closer to the bounce point.

6. An extreme backspin shot will rebound off my racket with a *down* action.

7. Two ways to reduce effectiveness of an opponent's underspin are: (a) hold the racket firmly and stroke with force and (b) wait until the underspin has worn off the shot—until rotary motion has slowed or died.

8. Drive back an opponent's chopped groundstrokes and serves.

9. On high bouncing backspin shots, hit back flat if there is still backspin on the ball. If I wait until the spin is worn off, I can chip it back.

10. When returning chopped shots with a volley, hit my volleys flatter (with less spin) than normal and allow for the *down* action, holding the racket firmly. There is more backspin on a chop before it bounces.

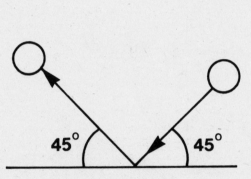

The angle of reflection equals the angle of incidence if there is no spin on the ball.

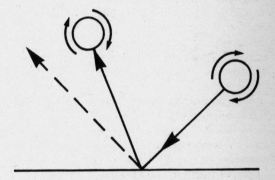

The angle of the rebound increases when there is underspin on the ball.

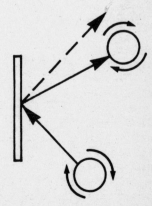

Backspin will rebound off the racket with more "down" than expected, whether the ball comes from above (left) or below (right). Backspin rebounds off the racket as topspin.

Lesson 34—About Those Sidespins

In the past, most tennis players thought of sidespin only in conjunction with groundstrokes. The author points out that what is ordinarily considered a "slice" serve is actually a stroke with sidespin. This is true. However, one must realize that the sidespin or slice SERVE bounces absolutely in the opposite direction from the sidespin GROUNDSTROKE.

Carol: On a service, how will I recognize that the server is going to use sidespin?

Teacher: Let's call that a slice service. And in answer to your question, the server will toss the ball out to his side. The right-handed server will throw his toss farther out to his right side. As you, the receiver, watch, it will be farther to your left. As the server hits the ball, he will curve around the ball, hitting the outside "edge" and following through on his left side.

Carol: It comes back to me from my serving lessons. I remember now. And the slice serve will almost duplicate the server's arm action. As receiver it will curve from my left to my right, and it will bounce to my right. The ball's rotation will be counter-clockwise.

Teacher: Correct. The linear momentum (the curve forward through the air), the rotation of the ball and the rebound off the court all go in the same direction—from left to right, viewed from the receiver's side. (Diagram 1)

Carol: Which way would the ball rebound off my racket?

Teacher: Here is the surprise: when receiving a slice service the ball will rebound off your racket to your left! It won't go to your right as it does off the court. It is the opposite response.

Carol: That is going to be hard to adjust to. That means, in the deuce court, a right-hander's slice service to my forehand tends to come off my racket straight—more "left" than expected. (Diagram 2)

Teacher: Correct. And in the ad court the slice serve into your backhand (or forehand) will also tend to go to your left—which could mean out beyond the sideline. (Diagram 3)

Carol: This is completely different from what I have been thinking. So, when I face a left-hander's slice serve, I have to allow for the pull of the ball to the right.

Teacher: You can sum it up by saying: slice service will come off your racket in the direction opposite to the way it bounces off the court.

Carol: I like that. Now tell me, how do I handle the service if it is a topspin slice?

Teacher: Remember to allow for the "up" action of the topspin as well.

Carol: I understand. When else will a player use a slice shot?*

Teacher: A player can use a slice shot in returning a wide, high ball, since it permits him to hit the outside "edge" of the ball and curve it back into the court. Usually he will follow through low, under the ball; therefore, this shot has some backspin on it as well. The ball will curve through the air (the direction of the curve is de-

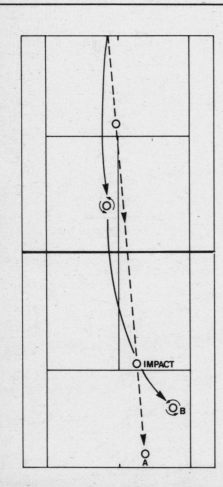

DIAGRAM 1—A right-hander's slice service (B) curves from the receiver's left to the right while rotating in a counter-clockwise direction. When the ball bounces it pulls sharply to the right. The path of a flat service is shown by the line of dashes (A).

*My definition of a slice is a long stroke (from high-to-low) with backspin or sidespin on it. It can also refer to a drive which has sidespin on it. However, to avoid confusion (that is, if you are not already confused), in this article I have referred to the latter type of shot as a "groundstroke with sidespin."

pendent upon whether it is a forehand slice or backhand slice), bounce low (due to the backspin) and to the side.

Carol: So the forehand slice would curve and bounce to my right. And an opponent's backhand slice would curve and bounce to my left. I would also have to allow for the "down" action of the backspin.

Teacher: Right. But remember, if an opponent comes down and under the ball without striking the outside "edge" of the ball, it is a backspin or underspin shot and would behave differently.

Carol: I hope I can learn to do all this on an instinctive basis fairly soon. It gets complicated.

Teacher: It doesn't take many shots to begin to "feel" it.

Carol: I want to go over the groundstrokes that are hit with sidespin.

Teacher: Although a sidespin groundstroke can have topspin, it usually has some amount of backspin. It is a long groundstroke, accomplished in the following manner: as the racket contacts the ball, the arm pulls the racket face across and behind the ball (see Diagram 3), making the ball spin sideways as it travels forward. The follow-through, very often, is on a plane level to the hit.

Carol: Then, if my opponent were hitting me a forehand sidespin shot, his ball would have clockwise spin on it, if viewed from above. And the ball's first flight through the air would curve slightly to my left.

Teacher: Yes. It would bounce and rebound to your left, and it would bounce low because of the backspin.

Carol: And I would have to allow for the rebound action off my racket to the right (Diagram 4) as well as for the "down" action of the backspin, depending upon how much backspin there was.

Teacher: Yes. You just reverse this when returning your opponent's sidespin backhand.

Carol: Let me recap today's lesson, including some information from our previous lessons. I hope we are going to be through with spins soon! It taxes me.

Teacher: Me, too; me, too. On both counts. However, we have yet to cover when we would use what spins. But more on that next week. Let's review the lesson.

Carol: Okay, here goes: 1. Watch the

opponent's stroke to anticipate the kind of spin he is imparting to the ball. (a) On the service, my right-handed opponent is going to slice the serve if he tosses the ball out to his right, thus enabling him to hit the outside "edge" of the ball in a curving motion. The ball will curve towards my right and bounce to my right. (b) On groundstrokes, my opponent is imparting sidespin to the ball if he "pulls" the stroke across his body. The ball's flight and bounce will be oppo-

site to the direction that his racket pulled across his body.

2. When preparing to return a sidespin shot, I should make allowance for the fact that the ball will bounce to the side.

3. A slice or sidespin shot will rebound off my racket in the opposite direction that it bounded off the court.

4. To counter the effect of the spin, I should hold my racket firmly and stroke with force. I can also wait until some of the spin is off the ball.

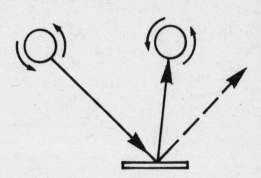

DIAGRAM 2—As viewed from above, a right-hander's slice service to the deuce court will tend to come off the racket more "left" than expected. Dashes show the angle of rebound of a flat serve.

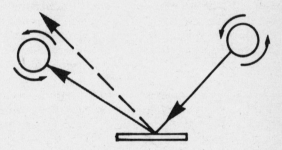

DIAGRAM 3—Also viewed from above, a right-hander's slice serve to the ad court will tend to shoot off the racket with more "left" than expected...thus going out of court. Dashes show rebound of flat serve.

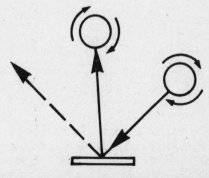

DIAGRAM 4—From above, a right-hander's forehand sidespin down-the-line shot will rebound off the racket more to the "right" than expected. The rebound is in the direction opposite to its bounce.

Lesson 35—Carol Learns When to Use Topspin

Carol: I have had it with spins. Can we go to something else this week?

Teacher: Not yet. There is a logical conclusion: when to use what spin.

Carol: That sounds helpful. When would I use topspin?

Teacher: That's a short question with a long answer. First, I would like you to review the characteristics and advantages of topspin.

Carol: Topspin is the spin that enables you to hit the ball hard and still have it land in. It is attacking and forcing. Topspin has a large margin of safety since it has a rather high trajectory over the net and, once it has reached its apex, it descends rapidly. In brief, it has speed, control and safety.

Teacher: So, it is useful for hitting the ball hard…

Carol: And for hitting the ball deep to the baseline.

Teacher: Generally speaking, use topspin on groundstrokes for depth, power, to keep errors to a minimum and to keep your opponent away from the net.

Carol: It can be helpful on a service return, particularly when the opponent has hit a serve which gives me time to take a backswing.

Teacher: Right, although it is difficult to execute on a fast service.

What about using topspin on approach shots?

Carol: Yes, that would be good. Topspin would enable me to hit the ball deep and hard; topspin wouldn't give my opponent time to get set for the shot.

Teacher: And it wouldn't give you much time either.

Carol: I would make allowances for that by running faster or coming up on the opponent's shorter balls.

Teacher: How about using topspin on the volley?

Carol: That's a trick question. There is no way to use topspin on net shots. There isn't time to take a backswing. I would meet the ball late, my shots would be wild and I wouldn't be able to return low volleys.

Teacher: We agree—no topspin on volleys. What if your opponent is at net? What would you use?

Carol: That is the perfect time to use topspin—as a passing shot. Topspin has speed and topspin descends so my drive will drop quickly after it has crossed the net, forcing my opponent to hit up.

Teacher: Good. Even if you can't pass the net man cold, you can force him to reach for the ball and/or hit it below the height of the net, both of which put him on the defensive.

Carol: If he is in mid-court, I could hit the ball at his feet, using my topspin.

Teacher: Yes. You don't always have to blast the ball. Play the topspin gently. Get him to hit up to you. Slug it when he gives you a high one. What if you decide not to pass him but to lob?

Carol: If I want to surprise him, not giving him enough time to get to the ball, then I should quick-lob him, using topspin.

Teacher: Even if he should run the ball down after it bounces, the topspin on the ball makes it difficult to hit since it will rebound quickly.

Carol: I'm going to use that quick-lob more often. There's still another time to use topspin—when returning low, short balls. By putting topspin on the ball, I will be able to get the ball over the net and still keep it in the court.

Teacher: Absolutely. Remember, anytime you want to attack and hit powerfully off a groundstroke, and when you want safety as well, use topspin.

Carol: That is SAD.

Teacher: Sad? What do you mean?

Carol: Yes, for Safety, Attack and Depth, use topspin.

Teacher: Enough! The lesson is over. Now I think I have had it with spins.

Lesson 36—Let's Talk About Backspin

Carol: I spent all of last week hitting topspin shots in all possible situations. Now I want to work on backspin shots and when to use them.

Teacher: Aren't you tired of spins?

Carol: I now know how useful they can be. I would like to know when to use backspin.

Teacher: Let's start by discussing net play. Would you use backspin on volleys? If so, why?

Carol: Yes. In the first place, I want

spin on my volleys because spin is control. Second, backspin makes the ball skid when it hits the ground and it enables me to volley back the low balls with safety. Third, I can impart backspin to my volleys with minimum backswing, which means I can still meet the ball in front of me. However, the higher the volley, the flatter I would hit it and, conversely, the lower the ball, the more underspin I would apply.

Teacher: You understand it. Since your volley would tend to skid and stay low, your opponent would be in the position of having to hit up to you, which is just what you want him to do.

Carol: So I can pounce and kill it!

Teacher: Now that we have covered the net situation, move back in the court. What would you do when returning a low, short ball—not the easy one, but the desperation, dive-for-it-before-it-bounces-twice shot?

Carol: I would hack at it—chop it. That's another situation where I would find the backspin useful. By coming down and under the ball with an open racket face, I can lift the ball up and over the net; granted it is not a forcing shot, but it is a save.

Teacher: And then, please, go to net behind it, because you are already close to the net. To stay at mid-court or to back up would be suicide.

Carol: This shot is also useful for drop shots since it stops cold after it bounces on the other side—if I get under the ball enough and put enough backspin on it, it will arch high over the net and then drop like a hair-pin just beyond the net.

Teacher: The drop shot is very effective, used properly. However, you can take the same ball from which you would drop shot and turn it into an approach shot, except you would hit the ball harder and deeper.

Carol: Hmmm. I can use backspins as approach shots?

Teacher: Yes. Backspin is effective as an approach shot since the spin makes the shot "drag," giving you time to get up to the net.

Carol: But doesn't it also give my opponent time to get to the ball?

Teacher: Yes, and that is one of its disadvantages. But this shot will bounce low and skid, forcing your opponent to hit up, once again, as on the volley returns. You do have to consider the options. Is it more important for you to have the time to get up to net? Will the time help him more than you? Does he have good passing shots? There is no clear answer here, just

intelligent choices

Carol: I can see it now. I'll be out there on the court with my slide rule, calculating the elements.

Teacher: What is another time to use backspin?

Carol: On the service return, using my chip shot. That works well. All I do, basically, is block the fast serves and just pull under the ball enough to give the ball backspin for control. And my opponent groans because I've used her speed to my advantage.

Teacher: Great!

Carol: I've also observed that it is much easier to return high balls to my backhand by pulling under them and applying backspin than by trying to drive them back. It takes work to learn to turn them into aggressive shots.

Teacher: True. Going from there, it is easy to see that when the ball gets behind you in the backcourt, it's preferable to lob it back with backspin; you need only come down under the ball. That's what we call the defensive lob.

Carol: I have found I do it more or less naturally.

Teacher: You mean you do it easily or not easily?

Carol: I do it unconsciously.

Teacher: There's another time to use chop—on regular backhand groundstrokes.

Carol: What? And give up my topspin backhand?

Teacher: Hold on a minute. There's nothing wrong with a chop backhand. It's easier to hit, requires less effort and gives you time, as we mentioned, to get up to the net or to get back to the

center. It's great when you are tired.

Carol: But it's not an attacking, forcing shot. It's basically a defensive shot.

Teacher: True. That's why it isn't good as a passing shot when your opponent is at net.

Carol: I know; the shot rises and gives the opponent a chance to get to the ball. It also gives her time to get to the ball since backspin doesn't carry a lot of speed.

Teacher: And chop does not have good margin over the net, so it is not the way to keep your opponent back.

Carol: What you are telling me is that I need both kinds of spin in my repertoire.

Teacher: Right. You have caught on. A well-rounded player needs different shots for different situations, and that includes different spins. Let me mention here that one very good use for spins is wrecking your opponent's timing by mixing up the spins you use.

Carol: Where does that leave the sidespin shot?

Teacher: As far as I am concerned the sidespin is only effective on a down-the-line shot since it pulls the opponent off the court. It has to be hit with power or you don't get the angled bounce.

Carol: I have a lot of thinking to do to assimilate all about spins.

Teacher: What, no acronym today?

Carol: Are you kidding? It's all I can do to remember that you can use backspin on: 1. service returns, 2. volleys, 3. approach shots, 4. high backhands, 5. drop shots, 6. lobs and 7. low shots.

Lesson 37—Don't Be Half-Baked on Half-Volleys

Carol: I would like to work on my half-volley today. I have never understood why it is called a half-volley. It is a misnomer since it isn't half a volley at all.

Teacher: I agree. It is a shot hit right off the bounce, before the ball has risen to its peak. It's really a half-drive off a ball that has bounced at or near your feet.

Carol: Can you execute a half-volley from all parts of the court?

Teacher: Yes, but it is usually hit from inside the service line. Consider the implications of this shot if the ball has bounced near your feet.

Carol: I would be connecting with the ball on the rise. Is my assumption correct that I want to meet the ball in my usual hitting zone, a little bit in front of me?

Teacher: Yes. You never want to let a ball get behind you. Try to meet all shots in the same hitting zone.

Granted, some balls will be high, some medium and some low, but you should be hitting all of them about the same distance in front and out to the side. That being the case, then how high would the ball be when you hit it?

Carol: The ball will be low when I'm hitting a half-volley.

Teacher: Even if the ball came over high, like a lob?

Carol: Yes, because I am hitting it right off the bounce, before the ball has time to travel up in height.

Teacher: So this is a low shot which means what?

Carol: That I should return it like a short, low ball. Get low, swing low, stay low. But there is a difference in the timing.

Teacher: Yes. It is difficult to hit the ball on the rise, and that is the case with this shot. The ball isn't sitting there, at the peak, as on a normal shot.

Carol: What is the answer?

Teacher: Start your forward swing as the ball *starts* to bounce. On a half-volley you do not wait until the ball has come up from the bounce and is at the peak before you swing.

Carol: That means I should have a very short backswing.

Teacher: Right. And what else?

Carol: A very low backswing be-cause the ball is going to be low.

Teacher: And?

Carol: The follow-through will be short.

Teacher: Right. The closer to the net, the shorter the follow-through. And?

Carol: I should be stroking this shot, not chopping it.

Teacher: Right. Let's give you some shots now.

Carol: It's working better, but I still have trouble hitting the ball squarely. Sometimes I swing and miss completely.

Teacher: Are you watching the ball?

Carol: Yes. And watching the ball means: (a.) watch the ball as I hit and (b.) keep my eyes on the spot in the air where the ball and racket met (the contact point) until I finish my follow-through. In other words, I *don't* watch the ball for a split-second after I hit it.

Teacher: Very good.

Carol: If it is so good, why am I missing the ball when I do this on the half-volleys?

Teacher: Are you ready for this? Maybe you had better sit down.

Carol: What are you going to tell me? That I am not supposed to watch the ball on this shot?

Teacher: Right.

Carol: Maybe I'd better sit down. I've spent three years working on watching the ball and it comes to this.

Teacher: The mark of a mature mind is the ability to assimilate contradictions.

Carol: If I am not supposed to watch the ball, what should I watch?

Teacher: Please remember that this is the exception. It has to do with the fact that the ball is bouncing so close to you and that the whole procedure occurs so rapidly that your eyes cannot move quickly enough from bounce point to contact point with the racket.

Carol: It is coming to me. I am supposed to watch the ground, the bounce point.

Teacher: Yes, but do this only on those shots that bounce at your feet. On all other shots you do watch the ball as you hit it.

Carol: So by watching the bounce point on half-volleys I will get a clean hit and it will keep me from popping up as well. It makes sense. Let me hit some more shots now. Hey, I am beginning to get the feel!

Teacher: You are ready to sum up the lesson now.

Carol: Finally! Don't think this lesson has been easy.

1. Get low, swing low, stay low.
2. Short backswing, short forward swing.
3. Start forward swing as ball starts to bounce.
4. Watch the bounce spot on the ground, not the ball. A half-volley is the exception to the rule.

Teacher: I will see you next week—when you are no longer stunned.

Depending on where you are in relation to where the ball bounces, you will hit the ball at one of points B, C, D or E. When hitting a half-volley, remember to watch the bounce point (A) in order to get a clean hit and to keep from popping the ball up.

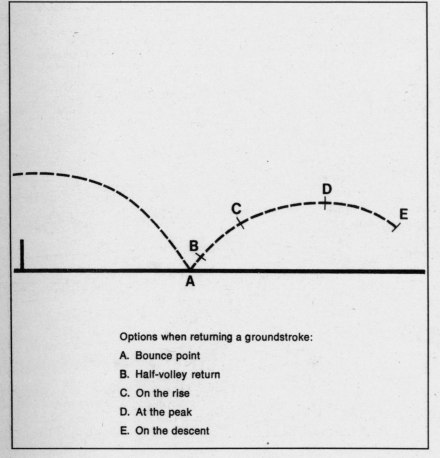

Options when returning a groundstroke:

A. Bounce point

B. Half-volley return

C. On the rise

D. At the peak

E. On the descent

Lesson 38—A Two-Handed Backhand

Carol: I almost didn't come today because my elbow is killing me.

Teacher: It's only been a week since I've seen you. What did you do?

Carol: I've been working hard on my backhand. Evidently I am doing something wrong.

Teacher: Let me watch you hit. Wow, I'll say you've been doing something wrong. Ouch! It pains me just to watch you.

Carol: What am I doing? It hurts so much I can hardly hold the racket.

Teacher: First, you might want to see your doctor so that we can rule out the possibility of serious injury to that elbow.

Carol: Good idea.

Teacher: Now for the backhand. Everytime you hit the ball, you are snapping your elbow straight. That's like doing a judo hold on yourself with every shot.

Carol: Teach me to stop.

Teacher: You'll have to wait until that arm isn't so sore and tender.

Carol: Does that mean I have to quit playing?

Teacher: No.

Carol: Run around my backhand?

Teacher: No.

Carol: Hit a left-handed forehand?

Teacher: In a sense.

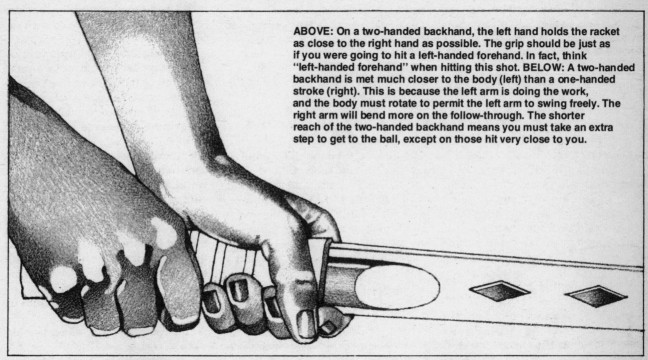

ABOVE: On a two-handed backhand, the left hand holds the racket as close to the right hand as possible. The grip should be just as if you were going to hit a left-handed forehand. In fact, think "left-handed forehand" when hitting this shot. BELOW: A two-handed backhand is met much closer to the body (left) than a one-handed stroke (right). This is because the left arm is doing the work, and the body must rotate to permit the left arm to swing freely. The right arm will bend more on the follow-through. The shorter reach of the two-handed backhand means you must take an extra step to get to the ball, except on those hit very close to you.

Carol: You mean a two-handed backhand?

Teacher: Right. You can leave the lesson today hitting acceptable shots with a two-handed backhand.

Carol: I don't believe it. You're advocating a two-handed backhand?

Teacher: Not exactly. I prefer the one-handed backhand, but in a case like yours, it is the expedient thing to do. I'm not a purist. The reason I want you to try it is it will take the strain off that poor, sore right arm, letting it heal while you still enjoy your tennis.

Carol: Let's get to work.

Teacher: In your ready position, hold your left hand in a left-handed forehand grip as close to your right hand as possible.

Carol: What grip should my right hand have?

Teacher: The forehand. When you see it is a forehand, you release your left hand when you pivot. When you see it is a backhand, you let your left hand pull the racket back. It is optional if you want to change the right hand to the backhand grip.

Carol: I'm going to hit this backhand shot with a forehand grip?

Teacher: Let me tell you a secret about this shot: you are not really going to be hitting a backhand; you'll be hitting a left-handed forehand. You've got to think forehand or you won't hit the shot well. Keep your right hand loose and the right arm very relaxed so there is no tension or strain on it. The right arm is coming along for the ride; it is assisting your left arm by giving it a little added strength.

Carol: Hit me some. Oh, I missed that completely! It was farther away than I thought. Hit me another. I've got to connect with the ball much closer to me.

Teacher: Right. You have less reach in all directions when you have two hands on the racket. You cannot reach as high, as low, as far in front or as far to the side.

Carol: Something is becoming clear to me. The disadvantage of the two-handed backhand is the lack of reach.

Teacher: I'll take that one more step and say that you have to go one step farther on all backhands that you hit two-handed, except for balls close to you. On a one-handed backhand where you would take one step to reach the ball, you will now have to take two.

Carol: It's a good thing I've been jumping rope and staying in shape.

Teacher: There are advantages to this shot. You get a lot of power and more accuracy. At least I did.

Carol: You used to hit a two-handed backhand? Why?

Teacher: I used it temporarily for the same reason as you but a different cause.

Carol: That makes me feel better. At least you understand what I'm going through.

Teacher: I'm going to hit a few to you. Remember, keep a loose right arm and think "left hand."

Carol: I feel the power. This is amazing. But why are they sailing out?

Teacher: You're taking the racket head back too high. Let it get down level with your hands and under the height at which you are going to hit the ball.

Carol: You mean the low-to-high swing. Ah, much better.

Teacher: Follow through with both hands about chin high, the racket head about head high, your left arm almost straight and the right arm bent. Remember, we are keeping that right arm loose.

Carol: That puts some nice topspin on the ball. These shots feel good now.

Ooops. That one went wild.

Teacher: Remember your basics: watch the ball, keep your balance, stay with the ball.

Carol: Stay with the ball?

Teacher: Yes, don't change your plane (your level) while you swing. It also means to follow through, keeping the ball on your strings.

Carol: It all comes back to me. Don't pop up while I hit, watch the contact point, follow through. I'm going to like this shot. It's taking me a little while to adjust to my new hitting zone. It really blows my mind that this shot is really a left-handed forehand.

Teacher: Let's sum up the lesson. A good interim shot for a person with a sore elbow is the two-handed backhand. Remember:

(1) Waiting position...grip racket with both hands together, left hand in forehand grip and right hand in forehand grip.

(2) Think left-handed forehand.

(3) Get racket back low, right hand can change to backhand grip if desired and swing low-to-high.

(4) Right arm l-o-o-o-s-e during entire swing and bent on follow through.

(5) Get one step closer to the ball than on a one-handed backhand.

(6) Get rid of the extra ball or put it in a pocket.

Carol: What do you mean by that last tip?

Teacher: You no longer have a free left hand, so how can you hold that second service ball after you have served?

Carol: I understand. You forgot to mention that under the "disadvantage" list.

Teacher: Right.

Carol: I'm so glad that I can still play tennis while I'm recuperating. And to think I didn't want to come for my lesson today.

Lesson 39—An Introduction to Doubles

Carol: I've concentrated almost totally on singles. Now I want to learn all about doubles strategy.

Teacher: Doubles is a different game from singles. Don't think it is singles with four people. In singles, the court is 27 feet wide; in doubles, the court is 36 feet wide, only nine feet wider, thereby giving each partner only 18 feet of court to cover, which is nine feet less than a player has to protect in singles. Does this give you some hint as to why you have to consider a different strategy for doubles than singles?

Carol: I never thought of it that way before. Neither partner has to move very far to run down the ball. It would be comparable to playing singles on a court only 18 feet wide. Now I understand why I have had so much difficulty slugging the ball by my doubles opponents.

Teacher: Then what is your conclusion on strategy?

Carol: That you aren't going to win in doubles by speed and power. You are going to need finesse, patience and smarts.

Teacher: All of which you have in abundance.

Carol: I must or I wouldn't be coming to you for lessons.

Teacher: And you are going to need a net game. Good doubles is won at the net. Only when you are on top of the ball are you close enough to your opponents to hit it past them, either with power or with angles. Only by being on top of the ball can you neutralize the disadvantage of one person having only 18 feet to cover; then they don't have time to run down the ball. There is another way to win in doubles and that is through your opponents' errors. They will make many more errors if you play the net and put the pressure on them.

Carol: I get the message. Is it the net man's job to cover the short balls while the backcourt man handles the deep shots?

Teacher: No. The basic approach is to divide the court in half the long way, which means that one person covers the left half of the court while the other one protects the right half. However, at times the backcourt man will cross out of his territory to retrieve a shot his partner at net couldn't reach (i.e. a lob), and at other times the net man will poach, going out of his territory.

Carol: Can we get into the actual play now?

Teacher: Not yet. We have to go over the four positions and their roles. Each player has important things to remember, and they vary depending upon the position he is playing.

Carol: Let's start with the server. What should he concentrate on?

Teacher: His job is to get his first service in. If he can do that consistently, his second priority is to place the

service to the opponent's weaker side, which is generally the backhand. That being the case, look at Diagram C and tell me where the server should position himself in the deuce court?

Carol: The obvious answer is S-1.

Teacher: But then he wouldn't be prepared to return the next shot.

Carol: Why?

Teacher: The server has to protect the wide corner since, other than a lob, a crosscourt is the only shot the receiver can hit that will keep the ball away from the net man. If the return goes straight, the server's partner (the net man) will hit it. The crosscourt shot is the one the server has to cover and it will bounce wide, on an angle, since it came from an angle. (Diagram D)

Carol: Back to Diagram C. S-1 has a disadvantage. If the server stands at S-3, he does not have a good chance of getting his service in to their backhand regularly (the angle is too small). So that leaves S-2 as the place to serve from in the deuce court.

Teacher: Right. The answer is not a cut and dried one. S-2 is a good compromise between accuracy to their backhand and protecting against the return. But you have to know your opponent and make adjustments accord-

ingly. Another advantage of S-2 is that it puts you in a good position to serve and rush net. It's the shortest distance to the service line, which is the first volley position.

Carol: Regarding the ad court, I can see that S-6 is the most advantageous. I not only have the best angle to the receiver's backhand but I am also in the best position for the return.

Teacher: That is true except when you want to run to net. S-6 is the spot to serve in the ad court. Again you have to make adjustments based upon your opponent. If you were going to serve and run up, you would serve from S-5

Carol: Okay, I have it. Tell me the role of the receiver.

Teacher: His object is to return the ball away from the net man. Doubles is won at the net and lost on errors. Errors are defined here as: (a) any shot that lands in the net or goes out, and (b) a shot that sets up for the opponents. Hitting to a net man is a setup for your opponents, which means an error for you.

Carol: What about a lob or passing shot?

Teacher: Briefly, since I want to save discussion of those shots for another lesson, those shots fall in the

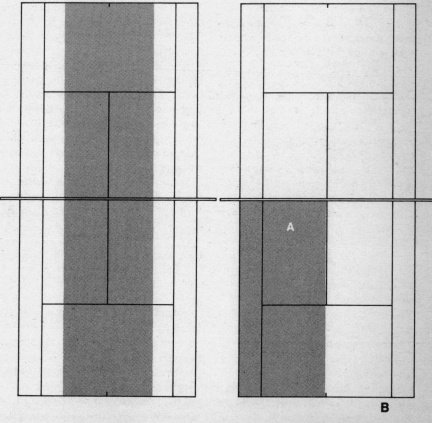

DIAGRAM A: The shaded portion of the court shows the width of court a doubles player has to cover as opposed to the amount of court a singles player must cover—18 feet vs. 27 feet.

DIAGRAM B: Partner A is responsible for shaded half of the court while B protects the other side.

DIAGRAM A

DIAGRAM B

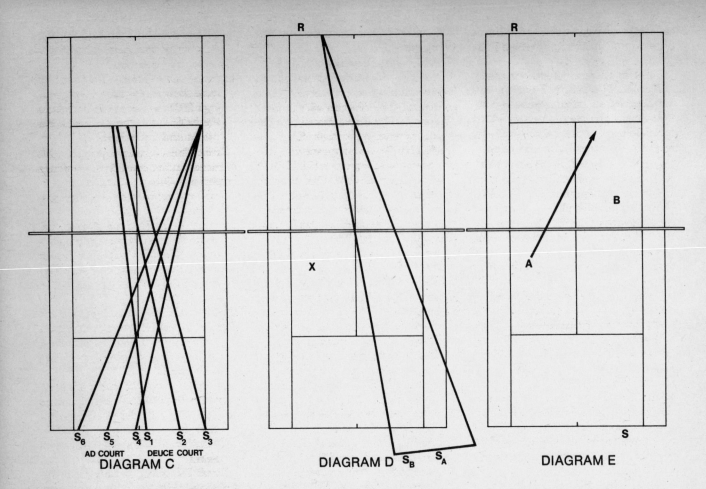

S₆   S₅   S₄ S₁   S₂   S₃
AD COURT   DEUCE COURT
DIAGRAM C

DIAGRAM D S_B   S_A

DIAGRAM E

DIAGRAM C: Lines indicate the advantages and drawbacks of serving from the different positions.

DIAGRAM D: After serving, the server places himself in the "center of possible returns." On this service it will be near S-a; if the opponent lobs down-the-line frequently and the server has to run that shot down, his center would be closer to S-b. Calculate opponents' oft-used shots into the "center of possible returns."

DIAGRAM E: Server's partner, A, tries to cut off the service return (or any shot from R) and volley it for a winner into the gap.

category of "hitting it away from the net man." The passing shot is a low percentage shot and should be used judiciously. Too often it just becomes a setup for the net man and therefore your error. For purposes of today's lesson, let's keep the message very simple—return service with a crosscourt.

Carol: I get it. I can see another advantage of the crosscourt return. It is traveling over the lowest part of the net, which will reduce errors.

Teacher: True. Remember the crosscourt return is the receiver's bread and butter shot. Now let me ask you where the receiver should position himself.

Carol: Basically, he would stand near the corner on either service court and as close to the baseline as possible. He would adjust his receiving position based upon what the server is doing. If I were the receiver, and the server hit to my backhand too often, or if I were making poor returns off my backhand, I would move over to my left. And the converse is true. If I were missing points because of wide serves to my forehand, I would move to my right. If I found I needed more time, I would back up.

Teacher: Don't forget about moving up and waiting for the service inside the baseline if the opponent has a poopy serve. Most people ease up on second service, so take at least a couple of steps in when a first serve is missed.

Carol: After I receive, I am going to recover.

Teacher: For now, recover in a comparable position to where the server recovers. (Diagram D) This will be protecting the crosscourt side and about 3 to 4 feet behind the baseline.

Carol: In other words, in the "center of possible returns."

Teacher: Again, play your opponent. If he tends to give you only short balls, play up closer. Generally you want to stay out of no-man's-land, that area between the baseline and the service line.

Carol: Where should the server's partner stand?

Teacher: I can give you some guidelines, but you must use some common sense on the spot. Try to be as near as possible to the net and to the center service line without losing too many points. I recommend 7 to 9 feet from the net and 7 to 9 feet from the doubles sideline to start with. You learn later where and when to move. For the present, if you find yourself volleying from below the net height a lot, you are too far back. If you anticipate a short return, move closer to the net. If the opposing team charges net, fade back a little to leave more room between you and them. At the present time, stick to 7 to 9 feet from net and doubles sideline and you won't go wrong.

Carol: What is the aim of the server's partner?

Teacher: His goal is to see if he can

cut off the service return and volley it for a winner in the gap between the players. (Diagram E)

Carol: Is there a defense for that?

Teacher: Not really. Later on you will find out about an advanced position for the receiver's partner which will help some. The error lies with the receiver in setting up the net man.

Carol: You mentioned the receiver's partner. Where should he stand?

Teacher: A beginning player and a beginning doubles player, when he is the receiver's partner, should stand in the 7 to 9 feet spot from net and doubles sideline. Then he is at net, ready to take advantage of any balls which come close.

Carol: I assume his goal is to grab a shot and zap it in an open area between his doubles opponents.

Teacher: Right on. Now that we have covered all four positions and the role of each, let me give you a stylized routine I want you to work on this week. In doubles there are several good plays to use, and they all start off with playing it safe. Remember if you get the ball back over the net, your opponents have one more chance to miss it.

Carol: You mean if I learn these routines, I will play good doubles?

Teacher: If you learn and execute them, yes.

Carol: This is exciting.

Teacher: Complicated as today's lesson sounded, we kept it simple by reducing the options of the four players and by concentrating on the most common, basic shots that occur in doubles. We are not permitting lobs or down-the-alley shots for now. If, this week, when playing doubles, these or other shots not covered do come up, don't worry about them because we will introduce them as you improve.

Carol: How do you want me to practice this week?

Teacher: I want you to be specific and stick to this play pattern at each position:

(1) Server—Get your first service in, preferably to the opponent's backhand, then recover behind the baseline and towards the corner. Return all balls crosscourt away from the net man.

(2) Receiver—Keep the ball away from the net man. Return the service (and all balls) crosscourt and recover behind the baseline and towards the corner.

(3) Server's Partner—Watch the receiver, not the server. Try to inter-

cept some shots and go for the winner in the gap between receiver and net man.

(4) Receiver's Partner—Try to cut off some shots and go for winning volleys. If the server's partner gets to the ball, watch the ball leave his racket and try to block it.

Carol: This is going to require a lot of concentration, but I have a definite pattern to follow.

Teacher: Let me mention a few general items.

(1) Don't keep score when you practice this week. Play several points in a row from the same position so you can easily get the hang of it.

(2) No lobbing and no down-the-line shots this week.

(3) See how many times you can hit the ball over the net without an error. In most doubles matches, the ball doesn't get over the net three times.

(4) A net man should watch his partner only out of the corner of his eye. The partner of the server should not watch him serve. Watch the ball leave the receiver's racket.

Carol: I'm going to be very busy. And I thought doubles was a lazy man's game of singles.

Lesson 40—Serve and Run Up in Doubles

Carol: Last week's doubles lesson was excellent because there was so much information to absorb.

Teacher: I take it you worked on the pattern of play we discussed.

Carol: Yes. The server concentrated on getting his first serve in and to the backhand, and then on returning the other shots crosscourt, away from the opposing net man. The receiver tried to return the service and the other shots crosscourt, away from the net man. The two net men tried to cut off any returns and volley the ball for a winner.

Teacher: What were your observations?

Carol: In the beginning we were making many errors and the points were over after one or two hits. But by the end of the week we were having

some long rallies because we were eliminating our errors and not setting up the opposing team. At that point, because we were doing what we were supposed to, it became a crosscourt rally between the two backcourt men and that, frankly, is rather boring.

Teacher: Today I am going to show you a way of breaking up a backcourt rally. You still are not permitted to lob—not for a while. In this lesson let's concentrate on getting you up to net behind serve and then, if you are the receiver, defending against the server's attack. For every...

Carol: I know, I know: for every offense, there is a good defense.

Teacher: Let's start by having the server run up behind serve. If you are serving from the deuce court, you will place yourself at position S-d (Dia-

gram A). When serving from the ad court, use position S-a. A word to the wise, now that you are adding this routine to your game: don't fall into the trap of standing wide every time you are going to serve and stay back, and then moving towards the center every time you intend to serve and run up.

Carol: I see that. Can I assume that the method for serving and rushing net is the same as for singles?

Teacher: Right, except that you move to the "center of possible returns" for doubles. What do you remember about serving and moving up?

Carol: I'm going to take at least three steps, counting my right foot (because I'm right-handed) as it crosses over into the court as one step, and the last step is my "hopscotch" step, where both feet land on the ground at the same time, on the balls of my feet.

Teacher: If you have time to take four steps, fine. But you have to stop or pause just before your opponent hits so that you can change direction, if need be. Since most people have trouble pausing in time, a good gimmick is to pause when the ball bounces.

Carol: I like that, and even though I might hopscotch a little bit too soon, at least I won't be running when the opponent is swinging.

Teacher: A few other items to mention here: 1. Toss your service ball farther in front. 2. Come in on your first service only; this routine works when the service is strong enough to elicit a weak return. 3. Don't wait to see if the service is good: serve, move up and *then* find out if the serve was in. 4. A spin service will allow you more time to move up; a fast serve comes back too quickly.

Carol: It looks as though I won't make it all the way up to the service line before the opposition hits.

Teacher: No, you probably won't. It is much better if you can, of course. But if not, this is one time you stop (it should always be more of a pause rather than a stop) in no-man's-land while you wait and watch your opponent as he hits. Then you will move in to meet the ball (assuming the opponent hasn't lobbed) somewhere in the service line vicinity. Don't feel that because you have stopped behind the service line you can't move forward to volley the return. If you don't move up, you're dead; your opponents will have a good chance of hitting the ball at your feet, which means you have to hit up.

Carol: And then they can volley down for the winner.

Teacher: Correct. Now where are you going to put your first volley—the mid-court volley?

Carol: I know that answer. I'm going to put it back deep to the receiver since then I am keeping it away from the net man, I am keeping the back court man back, and I am hitting a good percentage shot. I am aiming over the lowest part of the net and into the "fat" part of the court.

Teacher: Good. Go for the angle volleys *only* when you are on top of the net. Or to phrase it differently, only try for the angle when you can see that

part of the court *over* the net, not through it.

Carol: That's certainly specific. After I hit the first volley, do I go all the way up to net?

Teacher: You could. The pros play "both up," in the center of the service box.

Carol: It looks great, but if my partner and I did it we would be lobbed.

Teacher: Aha! That's the disadvantage of "both up." I prefer what I call a "staggered" net position. (See Diagram B) One player is on the service line and the other is close up. The player who is farther back is in a better position to get the deep lobs, yet this formation has the advantage of

presenting two net men to the opponents.

Carol: What if I am on the service line and a short ball comes to me? Should I move up on it or wait until it comes to me?

Teacher: Carol, I'm surprised at you. Of course move up. Get the ball at its highest point—at the peak of its arc—so you can hit down on the ball and make a winner. *Never* take a ball below the height of the net if you can move in and hit it at a spot higher than the net.

Carol: But if I'm up, how can we protect against the lob?

Teacher: I'm answering this question assuming you haven't made the

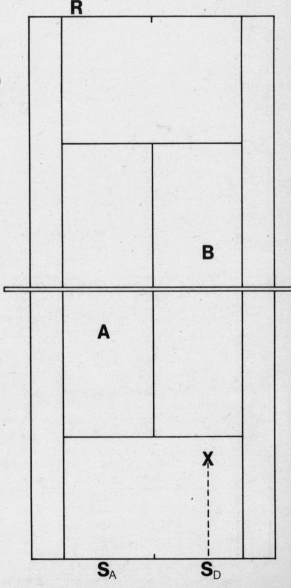

DIAGRAM A
In the deuce court, serve from position S-d, move up to X and split-step; pause and watch the opponent hit, then move up for the first volley. In the ad court, serve from S-a—the path to the net is the same.

winner off that volley. When you move in close to the net, your partner fades back towards the service line. This means your team is in a constant state of flux, shifting up and back, based upon the kinds of shots you have received, where you have to move to get the ball, and the kinds of shots you have hit.

Carol: So if our opponents never lob, we both play close to net.

Teacher: Absolutely. Play your opponents and know their abilities and patterns.

Carol: I'm going to be exhausted if I serve and run up on every point.

Teacher: Don't do it on every point yet. Mix it up. Stay back sometimes.

The two-fold advantage is that you conserve your energy and the opponents don't know what kind of shot to hit.

Carol: How is that?

Teacher: Let's go into the receiver's role and it will become clear. The job of the receiver is what?

Carol: To return the ball away from the net man.

Teacher: What kind of shot should he hit against an incoming server?

Carol: One that lands at his feet or a lob over the net man.

Teacher: Right on both counts. But once again, we are not permitting lobs yet.

Carol: So, for today, the receiver is

going to hit at the net man's feet—a dink return.

Teacher: That's a great return if the server does follow his serve in. But if he stays back, the receiver has sent over a short ball which...

Carol: Which means he has given the server an opportunity to come up to net in another fashion, namely behind a short ball. He will drive and then follow that ball to net. I see what you mean. Staying back is sometimes a smart move for the server. But what is the receiver to do?

Teacher: It is difficult for the receiver. He can't be watching the server to see what he's doing and still watch the ball.

Carol: That's why I get some flub shots. But, if I am the receiver and the server stays back consistently, my best return would be to hit it back deep, which means it goes over the net about five feet high, and this would keep the server away from the net. However, if I do this regularly and the server rushes net, what I have given him is a ball that will be very easy to volley, about shoulder high. How does the receiver handle a server who varies running up and staying back?

Teacher: One tactic is to lob, but we are not going to introduce that for a while. So the answer for the receiver is to know the opponent. Being observant helps—watching to see if he is tossing his ball way in front, noticing if this is his first or second service and remembering if he runs in a lot or seldom.

Carol: Some of those tips are so simple.

Teacher: But often neglected. If the server runs in a lot on his service just aim the shots short, dinky and soft. If he serves and stays back most of the time, return deep. If the server mixes it up, you might hit them all short, on the theory he's going to get up anyway so don't give him a ball to volley. Try moving in on the service and take it on the rise, which gives him less time to run in and leaves him in a bad position from which to hit your return. This could discourage him from running in on his service so frequently. Or you might hit the return harder, which also gives him less time to get set.

Carol: What about trying to make my returns short and wide into the crosscourt doubles alley?

Teacher: Terrific! That's going to make him stretch wide for the ball,

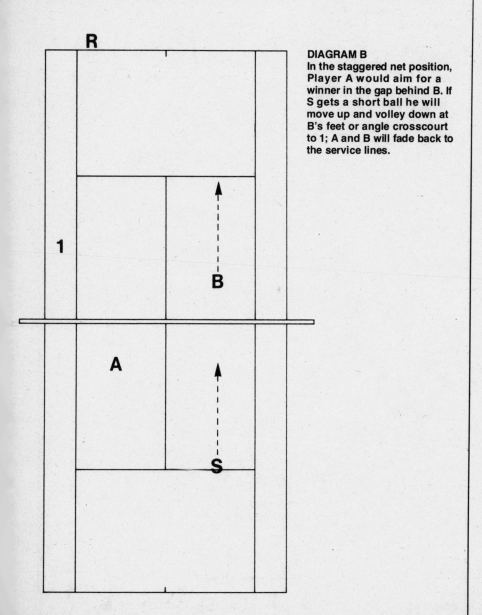

DIAGRAM B
In the staggered net position, Player A would aim for a winner in the gap behind B. If S gets a short ball he will move up and volley down at B's feet or angle crosscourt to 1; A and B will fade back to the service lines.

which means he's going to have to hit more to your partner at the net.* A great ploy to use when you have the opportunity. Remember, it will require working on your crosscourt returns.

Carol: What is the planned practice

for this week?

Teacher: Still no lobbing and no down-the-line returns. Concentrate on these items:

1. Server will come to net, either behind his service or off a short ball. He will concentrate on getting his first service in, to the backhand. His returns, whether they be volleys or drives, go crosscourt, deep and away from the opposing net man.
2. Receiver hits the ball away from

the opposing net man and aims at the feet of the incoming server, or wide and short. If the receiver can anticipate the server staying back, he will return deep crosscourt.

3. Server's partner tries to intercept a shot and go for the winning volley.
4. Receiver's partner also tries to intercept a shot and put it away. (His home position, for the present, is up, close to the net.)

---

*When you meet the ball wide, you must connect with it farther behind you. It is difficult to hit such a shot crosscourt. Therefore the odds are that the ball will go down-the-line.

Lesson 41—Doubles Can Be Complicated

Teacher: How do you like serving and running up to net?

Carol: It was great. I mixed it up with serving, staying back for one shot and then approaching. Both plays

worked very well. It makes doubles much more exciting.

Teacher: I hope that when the server moved in behind his serve he got as far in as possible.

Carol: Absolutely, but I have a question regarding the partner of the receiver. When I played that position, up at net, against a server who ran up, and my partner sent back a semi-high

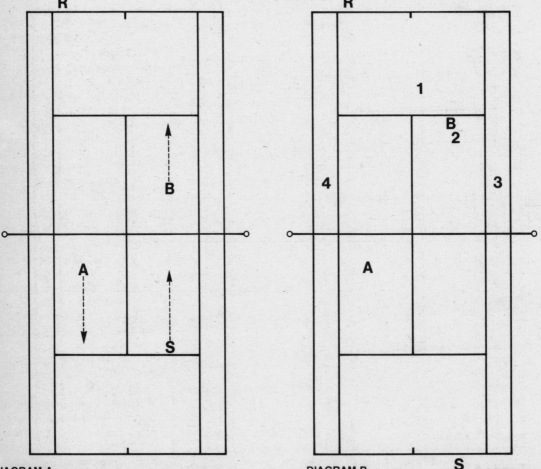

DIAGRAM A
Player B should fade back against an incoming volleyer who has a ball higher than the net. Player A should also shift to maintain the staggered position. This enables Player A to run down any lobs.

DIAGRAM B
By waiting on the service line, Player B reduces the opening available to Player A should R return the ball to A. If A gets the ball his options would be hitting to Points 1, 2, 3 and 4.

crosscourt return, I felt much more comfortable fading back so I wasn't nose-to-nose with him. Is that right?

Teacher: That is perfectly legitimate. If you are too close against his high volley, you won't be able to react quickly enough.* (Diagram A) I think it is time to introduce the more advanced position for the partner of the receiver. He should stand with his heels on the service line. This has the two-fold purpose of 1) putting him in a good position to call the service and 2) helping him cut off the gap should the opposing net man volley the service return. (See Diagram B)

Carol: I can see that. But it is still extremely difficult for Player B to cut off the net man's volley.

Teacher: Oh, this is no guarantee that he *will* return the volley; it just increases his odds a little and puts a little more pressure on the net man to be accurate.

_____

*The close net position is 7-9 feet from the net and 7-9 feet from the doubles sideline.

Carol: I see.

Teacher: The receiver's partner watches the serve and then the service return. He determines if the opposing net man will be able to volley the return. (Diagram C) If Player A is able to get to it, B will stay put and make every effort to block the return. However, if the service return gets by Player A, then Player B will move to his closeup net position before the backcourt man starts to hit the ball.

Carol: What if the server has come in behind his service? Should the partner of the receiver still move in?

Teacher: That's a good question. Player B will have to evaluate the return. If it is a shot which puts the incoming server on the defensive (a ball at his feet, a wide low ball), then the answer is yes. If, on the other hand, the receiver has sent over a semi-high crosscourt ball higher than the net, then Player B better stay put.

Carol: This is going to take quite a bit of time to absorb and master.

Teacher: For purposes of learning,

we are going to have the server stay back today. Otherwise, the partner of the receiver has too much to think about.

Carol: Good.

Teacher: This maneuver is a little rough at first, but it is a very effective play.

Carol: Is there more that I have to concentrate on for today?

Teacher: Yes. The server will serve wide on both courts and stay back; the net man (his partner) moves over toward the sideline to protect against a down-the-line return. (Diagram D) The rule when playing net is "follow the ball" since this will put you in the "Center of Possible Returns."

Carol: Oh. That's why I have been getting passed down-the-line so much.

Teacher: Now you know.

Carol: If the serve does not go wide, I stay where I am. Is that correct?

Teacher: Yes.

Carol: If the service goes wide and I, as partner of the server, have moved over and the receiver has returned it

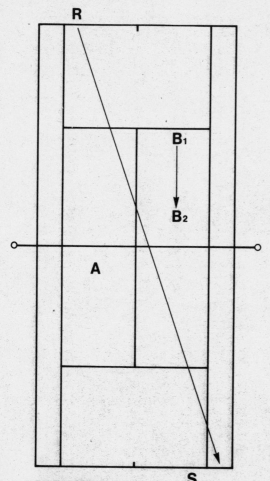

DIAGRAM C
If Receiver R returns the ball past
Player A, Player B will move toward the net.
B will also move up if R lobs
successfully over Player A.

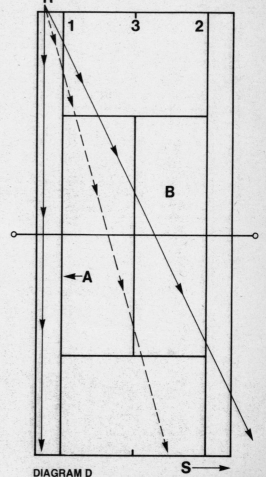

DIAGRAM D
On a wide serve, A moves to the ball to protect
against down-the-line returns. Server S shifts in the
opposite direction. The center shot (broken line),
if it passes A, will reach S as a crosscourt.

crosscourt past me, where do I go then?

Teacher: Return to your "home base" and then wait and watch to see what kind of shot your partner sends over. You "follow the ball" all over again.

Carol: You mean I don't stand still?

Teacher: Poor doubles players do. Good doubles players are continually shifting, modifying their position based upon where the ball is hit.

Carol: That means if my partner returns a ball wide, with her forehand crosscourt to Position 1 (see Diagram D) to the receiver again, I again move toward my alley. If my partner hits to Position 3, I will stay where I am. And if my partner hits the ball to Position 2, I will move a few steps to my right.

Teacher: You've got it. It takes constant re-evaluation.

Carol: As for the partner of the receiver, once he is up at net, obviously he is going through the same constant evaluation process and shifting left or right as the ball dictates.

Teacher: Absolutely. Don't forget the two back men are also going through a shifting process, but instead of "following the ball," they move to the opposite side by a step or two.

Carol: Yes, because an angled ball will move beyond the width of the court after the bounce point, whereas that same shot has to cross the net quite near the center of the net or else it would be out. I remember from the last lesson that the net men also shift forward and back depending on the shots received and hit.

Teacher: Yes, so this shifting process takes place in four directions for the net men—up, back, left and right.

Carol: Regarding the server, how, in the deuce court, can he pull the service wide?

Teacher: Hit the ball more on the right edge of the ball; give it some slice. Try not to stand in a different place or you will telegraph your intent. In addition, try not to toss the ball significantly farther to the right or that will also signal your goal.

Carol: The receiver should still return service crosscourt?

Teacher: Generally, yes, but he may hit one out of 10 shots down-the-line to keep the net man alert and even, perhaps, win a point or two. An occasional down-the-alley shot keeps the net man from too much poaching.

Carol: He goes down-the-line seldom?

Teacher: Yes. It is a low-percentage shot. If the net man gets it, you have lost the point since he will volley for a winner nine times out of 10. Also, the net is at its highest point there. Of course if the net man refuses to cover his alley, then pass him all the time.

Carol: If I am the partner of the server, who should I watch? The server or the receiver?

Teacher: Watch the receiver. See where he moves. This will tell you where to go. If you try to watch the server, you will have to turn your head to follow the ball over the net and you will have difficulty trying to focus on the ball. Try this tip: watch the eyes of the receiver. A lot of times, when the receiver is going to go down-the-line, he will glance there just before the ball is served.

Carol: How else will he know where the alley is?

Teacher: Carol! You know better.

Carol: Just kidding.

Teacher: I'll tell you a secret: the lines haven't moved since they were painted, but the ball does. So the receiver should look at the court as a whole, make up his mind and look only at the ball.

Carol: I knew that all along.

Teacher: We've covered a lot of material for today. Let's review what your play pattern will be this week.

1. Server: Serves wide into both service courts and stays back. Returns most shots crosscourt. Occasionally tries a down-the-line passing shot. Remember to shift to the opposite side of where the ball was hit by your team.

2. Receiver: Generally returns service crosscourt away from the opposing net man. Occasionally goes for the down-the-line shot which is more effective off a wide ball. Like any backcourt man, he shifts to the opposite side of the ball.

3. Server's Partner: "Follows the ball," left or right, up or back, as the ball dictates.

4. Receiver's Partner: Waits on service line. If service return gets by opposing net man, he will move up close to the net. He, too, will shift left or right, up or back, depending on the ball.

Carol: And we are still not lobbing, I assume.

Teacher: No lobs and no rushing net. Let's give the receiver's partner a chance to get used to his advanced move.

Lesson 42—Keys to Doubles Strategy: Play The Odds

Carol: I like the play we worked on last week where the partner of the receiver waits on the service line and then moves up if the ball gets by the opposing net man.

Teacher: It's effective. Moving up puts him in a position to attack with his volleys. If he were to stay on the service line, his volleys would not be winners since he is too far back; the balls would probably be at his feet, preventing him from hitting down. He would be forced to hit up, giving the

opposition a chance to pounce on the ball and kill it.

Carol: Who should receive from which service court?

Teacher: Rather than thinking of who has the best stroke, consider the weakest link. The stronger player should receive in the ad court. Obviously you will have to weigh the factors and make a decision as to which way the team will lose the fewest points through errors vs. winning the most through strong play. When you

only evaluate the strongest stroke, you are giving greater value to winners. Since tennis is 80% errors and 20% winners, you have to give greatest consideration to errors.

Carol: Which is what you have been teaching in our doubles play all along: play the odds, make the high-percentage shots and avoid the moves that lose points.

Teacher: Don't be afraid to experiment. There are always exceptions. Conditions vary with every team you play. If you are losing, change the receiving courts at the end of a set. Look at Diagram A and see how you can protect a stroke weakness. Also, notice where to position yourself if you must play the deuce court with a weak forehand or the ad court with a weak backhand.

Carol: Speaking of the receiver, I have been moving up one or two steps when receiving second serve.

Teacher: Good. The server eases up on his second delivery, so take advantage of it. Put the pressure on him by taking the second serve sooner and giving him less time to prepare for the return.

Carol: Shouldn't the server use spin on most of his serves, even when he is not coming to net?

Teacher: Yes. In doubles you win at net through your opponents' errors. You lose if you make more errors than your opponents. A spin service gives you a large margin for error. It enables you to get the first serve in. Wherever you serve a second ball, you are at a disadvantage. It's going to be an error if you set up the opponents with a weak service. The pressure is on; you must get the service in or you will double-fault. Naturally you will tend to "push" that serve.

Carol: I'm going to keep that in mind. Needing a second service is an error.

Teacher: Obviously you can't get all first serves in, but by utilizing spin you can increase your chances.

Carol: Who says doubles is easy?

Teacher: You are constantly building on what you have learned so far. Today the server will vary serving and rushing net with serving and staying back. He will also mix up his placements.

Carol: How does this affect the receiver?

Teacher: The receiver will not only concentrate on keeping the ball away from the opposing net man, but he will try to hit low to the incoming server's feet. Otherwise, he has made his partner a sitting duck.

Carol: Last week the receiver's partner waited on the service line while the ball was served. He moved up if the return got past the opposing net man. Now he will have to determine whether or not the server is coming in, then move up to the close net position only if his partner has hit a low shot. (See Diagram B.)

Teacher: I am still not permitting

DIAGRAM A
1) In the deuce court, if the receiver has a weak forehand he should shift in and to the right. He stands in to cut off the angle of the wide serve. 2) In the ad court, if the receiver has a weak backhand he moves to the left and in to return service. If he waited behind the baseline he would have to move farther to reach a wide serve. 3) In the ad court, if the receiver has a weak forehand he should position himself more to the right. 4) When playing in the deuce court, a receiver with a weak backhand should move to the left. A late backhand is a good shot from the deuce court because it will go crosscourt, away from the opposing netman.

the lob, but a lob over the net man's head would also be a shot that the receiver's partner could move to net on.

Carol: If the server stays back, the important thing is "Did the return get by the opposing net man?" If the server moves in, the receiver's partner then asks, "Will the shot force the server to hit defensively?"

Teacher: In both cases, if the answer is yes, the partner of the receiver will move in. If the answer is no, he will stay put and try to cut off the return.

Carol: Then, generally anytime the receiver hits a low ball by the net man, it's proper for the receiver's partner to move in.

Teacher: Right.

Carol: What is the program for today? What is our planned practice?

Teacher: The server is going to be quite busy. He is going to provide the element of surprise by mixing up placements. No matter how good the server, if the receiver knows where and how the ball is coming, he can get set for the shot.

1. The server has these options—on deuce court: serve to backhand and come up; serve to backhand and stay back; serve wide to forehand and come up; serve wide to forehand and stay back. On ad court: serve to backhand and come up; serve to backhand and

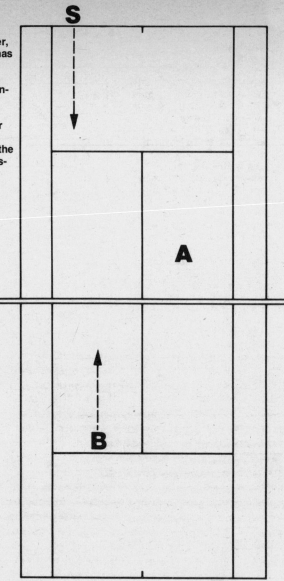

DIAGRAM B
Against an incoming server, B will move up if, first, R has returned the ball past the opposing net man, and second, S is hitting a defensive shot. The two shots meeting these conditions are a low ball or a lob over the net man's head. Reminder: if R had returned the service wide into the crosscourt alley, B would have moved up and to his left (the net man follows the ball).

stay back; serve to forehand and come up; serve to forehand and stay back. Remember to come in behind first service only; stay back on second service. The server should come up to net behind any short ball. He will return drives and volleys crosscourt, away from the opposing net man except when he can go for a down-the-line winner or make a put-away volley. (The put-away volley can be crosscourt.)

2. The receiver returns the ball crosscourt away from the net man. He aims at the incoming server's feet. He goes for the down-the-line passing shot when pulled wide and an opening exists. He moves inside one baseline when returning second serve.

3. The server's partner plays in "home base" net position close to the net. He goes for the winner when he can reach the ball. If the serve or any shot is wide, he will "follow the ball" by moving in that direction to await the return.

4. The receiver's partner waits on the service line. If the ball gets by one opposing net man and if the server either stays back or is hitting from a defensive position, he moves up close to net, hoping to cut off the return with a winning volley

Carol: And no lobbing. All players shift their waiting positions during the play of a point—left, right, up or back—as the ball dictates.

Teacher: Good, I'm glad you mentioned that. Have fun this week.

Lesson 43—Get Up to Net!

Carol: I feel like I'm a walking compendium of doubles. I never knew doubles could involve so much thought. I used to think I could loaf through a set.

Teacher: Not if you are my partner.

Carol: What's the program today?

Teacher: Concentration on "receiving service and moving up." You'll only do it off a serve when you are in charge, not off a serve that puts you on

the defensive.

Carol: Since the service has to bounce short—well within the service line—this will be the same maneuver as coming to net off a short ball.

Teacher: Right. Where is your return going to go?

Carol: If I didn't know that answer by now, I would flunk this doubles course. I'll hit it away from the net man and crosscourt. When will the re-

ceiver be allowed to do something other than the crosscourt or an occasional down-the-line?

Teacher: Next week. If you get impatient with the crosscourt return, you will lose points in doubles. It's the bread-and-butter play in doubles.

Carol: I get the message. The receiver returns crosscourt and if the ball gets by the net man, he runs to the service line and "splitsteps" with a

DIAGRAM A: The receiver (R) returns service crosscourt and if the ball gets by the net man (A), he runs to the service line (R-2) and "split-steps" with a hopscotch motion just as the opponent starts his forward swing. The partner of the receiver (B-1) also moves in, all the way up to the net (B-2). If the return had been more to the left, B and R would have shifted left.

DIAGRAM B: If the server (S) comes up and the receiver (R) comes up, each team holds its position. If S gets a short ball and moves in, A will fade back.

DIAGRAM C: When S gets a short ball, he will move up and A will fade back. B, to avoid getting hit, will also fade back. If S does not make a winner (shame!), then B or R will try to get up close to the net again as soon as possible. If B is an excellent volleyer with fast reflexes, he may elect to hold his ground.

DIAGRAM D: If the B-R team hits the ball down the center, each of them will "follow the ball" and move towards the center. Their moves enable them to cover S-A's best return, while forcing S-A to go for the tougher angle shots.

DIAGRAM E: Hitting the ball wide to S-A splits their team. S moves over to protect the vast expanse of open court. B-R follow the ball to their right, leaving A the difficult crosscourt angle and choking off A's preferred shots, i.e., down the middle or down-the-line.

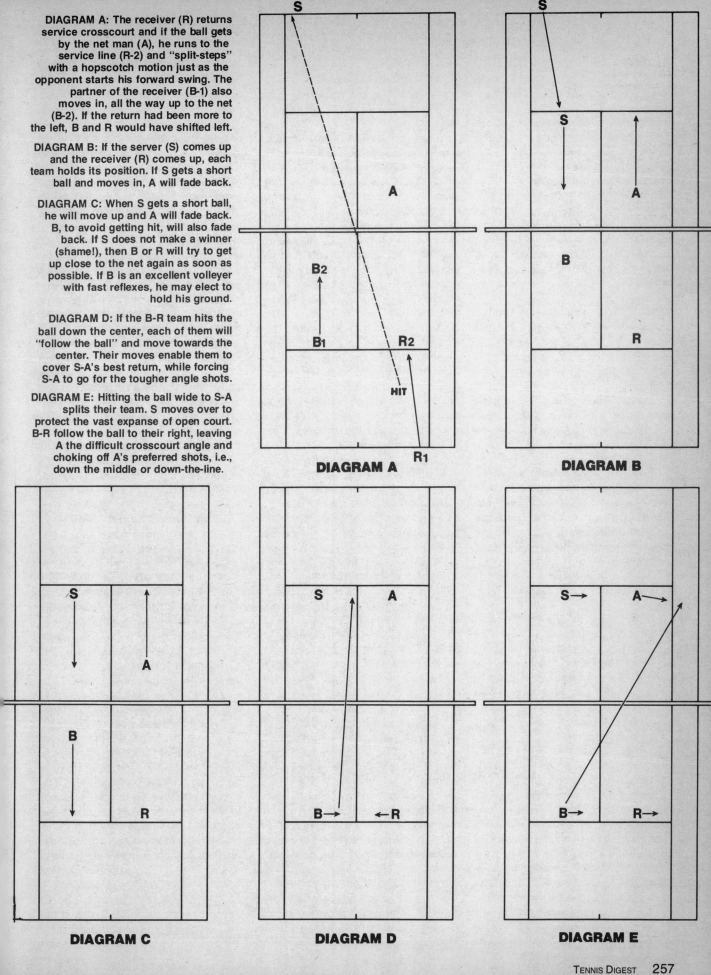

DIAGRAM A

DIAGRAM B

DIAGRAM C

DIAGRAM D

DIAGRAM E

hopscotch motion just as his opponent starts his forward swing.

Teacher: What else is happening simultaneously?

Carol: The partner of the receiver is also moving in, only he is moving all the way to net. (Diagram A.)

Teacher: When the two of you storm the net, it's going to shake up quite a few opponents.

Carol: Aren't we then in a perfect position to be lobbed?

Teacher: Yes, but you have a staggered net position just for that reason, to protect against lobs. The man farther back is responsible for the lob. Additionally, the "splitstep" enables you to change direction. However, there will be no lobbing for one more week.

Carol: I'll also have to remember that we, the net men, are still "following the ball." If one of us volleys to the left, we both shift left; if my partner volleys to the right, we both shift right.

Teacher: But if the receiver does not come in, he will shift to the opposite direction from where the ball went.

Carol: Yes, the good old COPR—Center of Possible Returns. Speaking of "Center," who should take the center balls when both partners are at net? I've heard several theories: the one who can take the ball with his forehand volley should take it; the person closer to the net should take it; and the person who is crosscourt to the ball should take it since the ball is coming towards him, not away from him.

Teacher: All have their merits and drawbacks. The biggest drawback is the time it takes to figure out whose forehand is down the middle or who is closer to the net or who is crosscourt to the ball. I have another suggestion which leads to losing the fewest points on these shots.

Carol: Tell me.

Teacher: The person who hits the last shot should take the center ball.

Carol: Why?

Teacher: That's the person with the momentum. You don't have to stop and figure out who, what and where. That person is already in motion. But there are always going to be exceptions to any rule. Each team will have

to work out what is the best rule. For example, if one partner does not have a put-away volley, the stronger net man will take the middle shots.

Carol: If we, as the receiving team, are at net and the opposing team comes up on a short ball, should we go back?

Teacher: No, hold your ground. (Diagram B.) Hit the ball low to the feet of the back net man. You don't want to hit the ball shoulder-high since they can hit it down for the winner. Get them to hit the ball semi-high to YOU. Remember when you are in your staggered net position, you are not only "following the ball" but you are also going to move in or fade back depending upon the situation. If you are the close net man and your partner moves up for a short ball, you will fade back to the service line to protect for a lob. Of course your partner should make a winner off that volley. If your team hits them a short or low lob and you are the close net man, you will generally move back to increase your chances of returning that ball and to decrease the possibility of your getting hit. (Diagram C.)

Carol: How come we often see four good players all on the service line?

Teacher: Because the action is so fast they need a little more distance for reflex action. Let's talk about the play patterns when all four of you are on the service line. What are you going to do if your team hits the ball down the center of the court?

Carol: Since the net men have to "follow the ball," I think we would both move towards the ball, towards our center. This would close the gap down the middle, leaving them only the angle shots to try for. (Diagram D.)

Teacher: You're getting very knowledgeable. The only time to try for a shot between your opponents—a straight shot down the middle—is when both of your opponents are at net. If one of them is in the backcourt, it's a very risky shot. The net man gets a chance to volley it for a winner, and the backcourt man could always run it down anyway, even if it does get by the net man.

Carol: What is the best play when all four of us are at net, on the service line?

Teacher: Again, there are advantages and disadvantages to the possibilities. If you go for the angles, you are splitting their team, thus giving you an opening down the middle, off their return. (Diagram E.) But if you pull them wide, they then have a better angle against your team. Also, placing low shots wide is difficult. Angled low volleys and half-volleys are tricky, for you and for them.

The second approach is to place the balls down the middle, low, until they give you a shoulder high ball, one higher than the net, that you can then angle for a winner. There are fewer errors when you aim down the middle since the net is lower. Also you don't give them a good angle to shoot for.

The third approach is to play to their stroke weakness rather than to their court position as in the first two plays. You could play the guy with the weak backhand volley or the one who misses the low shots. You have to know your team's abilities and your opponents' and act accordingly.

Generally, I prefer going for low middle shots. What happens is that you use all three of these plans, but in varying degrees, and you mix them up by throwing in a lob at every opportunity. But we'll discuss that next week.

Carol: I'm looking forward to our lobbing day. Now I would like to go over today's lesson.

Teacher: This week's play pattern emphasizes "receive and move up" with lobs forbidden. The points to remember are: 1) move to net behind a good service return. Hit the ball crosscourt. If the serve is strong, wait for the first good opportunity and then move up; 2) the receiver's partner will move to the close net position if the service return gets by the opposing net man; 3) when both partners are at net, the one who hit the last ball should take the center ball; 4) if all players are at net, play on the service line or just inside; 5) when at net, remember to "follow the ball" left or right and to move forward or back as play dictates; 6) when both partners are at net and one has volleyed down the middle, both move towards the center of their court, and 7) aim low, at the net man's feet. ●

Good Afternoon, Folks- Welcome to The U.S. Open Of 2001

by BUD COLLINS

...and now, ladies and gentlemen of the listening audience, Station WREK—always first in bringing you the new, novel, nutty and newsworthy—takes you direct to Death Valley, California, for a revival of the U.S. Open Tennis Championships...on the scene and at the WREK microphone, as ever, is our ace sports director...that irrepressible sports maniac who says, "You don't have to play a sport to appear in court!" ...You know his mellifluous voice so well from his nightly descriptions of the rat races at Rodent Downs in Reno...here he is—Howdy Gosell ...Come in Howdy...

Thanks, Ed, and good afternoon fun-and-games fans, this is old Liberated Lips himself, Howdy Gosell, feeling a little like an archaeologist today because we've dug up a sports event like nothing we've ever broadcast on Radio Station WREK. It's called tennis, folks, and don't turn me off just 'cause you've never heard of it. Could be fun. Looks like fun, and I'll try to call it for you just the way it looks, which is basically people hitting a ball over a net with a racket that's like a kind of shovel. The ball bounces pretty good and there's plenty of running involved. It don't look easy at all, and with the temperature 137 here today, you know these athletes—these men and women—are gonna really test themselves.

I hope you'll agree that any championship of these United States in any kind of sport is worth putting on the air for you folks listening back in Reno and Storey County—even if it's an unknown game like this, which obviously few people are aware of, or play. Could become popular. It was once, which I'll get into in a minute. And WREK, in keeping with its innovative policy in sports coverage—remember that stomach-gripping, cactus-eating tournament we put on the airwaves from Winnemucca last month?—is ready to zoom into your ears with another possible fad: tennis.

One thing you may like about today's program is there's no commercials. Despite the fact we couldn't get any sponsorship for something as new, maybe radical, as this U.S. Open Tennis, Station WREK—dedicated to you listeners—is carrying this show as a public service. Write in and let us know what you think. If you got a business,

and you like what you hear—and you'd be willing to underwrite a few commercials—maybe we can put some more tennis on the air. They tell me this game was once as big as bicycle racing in the 1890s, although for the life of me I don't see how.

But...but...but I'm as willing as the next guy to look at something new, and try to be objective about it. That's my job, and I must admit I had my doubts about the rat races at Rodent Downs before the sport of kinks was fully organized, and we began airing the thrilling competition of our furry four-footed friends. Remember, competition's the thing. That's what makes rat races. Maybe it could make this game of tennis. I don't know.

But let's keep an open mind on it, friends. You might become a tennis player someday yourself, and it might be you'll look back on this historic broadcast as your inspiration. Well, don't blame or praise me. I'm just doing my job for WREK—first with the new, novel, nutty and newsworthy. Today it's tennis. Tomorrow it'll be the first annual Gila Derby at Monster Park in Tonopah. I guess the gila promoters over there think they can rival our rats in Reno by breeding and racing thoroughbred monsters. More power to 'em. The public needs entertainment in these difficult days, so maybe even tennis could serve a need. Anyway—as you know—we'll put anything on the air, and today it's the U.S. Open Championships of 2001.

It's a regular kind of tournament, which was entered by four men in the one event and six women in the other. Now they're down to two finalists, whose names wouldn't mean anything to you—Chrissie Scaggs against Billie Jean Scaggs, and Rodney George Scaggs against Jimmy Scaggs. In fact everybody entered was named Scaggs. They're all cousins and a couple of brothers and sisters from a family over on Mt. Lena, Utah, that apparently preserved this game which is supposed to have started in 1874 and had its high point a hundred years after that. I'm told they learned the game from an old man named Rosewall, who escaped from Australia just before it sank, floated to the West Coast on his wallet and made his way to Utah where, as you know, a lot of the re-settling has gone on. I can't tell you nothing about the contestants or the rules. I'll just have to

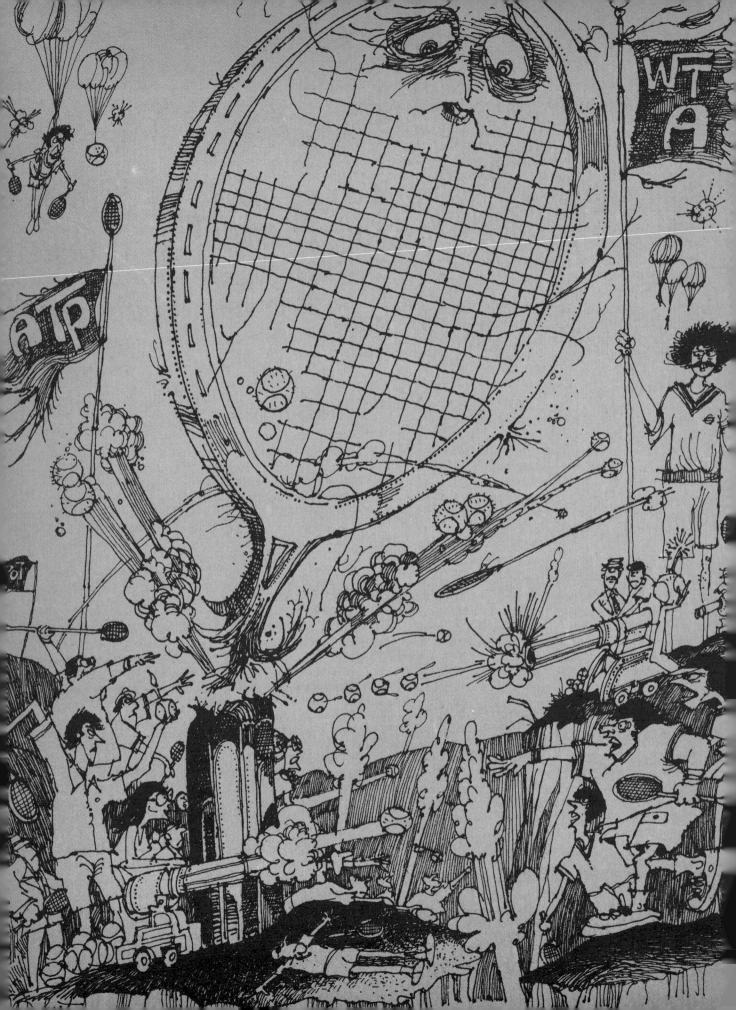

try to tell you how they look and what happens as it goes along, so bear with me, if you will, folks.

But I do have some notes on the background of this game which seems to have started going down the drain in 1975, even though it was allegedly played by millions and seen by millions more on television back when the government permitted television. I don't see how this could have been, but I'm just quoting from the notes given me by historian Jimmy Van Scaggs, the patriarch of this family, and...remember...this period of tennis vogue I'm talking about was back in a time that's hazy to us...back before the Big Daddy Depression of '76...before the Limited Nuclear Wars when our East Coast was farther east than the Mississippi...a few years before the Army elected H. R. Haldeman as Presidential Brother in 1984.

That's real heavy thinking, ain't it—going back so far—for us strontium-warped folks of the present day? But I find delving in the dark past kind of interesting, and I hope I don't bore you with a little history—seeing as how I got to fill the airspace that would usually be devoted to commercials and messages from H. R. Haldeman. Presidential Brother has graciously relinquished his daily air time so we can devote more hours to tennis because, actually, the U.S. Open has been revived to call attention to the government housing projects in this Death Valley resettlement area. The joys of living in these modern 90-story walk-ups haven't yet been transmitted to the general public. But Presidential Brother feels that if this becomes a tennis center, and the game gets a little of what they used to call charisma—well, Death Valley will thrive. The Valley game will be good for everybody. Presidential Brother Haldeman and his associates were tennis players, so the story goes, long ago in Washington, D.C.—when there was a Washington and it was the capital. That was prior to the event we now commemorate with the Feast of the Watergate Persecution, when Presidential Brother went to jail for his beliefs in executive freedom.

That's getting away from sports, though, folks, and your old pal, Howdy Gosell, is here to tell you about tennis, and about this open championship of our country that was last played in 1974 at a place called Forest Hills in New York City. Long gone now, of course, but they played on grass, which as you know is extinct throughout the world. Hasn't grown anywhere for decades.

As I've said, this tennis reached a stature where, amazingly enough, it was considered the No. 1 sport in the U.S., even though the player mortality rate was low. Oh, there were occasional fatal bludgeonings with metal rackets, which were eventually outlawed. The culprits who knocked off their opponents alibied that "the pressure" got to them. The appeal of the game was not really brutality. Nevertheless it climbed ahead of hockey and football in popularity, according to shocked poll-takers.

Supposedly the trouble began at the highest level, with professionals who got paid (honest!) to play tennis. Problems, difficulties, unrest filtered down to the masses who were using the game as dope to escape reality. Poof—it all collapsed in about 1980. But the so-called Sport of the Seventies began to disintegrate when labor strife cancelled the Open of 1975. It was never resumed until this week in Death Valley.

There had been rumblings of trouble in 1974 when the men's union, called ATP, and the women's union, called WTA, went at each other with the tournament in the middle. They were all demanding more money. Plus, the women wanted as much as the men, and the men didn't like that. But they all wanted more and they got it, which was an attitude characterizing the professionals in that era. Now that we've abolished professionalism, we're a lot happier, don't you think? Our rats in Reno are doing their running for room and board, happy knowing that the public is entertained. But I guess the athletes back then weren't so civic-spirited.

Anyway, in 1975 the dispute over the Open was fiercer. There was another union to contend with called RCA—the Riordan-Connors Alliance—whose only member, Jimmy Connors, was the defending champion. His agents asked a $100,000 appearance fee for his union. And the WTA and ATP were asking $500,000 each in prize money—even though they couldn't guarantee any of their members would show up, since most of them were tired, and a lot were playing for city clubs in something called World Team Tennis. This WTT had expanded its season to 51 weeks (giving one week off to a tournament called Wimbledon, which was asked to compress its schedule).

If that seems confusing to you, try to imagine another league of cities being formed called POT (Planet of Tennis), containing 44 teams from Ashtabula to Zululand. Which is what did happen. Thus there was a bidding war between POT and WTT. Not only for men and women. POT's format also included matches for juniors, and the national 12-year-old champs, Ben Testerman and Tracy Austin, signed a package deal for $3 million guaranteed over three years to play for Berea, Ohio. It was a tremendous publicity score for Berea, a territorial rival of the Cleveland Nets, and the new coach, Jack Frost, said, "No team can match our infant-ry—get it?" But the difficulty was the whole town wasn't worth $3 million. The franchise folded after one match in which Berea beat Katmandu 408-407 on a doubtful call against Martin Cornica in the over-80 set that concluded the two-day program. Testerman and Austin were stuck with a meaningless contract, and had to settle for the deed to city hall, which they ran as a rooming house.

Meanwhile with POT and WTT at each other's throats on year-around schedules, the regular professional circuits had to go back to contracts and guarantees to assure themselves of any players at all. These circuits were World Championship Tennis, the Riordan Universal Title, the Commercial Union Grand Prix plus the Virginia Slims for women. Matters got more complicated when Mail Pouch Chewing Tobacco entered tennis to sponsor an alternate women's circuit. They were impressed with what a slogan—"You've Come a Long Way Baby"—had done for Slims cigarette sales. So Mail Pouch came up with "You're the Spittin' Image of a Champ, Ms." to help promote chewing among women. It worked pretty well, but then Mail Pouch, Slims, WTT and POT were battling each other for the leading women's services. Prices soared. Sponsors screeched. However, they were assured by the unions that nobody was greedy. These were just inflationary times and guarantees and prize money had to go up progressively and logically to an annual high of $2.5 billion in 1976.

Several players, in the interest of fairness to all, signed with WCT, CUGP, RUT, WTT and POT and played every circuit they could find. That meant tennis every day of the year, but so what, they said. They said a professional came to play. A geezer named Hamilton Richardson emerged from retirement and made $583,610 in 1976 even though he didn't win a single point. By then the unions had done away with games and sets and were playing best-of-three tie-breaker matches. All you had to do was win 10 points to win a match, whatever that meant. It reduced wear and tear on the players. They kept moaning they were worn out, but they entered more and more tournaments and played more and more matches with WTT and POT.

So it went until the sponsors of tournaments started to drop away because they never knew which players would show up. Players began to jump contracts from one league to another, and from WCT to RUT, and VS to MP and back again, starting a chain of lawsuits as bad as those in other professional sports. Commercial Union Assurance, one of the big sponsors, collapsed in a sea of lawsuits and escalated bonuses in an effort to lure the best men and women to the Grand Prix.

There also was another competition, between countries, called the Davis Cup, which fell apart in 1977 in a mishmash of outraged protests against the United States. Numerous countries refused to play against the U.S. because that's where all the player-corrupting money came from. Poland, Mexico and South Vietnam went bankrupt trying to support their Davis Cup teams, whose demands finally couldn't be met. With all the protests, money problems and defaults, the 1977 Cup was won by Paraguay over Monaco in the final.

Then there were betting scandals. Several great players got caught and put in jail for fixing matches and shaving points after New York's Off-Track Betting system put tennis on the board along with horseracing in 1978.

I know this sounds incredible, folks, truly unbelievable, and you probably think I'm just filling time until our first match starts. But this is history I'm quoting from. It makes our rat races over at Rodent Downs sound pretty tame, don't it? It's impossible to imagine a little game of people batting a ball back and forth being taken so seriously, ain't it? But I'm telling you this was a long time ago when they were going through the Silly Age.

Anyhow, it was just about 1981 that the U.S. government had enough and they banned tennis. Not just the professionals who suddenly had to go to work for a living. All tennis—because that's all anybody wanted to do was play tennis. That's about the time the depressions and the famines began to really hit the country, and the government had to take over the millions of indoor courts to use them for soup kitchens and emergency housing. By that time, I'm led to believe, there were indoor tennis centers on nearly every city block. Wow, those folks must have been loonier than a gila that falls in love with a copperhead!

But that was America the Boobyful in the 1970s from what I've heard. Maybe history will teach us a lesson although I guess it never does. But I know a couple of things: the government we got now ain't gonna let this tennis revival run away with us, and it don't look like a game that would appeal to many sensible folks anyway.

Well, I see Billie Jean Scaggs and Chrissie Scaggs are just about ready to play our first final of the day. This is Howdy Gosell right here ready to give you all the action on WREK just as soon as we pause for station identification...

●

"Great Game!"

Thru the Years with Rod Laver

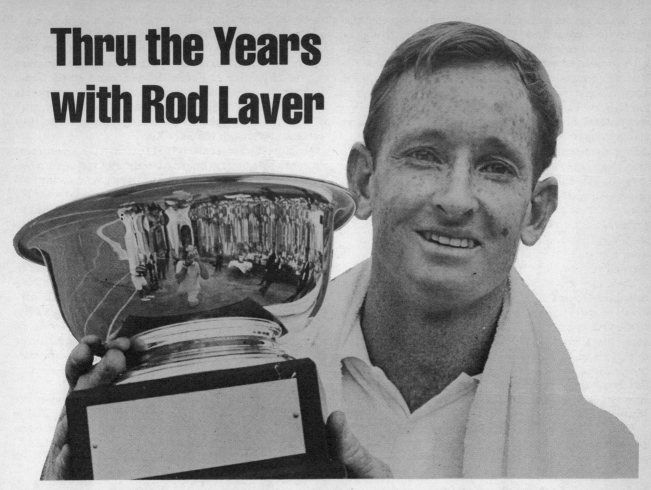

Second of Laver's five U.S. Pro titles is captured in Boston, 1966, in a final victory over Ken Rosewall.

Above—Rice and rackets—Rod and Mary Laver's wedding in 1966. Identifiable colleagues, from right, Ken Rosewall, Andres Gimeno, Butch Buchholz.

Left—Hello America: Rod's first trip away from Australia was in 1956 when he won the U.S. Junior championship at Kalamazoo, Mich.

Above—Unexpected respectability—In 1965 when the pros were at loose ends, millionaire Jimmy Van Alen invited them to Newport to play a $10,000 tourney using his radical VASSS scoring system at the hallowed Casino, site of the first U.S. championship. This troupe was just about all there was to pro tennis in those days, from left, Andres Gimeno, Pancho Segura, Luis Ayala, Laver, Joanne MacKay, Barry MacKay, Van Alen, Mal Anderson, Marilyn Buchholz, Butch Buchholz, Mike Davies.

Right—Amateur days at Forest Hills, Rod with Frank Froehling, quarter-final victim during Laver's last leg run on the 1962 Grand Slam.

Below—Out on the street: in the uncertain days of pro tennis (this was 1964) they'd do anything to attract attention, like playing on a St. Louis thoroughfare. From left, Pancho Gonzalez, Laver, Butch Buchholz, Barry MacKay. Seldom did this many spectators show for the tournaments.

Above—Quartet of barnstormers in Rod's early pro days, from left, Ken Rosewall, Pancho Gonzalez, Andres Gimeno.

Left—A heavy check, especially in 1969, was the $15,000 Rod grabbed for winning a pro tourney at Madison Square Garden.

Below—Receiving sportsmanship award from U.S. Tennis Writers in 1962, year of the first Grand Slam. The elderly man at Laver's right is the late Sir Norman Brookes, the first great Aussie and a lefty himself.

Above—Return to the upper world: Laver grips the big one, the trophy for the first open Wimbledon in 1968, following victory over Tony Roche.

Right—Extra kick in a smash—Rod during his last Wimbledon appearance in 1971, losing a quarter-final to Tom Gorman.

A Pedal Nudist on the Joys and Trials of a Barefoot Contester

by BUD COLLINS

NUDITY ISN'T that big a deal any more. Not even pedal nudity—an aberration to which I confess—is likely to outrage or titillate much of the populace in this day of "Deep Throat" and "Last Tango in Paris" at the cinema and *Playboy* and *Oui* on the newsstands. Bottomless-at-the-baseline might be a condition to attract the vice squad to the tennis court, until they discover me bottomless in the truest form: no shoes and socks.

After you've seen the voluptuous toes of Linda Lovelace and Maria Schneider, what is a glimpse of Collins' instep going to do for you? Nevertheless, there is something about disrobing the feet in public to play tennis that arouses suspicion, derision, even indignation and antagonism. Nobody minds if you go swimming barefoot, but the sneaker lobby grumbles whenever I break the no-shoe taboo. Lawyers for Adidas, Converse, Keds, Puma, Tretorn, Head, Nike et al are seeking an injunction forbidding me to expose my lowest flesh.

If I bare my soles, numerous guardians of tennis morals accuse me of breaking the sacred code of dress, dating back to King Louis X of France who, while chasing his cook, Madeleine, around the kitchen, fell in a barrel of flour. Since he was late for his daily game of tennis and had no time to change, Louis accidentally inaugurated the custom of all-white costume for the court. I respect that legend, but I hasten to tell sticklers for proper white attire that Louis would indeed have played *his* game barefoot if he'd caught up with the cook.

"Put on shoes, please," is the directive at such clubs as Merion Cricket, Essex County, Badminton & Tennis and several more where you may not be pedally naked. Yet at Wimbledon Cricket (across the street from the All England Club), although you must not remove your shirt to sunbathe while lolling near the courts (during the two or three minutes of sunshine each year) there are no barefoot hang-ups. As I pad onto the court, Derek, the overseer, mutters, "Oh, the crazy American is back."

Sir Reginald Brace, Boswell to Roger Taylor, scowls, "Bloody Yank will get his bloody feet bloody if he plays on the shale courts. Then he'll expect us to take care of him on the National Health."

I have been blessed with feet as hard as my head, treads as heavy as my prose. Thus my feet have gamboled starkers on the courts of six continents. Unclothed, they have provoked frowns, puzzlement, guffaws, disdain and once—yes, once in Bangkok—lust. Unknown to me, a colony of red ants inhabited a grass court where Donald Dell and I were having a hit one hot morning during a Davis Cup team tour of Southeast Asia. And they wanted my feet. Madly. To these ants my feet were great sex objects to be swarmed in a gang bite. For a while I thought the grass was merely unusually warm and itchy. Presently their nibbles drove we wild, but not with ecstasy. Although I seemed everything they desired, I ran screaming for the shower. Their little love bites haunted me for days.

I do not advise barefootin' in Bangkok.

Indeed, why do I do it at all? My reply is that of a character in a forgotten book called "Harry Vernon at Prep." A shameless rake, this character was being scolded for engaging in another pleasure of the flesh.

"How can you do this to her, a married woman?" went the rebuke from his mortified friend.

"It feels good."

That's it. Sybaritic pleasure. Hedonism. Cast off all restraints of sock and shoe. Take them off…all off…and let your toes bump and grind against Mother Earth in a forbidden frolic.

Hold it, don't call the cops. I'm not saying this is right for you. Don't book me for attempting to corrupt a metatarsal. Possibly there are some redeeming social features of barefootin', but I'm not trying to set myself up as a pusher. It works for me, see, but if it's against your religion or the obscenity laws in your locale, forget I mentioned it. I'm no Timothy Leary urging you to tune in to pedal nudity, turn on your sporting goods salesman, and drop out of sneakers.

Maybe your feet weren't meant to escape their Victorian binding and breathe. That's OK. These sensual pleasures aren't for all of us. Podiatric Lib isn't my cause, just my choice. I cannot envision a place for me in history alongside those earlier sartorial-freedom fighters, Billie Tapscott and Henry Austin. Billie liberated the female leg in 1929 by appearing stockingless at Wimbledon, parading calves in full view. Not long thereafter, Austin freed the male knee from flannel incarceration with a scissors, creating the first shorts to startle the All England Club. Bless them both. Their radicalism born of practicality—stockings and trousers were too hot and hampering—has been *de rigeur* ever since.

But will we ever shed our shoes en masse as we rush to the courts? I think not. Shoes seem to represent security (remember running Sammy Glick?) and status. Tennis equipment becomes more elaborate, attractive, specialized and expensive. Not many would care to decrease the amount of gear or part with their $25 leather sneaks. Moreover, I should say tennis shoes are becoming more chic and interesting (have you seen the gleaming Nikes in scarlet or navy on Valerie Ziegenfuss?)

No, barefootin' won't sweep the tennis universe. It is an exotic taste, confined to the handful who would dare the odds on stubbing a toe, or maiming several with a metal racket on the service follow-through. The latter happens to me about once a year, whereupon my doubles partner, R. B. (Death House) Wogan, shakes his head at the gush of blood. From across the net Z. Paul Callahan screeches: "No transfusions. Play is continuous!"

Grass is by far the most receptive ground for skinnydipping heels and toes. The most celebrated instance occurred, unpremeditated, in 1947 during the Davis Cup Challenge Round at Forest Hills. Ted Schroeder coped with a slippery court and Australian Dinny Pails by discarding shoes and socks in winning the deciding match in five sets, apologizing to Pails for exposing himself below the ankles.

John Kroel, the venerable linesman, tells me he used to win Senior tournaments barefoot. Pro Tom Leonard tried shoelessness in the National Amateur of 1969 but lost to Ray Keldie.

Five years before that on the same court at Longwood in Boston, Alex Olmedo staged a gradual strip in overcoming Sammy Giammalva, 12-14, 7-5, 6-2, in the first round of the U.S. Pro. It was damp, misty and mushy as The Chief struggled to stay in the match. First he shed shoes. Stocking feet didn't help. So he got right down to the toenails and hung on by them. "Nobody got better gripping toenails than an Inca," said Olmedo. They pulled him through, kept him upright and attacking through the slop.

Olmedo was my inspiration. Above all Peruvian players he was my favorite, and I sought to emulate his dazzling digital display. The idea had occurred to me a few years prior when a handsome blonde named Eileen Reardon got down to essentials on an adjoining court at Longwood.

"What's it like bare?" I ventured.

"Divine," she replied, her eyes slightly glazed. She was high on ordinary grass, but I still didn't have the nerve to try until Olmedo trod on convention and Giammalva in that pro tournament. From that point, there would be no walking back.

Ridicule and censure have been my lot. (Fred Stolle always sneers, "Are things that bad, Hacker? Can we chip in to get you a pair of shoes?") But nothing can destroy the happiness of my toes. Oh, occasionally I must resort to shoes, particularly indoors or on an abrasive surface. They feel cumbersome and restrictive.

Six years ago I lost faith momentarily. Denny Ralston, desperate for somebody to practice with, asked me if I could protect myself while he rapped a few at me. Great. "Hey, where are your shoes?" Denny asked as we picked out a grass court at Longwood.

"Don't wear any. I was a Depression baby."

"Listen, you'll ruin your feet if you keep that up. Go put some on, will you?" he said, considerately. So I did.

A few days later Pierre Barthes asked, "Why you wear shoes, mon ami? This isn't like you."

I told him Ralston had convinced me feet weren't meant to take that kind of action.

"Were you born with shoes on?" Barthes asked.

That brought it back into perspective. If the Lord had meant me to be sneakered…

Just to be sure, I checked with Dr. Syd Brass, the podiatrist who tends Arthur Ashe's Haglund's Disease (a spur on Arthur's left heel). Brass, a respectable player himself, said, "On elastic surfaces, grass and clay, playing barefoot is good for you, especially grass where your toes dig in. Strengthens the calf musculature. Of course on clay you have to watch out for the tapes, calcium chloride which can burn, and foreign objects anywhere. If you stub a toe or step on a sliver of glass in the grass, it isn't so good, is it?

"Playing barefoot is fine. The inelastic surfaces—hard courts—are a different proposition. You need shock absorbing shoes and two pairs of socks there. Unfortunately the trend is to hard surfaces, which means more foot and leg injuries."

Thanks, Doc.

His report hasn't prevented groundskeepers Joe Leandra at Newport (R.I.) Casino, Walter Chambers at Longwood and Ownie Sheridan at Forest Hills from accusing me of spreading athlete's foot throughout their precious lawns. "You're worse than Typhoid Mary," says Leandra, curator of the Hall of Fame courts. "See those brown patches? We call that Fungus Collinsis."

It's nice to have a niche at the Hall of Fame.

"Well, I don't think you can hurt the clay," said Sheridan at Forest Hills last year. That was before I left footprints on a wet court. "Go track up somebody's livingroom, will you?" Ownie pleaded.

Once I played in the National Mixed with Joyce Williams. A well-mannered Scotswoman, Joyce was sporting enough to go through with it, although fearing she might lose her Wightman Cup scholarship for accompanying a partially clad male. "I can't take my eyes off your feet," she kept saying.

"Do they excite you?" I said hopefully, thinking maybe she was a foot fetishist.

"Heavens, no," she said. "I just keep thinking that if they were Neale Fraser's feet we might have a chance in this match. But as long as you keep standing in one place, you won't harm the court, will you?"

The next year I played with Gail Hansen against Linda Tuero and Mike Estep. Gail and Linda giggled all the way.

"What's the matter? Didn't you ever see a man's feet before?" I was getting impatient. "Didn't your mothers ever tell you the facts of life?"

They just giggled. At last—before she smashed an overhead off my left big toe—Linda managed a sentence: "Don't your feet hurt?"

"Only when you laugh."

Barefootin' has its hazards: red ants, calcium chloride, pebbles, protruding line tapes, metal stripping from ball cans, thistles, uncurbed dogs (yikes, now I've really put my foot in it), broken glass, splinters, ungainly partners who walk on you. Not to mention the scorn of traditionalists.

Nonetheless, the rewards of getting down to the nitty gritty, right down to the grass roots of the game—to beat your feet on the Mississippi mud, so to speak—make it all worth while. Whenever I'm dismayed by the conditions or the calumny, I remember Pierre Barthes telling me, "If God wanted you to wear tennis shoes, you would have been born with them on."

He's right, even though I'll never convince the majority who are repelled, frightened or shocked by pedal nudity. Still, I'm always comforted by Pierre's words, and this thought that came to me not long ago:

"I complained when I had no shoes... until I met a man who had no backhand." ●

Where Angels Fear to Tread

by CANDACE MAYERON

IT'S BEEN SAID, "Those who can't, teach." Whoever said that couldn't possibly have been thinking of tennis, as it still takes a certain amount of physical prowess to teach. For those of us who only gird our loins in Maidenform to keep the sinew from sagging, teaching is out of the question. So, those who can't teach, write.

Unquestionably this is the category I fall into. Even without the advice of all my good friends, I knew I'd never make it as a professional player. Starting the game at age 24 doesn't make for a future Wimbledon champion. And to teach tennis I would have to forego my daily intake of cigarettes. Somehow it was a lot easier to give up any aspirations to teach tennis than to quit smoking. That left journalism. Actually I am rather well suited to writing about tennis. *That* I can do sitting down, smoking a cigarette.

God knows I'm no sportswoman anyway. Whenever I feel the urge for physical exercise, I lie down until the feeling passes. For most my life the most physical activity I got was turning the page of a book.

As a child, I was sent to a very expensive girls' camp. My parents hoped I would learn some socially useful sport. "You'll love it," they said. "They have swimming, sailing, horseback riding, hiking, canoeing and all sorts of fun things." The bus ride alone tired me out. Arriving at camp the first thing I saw was 20 mattresses spread in a line, and 20 girls lying flat prone on each mattress. "I don't know what it is, but THAT'S for me!" It turned out to be riflery, and I spent seven hours a day on the rifle range. I have a great natural talent for lying down.

My parents were not thrilled. "What are you going to do with boys? Ask them to go out *shooting?!*" Somehow I managed to overcome this deficiency, and as I grew up I found plenty of things to do with boys.

On the whole I was a war-boom baby, not a tennis-boom baby. Tennis courts did not exist in the frozen tundra of Minnesota where I grew up. In fact I never even saw a tennis court until I moved to California. Once I tried it, I found much to my shock that I really loved playing tennis, and have been playing steadily for almost two years.

To be sure, I don't play a terrific game. I'm quite lazy. I

don't like to have to move my feet around too much or too quickly, and would rather have the ball hit directly to me. A thorough knowledge of the rules is my chief asset. I get a lot of points off opponents who catch the kind of ball that is "obviously" going out—BEFORE it bounces. But at least tennis is a sport where one can remain feminine in appearance and not worry about breaking a fingernail or losing an eyelash.

One thing though about tennis reporting—watching the pros makes one hungry to get out on the court and play. This year I decided to take the plunge. I entered the Women's Singles of the Pacific Southwest.

When my little green acceptance card arrived in the mail I looked at it with trepidation. The PSW is after all, no small tournament. It is one of the most important tourneys on the USLTA circuit. For the men that is. For the women it is nothing. There is no prize money, no points. For that reason one can enter the Women's Singles merely by signing up. Of course only other tennis players would know that, my friends and parents didn't, and they were sufficiently impressed that I'd actually been "accepted" for the event.

The card stated I was to play my first match Sunday at 10:00 AM. Ten in the MORNING?! I haven't seen 10 AM in many years. As a journalist my hours are my own, and I frequently and most enjoyably abuse my body. I smoke to excess and stay up late. My day begins at the conclusion of other people's lunch hour.

On Saturday I went to the Los Angeles Tennis Club where the tournament is held, to look at the draw. I'd received a bye for the qualifying round. As no one at the club was familiar with my tennis game, they had probably assumed since I write about tennis I can play too. For the first round I was to play a girl named Lindsay Morse. The #3 seed. Damn! Surely there had to be other girls of my caliber in the tournament, and I wanted to play one of them. But then I reminded myself there is less shame in losing to a good player than a bad one, and certainly more glory in winning. And I had every intention of winning. I do not attempt anything with a defeatist attitude.

I figured if nothing else I had the element of surprise on my side. Lindsay knew nothing about me. For all she knew I might be some hot-shot from out of town. And I also knew that her first sight of me would scare the hell out of her. At 5'9" and with dark features, I can be very intimidating merely by pulling my eyebrows together in a way to make my mother cringe ("Don't DO that, Dear, you'll make wrinkles in that pretty face!")

I also planned to forego the warmup. That would surely throw her off balance. It would also avoid giving her advance notice of just how bad a player I really am.

My preparations for the match were elaborate. On advice from John Newcombe I packed a bag containing any paraphenalia I could conceivably need: powder, thermos, stopwatch, extra tennis shoes, extra shoelaces, towel, salt tablets. I stopped just short of spikes. What I really needed was a gun, but under the current USLTA rules it is not allowed. Like my heroine, Billie Jean King, I took time working up a good hate for my as yet unknown opponent.

But Lindsay Morse did not turn out to be a greeneyed nine-headed Hydra that I could cheerfully hate. Nor, sad to say, was she a midget to be intimidated by my height. Lindsay is a tall girl herself. She has the face of an angel.

Although she is a blonde, and I've always hated blondes— they do have more fun—I liked her immediately. While I arrived burdened like a pack mule, Lindsay brought only a racket and her mother. She was so unassuming I even found myself offering her drinks from my thermos.

I won the spin and elected to serve. I lost it to love. From there things went downhill.

As we changed sides after the first game, I sat down determined to use my full 60 seconds. Lindsay, with the braggadocio of youth, swaggered immediately to the other side. To show I was just as fit, I bounced right over to my side of the court and prepared to receive.

My ready position—a cross between Tom Okker and the Hunchback of Notre Dame—must have thrown her: she double faulted. I loved it. I was on my way to a break!

But her following serves surprised me. They twisted about in a manner I'd never experienced before, and I had trouble even getting my racket on the ball. I returned just one.

My serve followed, and I was down 0-3. This time I really needed that 60 second rest. I was beginning to breathe heavily (those damn cigarettes!) and sat down plowing through my bag looking for something to change, take or imbibe.

At the 0-5 change-over I debated changing rackets. But as the other racket I'd brought with me—it was just for show—had no strings, I discarded that idea. I don't think it would have affected the outcome very much anyway.

Pros don't speak to one another during the change overs, but now I had to save some face. I knew I wasn't going to save face by winning a few games so I did the next best thing. I confessed. "This is my first tournament," I said rather lamely. Lindsay very sweetly pretended surprise. While my confession didn't cause her to let up any, at least she didn't start giving me pointers during play.

I glanced at her mother. (It wasn't hard to pick her out. She was the only spectator.) No longer nervous for her daughter, she was discussing with a friend Lindsay's next match. "What makes her so goddamn sure there's going to be a next match?" I wondered.

Zip. Zip. Whiz. The balls sizzled past. I'd never seen such aim, such accuracy. Lindsay's shots skipped by, skimming the lines. She daintily reached for an overhead. Remembering how bad women are with overheads, I relaxed, knowing I'd get this point at least. She smashed it away. "It's the first good one I've hit all week," she said. My luck.

No longer perspiring, I was now sweating profusely from my efforts. At each change over I put on new wrist bands. When I play socially I only play one set. I'd never before played two sets (and we might go to three!) and I was finding it a bit difficult to breathe.

At 0-6, 0-3 I knew I had her psychologically right where I wanted her. After all, I was only down a set and a break.

I began to have fun with the match, enjoying myself. It isn't often I have a chance to play someone this good, and I decided I might as well use it as a learning experience. Actually I wasn't playing badly—for me. But next year I'm going to warm up before I play!

To do myself justice, I must say I once had game point on her serve, and another game even went to deuce. So even though the final score was 6-0, 6-0; it was clearly another case of "the score not really reflecting the quality of the play!" ●

Championship Rolls
USLTA & Wimbledon Winners

William Tilden

U.S. CHAMPIONS

Men's Singles

YEAR	CHAMPION	RUNNER-UP	SCORE
1881	R. D. Sears	W. E. Glyn	6-0, 6-3, 6-2
1882	R. D. Sears	C. M. Clark	6-1, 6-4, 6-0
1883	R. D. Sears	J. Dwight	6-2, 6-0, 9-7
1884	R. D. Sears	H. A. Taylor	6-0, 1-6, 6-0, 6-2
1885	R. D. Sears	G. M. Brinley	6-3, 4-6, 6-0, 6-3
1886	R. D. Sears	R. L. Beeckman	4-6, 6-1, 6-3, 6-4
1887	R. D. Sears	H. W. Slocum, Jr.	6-1, 6-3, 6-2
1888	H. W. Slocum, Jr.	H. A. Taylor	6-4, 6-1, 6-0
1889	H. W. Slocum, Jr.	Q. A. Shaw	6-3, 6-1, 4-6, 6-2
1890	O. S. Campbell	H. W. Slocum, Jr.	6-2, 4-6, 6-3, 6-1
1891	O. S. Campbell	C. Hobart	2-6, 7-5, 7-9, 6-1, 6-2
1892	O. S. Campbell	F. H. Hovey	7-5, 3-6, 6-3, 7-5
1893	R. D. Wrenn	F. H. Hovey	6-4, 3-6, 6-4, 6-4
1894	R. D. Wrenn	M. F. Goodbody	6-8, 6-1, 6-4, 6-4
1895	F. H. Hovey	R. D. Wrenn	6-3, 6-2, 6-4
1896	R. D. Wrenn	F. H. Hovey	7-5, 3-6, 6-0, 1-6, 6-1
1897	R. D. Wrenn	W. V. Eaves	4-6, 8-6, 6-3, 2-6, 6-2
1898	M. D. Whitman	D. F. Davis	3-6, 6-2, 6-2, 6-1
1899	M. D. Whitman	J. P. Paret	6-1, 6-2, 3-6, 7-5
1900	M. D. Whitman	W. A. Larned	6-4, 6-1, 6-2, 6-2
1901	W. A. Larned	B. C. Wright	6-2, 6-8, 6-4, 6-4
1902	W. A. Larned	R. F. Doherty	4-6, 6-2, 6-4, 8-6
1903	H. L. Doherty	W. A. Larned	6-0, 6-3, 10-8
1904	Holcombe Ward	W. J. Clothier	10-8, 6-4, 9-7
1905	B. C. Wright	Holcombe Ward	6-2, 6-1, 11-9
1906	W. J. Clothier	B. C. Wright	6-3, 6-0, 6-4
1907	W. A. Larned	Robert LeRoy	6-2, 6-2, 6-4
1908	W. A. Larned	B. C. Wright	6-1, 6-2, 8-6
1909	W. A. Larned	W. J. Clothier	6-1, 6-2, 5-7, 1-6, 6-1
1910	W. A. Larned	T. C. Bundy	6-1, 5-7, 6-0, 6-8, 6-1
1911	W. A. Larned	M. E. McLoughlin	6-4, 6-4, 6-2
1912	M. E. McLoughlin	W. F. Johnson	3-6, 2-6, 6-2, 6-4, 6-2
1913	M. E. McLoughlin	R. N. Williams	6-4, 5-7, 6-3, 6-1
1914	R. N. Williams	M. E. McLoughlin	6-3, 8-6, 10-8
1915	Wm. M. Johnston	M. E. McLoughlin	1-6, 6-0, 7-5, 10-8
1916	R. N. Williams	Wm. M. Johnston	4-6, 6-4, 0-6, 6-2, 6-4
1917	R. L. Murray	N. W. Niles	5-7, 8-6, 6-3, 6-3
1918	R. L. Murray	Wm. T. Tilden	6-3, 6-1, 7-5
1919	Wm. M. Johnston	Wm. T. Tilden	6-4, 6-4, 6-3
1920	Wm. T. Tilden	Wm. M. Johnston	6-1, 1-6, 7-5, 5-7, 6-3
1921	Wm. T. Tilden	Wallace F. Johnston	6-1, 6-3, 6-1
1922	Wm. T. Tilden	Wm. M. Johnston	4-6, 3-6, 6-2, 6-3, 6-4
1923	Wm. T. Tilden	Wm. M. Johnston	6-4, 6-1, 6-4
1924	Wm. T. Tilden	Wm. M. Johnston	6-1, 9-7, 6-2
1925	Wm. T. Tilden	Wm. M. Johnston	4-6, 11-9, 6-3, 4-6, 6-3
1926	Rene Lacoste	Jean Borotra	6-4, 6-0, 6-4
1927	Rene Lacoste	Wm. T. Tilden	11-9, 6-3, 11-9
1928	Henri Cochet	Francis T. Hunter	4-6, 6-4, 3-6, 7-5, 6-3
1929	Wm. T. Tilden	Francis T. Hunter	3-6, 6-3, 4-6, 6-2, 6-4
1930	John H. Doeg	Francis X. Shields	10-8, 1-6, 6-4, 16-14
1931	H. Ellsworth Vines	George M. Lott, Jr.	7-9, 6-3, 9-7, 7-5

YEAR	CHAMPION	RUNNER-UP	SCORE
1932	H. Ellsworth Vines	Henri Cochet	6-4, 6-4, 6-4
1933	Frederick J. Perry	John H. Crawford	6-3, 11-13, 4-6, 6-0, 6-1
1934	Frederick J. Perry	Wilmer L. Allison	6-4, 6-3, 3-6, 1-6, 8-6
1935	Wilmer L. Allison	Sidney B. Wood	6-2, 6-2, 6-3
1936	Fred Perry	J. Donald Budge	2-6, 6-2, 8-6, 1-6, 10-8
1937	J. Donald Budge	Baron G. von Cramm	6-1, 7-9, 6-1, 3-6, 6-1
1938	J. Donald Budge	C. Gene Mako	6-3, 6-8, 6-2, 6-1
1939	Robert Riggs	S. Welby Van Horn	6-4, 6-2, 6-4
1940	Donald McNeill	Robert L. Riggs	4-6, 6-8, 6-3, 6-3, 7-5
1941	Robert L. Riggs	Francis Kovacs, 2nd	5-7, 6-1, 6-3, 6-3
1942	Frederick R. Schroeder, Jr.	Frank Parker	8-6, 7-5, 3-6, 4-6, 6-2
1943	Lt. Joseph R. Hunt	Seaman John A. Kramer	6-3, 6-8, 10-8, 6-0
1944	Sgt. Frank A. Parker	William F. Talbert	6-4, 3-6, 6-3, 6-3
1945	Sgt. Frank A. Parker	William F. Talbert	14-12, 6-1, 6-2
1946	John A. Kramer	Tom Brown, Jr.	9-7, 6-3, 6-0
1947	John A. Kramer	Frank A. Parker	4-6, 2-6, 6-1, 6-0, 6-3
1948	Richard A. Gonzales	Eric W. Sturgess	6-2, 6-3, 14-12
1949	Richard A. Gonzales	Frederick R. Schroeder, Jr.	16-18, 2-6, 6-1, 6-2, 6-4
1950	Arthur Larsen	Herbert Flam	6-3, 4-6, 5-7, 6-4, 6-3
1951	Frank Sedgman	E. Victor Seixas, Jr.	6-4, 6-1, 6-1
1952	Frank Sedgman	Gardnar Mulloy	6-1, 6-2, 6-3
1953	Tony Trabert	E. Victor Seixas, Jr.	6-3, 6-2, 6-3
1954	E. Victor Seixas, Jr.	Rex Hartwig	3-6, 6-2, 6-4, 6-4
1955	Tony Trabert	Ken Rosewall	9-7, 6-3, 6-3
1956	Kenneth Rosewall	Lewis Hoad	4-6, 6-2, 6-3, 6-3
1957	Malcolm J. Anderson	Ashley J. Cooper	10-8, 7-5, 6-4
1958	Ashley J. Cooper	Malcolm J. Anderson	6-2, 3-6, 4-6, 10-8, 8-6
1959	Neale Fraser	Alejandro Olmedo	6-3, 5-7, 6-2, 6-4
1960	Neale Fraser	Rodney Laver	6-4, 6-4, 9-7
1961	Roy Emerson	Rodney Laver	7-5, 6-3, 6-2
1962	Rodney Laver	Roy Emerson	6-2, 6-4, 5-7, 6-4
1963	Rafael Osuna	Frank Froehling, III	7-5, 6-4, 6-2
1964	Roy Emerson	Fred Stolle	6-4, 6-1, 6-4
1965	Manuel Santana	Cliff Drysdale	6-2, 7-9, 7-5, 6-1
1966	Fred Stolle	John Newcombe	4-6, 12-10, 6-3, 6-4
1967	John Newcombe	Clark Graebner	6-4, 6-4, 8-6
1968	Arthur Ashe	Robert Lutz	4-6, 6-3, 8-10, 6-0, 6-4
1968*	Arthur Ashe	Tom Okker	14-12, 5-7, 6-3, 3-6, 6-3

Arthur Ashe

Jimmy Connors

YEAR	CHAMPION	RUNNER-UP	SCORE
1969	Stan Smith	Robert Lutz	9-7, 6-3, 6-1
1969*	Rod Laver	Tony Roche	7-9, 6-1, 6-3, 6-2
1970*	Ken Rosewall	Tony Roche	2-6, 6-4, 7-6, 6-3
1971*	Stan Smith	Jan Kodes	3-6, 6-3, 6-2, 7-6
1972*	Ilie Nastase	Arthur Ashe	3-6, 6-3, 6-7, 6-4, 6-3
1973*	John Newcombe	Jan Kodes	6-4, 1-6, 4-6, 6-2, 6-3
1974*	Jimmy Connors	Ken Rosewall	6-1, 6-0, 6-1

*Open Champion

Men's Doubles

YEAR	WINNERS	RUNNERS-UP
1881	C. M. Clark-F. W. Taylor	A. Van Rensselaer-A. E. Newbold
1882	R. D. Sears-J. Dwight	W. Nightingale-G. M. Smith
1883	R. D. Sears-J. Dwight	A. Van Rensselaer-A. E. Newbold
1884	R. D. Sears-J. Dwight	A. Van Rensselaer-W. V. R. Berry
1885	R. D. Sears-J. S. Clark	H. W. Slocum, Jr.-W. P. Knapp
1886	R. D. Sears-J. Dwight	H. A. Taylor-G. M. Brinley
1887	R. D. Sears-J. Dwight	H. A. Taylor-H. W. Slocum, Jr.
1888	O. S. Campbell-V. G. Hall	C. Hobart-E. P. MacMullen
1889	H. W. Slocum, Jr.-H. A. Taylor	V. G. Hall-O. S. Campbell
1890	V. G. Hall-C. Hobart	J. W. Carver-J. A. Ryerson
1891	O. S. Campbell-Robt. P. Huntington, Jr.	V. G. Hall-Clarence Hobart
1892	O. S. Campbell-Robt. P. Huntington, Jr.	V. G. Hall-Edward L. Hall
1893	Clarence Hobart-Fred H. Hovey	O. S. Campbell-Robt. P. Huntington, Jr.
1894	Clarence Hobart-Fred H. Hovey	C. B. Neel-Samuel R. Neel
1895	M. G. Chace-R. D. Wrenn	J. Howland-A. E. Foote
1896	Carr B. Neel-Samuel R. Neel	Robert D. Wrenn-M. G. Chace
1897	Leo E. Ware-Geo. P. Sheldon, Jr.	Harold S. Mahony-H. A. Nisbet
1898	Leo E. Ware-Geo. P. Sheldon, Jr.	Holcombe Ward-Dwight F. Davis
1899	Holcombe Ward-Dwight F. Davis	Leo E. Ware-Geo. P. Sheldon, Jr.
1900	Holcombe Ward-Dwight F. Davis	Fred B. Alexander-Raymond D. Little
1901	Holcombe Ward-Dwight F. Davis	Leo E. Ware-Beals C. Wright
1902	Reginald F. Doherty-Hugh L. Doherty	Holcombe Ward-Dwight F. Davis
1903	Reginald F. Doherty-Hugh L. Doherty	Kreigh Collins-L. Harry Waidner
1904	Holcombe Ward-Beals C. Wright	Kreigh Collins-Raymond D. Little
1905	Holcombe Ward-Beals C. Wright	Fred B. Alexander-Harold H. Hackett
1906	Holcombe Ward-Beals C. Wright	Fred B. Alexander-Harold H. Hackett
1907	Fred B. Alexander-Harold H. Hackett	Nat Thornton-B. M. Grant
1908	Fred B. Alexander-Harold H. Hackett	Raymond D. Little-Beals C. Wright
1909	Fred B. Alexander-Harold H. Hackett	Maurice E. McLoughlin-George J. Janes
1910	Fred B. Alexander-Harold H. Hackett	Thos. C. Bundy-Trowbridge W. Hendrick
1911	Raymond D. Little-Gustave F. Touchard	Fred B. Alexander-Harold H. Hackett
1912	Maurice E. McLoughlin-Thomas C. Bundy	Raymond D. Little-Gustave F. Touchard
1913	Maurice E. McLoughlin-Thomas C. Bundy	John R. Strachan-Clarence J. Griffin
1914	Maurice E. McLoughlin-Thomas C. Bundy	George M. Church-Dean Mathey
1915	William M. Johnston-Clarence J. Griffin	Maurice E. McLoughlin-Thomas C. Bundy
1916	William M. Johnston-Clarence J. Griffin	Maurice E. McLoughlin-Ward Dawson
1917	Fred B. Alexander-Harold A. Throckmorton	Harry C. Johnson-Irving C. Wright
1918	William T. Tilden, 2nd-Vincent Richards	Fred B. Alexander-Beals C. Wright
1919	Norman E. Brookes-Gerald Patterson	William T. Tilden, 2nd-Vincent Richards
1920	William M. Johnston-Clarence J. Griffin	Willis F. Davis-Roland E. Roberts
1921	William T. Tilden, 2nd-Vincent Richards	R. N. Williams, 2nd-W. M. Washburn
1922	William T. Tilden, 2nd-Vincent Richards	Gerald L. Patterson-Pat O'Hara Wood
1923	William T. Tilden, 2nd-Brian I. C. Norton	R. N. Williams, 2nd-W. M. Washburn
1924	Howard Kinsey-Robert Kinsey	Gerald L. Patterson-Pat O'Hara Wood
1925	R. Norris Williams, 2nd-Vincent Richards	Gerald Patterson-John B. Hawkes

YEAR	WINNERS	RUNNERS-UP
1926	R. N. Williams, 2nd-Vincent Richards	Wm. T. Tilden, 2nd-Alfred H. Chapin, Jr.
1927	Wm. T. Tilden, 2nd-Francis T. Hunter	Wm. M. Johnston-R. Norris Williams, Jr.
1928	George M. Lott, Jr.-John Hennessey	Gerald L. Patterson-John B. Hawkes
1929	George M. Lott, Jr.-John H. Doeg	Berkeley Bell-Lewis N. White
1930	George M. Lott, Jr.-John H. Doeg	John Van Ryn-Wilmer Allison
1931	Wilmer Allison-John Van Ryn	Gregory Mangin-Berkeley Bell
1932	H. Ellsworth Vines, Jr.-Keith Gledhill	Wilmer Allison-John Van Ryn
1933	George M. Lott, Jr.-Lester R. Stoefen	Francis X. Shields-Frank A. Parker
1934	George M. Lott, Jr.-Lester R. Stoefen	Wilmer L. Allison-John Van Ryn
1935	Wilmer L. Allison-John Van Ryn	J. Donald Budge-C. Gene Mako
1936	J. Donald Budge-C. Gene Mako	Wilmer L. Allison-John Van Ryn
1937	Baron G. von Cramm-Henner Henkel	J. Donald Budge-C. Gene Mako
1938	J. Donald Budge-C. Gene Mako	Adrian K. Quist-John Bromwich
1939	Adrian K. Quist-John E. Bromwich	John A. Crawford-Harry C. Hopman
1940	John A. Kramer-Frederick R. Schroeder, Jr.	Gardnar Mulloy-Henry J. Prussoff
1941	John A. Kramer-Frederick R. Schroeder, Jr.	Wayne Sabin-Gardnar Mulloy
1942	Lt. Gardnar Mulloy-William Talbert	Frederick Schroeder, Jr.-Sidney B. Wood, Jr.
1943	J. A. Kramer-Frank A. Parker	William Talbert-David Freeman
1944	Lt. W. Donald McNeill-Robert Falkenburg	William Talbert-Francisco Segura
1945	Lt. Gardnar Mulloy-William Talbert	Robert Falkenburg-Jack Tuero
1946	Gardnar Mulloy-William Talbert	Donald McNeill-Frank Guernsey
1947	John A. Kramer-Frederick R. Schroeder, Jr.	William Talbert-William Sidwell
1948	Gardnar Mulloy-William Talbert	Frank A. Parker-Frederick R. Schroeder, Jr.
1949	John Bromwich-William Sidwell	Frank Sedgman-George Worthington
1950	John Bromwich-Frank Sedgman	William Talbert-Gardnar Mulloy
1951	Kenneth McGregor-Frank Sedgman	Don Candy-Mervyn Rose
1952	Mervyn Rose-E. Victor Seixas, Jr.	Kenneth McGregor-Frank Sedgman
1953	Rex Hartwig-Mervyn Rose	Gardnar Mulloy-William F. Talbert
1954	E. Victor Seixas, Jr.-Tony Trabert	Lewis Hoad-Ken Rosewall
1955	Kosei Kamo-Atsushi Miyagi	Gerald Moss-William Quillian
1956	Lewis Hoad-Kenneth Rosewall	Hamilton Richardson-E. Victor Seixas, Jr.
1957	Ashley J. Cooper-Neale Fraser	Gardnar Mulloy-Budge Patty
1958	Alex Olmedo-Hamilton Richardson	Sam Giammalva-Barry MacKay
1959	Neale Fraser-Roy Emerson	Alex Olmedo-Earl Buchholz, Jr.
1960	Neale Fraser-Roy Emerson	Rod Laver-Bob Mark
1961	Charles McKinley-Dennis Ralston	Rafael Osuna-Antonio Palafox
1962	Rafael Osuna-Antonio Palafox	Charles McKinley-Dennis Ralston
1963	Charles McKinley-Dennis Ralston	Rafael Osuna-Antonio Palafox
1964	Charles McKinley-Dennis Ralston	Graham Stilwell-Mike Sangster
1965	Roy Emerson-Fred Stolle	Frank Froehling, III-Charles Pasarell
1966	Roy Emerson-Fred Stolle	Clark Graebner-Dennis Ralston
1967	John Newcombe-Tony Roche	William Bowrey-Owen Davidson
1968	Robert Lutz-Stan Smith	Robert Hewitt-Ray Moore
1968*	Robert Lutz-Stan Smith	Arthur Ashe-Andres Gimeno
1969	Richard Crealy-Alan Stone	William Bowrey-Charles Pasarell
1969*	Ken Rosewall-Fred Stolle	Charles Pasarell-Dennis Ralston
1970*	Pierre Barthes-Nicki Pilic	Roy Emerson-Rod Laver
1971*	John Newcombe-Roger Taylor	Stan Smith-Erick Van Dillen
1972*	Roger Taylor-Cliff Drysdale	John Newcombe-O. K. Davidson
1973*	John Newcombe-O.K. Davidson	Rod Laver-Ken Rosewall
1974*	Robert Lutz-Stan Smith	Patricio Cornejo-Jaime Fillol

*Open Champions

Women's Singles

YEAR	WINNER	RUNNER-UP	SCORE
1887	Ellen Hansell	Laura Knight	6-1, 6-0
1888	Bertha B. Townsend	Marion Wright	6-2, 6-2
1889	Bertha B. Townsend	Louise D. Voorhes	7-5, 6-2
1890	Ellen C. Roosevelt	Grace W. Roosevelt	6-3, 6-1
1891	Mabel Cahill	Elisabeth H. Moore	5-7, 6-3, 6-4, 4-6, 6-2
1892	Mabel Cahill	Bessie Moore	
1893	Aline Terry	Mabel Cahill	default
1894	Helen Helwig	Aline Terry	7-5, 3-6, 6-0, 3-6, 6-3
1895	Juliette P. Atkinson	Helen Helwig	6-4, 6-2, 6-1
1896	Elisabeth Moore	Juliette Atkinson	6-4, 4-6, 6-3, 6-2
1897	Juliette Atkinson	Bessie Moore	6-3, 6-3, 4-6, 3-6, 6-3
1898	Juliette Atkinson	Marion Jones	6-3, 5-7, 6-4, 2-6, 7-5
1899	Marion Jones	Juliette Atkinson	default
1900	Myrtle McAteer	Marion Jones	default
1901	Elisabeth Moore	Myrtle McAteer	6-4, 3-6, 7-5, 2-6, 6-2
1902	Marion Jones	Elisabeth Moore	6-1, 1-0, default
1903	Elisabeth Moore	Marion Jones	7-5, 8-6
1904	May Sutton	Elisabeth Moore	6-1, 6-2
1905	Elisabeth Moore	Helen Homans	6-4, 5-7, 6-1
1906	Helen Homans	Elisabeth Moore	default
1907	Evelyn Sears	Carrie Neely	6-3, 6-2
1908	Mrs. Maud Barger-Wallach	Evelyn Sears	6-2, 1-6, 6-3
1909	Hazel Hotchkiss	Mrs. Barger-Wallach	6-0, 6-1
1910	Hazel Hotchkiss	Louise Hamond	6-4, 6-2
1911	Hazel Hotchkiss	Florence Sutton	8-10, 6-1, 9-7
1912	Mary K. Browne	Eleonora Sears	6-4, 6-2
1913	Mary K. Browne	Dorothy Green	6-2, 7-5
1914	Mary K. Browne	Miss Marie Wagner	6-2, 1-6, 6-1
1915	Molla Bjurstedt	Mrs. H. Wightman	4-6, 6-2, 6-0
1916	Molla Bjurstedt	Mrs. E. Raymond	6-0, 6-1
1917	Molla Bjurstedt	Marion Vanderhoef	4-6, 6-0, 6-2
1918	Molla Bjurstedt	Eleanor E. Goss	6-4, 6-3
1919	Mrs. H. Wightman	Marion Zinderstein	6-1, 6-2
1920	Mrs. M. Mallory	Marion Zinderstein	6-3, 6-1
1921	Mrs. M. Mallory	Mary K. Browne	4-6, 6-4, 6-2
1922	Mrs. M. Mallory	Helen Wills	6-3, 6-1
1923	Helen Wills	Mrs. M. Mallory	6-2, 6-1
1924	Helen Wills	Mrs. M. Mallory	6-1, 6-2
1925	Helen Wills	Kathleen McKane	3-6, 6-0, 6-2
1926	Mrs. M. Mallory	Elizabeth Ryan	4-6, 6-4, 9-7
1927	Helen Wills	Betty Nuthall	6-1, 6-4
1928	Helen Wills	Helen H. Jacobs	6-2, 6-1
1929	Helen Wills	Mrs. M. Watson	6-4, 6-2
1930	Betty Nuthall	Mrs. L. A. Harper	6-4, 6-1
1931	Mrs. Helen Wills Moody	Mrs. E. B. Whittingstall	6-4, 6-1
1932	Helen H. Jacobs	Carolin A. Babcock	6-2, 6-2
1933	Helen H. Jacobs	Mrs. Helen Wills Moody	8-6, 3-6, 3-0, default
1934	Helen H. Jacobs	Sarah H. Palfrey	6-1, 6-4
1935	Helen H. Jacobs	Mrs. Sarah P. Fabyan	6-1, 6-4
1936	Alice Marble	Helen H. Jacobs	4-6, 6-3, 6-2
1937	Anita Lizana	Pauline Betz	6-1, 6-4
1938	Alice Marble	Louise Brough	4-6, 6-1, 6-4
1939	Alice Marble	Louise Brough	6-3, 5-7, 6-3
1940	Alice Marble	Margaret Osborne	6-3, 8-6
1941	Mrs. Sarah Palfrey Cooke	Pauline Betz	3-6, 8-6, 6-4

YEAR	WINNER	RUNNER-UP	SCORE
1942	Pauline Betz	Jadwiga Jedrzejowska	6-4, 6-2
1943	Pauline Betz	Nancy Wynne	6-0, 6-3
1944	Pauline Betz	Helen Jacobs	6-0, 8-10, 6-4
1945	Mrs. Sarah Palfrey Cooke	Helen Jacobs	6-2, 6-3
1946	Pauline Betz	Doris Hart	11-9, 6-3
1947	Louise Brough	Margaret Osborne	8-6, 4-6, 6-1
1948	Mrs. Margaret Osborne duPont	A. Louise Brough	4-6, 6-4, 15-13
1949	Mrs. Margaret Osborne duPont	Doris Hart	6-4, 6-1
1950	Mrs. Margaret Osborne duPont	Doris Hart	6-3, 6-3
1951	Maureen Connolly	Shirley Fry	6-3, 1-6, 6-4
1952	Maureen Connolly	Doris Hart	6-3, 7-5
1953	Maureen Connolly	Doris Hart	6-2, 6-4
1954	Doris Hart	A. Louise Brough	6-8, 6-1, 8-6
1955	Doris Hart	Patricia Ward	6-4, 6-2
1956	Shirley J. Fry	Althea Gibson	6-3, 6-4
1957	Althea Gibson	A. Louise Brough	6-3, 6-2
1958	Althea Gibson	Darlene Hard	3-6, 6-1, 6-2
1959	Maria Bueno	Christine Truman	6-1, 6-4
1960	Darlene R. Hard	Maria E. Bueno	6-4, 10-12, 6-4
1961	Darlene R. Hard	Ann Haydon	6-3, 6-4
1962	Margaret Smith	Darlene Hard	9-7, 6-4
1963	Maria E. Bueno	Margaret Smith	7-5, 6-4
1964	Maria E. Bueno	Mrs. Carole C. Graebner	6-1, 6-0
1965	Margaret Smith	Billie Jean Moffitt	8-6, 7-5
1966	Maria E. Bueno	Nancy Richey	6-3, 6-1
1967	Billie Jean King	Mrs. Ann H. Jones	11-9, 6-4
1968	Margaret S. Court	Maria Bueno	6-2, 6-2
1968*	Virginia Wade	Mrs. Billie Jean King	6-4, 6-4
1969	Margaret S. Court	Virginia Wade	4-6, 6-3, 6-0
1969*	Margaret S. Court	Nancy Richey	6-2, 6-2
1970*	Margaret S. Court	Rosemary Casals	6-2, 2-6, 6-1
1971*	Billie Jean King	Rosemary Casals	6-4, 7-6
1972*	Billie Jean King	Kerry Melville	6-3, 7-5
1973*	Margaret Court	Evonne Goolagong	7-6, 5-7, 6-2
1974*	Billie Jean King	Evonne Goolagong	3-6, 6-3, 7-5

*Open Champion

Billie Jean King

Virginia Wade

Women's Doubles

YEAR	WINNERS
1890	Ellen C. Roosevelt-Grace W. Roosevelt
1891	Mabel E. Cahill-Mrs. W. Fellowes Morgan
1892	Mabel E. Cahill-A. M. McKinley
1893	Aline M. Terry-Hattie Butler
1894	Helen R. Helwig-Juliette P. Atkinson
1895	Helen R. Helwig-Juliette P. Atkinson
1896	Elisabeth H. Moore-Juliette P. Atkinson
1897	Juliette P. Atkinson-Kathleen Atkinson
1898	Juliette P. Atkinson-Kathleen Atkinson
1899	Jane W. Craven-Myrtle McAteer
1900	Edith Parker-Hallie Champlin
1901	Juliette P. Atkinson-Myrtle McAteer
1902	Juliette P. Atkinson-Marion Jones
1903	Elisabeth H. Moore-Carrie B. Neely
1904	May G. Sutton-Miriam Hall
1905	Helen Homans-Carrie B. Neely
1906	Mrs. L. S. Coe-Mrs. D. S. Platt
1907	Marie Weimer-Carrie B. Neely
1908	Evelyn Sears-Margaret Curtis
1909	Hazel V. Hotchkiss-Edith E. Rotch
1910	Hazel V. Hotchkiss-Edith E. Rotch
1911	Hazel V. Hotchkiss-Eleonora Sears
1912	Dorothy Green-Mary K. Browne
1913	Mary K. Browne-Mrs. R. H. Williams
1914	Mary K. Browne-Mrs. R. H. Williams
1915	Mrs. Hazel Hotchkiss Wightman-Eleonora Sears
1916	Molla Bjurstedt-Eleonora Sears
1917	Molla Bjurstedt-Eleonora Sears
1918	Marion Zinderstein-Eleanor Goss
1919	Marion Zinderstein-Eleanor Goss

Hazel Hotchkiss Wightman today.

YEAR	WINNERS
1920	Marion Zinderstein-Eleanor Goss
1921	Mary K. Browne-Mrs. R. H. Williams
1922	Mrs. Marion Zinderstein Jessup-Helen N. Wills
1923	Kathleen McKane-Mrs. B. C. Covell
1924	Mrs. Hazel Hotchkiss Wightman-Helen N. Wills
1925	Mary K. Browne-Helen N. Wills
1926	Elizabeth Ryan-Eleanor Goss
1927	Mrs. Kathleen McKane Godfree-Ermyntrude Harvey
1928	Mrs. Hazel Hotchkiss Wightman-Helen N. Wills
1929	Mrs. Phoebe Watson-Mrs. L. R. C. Michell
1930	Betty Nuthall-Sarah Palfrey
1931	Betty Nuthall-Mrs. Eileen Bennett Whittingstall
1932	Helen Jacobs-Sarah Palfrey
1933	Betty Nuthall-Freda James
1934	Helen Jacobs-Sarah Palfrey
1935	Helen Jacobs-Mrs. Sarah Palfrey Fabyan
1936	Mrs. Marjorie Gladman Van Ryn-Carolin Babcock
1937	Mrs. Sarah Palfrey Fabyan-Alice Marble
1938	Mrs. Sarah Palfrey Fabyan-Alice Marble
1939	Mrs. Sarah Palfrey Fabyan-Alice Marble
1940	Mrs. Sarah Palfrey Fabyan-Alice Marble
1941	Mrs. Sarah Palfrey Cooke-Margaret E. Osborne
1942	A. Louise Brough-Margaret E. Osborne
1943	A. Louise Brough-Margaret E. Osborne
1944	A. Louise Brough-Margaret E. Osborne
1945	A. Louise Brough-Margaret E. Osborne
1946	A. Louise Brough-Margaret E. Osborne
1947	A. Louise Brough-Margaret E. Osborne
1948	A. Louise Brough-Mrs. Margaret Osborne duPont
1949	A. Louise Brough-Mrs. Margaret Osborne duPont
1950	A. Louise Brough-Mrs. Margaret Osborne duPont
1951	Shirley Fry-Doris Hart
1952	Shirley Fry-Doris Hart
1953	Shirley Fry-Doris Hart
1954	Shirley Fry-Doris Hart
1955	A. Louise Brough-Mrs. Margaret Osborne duPont
1956	A. Louise Brough-Mrs. Margaret Osborne duPont
1957	A. Louise Brough-Mrs. Margaret Osborne duPont
1958	Jeanne M. Arth-Darlene R. Hard
1959	Jeanne M. Arth-Darlene R. Hard
1960	Maria E. Bueno-Darlene R. Hard
1961	Darlene R. Hard-Lesley Turner
1962	Darlene R. Hard-Maria Bueno
1963	Robyn Ebbern-Margaret Smith
1964	Billie Jean Moffitt-Mrs. Karen H. Susman
1965	Mrs. Carole Caldwell Graebner-Nancy Richey
1966	Maria E. Bueno-Nancy Richey
1967	Rosemary Casals-Mrs. Billie Jean King
1968	Maria Bueno-Mrs. Margaret S. Court
1968*	Maria Bueno-Mrs. Margaret S. Court
1969	Margaret S. Court-Virginia Wade
1969*	Francoise Durr-Darlene Hard
1970*	Margaret S. Court-Judy T. Dalton
1971*	Rosemary Casals-Judy T. Dalton
1972*	Francoise Durr-Betty Stove
1973*	Margaret S. Court-Virginia Wade
1974*	Billie Jean King-Rosemary Casals

*Open Champions

WIMBLEDON CHAMPIONS

Men's Singles

YEAR	WINNER	RUNNER-UP	SCORE
1877	Spencer W. Gore	W. C. Marshall	6-1, 6-2, 6-4
1878	P. F. Hadow	Spencer W. Gore	7-5, 6-1, 9-7
1879	J. T. Hartley	V. St. Leger Gould	6-2, 6-4, 6-2
1880	J. T. Hartley	H. F. Lawford	6-0, 6-2, 2-6, 6-3
1881	William Renshaw	J. T. Hartley	6-0, 6-2, 6-1
1882	William Renshaw	Ernest Renshaw	6-1, 2-6, 4-6, 6-2, 6-2
1883	William Renshaw	Ernest Renshaw	2-6, 6-3, 6-3, 4-6, 6-3
1884	William Renshaw	H. F. Lawford	6-0, 6-4, 9-7
1885	William Renshaw	H. F. Lawford	7-5, 6-2, 4-6, 7-5
1886	William Renshaw	H. F. Lawford	6-0, 5-7, 6-3, 6-4
1887	H. F. Lawford	Ernest Renshaw	1-6, 6-3, 3-6, 6-4, 6-4
1888	Ernest Renshaw	H. F. Lawford	6-3, 7-5, 6-0
1889	William Renshaw	Ernest Renshaw	6-4, 6-1, 3-6, 6-0
1890	W. J. Hamilton	William Renshaw	6-8, 6-2, 3-6, 6-1, 6-1
1891	Wilfred Baddeley	Joshua Pim	6-4, 1-6, 7-5, 6-0
1892	Wilfred Baddeley	Joshua Pim	4-6, 6-3, 6-3, 6-2
1893	Joshua Pim	Wilfred Baddeley	3-6, 6-1, 6-3, 6-2
1894	Joshua Pim	Wilfred Baddeley	10-8, 6-2, 8-6
1895	Wilfred Baddeley	Wilberforce V. Eaves	4-6, 2-6, 8-6, 6-2, 6-3
1896	H. S. Mahoney	Wilfred Baddeley	6-2, 6-8, 5-7, 8-6, 6-3
1897	Reggie F. Doherty	H. S. Mahony	6-4, 6-4, 6-3
1898	Reggie F. Doherty	H. Laurie Doherty	6-3, 6-3, 2-6, 5-7, 6-1
1899	Reggie F. Doherty	Arthur W. Gore	1-6, 4-6, 6-2, 6-3, 6-3
1900	Reggie F. Doherty	Sidney H. Smith	6-8, 6-3, 6-1, 6-2
1901	Arthur W. Gore	Reggie F. Doherty	4-6, 7-5, 6-4, 6-4
1902	H. Laurie Doherty	Arthur W. Gore	6-4, 6-3, 3-6, 6-0
1903	H. Laurie Doherty	Frank L. Riseley	7-5, 6-3, 6-0
1904	H. Laurie Doherty	Frank L. Riseley	6-1, 7-5, 8-6
1905	H. Laurie Doherty	Norman E. Brookes	8-6, 6-2, 6-4
1906	H. Laurie Doherty	Frank L. Riseley	6-4, 4-6, 6-2, 6-3
1907	Norman E. Brookes	Arthur W. Gore	6-4, 6-2, 6-2
1908	Arthur W. Gore	H. Roper Barrett	6-3, 6-2, 4-6, 3-6, 6-4
1909	Arthur W. Gore	M. J. G. Ritchie	6-8, 1-6, 6-2, 6-2, 6-2
1910	Anthony F. Wilding	Arthur W. Gore	6-4, 7-5, 4-6, 6-2
1911	Anthony F. Wilding	H. Roper Barrett	6-4, 4-6, 2-6, 6-2 def.
1912	Anthony F. Wilding	Arthur W. Gore	6-4, 6-4, 4-6, 6-4
1913	Anthony F. Wilding	Maurice E. McLoughlin	8-6, 6-3, 10-8
1914	Norman E. Brookes	Anthony F. Wilding	6-4, 6-4, 7-5
1915-18	not held		
1919	Gerald L. Patterson	Norman E. Brookes	6-3, 7-5, 6-2
1920	William T. Tilden	Gerald L. Patterson	2-6, 6-3, 6-2, 6-4
1921	William T. Tilden	Brian I. C. Norton	4-6, 2-6, 6-1, 6-0, 7-5
1922	Gerald L. Patterson	Randolph Lycett	6-3, 6-4, 6-2
1923	William M. Johnston	Francis T. Hunter	6-0, 6-3, 6-1
1924	Jean Borotra	Rene Lacoste	6-1, 3-6, 6-1, 3-6, 6-4
1925	Rene Lacoste	Jean Borotra	6-3, 6-3, 4-6, 8-6
1926	Jean Borotra	Howard Kinsey	8-6, 6-1, 6-3
1927	Henri Cochet	Jean Borotra	4-6, 4-6, 6-3, 6-4, 7-5
1928	Rene Lacoste	Henri Cochet	6-1, 4-6, 6-4, 6-2
1929	Henri Cochet	Jean Borotra	6-4, 6-3, 6-4
1930	William T. Tilden	Wilmer Allison	6-3, 9-7, 6-4

Alex Metreveli (left) and Rod Laver (above)

YEAR	WINNER	RUNNER-UP	SCORE
1931	Sidney Wood	Frank X. Shields	default
1932	Ellsworth Vines	Wilfred Austin	6-4, 6-2, 6-0
1933	Jack Crawford	Ellsworth Vines	4-6, 11-9, 6-2, 2-6, 6-4
1934	Fred J. Perry	Jack Crawford	6-3, 6-0, 7-5
1935	Fred J. Perry	Gottfried von Cramm	6-2, 6-4, 6-4
1936	Fred J. Perry	Gottfried von Cramm	6-1, 6-1, 6-0
1937	Donald Budge	Gottfried von Cramm	6-3, 6-4, 6-2
1938	Donald Budge	Wilfred Austin	6-1, 6-0, 6-3
1939	Bobby Riggs	Elwood Cooke	2-6, 8-6, 3-6, 6-3, 6-2
1940-45	not held		
1946	Yvon Petra	Geoff E. Brown	6-2, 6-4, 7-9, 5-7, 6-4
1947	Jack Kramer	Tom P. Brown	6-1, 6-3, 6-2
1948	Bob Falkenburg	John Bromwich	7-5, 0-6, 6-2, 3-6, 7-5
1949	Ted Schroeder	Jaroslav Drobny	3-6, 6-0, 6-3, 4-6, 6-4
1950	Budge Patty	Frank Sedgman	6-1, 8-10, 6-2, 6-3
1951	Dick Savitt	Ken McGregor	6-4, 6-4, 6-4
1952	Frank Sedgman	Jaroslav Drobny	4-6, 6-3, 6-2, 6-3
1953	Vic Seixas	Kurt Nielsen	9-7, 6-3, 6-4
1954	Jaroslav Drobny	Ken Rosewall	13-11, 4-6, 6-2, 9-7
1955	Tony Trabert	Kurt Nielsen	6-3, 7-5, 6-1
1956	Lew Hoad	Ken Rosewall	6-2, 4-6, 7-5, 6-4
1957	Lew Hoad	Ashley Cooper	6-2, 6-1, 6-2
1958	Ashley Cooper	Neale Fraser	3-6, 6-3, 6-4, 13-11
1959	Alex Olmedo	Rod Laver	6-4, 6-3, 6-4
1960	Neale Fraser	Rod Laver	6-4, 3-6, 9-7, 7-5
1961	Rod Laver	Chuck McKinley	6-3, 6-1, 6-4
1962	Rod Laver	Martin Mulligan	6-2, 6-2, 6-1
1963	Chuck McKinley	Fred Stolle	9-7, 6-1, 6-4
1964	Roy Emerson	Fred Stolle	6-4, 12-10, 4-6, 6-3
1965	Roy Emerson	Fred Stolle	6-2, 6-4, 6-4
1966	Manuel Santana	Dennis Ralston	6-4, 11-9, 6-4
1967	John Newcombe	Wilhelm Bungert	6-3, 6-1, 6-1
1968*	Rod Laver	Tony Roche	6-3, 6-4, 6-2
1969*	Rod Laver	John Newcombe	6-4, 5-7, 6-4, 6-4
1970*	John Newcombe	Ken Rosewall	5-7, 6-3, 6-2, 3-6, 6-1
1971*	John Newcombe	Stan Smith	6-3, 5-7, 2-6, 6-4, 6-4
1972*	Stan Smith	Ilie Nastase	4-6, 6-3, 6-3, 4-6, 7-5
1973*	Jan Kodes	Alex Metreveli	6-1, 9-8, 6-3
1974*	Jimmy Connors	Ken Rosewall	6-1, 6-1, 6-4

*Open Championship

Men's Doubles

YEAR	WINNERS	RUNNERS-UP
1879	L. R. Erskine-H. F. Lawford	F. Durant-G. E. Tabor
1880	William-Ernest Renshaw	O. E. Woodhouse-C. J. Cole
1881	William-Ernest Renshaw	W. J. Down-H. Vaughan
1882	J. T. Hartley-R. T. Richardson	J. G. Horn-C. B. Russell
1883	C. W. Grinstead-C. E. Welldon	C. B. Russell-R. T. Milford
1884	William-Ernest Renshaw	E. W. Lewis-E. L. Williams
1885	William-Ernest Renshaw	C. E. Farrar-A. J. Stanley
1886	William-Ernest Renshaw	C. E. Farrar-A. J. Stanley
1887	Herbert W. Wiberforce-P. B. Lyon	J. Hope Crips-Barratt Smith
1888	William-Ernest Renshaw	Herbert W. Wiberforce-P. B. Lyon
1889	William-Ernest Renshaw	E. W. Lewis-G. W. Hillyard
1890	Joshua Pim-F. O. Stoker	E. W. Lewis-G. W. Hillyard
1891	Wilfred-Herbert Baddeley	Joshua Pim-F. O. Stoker
1892	E. W. Lewis-H. S. Barlow	Wilfred-Herbert Baddeley
1893	Joshua Pim-F. O. Stoker	E. W. Lewis-H. S. Barlow
1894	Wilfred-Herbert Baddeley	H. S. Barlow-C. H. Martin
1895	Wilfred-Herbert Baddeley	E. W. Lewis-W. V. Eaves
1896	Wilfred-Herbert Baddeley	Reggie F. Doherty-H. A. Nisbet
1897	Reggie F.-H. Laurie Doherty	Wilfred-Herbert Baddeley
1898	Reggie F.-H. Laurie Doherty	H. A. Nisbet-C. Hobart
1899	Reggie F.-H. Laurie Doherty	H. A. Nisbet-C. Hobart
1900	Reggie F.-H. Laurie Doherty	H. Roper Barrett-H. A. Nisbet
1901	Reggie F.-H. Laurie Doherty	Dwight Davis-Holcombe Ward
1902	Sidney H. Smith-Frank Riseley	Reggie F.-H. Laurie Doherty
1903	Reggie F.-H. Laurie Doherty	H. S. Mahony-M. J. G. Ritchie
1904	Reggie F.-H. Laurie Doherty	Sidney H. Smith-Frank Riseley
1905	Reggie F.-H. Laurie Doherty	Sidney H. Smith-Frank Riseley
1906	Sidney H. Smith-Frank Riseley	Reggie F.-H. Laurie Doherty
1907	Norman E. Brooks-Anthony F. Wilding	Beals C. Wright-Karl Behr
1908	Anthony F. Wilding-M. J. G. Ritchie	Arthur W. Gore-H. Roper Barrett
1909	Arthur W. Gore-H. Roper Barrett	Stanley Doust-H. A. Parker
1910	Anthony F. Wilding-M. J. G. Ritchie	Arthur W. Gore-H. Roper Barrett
1911	Andre Gobert-Max Decugis	Anthony F. Wilding-M. J. G. Ritchie
1912	H. Roper Barrett-Charles P. Dixon	Andre Gobert-Max Decugis
1913	H. Roper Barrett-Charles P. Dixon	F. W. Rahe-H. Kleinschroth
1914	Norman E. Brookes-Anthony F. Wilding	H. Roper Barrett-Charles P. Dixon
1915-18	not held	
1919	R. V. Thomas-Pat O'Hara Wood	Randolph Lycett-R. W. Heath
1920	R. N. Williams-C. S. Garland	A. R. F. Kingscote-J. C. Parke
1921	Randolph Lycett-Max Woosnam	Arthur H.-Frank G. Lowe
1922	J. O. Anderson-Randolph Lycett	Gerald Patterson-Pat O'Hara Wood
1923	Leslie A. Godfree-Randolph Lycett	Count de Gomar-E. Flaquer
1924	Frank Hunter-Vincent Richards	R. N. Williams-W. M. Washburn
1925	Jean Borotra-Rene Lacoste	J. Hennessey-R. Casey
1926	Jaques Brugnon-Henri Cochet	H. Kinsey-Vincent Richards
1927	Frank Hunter-William T. Tilden	Jaques Brugnon-Henri Cochet
1928	Jaques Brugnon-Henri Cochet	Gerald Patterson-J. B. Hawkes
1929	Wilmer Allison-John Van Ryn	J. Colin Gregory-Ian G. Collins
1930	Wilmer Allison-John Van Ryn	John H. Doeg-George M. Lott
1931	George M. Lott-John Van Ryn	Jaques Brugnon-Henri Cochet
1932	Jean Borotra-Jaques Brugnon	Fred J. Perry-G. Pat Hughes
1933	Jean Borotra-Jaques Brugnon	R. Nunoi-J. Satoh
1934	George M. Lott-Lester R. Stoefen	Jean Borotra-Jaques Brugnon
1935	Jack Crawford-Adrian Quist	Wilmer Allison-John Van Ryn
1936	G. Pat Hughes-Raymond Tuckey	Charles Hare-Frank Wilde

YEAR	WINNERS	RUNNERS-UP
1937	Don Budge-Gene Mako	G. Pat Hughes-Raymond Tuckey
1938	Don Budge-Gene Mako	Henner Henkel-G. von Metaxa
1939	Ellwood Cooke-Bobby Riggs	Charles Hare-Frank Wilde
1940-45	not held	
1946	Tom Brown-Jack Kramer	Geoff Brown-Dinny Pails
1947	Bob Falkenburg-Jack Kramer	Tony Mottram-O. W. Sidwell
1948	John Bromwich-Frank Sedgman	Tom Brown-Gardnar Mulloy
1949	Richard Gonzales-Frank Parker	Gardnar Mulloy-Ted Schroeder
1950	John Bromwich-Adrian Quist	Geoff Brown-O. W. Sidwell
1951	Ken McGregor-Frank Sedgman	Jaroslav Drobny-Eric Sturgess
1952	Ken McGregor-Frank Sedgman	Vic Seixas-Eric Sturgess
1953	Lew Hoad-Ken Rosewall	Rex Hartwig-Mervyn Rose
1954	Rex Hartwig-Mervyn Rose	Vic Seixas-Tony Trabert
1955	Rex Hartwig-Lew Hoad	Neale Fraser-Ken Rosewall
1956	Lew Hoad-Ken Rosewall	Nicola Pietrangeli-Orlando Sirola
1957	Budge Patty-Gardnar Mulloy	Neale Fraser-Lew Hoad
1958	Sven Davidson-Ulf Schmidt	Ashley Cooper-Neale Fraser
1959	Roy Emerson-Neale Fraser	Rod Laver-Bob Mark
1960	Rafael Osuna-Dennis Ralston	Mike Davies-Bobby Wilson
1961	Roy Emerson-Neale Fraser	Bob Hewitt-Fred Stolle
1962	Bob Hewitt-Fred Stolle	Boro Jovanovic-Nikki Pilic
1963	Rafael Osuna-Antonio Palafox	Jean Claude Barclay-Pierre Darmon
1964	Bob Hewitt-Fred Stolle	Roy Emerson-Ken Fletcher
1965	John Newcombe-Tony Roche	Ken Fletcher-Bob Hewitt
1966	Ken Fletcher-John Newcombe	Bill Bowrey-Owen Davidson
1967	Bob Hewitt-Frew McMillan	Roy Emerson-Ken Fletcher
1968*	John Newcombe-Tony Roche	Ken Rosewall-Fred Stolle
1969*	John Newcombe-Tony Roche	Tom Okker-Marty Riessen
1970*	John Newcombe-Tony Roche	Ken Rosewall-Fred Stolle
1971*	Roy Emerson-Rod Laver	Arthur Ashe-Dennis Ralston
1972*	Bob Hewitt-Frew McMillan	Stan Smith-Erik van Dillen
1973*	Jimmy Connors-Ilie Nastase	John Cooper-Neale Fraser
1974*	John Newcombe-Tony Roche	Robert Lutz-Stan Smith

*Open Championships

Nikki Pilic (above) and Ilie Nastase (right)

Women's Singles

YEAR	WINNER	RUNNER-UP	SCORE
1884	Maud Watson	Lillian Watson	6-8, 6-3, 6-2
1885	Maud Watson	Blanche Bingley	6-1, 7-5
1886	Blanche Bingley	Maud Watson	6-3, 6-3
1887	Lottie Dod	Blanche Bingley	6-2, 6-0
1888	Lottie Dod	Blanche Bingley-Hillyard	6-3, 6-3
1889	Blanche Bingley-Hillyard	L. Rice	4-6, 8-6, 6-4
1890	L. Rice	L. Jacks	6-4, 6-1
1891	Lottie Dod	Blanche Bingley-Hillyard	6-2, 6-1
1892	Lottie Dod	Blanche Bingley-Hillyard	6-1, 6-1
1893	Lottie Dod	Blanche Bingley-Hillyard	6-8, 6-1, 6-4
1894	Blanche Bingley-Hillyard	L. Austin	6-1, 6-1
1895	Charlotte Cooper	H. Jackson	7-5, 8-6
1896	Charlotte Cooper	Mrs. W. H. Pickering	6-2, 6-3
1897	Blanche Bingley-Hillyard	Charlotte Cooper	5-7, 7-5, 6-2
1898	Charlotte Cooper	L. Martin	6-4, 6-4
1899	Blanche Bingley-Hillyard	Charlotte Cooper	6-2, 6-3
1900	Blanche Bingley-Hillyard	Charlotte Cooper	4-6, 6-4, 6-4
1901	Charlotte Cooper-Sterry	Blanche Bingley-Hillyard	6-2, 6-2
1902	M. E. Robb	Charlotte Cooper-Sterry	7-5, 6-1
1903	Dorothea Douglas	E. W. Thomson	4-6, 6-4, 6-2
1904	Dorothea Douglas	Charlotte Cooper-Sterry	6-0, 6-3
1905	May Sutton	Dorothea Douglas	6-3, 6-4
1906	Dorothea Douglas	May Sutton	6-3, 9-7
1907	May Sutton	Dorothea Douglas-Lambert-Chambers	6-1, 6-4
1908	Charlotte Cooper-Sterry	A. M. Morton	6-4, 6-4
1909	Dora Boothby	A. M. Morton	6-4, 4-6, 8-6
1910	Dorothea Douglas-Lambert-Chambers	Dora Boothby	6-2, 6-2
1911	Dorothea Douglas-Lambert-Chambers	Dora Boothby	6-0, 6-0
1912	E. W. Thomson-Larcombe	Charlotte Cooper-Sterry	6-3, 6-1
1913	Dorothea Douglas-Lambert-Chambers	Mrs. R. J. McNair	6-0, 6-4
1914	Dorothea Douglas-Lambert-Chambers	E. W. Thomson-Larcombe	7-5, 6-4
1915-18	not held		
1919	Suzanne Lenglen	Dorothea Douglas-Lambert-Chambers	10-8, 4-6, 9-7
1920	Suzanne Lenglen	Dorothea Douglas-Lambert-Chambers	6-3, 6-0
1921	Suzanne Lenglen	Elizabeth Ryan	6-2, 6-0
1922	Suzanne Lenglen	Molla Mallory	6-2, 6-0
1923	Suzanne Lenglen	Kitty McKane	6-2, 6-2
1924	Kitty McKane	Helen Wills	4-6, 6-4, 6-4
1925	Suzanne Lenglen	Joan Fry	6-2, 6-0
1926	Kitty McKane-Godfree	Lili Alvarez	6-2, 4-6, 6-3
1927	Helen Wills	Lili Alvarez	6-2, 6-4
1928	Helen Wills	Lili Alvarez	6-2, 6-3
1929	Helen Wills	Helen Jacobs	6-1, 6-2
1930	Helen Wills-Moody	Elizabeth Ryan	6-2, 6-2
1931	Cilly Aussem	Hilda Krahwinkel	6-2, 7-5
1932	Helen Wills-Moody	Helen Jacobs	6-3, 6-1
1933	Helen Wills-Moody	Dorothy Round	6-4, 6-8, 6-3
1934	Dorothy Round	Helen Jacobs	6-2, 5-7, 6-3
1935	Helen Wills-Moody	Helen Jacobs	6-3, 3-6, 7-5
1936	Helen Jacobs	Hilda Krahwinkel-Sperling	6-2, 4-6, 7-5
1937	Dorothy Round	Jadwiga Jedrzejowska	6-2, 2-6, 7-5
1938	Helen Wills-Moody	Helen Jacobs	6-4, 6-0
1939	Alice Marble	Kay Stammers	6-2, 6-0
1940-45	not held		
1946	Pauline Betz	Louise Brough	6-2, 6-4

Chris Evert

YEAR	WINNER	RUNNER-UP	SCORE
1947	Margaret Osborne	Doris Hart	6-2, 6-4
1948	Louise Brough	Doris Hart	6-3, 8-6
1949	Louise Brough	Margaret Osborne-duPont	10-8, 1-6, 10-8
1950	Louise Brough	Margaret Osborne-duPont	6-1, 3-6, 6-1
1951	Doris Hart	Shirley Fry	6-1, 6-0
1952	Maureen Connolly	Louise Brough	7-5, 6-3
1953	Maureen Connolly	Doris Hart	8-6, 7-5
1954	Maureen Connolly	Louise Brough	6-2, 7-5
1955	Louise Brough	Beverly Baker-Fleitz	7-5, 8-6
1956	Shirley Fry	Angela Buxton	6-3, 6-2
1957	Althea Gibson	Darlene Hard	6-3, 6-2
1958	Althea Gibson	Angela Mortimer	8-6, 6-2
1959	Maria Bueno	Darlene Hard	6-4, 6-3
1960	Maria Bueno	Sandra Reynolds	8-6, 6-0
1961	Angela Mortimer	Christine Truman	4-6, 6-4, 7-5
1962	Karen Hantze-Susman	Vera Puzejova-Sukova	6-4, 6-4
1963	Margaret Smith	Billie Jean Moffitt	6-3, 6-4
1964	Maria Bueno	Margaret Smith	6-4, 7-9, 6-3
1965	Margaret Smith	Maria Bueno	6-4, 7-5
1966	Billie Jean King	Maria Bueno	6-3, 3-6, 6-1
1967	Billie Jean King	Ann Haydon-Jones	6-3, 6-4
1968*	Billie Jean King	Judy Tegart	9-7, 7-5
1969*	Ann Haydon-Jones	Billie Jean King	3-6, 6-3, 6-2
1970*	Margaret Smith Court	Billie Jean King	14-12, 11-9
1971*	Evonne Goolagong	Margaret Smith Court	6-4, 6-1
1972*	Billie Jean King	Evonne Goolagong	6-3, 6-3
1973*	Billie Jean King	Chris Evert	6-0, 7-5
1974*	Chris Evert	Olga Morozova	6-0, 6-4

Open Championships

Women's Doubles

YEAR	WINNERS	RUNNERS-UP
1913	Mrs. R. J. McNair-Dora Boothby	Charlotte Cooper Sterry-Dorothea Douglas Lambert Chambers
1914	A. M. Morton-Elizabeth Ryan	E. W. Thomson Larcombe-Mrs. Hannam
1915-18	not held	
1919	Suzanne Lenglen-Elizabeth Ryan	E. W. Thomson Larcombe-Dorothea Douglas Lambert Chambers

YEAR	WINNERS	RUNNERS-UP
1920	Suzanne Lenglen-Elizabeth Ryan	E. W. Thomson Larcombe-Dorothea Douglas Lambert Chambers
1921	Suzanne Lenglen-Elizabeth Ryan	Geraldine Beamish-Mrs. G. Peacock
1922	Suzanne Lenglen-Elizabeth Ryan	Kitty McKane-Mrs. A. D. Stocks
1923	Suzanne Lenglen-Elizabeth Ryan	Joan Austin-Edith Colyer
1924	Hazel Wightman-Helen Wills	Phyllis Covel-Kitty McKane
1925	Suzanne Lenglen-Elizabeth Ryan	Mrs. A. V. Bridge-Mrs. C. G. McIlquham
1926	Mary K. Browne-Elizabeth Ryan	Kitty McKane-Godfree-Edith Colyer
1927	Helen Wills-Elizabeth Ryan	Mrs. G. Peacock-Bobbie Heine
1928	Peggy Saunders-Phyllis Watson	Ermyntrude Harvey-Eileen Bennett
1929	Peggy Michell-Phyllis Watson	Phyllis Covel-Dorothy Shepherd Barron
1930	Helen Wills Moody-Elizabeth Ryan	Eleanor Cross-Sarah Palfrey
1931	Phyllis Mudford-Dorothy Shepherd Barron	Doris Metaxa-Josane Sigart
1932	Doris Metaxa-Josane Sigart	Helen Jacobs-Elizabeth Ryan
1933	Simone Mathieu-Elizabeth Ryan	Freda James-Billie Yorke
1934	Simone Mathieu-Elizabeth Ryan	Dorothy Andrus-Sylvia Henrotin
1935	Freda James-Kay Stammers	Simone Mathieu-Hilda Krahwinkel Sperling
1936	Freda James-Kay Stammers	Helen Jacobs-Sarah Palfrey Fabyan
1937	Simone Mathieu-Billie Yorke	Phyllis Mudford King-Elsie Pittman
1938	Sarah Palfrey Fabyan-Alice Marble	Simone Mathieu-Billie Yorke
1939	Sarah Palfrey Fabyan-Alice Marble	Helen Jacobs-Billie Yorke
1940-45	not held	
1946	Louise Brough-Margaret Osborne	Pauline Betz-Doris Hart
1947	Pat Todd-Doris Hart	Louise Brough-Margaret Osborne
1948	Louise Brough-Margaret Osborne duPont	Pat Todd-Doris Hart
1949	Louise Brough-Margaret Osborne duPont	Pat Todd-Gussie Moran
1950	Louise Brough-Margaret Osborne duPont	Doris Hart-Shirley Fry
1951	Doris Hart-Shirley Fry	Louise Brough-Margaret Osborne duPont
1952	Doris Hart-Shirley Fry	Louise Brough-Maureen Connolly
1953	Doris Hart-Shirley Fry	Julie Sampson-Maureen Connolly
1954	Louise Brough-Margaret Osborne duPont	Doris Hart-Shirley Fry
1955	Angela Mortimer-Anne Shilcock	Shirley Bloomer-Pat Ward
1956	Angela Buxton-Althea Gibson	Daphne Seeney-Fay Muller
1957	Althea Gibson-Darlene Hard	Thelma Long-Mary Hawton
1958	Maria Bueno-Althea Gibson	Margaret Osborne duPont-Margaret Varner
1959	Jean Arth-Darlene Hard	Beverly Baker Fleitz-Christine Truman
1960	Maria Bueno-Darlene Hard	Sandra Reynolds-Renee Schuurman
1961	Karen Hantze-Billie Jean Moffitt	Jan Lehane-Margaret Smith
1962	Billie Jean Moffitt-Karen Hantze Susman	Sandra Reynolds Price-Renee Schuurman
1963	Maria Bueno-Darlene Hard	Robyn Ebbern-Margaret Smith
1964	Margaret Smith-Lesley Turner	Billie Jean Moffitt-Karen Hantze Susman
1965	Maria Bueno-Billie Jean Moffitt	Francoise Durr-Janine Lieffrig
1966	Maria Bueno-Nancy Richey	Margaret Smith-Judy Tegart
1967	Rosemary Casals-Billie Jean King	Maria Bueno-Nancy Richey
1968*	Rosemary Casals-Billie Jean King	Francoise Durr-Ann Haydon Jones
1969*	Margaret Smith Court-Judy Tegart	Patti Hogan-Peggy Michel
1970*	Rosemary Casals-Billie Jean King	Francoise Durr-Virginia Wade
1971*	Rosemary Casals-Billie Jean King	Margaret S. Court-Evonne Goolagong
1972*	Billie Jean King-Betty Stove	Judy T. Dalton-Francoise Durr
1973*	Billie Jean King-Rosemary Casals	Francoise Durr-Betty Stove
1974*	Evonne Goolagong-Peggy Michel	Helen Gourlay-Karen Krantzcke

*Open Championships

AMERICA'S TENNIS IMMORTALS

Since 1955, 51 men and 24 women have been selected to reside in the National Lawn Tennis Hall of Fame at Newport. Here they are listed alphabetically, with the years encompassing their prominence, along with their U.S. adult championships won in singles and doubles (S and D).

Women

Mrs. Pauline Betz Addie, 1939-46 (10-S, 9-D)
Mrs. Ellen Hansell Allerdice, 1887 (1-S)
Juliette Atkinson, 1894-1902 (3-S, 10-D)
Mrs. Maureen Connolly Brinker, 1950-54 (5-S, 1-D)
Mrs. Maude Barger-Wallach, 1908-16 (1-S)
Mary K. Browne, 1912-25 (4-S, 10-D)
Mrs. May Sutton Bundy, 1904-28 (2-S, 1-D)
Mrs. Louise Brough Clapp, 1941-57 (1-S, 17-D)
Mrs. Sarah Palfrey Fabyan Cooke Danzig, 1928-45
  (4-S, 19-D)
Mrs. Althea Gibson Darben, 1952-58 (3-S, 2-D)
Mrs. Margaret Osborne duPont, 1938-60
  (3-S, 23-D)
Darlene Hard, 1955-69 (4-S, 12-D)
Doris Hart, 1942-55 (4-S, 16-D)
Mrs. Shirley Fry Irvin, 1944-56 (1-S, 5-D)
Helen Jacobs, 1927-41 (4-S, 4-D)
Mrs. Molla Bjurstedt Mallory, 1915-28 (15-S, 9-D)
Alice Marble, 1932-40 (5-S, 8-D)
Elisabeth Moore, 1891-1909 (4-S, 6-D)
Mrs. Helen Wills Moody Roark, 1922-38 (7-S, 6-D)
Elizabeth Ryan, 1914-34 (1-S, 3-D)
Eleonora Sears, 1911-17 (5-D)
Bertha Townsend, 1888-89 (2-S)
Marie Wagner, 1908-22 (6-S, 4-D)
Mrs. Hazel Hotchkiss Wightman, 1909-43
  (6-S, 28-D)

Men

Fred Alexander, 1901-18 (1-S, 12-D)
Wilmer Allison, 1927-35 (2-S, 5-D)
Karl Behr, 1906-15 (0)
Don Budge, 1934-38 (4-S, 10-D)
Oliver Campbell, 1888-92 (3-S, 5-D)
Malcolm Chace, 1892-95 (3-S, 4-D)
Joseph Clark, 1883-89 (1-S, 2-D)
William Clothier, 1901-14 (2-S)
Dwight Davis, 1898-1901 (1-S, 4-D)
John Doeg, 1927-31 (1-S, 2-D)
Dr. James Dwight, 1882-88 (5-D)

Bob Falkenburg, 1943-48 (1-S, 3-D)
Chuck Garland, 1917-20 (1-S, 3-D)
Pancho Gonzalez, 1948-70 (13-S, 6-D)
Bitsy Grant, 1930-41 (3-S, 1-D)
Clarence Griffin, 1913-24 (1-S, 4-D)
Harold Hackett, 1906-12 (9-D)
Frank Hunter, 1922-30 (2-S, 4-D)
Fred Hovey, 1890-96 (3-S, 3-D)
Joe Hunt, 1936-43 (2-S, 2-D)
Bill Johnston, 1913-27 (3-S, 5-D)
Jack Kramer, 1939-47 (4-S, 9-D)
Bill Larned, 1892-1911 (8-S)
Art Larsen, 1949-56 (5-S, 4-D)
George Lott, 1924-34 (1-S, 13-D)
Gene Mako, 1933-39 (1-S, 8-D)
Maurice McLoughlin, 1909-15 (2-S, 3-D)
Don McNeill, 1937-50 (5-S, 6-D)
Gardnar Mulloy, 1939-57 (7-D)
R.L. Murray, 1914-18 (3-S)
Frank Parker, 1933-49 (8-S, 3-D)
Theodore Pell, 1905-15 (3-S, 5-D)
Vinnie Richards, 1918-26 (7-S, 20-D)
Bobby Riggs, 1936-41 (9-S, 7-D)
Fred Schroeder, 1940-51 (5-S, 9-D)
Dick Sears, 1881-87 (7-S, 6-D)
Vic Seixas, 1942-66 (3-S, 10-D)
Frank Shields, 1928-45 (0)
Henry Slocum, Jr., 1886-90 (2-S, 1-D)
Bill Talbert, 1941-54 (2-S, 19-D)
Bill Tilden, 1913-29 (16-S, 18-D)
Tony Trabert, 1951-55 (8-S, 7-D)
John Van Ryn, 1927-37 (4-D)
Elsworth Vines, 1930-32 (4-S, 3-D)
Holcombe Ward, 1899-1906 (2-S, 7-D)
Watson Washburn, 1913-22 (2-D)
Malcolm Whitman, 1896-1902 (4-S, 2-D)
Dick Williams, 1912-26 (6-S, 5-D)
Sidney Wood, 1930-45 (0)
Bob Wrenn, 1891-97 (4-S, 3-D)
Beals Wright, 1899-1910 (1-S, 3-D)